MATHEMATICS
for year 7

second edition

Stan Pulgies
Robert Haese
Sandra Haese

Haese & Harris Publications

MATHEMATICS FOR YEAR 7
SECOND EDITION

Stan Pulgies   M.Ed., B.Ed., Grad.Dip.T.
Robert Haese   B.Sc.
Sandra Haese   B.Sc.

Haese & Harris Publications
3 Frank Collopy Court, Adelaide Airport SA 5950
Telephone: (08) 8355 9444, Fax: (08) 8355 9471
email: info@haeseandharris.com.au
web: www.haeseandharris.com.au

National Library of Australia Card Number & ISBN 978-1-876543-56-3

© Haese & Harris Publications 2003

Published by Raksar Nominees Pty Ltd, 3 Frank Collopy Court, Adelaide Airport SA 5950

First Edition   1998
Second Edition   2003   *Reprinted*   2005 twice, 2007 twice, 2008, 2010

Cartoon artwork by John Martin and Chris Meadows.
Artwork by Piotr Poturaj, Joanna Poturaj and David Purton
Cover design by Piotr Poturaj.
Cover photograph: © Nicholas Birks, *Wildflight Australia Photography*
Computer software by David Purton and Eli Sieradzki
Typeset in Australia by Susan Haese (Raksar Nominees). Typeset in Times Roman $10\frac{1}{2}/11\frac{1}{2}$

This book is copyright. Except as permitted by the Copyright Act (any fair dealing for the purposes of private study, research, criticism or review), no part of this publication may be reproduced, stored in a retrieval system, or transmitted in any form or by any means, electronic, mechanical, photocopying, recording or otherwise, without the prior permission of the publisher. Enquiries to be made to Haese & Harris Publications.

Copying for educational purposes: Where copies of part or the whole of the book are made under Part VB of the Copyright Act, the law requires that the educational institution or the body that administers it has given a remuneration notice to Copyright Agency Limited (CAL). For information, contact the Copyright Agency Limited.

Acknowledgements: the descriptors listed at the beginning of each chapter are taken from the *R-7 SACSA Mathematics Teaching Resource* published by the Department of Education and Children's Services. The Publishers also wish to acknowledge The Royal Agricultural & Historical Society of S.A. Inc. for permission to include the map of the Royal Adelaide Show.

FOREWORD

Mathematics for Year 7 (second edition) offers a comprehensive and rigorous course of study at Year 7 level. Through its worked examples, exercises, activities and answers, and the support of the interactive Student CD, the book provides students with the structure and content to work efficiently at their own rate.

The book and CD package is designed to supplement classroom practice and give teachers time to explore other creative strategies, depending on the needs of their students. It is not the Year 7 Mathematics Curriculum, nor does it proclaim to provide the most effective teaching program.

The knowledge, skills and understandings listed at the beginning of each chapter incorporate the descriptors used in the *R-7 SACSA Mathematics Teaching Resource* for Middle Years. We have listed the descriptors in the hope that this will be a helpful guide for Year 7 teachers who may wish to use the book to support their teaching practice.

About this second edition: the second edition is an extensive revision and updating of the original text, with considerable reorganisation of chapters. Changes include:

- revised sections on addition, subtraction, multiplication and division of whole numbers, with a new section on two step problem solving, in Chapter 1
- coverage of four problem solving techniques is included in Chapter 2: 'Trial and Error', 'Making a Table and Looking for a Pattern', 'Modelling or Drawing a Picture', and 'Working Backwards'
- Chapter 3 Shapes and Solids combines the two chapters 'Geometric Figures' and 'Angles' from the first edition
- a section on GST is among the new sections in Chapter 6 Percentage
- Measurement has been split into two chapters: 'Length and Mass' and 'Area and Volume'
- much of the old Statistics chapter is included in a new chapter, Data Collection and Representation
- a new chapter on Transformation and Location includes a section on 'Bearings and Directions'
- the inclusion of an interactive Student CD

In the table of contents, page numbers for corresponding sections in the first edition are given in brackets. This is intended as a guide for teachers who may have to use the first and second editions within the same classroom. A glance at the contents pages will show how both books correlate (the absence of a page number in brackets denotes the introduction of a new section).

About the interactive Student CD: the CD contains the text of the book. Students can leave the textbook at school and keep the CD at home, to save carrying a heavy textbook to and from school each day. But more than that, by clicking on the 'active icons' within the text, students can access a range of interactive features: graphing and geometry software, spreadsheets, video clips, computer demonstrations and simulations, and worksheets.

The CD is ideal for independent study. Students can revisit concepts taught in class and explore new ideas for themselves. It is fantastic for teachers to use for demonstrations and simulations in the classroom. In summary, the book offers structure and rigour, and the CD makes maths come alive.

We have endeavoured to provide as broad a base of activity and learning styles as we can, but we also caution that no single book should be the sole resource for any classroom teacher.

We welcome your feedback.

Email: info@haeseandharris.com.au
Web: www.haeseandharris.com.au

SP
RCH
SHH

TABLE OF CONTENTS

Numbers in brackets denote pages in the first edition. They have been included to assist teachers using the first and second editions in the same classroom.

1 WHOLE NUMBERS — 9 (9)

A	Different number systems	10	(10)
B	Our number system	16	(16)
C	Rounding numbers	19	(19)
D	Adding and subtracting whole numbers	21	
E	Multiplying and dividing whole numbers	23	
F	Estimation and approximation	27	(21)
G	How big is one million?	32	(32)
H	Numbers beyond one million	36	(37)
I	Two step problem solving	39	
J	Number opposites	41	
	Review Set A (Chapter 1)	44	
	Review Set B (Chapter 1)	45	
	Review Set C (Chapter 1)	46	

2 NUMBER PROPERTIES — 47 (83)

A	Operating with numbers	48	(84)
B	Order of operations	51	(87)
C	Factors of natural numbers	53	(94)
D	Multiples of natural numbers	57	(98)
E	Divisibility rules	59	(102)
F	Powers of numbers	61	(104)
G	Powers with base 10	63	(106)
H	Square and cube numbers	64	(100)
I	Problem solving	68	
	Method 1: Trial and error	68	
	Method 2: Making a table and looking for a pattern	69	
	Method 3: Modelling or drawing a picture	71	
	Method 4: Working backwards	72	
	Review Set A (Chapter 2)	73	
	Review Set B (Chapter 2)	73	
	Review Set C (Chapter 2)	74	

3 SHAPES AND SOLIDS — 75 (61)

A	Points and lines	77	(63)
B	Angles	81	(150)
C	Angles of a triangle	87	(155)

D	Angles of a quadrilateral	89	(157)
E	Polygons	91	(66)
F	Triangles and quadrilaterals	93	(69)
G	Constructing a triangle	97	(157)
H	Bisecting and constructing angles	100	(160)
I	Polyhedra	104	(72)
J	Nets of solids	106	(74)
K	Drawing solids	108	(77)
L	Constructing block solids	110	(78)
M	Freehand drawings of solids	111	(77)
N	Circles	114	(248)
	Review Set A (Chapter 3)	115	
	Review Set B (Chapter 3)	116	
	Review Set C (Chapter 3)	117	

4 FRACTIONS — 119 (111)

A	Fractions are everywhere	120	(112)
B	Representation of fractions	121	(113)
C	Fractions of regular shapes	123	(114)
D	Equal (equivalent) fractions	125	(121)
E	Lowest terms	129	(126)
F	Fractions of quantities	130	(117)
G	Comparing fraction sizes	134	(125)
H	Improper fractions and mixed numbers	136	(120)
I	Adding fractions	138	(128)
J	Subtracting fractions	141	(130)
K	Multiplying fractions	143	(132)
L	Problem solving	146	(138)
	Review Set A (Chapter 4)	147	
	Review Set B (Chapter 4)	148	

5 DECIMALS — 149 (171)

A	Representing decimals	150	(172)
B	Place value	157	(182)
C	Rounding decimal numbers	160	(202)
D	Large decimal numbers	162	(181)
E	Fraction and decimal interchange	164	
F	Ordering decimals	166	(186)
G	Adding and subtracting decimals	168	(188)
H	Multiplying/dividing by powers of 10	170	(190)
I	Multiplying decimal numbers	173	(192)
J	Dividing decimals by whole numbers	177	

K	Terminating and recurring decimals	179	(198)
L	Converting decimals to fractions	182	(201)
M	Using a calculator for decimal numbers	182	
	Review Set A (Chapter 5)	184	
	Review Set B (Chapter 5)	185	
	Review Set C (Chapter 5)	186	

6 PERCENTAGE — 187 (207)

A	Percentage	189	(209)
B	Fractions to percentages	191	(210)
C	Percentages to fractions	195	(219)
D	Converting decimals to percentages	196	
E	Converting percentages into decimals	197	
F	Plotting numbers on a number line	199	(212)
G	Percentages are all around us	200	(215)
H	One quantity as a percentage of another	205	(223)
I	Finding percentages of quantities	207	(225)
J	Percentages and money	208	(227)
K	Who uses percentages?	210	
L	Problem solving with percentages	213	
M	Discount	215	(230)
N	Goods and services tax (GST)	216	
O	Simple interest	217	(215)
	Review Set A (Chapter 6)	218	
	Review Set B (Chapter 6)	219	
	Review Set C (Chapter 6)	220	

7 MEASUREMENT (LENGTH AND MASS) — 221 (237)

A	Units of measurement	223	(239)
B	Reading scales	225	(240)
C	Length conversions	228	(243)
D	Perimeter	231	(245)
E	Scale diagrams	235	(251)
F	Mass	239	(254)
G	Qualitative data	241	
H	Problem solving with length and mass	242	(256)
	Review Set A (Chapter 7)	247	
	Review Set B (Chapter 7)	248	
	Review Set C (Chapter 7)	249	

8 MEASUREMENT (AREA AND VOLUME) — 251 (343)

A	Area units	252	(344)

	B	Area of a rectangle	258	(350)
	C	Area of a triangle	263	(357)
	D	Volume and capacity	267	(361)
	E	Volume	271	(364)
	F	Capacity	277	(372)
	G	Problem solving	279	(374)
		Review Set A (Chapter 8)	282	
		Review Set B (Chapter 8)	283	

9 DATA COLLECTION AND REPRESENTATION — 285

	A	Samples and populations	286	(284)
	B	Organising categorical data	290	(286)
	C	Graphing categorical data with technology	293	
	D	Interpreting graphs of categorical data	295	(289)
	E	Numerical data	299	(294)
	F	Mean and median	303	(291)
	G	Line graphs and time series	307	(298)
		Review Set A (Chapter 9)	309	
		Review Set B (Chapter 9)	310	
		Review Set C (Chapter 9)	311	

10 TIME AND TEMPERATURE — 313 (265)

	A	Time lines	315	(267)
	B	Units of time	317	(268)
	C	Differences in time	319	(271)
	D	Reading clocks and watches	322	(273)
	E	Timetables	325	(275)
	F	Time zones (extension)	328	(277)
	G	Average speed	331	(255)
	H	Temperature	333	
		Review Set A (Chapter 10)	334	
		Review Set B (Chapter 10)	335	
		Review Set C (Chapter 10)	335	

11 ALGEBRA — 337 (45)

	A	Geometric patterns	338	(48)
	B	Number patterns	340	(46)
	C	Formulae and variables	342	(50)
	D	Discovering formulae	346	(53)
	E	Practical problems using formulae	348	
	F	Linear graphs	351	
	G	Solving equations	352	(317)

H	Graphs of real life situations	355	
	Review Set A (Chapter 11)	357	
	Review Set B (Chapter 11)	358	
	Review Set C (Chapter 11)	359	

12 TRANSFORMATION AND LOCATION 361

A	Number planes	363	(91)
B	Transformations	367	
C	Using ratios	376	(143)
D	Bearings and directions	378	(163)
E	Activities	384	
	Review Set A (Chapter 12)	385	
	Review Set B (Chapter 12)	387	
	Review Set C (Chapter 12)	388	

13 CHANCE 389 (325)

A	Describing chance	390	(326)
B	Assigning numbers to chance	393	(328)
C	Defining probability	395	(330
D	Tree diagrams	399	
E	Making your own probability generators	401	(333)
F	Expectation	402	(333)
G	Gambling systems	405	(337)
	Review Set A (Chapter 13)	407	
	Review Set B (Chapter 13)	408	

ANSWERS 409

INDEX 445

Chapter 1
Whole numbers

Knowledge, skills and understandings

By the end of this chapter you should be able to

- develop an understanding of number systems across time and place (e.g., Mayan, Chinese)
- recognise, use and write in words and numbers beyond 1 000 000
- identify place value of numbers over 1 000 000
- compare numbers and use symbols (e.g., $\approx$, (), $\geqslant$, $\leqslant$)
- write numbers over 100 000 in ascending and descending order
- identify large numbers in everyday use (e.g., comparing populations)
- solve a given 2 step number or word problem (e.g., "A school has a total of 854 students. 102 boys and 84 girls leave. How many students are left at the school?")
- multiply a 3 digit number by a 2 digit number using the extended form (long multiplication)
- divide a number with 3 or more digits by a single digit or multiples of 10 (with a remainder expressed as a decimal)
- recognise the existence of negative numbers (e.g., profit and loss)

A DIFFERENT NUMBER SYSTEMS

The number system we use is called the **Hindu-Arabic System**.

Over the next few pages, a brief look at four different number systems is presented. These were some of the systems being used by different cultures in various parts of the world.

As travel and communication between countries and cultures was limited by distance and other boundaries there was little opportunity to share and develop ideas.

A more detailed look at various number systems is provided through the activities.

THE EGYPTIAN NUMBER SYSTEM

There is archaeological evidence that as long ago as 3600 BC the Egyptians were using a detailed number system. The symbols used to represent numbers were pictures of everyday things. These symbols are called hieroglyphics which means sacred picture writings.

The Egyptians had developed a tally system based on ten. Ten of one symbol could be replaced by one of another symbol. We call this a base ten system.

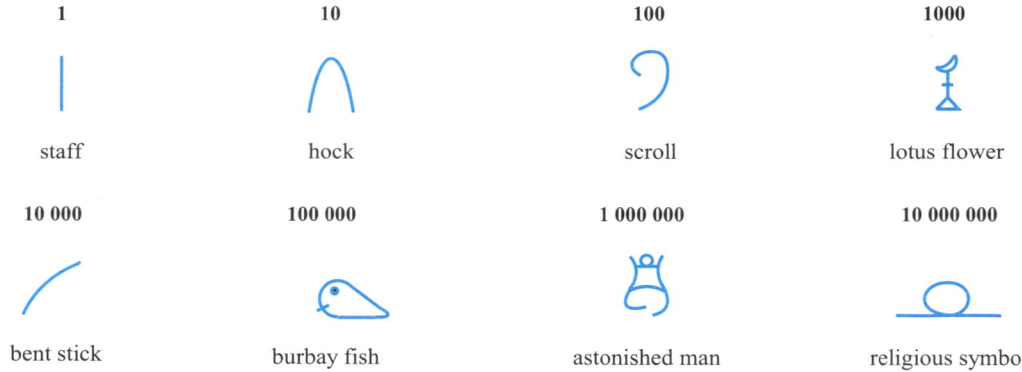

The order in which the symbols were written down did not affect the value of the numerals. The value of the numerals could be found by adding the value of the symbols used.

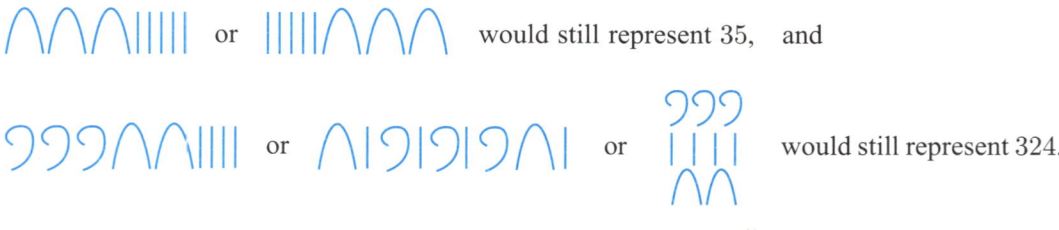

Whereas in our system 35 could not be represented as 53 or $\frac{5}{3}$,

nor could 324 be represented as 432 or 342 or 423 or 234 or $\begin{smallmatrix}2\\3\\4\end{smallmatrix}$.

Simply put, the **Egyptian system** did not have **place values** as our system does.

EXERCISE 1A.1

1 a In our number system, 3 symbols are used to write the number 999. How many Egyptian symbols are needed to write our 999?

  b Write the Egyptian symbols for 728 and 234 124.

2 Change these symbols to our numerals:

  a   **b**

ROMAN NUMERALS

The Romans developed a system which used a combination of symbols.

The first four numbers could be represented by the fingers on one hand.

The V formed by the thumb and forefinger of an open hand represented 5.

Two Vs joined together became two lots of 5 i.e., ten or X.

C represented one hundred, and half a i.e., L became 50.

One thousand was represented by an . With a little imagination you should see that an split in half and turned 90° would look like a which became half a thousand or 500.

1	2	3	4	5	6	7	8	9	10
I	II	III	IV	V	VI	VII	VIII	IX	X
20	30	40	50	60	70	80	90	100	500	1000
XX	XXX	XL	L	LX	LXX	LXXX	XC	C	D	M

Unlike the Egyptian system, this system did have to be written in order as the value would change if the order changed. For example:

	IV stands for 1 before 5	i.e., 4
whereas	VI stands for 1 after 5	i.e., 6
and	XC stands for 10 before 100	i.e., 90
whereas	CX stands for 10 after 100	i.e., 110.

These were the rules for the order in which symbols could be used:
- The I could only appear before V or X.
- The X could only appear before L or C.
- C could only appear before a D or an M.

One less than a thousand therefore could not be written as IM but as CMXCIX.

Larger numerals were formed by placing a stroke above the symbol which made the number 1000 times as large.

5000	10 000	50 000	100 000	500 000	1 000 000
$\overline{V}$	$\overline{X}$	$\overline{L}$	$\overline{C}$	$\overline{D}$	$\overline{M}$

EXERCISE 1A.2

1 What numbers are represented by the following symbols?
- **a** DCCLXVIII
- **b** CDXXIX
- **c** MMDCCXVI
- **d** $\overline{X}\overline{X}\overline{V}$MCCCL
- **e** $\overline{D}\overline{L}\overline{V}$DLV
- **f** $\overline{M}\overline{M}\overline{C}\overline{C}$

2 Write the following numbers in Roman numerals:
- **a** 89
- **b** 347
- **c** 654
- **d** 5650
- **e** 75 942
- **f** 954 000

3 Which Roman numeral less than one thousand has the greatest number of symbols?
Hint: Which Roman numeral less than X has the greatest number of symbols?

ACTIVITY   IF YOU LIVED IN ROMAN TIMES

What to do:

Use Roman numerals to write:

1. your house number and postcode
2. the family's car registration number
3. your height in centimetres
4. the school's phone number
5. your phone number
6. the cost of a home delivered pizza
7. your water meter reading
8. the speedometer reading in a car
9. today's date in the day, month and year pattern
10. the scores in a recent school or league sporting competition.

That's MXXII plus CDL minus CXIX.

ZERO

Neither the Egyptians nor the Romans had a symbol to represent nothing.

The symbol 0 was called **zephirum** in Arabic. Our word **zero** comes from this.

In the Hindu-Arabic System, the digit for **zero** is used as a place holder in numerals.

For example, in 470 the 0 is a place holder for units to show that the 7 means 7 tens and there are no single units. Also, in the number 2094 the 0 shows that there are no hundreds. However, because of the place that the zero takes, the digit to the left of it acquires the value of 'thousands'.

With whole numbers the zero is never placed before any other digit, unless there is a very special reason.

The **rules** for **operating with zero** are:

- Any number $+ \ 0 =$ the same number   Example: $8 + 0 = 8$
- Any number $- \ 0 =$ the same number   Example: $9 - 0 = 9$
- Any number $\times 0 = 0$ Example: $6 \times 0 = 0$
- $0 \div$ any number $= 0$ Example: $0 \div 4 = 0$
- Any number $\div 0$ has no answer   Example: $2 \div 0$ has no answer

MAYAN SYSTEM

Mayans used pebbles and sticks to represent numbers which they recorded as dots and strokes.

1 2 3 4 5 6 7 8 9 10

11 12 13 14 15 16 17 18 19 20

However, unlike the Egyptians and Romans the Mayans created a place value by placing one symbol above the other. You could almost say that their system was a multiplication or 'lots of' system.

Using our base 10 system, the number 172 is 17 'lots of' 10 and 2 'lots of' 1.

The Mayans used base 20.   Consider

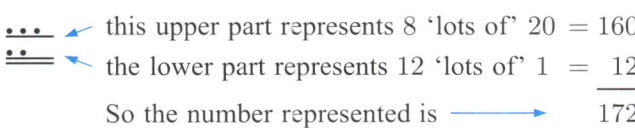

this upper part represents 8 'lots of' $20 = 160$
the lower part represents 12 'lots of' $1 = \underline{12}$
So the number represented is $\longrightarrow$ 172

The Mayans also saw the need to have a symbol to show the difference between 'lots of 1' and 'lots of 20'. The symbol   which represented a mussel shell, works like our zero.

Compare these symbols:

43	40	68	60	149	100	
..	..	...	...	..	—	lots of 20
...	🛎	...	🛎	....	🛎	lots of 1

EXERCISE 1A.3

1 Make these numbers into Mayan symbols:
   a 23   **b** 50   **c** 99   **d** 105   **e** 217   **f** 303

2 Convert these Mayan symbols into our numbers:

CHINESE - JAPANESE

The Chinese and Japanese also use a system similar to the multiplication or 'lots of' system.

1	2	3	4	5	6
一	二	三	四	五	六

Their symbols look like these:

7	8	9	10	100	1000
七	八	九	十	百	千

This is how 4983 would be written:

四千　} 4 'lots' of 1000
　　　＋
九百　} 9 'lots' of 100
　　　＋
八十　} 8 'lots' of 10
　　　＋
三　　　3

EXERCISE 1A.4

1 What are the numbers represented by these symbols?
   a 七百六十五   **b** 三千二百四十八   **c** 九千九百九十九

2 Write these numbers using the Chinese-Japanese system:
   a 497   **b** 8400   **c** 1111

3 Draw this grid in your book and complete the missing symbols:

	Words	Hindu-Arabic	Roman	Egyptian	Mayan	Chinese-Japanese
a	thirty seven	37				
b				⌒||||		
c			CLIX			
d					••••⌢	

ACTIVITY — UNDERSTANDING NUMBER SYSTEMS

What to do:

1 Using the *History of Number* as your topic, research and prepare a short talk in which you use and explain the words **archaeologists**, **cultures**, **anthropologists**, **hieroglyphics**, **BC**, **AD** and **tally**.

2 Suggest reasons for the different markings Egyptians, Romans, Mayans, Chinese and Japanese used in their number systems. Check your suggestions by researching.

3 From your understanding of ancient times, list the different reasons, situations, methods and materials different groups of people may have used as a method for counting. For example:

Knots on the rope — Notches cut on the branch — Pebbles on sand — Scratches on a cave wall

4 The most portable method for counting or measuring a quantity involved using parts of the body. Today we still use "a pinch of salt", "a handful of peanuts" and a "a sip of medicine". The height of a horse is still measured in "hands".

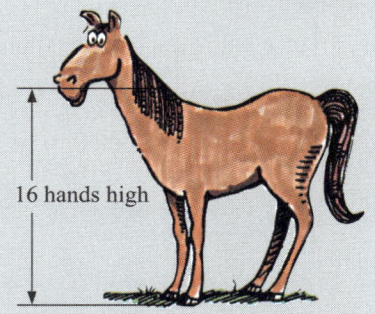

16 hands high

  a In groups list other ways the body is used for counting.

  b Research other systems to find out how the body was/is used for counting. Present your findings.

5 Match these numbers! Use matchsticks to solve these puzzles.

  a Move just one matchstick to make this correct.

  b Move one matchstick to make this correct.

  c Arrange 4 matchsticks to make a total of 15.

  d Make it work without removing any matchsticks.

  e Remove 3 matchsticks from this sum to make the equation correct.

$$IV - II = V$$
$$III - II = IV$$
$$XI + I = X$$
$$VII + I = I$$

B OUR NUMBER SYSTEM

The method of writing numbers is called a **number system**. The system we use was developed in India 2000 years ago, and was introduced by Arab traders about 1000 years ago. We therefore call our system the **Hindu-Arabic System**.

The marks we use to represent numbers are called **numerals**. They are made up by using the symbols 1, 2, 3, 4, 5, 6, 7, 8, 9 and 0. These symbols are called **digits**.

The digits 4 and 7 can be used to form the numeral '47' for number 'forty seven' and numeral '74' for number 'seventy four'.

In Latin '*numerus*' means **number**.

In most of our work we are not concerned about the difference between numeral and number. We use the word number on most occasions.

The numbers we use for counting are called **natural numbers**. The possible combination of natural numbers is endless. There is no largest natural number. We say the set of all natural numbers is **infinite**. Natural numbers are also called **counting numbers**. If we include in our set of numbers the number zero, 0, then our set now has a new name, the set of **whole numbers**.

The Hindu-Arabic system is more useful and more efficient than the systems used by the Egyptians, Romans or Mayans.

- It uses only 10 digits to construct all the natural numbers.
- It uses the digit 0 or zero to show an empty place value.
- It has a place value system where digits represent different numbers when placed in different place value columns.

Example 1

What number is represented by the digit 3 in the numeral 4389?

Three hundred or 300.

EXERCISE 1B

1 What number is represented by the digit 8 in the following?
   - a 38
   - b 81
   - c 458
   - d 847
   - e 1981
   - f 8247
   - g 2861
   - h 28 902
   - i 60 008
   - j 84 019
   - k 78 794
   - l 189 964

2 What is the place value of the digit 7 in the following?
   - a 497
   - b 37 482
   - c 856 784
   - d 755 846

3 Write down the place value of the 3, the 5 and the 8 in each of the following:
   - a 53 486
   - b 3580
   - c 50 083
   - d 805 340

4
   - a Use the digits 6, 4 and 8 once only to make the largest number you can.
   - b Write the largest number you can using the digits 4, 1, 0, 7, 2 and 9 once only.
   - c What is the largest 6 digit numeral you can write using each of the digits 2, 7 and 9 twice?
   - d How many different numbers can you write using the digits 3, 4 and 5 once only?

5 Put the following numbers in ascending order (beginning with the smallest):
   - a 57, 8, 75, 16, 54, 19
   - b 660, 60, 600, 6, 606
   - c 1080, 1808, 1800, 1008, 1880
   - d 45 061, 46 510, 40 561, 46 051, 46 501
   - e 236 705, 227 635, 207 653, 265 703
   - f 554 922, 594 522, 545 922, 595 242

6 Write the following numbers in descending order (largest first):
   - a 361, 136, 163, 613, 316, 631
   - b 7789, 7987, 9787, 8779, 8977, 7897, 9877
   - c 498 231, 428 931, 492 813, 428 391, 498 321
   - d 563 074, 576 304, 675 034, 607 543, 673 540

Example 2

a Express $3 \times 10\,000 + 4 \times 1000 + 8 \times 10 + 5 \times 1$ in simplest form.
b Write 9602 in expanded form.

---

a $3 \times 10\,000 + 4 \times 1000 + 8 \times 10 + 5 \times 1 = 34\,085$

b $9602 = 9 \times 1000 + 6 \times 100 + 2 \times 1$

7 Express the following in simplest form:
   - a $8 \times 10 + 6 \times 1$
   - b $6 \times 100 + 7 \times 10 + 4 \times 1$
   - c $9 \times 1000 + 6 \times 100 + 3 \times 10 + 8 \times 1$
   - d $5 \times 10\,000 + 2 \times 100 + 4 \times 10$

    e $2 \times 10\,000 + 7 \times 1000 + 3 \times 1$
    f $2 \times 100 + 7 \times 10\,000 + 3 \times 1000 + 9 \times 10 + 8 \times 1$
    g $3 \times 100 + 5 \times 100\,000 + 7 \times 10 + 5 \times 1$
    h $8 \times 100\,000 + 9 \times 1000 + 3 \times 100 + 2 \times 1$

8 Write in expanded form:
    a 975   **b** 680   **c** 3874   **d** 9083
    e 56 742   **f** 75 007   **g** 600 829   **h** 354 718

Example 3

Write in numeral form the number "seven thousand four hundred and eight".

7408

---

9 Write the following in numeral form:
    a twenty seven
    b eighty
    c six hundred and eight
    d one thousand and sixteen
    e eight thousand two hundred
    f nineteen thousand five hundred and thirty eight
    g seventy five thousand four hundred and three
    h six hundred and two thousand eight hundred and eighteen.

10 What number is:
    a one less than eight
    b two greater than eleven
    c four more than seventeen
    d one less than three hundred
    e seven greater than four thousand
    f 3 less than 10 000
    g four more than four hundred thousand
    h 26 greater than two hundred and nine thousand?

Remember:
    $=$ reads "is equal to"
    $\doteq$ or $\approx$ reads "is approximately equal to"
    $>$ reads "is greater than"
    $<$ reads "is less than"

11 In the following replace $\square$ by $=$ or $\doteq$:
    a $375 + 836 \,\square\, 1200$
    b $79 \times 8 \,\square\, 640$
    c $978 - 463 \,\square\, 515$
    d $7980 \div 20 \,\square\, 400$
    e $455 + 544 \,\square\, 999$
    f $50 \times 400 \,\square\, 20\,000$
    g $2000 - 1010 \,\square\, 990$
    h $3000 \div 300 \,\square\, 10$

12 In the following replace $\triangle$ by $>$ or $<$:
    a $5268 - 3179 \,\triangle\, 4169$
    b $29 \times 30 \,\triangle\, 900$
    c $672 + 762 \,\triangle\, 1444$
    d $720 \div 80 \,\triangle\, 8$
    e $20 \times 80 \,\triangle\, 160$
    f $700 \times 80 \,\triangle\, 54\,000$
    g $5649 + 7205 \,\triangle\, 12\,844$
    h $6060 - 606 \,\triangle\, 5444$

C ROUNDING NUMBERS

Often we are not really interested in the exact value of a number, but rather we want a reasonable estimate of it.

For example:

the number of spectators at an AFL match at the MCG was 43 759. We are only interested in an approximate number, possibly to the nearest thousand, and 43 759 ≑ 44 000. There were approximately 44 000 spectators. We have rounded off the number.

We may round off numbers by making them into, for example, the nearest number of tens:

    258 is roughly 26 tens or 260

    253 is roughly 25 tens or 250.

We say 258 is rounded up to 260 and 253 is rounded down to 250. When we say 258 is roughly or approximately equal to 26 tens we can use the symbol ≑ or ≈ to mean "is approximately equal to".

So, 258 ≑ 260.

≑ and ≈ are both used to represent the phrase "is approximately equal to".

When a number is halfway between tens we always round up, so 255 ≑ 260.

Rules for rounding off are:

- If the digit after the one being rounded off is **less than 5** (i.e., 0, 1, 2, 3 or 4) we round **down**.
- If the digit after the one being rounded off is **5 or more** (i.e., 5, 6, 7, 8, 9) we round **up**.

Example 4

Round off the following to the nearest 10:
  a 48   **b** 583   **c** 5705

a 48 ≑ 50   {Round up, as 8 is greater than 5}

b 583 ≑ 580   {Round down, as 3 is less than 5}

c 5705 ≑ 5710   {Round up, halfway is always rounded up}

EXERCISE 1C

1 Round off to the nearest 10:

  a 75   **b** 78   **c** 298   **d** 2379
  e 3994   **f** 1651   **g** 9797   **h** 61 015
  i 49 566   **j** 30 942   **k** 999 571   **l** 128 674

20　WHOLE NUMBERS　(CHAPTER 1)

> **Example 5**
>
> Round off the following to the nearest 100:　**a** 452　　**b** 37 239
>
> **a**　452 ≑ 500　　{Round up for 5 or more}
> **b**　37 239 ≑ 37 200　{Round down, as 3 is less than 5}

2 Round off to the nearest 100:
- **a** 78
- **b** 468
- **c** 998
- **d** 2954
- **e** 25 449
- **f** 14 765
- **g** 130 009
- **h** 43 951

> **Example 6**
>
> Round off the following to the nearest 1000:
> **a** 873　**b** 3500　**c** 33 407
>
> **a**　873 ≑ 1000　　{Round up, as 8 is greater than 5}
> **b**　3500 ≑ 4000　　{Round up for 5 or more}
> **c**　33 407 ≑ 33 000　{Round down, as 4 is less than 5}

3 Round off to the nearest 1000:
- **a** 748
- **b** 5500
- **c** 9990
- **d** 43 743
- **e** 65 438
- **f** 123 456
- **g** 434 576
- **h** 570 846

4 Round off to the accuracy given:
- **a** $45 387 (to the nearest $1000)
- **b** 328 kg (to the nearest ten kg)
- **c** a weekly wage of $485 (to the nearest $100)
- **d** a distance of 4753 km (to the nearest 100 km)
- **e** the annual amount of water used in a household was 362 498 litres (to the nearest kilolitre)
- **f** the profit of a company was $487 374 (to nearest $10 000)
- **g** the population of a town is 37 495 (to nearest one thousand)
- **h** the population of a city is 637 952 (to nearest hundred thousand)
- **i** the number of times the average heart will beat in one year is 35 765 280 times (to nearest million)
- **j** a year's loss by a large mining company was $1 517 493 826 (to nearest billion).

HOME RESEARCH — ROUNDING

Use resources around your home to find the following and then round off to the accuracy requested:

1. The number of local telephone calls your household made in one year (to nearest 10).
2. The number of litres of water your household used in one year (nearest kilolitre).
3. The distance the family car travelled in one year (nearest 1000).
4. The distance in kilometres you travelled to school and back in one year (nearest 10).
5. The number of times your heart beats in one day (nearest ten thousand).
6. The number of hours you spend each year watching television or playing computer games (nearest 100).

LIBRARY RESEARCH — ROUNDING

Research the following and round off to the accuracy requested. Do not forget to record the name and date of publication of the reference (book/magazine title, CD-ROM), the value given in the reference and your rounded value.

1. The population of your nearest capital city (nearest 10 000).
2. The speed of light (nearest 1000 km per hour).
3. The railway distance between Adelaide and Perth (nearest 100 km).
4. The population of Australia (nearest 100 000).
5. The population of the world (nearest billion).
6. The distance to the sun (nearest million km).

D ADDING AND SUBTRACTING WHOLE NUMBERS

In this section we will review the operations between numbers.

ADDITION

Example 7

Find: $32 + 427 + 3274$

We rewrite in columns where we can add the units digits, the 10's digits, etc.

$$\begin{array}{r} 32 \\ 427 \\ +\ 3274 \\ \underline{1\ 1} \\ 3733 \end{array}$$

EXERCISE 1D

1 Do these additions:

a 392
 + 415

b 601
 + 729

c 1917
 + 2078

d 913
   24
 + 707

e 217
   106
 + 1274

f 9004
   216
   23
 + 3816

2 Find:

a 42 + 37
b 72 + 35
c 421 + 327
d 624 + 72
e 921 + 1234
f 6214 + 324 + 27
g 90 + 724
h 32 + 627 + 4296
i 912 + 6 + 427 + 3274

SUBTRACTION

Example 8

Find: a 207 − 128   b 4200 − 326

a $\overset{1\ 9\ 17}{2\ 0\ 7}$
 − 1 2 8
   ───
    7 9

b $\overset{3\ 11\ 9\ 10}{4\ 2\ 0\ 0}$
 −   3 2 6
   ─────
   3 8 7 4

3 Do these subtractions:

a 97
 − 15

b 63
 − 19

c 247
 − 138

d 602
 − 149

e 713
 − 48

f 6005
 − 2349

4 Find:

a 47 − 13
b 62 − 14
c 33 − 27
d 40 − 18
e 214 − 32
f 623 − 147
g 503 − 127
h 5003 − 1236

WORD PROBLEMS

We will now look at solving some **word problems** where the solution depends on **addition** or **subtraction**.

A number sentence is needed in order to answer the problem.

Example 9

John filled a wheelbarrow with 5 kg of potatoes, 3 kg of carrots, 7 kg of onions and 25 kg of pumpkin. What was the total weight of John's vegetables?

Total weight $= 5 + 3 + 7 + 25$
$\phantom{\text{Total weight }}= 40$ kg

5 **a** Jack bought 4 separate lengths of timber. Their lengths were as follows: 5 m, 1 m, 7 m, and 9 m. If all four lengths of timber were put end to end how long would the total length be?

b Jenny bought a play station for $255. She also purchased another controller for $50, a play station game for $95 and a bag to store these in for $32. How much did she pay altogether?

c Kerry needed to lose some weight to be chosen in a light weight rowing team. He weighed 60 kg but needed to weigh 54 kg. How much weight did he need to lose?

d Stephen made $72 worth of phone calls in one month. His parents said they would only pay $31 of this. How much did Stephen have to pay?

e Miki had 65 minutes of time left on her prepaid cellphone. She made a 10 minute call to Rupesh, a 7 minute call to her mother and a 26 minute call to her boyfriend Michael. How many minutes did she have left after making these calls?

f Rima went on an overseas trip that required three plane flights. The first flight was 2142 km long, the next one was 732 km long and the third one was 1049 km long. How long was her flight in total?

g Bill measured out a straight line that was 6010 cm long on the school grounds. He actually went too far. The line should have been 4832 cm long. How much of the line will he need to rub out?

E   MULTIPLYING AND DIVIDING WHOLE NUMBERS

MULTIPLYING BY POWERS OF 10   (REVIEW)

When we multiply by   10   we make a number 10 times larger
100 we make a number 100 times larger
1000 we make a number 1000 times larger

24 WHOLE NUMBERS (CHAPTER 1)

Example 10

Find: **a** 23×10 **b** 89×100 **c** 381×1000

a 23×10
      $= 230$

b 89×100
      $= 8900$

c 381×1000
      $= 381\,000$

The first three powers of 10 are 10, 100 and 1000.

Notice that multiplying by 100 (1 with *two* 0s) shifts the decimal point *two* places to the right.

$$89 \times 100 = 89.00$$
$$= 8900$$

EXERCISE 1E

1 Find: (You could do these mentally.)

a 50×10	**b** 50×100	**c** 50×1000
d 69×100	**e** 69×1000	**f** $69 \times 10\,000$
g 123×100	**h** 246×1000	**i** 960×100
j $49 \times 10\,000$	**k** 490×100	**l** 4900×100

DIVIDING BY POWERS OF 10 (REVIEW)

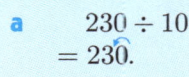

When we divide by 10 we make a number 10 times smaller
                  100 we make a number 100 times smaller
                  1000 we make a number 1000 times smaller

Example 11

Find: **a** $230 \div 10$ **b** $230 \div 100$ **c** $230 \div 1000$

a $230 \div 10$
      $= 230.$
      $= 23$

b $230 \div 100$
      $= 230.$
      $= 2.3$

c $230 \div 1000$
      $= 230.$
      $= 0.23$

Notice that in **b** the answer 2.3 is 2 with remainder 0.3

2 Find: (You could do these mentally.)

a $2000 \div 10$	**b** $2000 \div 100$	**c** $2000 \div 1000$
d $570 \div 10$	**e** $570 \div 100$	**f** $570 \div 1000$
g $243 \div 10$	**h** $243 \div 100$	**i** $243 \div 1000$
j $4500 \div 10$	**k** $4500 \div 100$	**l** $4500 \div 1000$
m $72 \div 10$	**n** $72 \div 100$	**o** $72 \div 1000$
p $6 \div 10$	**q** $6 \div 100$	**r** $6 \div 1000$

MULTIPLYING LARGER WHOLE NUMBERS

Example 12

Find: a 67×4 b 53×16 c 428×54

a
```
    6 7
  ×   4
  ─────
    2 6 8
```

b
```
      5 3
  ×   1 6
  ───────
      3 1 8
      5 3 0
  ───────
      8 4 8
```

c
```
        4 2 8
    ×    5 4
    ─────────
        1 7 1 2
      2 1 4 0 0
    ─────────
      2 3 1 1 2
```

3 Find:

a 24×5 b 37×4 c 62×8 d 53×24
e 27×15 f 56×49 g 324×45 h 642×36
i 274×21 j 958×47 k 117×89 l 368×73

DIVISION BY A SINGLE DIGIT NUMBER

Example 13

Find: a $256 \div 4$ b $325 \div 5$ c $2502 \div 6$

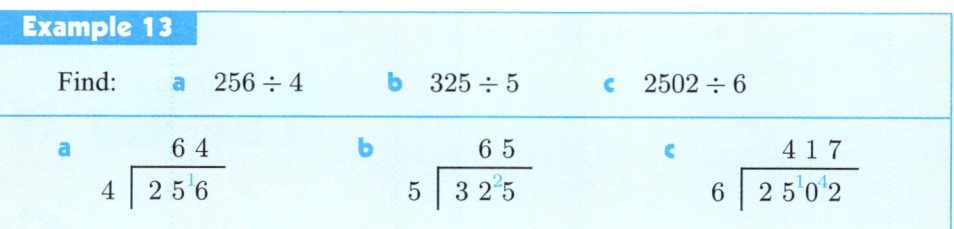

4 Do these divisions:

a $3\overline{\smash{)}42}$ b $4\overline{\smash{)}216}$ c $8\overline{\smash{)}168}$
d $5\overline{\smash{)}375}$ e $7\overline{\smash{)}6307}$ f $11\overline{\smash{)}6809}$

5 Find:

a $24 \div 4$ b $125 \div 5$ c $312 \div 6$
d $240 \div 5$ e $624 \div 3$ f $7353 \div 9$

Example 14

Find: a $1268 \div 5$ b $351 \div 4$

a
```
         2 5 3 . 6
    5 ) 1 2 ²6 ¹8 .³0
```
So, $1268 \div 5 = 253.6$

b
```
          8 7 . 7 5
    4 ) 3 5 ³1 .³0 ²0
```
So, $351 \div 4 = 87.75$

6 Find:

- **a** 45 ÷ 2
- **b** 63 ÷ 4
- **c** 81 ÷ 5
- **d** 97 ÷ 8
- **e** 143 ÷ 2
- **f** 275 ÷ 4
- **g** 439 ÷ 5
- **h** 661 ÷ 8
- **i** 955 ÷ 2
- **j** 1033 ÷ 4
- **k** 1201 ÷ 5
- **l** 4699 ÷ 8
- **m** 7349 ÷ 2
- **n** 8463 ÷ 4
- **o** 7999 ÷ 5

> **Example 15**
>
> Jason buys 217 baskets of fresh cherries for a supermarket chain at $38 a basket. What will be the total cost?
>
> Total cost = 217 × $38
> = $8246
>
> ```
>       2 1 7
>   ×  ₁3 8
>       ₂₅
>     1 7 3 6
>     6 5 1 0
>      ₁
>     8 2 4 6
> ```

7

a Carlo lifted five 18 kg bags of potatoes onto a truck. How many kg of potatoes did he lift altogether?

b My three brothers and I received a gift of $320. If we shared the money equally amongst ourselves how much did each person receive?

c A relay team of nine people took 738 minutes to complete a relay race. If each team member took exactly the same time how long did each team member take?

d This maths textbook is 245 mm long. If I put 10 books end to end how far would they stretch?

e 24 people each travelled 28 km to play sport. How far in total did they travel?

f If I write 8 words per minute how long would it take me to write 648 words?

g How much would June pay for 8 iced buns if 3 buns cost her 54 cents?

ESTIMATION AND APPROXIMATION

Calculators and computers are part of everyday life. They save lots of time, energy and money by the speed and accuracy with which they complete different operations.

However the people operating the computers and calculators can and do make mistakes when keying in the information.

It is very important that when we use calculators we have a strategy for making an **estimate** of what the answer should be. An estimate is not a guess. It is a quick and easy **approximation** of the correct answer.

By making an estimate we can tell if our calculated or computed answer is **reasonable**.

ROUNDING SMALLER AMOUNTS OF MONEY

In Australia, although we still price goods in cents, most businesses round to the nearest 5 cents.

For example, $2.87 would be rounded down to $2.85 and $2.88 would be rounded up to $2.90.

However for the purpose of estimation, money is rounded to the nearest whole dollar. Amounts between $1.00 and $1.49 are rounded to one dollar, and amounts $1.50 and up to $1.99 are rounded to $2.00.

When estimating sums, products, quotients and differences we usually round the first digit (from the left) and put zeros in other places.

For example:
- 59 would round to 60
- 178 would round to 200
- 3431 would round to 3000
- and 51 974 would round to 50 000.

Round each number to one figure before multiplying. For example: $41 \times 287 \doteqdot 40 \times 300$

Example 16

Estimate the cost of 19 pens at $1.95 each.

$19 \times \$1.95 \doteqdot 20 \times \$2$
$\doteqdot \$40$

EXERCISE 1F

1 Estimate the cost of:
- **a** 195 exercise books at 98 cents each
- **b** 27 sweets packets at $2.15 a packet
- **c** 18 show bags at $3.45 each
- **d** 12 bottles of drink at $2.95 a bottle
- **e** 4 dozen iceblocks at $1.20 each
- **f** 3850 football tickets at $6.50 each.

ACTIVITY — COSTLESS SHOPPING

What to do:

a How well can you estimate the prices in shops? Before you enter a store, have a friend nominate 10 items for you to estimate the price. You also nominate 10 different items for your friend to estimate.

Write down these estimations. As you walk through the store, compare your estimates with the actual costs. The winner is the one with the most best estimates.

b Play similar games in variety stores, electrical stores, fast food outlets and car yards.

The more accurate you become the more aware you will be of the value of goods.

2 Use estimates of each item to the nearest $10.

  a Estimate the total cost of a game console, a game controller and a skateboard.

  b What is the approximate total cost of a pair of track pants, roller blades, a crash helmet and the latest video movie?

  c Would $300 be enough for the game console and the women's track shoes?

  d Approximately how much change from $200 would you have if you bought the bike, the netball and the clock radio?

Skateboard $38.99
Roller Blades $42.99
Crash Helmet $24.95
50cm BMX Bike $113
Game Console $187

Netball $19.99

Latest Movie Releases $19.95

Clock Radio $34.90

Track Pants $39.99

Portable CD Player $229

Game Controller $48.95

Women's Track Shoes $119.99

ONE FIGURE APPROXIMATIONS

> **Rules:**
> - Leave single digit numbers as they are.
> - Round all other numbers to single figure approximations.

For example, 3785×7
$\doteq 4000 \times 7$
$\doteq 28\,000$

Example 17

Estimate the product: **a** 57×8 **b** 537×6

a Round off to the first digit; put zeros in the other places.
57×8
$\doteq 60 \times 8$
$\doteq 480$

b Round off to the first digit; put zeros in other places.
537×6
$\doteq 500 \times 6$
$\doteq 3000$

3 Estimate the following products:
- **a** 79×4
- **b** 47×8
- **c** 62×7
- **d** 88×6
- **e** 55×3
- **f** 37×5

4 Multiply the following. Use estimation to check that your answers are reasonable.
- **a** 59×7
- **b** 83×9
- **c** 75×5

5 Estimate the products:
- **a** 284×3
- **b** 617×7
- **c** 408×9
- **d** 494×6
- **e** 817×8
- **f** 2094×7

6 Multiply the following. Use estimation to check that your answers are reasonable.
- **a** 679×7
- **b** 445×8
- **c** 3759×9

Example 18

Estimate the product: 623×69

Round off to the first digit; put zeros in the other places.
623×69
$\doteq 600 \times 70$ {3 zeros in the question}
$\doteq 42\,000$ {3 zeros in the answer}

The estimate tells us the correct answer should have 5 digits in it.

The sum of the number of zeros is the number of zeros which should appear in the product, unless the product of two digits ends in zero.

Example 19

Estimate the product: 387 × 891

Round off to the first digit; put zeros in the other places.
$$387 \times 891$$
$$\approx 400 \times 900 \quad \{4 \text{ zeros in the question}\}$$
$$\approx 360\,000 \quad \{4 \text{ zeros in the answer}\}$$
In this case notice that the rounded numbers were both higher than the real value. We expect the answer to have 6 digits and it will be less than 360 000.

7 Estimate the following products using 1 figure approximations:
- **a** 57 × 42
- **b** 73 × 59
- **c** 85 × 98
- **d** 275 × 54
- **e** 389 × 73
- **f** 4971 × 32
- **g** 3079 × 29
- **h** 40 989 × 9
- **i** 880 × 750

Example 20

Find the approximate value of the quotient of 3946 ÷ 79.

$$3946 \div 79 \approx 4000 \div 80$$
$$\approx 400 \div 8$$
$$\approx 50$$

8 Estimate the following quotients using 1 figure approximations:
- **a** 397 ÷ 4
- **b** 6849 ÷ 7
- **c** 79 095 ÷ 8
- **d** 6000 ÷ 19
- **e** 80 000 ÷ 37
- **f** 18 700 ÷ 97
- **g** 549 ÷ 49
- **h** 3038 ÷ 28
- **i** 5899 ÷ 30
- **j** 2780 ÷ 41
- **k** 48 097 ÷ 243
- **l** 798 450 ÷ 399

9 Use estimation only to find which of these calculator answers is reasonable:

- **a** 489 × 19   9291   96 081   92 901
- **b** 843 × 74   56 382   560 382   62 38
- **c** 3907 × 89   347 723   5 361 243   35 723
- **d** 3132 ÷ 87   3600   36   306

10 In the following questions, round the given data to one figure to find the approximate value asked for:

- **a** In her bookcase Lynda has 12 shelves. Estimate the number of books in the bookcase if there are approximately 40 books on each shelf.
- **b** Miki reads 217 words in a minute. Estimate the number of words she can read in one hour.

c A bricklayer lays 115 bricks each hour. If he works a $37\frac{1}{2}$ hour week, approximately how many bricks will he lay in one month?

d If Joe can type at 52 words per minute, find an approximate time for him to type a document of 3820 words.

e In a vineyard there are 189 vines in each row. There are 54 rows. Find the approximate number of vines in the vineyard.

f One of South Australia's largest wineries bottles 480 000 cases of wine each year. If each case holds one dozen bottles, approximately how many bottles of wine are produced each year?

g If a trip of 1423 km from Adelaide to Sydney took 19 hours, find the approximate average speed in kilometres per hour.

h An electricity supply company employs 19 people to read meters. If each reader takes approximately 3 minutes to read one meter, estimate how many meters are read each hour.

ESTIMATION OF NUMBERS OF OBJECTS

We may not need an exact answer when counting, for example, the number of people in a crowd as seen on a photograph. The method shown in the next example could be used.

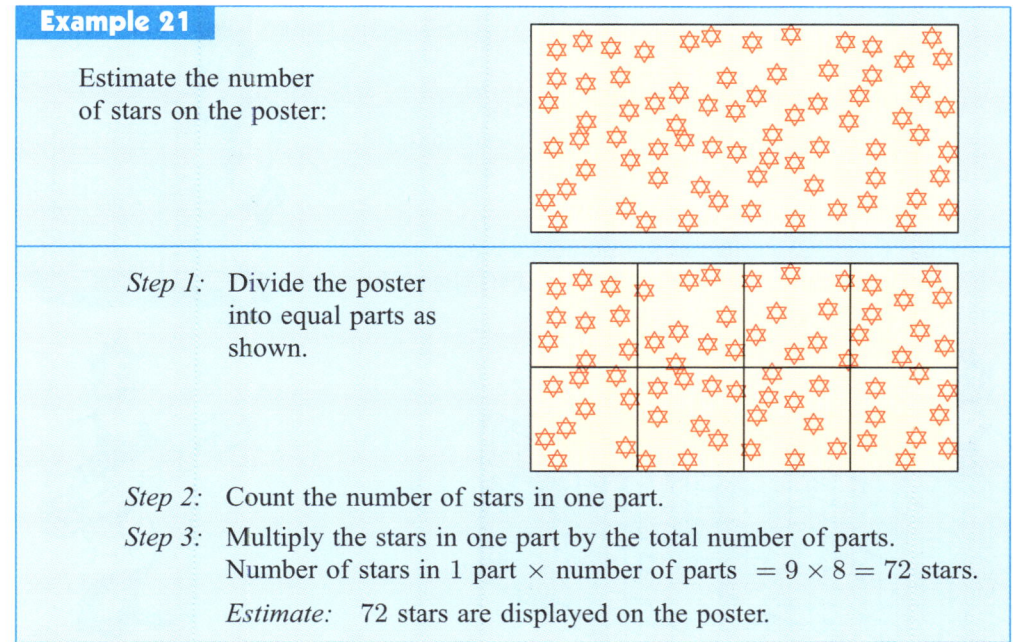

Example 21

Estimate the number of stars on the poster:

Step 1: Divide the poster into equal parts as shown.

Step 2: Count the number of stars in one part.

Step 3: Multiply the stars in one part by the total number of parts.
Number of stars in 1 part × number of parts $= 9 \times 8 = 72$ stars.

Estimate: 72 stars are displayed on the poster.

11 Estimate the number of objects in:

a

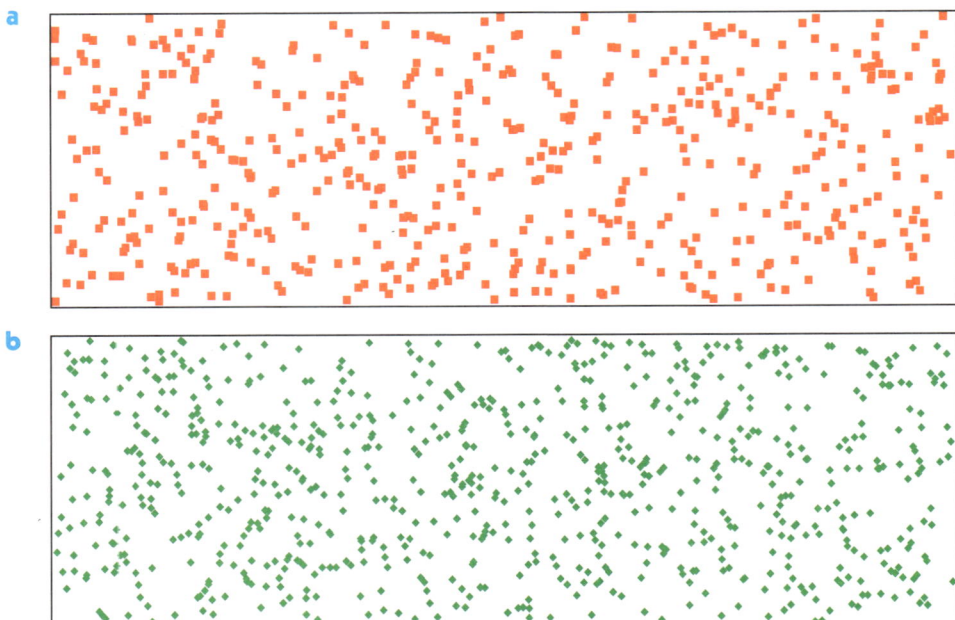

b

12 Click on the icon to bring up objects to be estimated. Play with the software to improve your estimating skills. Note that the coloured square which appears is chosen at random by the computer.

RANDOM COUNTING

G   HOW BIG IS ONE MILLION?

One million is written 1 000 000.

If we had enough timber to make a place value block to represent 1 million unit blocks and then had the strength to lift it into the classroom it would look like this.

Each of the 'flats' (B) in the million unit cube would contain 100 000 unit blocks. (There would be 10 flats (B) each containing 100 000 unit blocks.)

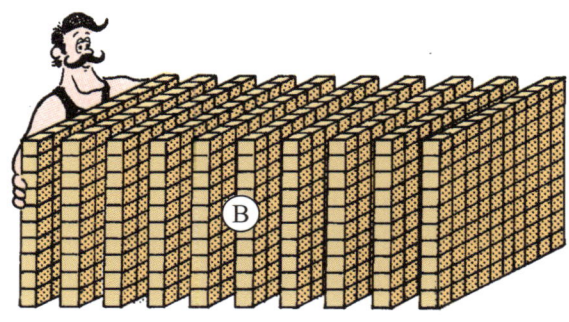

Each of the 'longs' (C) in each of the flats (B) would contain 10 000 unit blocks.

There would be 10 longs (C) in each flat (B) and $10 \times 10\,000 = 100\,000$.

There would be 100 longs (C) in each cube (A), each containing 10 000 unit blocks and $100 \times 10\,000 = 1\,000\,000$.

ACTIVITY   ONE MILLION CUBES

What to do:

1. Collect 10 of your school's 1000 unit cube blocks and arrange them into a long (C). How many of your school's 1000 blocks would be needed to have 1 000 000 units? How could you show this in the classroom?

2. How much would 1 million MA unit blocks weigh? Describe the most accurate way you could find their weight. Remember that your 1000 unit blocks may not be made of solid wood.

3. Look at a single unit cube. Measure it with a ruler. You should find that it is 10 mm long. It is also 10 mm wide and 10 mm deep.

   In fact one centicube is 10 mm × 10 mm × 10 mm i.e., 1000 mm^3 or 1000 cubic millimetres.

   One thousand centicubes is
   1000×1000 mm$^3 = 1\,000\,000$ mm^3.

   Find the block which has 1000 unit cubes. This is also the block which represents 1 000 000 cubic millimetres (mm^3).

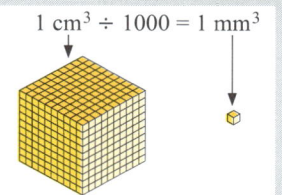

$1 \text{ cm}^3 \div 1000 = 1 \text{ mm}^3$

FACTS ABOUT 'A MILLION'

Example 22

How far would 1 million one dollar coins, placed side by side, stretch?
Note: $1 \text{ km} = 1000 \text{ m} = 100\,000 \text{ cm}$

2.5 cm

    1 million × 2.5 cm
$= 2.5 \times 1\,000\,000$ cm
$= 2\,500\,000$ cm
$= (2\,500\,000 \div 100\,000)$ km
$= 2\,500\,000$.
$= 25$ km

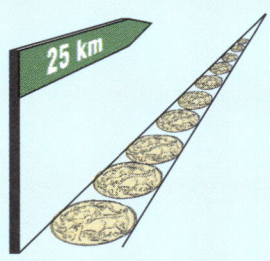

EXERCISE 1G

1. How long would a motor cyclist travelling non-stop at 50 kilometres per hour take to travel one million kilometres?

2. How many hours would a jumbo jet, flying non-stop at 500 kilometres per hour, take to fly 1 million kilometres? Give your answer in days and hours.

3. How long would a car, travelling non-stop at 100 kilometres per hour, take to travel a million kilometres?

4. A $5 note is 135 mm long.
   a. How far would one million $5 notes laid out end to end in a straight line stretch?
   b. If you walked from one end of the line to the other at a walking speed of 5 kmph, how long would it take?

5. How long would a satellite orbiting the earth at 8000 kmph take to fly 1 million kms?

6. One million one dollar coins stacked on top of one another would be 2700 metres high. That is about 8 times higher than Auckland's Sky Tower, 9 times higher than Sydney's Centrepoint Tower and over 4 times higher than the world's tallest tower, the Canadian National Tower in Toronto, Canada.

   How many coins are there for:
   a. one metre (to the nearest 10 coins)
   b. each of the illustrated buildings (to the nearest 1000 coins)?

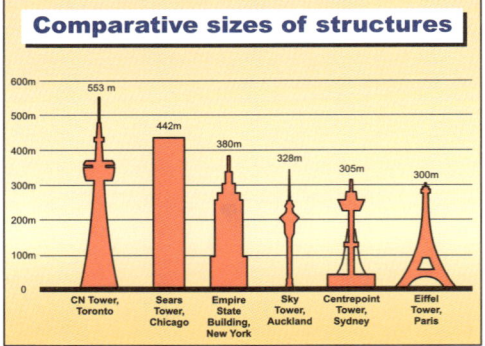

Example 23

How many capacity crowds of 100 000 would the Melbourne Cricket Ground need to reach 1 million spectators?

Number of times
= 1 000 000 ÷ 100 000
= 10

7 In the following questions, how many times does the given container need to be filled to hold 1 000 000 units?

- **a** fuel tank holding 50 litres
- **b** packet containing 250 sugar cubes
- **c** school hall seating 400 students
- **d** rainwater tank holding 2000 litres
- **e** case packed with 100 oranges
- **f** carriage for 80 passengers
- **g** restaurant feeding 125 diners
- **h** computer disk cartridges with 40 disks
- **i** crates holding 160 cans
- **j** stackers storing 8 CDs

Did you know?

The milk from 1 000 000 litre cartons would fill a 50 metre long by 20 metre wide pool to a depth of 1 metre.

8 Use your calculator to complete the following:

- **a** 1 000 000 seconds = ... minutes = ... hours = ... days
- **b** 1 000 000 minutes = ... hours = ... days = ... weeks
- **c** 1 000 000 hours = ... days = ... weeks = ... years
- **d** 1 000 000 days = ... years
- **e** 1 000 000 years = ... centuries = ... millenniums

You will need to know your time facts.

ACTIVITY — A MILLION

What to do:

1 Find out the seating capacity of your school hall. Determine how many such halls would need to be filled to seat one million people.

2 Look at the clock or your watch now. Record the time to the nearest 15 minutes. For example, if it is 11 minutes and 30 seconds past 10, record it as 10:15.

Use a calendar to work out what the day, date and time was 1 000 000 seconds ago. What will be the day, date and time 1 million seconds from now?

Try working out the day, date and time:

- **a** a million minutes into the future
- **b** a million hours back into the past.

3 The White Pages of the telephone directory lists telephone numbers alphabetically in 5 columns per page. Each column has approximately 100 telephone numbers. One million telephone listings would need 2500 pages, as $\dfrac{1\,000\,000}{5 \times 100} = 2000$.

Approximately how many numbers are listed in your area's White Pages?

4 Without actually counting one million grains of rice, outline the steps you would take to see what the volume, mass or area one million grains of rice would measure.

    a Using the steps you have suggested, find out:
        i the volume of 1 000 000 grains of rice
        ii the mass of 1 000 000 grains of rice
        iii the area, to a depth of one grain of rice, that one million grains of rice would cover.
    b Compare your measurements and calculations with your classmates.
    c List the reasons your results may be different.
    d How could you have improved the accuracy of your measurements?

5 A jogger starts running at midday Monday on the day of his thirteenth birthday which is the first of January in a leap year.

    a How old will he be if he runs non-stop at 10 kilometres per hour for one million kilometres?
    b What will be the day and month at the end of his run?
    c If he rests for twelve hours each day and runs at 10 kmph for the other twelve hours:
        i how old will he be at the end of one million kilometres
        ii what will be the day and month at the end of his run?

H   NUMBERS BEYOND ONE MILLION

Commas (,) were once used to make it easier to read numbers greater than 3 digits. For example, 2,954 two thousand, nine hundred and fifty four and 4,234,685 four million, two hundred and thirty four thousand, six hundred and eighty five would have been much easier to read than 2954 and 4234685.

Now a space has replaced the comma. Can you suggest some reasons for this?

Millions			Thousands			Units		
hundreds	tens	units	hundreds	tens	units	hundreds	tens	units
	5	3	4	7	9	6	8	2

The number displayed in the place value chart is 53 million, 479 thousand, 682. To make the number easier to read the digits are arranged into the units, the thousands and the millions. With spaces now used to separate the groups, the number on the place-value chart is written 53 479 682.

4,234,685 out   4 234 685 in

EXERCISE 1H

1 In the number shown on the chart above, the digit 9 has the value 9000 and the digit 3 has the value 3 000 000. Give the value of the:
   a 8   **b** 5   **c** 6   **d** 4   **e** 7   **f** 2

2 Write the value of each digit in the following numbers:
   a 3 648 597   **b** 34 865 271

3 Read the following stories about large numbers. Write each large number using figures.
   a A heart beating at a rate of 70 beats per minute would beat about thirty seven million times in a year.
   b Australia's largest hamburger chain bought two hundred million bread buns and used seventeen million kilograms of beef in one year.
   c The Jurassic era was about one hundred and fifty million years ago.
   d One hundred and eleven million, two hundred and forty thousand, four hundred and sixty three dollars and ten cents was won by two people in a Powerball Lottery in Wisconsin USA in 1993.
   e A total of twenty one million, two hundred and forty thousand, six hundred and fifty seven Volkswagen 'Beetles' had been built to the end of 1995.
   f In a lifetime the average person will blink four hundred and fifteen million times.
   g One Megabyte of data is one million, forty eight thousand, five hundred and seventy six bytes.

4 Arrange these planets in order of their distance from the Sun starting with the closest.

Venus	108 200 000 kms
Saturn	1 427 000 000 kms
Earth	149 600 000 kms
Uranus	2 870 000 000 kms
Mercury	57 900 000 kms
Jupiter	778 300 000 kms
Pluto	5 900 000 000 kms
Neptune	4 497 000 000 kms
Mars	227 900 000 kms

5 Answer the following questions about the given table.
   a Which continent has the greatest area?
   b Name the continents with an area greater than 20 million square kilometres.
   c Find out which continents are completely in the Southern Hemisphere.

Continent	Area in square km
Africa	30 271 000
Antarctica	13 209 000
Asia	44 026 000
Australia	7 682 000
Europe	10 404 000
North America	24 258 000
South America	17 823 000

HOW MUCH BIGGER IS ....?

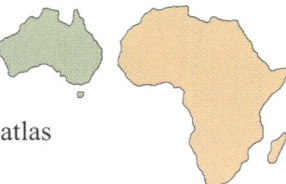

How much bigger is Africa than Australia?

Questions like this are easily answered using tabled facts from an atlas or text book or from the internet.

You could use: **The number of times A is bigger than B = size of A ÷ size of B**

A calculator is advisable.

Using the table of question **5**, the number of times Africa is bigger than Australia is

$\quad$ 30 271 000 ÷ 7 682 000

$\quad \doteqdot 3.94$

So, Africa is almost four times bigger than Australia.

6 Use a calculator to find how many times:

$\quad$ **a** Mount Everest (8848 m) is higher than Mount Kościuszko (2228 m)

$\quad$ **b** the river Nile (6695 km) is longer than the river Murray (2590 km)

$\quad$ **c** Asia is bigger in area than Europe

$\quad$ **d** the population of China (1 261 800 000) was larger than the population of Australia (19 800 000) at the start of the millenium

$\quad$ **e** Pluto is further than Earth from the Sun.

NUMBER SEARCH PROBLEMS

Number searches are like crossword puzzles with numbers going across and down.

The aim is to fit all of the numbers into the grid. There is only one way in which all the numbers will fit.

Draw or click on the icon to print these grids. Place the given numbers on them so that they fit properly.

Search 1:

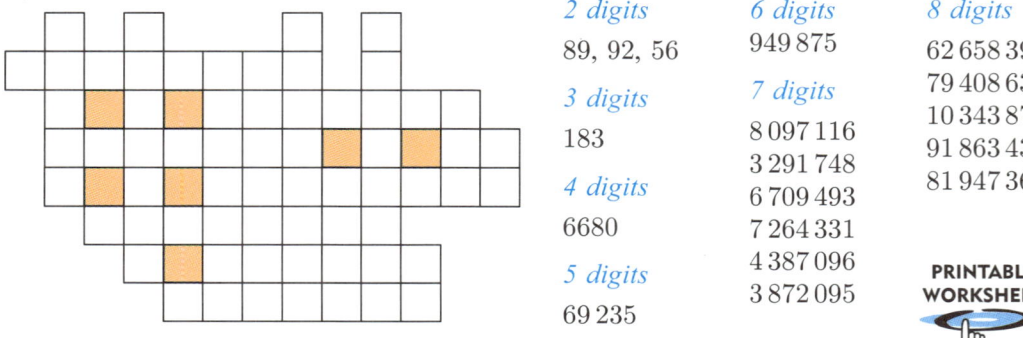

2 digits
89, 92, 56

3 digits
183

4 digits
6680

5 digits
69 235

6 digits
949 875

7 digits
8 097 116
3 291 748
6 709 493
7 264 331
4 387 096
3 872 095

8 digits
62 658 397
79 408 632
10 343 879
91 863 432
81 947 368

PRINTABLE WORKSHEET

Search 2:

- seven hundred and nine
- five hundred and eighty six
- sixty thousand, two hundred and eighty four
- seven hundred and ninety three thousand and forty two
- four hundred and forty nine thousand, seven hundred and sixty eight
- three million eight hundred and two thousand, seven hundred and forty eight
- two million six hundred and eighty three thousand, one hundred and forty eight
- seventy million, two hundred and eighty three thousand, six hundred and forty two
- nineteen million, three hundred and eighty four thousand, and three
- five hundred and eighty three million, seventy nine thousand, six hundred and forty six
- three hundred and forty five million, six hundred and ninety seven thousand and fifty one

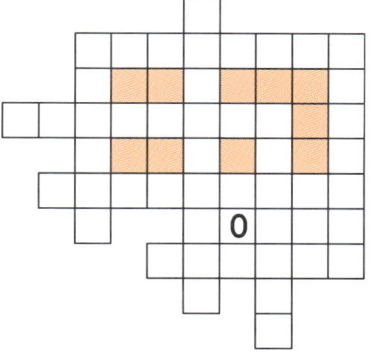

I TWO STEP PROBLEM SOLVING

Two steps are sometimes necessary to solve a problem.

For example, how much change from $50 would you receive after buying three bags of potatoes at $14 a bag?

$$\text{Step 1:} \quad \text{Total cost of potatoes} = \$14 \times 3 = \$42$$

$$\text{Step 2:} \quad \text{So, change is} \quad \$50 - \$42 = \$8$$

Example 24

Each week Clancy is paid $350 a week as a retainer and $65 for each vacuum cleaner he sells. How much does Clancy earn if he sells 13 vacuum cleaners in a week?

$$\text{Money from sales} = \$65 \times 13 = \$845$$

$$\text{So, total earned} = \$845 + \$350 = \$1195$$

```
      6 5
    × 1 3
      ¹
    1 9 5
    6 5 0
    ¹
    8 4 5
```

EXERCISE 1I

1 Sara bought a shirt costing $29 and a pair of jeans costing $45. How much change did she get from $100?

2 Glen bought three T-shirts costing $42 each and a pair of shoes costing $75. Find the total cost of his purchases.

3 Maria bought five 3 kilogram bags of oranges. The numbers of oranges in the bags were: 10, 11, 12, 12 and 10. Find the average number of oranges in a bag.

4 Lachlan had a herd of 183 goats. He put 75 in his largest paddock and divided the rest equally between two smaller paddocks. How many goats were put in each of the smaller paddocks?

5 George had $436 in his bank and was given $30 cash for his birthday. How much money did he have left if he bought a bicycle costing $455?

6 The cost of placing an advertisement in the local paper is $10, plus $4 for each line of type. If my advertisement takes 5 lines, how much will I pay?

7 A football team had kicked 12 goals 13 points. They had another kick for goal as the siren sounded. Their final score was 91 points. Did the last kick score a goal or a point? (1 goal = 6 points)

8 Marcia saved $620 during the year and her sister saved twice that amount. How much money did they save in total?

9 Anna had $463 in her savings account and decided to bank $20 a week for 14 weeks. How much was in the account at the end of that time?

10 Tony's wages for the week were $496. He was also paid for 3 hours overtime at $18 per hour. How much did he earn in total?

11 Alicia ran 6 km each day from Monday to Saturday and 12 km on Sunday. How far did she run during the week?

12 A plastic crate contains 100 boxes of ball point pens. The boxes of pens each weigh 86 grams. If the total mass of the crate and pens is 9200 g, find the mass of the crate.

J NUMBER OPPOSITES

The following problems all involve **opposites**.

These are:
- *Having money in a bank account* and *owing money to a bank account.*
- *Temperature above zero* and *temperature below zero.*
- *Height above sea level* and *height below sea level.*

DISCUSSION

 Prepare a list of *ten* opposites.

These opposites must involve numerical quantities, i.e., quantities which involve numbers.

Instead of distinguishing between opposites by using words, we can use **positive** and **negative** numbers.

NEGATIVE NUMBERS

All of the ideas
- 10 metres below sea level
- owing $30
- 3 floors below ground level
- 5 degrees below freezing
- a loss of $4500

can be represented using **negative numbers**.

Negative numbers are written with a **negative sign (−)** before the number.

For instance:
- '10 metres below sea level' would be represented by -10 (or $^-10$)
- 'owing $30' would be represented by -30
- '3 floors below ground level' would be represented by -3.

In each case, a measurement is being taken from a reference position of zero, for instance, sea level or ground level.

POSITIVE NUMBERS

Positive numbers are the opposite of negative numbers.

They can be written with a **positive sign (+)** before the number, or with no sign at all (in which case we assume the number is positive).

For instance:
- 10 metres above sea level would be written as $+10$ (or $^+10$) or just 10
- having $30 would be written as $+30$
- 3 floors above ground level would be written as $+3$.

Again, the measurement is being taken from a zero reference position.

Referring to our three opening problems:

- Owing the bank $5 would be represented as −5, whereas having a deposit of $5 would be represented as +5 or just 5.
- A temperature of 21°C above zero would be 21, whereas 3°C below zero would be −3.
- A height of 16 m below sea level would be −16, whereas 8848 m above sea level would be 8848.

Some common uses of positive and negative signs are listed in the given table:

Positive (+)	Negative (−)
above	below
increase	decrease
profit	loss
right	left
fast	slow
win	loss
north	south

Positive and negative numbers are called **directed numbers**.

Example 25

Write the positive or negative number or zero for the position of each object. The reference position is the water level.

a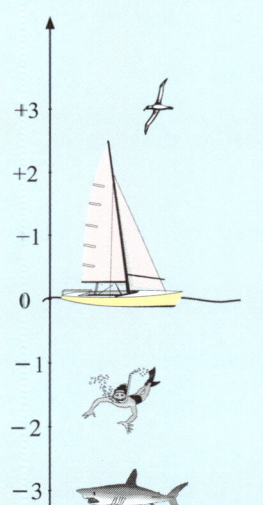

b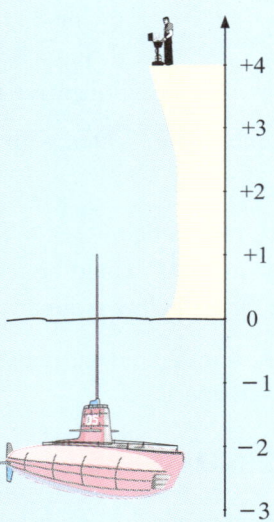

a Positions *above* the water level are marked off with *positive numbers*, so the bird is at +3.

The boat is level with the water, so it is at 0.

Positions *below* the water level are marked off with *negative numbers*. The diver is at −1.5 and the shark is at −3.

b The clifftop is at +4, the periscope is at +1, the water is at 0, the submarine is at −2.

EXERCISE 1J

1 Copy and complete the following table:

	Statement	Directed number	Opposite to statement	Directed number
a	20 m above sea level	+20	20 m below sea level	−20
b	45 km south of the city			
c	a loss of 2 kg in weight			
d	a clock is 2 min fast			
e	she arrives 5 min early			
f	a profit of $4000			
g	2 floors above ground level			
h	10°C below zero			
i	an increase of $400			
j	winning by 34 points			

2 Write positive or negative numbers for the position of the lift, the car, the parking attendant and the rubbish skip.

(Use the bottom of each object.)

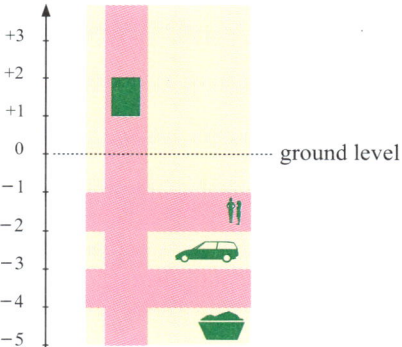

3 If right is positive and left is negative, write the numbers for the positions of A, B, C, D and E using zero as the reference position.

4 Write these temperatures as positive or negative numbers. Zero degrees is the reference point.
- **a** 11° above zero
- **b** 6° below zero
- **c** 8° below zero
- **d** 29° above zero
- **e** 14° below zero

5 Write these gains or losses as positive or negative numbers:
- **a** $30 loss
- **b** $200 gain
- **c** $431 loss
- **d** $751 loss
- **e** $809 gain

6 If north is the positive direction, write these directions as positive or negative numbers:
- **a** 7 metres north
- **b** 15 metres south
- **c** 115 metres south
- **d** 362 metres north
- **e** 19.6 metres south

7 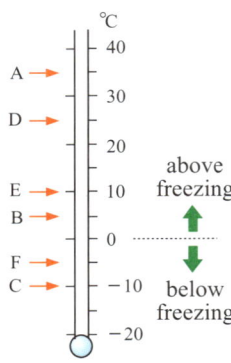 The temperatures of cities A, B, C, D, E and F were recorded at 12 noon on a certain day last year.

    a What was the temperature of each of the cities?

    b How many °C is city D warmer than city:
        i E   **ii** B   **iii** F   **iv** C?

    c How many °C is city C cooler than city:
        i A   **ii** E   **iii** F   **iv** B?

    d What is the difference in temperature between:
        i A and B   **ii** D and E
        iii E and C   **iv** F and C
        v B and F   **vi** D and F?

ADDING AND SUBTRACTING

$4 + 7 = 11$ whereas $4 - 7 = -3$

This can be seen by movement along the number line:

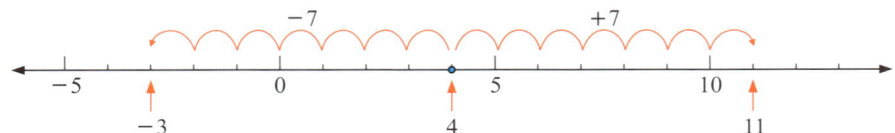

8 If necessary, use the number line to find:

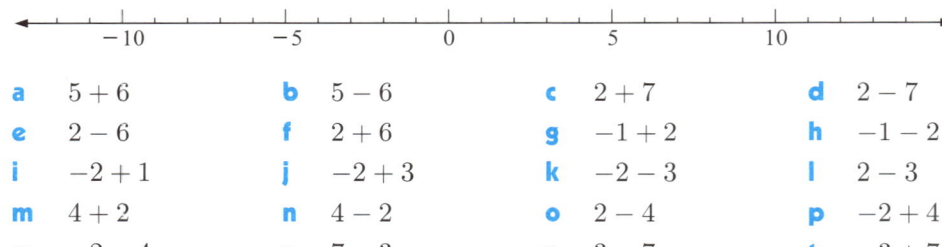

a	$5 + 6$	**b**	$5 - 6$	**c**	$2 + 7$	**d**	$2 - 7$
e	$2 - 6$	**f**	$2 + 6$	**g**	$-1 + 2$	**h**	$-1 - 2$
i	$-2 + 1$	**j**	$-2 + 3$	**k**	$-2 - 3$	**l**	$2 - 3$
m	$4 + 2$	**n**	$4 - 2$	**o**	$2 - 4$	**p**	$-2 + 4$
q	$-2 - 4$	**r**	$7 - 3$	**s**	$3 - 7$	**t**	$-3 + 7$

REVIEW SET A   CHAPTER 1

1 Write T(true) or F(false) to the following statements:

    a Counting from one to one million in units would take about one million seconds.

    b $1\,000\,000 = 100 \times 100 \times 100$

    c $10\,000\,000 = 10 \times 100 \times 1000$

    d $468\,751 > 468\,577$

    e $1000 \times 4612 \neq 2306 \times 2000$

2 Write in ascending order (smallest number first):

    $673\,502, \;\; 674\,551, \;\; 654\,662, \;\; 765\,442, \;\; 750\,467$

3 Write the numeral for $126\,350$ greater than four million.

4 Simplify $4 \times 25 \times 7 \times 0 \times 10$.

5 What is half the difference between 198 and 374?

6 Find an approximate value for 687×231.

7 Find $7686 \div 7$.

8 Find the cost of 24 concert tickets at $112 each.

9 During 3 days of practice, a golfer hit 24 more balls each day than the previous day. How many golf balls did she hit in the 3 days if she hit 376 on the first day?

10 **a** Round $39 758 to the nearest $100.

b Round 560 823 to the nearest 100 000.

11 Damien bought a pair of jeans for $39 and a T-shirt for $32. How much change did he get from $100?

12 **a** Write the opposite of *a withdrawal of $30* from the bank.

b Find **i** $2 - 5$ **ii** $-2 - 5$

13 The population of Australia is approximately 20 000 000 and the population of New Zealand is approximately 4 000 000.

a What is the difference in population size?

b How many times larger is the population of Australia than the population of New Zealand?

REVIEW SET B — CHAPTER 1

1 Write T (true) or F (false) in the following statements:

a $4 863 663 < 4 863 363$

b $8703 - 6679 = 2124$

c The place value of the 6 digit in the following number, 526 947 857, is a million.

d $504 \times 1998 \doteqdot 1 000 000$

2 How many times larger is the first 6 than the second in 63 264?

3 Round 37 439 to the nearest 10 000.

4 Find the approximate value of 197×234.

5 Write in descending order (largest number first):

680 969,   608 699,   6 080 699,   698 096,   968 099

6 What is the difference between 2783 and 4368?

7 A recycle depot pays 5 cents for each empty bottle. How much would a school's fundraising committee get if it collects and fills 154 crates which had two dozen bottles each?

8 Kathryn was paid wages of $608 for the week. She also earned $24 an hour for 5 hours overtime. How much did Kathryn earn in total?

9 a Write the opposite of *a rise in temperature of 5°C*.
  b On a very cold winter's day the temperature was −2°C at 8 am. By 10 am the temperature had risen 7°. What was the temperature at 10 am?

10 The area of Africa is approximately 30 271 000 km², and the area of Europe is approximately 10 404 000 km². Approximately how many times larger than Europe is Africa?

11 Nine office workers form a syndicate and buy lottery tickets. If they win $4275, how much does each person receive?

REVIEW SET C — CHAPTER 1

1 Replace □ by > or <:
  a 60 × 1000 □ 59 000
  b 499 994 □ 499 949

2 Use the digits 3, 8, 0, 4, 1, 7 to make the largest number you can.

3 What is the place value of the 8 in the following numbers?
  a 3894
  b 508 415
  c 856 042
  d 38 475 042

4 Round off:
  a 35 to the nearest 10
  b 4384 to the nearest 1000
  c 463 994 to one figure.

5 Write the numbers that are:
  a thirty seven greater than one hundred and ninety four thousand two hundred and twenty
  b the product of 395 and 49
  c fifty seven multiplied by zero.

6 Find the approximate mass of one can of cat food if a carton containing 96 cans weighs 18 kilograms. (1 kilogram = 1000 grams)

7 Would $200 be enough to pay for a $69 'Cheap Deal' flight to Melbourne, a $114 return ticket and an $18 ticket to the football? Show your working.

8 Write these numbers in ascending order (smallest first):
  569 207, 96 572, 652 097, 795 602, 79 562

9 a Write the opposite of *losing by 2 goals*.
  b On the weather report Philip noticed that the temperature was 25° C in Adelaide, −1° C in London and −5° C in Berlin.
    i How much warmer was it in Adelaide than London?
    ii How much colder was it in Berlin than London?

Chapter 2

Number properties

Knowledge, skills and understandings

By the end of this chapter you should be able to

- write numbers up to 1 000 000 in expanded form (e.g., using powers of 10)
- use powers or index (exponents) notation
- identify factors, common factors, prime factors, highest common factor and lowest common multiple
- use arrays and divisibility rules
- identify triangular and cubic numbers
- apply square root to square numbers and use symbol $\sqrt{}$
- understand the order of operations using BEDMAS (Brackets, Exponents, Division, Multiplication, Addition, Subtraction)

- use and explain appropriate strategies in problem solving (e.g., trial and error, working backwards, looking for patterns)
- use calculators to solve problems where the numbers are outside mental and written limits
- identify the operations required to solve more complex problems within your experiences (e.g., deposits and withdrawals in banking, and other everyday use)

A OPERATING WITH NUMBERS

There are four basic operations that are carried out with numbers.

They are: addition (+), subtraction (−), multiplication (×) and division (÷).

Here are some words which are frequently used with these operations:
- sum
- difference
- product
- quotient

SUMS AND DIFFERENCES

- To find the **sum** of two or more numbers, we **add** them.
  For example, the sum of 8 and 17 is $8 + 17 = 25$.

- To find the **difference** between two numbers, we **subtract the smaller from the larger**.
  For example, the difference between 8 and 17 is $17 - 8 = 9$.

PRODUCTS AND QUOTIENTS

- To find the **product** of two or more numbers we multiply them.
  For example, the product of 3 and 5 is $3 \times 5 = 15$.

- To find the **quotient** of two numbers we divide the first one mentioned by the second.
  For example, the quotient of 15 and 3 is $15 \div 3 = 5$.

Example 1

a Find the sum of 7, 9 and 13.
b Find the difference between 6 and 13.
c Find the product of 5 and 8.
d Find the quotient of 32 and 4.

a The sum of 7, 9 and 13 is $7 + 9 + 13 = 29$.
b The difference between 6 and 13 is $13 - 6 = 7$.
c The product of 5 and 8 is $5 \times 8 = 40$.
d The quotient of 32 and 4 is $32 \div 4 = 8$

Product means multiplication.

EXERCISE 2A

1 Solve the following problems:
   a Find the sum of 23 and 37.
   b Find the difference between 37 and 56.
   c Find the product of 14 and 28.
   d Calculate the quotient of three hundred and seventy four and seventeen.
   e By how much is the sum of 90 and 50 greater than the difference between 90 and 50?

f What is the product of the first 5 even numbers?

g Find the sum of the first 10 odd numbers.

2 Solve the following problems:

a Mount Cook in New Zealand is 3765 m above sea level, whereas Mount Kościuszko in Australia is 2231 m high. How much higher is Mount Cook than Mount Kościuszko?

b A couple saved $12 654 towards the cost of their first home. How much would they need to borrow if they are to purchase a home for $109 850?

c What is the difference between the AFL's prediction of 120 000 for the first three games in July and the actual attendances of 36 287, 27 615 and 32 974?

d Four friends shared a Lotto payout of $13 828. How much each did they collect?

e A gambler bets $35 on a winning horse. How much does she collect if the dividend paid is $10.20 for each dollar bet?

f The organisers of a concert set out four identical blocks of seating. If each block has 35 rows, each with 40 seats, how many people can be seated?

g A softdrink company fills and packs 540 dozen cans of drink every hour. How many cans are filled and packed in an 8 hour day?

h All rooms of a hotel cost $88 per day to rent. The hotel has 5 floors and 37 rooms per floor. What is the total rental received per day if the hotel is fully occupied?

i An investor bought 5000 shares at $2.15 each on the stock market. He sold half of them at $2.65 each. A few weeks later he sold the rest at $2.85 each. What was his total profit?

j A basketball team scores the following goals in their season of 10 games: 24, 15, 108, 26, 35, 23, 31, 19, 27, 50. What is their total goal score for the season?

k Jacob's nursery sells 145 dozen flower plants each week. How many plants do they sell in 16 weeks?

l The aeroplanes in use seat 143 passengers. If 19 full aircraft leave Adelaide each day, how many passengers are carried?

m If each carton holds 8 books, how many cartons can be filled from 912 books?

n The force of gravity on the moon is about one sixth of that on Earth. What is the weight on the moon of a man who weighs 90 kg on Earth?

o A paper girl has to deliver 80 papers each weighing 150 grams. What is the total weight of the 80 papers?

p The stadium was almost full when you arrived. The turnstile counter was at number 16 384 when you went through at 6 pm. How many people went through the turnstile in two hours if the counter was at 25 897 at 8 pm?

ACTIVITY — CROSS-PRODUCTS

In each of the following cross diagrams you must put a different number in each circle so that the three numbers going across, multiplied together, equal the same product as the three numbers going down.

The product is given to you each time. You can choose numbers from 0, 1, 2, 3, 4, 5, 6, 7, 8, 9, 10 only and remember each number can be used only once.

One number is given to you.

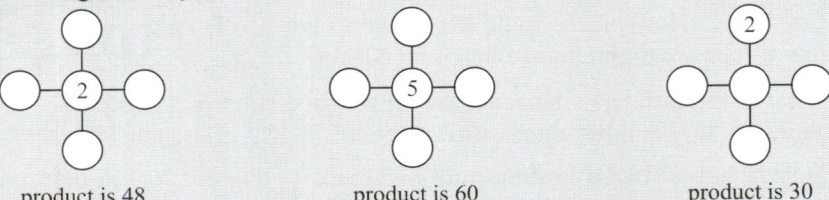

product is 48   product is 60   product is 30

Make one or two of your own cross diagrams and get your partner to try them.

ACTIVITY — BALANCING

In each of the mobiles the sum of the numbers on each arm must balance the other side.

For example:

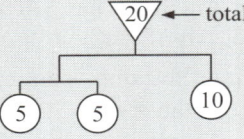   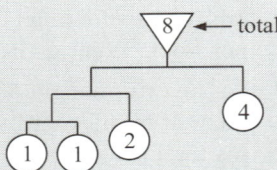

Copy the following mobiles and fill in the circles with whole numbers so that the mobile is balanced. The total of each mobile must be maintained, i.e., $5 + 5 + 10 = 20$, etc.

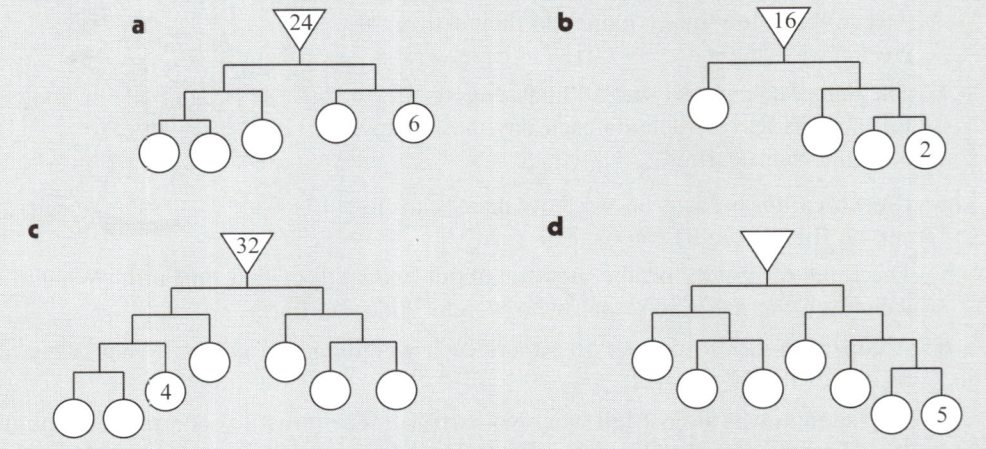

Make up a mobile of your own choosing and get your partner to try it.

B ORDER OF OPERATIONS

Just as the order in which you do things in everyday life is important, so is the order in which mathematical operations are carried out.

Different answers can result depending on the **order** in which the operations are performed.

For example, calculate: $15 - 9 \div 3$

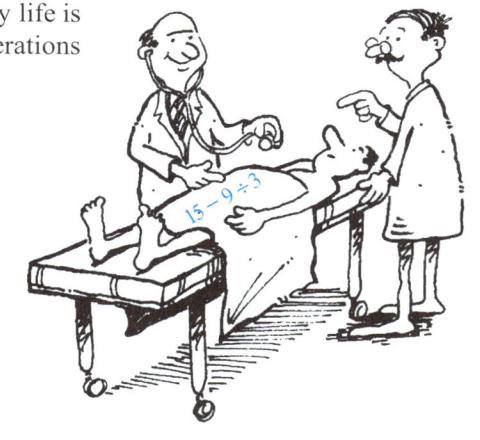

Method 1:
subtract first,
then divide
$15 - 9 = 6$
$6 \div 3 = 2$
Answer: 2

Method 2:
divide first,
then subtract
$9 \div 3 = 3$
$15 - 3 = 12$
Answer: 12

Which answer is correct, 2 or 12?

To avoid this problem, a set of rules, which states the order of performing operations, has been agreed upon by all mathematicians.

Using these rules, **method 2** is correct in the previous example, and

$$15 - 9 \div 3 = 12$$

Rules of order of performing mathematical operations

B	operate within the **brackets** first
E	do **exponents** (or powers) next
D	**division** and
M	**multiplication** } (left to right)
A	**addition** and
S	**subtraction** } (left to right)

Example 2

Evaluate: $48 - 16 \div 2 \times 4 + 7$

$48 - 16 \div 2 \times 4 + 7$
$= 48 - 8 \times 4 + 7$ {÷ left to right}
$= 48 - 32 + 7$ {× next}
$= 16 + 7$ {− and + last}
$= 23$

BEDMAS is a mnemonic. A mnemonic is an aid to help you to remember something.

EXERCISE 2B

1 Evaluate the following:

a $6 + 9 - 7$
b $7 \times 6 + 4$
c $18 + 9 \times 3$
d $18 \div 3 + 9$
e $50 + 6 - 7$
f $7 + 8 \div 2$
g $8 \div 2 + 7$
h $5 + 4 \times 3 - 1$
i $24 \div 6 + 4 \times 5$
j $4 + 5 - 3 \times 2$
k $7 \times 9 \div 3$
l $4 + 3 \times 8 \div 4$
m $5 \times 3 \times 2 - 1$
n $7 \times 9 - 3 \times 9$
o $8 + 6 \div 3 \times 4$

Example 3

Evaluate: $2 \times (3 \times 6 - 4) + 7 - 12 \div 6$

$$2 \times (3 \times 6 - 4) + 7 - 12 \div 6$$
$$= 2 \times (18 - 4) + 7 - 12 \div 6 \quad \{\text{inside brackets } \times\}$$
$$= 2 \times 14 + 7 - 12 \div 6 \quad \{\text{inside brackets } -\}$$
$$= 28 + 7 - 2 \quad \{\div, \times, \text{next}\}$$
$$= 35 - 2$$
$$= 33$$

2 Evaluate the following: (Remember to complete the brackets first.)
- a $(9 + 6) \times 2$
- b $(23 - 7) \times 2$
- c $(16 + 4) \div 10$
- d $4 \times (7 + 5)$
- e $26 - (7 - 5) \times 4$
- f $(27 + 5) \times 3$
- g $(27 - 27) \times 9$
- h $5 + 4 \times 6 + 30 \div 5$
- i $(13 - 7 + 5) \times 8$
- j $32 - (6 \times 3) \div 9$
- k $(15 + 5) \div (10 - 6)$
- l $3 \times (9 - 4) + 8$

3 Make the following statements true by putting in brackets where necessary:
- a $6 + 3 \times 2 = 18$
- b $21 - 7 \times 3 = 0$
- c $8 + 4 - 3 \times 2 = 6$
- d $50 \div 5 + 5 = 5$
- e $5 \times 3 - 1 + 7 = 17$
- f $4 + 4 \times 4 \div 16 = 2$
- g $50 \div 5 + 5 = 15$
- h $9 \times 7 + 5 + 2 = 110$
- i $9 \times 7 + 5 - 2 = 66$

4 Put brackets where necessary into these evaluations to make each answer correct:
- a $96 \div 4 + 8 \times 10 - 9 = 71$
- b $96 \div 4 + 8 \times 10 - 9 = 32$
- c $96 \div 4 + 8 \times 10 - 9 = 95$
- d $96 \div 4 + 8 \times 10 - 9 = 8$

5 State whether the following equations are true or false:
- a $(3 + 2) \times 6 \div 10 = 3$
- b $18 \div (3 \times 2) + 5 = 17$
- c $(3 + 6 \div 2) \div 3 = 2$
- d $3 + 6 \times 4 \div 2 = 18$
- e $5 + 5 \times 5 \div 10 = 5$
- f $40 \div 10 \times 4 + 4 = 20$
- g $18 + 7 - 3 + 4 = 27$
- h $3 \times (5 + 7) \div 12 = 3$
- i $54 = 3 + 6 \times 3$

6 Evaluate the following: (Remember the rules.)
- a $3 \times 2 - 12 \div (3 \times 2)$
- b $10 \div 5 + 20 \div (4 + 1)$
- c $6 + (4 \times 0)$
- d $48 - 9 \div 3 \times 7$
- e $(2 \times 3 - 4) + (33 \div 11 + 5)$
- f $7 + (4 - 3) \times 2$
- g $84 \div (3 + 9) \times (15 - 11)$
- h $(45 \div 5 + 6) - (9 \times 2 - 4)$

C FACTORS OF NATURAL NUMBERS

A **factory** makes or produces goods from parts. The goods which leave the factory are a product of the factory.

> The **factors** of a natural number are the natural numbers whose product produces the number.

For example, the factors of 8 are 1, 2, 4 and 8 since
$$8 = 8 \times 1$$
$$8 = 2 \times 4$$
$$8 = 4 \times 2$$
$$8 = 1 \times 8$$

Conversely a factor is a natural number (i.e., a "part") which has been multiplied by another factor (another "part") to make (or produce) a larger number.

For example, $24 \times 96 = 2304$ which means that 24 and 96 are factors of 2304, and 2304 is the product.

This is true in the previous example since **pairs of factors** can be multiplied together to give the natural number and these are $1 \times 8 = 8$ and $2 \times 4 = 8$.

A number can have many factors. When we write the number as a product of factors we say it is **factorised**.

8 may be factorised as a product of two factors in two ways: 1×8 or 2×4.

12 has factors 1, 2, 3, 4, 6, 12 and can be factorised into two factors in three ways. These are 1×12, 2×6, 3×4 ($1 \times 12 = 12 \times 1$ so we only count this once).

DEMO

EXERCISE 2C

1 **a** List all the factors of 15.   **b** List all the factors of 16.
   c Complete this equation: $16 = 2 \times \ldots$
   d Write all pairs of factors which multiply to give 16.

2 List all the factors of each of the following numbers:

   a 8   **b** 36   **c** 40   **d** 42
   e 48   **f** 63   **g** 30   **h** 84
   i 39   **j** 35   **k** 60   **l** 81

3 Copy and complete the factorisations below:

   a $33 = 3 \times \ldots$ **b** $55 = 5 \times \ldots$ **c** $28 = 4 \times \ldots$
   d $50 = 10 \times \ldots$ **e** $27 = 9 \times \ldots$ **f** $42 = 2 \times \ldots$
   g $35 = 5 \times \ldots$ **h** $72 = 8 \times \ldots$ **i** $99 = 11 \times \ldots$
   j $49 = 7 \times \ldots$ **k** $121 = 11 \times \ldots$ **l** $48 = 6 \times \ldots$
   m $64 = 16 \times \ldots$ **n** $108 = 12 \times \ldots$ **o** $88 = 2 \times \ldots$

4 Write the largest factor (not itself) of each of the following numbers:
  a 12   **b** 18   **c** 27   **d** 48
  e 44   **f** 75   **g** 90   **h** 39

PRIMES AND COMPOSITES

Some numbers can be written as the product of **two factors** only.

For example, the only two factors of 5 are 5 and 1, and the only two factors of 13 are 13 and 1.

Numbers of this type are called **prime numbers**.

> A **prime number** is a natural number which has exactly two factors, 1 and itself.
> A **composite number** is a natural number which has more than two factors.

For example, 6 is a **composite number** since it has four factors: 1, 6, 2, 3.

Notice that one pair of factors of 6, namely 2 and 3, are both prime numbers.

In fact, all composite numbers can be written as the product of prime factors.

From the definition of prime and composite numbers we can see that the number **1 is neither prime nor composite**!

EXERCISE 2C (continued)

5 List all the prime numbers less than 100.

6 Are there patterns in the way prime numbers occur? Copy the table into your book and count the number of primes in each set of numbers. Is there a pattern?

Set of Numbers	Total Number of Prime Numbers
0 - 9	
10 - 19	
20 - 29	
30 - 39	
40 - 49	
50 - 59	
60 - 69	

PRIME FACTORS

To find the prime factors of a composite number we divide the number by the prime numbers which are its factors, starting with the smallest.

These divisibility rules may help you decide if a composite number has particular numbers as factors.

Divisibility Rules:

The following **divisibility rules** may prove useful in this exercise.

- A number is divisible by the prime number 2 if the **last digit is even or zero**.
- A number is divisible by the prime number 3 if the **sum of its digits is divisible by** 3.
- A number is divisible by 5 if the **last digit is 0 or 5**.

Example 4

Use a factor tree to show **a** 18 **b** 48 as the product of its prime factors.

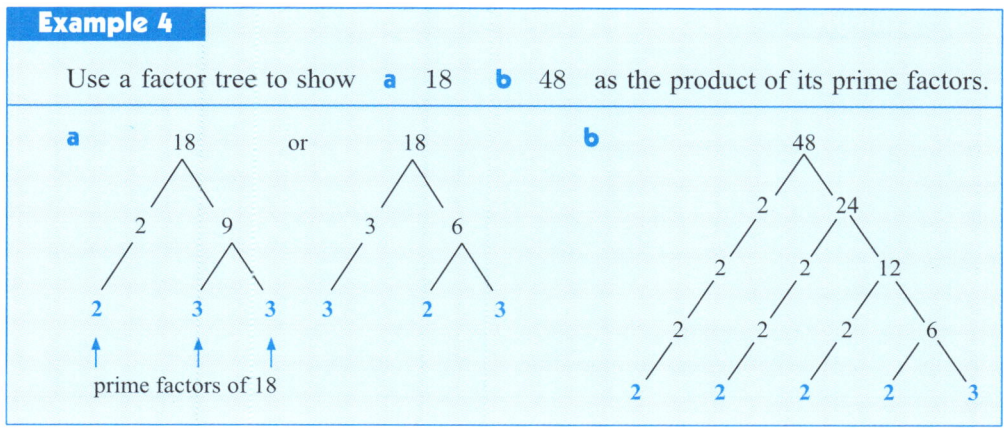

7 Copy and complete the following factor trees:

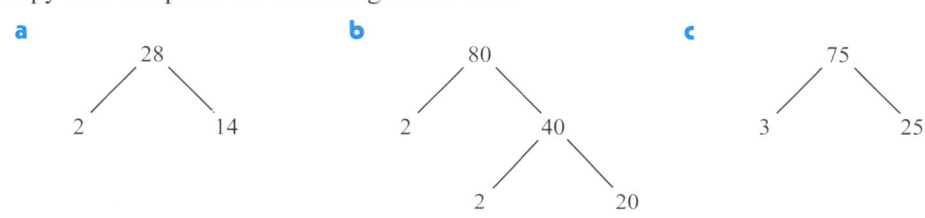

Example 5

Express 180 as the product of its prime factors.

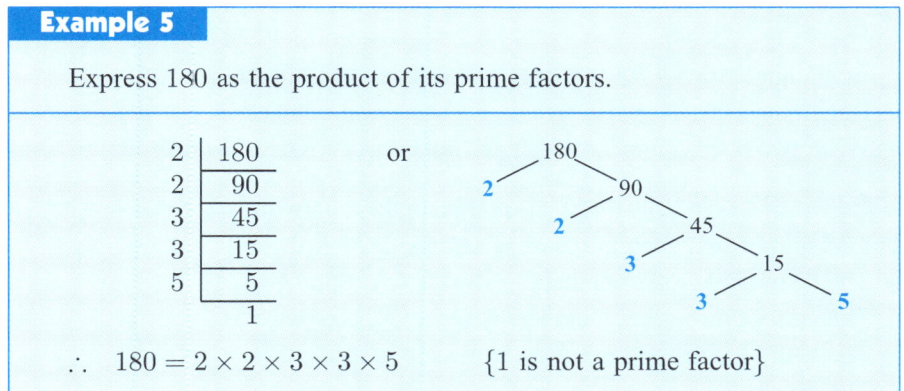

∴ $180 = 2 \times 2 \times 3 \times 3 \times 5$ {1 is not a prime factor}

8 Express each of the following numbers as the product of prime factors:
   a 16   **b** 36   **c** 28   **d** 56   **e** 63
   f 75   **g** 168   **h** 252   **i** 305   **j** 392

HIGHEST COMMON FACTOR

A number which is a factor of two or more other numbers is called a **common factor** of these numbers.

For example, 9 is a common factor of 18 and 27.

We use the method of finding prime factors to find the **highest common factor (HCF)** of two or more natural numbers.

Example 6

Find the highest common factor (HCF) of 18 and 24.

```
2 | 18        2 | 24
3 |  9        2 | 12      18 = **2 × 3** × 3
3 |  3        2 |  6      24 = **2** × 2 × 2 × **3**
       1      3 |  3
                     1
```

2×3 is common to both and $2 \times 3 = 6$

∴ 6 is the highest common factor of 18 and 24.

9 Find the highest common factor of:
- **a** 9, 15
- **b** 7, 28
- **c** 18, 30
- **d** 21, 28
- **e** 27, 45
- **f** 25, 50
- **g** 40, 80
- **h** 27, 108
- **i** 60, 132

EVEN OR ODD

A natural number is **even** if it has at least one factor of two (if it is divisible by 2).
A natural number is **odd** if it is not divisible by 2.

10
- **a** Beginning with 14, write three consecutive even numbers.
- **b** Beginning with 35, write five consecutive odd numbers.
- **c** Write two even numbers which are not consecutive and which add to 10.

11 Use the words "even" and "odd" to complete the following sentences correctly:
- **a** The sum of two even numbers is always .....
- **b** The sum of two odd numbers is always .....
- **c** The sum of three even numbers is always .....
- **d** The sum of three odd numbers is always .....
- **e** The sum of an odd number and an even number is always .....
- **f** When an even number is subtracted from an odd number the result is .....
- **g** When an odd number is subtracted from an even number the result is .....
- **h** The product of two odd numbers is always .....
- **i** The product of an even and an odd number is always .....

There is only one even prime number.

How odd!

INVESTIGATION   THE SIEVE OF ERATOSTHENES

Eratosthenes (pronounced Erra-toss-tha-nees) was a Greek mathematician and geographer who lived between 275 BC and 194 BC. He is credited with many useful mathematical discoveries and calculations.

Eratosthenes was probably the first person to make a calculation of the circumference of the earth by using lengths of shadows. His calculation was in terms of 'stadia' which were the units of length in his day. When converted to metres, his calculation was found to be very close to modern day calculations.

Eratosthenes also found a method for 'sieving' out composite numbers from the set of naturals from 1 to 100 to leave only the primes. The method was to cross out 1, then all evens except 2, then all multiples of 3 except 3, then all multiples of 5 except 5, then all multiples of 7 except 7.

1	2	3	4	5	6	7	8	9	10
11	12	13	14	15	16	17	18	19	20
21	22	23	24	25	26	27	28	29	30
31	32	33	34	35	36	37	38	39	40
41	42	43	44	45	46	47	48	49	50
51	52	53	54	55	56	57	58	59	60
61	62	63	64	65	66	67	68	69	70
71	72	73	74	75	76	77	78	79	80
81	82	83	84	85	86	87	88	89	90
91	92	93	94	95	96	97	98	99	100

What to do:

Write out as shown, the naturals from 1 to 100 and use Eratosthenes' method to discover the primes between 1 and 100.

D   MULTIPLES OF NATURAL NUMBERS

The multiples of 10 are   10, 20, 30, 40, 50, ...

These are found by multiplying each of the natural numbers by 10,   i.e., $1 \times 10 = 10$
$2 \times 10 = 20$
$3 \times 10 = 30$
$4 \times 10 = 40.$

The multiples of 15 are   15, 30, 45, 60, 75, ...   i.e., $1 \times 15 = 15$
$2 \times 15 = 30$
$3 \times 15 = 45$
$4 \times 15 = 60.$

The number 30 is a multiple of both 10 and 15, so we say 30 is a **common multiple** of 10 and 15. (10 and 15 are both factors of 30.) In fact 30 has several factors including 2, 3, 5, 10 and 15. 30 is a **common multiple** of each of its factors.

Example 7

Find common multiples of 4 and 6 between 20 and 40.

Multiples of 4 are   4, 8, **12**, 16, 20, **24**, 28, 32, **36**, 40, ...
Multiples of 6 are   6, **12**, 18, **24**, 30, **36**, 42, ...
∴ the common multiples between 20 and 40 are   24 and 36.

LOWEST COMMON MULTIPLE

> The **Lowest Common Multiple (LCM)** of two or more numbers is the smallest number which has **each** of these numbers as a **factor**.

Example 8

Find the lowest common multiple of 9 and 12.

Multiples of 9 are: 9, 18, 27, **36**, 45, 54, 63, **72**, 81, ...

Multiples of 12 are: 12, 24, **36**, 48, 60, **72**, 84, ...

∴ the common multiples are 36, 72, ... and 36 is the smallest of these.

∴ the LCM is 36.

Consider the following alternative method for finding LCM's.

For example,

Find the LCM of 9 and 12.

```
3 | 9        2 | 12
3 | 3        2 | 6
    1        3 | 3
                 1
```

Prime factors of 9: $\quad 3 \times 3$

Prime factors of 12: $\quad 2 \times 2 \times 3$

Total prime factors of LCM: $\quad 2 \times 2 \times 3 \times 3$

∴ LCM = 36

EXERCISE 2D

1 List the numbers from 1 to 30.
  a Put a circle around each multiple of 3.
  b Put a square around each multiple of 4.
  c List the common multiples of 3 and 4 which are less than 30.

2 In the question following use the list of multiples of 15 given:
  15   30   45   60   75   90   105   120   135   150
  State which of these numbers are common multiples of both:
  a 15 and 10   **b** 15 and 9   **c** 20 and 30   **d** 4 and 30

3 Find the lowest common multiples of the following sets:
  a 3, 6   **b** 4, 6   **c** 5, 8   **d** 12, 15
  e 6, 8   **f** 2, 4, 6   **g** 15, 12   **h** 3, 4, 5

4 A piece of rope is either to be cut exactly into 12 metre lengths or exactly into 18 metre lengths. Find the shortest length of rope satisfying these requirements.

5 Two bells toll at intervals of 6 and 9 seconds respectively. If they start to ring at the same instant, how long will it take before they will again ring together?

6 Two different arcade games cost 4 and 5 tokens respectively. Two brothers each play one of the games and spend the same amount. How many tokens will they each need?

Harder:

7 Three long distance runners train to drink at 3, 5 and 6 kilometre intervals respectively. At what distance will they all drink?

8 Four students each have a special bar to play.

The piano player repeats his piece every 4th bar, the saxophone player every 5th bar, the drummer every 6th bar and the xylophone player every 10th bar.

If the piece of music contains 100 bars, at what stages will they all play together?

E DIVISIBILITY RULES

A number is **divisible** by another if we get a whole number when we divide the first number by the second.

For example: 16 is divisible by 2 because $16 \div 2 = 8$,   but
16 is not divisible by 3 as $16 \div 3 = 5$ remainder 1.

We may wish to quickly decide whether one number is divisible by another (from 2 to 9).

This can be done using a calculator, but there are often simple rules we can follow to find whether one number is divisible by another, without actually doing the division!

For example, we know that any even number is divisible by 2 and so it must end (last digit) in an even number (0, 2, 4, 6, 8).

INVESTIGATION   DIVISIBILITY BY 4 AND 9

One of the joys of mathematics comes from investigating and discovering things for yourself. In this investigation you should discover rules for divisibility by 4 and by 9.

What to do:

1 Copy the following table:

Number	Divisibility by 4 (Yes/No)	Last 2 digits
81		
252		
3624		
81 234		

2 Fill out the second column using your calculator (or using simple division) and fill out the third column, writing down the last two digits of each number.

3 Copy and complete: "A natural number is divisible by 4 if ……".

4 Copy and complete the following table:

Number	Divisibility by 9 (Yes/No)	Sum of its digits
81		$8 + 1 = 9$
154		
252		
3624		
18 268		
81 234		

5 Copy and complete: "A natural number is divisible by 9 if ......".

STANDARD DIVISIBILITY TESTS

Number	Divisibility Test
2	If the last digit is 0 or even, then the original number is divisible by 2.
3	If the sum of the digits is divisible by 3, then the original number is divisible by 3.
4	If the last two digits of a number are divisible by 4 then the original number is divisible by 4.
5	If the last digit is 0 or 5 then the number is divisible by 5.
6	If the number is even **and** divisible by 3 then it is divisible by 6.
8	Write down the last 3 digits as a number. If this is divisible by 8, then the original number is divisible by 8.
9	If the sum of the digits of a number is divisible by 9 then the original number is divisible by 9.

There is a test for divisibility by 7 but it is too difficult to use.

Example 9

a Is 2328 divisible by 3?

b 23☐8 is divisible by 3. What digits can ☐ be replaced by?

a $2 + 3 + 2 + 8 = 15$
and 15 is divisible by 3
So 2328 is divisible by 3

b $2 + 3 + ☐ + 8$
$= ☐ + 13$
which is divisible by 3 when
$☐ = 2, 5$ or 8

EXERCISE 2E

1 Answer *true* or *false* for the following:
- **a** 45 is divisible by 5
- **b** 75 is divisible by 2
- **c** 92 is divisible by 3
- **d** 126 is divisible by 3
- **e** 56 235 is divisible by 3
- **f** 1042 is divisible by 8
- **g** 1088 is divisible by 8
- **h** 2120 is divisible by 8

2 Which of the following are divisible by 3?
- **a** 75
- **b** 96
- **c** 186
- **d** 254
- **e** 509
- **f** 816
- **g** 9657
- **h** 8433
- **i** 817 203
- **j** 246 642
- **k** 123 456 789
- **l** 124 124 124

3 Find all the possible values of the missing digit if the following are divisible by 3:
- **a** 3☐
- **b** 2☐4
- **c** 1☐82
- **d** 6☐34
- **e** 5☐87
- **f** 45☐7
- **g** 89☐216
- **h** 348☐10

4 Decide whether the following are divisible by 4:
- **a** 3784
- **b** 8804
- **c** 6794
- **d** 32 418

5 Decide whether the following are divisible by 9:
- **a** 496
- **b** 7862
- **c** 34 191
- **d** 361 908

F — POWERS OF NUMBERS

A **power** or **index** number shows that a number is been multiplied by itself several times.

For example, 3^4 is a quick way of writing $3 \times 3 \times 3 \times 3$ $(= 81)$

which is **not** the same as 3×4 $(= 12)$.

The quick way for writing $6 \times 6 \times 6 \times 6$ would be 6^4. This is read as either six to the fourth power or six to the power of four.

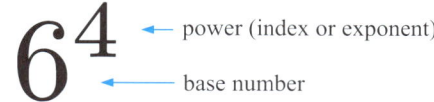

The power 4 says how many times the base number 6 is multiplied together.

When 2 is the index or exponent as in 7^2 we read it as seven to the 'power of two' or seven to the 'second power' or seven 'squared'.

When 3 is the index or exponent as in 7^3 we read it as seven to the 'power of three' or seven to the 'third power' or seven 'cubed'.

We can represent these exponents using MA blocks.

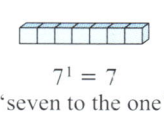

$7^1 = 7$
'seven to the one'

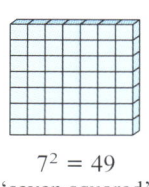

$7^2 = 49$
'seven squared'

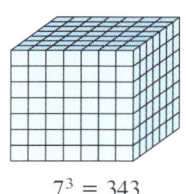

$7^3 = 343$
'seven cubed'

> **Example 10**
>
> Write in power form:
> $2 \times 2 \times 2 \times 2 \times 3 \times 3 \times 3$
>
> $2 \times 2 \times 2 \times 2 \times 3 \times 3 \times 3$
> $= 2^4 \times 3^3$

> **Example 11**
>
> Write $9^4 \times 3^5$ in expanded form and use a calculator to find its value.
>
> $9^4 \times 3^5$
> $= 9 \times 9 \times 9 \times 9 \times 3 \times 3 \times 3 \times 3 \times 3$
> $= 6561 \times 243$
> $= 1\,594\,323$

EXERCISE 2F

1 Write each number in exponent form:
- **a** $6 \times 6 \times 6 \times 6$
- **b** $4 \times 4 \times 4 \times 4 \times 4 \times 4$
- **c** $13 \times 13 \times 13 \times 13 \times 13$
- **d** $5 \times 5 \times 5 \times 3 \times 3$
- **e** $9 \times 9 \times 2 \times 2 \times 2 \times 2$
- **f** $8 \times 8 \times 8 \times 3 \times 3 \times 3$
- **g** $2 \times 2 \times 4 \times 4 \times 4 \times 5 \times 5$
- **h** $11 \times 11 \times 11 \times 3 \times 3 \times 6$
- **i** $3 \times 3 \times 3 \times 5 \times 5 \times 9 \times 9$

2 Convert into a single whole number without using a calculator:
- **a** $2 \times 3 \times 5$
- **b** $2^2 \times 3$
- **c** $3^3 \times 2$
- **d** $2 \times 3^2 \times 5$
- **e** $2^2 \times 3^2 \times 11$
- **f** $2^3 \times 5^2 \times 11$
- **g** $3 \times 4^2 \times 10$
- **h** $2^5 \times 3^2 \times 10$
- **i** $1^2 \times 2^3 \times 3^4$

3 Without using a calculator, work out the difference between the following pairs of values:
- **a** 2^5 and 5^2
- **b** 3^4 and 4^3
- **c** 6^3 and 3^6
- **d** 9×2 and 9^2
- **e** 3^5 and 3×5
- **f** 8^4 and 8^3
- **g** 2^{10} and 10^2
- **h** 5^3 and 3×5
- **i** 50^3 and $50 \times 50 \times 50$

4 Write the following in expanded form and use a calculator to find the value:
- **a** 5^4
- **b** 7^3
- **c** 3^7
- **d** 12^5
- **e** 100^3
- **f** 14^5

5 Arrange these power expressions in ascending order:
- **a** $3^8,\ 6^5,\ 2^{10},\ 8^4,\ 5^7,\ 10^4$
- **b** $5^8,\ 9^5,\ 27^3,\ 100^3,\ 1^{27},\ 1000^2$

6 Work out in simplest form the answers to the following pattern of numbers:

$1^2 =$
$11^2 =$
$111^2 =$
$1111^2 =$
$11\,111^2 =$
$111\,111^2 =$
$1\,111\,111^2 =$

What does the resulting pattern of answers have in common with the following words:

"eye", "dad", "mum", "radar", "racecar", "rotator"?

POWERS WITH BASE 10

When using base ten the power shows the place value or number of zeros following the one.

	Tens of millions	Millions	Hundred thousands	Ten thousands	Thousands	Hundreds	Tens	Units
10^1							1	0
$10^2 = 10 \times 10 =$						1	0	0
$10^3 = 10 \times 10 \times 10 =$					1	0	0	0
$10^4 = 10 \times 10 \times 10 \times 10 =$				1	0	0	0	0
$10^5 = 10 \times 10 \times 10 \times 10 \times 10 =$			1	0	0	0	0	0
$10^6 = 10 \times 10 \times 10 \times 10 \times 10 \times 10 =$		1	0	0	0	0	0	0
$10^7 = 10 \times 10 \times 10 \times 10 \times 10 \times 10 \times 10 =$	1	0	0	0	0	0	0	0

EXPANDED NOTATION

In expanded notation we write the number as the sum of its place values.

For example, $5042 = (5 \times 1000) + (4 \times 10) + (2 \times 1)$.

Example 12

Write the simplest numeral for these numbers:
$(8 \times 10^4) + (7 \times 10^3) + (5 \times 10^2) + (3 \times 10^1) + (9 \times 1)$

$(8 \times 10^4) + (7 \times 10^3) + (5 \times 10^2) + (3 \times 10^1) + (9 \times 1)$
$= (8 \times 10\,000) + (7 \times 1000) + (5 \times 100) \times (3 \times 10) + (9 \times 1)$
$= 87\,539$

EXERCISE 2G

1 Write the simplest numerals for each of the following:
  a $(8 \times 100\,000) + (6 \times 10\,000) + (2 \times 1000) + (9 \times 100) + (5 \times 10) + (3 \times 1)$
  b $(6 \times 1\,000\,000) + (9 \times 100\,000) + (8 \times 10\,000) + (7 \times 1000) + (9 \times 10) + (6 \times 1)$
  c $(3 \times 1\,000\,000) + (5 \times 10\,000) + (7 \times 100) + (9 \times 1)$
  d $(4 \times 10^6) + (8 \times 10^5) + (9 \times 10^4) + (2 \times 10^3) + (2 \times 10^2) + (6 \times 10^1)$
  e $(2 \times 10^7) + (3 \times 10^5) + (6 \times 10^4) + (9 \times 10^3) + (6 \times 10^1) + (8 \times 1)$
  f $(10^6) + (10^4) + (10^3) + (10^2) + (9 \times 10^1)$
  g 9 thousands and 8 hundreds and 3 tens and 6 units
  h 8 hundred thousands + 9 ten thousands + 6 hundreds + 3 tens and seven units
  i 5 ten millions − 8 hundred thousands + seven ten thousands + 5 thousands

Example 13

Expand 952 473 using power notation.

952 473
$= (9 \times 100\,000) + (5 \times 10\,000) + (2 \times 1000) + (4 \times 100) + (7 \times 10) + (3 \times 1)$
$= (9 \times 10^5) + (5 \times 10^4) + (2 \times 10^3) + (4 \times 10^2) + (7 \times 10^1) + (3 \times 1)$

2 Write these numbers using expanded notation:
- **a** 9738
- **b** 29 782
- **c** 40 404
- **d** 657 931
- **e** 800 388
- **f** 1 247 091
- **g** 49 755 400
- **h** 6 777 777

3 Expand these numbers using power notation:
- **a** 658
- **b** 3874
- **c** 95 636
- **d** 100 100
- **e** 505 750
- **f** 1 274 947
- **g** 36 600 000
- **h** 4 293 375
- **i** four hundred thousand six hundred and eighty seven
- **j** twenty three million, six hundred and ninety seven thousand five hundred

H SQUARE AND CUBE NUMBERS

SQUARE NUMBERS

The product of two identical whole numbers is a **square number**.

For example, $1 \times 1 = 1$, $2 \times 2 = 4$, $3 \times 3 = 9$, $12 \times 12 = 144$
$1^2 = 1$, $2^2 = 4$, $3^2 = 9$, $12^2 = 144$

1, 4, 9 and 144 in the example above are square numbers.

Multiplying a whole number by itself produces a square number.

EXERCISE 2H

1 Find the value of:
- **a** 4^2
- **b** 5^2
- **c** 7^2
- **d** 10^2
- **e** 32^2
- **f** 72^2
- **g** $5^2 - 2^2$
- **h** $(5-2)^2$
- **i** $2^2 + 4^2$
- **j** $(2+4)^2$

2 Use a calculator to find:
- **a** 136^2
- **b** 408^2
- **c** 1167^2
- **d** 2305^2

3 $4^2 = 16$ ends in a 6 and $5^2 = 25$ ends in a 5.

   a List all the possible numbers that a square number could end in.

   b Is $638\,254\,916\,823\,620\,058$ a square number?

SQUARE ROOTS

The square root of the square number 9 is written as $\sqrt{9}$.
It is the positive number which when squared gives 9.

So, as $3^2 = 9$ then $\sqrt{9} = 3$.

   Likewise as $2^2 = 4,\quad 5^2 = 25,\quad 11^2 = 121,\quad 15^2 = 225$

   then $\sqrt{4} = 2,\quad \sqrt{25} = 5,\quad \sqrt{121} = 11,\quad \sqrt{225} = 15$.

4 Find the square root of:

   a 1   **b** 16   **c** 36   **d** 81   **e** 144

5 Find:

   a $\sqrt{49}$ **b** $\sqrt{64}$ **c** $\sqrt{100}$ **d** $\sqrt{0}$ **e** $\sqrt{400}$

CUBE NUMBERS

> A **cube number** is a result of cubing a whole number.

For example, 8 is a cube number as $2^3 = 8$.

6 Find the first 10 cube numbers, beginning with $1^3 = 1$.

7 Find:

   a $2^3 - 2^2$ **b** $5^3 - 5$ **c** $4^3 + 2^3$ **d** $7^3 - 7^2$

8 , 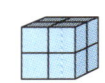 , 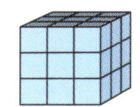 , etc. represents the first 3 cube numbers.

   a Draw a sketch of the representation of 4^3.

   b Explain why these diagrams do represent 1^3, 2^3, 3^3 and 4^3.

9 Paul believes that the following number forms are always divisible by 6.

   $2^3 - 1^3 - 1$
   $3^3 - 2^3 - 1$
   $4^3 - 3^3 - 1$
   $5^3 - 4^3 - 1$
   $\vdots$
   etc.

   a Check that the first four of them are divisible by 6.

   b Check that these are divisible by 6:

   i $10^3 - 9^3 - 1$

   ii $53^3 - 52^3 - 1$

ACTIVITY — MORE SQUARE NUMBERS

What to do:

1 Use graph paper to guide you.

Near the top left hand corner of the page, shade in one square region i.e., $1 \times 1 = 1^2$.

Leave two squares of space and shade another square region $2 \times 2 = 2^2 = 4$ squares.

Continue this pattern i.e., $3 \times 3, 4 \times 4, ...$ until you cannot fit any more on the page without overlapping.

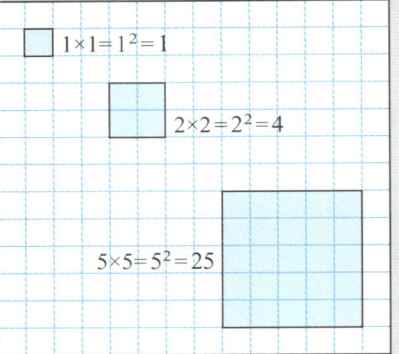

Write the rule which explains how the square number was produced.

2 Use graph paper. Construct overlapping squares as shown.

On the top right corner of each square, write down the **total** number of squares enclosed by the larger square.

On your piece of paper, what is the largest number of smaller squares that you can enclose with a larger square?

List your square numbers in ascending order.

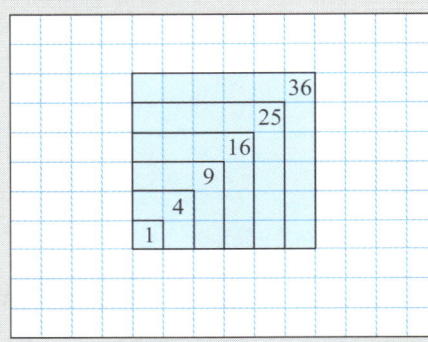

3 A B C

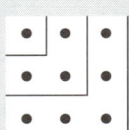 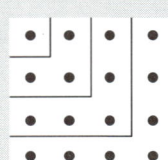 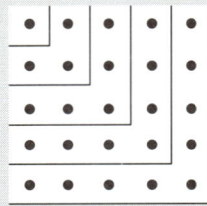

Diagram

A shows that the sum of the first 3 odd numbers is 3^2 i.e., $1 + 3 + 5 = 9$

B shows that the sum of the first 4 odd numbers is 4^2 i.e., $1 + 3 + 5 + 7 = 16$

C shows that the sum of the first 5 odd numbers is 5^2 i.e., $1 + 3 + 5 + 7 + 9 = 25$.

a Draw the next two diagrams in this pattern.

b Write down the next three lines in this pattern.

c Complete the first two lines.

d Add the first and last number in each sum then divide it by 2. What do you find?

e What numbers when squared are equal to these sums?

i $1 + 3 + 5 + 7 + ... + 21 =$ **ii** $1 + 3 + 5 + 7 + ... + 23 =$
iii $1 + 3 + 5 + 7 + ... + 35 =$ **iv** $1 + 3 + 5 + 7 + ... + 39 =$

4 Use the following formula to complete the exercises. A **square number** results from one being added to the product of any four consecutive whole numbers.

$1 \times 2 \times 3 \times 4 + 1 = 25 = 5^2$ $2 \times 3 \times 4 \times 5 + 1 = 121 = 11^2$

a $3 \times 4 \times 5 \times 6 + 1 = ... = 19^2$ **b** $4 \times 5 \times 6 \times 7 + 1 = ... = \Box^2$

c $5 \times 6 \times 7 \times 8 + 1 = ... = n^2$ **d** $6 \times 7 \times 8 \times 9 + 1 = ... = \Delta^2$

e $7 \times 8 \times 9 \times 10 + 1 = ... = \bigcirc^2$

Use any four consecutive whole numbers to show that the formula works.

5 Find other patterns and formulae using square numbers to share with the class.

TRIANGULAR NUMBERS

There are 133 members of a tennis club and each member must shake hands with every other member. How many handshakes must be made?

Too hard! Impossible! How can we do this?

Try the following investigation and find out how!

INVESTIGATION   TRIANGULAR NUMBERS

The numbers 1, 3, 6, 10, etc. are called **triangular numbers** as each can be represented by a triangle of dots.

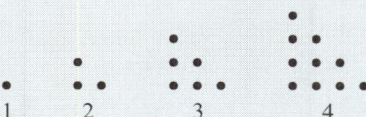

are the first 4 representations.

What to do:

1 Draw the next 3 triangular number representations and record the number of dots in a table like the one given:

Triangular number (n)	1st	2nd	3rd	4th	5th	6th	7th
Number of dots (D)							

2 What are the 8th, 9th and 10th triangular numbers?

3 Copy and complete: $\dfrac{1 \times 2}{2} = ...,$ $\dfrac{2 \times 3}{2} = ...,$ $\dfrac{3 \times 4}{2} = ...,$ $\dfrac{4 \times 5}{2} = ...,$

and hence state a formula connecting D and n for the tabled values in **1**.

4 When Alan, Bonny, Claudia and Daniel shake hands in all possible ways we notice that 6 handshakes have taken place.

These are: AB, AC, AD, where AB represents the Alan - Bonny hand-shake.
            BC, BD,
            CD

Copy and complete:

Number of people (P)	2	3	4	5	6
Number of handshakes (H)					

    a   State in words, the connection between the number of handshakes H, the number of people P, and the nth triangular number.

    b   State a formula connecting H and P.

    c   How many possible handshakes take place with a group of 20 people?

5 How many possible handshakes take place when all 142 representatives of the United Nations countries shake hands with each other?

PROBLEM SOLVING

You need to become familiar with a variety of problem solving techniques so you can feel confident when confronted by new problem situations. To enable you to become familiar with some techniques you need to experience them. The following exercises introduce you to some suitable techniques in an organised manner.

You need to be aware that any one problem can be solved in a variety of ways and the following examples are only possible solving techniques.

METHOD 1: TRIAL AND ERROR

This is the most common method used by students at your level. It is self-explanatory in its name but you need to be taught the check part of the method.

Example: On a farm there are some chickens and some cows. An observer counts 19 heads and 62 feet. Assuming each creature has only one head, cows have 4 feet and chickens have 2 feet, how many chickens and how many cows are on the farm?

A student answering this by the trial and error method would do something like the following:

Guess the number of chickens to be 5. Therefore the number of cows would need to be 14 since $5 + 14 = 19$.

Then check the total number of feet as follows:
$$5 \times 2 = 10$$
$$14 \times 4 = 56$$
$$\text{total} = 66$$

which does not equal the required 62 so another guess is needed. Hopefully the student can see that more chickens are needed and fewer cows.

The student continues in this manner until the correct answer is found.

It is important that the student is encouraged to show all working and that at the end a statement is written such as: "There are 7 chickens and 12 cows on the farm."

EXERCISE 21.1

Solve these problems using the trial and error method. Write your answer clearly.

1 Find consecutive whole numbers that add up to 51. (Consecutive numbers are numbers that follow each other, for example, 4 and 5 or 24 and 25.)

2 In a jar there are some spiders and beetles. If there are 13 creatures in total and the number of legs adds to 86 how many of each creature are in the jar?

3 How many two digit numbers are there in which the tens digit is less than the ones digit?

4 Using the digits 2, 3, 4 and 5 in that order and the symbols ×, −, + in any order, make a mathematical sentence that equals 9.

5 Hera paid for her $69 jeans with coins she had saved. She used only $2 and $1 coins and noticed she was able to pay using the same number of each coin. How many $1 coins did she use to pay for her jeans?

6 The sum on the right is not correct. By changing only one of the digits you can make it correct. Which one would you change?

$$\begin{array}{r} 386 \\ + \ 125 \\ \hline 521 \end{array}$$

7 What is the largest number of pieces you can cut a round pizza into using four straight cuts?

8 If $a \times b = 24$, $b \times c = 12$ and $c \times a = 18$, find values for a, b, and c.

9 Helen has three times as many brothers as sisters. Her brother John has two more brothers than he has sisters. How many boys and how many girls are there in the family?

10 Karen is two years older than Fred who is 6 years younger than Jill. Together their ages total 41 years. How old is each child?

METHOD 2: MAKING A TABLE AND LOOKING FOR A PATTERN (MAKING THE PROBLEM SIMPLER)

This method requires you to collect some information and organise it in table form so that some pattern can be seen. You then use the pattern to predict what may happen.

Example:

How many games in total would need to be played to complete a round robin tennis tournament if there were 20 players? A round robin tournament means that every player plays every other player once.

The solution to this can be found by trial and error but would take too long. You can solve this by making the problem simpler and forming a table as follows.

If there were only two players you would need 1 game. If there were only 3 players you would need 3 games (use counters to model this and count them).

If there were only 4 players you would need 6 games.

In table form this would look like

players	2	3	4	5	6
games	1	3	6	10	15
gap		2	3	4	5

From this table you can find a pattern and predict the result for 20 players - clearly this is easier than actually counting the number of games!

The pattern here is that the gap between the number of games played is increasing by one for every new player, so continuing this pattern gives 190 games for 20 players. There is another pattern here. Can you find it?

EXERCISE 21.2

Solve the following using **Method 2**.

1 How many different two course meals can I make with eight main courses and 16 desserts? **Hint:** Try with two mains and one dessert, then two mains and two desserts, etc and make a table of your findings and look for a pattern.

2 A club rugby team has three shirt colours (yellow, green and grey) and four shorts colours (black, white, blue and red). How many different uniforms are possible, if they have different colours for shorts and tops? (Remember to start with a smaller number of tops and shorts and look for a pattern.)

3 If there are 15 people in a room and everyone must shake hands with everyone else how many handshakes will there be in total? **Hint:** What if there were only two people in the room? Three people in the room? etc. Make a table and look for a pattern.

4 How many top and bottom rails would be needed to complete a straight fence if it has 55 posts?

5 How many diagonals would a 12-sided polygon have? (What is the name of a 12-sided polygon?) Remember that a diagonal is a straight line that joins two vertices of a polygon and is not a side of the polygon.

For example:  A rectangle has 2 diagonals. 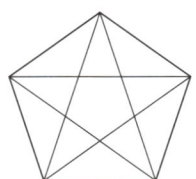 A pentagon has 5 diagonals.

6 The pizza problem met in the first section can also be solved by this patterning method. Use this method to find how many pieces you can cut a pizza into with ten straight cuts. Remember that each piece does not have to be the same size!

METHOD 3: MODELLING OR DRAWING A PICTURE

In this method you can act out the problem, draw pictures or use equipment to model the situation and then solve it.

Example:

If Jan has three different coloured tops and two different coloured skirts how many different combinations of skirts and tops can she wear?

It is possible to solve this by getting three different counters for the tops and two others for the skirts and actually pairing off the different combinations as you go. You are **modelling** the situation.

If you do it correctly you will get six different outfits she can wear! *or*

You can draw a picture of all the outfits she could wear. Again you should get six outfits.

EXERCISE 21.3

Do the following by modelling or drawing the picture. Remember to state your answer clearly and show any working you do.

1 A square table has four seats around it. In how many different ways can four people sit around the table?

2 This one can be modelled by counting seconds instead of minutes with a person/counter leaving the group at the correct time.

Year 7 and 8 students are doing the same orienteering course. A year 7 student leaves every 6 minutes and a year 8 student every 3.5 minutes. If the event begins at 9 am with one student from each year group leaving together, when is the next time a student from each year level will leave together?

3 Darren numbered the pages of his art folder using a packet of stickers. On each sticker there was one digit from 0 to 9. He started with page 1. When he finished he noticed he had used 77 stickers. How many pages were in his art folder?

4 When Bill and Karen went to a basketball game they had tickets for seats 93 and 94. They saw that the seat numbers followed a pattern as shown. In what row were their seats?

Row 3	11	12	13	14	15	16	17	18
Row 2		5	6	7	8	9	10	
Row 1			1	2	3	4		

5 When Stephen put 10 counters in a bag it was $\frac{1}{3}$ full.

When James put 13 in his bag it was $\frac{1}{2}$ full and when Blair put 7 in his bag it was $\frac{1}{4}$ full.

Who had the biggest bag?

METHOD 4: WORKING BACKWARDS

This method requires you to do the problem in reverse order, i.e., start at the answer given to find the required answer.

Example: I think of a number, add three to it, multiply this result by 2, subtract 4 then divide by 7.

The number I end up with is 2.

What was the number I first thought of?

To do this problem start with the result and work in reverse order.

    Start with 2   (your result)
    multiply by 7 to get 14   (the opposite of dividing by 7)
    add 4 to get 18   (the opposite of subtracting 4)
    divide by 2 to get 9   (the opposite of multiplying by 2)
    subtract 3 to get 6   (the opposite of adding 3)

The number I first thought of was 6. You should always check the answer by starting at 6 and ending up at 2.

EXERCISE 21.4

Attempt these problems using the working backwards method.

1. The number of rabbits in my rabbit farm double each month. At the end of last month there were 24 000 rabbits. When were there 1500 rabbits?

2. I think of a number and multiply it by 2, then add 2 and subtract 10. This result is then divided by 4. I end up with 4. What number did I think of originally?

3. I am trying to work out David's age. He told me that if I add 6 to his age, then multiply by 3, add another 17 then divide by 8 I will end up at his sister Susie's age which is twice his brother Bill's age which is 5 years old. How old is David?

4. Nikora left home at a certain time. He biked for 20 minutes, then walked for a further 15 minutes. He rested there for half an hour before continuing on to Sam's house which was a further 25 minutes walk away. Nikora played at Sam's house for 45 minutes before moving on to his grandmother's home which took him another 20 minutes. He arrived at his grandmother's home at noon, just in time for lunch. What was the time he left his home that morning?

5. Jillian enjoyed gardening and liked to keep a record of the height of her rose bush. After recording the starting height she noted that it grew a further 5 cm before halving in height when she pruned it by mistake. It then continued to grow nicely for another 20 cm before a hedge trimmer accidently cut one third off the height. At this stage Jillian recorded the height of the rose bush to be 24 cm. How high was the rose bush when she started measuring it?

REVIEW SET A — CHAPTER 2

1. **a** Find the difference between 10 and 2.
   b Decrease 10 by 2.
   c Find the quotient of 10 and 2.
   d Find 10 to the power of 2.

2. Evaluate the following:
   a $5 + 6 \times 3 - 9$
   b $(5 + 6) \times 3 - 9$
   c $5 + (6 \div 3 \times 9)$

3. Write the 4th prime number after 23.

4. **a** List all the factors of 56.
   b Determine the LCM of 4 and 10.
   c Find the highest common factor of 12 and 30.

5. In the following, is the first number divisible by the second number? (Answer yes or no.)
   a 3675, 10
   b 47 368, 4
   c 974 580, 5
   d 129 408, 3

6. Convert each number into natural form:
   a $3^2 \times 2^2 \times 10$
   b $2^4 \times 10^2 \times 2$
   c $10^2 \times 10^2 \times 10^2$

7. Simplify:
   a $5 \times 10^4 + 7 \times 10^2 + 3 \times 10$
   b $(4 \times 1\,000\,000) + (2 \times 10\,000) + (3 \times 100) + (5 \times 1)$

8. Find the value of: **a** 3^2 **b** 2^3 **c** $\sqrt{49}$

9. The quotation that I received for bathroom renovations was for $6850. When the bill came, an error had been made on it. I was charged $8650.

   How much was I being overcharged?

REVIEW SET B — CHAPTER 2

1. **a** Share 12 between 3.
   b Increase 12 by 3.
   c Find the product of 12 and 3.
   d $3\overline{\smash{)}12}^{\,4}$ The dividend is ......

2. Evaluate the following:
   a $6 + 8 \div 2 + 7$
   b $(6 + 8) \div 2 + 7$
   c $(27 \div 9) + (3 + 2) \times 2$

3. **a** List the factors of 110.
   b Find the highest common factor of 16 and 24.

4. For the set of numbers between 30 and 60, list all the:
   a multiples of 8
   b square numbers
   c prime numbers

5. A motorist has her oil, battery and radiator checked every 5000 km, her tyres rotated every 15 000 km and her engine tuned every 20 000 km. At what stage will all three services happen together?

6 Find the value of: **a** $3^3 - 4^2$ **b** $\sqrt{64} - \sqrt{36}$

7 Write the simplest numerals for these numbers:
 a $(4 \times 10^7) + (8 \times 10^5) + (3 \times 10^4) + (9 \times 10^2) + (6 \times 10^1)$
 b $(9 \times 100\,000) + (3 \times 10\,000) + (6 \times 100) + (4 \times 10) + (7 \times 1)$

8 List 4 consecutive powers of 10 after 100.

9 Marg and Don were buying a car costing $24 600. They were asked to pay a deposit of $\frac{1}{10}$ of its value, and to pay the balance when they collected the car. How much did they have to pay when they collected the car?

REVIEW SET C — CHAPTER 2

1 Simplify:
 a $3 \times 5 - 4 \times 2$ **b** $3 + 13 \times 2$
 c $12 \div 4 \times 2 + 7$ **d** $(3 + 4) \times 2 + 20 \div (9 - 4)$

2 The 4 game attendance at the local stadium was 5879, 6847, 6432 and 5907. What was the difference between the expected attendance of twenty five thousand and the actual attendance?

3 **a** List all the factors of 64.
 b List the prime numbers between 10 and 20.
 c Find the LCM of 15 and 21.
 d Express 120 as the product of prime factors.
 e Find the highest common factor of 18 and 45.

4 A long piece of licorice is to be cut exactly into 4, 6 and 9 cm lengths. Find the shortest length of licorice satisfying these requirements.

5 Complete the following:
 a $49 = \Box^2$ **b** $121 = \Delta^2$ **c** $\sqrt{81} = *$
 d $27 = \Delta^3$ **e** $\sqrt{400} = *$

6 Write the simplest numerals for these numbers:
 a $2^2 \times 5 \times 10^2$
 b $3^2 \times 7 \times 10^3$
 c $10 \times 10^2 \times 10^3$
 d $3 \times 10^4 + 7 \times 10^3 + 1 \times 10 + 2 \times 1$
 e $(6 \times 1\,000\,000) + (5 \times 100\,000) + (4 \times 1000) + (3 \times 100) + (8 \times 1)$

7 Find the total cost of 3 dozen jars of coffee priced at $9.95 each.

Chapter 3
Shapes and solids

Knowledge, skills and understandings

By the end of this chapter you should be able to

- use the terms lines, points, rays, segments, intersections, parallel and perpendicular when constructing diagrams (e.g., using drawing software to design a moving analogue clock)
- bisect angles using a compass
- construct triangles when only the length of sides is given
- draw a 2-D shape given a description of its side and angle properties, using geometric software or a ruler, protractor and set square
- identify the terminology of a circle - radius, diameter, circumference
- identify 2-D shapes within patterns across cultures and in nature (e.g., an investigation of Islamic design)
- classify solids in terms of their geometric properties (i.e., faces, edges, vertices and cross-sections)
- draw 3-D solids
- identify and name properties of polyhedra (e.g., tetrahedron, pentagonal prism, hexagonal prism)
- construct complex solids from nets (e.g., hexagonal-based pyramid)
- draw oblique and isometric projections of cubes using paper or drawing software
- recognise the properties of quadrilaterals
- construct, name and classify scalene, isosceles and equilateral triangles
- determine unknown angles in quadrilaterals and triangles

GEOMETRICAL SHAPES

Buildings and structures such as bridges and towers contain different geometrical shapes for visual appeal or strength features. Buildings show many square cornered shapes in the form of rectangles whilst triangles are especially common in bridges made of steel.

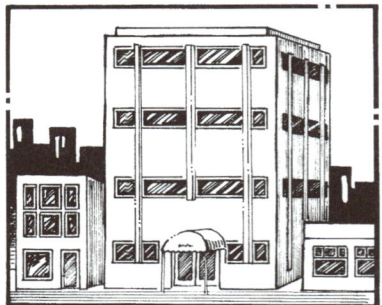

The word **geometry** originally came from two Greek words:

ge and **metron** meaning earth measure.

The study of geometry in mathematics involves considering the following:

- points
- lines
- angles
- surfaces
- solids

Notice that

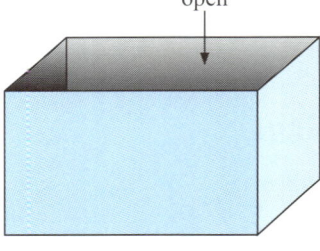

is a **container**

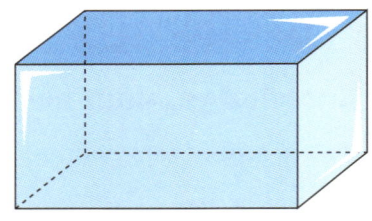

is a **solid**

ACTIVITY — GEOMETRICAL IDEAS

What to do:

1. Find in the classroom *two* examples of each of the following:
   - a point
   - a line
   - an angle
   - a solid
   - a flat surface
   - a curved surface
   - a container.

2. Consider two objects, a container and a solid, of the same shape.

Discussion:

a. Which of the objects occupies more space?
b. Which of the objects has more surface, i.e., is exposed to more air?
c. If they are made of the same material, which is heavier?
d. What special property does the container have compared with the solid?

SHAPES AND SOLIDS (CHAPTER 3)

A POINTS AND LINES

DISCUSSION — WHAT IS A POINT?

What to do:

In groups of 4 or 5, for at most 10 minutes, discuss the following questions.

1. What is meant by a *point*?
2. Give examples of things which could be used to represent a point.
3. How small can a point be?
4. Each group could make a brief report to the class.

POINTS IN GEOMETRY

Good examples of a point in the classroom are:
- the intersection of two side by side walls and the floor
- a speck of dust in the room at a particular instant in time.

In geometry, a point is represented by a small dot and to help identify it we name it with a capital letter.

Consider:

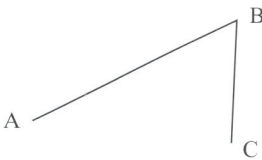

The letters A, B and C are useful because we can identify the point to which we are referring.

We can then make statements like "the distance from A to B is ....." or "the angle at B measures .....", etc.

To a mathematician,

> a **point** marks a position and does not have any size.

In order to see where a point is, we use a **dot** which has both size and colour.

FIGURES

A **figure** is a drawing which shows things we are interested in.

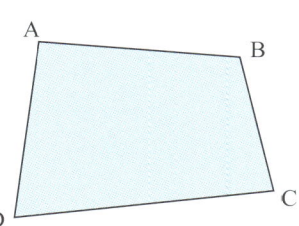

The figure alongside contains four points which have been labelled A, B, C and D.
These corner points are known as **vertices**.

(**Note:** Point B is a **vertex** of the figure.)

Vertices is the plural of vertex.

LINES

A **straight line** (usually just called a **line**) is a continuous infinite collection of points with no beginning and no end.

This line passes through points A and B. Notice that it continues indefinitely in both directions.

Because we cannot draw this line of infinite length, arrow heads are used to show that it continues endlessly.

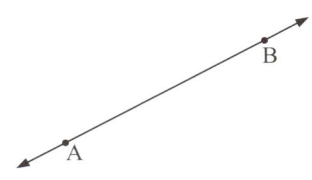

As with a point, a line has no width but in order to see it we give it thickness.

DISCUSSION — LINES

What to do:

In groups of 4 or 5, for at most 10 minutes, discuss the following questions.

1. How many different straight lines could be drawn through a single point which could, for example, be called A?

2. Suppose A and B are two separate points. How many straight lines could be drawn where each line passes through both A and B?

3. Suppose P, Q and R are three different points. How many straight lines can be drawn where each line passes through all of P, Q and R?

4. Each group could report their findings to the class.

Notation:

- The **line** passing through two separate (distinct) points A and B is represented by $\overleftrightarrow{AB}$ (or $\overleftrightarrow{BA}$).

- A **line segment** (or part line) connecting A and B is represented by $\overline{AB}$ or ($\overline{BA}$).

- A **ray** which starts at A and passes through B is represented by $\overrightarrow{AB}$.

PARALLEL AND INTERSECTING LINES

In a plane (flat surface), like a table top, two straight lines are either **parallel** or **intersecting**.

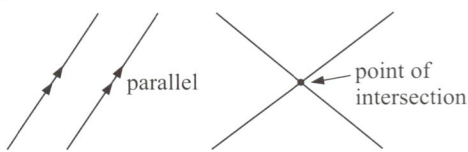

Parallel lines are lines which are always a fixed distance apart and so can never meet.

DISCUSSION

Look Dad, the parallel lines meet in the distance.

Oh yeah!

To the people in car A, the parallel lines (edges of the road) appear to meet in the distance.

Discuss this picture. Does it represent the real world?

EXERCISE 3A

1 Give two examples in the classroom which indicate:
   a a point   **b** a line

2 In geometry, what is meant by the word(s):
   a vertex   **b** point of intersection   **c** parallel lines?
   Draw diagrams to illustrate each.

3 Give all ways of naming the straight lines shown:
   a    **b**

   (**Hint:** In **b** there are 6 answers.)

4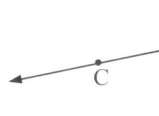

What is the intersection of:

a $\overleftrightarrow{AB}$ and $\overleftrightarrow{BC}$

b $\overrightarrow{CB}$ and $\overleftrightarrow{CA}$?

5 What is the intersection of:
   a $\overline{AB}$ and $\overline{BC}$
   b $\overline{AB}$ and $\overline{AC}$?

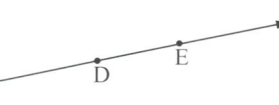

6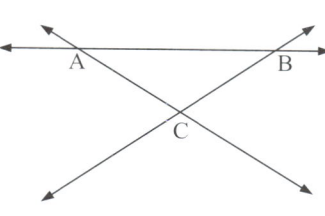

What is the intersection of:

a $\overline{PQ}$ and $\overleftrightarrow{PR}$ **b** $\overline{PQ}$ and $\overline{QS}$
c $\overline{QR}$ and $\overline{PS}$ **d** $\overline{PR}$ and $\overline{SQ}$?

7 For the given figure:

  a correctly name the line segments which form the sides

  b name the line segments which intersect at vertex M.

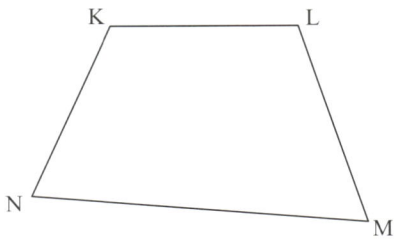

8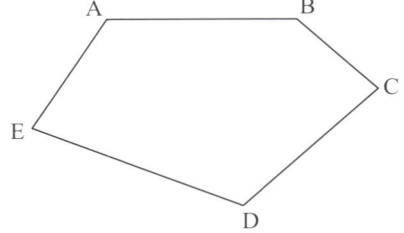

For the given figure:

  a name the line segments forming its sides

  b name the line segments which intersect at B

  c name 4 line segments (not all drawn) which could intersect at C.

ACTIVITY	STRAIGHT LINE SURPRISES

Part 1:

You will need: a sheet of blank paper, a ruler and a sharp pencil.

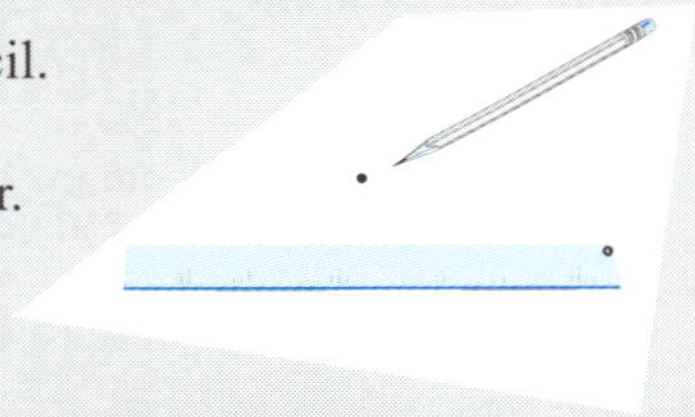

What to do:

1 Mark a point somewhere near the centre of the paper.

2 Line up one edge of your ruler so that it passes through the point. Draw a line along the *other* edge of the ruler across the paper.

3 Change the position of the ruler but still keep one edge passing through the point. Draw a second line so that it intersects with your first line.

4 Change the position of the ruler again, one edge passing through the point and the other edge allowing you to form a triangle. Draw the third line.

5 Rule lots more lines like this.

6 Describe what happens to the shape formed by the intersecting lines as more lines are drawn.

7 Why is this shape forming?

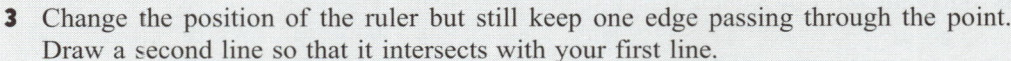

Part 2:

You will need: a sheet of 5 mm graph paper, a ruler, a sharp pencil.

What to do:

1 On graph paper, draw a horizontal base line and mark the numbers from 0 to 16 on it as shown in the diagram.

2 Draw a vertical line at O, and mark on it the numbers from 1 to 16 at the intersection of the horizontal lines, as shown.

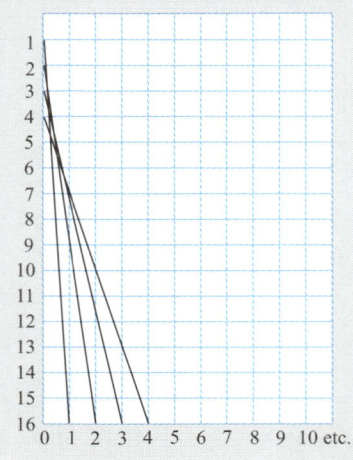

3 Rule a straight line from the intersection at vertical 1 to the intersection at horizontal 1.

4 Rule a straight line from the intersection at vertical 2 to the intersection at horizontal 2. Repeat this process until all the horizontal points have been joined.

5 Then draw a vertical line at 16 on the base line and repeat the pattern.

6 A real challenge is to turn the page upside down and repeat the pattern so that you have drawn 4 sets of straight lines.

B ANGLES

Whenever two lines or edges meet an **angle** is formed between them.

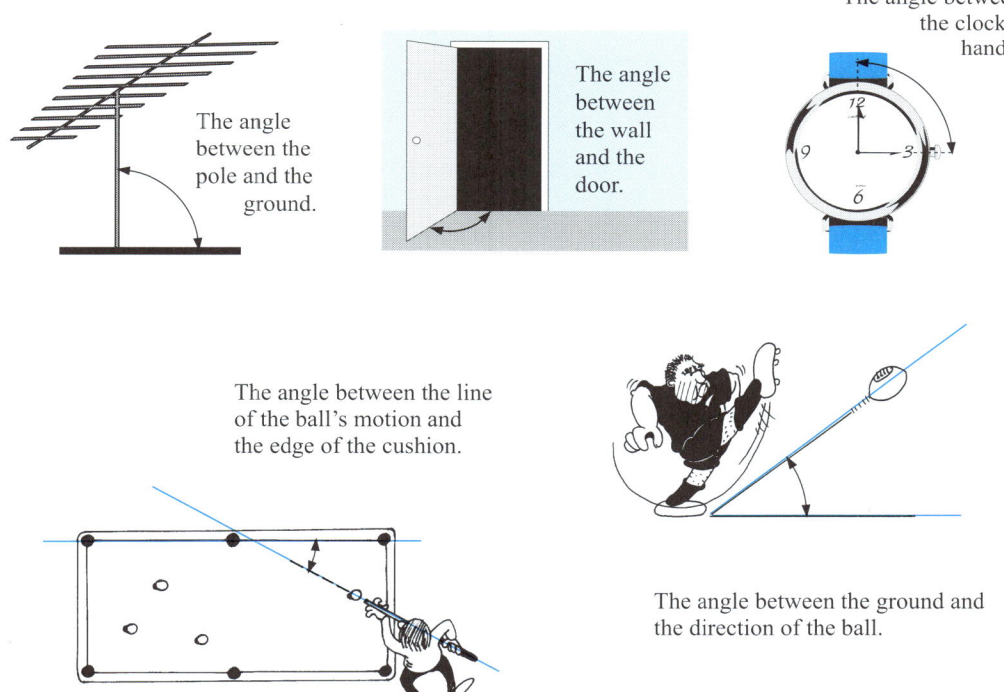

The angle between the pole and the ground.

The angle between the wall and the door.

The angle between the clock's hands.

The angle between the line of the ball's motion and the edge of the cushion.

The angle between the ground and the direction of the ball.

The **size of an angle** is the measure of the amount of rotation necessary to move one of the lines which makes up the angle onto the other one.

This is a small angle because only a small amount of turning is necessary for $\overline{AB}$ to turn about A until it fits onto $\overline{AC}$.

This is a large angle as a large amount of turning is necessary.

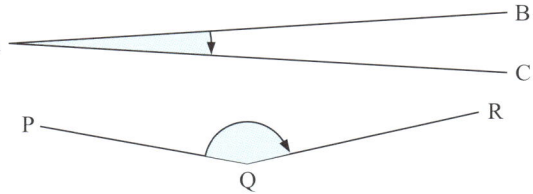

CLASSIFYING ANGLES

Below is a way of classifying (naming) angles according to the amount of turn:

Revolution	Straight Angle	Right Angle
One complete turn.	$\frac{1}{2}$ turn.	$\frac{1}{4}$ turn.
Acute Angle	**Obtuse Angle**	**Reflex Angle**
Less than a $\frac{1}{4}$ turn.	Between a $\frac{1}{4}$ turn and $\frac{1}{2}$ turn.	Between a $\frac{1}{2}$ turn and 1 turn.

Reminder: A small square where two lines meet indicates a right angle i.e.,

MEASURING ANGLES

To find the size of an angle accurately a unit of measurement is required. The unit chosen was the **degree**. There are 360 degrees in a full turn. 360 was probably chosen because it can be divided by 2, 3, 4, 5, 6, 8, 9, 10, 12, 15, etc. to give whole number answers.

So, a **straight angle** or **half turn** will measure $\frac{1}{2}$ of 360 degrees, i.e., 180 degrees.

We write this as $180°$. ← This small circle is used to indicate degrees and saves us writing the full word.

Also, a **right angle** or **quarter turn** will measure $\frac{1}{4}$ of $360°$, i.e., $90°$.

We can now classify angles in degree measure:

Name	Figure	Degrees
Revolution		$360°$
Straight angle		$180°$
Right angle		$90°$
Acute angle		between $0°$ and $90°$

Name	Figure	Degrees
Obtuse angle		between 90° and 180°
Reflex angle		between 180° and 360°

Two instruments that are used in schools for measuring angles are the **protractor** and the **geoliner**.

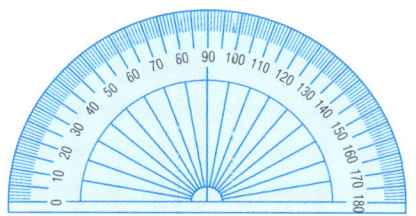 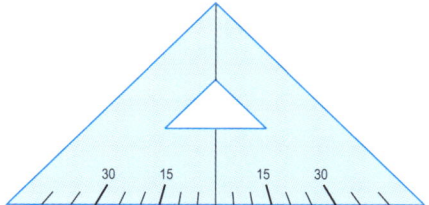

Protractors may be semi-circular (as above) or circular.

NAMING ANGLES (THREE POINT NOTATION)

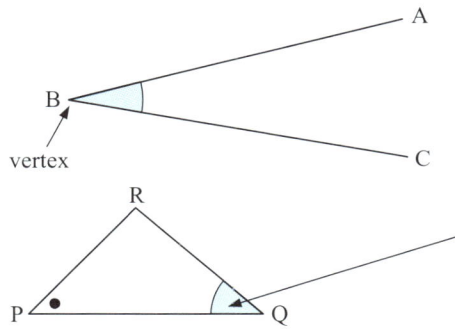

The angle shown is referred to as either:
- angle ABC   (or angle CBA),   or
- ∠ABC   (or ∠CBA)

Notice, that the angle is at vertex B and B is in the **middle** of the 3 given letters.

this angle is ∠PQR   (or ∠RQP)

It is wrong to call it ∠QPR, as this angle is the one marked •.

EXERCISE 3B.1

1 Draw a diagram to illustrate:
   a a $\frac{1}{2}$ turn   **b** a $\frac{1}{3}$ turn   **c** a full turn

2 Draw a diagram to illustrate:
   a a straight angle   **b** a right angle   **c** an obtuse angle

3 Use 3-point notation to name the following angles and state the type of angle in each case:

   a 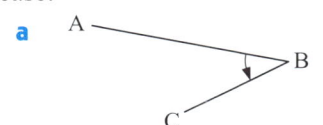   **b** 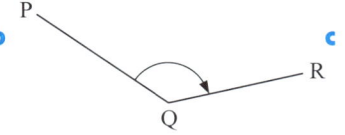   **c**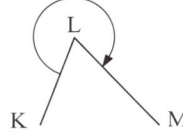

4 Draw an angle appropriate to the name:

   a ∠CDE   **b** ∠QPT   **c** angle MTD   **d** reflex ∠SNP.

5 The given figure contains many angles. Name all of them using 3-point notation.

Do not list ∠BAC as well as ∠CAB as these are the same angle.

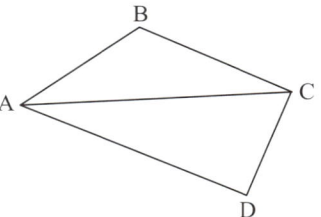

Extension:

6 The given diagram contains 3 acute angles ∠AOB, ∠BOC, ∠AOC within a right angle.

It contains 3 lines meeting at point O.

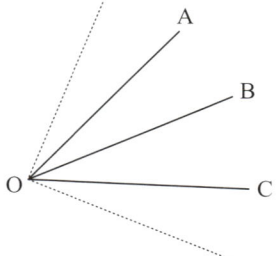

Copy and complete:

Number of lines meeting at O within a right angle	Number of acute angles formed
2	1
3	3
4	
5	
8	

USING A PROTRACTOR

Here is a picture of a protractor:

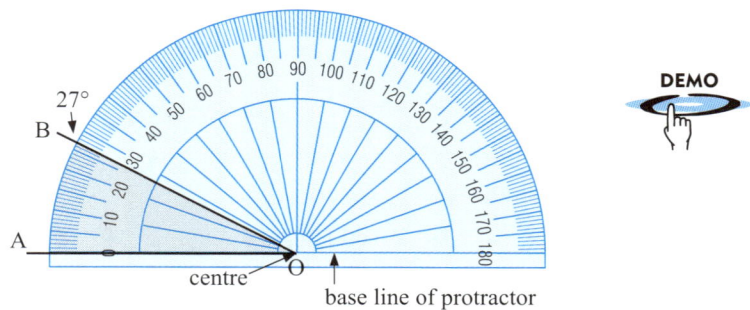

So, ∠AOB measures 27°.

Notice the centre of the semi-circle is placed at the vertex of the angle and the base line lies exactly on one arm of the angle.

Examples:

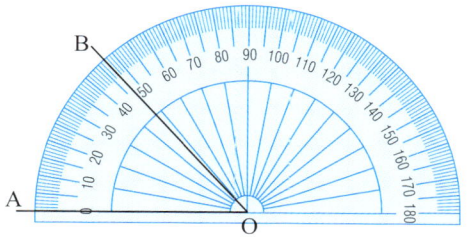 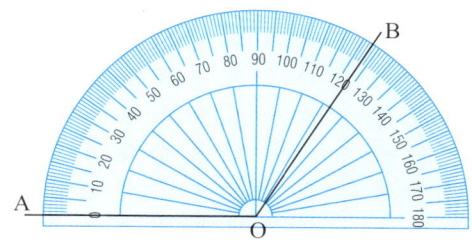

We say: the size of angle AOB is $47°$,
or $\angle AOB = 47°$.

We say: the size of angle AOB is $123°$,
or $\angle AOB = 123°$.

EXERCISE 3B.2

1 Find the degree measure of angle AOB for:

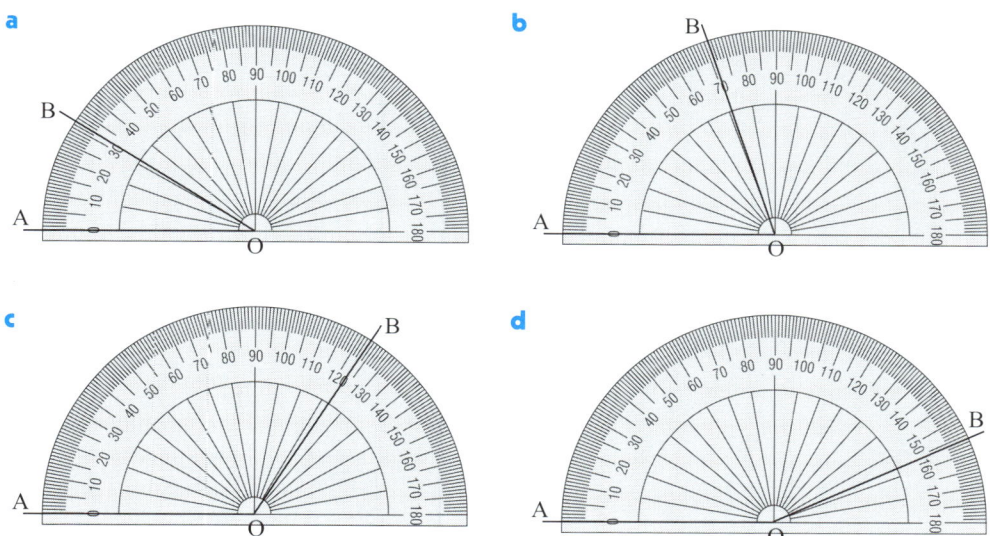

2 Measure all angles of the following triangles and use 3-point notation to write down your answers. For example $\angle PRQ = 38°$.

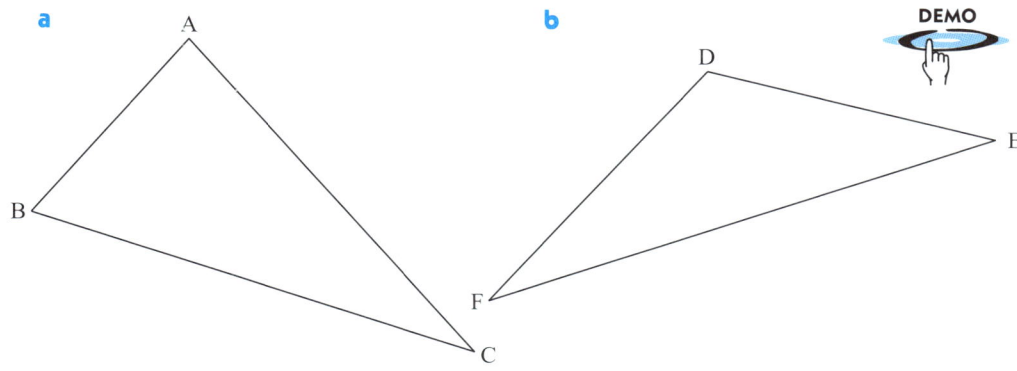

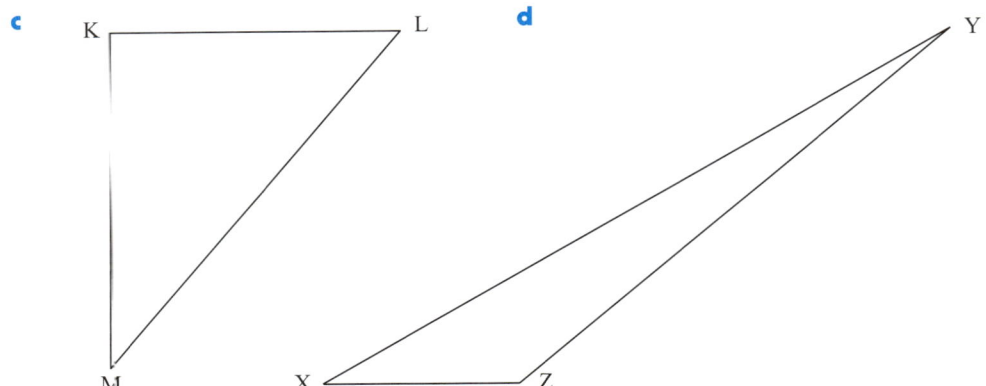

3 Measure all angles of the following figures and use 3-point notation to write down your answers:

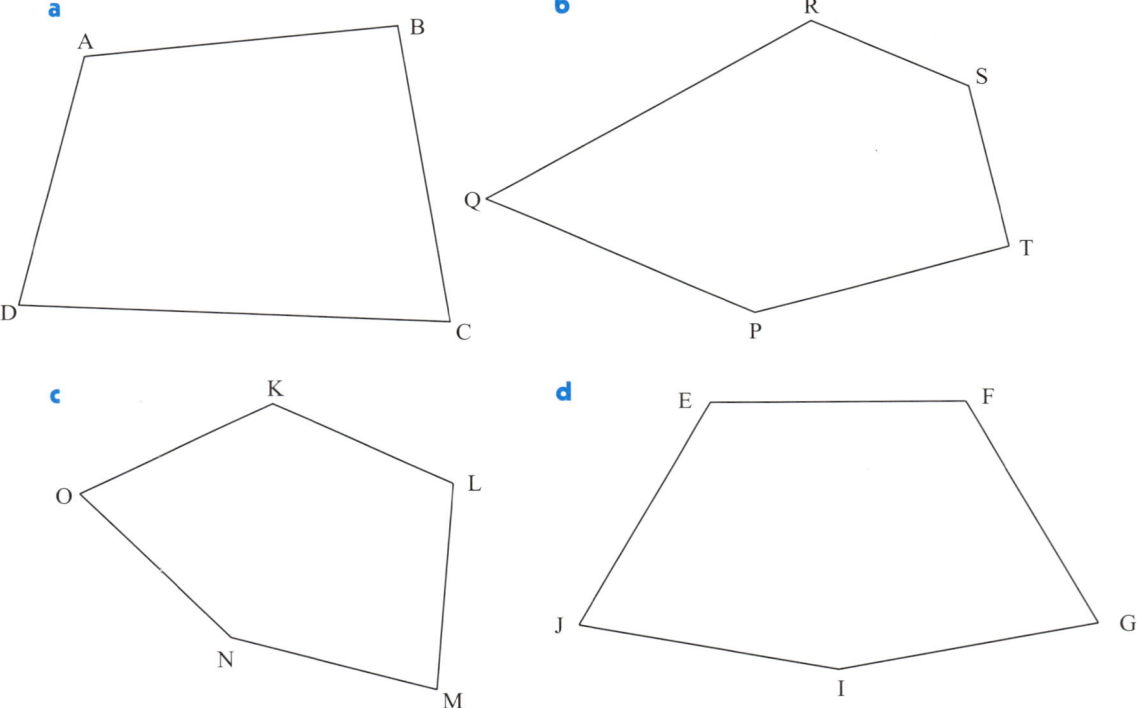

4 Estimate the size of the following angles then check how good (or bad) you are at estimating by using your protractor:

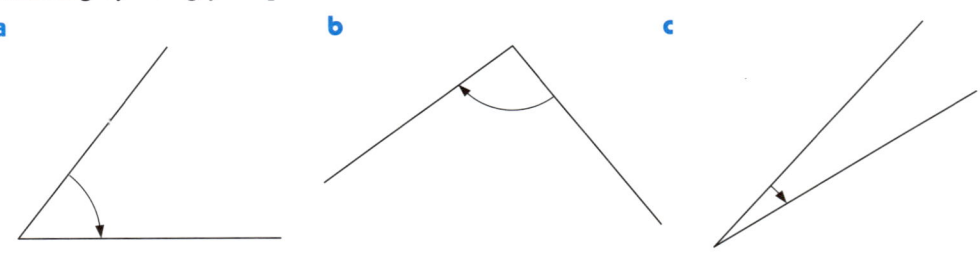

ACTIVITY — ANGLE GUESSING COMPETITION

Organise a competition between groups where 3 different angles are drawn. Each group guesses the size of each angle. The angles are then carefully measured with a protractor. A scoring system could be:

correct answer	±1°	5 points
correct answer	±2°	4 points
correct answer	±3°	3 points
correct answer	±4°	2 points
correct answer	±5°	1 point

C   ANGLES OF A TRIANGLE

INVESTIGATION — ANGLES OF A TRIANGLE

What to do:

1 Use a protractor to accurately measure (to the nearest degree) the sizes of the angles of triangle ABC:

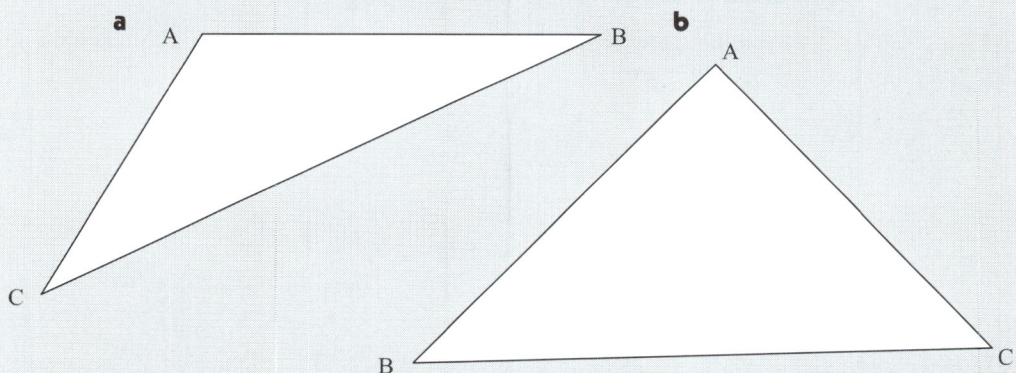

2 Copy and complete the following table using **a** and **b** results above and drawing *two* other triangles of your own choice (**c** and **d**) and measuring their angles:

	∠ABC	∠BCA	∠CAB	sum of the 3 angles
a				
b				
c				
d				

3 From your results in **2**, copy and complete:

   "The sum of the angles of a triangle is ......".

4 Now draw any triangle ABC and carefully cut it out.
   Fold down the angle at B to meet the side AC.
   Fold corner A along a vertical line to meet B.
   Fold corner C along a vertical line to meet B also.
   What do you notice?

   Repeat with another triangle of your choosing.

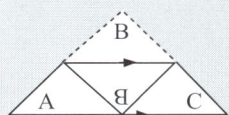

From the **Investigation** you should have noticed that:

> The sum of the angles of a triangle is always $180°$.

That is for 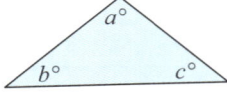 then $a + b + c = 180$.

We can also see this result by tearing the angles of the triangle and rearranging them to sit on a line.

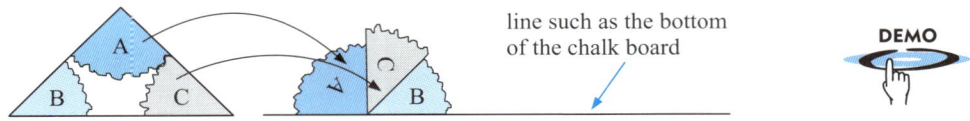

Example 1

Find the third angle of (i.e., find x):

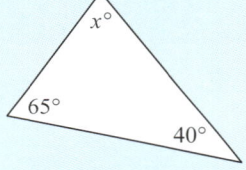

Since the angles add to $180°$, and $65 + 40 = 105$
then $x = 180 - 105$
$\therefore \quad x = 75$
and so the third angle measures $75°$.

EXERCISE 3C

1 Find the unknowns in the following which *have not been drawn accurately*:

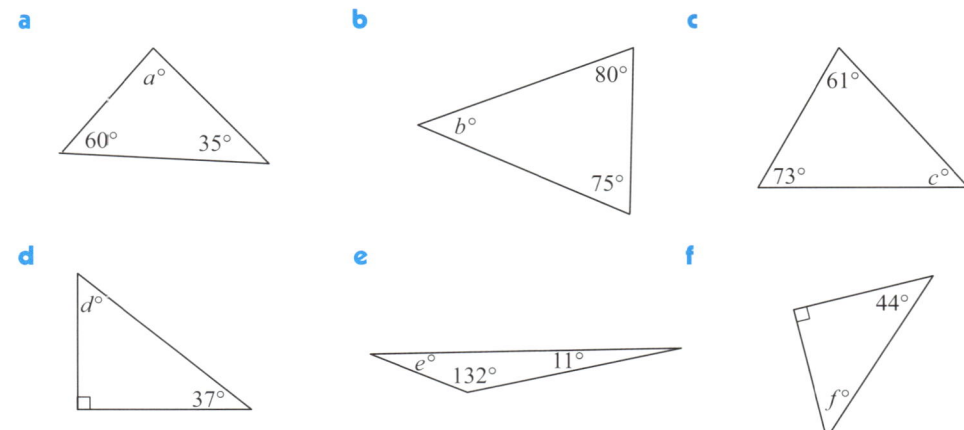

g   h   i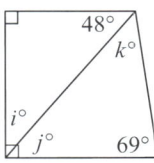

(triangle g: 67.2°, g°, right angle)
(triangle h: 36°, h°, 27°)

2 Write down a rule connecting the unknowns in:

a 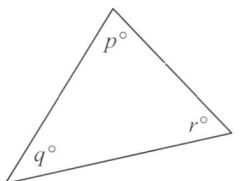 b 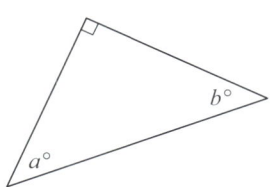 c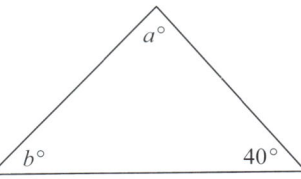

d 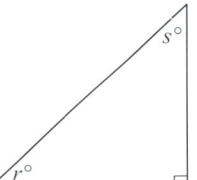 e 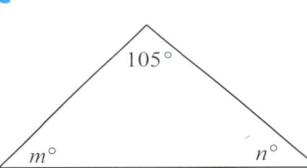 f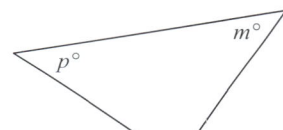

D ANGLES OF A QUADRILATERAL

INVESTIGATION   ANGLES OF A QUADRILATERAL

The purpose of this investigation is to discover any properties of the angles of quadrilaterals.

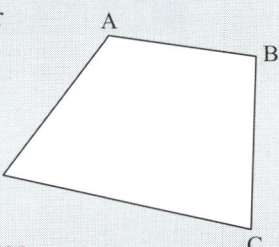

What to do:

1 Draw 4 half page size quadrilaterals and label the vertices A, B, C and D.

2 Accurately measure the angles at each vertex with a protractor.

3 Copy and complete the following recording sheet:

Diagram	∠DAB	∠ABC	∠BCD	∠CDA	sum of the angles
a					
b					
c					
d					

4 Using your recording sheet results, copy and complete:

"The sum of the angles in a quadrilateral is ......"

5 What other simple, special quadrilaterals support your answer in **4**?

6 Consider the given figure where AC is called a diagonal.

Copy and complete giving reasons at the end of each line in the bracket:

$b + c + d = \ldots\ldots$ {.................}

and $a + e + f = \ldots\ldots$ {.................}

$\therefore \ \angle DAB + \angle ABC + \angle BCD + \angle CDA$
$= (a + b) + c + (d + e) + f$
$=$
$=$

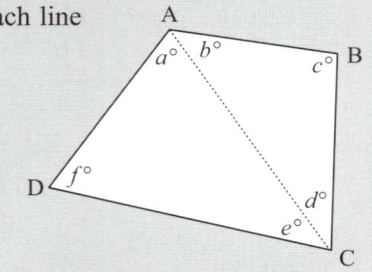

This successfully completed step-by-step argument should prove your statement in **4**.

From the **Investigation** you should have discovered that:

> The sum of the angles of a quadrilateral is always $360°$.

That is, if  then $a + b + c + d = 180$.

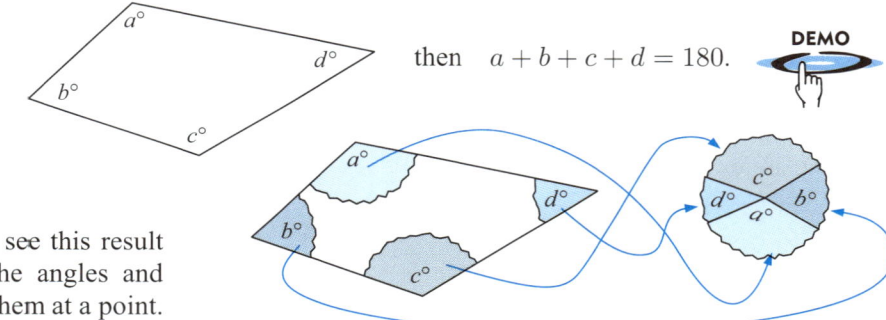

We can also see this result by tearing the angles and rearranging them at a point.

Example 2

Find the value of x in:

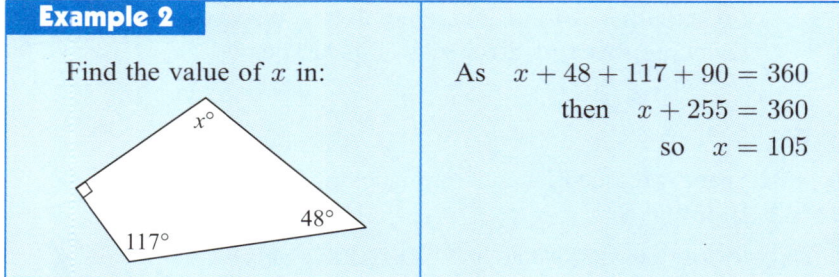

As $x + 48 + 117 + 90 = 360$
then $x + 255 = 360$
so $x = 105$

EXERCISE 3D

1 Find the unknowns in the following which *have not been drawn accurately*:

a 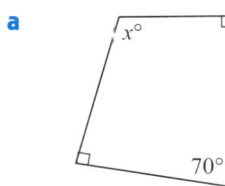 **b** 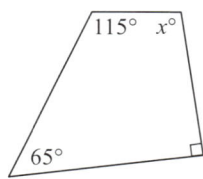 **c**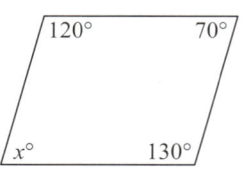

d 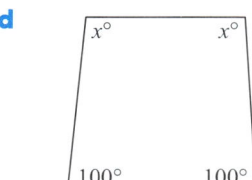   e 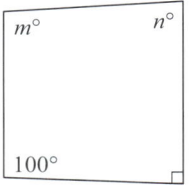   f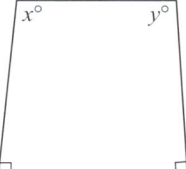

2 Write down a rule which connects the unknowns in:

a 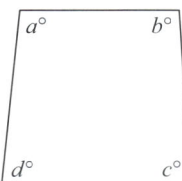   b 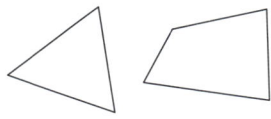   c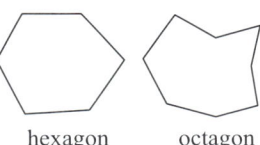

E   POLYGONS

Polygons are straight-sided closed figures that do not cross themselves and can only be drawn on a plane surface.

A **closed figure** has no gaps.

Following are examples of some simple polygons:

triangle   quadrilateral   pentagon   hexagon   octagon

An *n*-sided polygon is sometimes called an ***n*-gon**.

n stands for the number of sides.

So, an 8-sided polygon may be called an 8-gon or an octagon.

A **regular polygon** is a polygon with congruent sides and equal angles, i.e., sides the same length and angles the same size.

The polygons below are marked to show that they are regular:

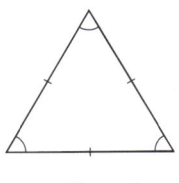   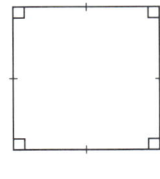   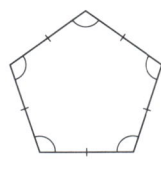   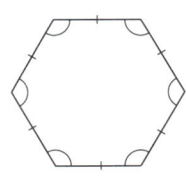

equilateral triangle   square   regular pentagon   regular hexagon

Equal sides are shown by using the same small markings on them. Equal angles are shown by using the same symbols (for example, ● or $a°$).

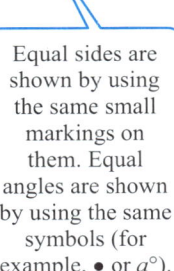

EXERCISE 3E

1 Give one reason why these are not polygons:

a 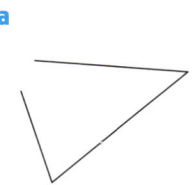 b 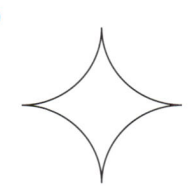 c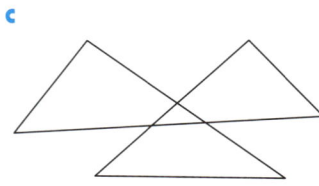

2 Which of the following are regular polygons?

a 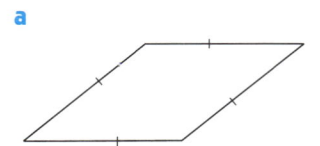 b  c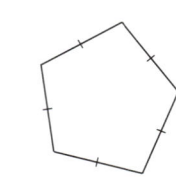

(**Note:** Angles marked with the same symbol are equal in size.)

3 Using the given code, name the polygons which follow:

tri-3, quad-4, penta-5, hexa-6, hepta-7, octa-8, nona-9, deca-10, dodeca-12

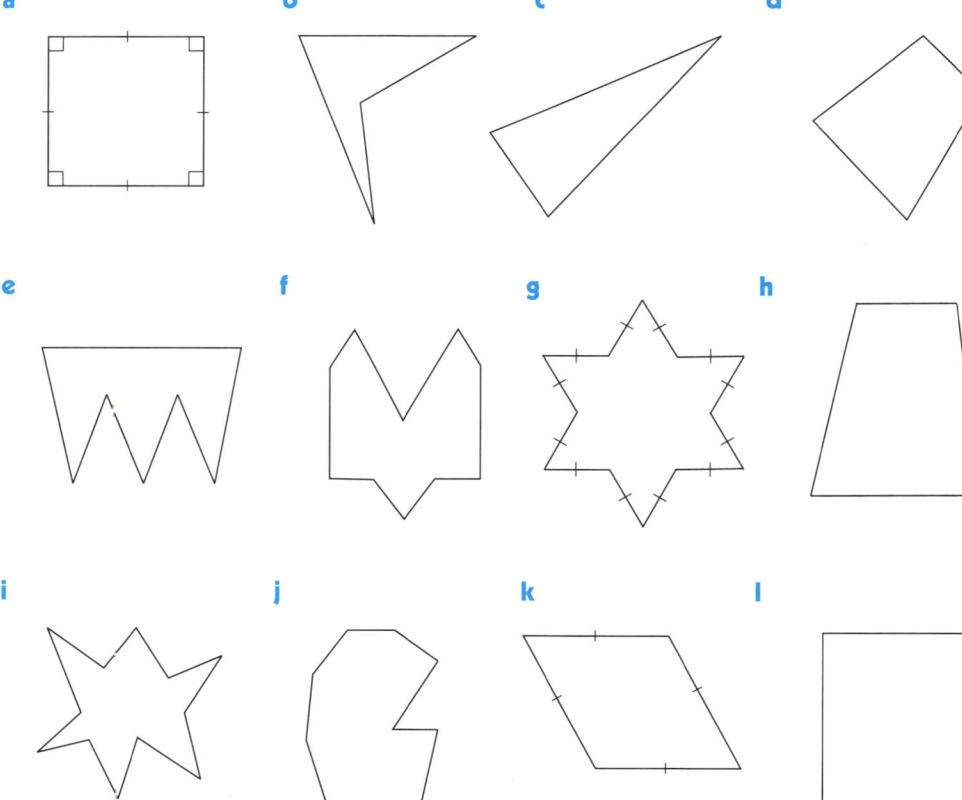

4 Draw an example of:
   a a quadrilateral   **b** an equilateral triangle   **c** a hexagon
   d a decagon   **e** a regular pentagon   **f** an octagon

5 Draw and name polygons with the following descriptions:
   a six equal sides and six equal angles   **b** three equal sides
   c five equal sides, but with unequal angles

6 Using a ruler and protractor, classify the following shapes as regular (R) or irregular (I) polygons:

a 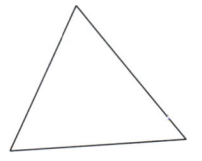   **b** 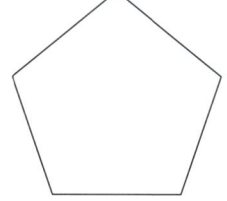   **c**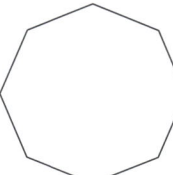

d 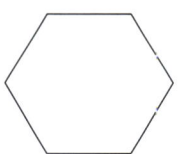   **e**    **f**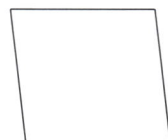

F   TRIANGLES AND QUADRILATERALS

TRIANGLES

> A **triangle** is a three-sided polygon.

There are 3 types of triangles which can be classified according to the number of sides which are equal in length. These are:

- **scalene**, where the 3 sides are of different length

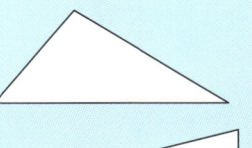

- **isosceles**, where 2 sides have the same length

- **equilateral**, where all 3 sides have the same length.

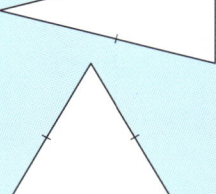

(Notice that an equilateral triangle is also isosceles.)

QUADRILATERALS

A **quadrilateral** is a four-sided polygon.

Parallel lines are shown using arrow heads

We can classify special quadrilaterals according to:
- the number of equal sides
- the number of parallel sides.

- A **trapezium** has exactly one pair of opposite sides which are parallel.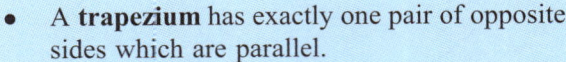

- A **parallelogram** has both pairs of opposite sides parallel.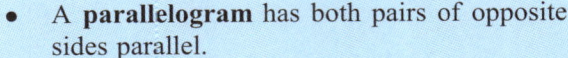

-  A **rectangle** has both pairs of opposite sides parallel and equal in length and the angles are right angles.

- A **rhombus** has both pairs of opposite sides parallel, and all four sides are equal in length.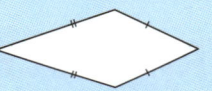

- 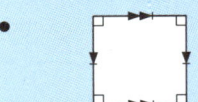 A **square** has both pairs of opposite sides parallel, all four sides are equal in length and the angles are all right angles.

- A **kite** has two pairs of adjacent sides which are equal in length.

FLOWCHART

The following **flowchart** may assist you in the classifying of quadrilaterals:

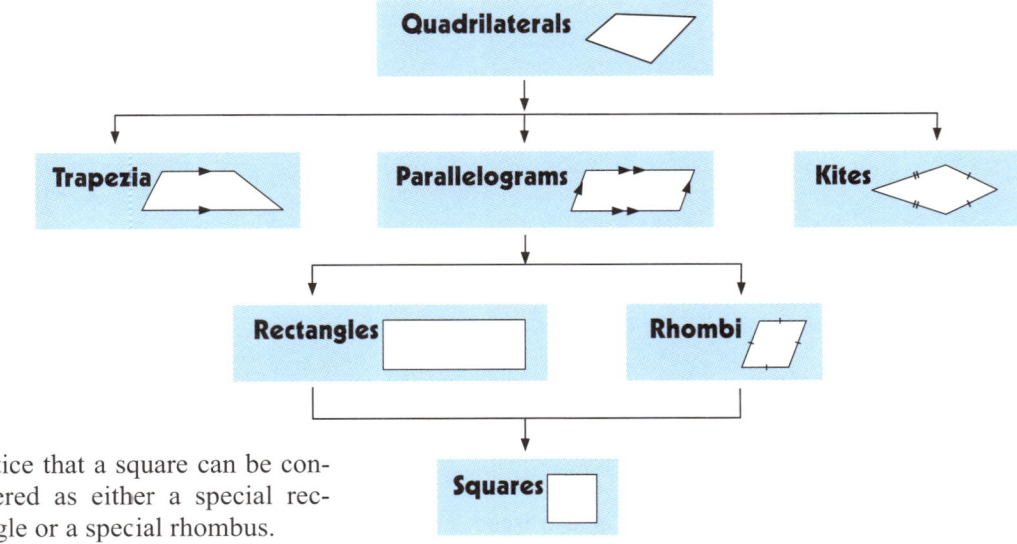

Notice that a square can be considered as either a special rectangle or a special rhombus.

EXERCISE 3F.1

1 Measure the length of the sides of the triangles and use these measurements to classify each as equilateral, isosceles or scalene:

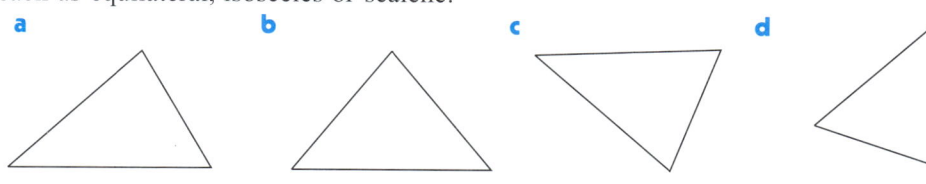

    a   b   c   d

2 Draw a fully labelled sketch of:
    a a parallelogram   **b** a rhombus   **c** a kite.

3 There are 3 special parallelograms. Name each of them.

4 Use a ruler to help classify the following:

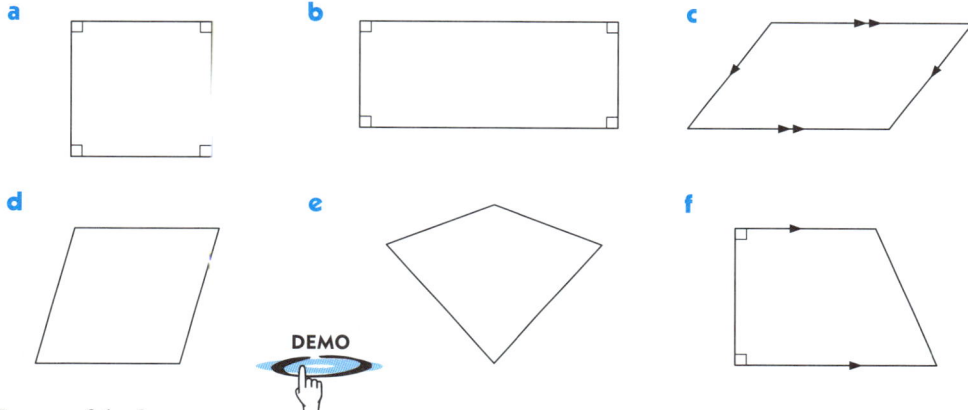

5 True or false?
    a A parallelogram is a quadrilateral which has opposite sides parallel.
    b A rectangle is a parallelogram with four equal angles of $90°$.
    c A rhombus is a quadrilateral in which all sides are equal (i.e., an equilateral quadrilateral).
    d A square is a rhombus with four equal angles of $90°$.
    e A trapezium is a quadrilateral which has a pair of parallel opposite sides.
    f A kite is a quadrilateral which has two pairs of adjacent sides equal.

PARALLEL AND PERPENDICULAR LINES

In the figure we notice that AB is parallel to DC.
We write this as AB $\parallel$ DC.

Also AD is perpendicular to DC.

We write this as AD $\perp$ DC.

So $\parallel$ reads *is parallel to*   and
    $\perp$ reads *is perpendicular to*.

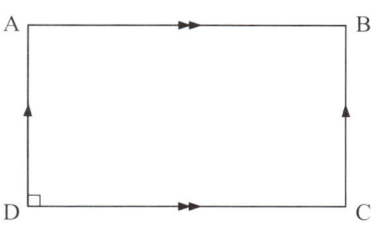

6 Using ∥ and ⊥, write statements about the following figures:

a [triangle PQR with right angle at Q]
b [trapezium ABCD with AB ∥ DC]
c [parallelogram HIJK with right angle at I]
d [lines KM and LN crossing]
e [square PQRS]
f [rectangle WXYZ]

7 Draw the figures from these instructions. A freehand labelled sketch is needed in each case.
  a AB is 4 cm long. BC is 3 cm long. AB ⊥ BC.
  b PQ is 5 cm long. RS is 4 cm long. RS ∥ PQ and RS is 3 cm from PQ.
  c ABCD is a quadrilateral in which BC ∥ AD and AB ⊥ AD.
  d ABCD is a quadrilateral where AB ∥ DC and AD ∥ BC and AB ⊥ BC.

INVESTIGATION — VERTICES, EDGES AND REGIONS

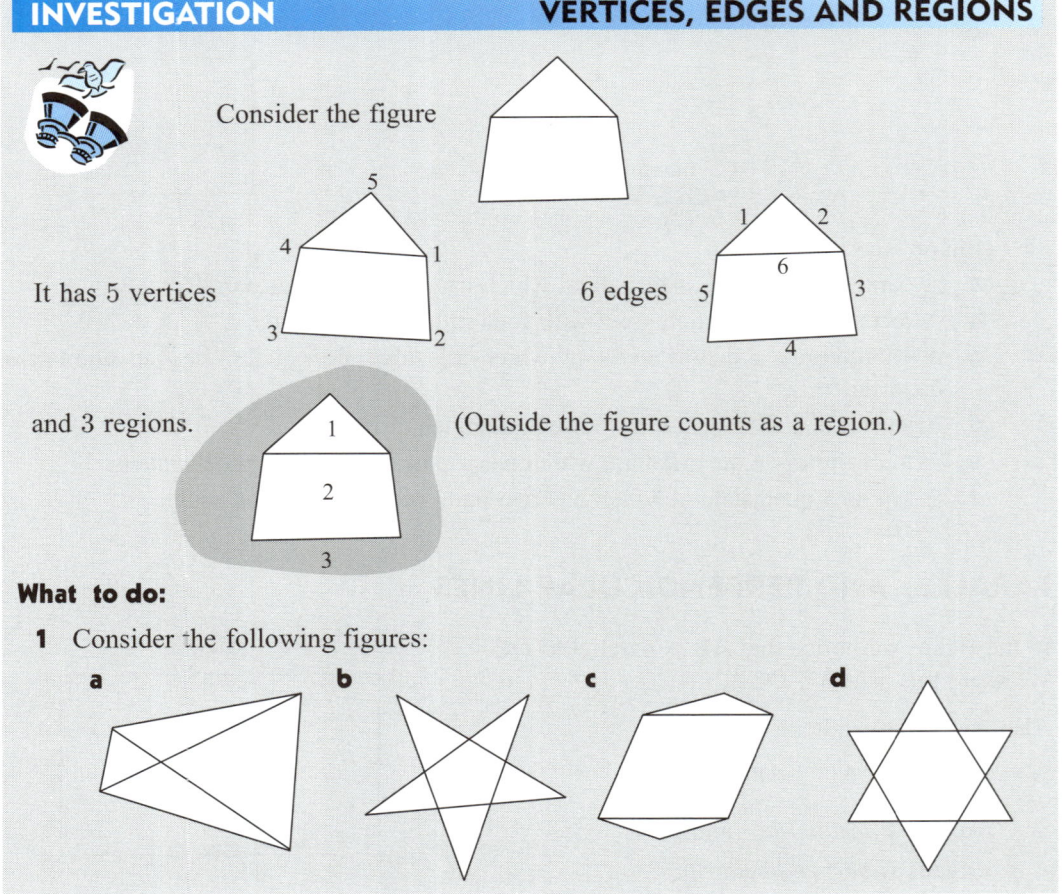

Consider the figure

It has 5 vertices   6 edges

and 3 regions.   (Outside the figure counts as a region.)

What to do:

1 Consider the following figures:

a   b   c   d

2 Copy and complete where **e** to **h** are for two diagrams like those above, but of your choice.

Figure	Vertices (V)	Regions (R)	Edges (E)	V + R − 2
given example	5	3	6	6
a				
b				
c				
d				
e				
f				
g				
h				

3 What is the most likely relationship (rule) between V, R and E?

EULER'S RULE

From the previous **Investigation** you should have discovered **Euler's Rule**.

> In any closed figure, the number of edges is always two less than the sum of the number of vertices and regions, i.e., $E = V + R - 2$.

Note:
- Euler is pronounced 'oiler'.
- Euler's Rule applies even if the edges are not straight lines.

For example,  has $V = 4$, $R = 5$ and $E = 7$
and $V + R - 2 = 9 - 2 = 7$, which checks.

EXERCISE 3F.2

1 Using Euler's Rule, determine the number of:
   a vertices of a figure with 7 edges and 3 regions
   b edges for a figure with 5 vertices and 4 regions
   c regions for a figure with 10 edges and 8 vertices.

2 Draw a possible figure for each of the cases in **1**.

3 Draw two *different* figures which have 5 vertices and 7 edges.

G CONSTRUCTING A TRIANGLE

Geometric constructions require the use of:
- a **ruler**, to provide a straight edge and a scale for measurement of length
- a **drawing compass** for drawing circles and arcs of circles
- a **sharp pencil** (preferably an HB or B) for the drawing of line segments
- a **protractor** for measuring angle sizes.

The instruction 'construct' a geometrical shape is different from 'sketch' or 'draw'.

Construct means you may use only a drawing compass and straight-edge. **Sketch** means a rough diagram is sufficient, and **draw** means you may use any instrument you wish such as a protractor, set square, etc.

Note: Construction lines should not be erased.

CONSTRUCTING A TRIANGLE

Aim: To construct a triangle with sides 4 cm, 3 cm and 2 cm long.

VIDEO CLIP

Step 1: Draw a line segment the length of one of the sides (say AB). It is often best to choose the longest side. Use this as the base of the triangle.

A ———— 4 cm ———— B

Step 2: Open your compass to a radius equal to the length of one of the other sides (say AC). Using this radius draw an arc from one end A, of the base line.

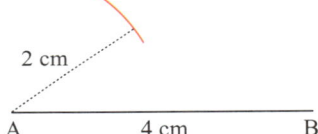

Step 3: Now open the compass to a radius equal to the length of the other side, BC. Draw another arc from B to intersect the first arc.

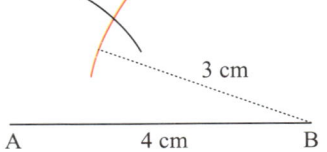

Step 4: Join A and B to the point of intersection of the two arcs C to form triangle ABC.

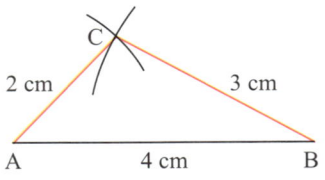

EXERCISE 3G

1 Accurately construct, with 'compass' and ruler:
   a a triangle with sides 4 cm, 5 cm and 6 cm
   b a triangle with sides 3 cm, 6 cm and 7 cm.

There are 6 parts to a triangle. Can you name them?

2 Draw AB of length 5 cm.

Set the compass points 5 cm apart. With centre A, draw an arc of a circle above AB.

Likewise with centre B draw an arc to intersect the other one.

Let C be the point where these arcs meet. Join AC and BC.

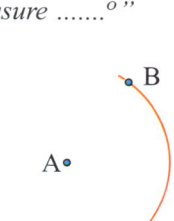

- **a** What type of triangle is ABC?   (Give a reason.)
- **b** Measure angles ABC, BCA, CAB using a protractor.
- **c** Copy and complete: *"All angles of an equilateral triangle measure ....°"*

3 With centre A, draw an arc of a circle of radius 5 cm. Choose any two points B and C on this arc (not too close together).

Join AB, BC and AC.

- **a** What type of triangle is ABC?   (Give a reason.)
- **b** Measure angles ABC and ACB using a protractor.
- **c** Copy and complete: *"In an isosceles triangle the angles opposite the equal sides are ...."*

4 Take a piece of clean paper and fold it down the middle.

Draw a straight line AB as shown, and with the two sheets pressed tightly together carefully cut through both of them.

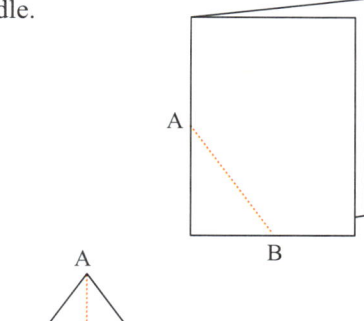

Open out the offcut. *You should now have:*

- **a** Explain why this triangle is isosceles.
- **b** Explain why the angles opposite the equal sides are equal in size.

You should not have to use a ruler and protractor.

5 Use a ruler and compass to construct:
- **a** an equilateral triangle with sides 6 cm long   (Use question **2**.)
- **b** an equilateral triangle with sides 4.8 cm long
- **c** an isosceles triangle with equal sides 6 cm long and third side 4 cm long
  (**Hint:** Use question **3**.)
- **d** an isosceles triangle with equal sides 4.4 cm long and third side 6 cm long.

Example 3

Find the value of the unknown in each figure:

Note: Sides marked with dashes are of equal length for that figure.

a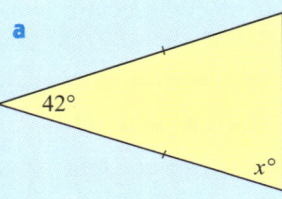

b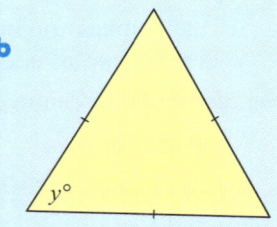

a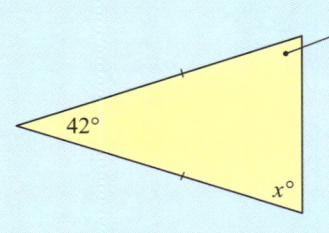

As the triangle is isosceles the angles opposite the equal sides are equal in size

∴ this angle is $x°$ as well.

But $x + x + 42 = 180$
∴ $x + x = 138$ {as $138 + 42 = 180$}
∴ $x = 69$ {as $69 + 69 = 138$}

b All angles of an equilateral triangle measure $60°$ ∴ $y = 60$.

6 Find the unknowns in the following which are *not drawn accurately*:

a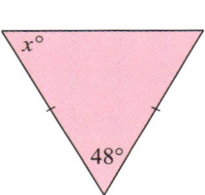

b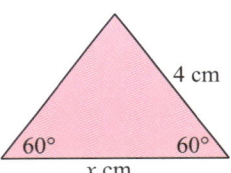

c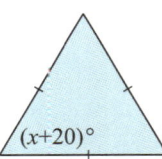

d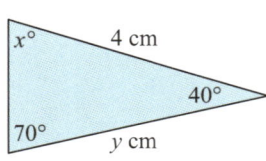

e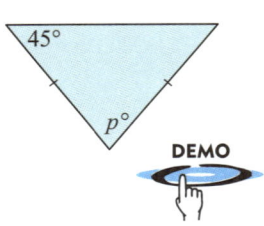

f

H BISECTING AND CONSTRUCTING ANGLES

If we are careful and accurate we can bisect a given angle without having to use a protractor.

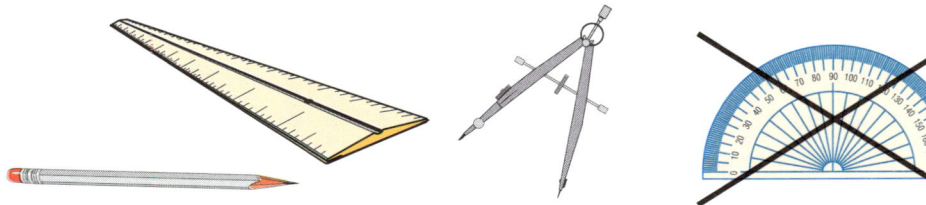

We use the following procedure:

SHAPES AND SOLIDS (CHAPTER 3) 101

BISECTING AN ANGLE

Aim: To bisect angle ABC.

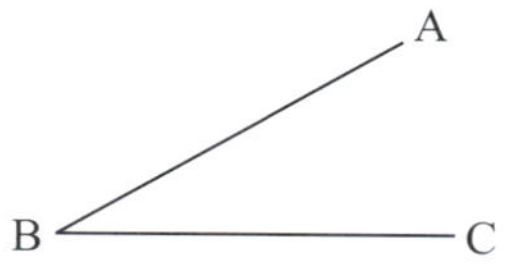

Step 1:	With centre at B, draw an arc which cuts BA at P and BC at Q.
Step 2:	With Q as centre, draw an arc within angle ABC.
Step 3:	Keep the **same** radius. With centre P draw another arc to intersect the previous one at M.
Step 4:	Join B to M. BM bisects angle ABC, i.e., $\angle ABM = \angle CBM$.

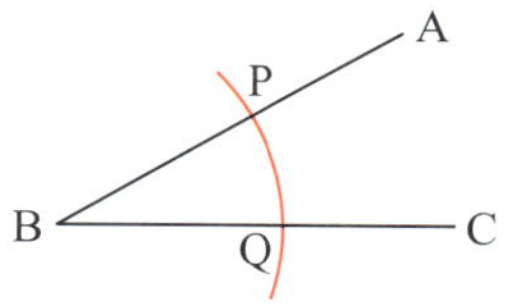

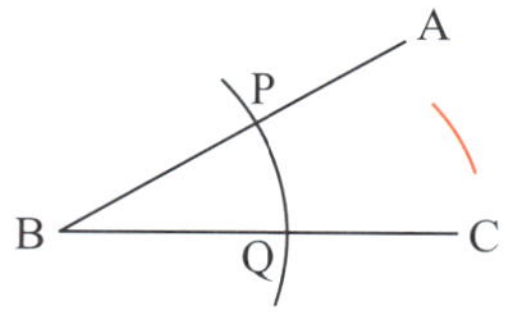

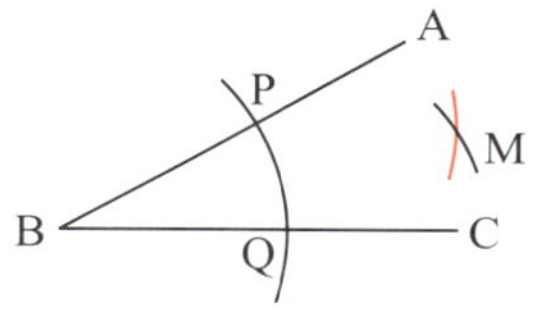

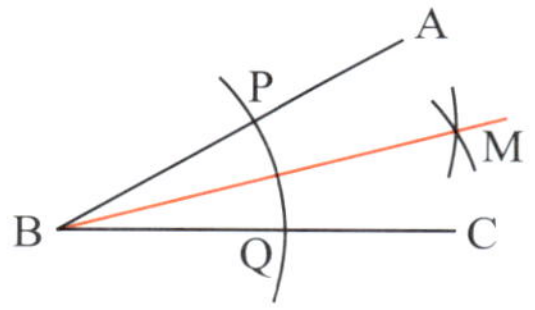

VIDEO CLIP

Constructing an angle of 60° at the end of a line segment is also straightforward.

CONSTRUCTING A 60° ANGLE

Aim: To construct a 60° angle at X on line segment XY.

Step 1:	On a line segment XY with centre X, draw an arc which cuts XY at Z.
Step 2:	With centre Z, and the same radius, draw an arc to cut the first one at W.
Step 3:	Draw the line from X through W. Angle WXY is 60°.

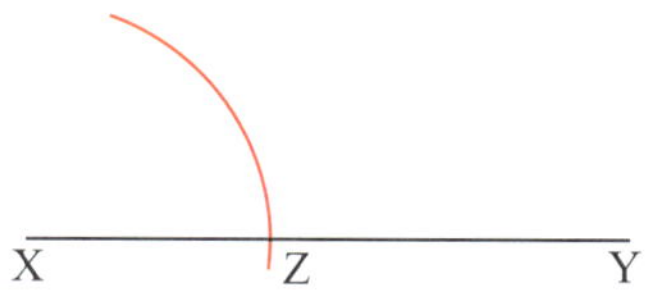

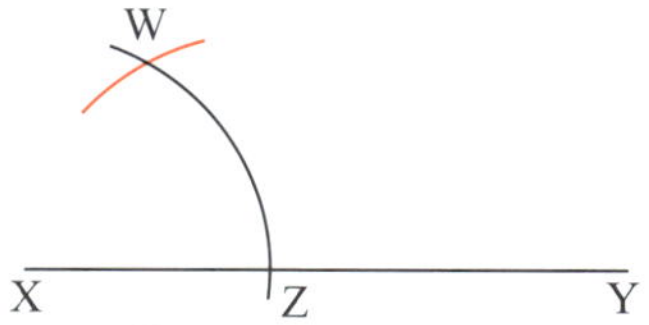

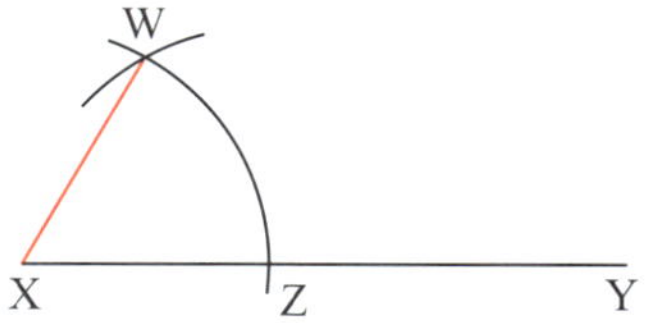

VIDEO CLIP

CONSTRUCTING A 90° ANGLE

Aim: To construct a 90° angle at X on line segment XY.

Step 1: With centre X, draw an arc which cuts XY at A.

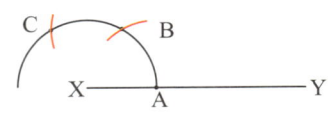

Step 2: Keep the same radius throughout. With centre A draw an arc which meets the first arc at B. With centre B draw another arc to meet the first arc at C.

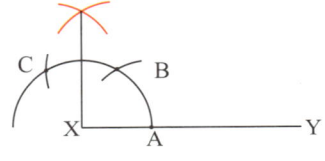

Step 3: With centres at B and C, draw arcs of equal radius above B and C to meet at Z. Join XZ. Angle YXZ is a right angle.

VIDEO CLIP

EXERCISE 3H

1 Draw 4 angles of your choice of different degree measure (2 acute and 2 obtuse). Bisect each angle using the given **bisecting an angle** method.

2 The last diagram in the **constructing a 60° angle** method is:

Explain how this figure enables you to decide that angle WXY measures 60°. A full explanation is necessary.

(**Hint:** Join WZ.)

Remember that construct means use a drawing compass and straight edge.

3 Construct a 90° angle at the end A of a 12 cm long line segment AB. If angle BAC is the right angle, put C so that AC is 5 cm long. Now join BC and measure its length. If you have been very accurate and have used a sharp pencil you should have found that BC is 13 cm long.

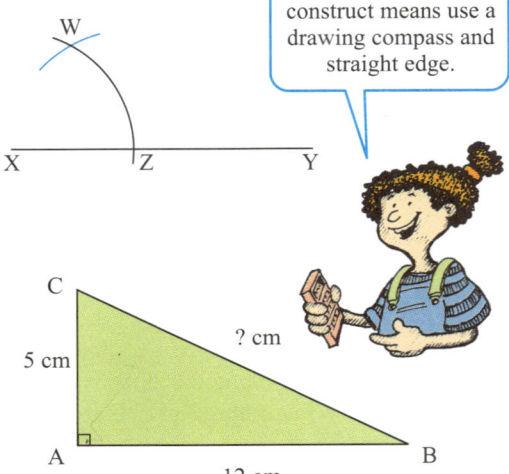

4 Extension: How can we construct an angle of 30° at the end of a line segment by using a ruler and compass construction (and no protractor or set square)? Write step-by-step instructions on how to do this, with suitable diagrams.

5 On the end of a line segment, construct an angle of:
   a 30°   **b** 45°   **c** 15°   **d** $22\frac{1}{2}°$

All construction lines must be visible.

6 Draw any triangle ABC with sides greater than 6 cm and bisect each of the angles using the compass method. What do you notice about the 3 angle bisectors?

Repeat with another different shaped triangle.

Copy and complete: *"The angle bisectors of any triangle appear to ..... point."*

7 Draw a circle of radius 3 cm and mark its centre at O. Draw a diameter AB through O meeting the circle at A and B.

Construct 60° angles at A on either side of AB.

Construct 60° angles at B on either side of AB.

Let these meet the circle at P, Q, R and S.
Join PS and QR.

Explain why AQRBSP is a regular hexagon.

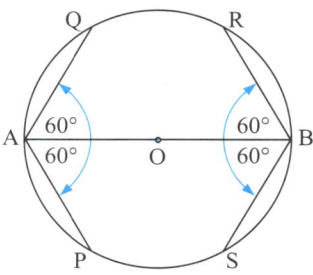

8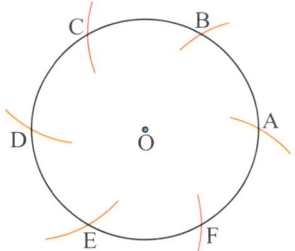

Another easier method of drawing a regular hexagon is to draw a circle (of radius 3 cm, say) and select point A on it.

Keeping the same radius as you used for the circle, with centre A, draw an arc meeting the circle at B. With centre B and same radius, draw an arc meeting the circle at C and continue this around the circle to obtain D, E and F.

If you have done this very accurately, a final arc will pass through A, the starting point.

Explain why ABCDEF is a regular hexagon.

ACTIVITY   IDENTIFYING SHAPES

Look at the following photograph of a house.

What to do:

1. Make a list of all the different shapes you can see in the photograph.
2. Write sentences to describe where you see
   - **a** parallel lines
   - **b** perpendicular lines.

ACTIVITY — ISLAMIC ART

Alongside is an example of Islamic art:

What to do:

1. Collect pictures of Islamic art from magazines, books or from the internet.
2. List shapes used in the designs.

POLYHEDRA

SOLIDS

> A **solid** is a body which occupies space.

These diagrams show some special solids. You should learn their names and be able to draw neat freehand sketches of them.

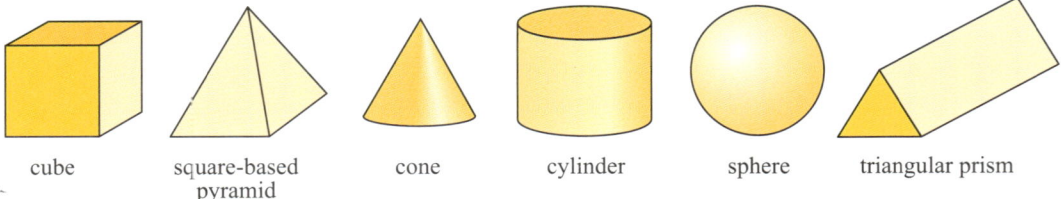

cube   square-based pyramid   cone   cylinder   sphere   triangular prism

The boundaries of a solid are called **surfaces**. These surfaces may be flat surfaces (or parts of planes), curved surfaces or a mixture of both. Which of the above solids have only flat surfaces, only curved surfaces or a combination of both types?

POLYHEDRA

> A **polyhedron** (plural polyhedra) is a solid which contains all flat surfaces.

Cubes are examples of polyhedra but spheres and cylinders are not.

Each flat surface of a polyhedron is called a **face** and has the shape of a polygon.

Each corner point of a polyhedron is called a **vertex**.

Each intersection of two faces is called an **edge**.

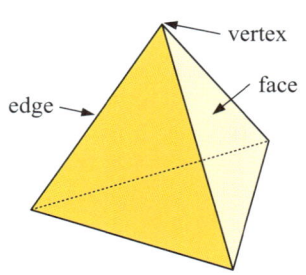

Notice that the drawing above is a triangular-based pyramid (often called a **tetrahedron**).

Labelling a figure helps describe its features.

For example:

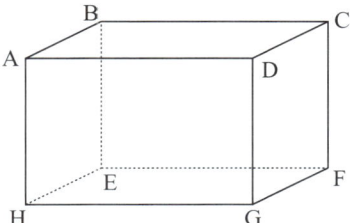

A, B, C, D, E, F, G and H are all vertices of this polyhedron.

ABCD is one face. There are five other faces.

AB is one edge. There are eleven other edges.

PRISMS

A **prism** is a solid whose cross-section is a regular polygon.

Examples of prisms:

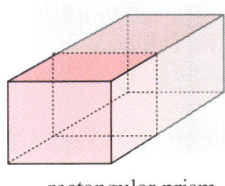
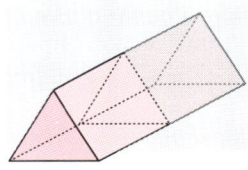
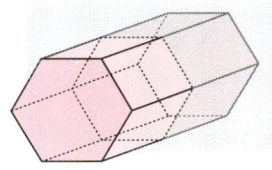

rectangular prism   triangular prism   hexagonal prism

PYRAMIDS

A **pyramid** is a solid with a polygon for a base and triangular faces which come from the base to meet at a point. A cone can be considered to be a special case of a pyramid.

Example of pyramids:

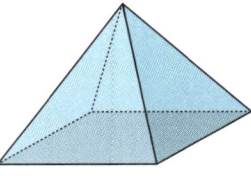
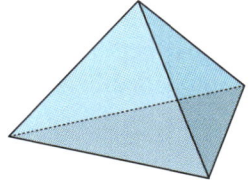

square-based pyramid   triangular-based pyramid

EXERCISE 31

1 Sketch a neat diagram to represent a:

- **a** cube
- **b** cone
- **c** cylinder
- **d** sphere
- **e** rectangular prism (cuboid)
- **f** triangular-based pyramid

2 Name the shape which best resembles:
    a a basketball   **b** the top part of a funnel   **c** a tennis ball container
    d a six-faced die   **e** a cornflakes packet   **f** a broom handle

3 Draw a neat diagram to represent:
    a a triangular prism   **b** a rectangular-based pyramid
    c an octagonal prism   **d** a hexagonal-based pyramid

4   **a** Name all the vertices of this cube.
       b Name all the faces of this cube.
       c Name all the edges of this cube.

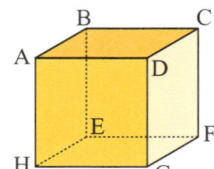

5 What shapes are the side faces of:
    a a prism   **b** a pyramid?

6 A tetrahedron is a triangular pyramid with all of its polygonal sides the same size. How many:
    a faces does a tetrahedron have   **b** edges does a tetrahedron have
    c vertices does a tetrahedron have?

J   NETS OF SOLIDS

A **net** is a two-dimensional shape which may be folded or shaped to form a solid.

For example, a **cube** is formed when the "net" shown is cut out and folded along the dotted lines.

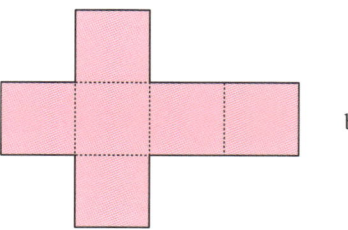 becomes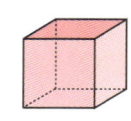

A **triangular-based pyramid** is formed when this "net" is cut out and folded along the dotted lines.

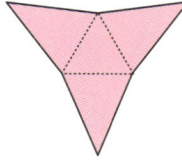 becomes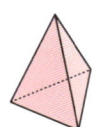

A **square-based pyramid** is formed when this "net" is cut out and folded along the dotted lines.

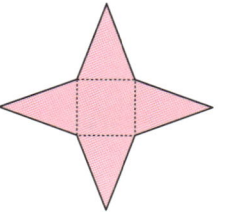 becomes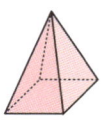

All the examples above are polyhedra and have **flat surfaces**. However, some solids with **curved surfaces** can also be made from nets. For example, the curved surface of a cone is formed when the following "net" is cut out and folded so the straight edges meet. A circle can then be cut out to add to the base of the cone.

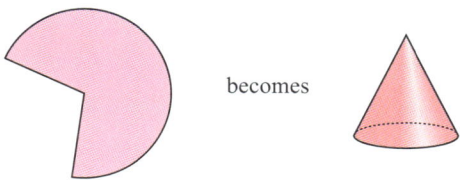
becomes

INVESTIGATION   MAKING CONES

The net for the curved surface of a cone is actually a sector of a circle.

What to do:

1 Draw two circles of radius 5 cm and one circle of radius 3 cm.
2 Cut the circles to produce the following sectors:

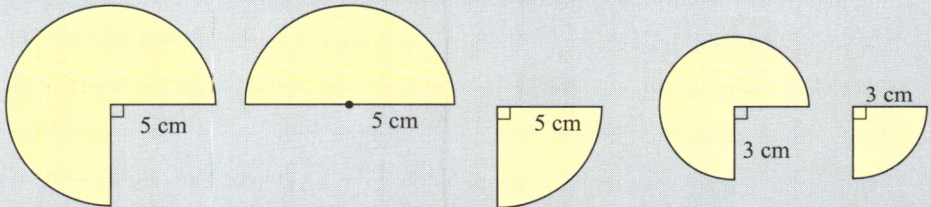

3 Using the above sectors as nets for the curved surface of cones, complete the following statements:

   a The radius of the sector affects the ...... of the cone.
   b The larger the sector cut from the circle, the .... the cone.

EXERCISE 3J

1 Match the net given in the first column with the correct solid and the correct name:

Net	Solid	Name
a	A	(1) Pentagonal-based pyramid
b	B	(2) Triangular prism
c	C	(3) Square-based pyramid
d	D	(4) Cylinder

108   SHAPES AND SOLIDS   (CHAPTER 3)

2 Make models of the solids in **1**, with gluing tabs, and construct each solid at a reasonable size.

3 Is [diagram] a possible net for a triangular-based pyramid?

ACTIVITY — WHICH CUBE IS IT?

What to do:

For each of the cases following:

1 Carefully study the nets and the sets of cubes given.

2 In **Case 1**, which cube can be made? In **Case 2**, which cube can not be made?

3 Construct an actual net and make the cube (with sides 2 cm), showing the **exact** same patterns on the faces, and check your answer to **2**.

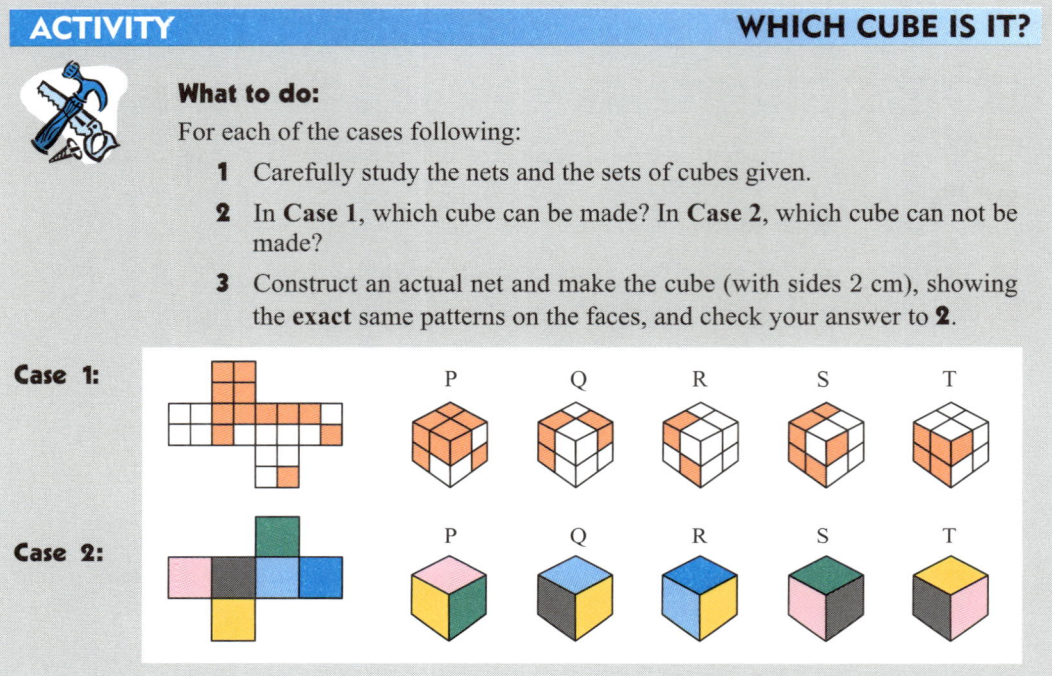

Case 1:

Case 3:

K DRAWING SOLIDS

We need to be able to draw three-dimensional shapes (solids) on a two-dimensional sheet of paper.

This can be done in two ways:
- by using a face to start with, or
- by using an edge to start the figure.

OBLIQUE PROJECTIONS

When drawing a rectangular object using an **oblique projection**, the lines which go back from the front face are inclined at $45°$ and lengths are shortened.

For example, to draw a cube we use:

Step 1: Draw the front face, a square.

Step 2: Draw edges back from the front face at $45°$ and shorter than those of the front face.

Step 3: Complete the cube.

Step 4: Draw in dotted lines which show the hidden edges,   i.e.,

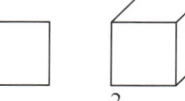 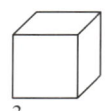 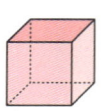

ISOMETRIC PROJECTIONS

When drawing a rectangular object using an **isometric projection**, lines go back at 30° and lengths of sides are maintained. Isometric graph paper is designed for drawing objects of this kind.

Here is a cube drawn this way.

Notice that the edge AB appears closest to us, and this is often the **starting edge** of the figure (the first edge drawn).

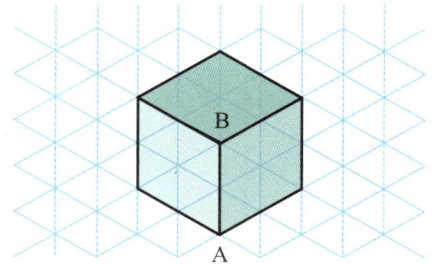

EXERCISE 3K

1. Draw an oblique projection diagram of a box which has sides 3 units by 1 unit by 2 units. (Start with a 3 unit by 2 unit front rectangle.)

2. Redraw the following figures on isometric graph paper:

   a    b    c

3. Copy these objects and then draw each of them as isometric projections.

   a 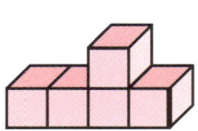   b    c

Example 4

On isometric graph paper, draw the only two different shapes which can be made from three cubes of the same size and which have at least one face in full contact with one of the other cubes.

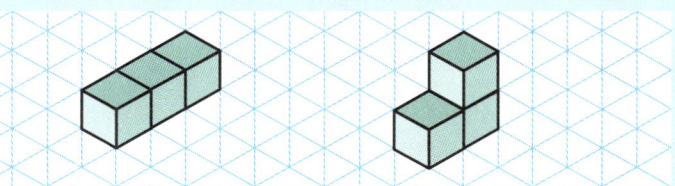

4. On isometric paper draw all possible different shapes which can be made from four cubes of the same size and which have at least one face in full contact with one of the other cubes.

   Note that 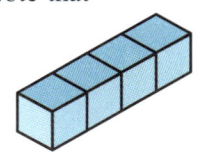 and 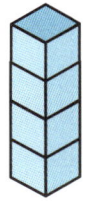 are the same.

110 SHAPES AND SOLIDS   (CHAPTER 3)

L CONSTRUCTING BLOCK SOLIDS

When an architect draws plans of a building, separate drawings are made from several viewing directions.

Consider:

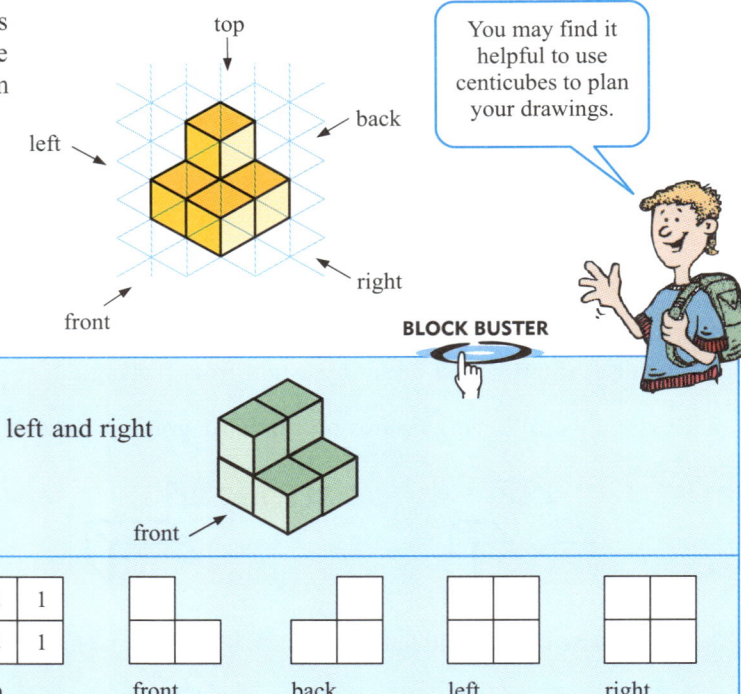

You may find it helpful to use centicubes to plan your drawings.

BLOCK BUSTER

Example 5

Draw top, front, back, left and right views of:

The views are:

2	1
2	1

top   front   back   left   right

EXERCISE 3L

1 Draw top, front, back, left and right views of:

   a   **b**   **c**

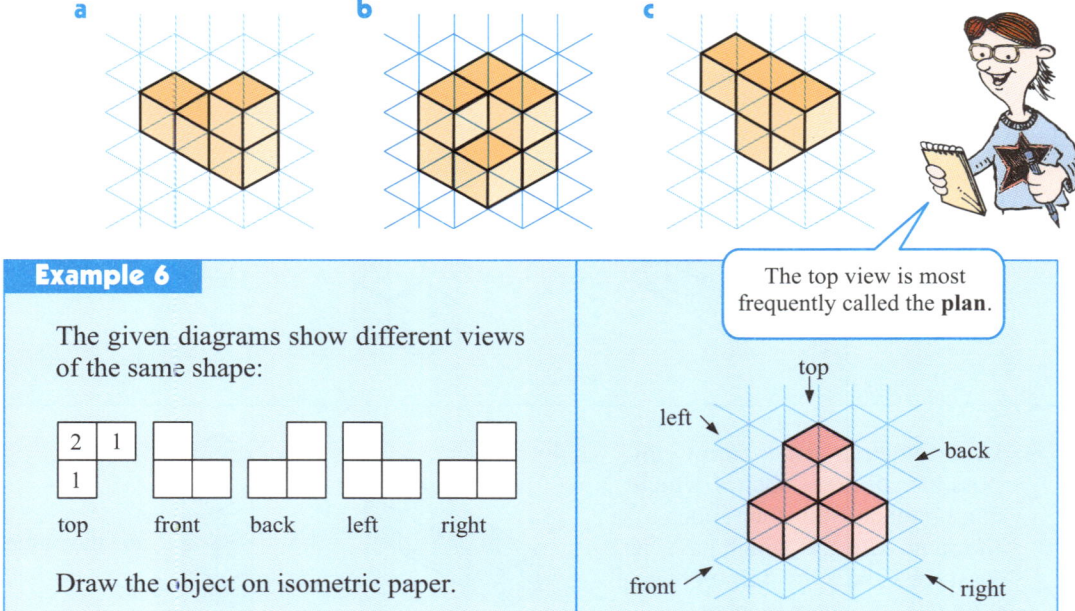

The top view is most frequently called the **plan**.

Example 6

The given diagrams show different views of the same shape:

2	1	
1		

top   front   back   left   right

Draw the object on isometric paper.

2 Draw the 3-dimensional object whose views are:

a

b

3 Draw five objects made from five cubes whose view from the top is  .

M FREEHAND DRAWINGS OF SOLIDS

Making freehand sketches of special solids is not easy. Following are step by step instructions on how to do them.

RECTANGULAR PRISM (OBLIQUE PROJECTION)

Step 1:

Draw a rectangle for the **front face**.

Step 2:

From each of the vertices draw lines back at an angle of $45°$ to create the edges. Their lengths are drawn slightly shorter than they would actually be.

Step 3:

Complete the drawing by joining the appropriate vertices, drawing in dotted lines which show the hidden edges.

Example 7

Draw an oblique projection for a rectangular box 2 units long by 1 unit wide by 1 unit high. $(2 \times 1 \times 1)$

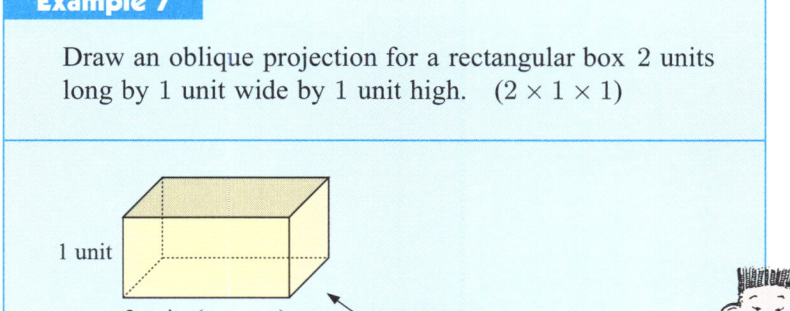

First measurement is length. Second measurement is width. Third measurement is height.

PYRAMIDS

In the picture of the pyramid alongside, only five edges, four vertices and two faces can be seen.

In fact, this pyramid has a square base and four triangular faces. To draw a pyramid we will use the following steps:

A pyramid does not have a uniform cross-section, so it is not a prism.

Step 1:

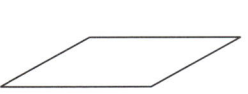

Draw a parallelogram to represent the base.

Step 2:

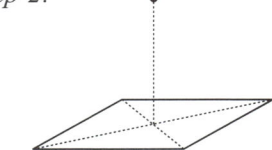

To find the centre of the parallelogram, draw the diagonals and find their point of intersection. Draw a point above the centre to represent the **apex** (or top) of the pyramid.

Step 3:

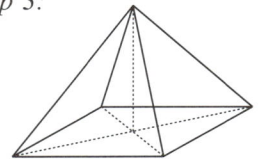

Join each vertex of the base to the apex to complete the pyramid.

Step 4:

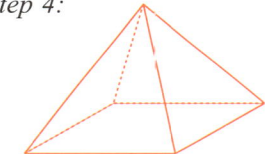

Looking at the picture of the pyramid above, not all edges can be seen at the one time. We draw invisible edges as dotted lines.

Note: When the pyramid is viewed from above, all edges can be seen as shown here.

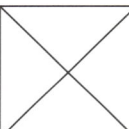

CYLINDERS

When looking at a can of food the front view looks like a rectangle. A view from directly above looks like a circle. A view from slightly above the end looks like an **ellipse**. (An oval is shaped like an ellipse.) To draw a cylinder, use the following steps.

Step 1:

Draw an ellipse to represent the base.

Step 2:

Draw the sides of the cylinder from the "ends" of the ellipse.

Step 3:

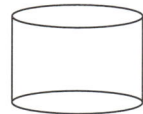

Complete the cylinder by drawing another ellipse on the top.

Step 4

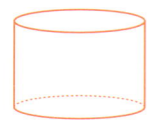

The picture shows us that not all drawn lines of the cylinder can be seen at once. So, we usually draw the cylinder as shown.

CONES

To draw a cone we can use the following steps.

Step 1:

Draw an ellipse to represent the base.

Step 2: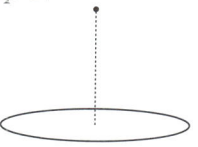

Mark a point directly above the centre of the ellipse (see diagram).

Step 3: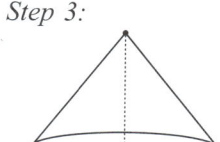

Join the "ends" of the ellipse to the point to complete the cone.

Step 4: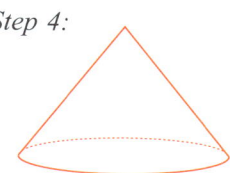

Again, the "back" of the ellipse cannot be seen. This can be shown by the dotted line.

EXERCISE 3M

1 Draw a freehand oblique projection for the following rectangular prisms:

    a $1 \times 1 \times 2$ prism   **b** $1 \times 2 \times 1$ prism   **c** $2 \times 2 \times 1$ prism

2 Draw freehand sketches of:

    a a square-based pyramid   **b** a tetrahedron
    c a cylinder   **d** a cone
    e an hexagonal-based pyramid   **f** a hexagonal prism

INVESTIGATION   MAKING MODELS OF SOLIDS

 Click on the icon of the model for which you wish to obtain a printable template. If possible print it on light card.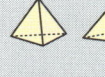

What to do:

1 Construct the solids from the nets provided.

2 Make a mobile from the solids to hang in your bedroom.

VISUAL ILLUSIONS

 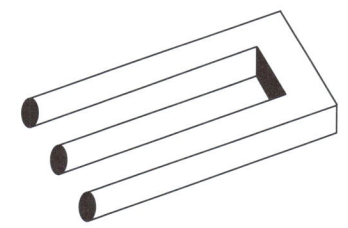 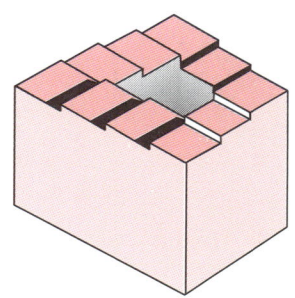

Trigon   Eat from this fork!   Ever-ascending steps?

CIRCLES

THE CIRCLE

All of the plane figures we have looked at so far have straight lines as sides.

Now consider the shapes of the following:

Each of these objects appears to have the same shape when we look at them and this shape is called a circle.

Note:
- For a wheel, the outside of the tyre is a circle and the centre of the circle is the axle.
- For the clock, the outside of the clock is the circle and the point about which the hands move is the centre.

FACTS ABOUT CIRCLES

Every circle has a centre which is inside it.

Every point on the circle is the same distance from the **centre**.

Any straight line from the centre to the circle is called a **radius**. Sometimes the length of this line is called the radius.

The **circumference** of a circle is the distance around the circle. That is, the circumference of a circle is its perimeter.

Any straight line which passes through the centre and starts and finishes on the circle is called a **diameter**.

An **arc** of a circle is part of the circle.

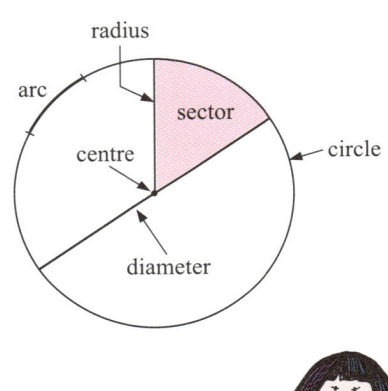

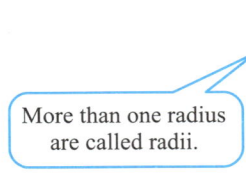 More than one radius are called radii.

ACTIVITY — DRAWING A CIRCLE USING A PIECE OF STRING

What to do:

1. Take a piece of string about 1 metre long and tie its ends together.

2. Place a peg at one end of the loop and a piece of chalk at the other end, as shown.

3. Hold the peg still. Keep the string taut while moving the chalk. The chalk will trace a circle. The peg will be the centre of the circle.

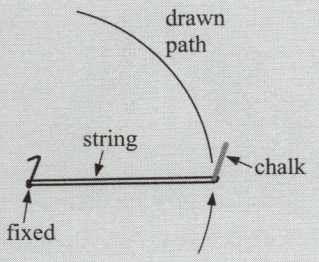

REVIEW SET A   CHAPTER 3

1 Name the intersection of:
   a $\overline{AC}$ and $\overline{BD}$
   b $\overline{BC}$ and $\overleftrightarrow{AD}$

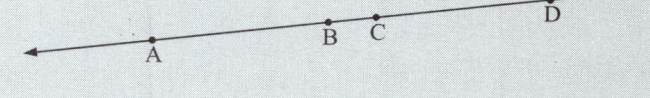

2 In the diagram shown alongside, what is represented by:
   a the double arrows
   b the dots
   c the ˋs?

3 What angle is formed inside the hands of the clock showing:
   a 3 o'clock
   b 6 o'clock?

4 Find the value of the missing angles in each of the following which *are not drawn accurately*:

   a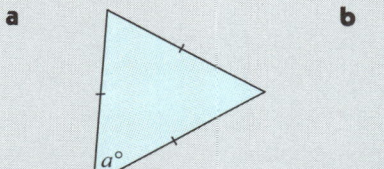
   b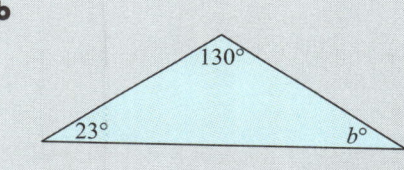

5 Use Euler's rule $E = V + R - 2$ to determine the number of:
   a vertices if there are 7 regions and 14 edges
   b regions if there are 12 edges and 8 vertices.

6 Draw the following polygons:
   a isosceles triangle
   b regular hexagon
   c rhombus

7 On isometric graph paper, draw 5 of the possible 8 arrangements of 4 blocks of the same size where every block is in full contact with at least one full face of another block.

8 Draw and name the solids which correspond to the following nets:

   a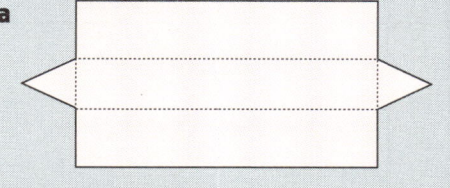
   b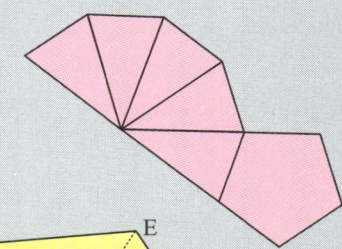

9 For the given figure, name:
   a all vertices
   b all edges
   c all faces.

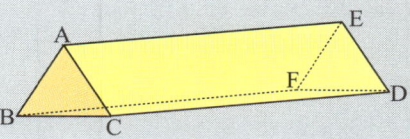

REVIEW SET B — CHAPTER 3

1 In the diagram alongside, what is represented by:
  a the arrows **b** $\overline{AB}$
  c $\overleftrightarrow{CD}$ **d** X?

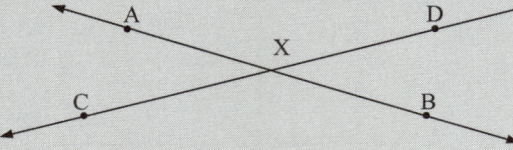

2 Name the following polygons:

  a  **b**  **c**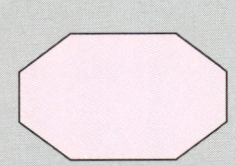

3 Accurately rule a line segment $\overline{AB}$ 6 cm long. Construct an angle of 90° at A with a line segment $\overline{AC}$ 8 cm. Join BC. Determine:
  a the length of $\overline{BC}$ **b** $\angle ABC$ **c** $\angle ACB$

4 Draw the following solids:
  a triangular prism **b** cylinder

5 Draw a net for:
  a a cube **b** a triangular-based pyramid

6 Find the value of the missing angles in each of the following which *are not drawn accurately*:

  a 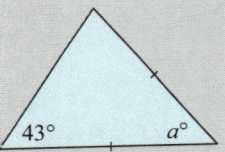 **b**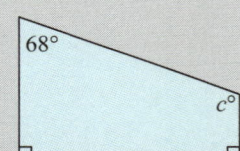

7 What is the aim of this construction?

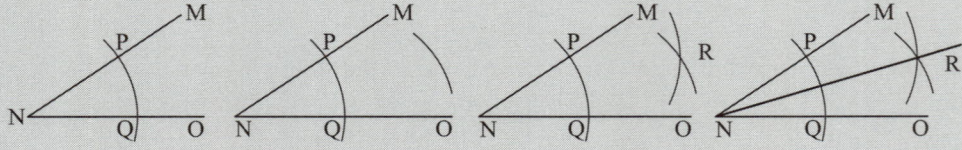

8 For the following views, draw an isometric diagram:

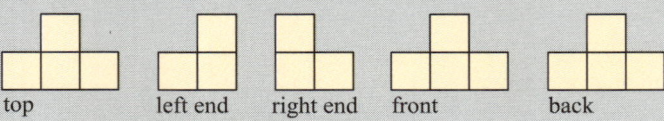

top   left end   right end   front   back

9 Draw oblique projections for:
  a a cube **b** a rectangular prism of $2 \times 3 \times 4$ units.

REVIEW SET C   CHAPTER 3

1 Classify the following triangles according to their sides by measurement:

   a    **b**    **c**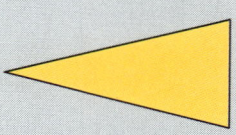

2 Find, giving reasons, the value of a in the following which *are not drawn accurately*.

   a 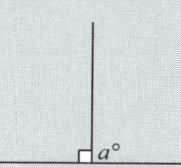   **b** 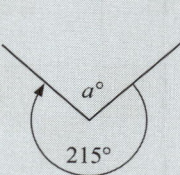   **c** 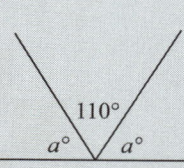   **d**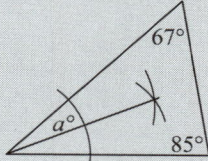

3 Find, giving reasons, the value of x in the following which *are not drawn accurately*.

   a 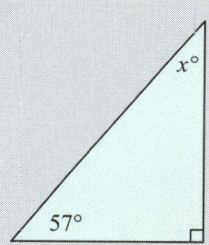   **b** 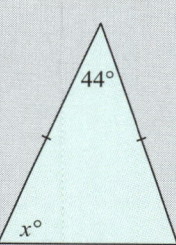   **c**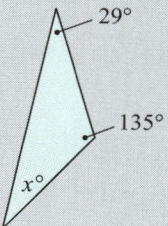

4 Draw a net for a rectangular prism.

5 Use Euler's rule $E = V + R - 2$ to determine the number of:

   a edges if there are 5 vertices and 11 regions

   b regions if there are 9 vertices and 17 edges.

6 Draw the following solids:

   a a cube   **b** a cone.

7 Draw a net for:

   a a cone   **b** a square-based pyramid.

8 For the following diagram, draw:

   a a top
   b a left
   c a right
   d a front
   e a back view.

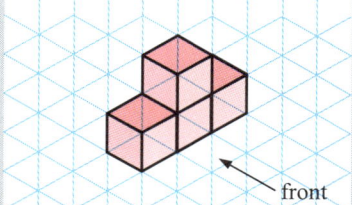

TRY THIS

ROMAN X-WORD

Using your knowledge of the information in **Chapters 1** and **2**, solve this puzzle:

PRINTABLE WORKSHEET

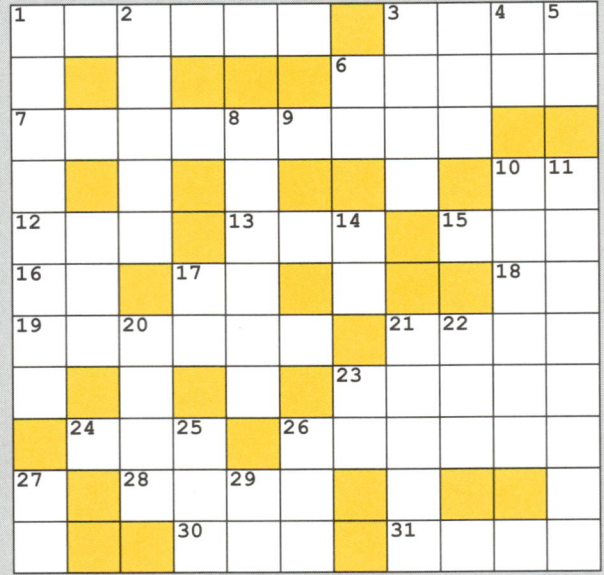

Write in Roman Numerals:

Across

1. One thousand six hundred and fifty six
3. 1509
6. One thousand subtract 404
7. $(8 \times 10^2) + (6 \times 10^1) + (7 \times 10^0)$
10. 2×10^3
12. The difference between 936 and 531
13. 9×5
15. The sum of 800 and six hundred
16. The product of fifty and four
17. Half of 1020
18. 999 999 − 999 909
19. Twelve times seven
21. Ten lots of (eleven times four)
23. 937, 948, ..., 970, 981
24. ...... the ingredients
26. 44 000 subtract 43 466
28. The dividend when the divisior is 2 and the quotient is 47
30. The quotient of 63 and 9
31. 12×2^3

Down

1. MMM minus CXL
2. (II times X^2) minus VI
3. Double DVII
4. XXXVI ÷ IX
5. V + VI
6. CCCII + CCIII
8. From C subtract XI
9. C divided by X
10. M + CX + XII
11. MM − CCCXXXIII
14. C − XC − IV
20. VII^2
21. The difference between M and LXXXI
22. The dividend when LXX and VIII are factors
25. LXXX, LXXXV, XC, ..., C, CV.
26. The sum of CCXCIX, CXLIII and LXIV
27. The product of CI and X
29. $I^2 + I^2$

Chapter 4
Fractions

Knowledge, skills and understandings

By the end of this chapter you should be able to

- compare the size of fractions (e.g., "Which is larger: $\frac{2}{5}$ or $\frac{1}{3}$?")
- compare and order fractions in ascending or descending order (e.g., $\frac{1}{3}, \frac{2}{5}, \frac{7}{8}$)
- add and subtract fractions with different denominators, including improper fractions and whole numbers
- multiply fractions including whole numbers and mixed numbers

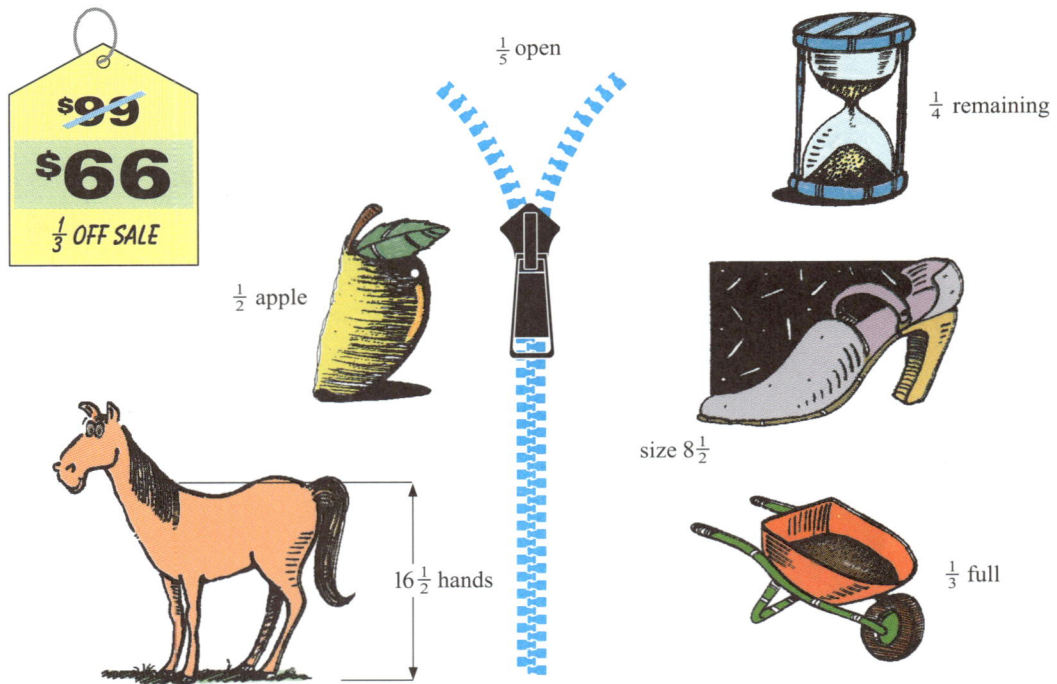

A   FRACTIONS ARE EVERYWHERE

Fractions are used constantly in everyday life. They can be seen in TV commercials, newspapers, magazines, brochures, books and music.

Here are just a few you may have read or heard:
- About half the population of Australia is female.
- About one quarter of the people living in Australia have parents who were born outside Australia.
- We spend about one third of our lives in bed.
- Two fifths of Australian children do not eat enough fruit.

Here are three diagrams which represent some everyday uses of fractions:

quarter to six

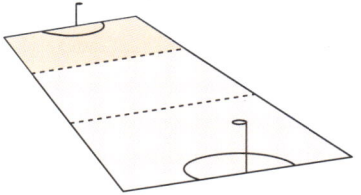

The netball goal-keeper defends one third of the court.

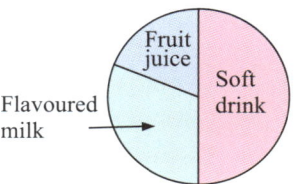

One sixth of students surveyed in a school prefer fruit juice with their lunch.

ACTIVITY   FRACTIONS WE ALL KNOW

What to do:

1 Copy and complete the following sketches to show:

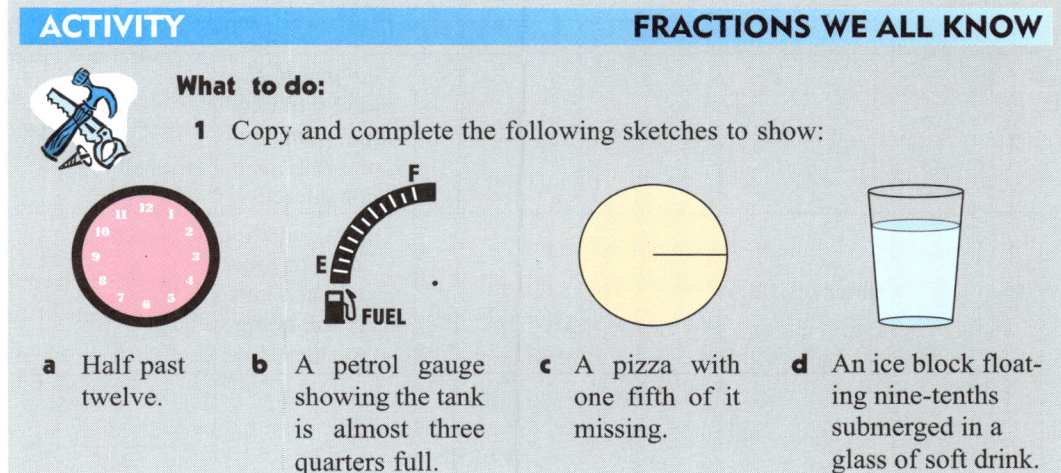

a Half past twelve.

b A petrol gauge showing the tank is almost three quarters full.

c A pizza with one fifth of it missing.

d An ice block floating nine-tenths submerged in a glass of soft drink.

B REPRESENTATION OF FRACTIONS

The fraction three eighths can be represented in a number of different ways:

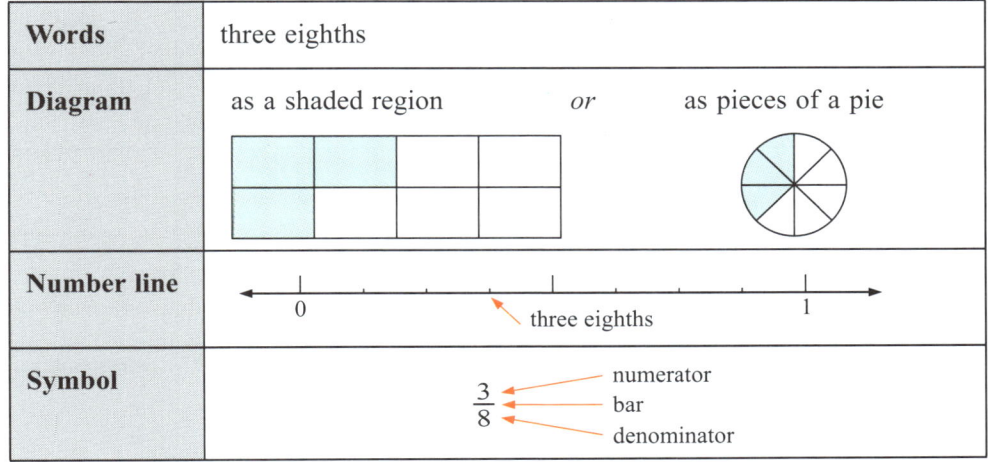

A fraction written in symbolic form with a bar is called a **common fraction**.

Note:
- $\dfrac{a}{b}$ — the **numerator** is the number of parts being considered
  — a ÷ sign (e.g., $\frac{4}{4} = 1$ and $4 \div 4 = 1$)
  — the **denominator** is the name of the fraction (e.g., 4 indicates quarters)
- A fraction represents a comparison of the numerator to the denominator.
- If a fraction is to have meaning, **the denominator cannot be zero**.
  (How can you divide something into zero parts?)

EXERCISE 4B

1 Copy and complete the following table:

	Symbol	Words	Numerator	Denominator	Meaning	Number Line
a		one half		2	One whole divided into two equal parts and one is being considered.	one half
b	$\frac{3}{4}$	three quarters			One whole divided into four equal parts and three are being considered.	three quarters
c	$\frac{2}{3}$		2	3		two thirds
d		two sevenths		7		
e					One whole divided into nine equal parts and seven are being considered.	
f			5	8		
g						

| ACTIVITY | FRACTION ESTIMATING |

What to do:

1 Make your own fraction wheel. Use a drawing compass to draw two identical circles on two different coloured pieces of cardboard.

Use your protractor to mark the fractions as shown on the second circle.

For example, $\frac{1}{10}$ is $(360° \div 10)$, $\frac{1}{8}$ is $(360° \div 8)$, $\frac{3}{8}$ is $(360° \div 8$ then $\times 3)$, etc.

Cut out both pieces. Mark and cut a radius on both circles as shown. Interlock the circles.

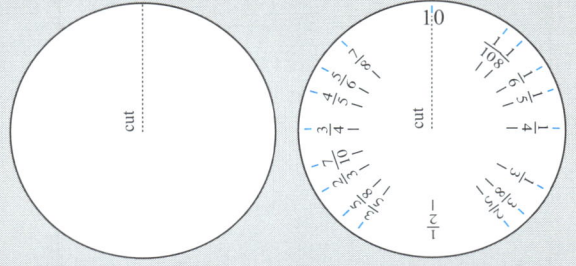

Challenge your partner to guess the fractions you make (the reverse side). Have your partner state two equivalent fractions for any fraction you make. Have your partner estimate the fraction which adds to yours to make one.

2 Click on the icon to bring up a fraction estimating game.
Play the game until your estimating ability is satisfactory.

C FRACTIONS OF REGULAR SHAPES

One of the most common ways to learn about fractions is to use regular two dimensional shapes.

EXERCISE 4C.1

1 Which of the following shaded shapes does not show five sixths?

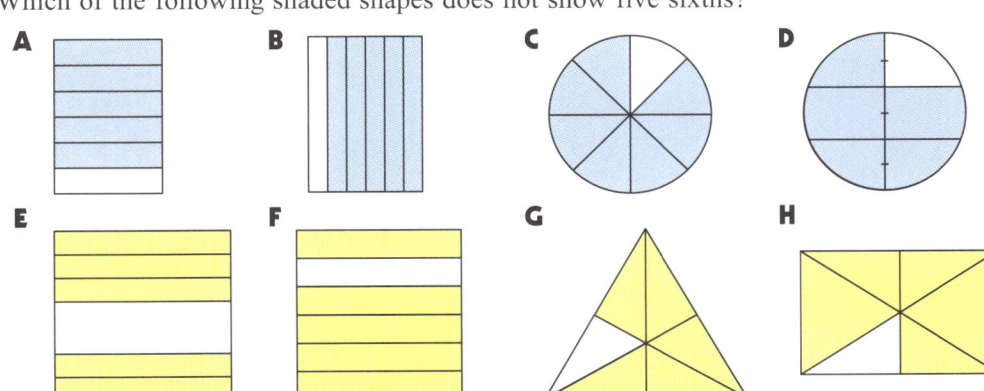

ACTIVITY FRACTIONS FROM REGULAR SHAPES

What to do: (click on the icon to obtain templates)

1. Copy the above examples which do show five sixths and change each into ten twelfths.

2. Carefully copy 3 identical sets of each of the following shapes. Complete and answer each question.

   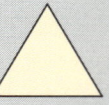 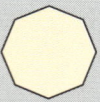

   a In the first set divide each whole shape into two equal parts. Each part is one half of the whole shape.

   b In the second set divide each whole shape into three equal parts. Each part is .....

   c In the third set divide each whole shape into four equal parts. Each part is .....

   d Which shapes were the most difficult to divide equally?

3. Copy and divide each of the following shapes into fifths:

  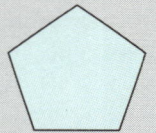  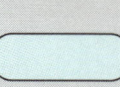 

   Which did you find most difficult to divide equally? Why?

4. Use pieces of paper large enough to allow you to increase by about 8 times any 6 of the above shapes. Carefully construct and cut out the shapes. See if you can fold the different pieces to create the fractions described in the exercises. Remember that the pieces must all be equal and must represent the number described in the denominator.

   a Which shapes allow you several different ways to fold and create the required fractions?

   b Which were the more difficult shapes to create the fractions with? Why?

5. List some reasons why the most popular shape for a pizza is a circle.

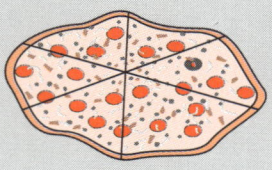

EXERCISE 4C.2

1 Copy the given shape exactly.

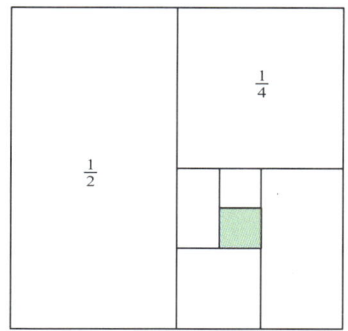

a If each rectangle is half of the one before it, how much of the shape is unshaded if the whole square is 1?

b Check your answer to **a** by drawing a grid within the large square. Use the boundaries of the shaded square as the dimensions of smallest squares in your grid.

c How many of the smallest squares fit into your large square?

Complete the shading of part **b** to make a chessboard and then answer the following:

d What fraction of the whole chessboard is the unshaded area?

e What fraction of the total chessboard is the first row?

f What fraction of the total chessboard are the unshaded squares in the first row?

2 Using identical square pieces of paper, make 2 copies of this tangram. Number the pieces on both sheets. Cut one of the sheets into its seven pieces. Use the pieces to help you work out the following:

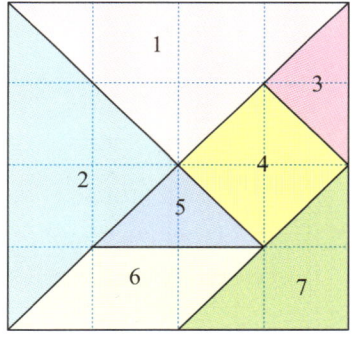

a How many triangles like piece 1 would fit into the largest square?

b What fraction of the largest square is piece 1?

c What fraction of piece 1 is piece 3?

d What fraction of the largest square is each tangram piece?

D EQUAL (EQUIVALENT) FRACTIONS

ACTIVITY   REPRESENTATIONS OF EQUAL (EQUIVALENT) FRACTIONS

What to do: (click on the icon to obtain templates)

1 Use grid paper to construct 6 identical squares with sides 4 cm long.

Use the grid lines on the paper to guide you.

TEMPLATE

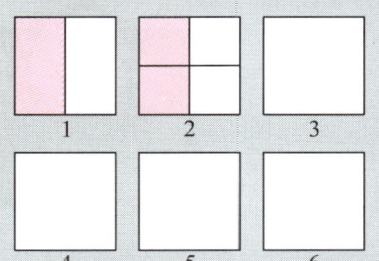

For this activity, use vertical and/or horizontal lines only.

a Divide the first square as shown into 2 equal parts. Each part is one half ($\frac{1}{2}$). One half has been shaded. Divide the second square as shown into quarters. Each half is now equivalent ($\equiv$) to two quarters ($\frac{2}{4}$). Shade in the same half as you did in the first square.

b Divide the third square into eighths. Shade in the one half which is equivalent to .....

c Divide the fourth square into sixteenths. One half is equivalent to .....

d In the fifth square show one half being equivalent to $\frac{16}{32}$.

e Using the pattern you have followed in the first five squares complete the last one. All the shaded areas should be equivalent to one half ($\frac{1}{2}$).

2 Try the same exercise constructing 6 identical 4 cm sided squares. This time, start with diagonal lines to create your halves and quarters. Name the equal fractions created in each square.

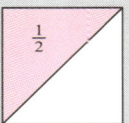 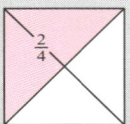    

3 Construct 4 identical rectangles to show $\frac{2}{5} = \frac{4}{10} = \frac{8}{20} = \frac{16}{40}$.

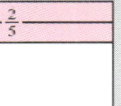   

4 a Use a protractor to outline 4 identical circles.

b From the centre of the first circle measure and rule 3 radii, 120° apart. Shade $\frac{2}{3}$.

c In the second circle using a similar method draw 6 radii 60° apart. Shade $\frac{4}{6}$.

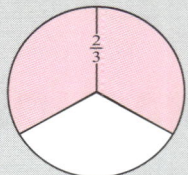 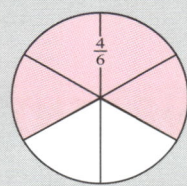  

d For the third circle, draw 12 radii .... degrees apart so that all three circles have equivalent areas shaded.

e What would you need to do for the fourth circle to make its shaded area equivalent to the previous three?

5 a Write the numbers 1 to 10 on one ice block stick, one centimetre apart.

b Write the multiples of 3 one centimetre apart on another stick.

1	2	3	4	5	6	7	8	9	10
3	6	9	12	15	18	21	24	27	30

c Place one stick directly above the other to show that
$\frac{1}{3}, \frac{2}{6}, \frac{3}{9}, \frac{4}{12}, ..., ..., ..., ..., ..., \frac{10}{30}$ are equal.

d On a third stick mark off the multiples of 5 from 5 to 50. Place the multiples of 3 stick directly above the multiples of 5 stick and complete these equivalent fractions $\frac{3}{5}, \frac{6}{10}, ..., ..., ..., ..., ..., ..., ..., \frac{30}{50}$.

Multiples of any numbers can be similarly presented to find equivalent fractions. By using the diagram method or the ice block stick method, or any of those mentioned earlier, you would see that:

$$\frac{4}{10} = \frac{2 \times 2}{5 \times 2} = \frac{2}{5}$$

$$\frac{8}{20} = \frac{2 \times 4}{5 \times 4} = \frac{2}{5}$$

$$\frac{24}{60} = \frac{2 \times 12}{5 \times 12} = \frac{2}{5} \quad \text{and so} \quad \frac{2}{5} = \frac{4}{10} = \frac{8}{20} = \frac{24}{60}$$

DEMO

We see that: Multiplying both the numerator and the denominator by the same non-zero number produces an equal (equivalent) fraction.

Also: Dividing both the numerator and the denominator by the same non-zero number produces an equal (equivalent) fraction.

Notice that $\frac{12}{18} = \frac{12 \div 2}{18 \div 2} = \frac{6}{9}$ and $\frac{6}{9} = \frac{6 \div 3}{9 \div 3} = \frac{2}{3}$ and so $\frac{12}{18} = \frac{6}{9} = \frac{2}{3}$

Example 1

Express with denominator 18:

a $\frac{7}{9}$ **b** $\frac{5}{6}$

a $\frac{7}{9}$

$= \frac{7 \times 2}{9 \times 2}$ {as $9 \times 2 = 18$}

$= \frac{14}{18}$

b $\frac{5}{6}$

$= \frac{5 \times 3}{6 \times 3}$ {as $6 \times 3 = 18$}

$= \frac{15}{18}$

Below is an example of how the same quantity of time can be represented by different names. Here both the numerators and the denominators change by the same multiple.

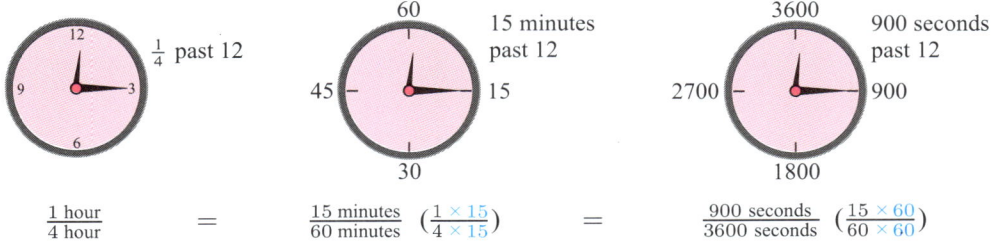

$\frac{1 \text{ hour}}{4 \text{ hour}} \quad = \quad \frac{15 \text{ minutes}}{60 \text{ minutes}} \left(\frac{1 \times 15}{4 \times 15}\right) \quad = \quad \frac{900 \text{ seconds}}{3600 \text{ seconds}} \left(\frac{15 \times 60}{60 \times 60}\right)$

EXERCISE 4D

1 Express with denominator 8:

   a $\frac{1}{4}$ **b** $\frac{1}{2}$ **c** $\frac{3}{4}$ **d** 1

2 Express with denominator 30:

   a $\frac{1}{2}$ **b** $\frac{4}{5}$ **c** $\frac{5}{6}$ **d** $\frac{3}{10}$

   e $\frac{1}{5}$ **f** $\frac{2}{3}$ **g** 1   **h** $\frac{3}{5}$

3 Express in sixteenths:

   a $\frac{1}{8}$ **b** $\frac{1}{4}$ **c** 1   **d** 0

   e $\frac{7}{8}$ **f** $\frac{3}{4}$ **g** $\frac{5}{8}$ **h** 2

4 Express in hundredths:

   a $\frac{1}{2}$ **b** $\frac{1}{4}$ **c** $\frac{4}{5}$ **d** $\frac{9}{10}$

   e $\frac{7}{25}$ **f** $\frac{13}{50}$ **g** 1   **h** $\frac{17}{20}$

5 Multiply to find equivalent fractions:

   a $\dfrac{5}{6} = \dfrac{5 \times 2}{6 \times \square} = \dfrac{10}{12}$ **b** $\dfrac{8}{9} = \dfrac{8 \times 3}{9 \times \square} = \dfrac{24}{\square}$

   c $\dfrac{5}{7} = \dfrac{5 \times \square}{7 \times 5} = \dfrac{25}{\square}$ **d** $\dfrac{3}{4} = \dfrac{3 \times 8}{4 \times \square} = \dfrac{\square}{32}$

   e $\dfrac{4}{5} = \dfrac{4 \times \square}{5 \times \square} = \dfrac{40}{50}$ **f** $\dfrac{7}{8} = \dfrac{7 \times \square}{\square \times \square} = \dfrac{28}{32}$

6 Divide to find equivalent fractions:

   a $\dfrac{6}{8} = \dfrac{6 \div 2}{8 \div \square} = \dfrac{3}{4}$ **b** $\dfrac{8}{10} = \dfrac{8 \div \square}{10 \div 2} = \dfrac{4}{\square}$

   c $\dfrac{10}{15} = \dfrac{10 \div 5}{15 \div \square} = \dfrac{\square}{3}$ **d** $\dfrac{18}{21} = \dfrac{18 \div 3}{21 \div \square} = \dfrac{\square}{\square}$

   e $\dfrac{15}{25} = \dfrac{\square \div 5}{25 \div \square} = \dfrac{\square}{5}$ **f** $\dfrac{18}{20} = \dfrac{\square \div \square}{20 \div \square} = \dfrac{9}{\square}$

7 Find $\square$ if:

   a $\dfrac{\square}{3} = \dfrac{7}{21}$ **b** $\dfrac{\square}{5} = \dfrac{12}{15}$ **c** $\dfrac{\square}{11} = \dfrac{56}{77}$

   d $\dfrac{15}{35} = \dfrac{\square}{7}$ **e** $\dfrac{27}{63} = \dfrac{\square}{7}$ **f** $\dfrac{27}{81} = \dfrac{\square}{3}$

   g $\dfrac{\square}{13} = \dfrac{9}{39}$ **h** $\dfrac{48}{72} = \dfrac{\square}{12}$

FRACTIONS (CHAPTER 4)

8 Find △ if:

a $\frac{4}{5} = \frac{16}{\triangle}$

b $\frac{5}{12} = \frac{50}{\triangle}$

c $\frac{6}{\triangle} = \frac{3}{4}$

d $\frac{15}{\triangle} = \frac{3}{5}$

e $\frac{7}{8} = \frac{35}{\triangle}$

f $\frac{63}{\triangle} = \frac{7}{9}$

g $\frac{21}{23} = \frac{63}{\triangle}$

h $\frac{48}{\triangle} = \frac{8}{11}$

E LOWEST TERMS

Arrange your ice block sticks like this example:

2 4 6 8 10 12 14 16 18 20

5 10 15 20 25 30 35 40 45 50

Choose any fraction, for example, $\frac{14}{35}$.

A simpler form of this is any fraction to the left of it. For example, $\frac{12}{30}$, $\frac{10}{25}$ etc.

However, the simplest form for $\frac{14}{35}$ is $\frac{2}{5}$.

The **simplest form** of a fraction is where there are no common factors in the numerator and denominator. Simplest form is also referred to as reducing the fraction to **lowest terms**.

Example 2

Reduce to lowest terms: a $\frac{32}{72}$ b $\frac{175}{125}$

a $\frac{32}{72}$

$= \frac{32 \div 8}{72 \div 8}$ {8 is the highest common factor of both 32 and 72}

$= \frac{4}{9}$

b $\frac{175}{125}$

$= \frac{175 \div 25}{125 \div 25}$ {25 is the highest common factor of both 175 and 125}

$= \frac{7}{5}$

EXERCISE 4E

1 Reduce to lowest terms:

a $\frac{8}{10}$
b $\frac{9}{36}$
c $\frac{21}{28}$
d $\frac{15}{35}$
e $\frac{24}{42}$
f $\frac{55}{77}$
g $\frac{48}{84}$
h $\frac{6}{30}$
i $\frac{123}{300}$
j $\frac{625}{1000}$

2 Reduce to lowest terms:

a $\frac{12}{15}$ b $\frac{18}{20}$ c $\frac{72}{96}$ d $\frac{35}{49}$ e $\frac{49}{91}$

f $\frac{39}{52}$ g $\frac{60}{80}$ h $\frac{15}{55}$ i $\frac{246}{600}$ j $\frac{875}{1000}$

3 Simplify:

a $\frac{56}{77}$ b $\frac{45}{80}$ c $\frac{12}{20}$ d $\frac{15}{45}$ e $\frac{250}{1000}$

f $\frac{3}{51}$ g $\frac{24}{81}$ h $\frac{45}{180}$ i $\frac{24}{360}$ j $\frac{135}{360}$

4 Which of these are lowest terms fractions?

a $\frac{15}{20}$ b $\frac{1}{3}$ c $\frac{13}{24}$ d $\frac{132}{144}$ e $\frac{6}{9}$

f $\frac{21}{28}$ g $\frac{22}{24}$ h $\frac{5}{6}$ i $\frac{75}{100}$ j $\frac{14}{15}$

k $\frac{9}{100}$ l $\frac{39}{52}$

F   FRACTIONS OF QUANTITIES

Remember that fractions are everywhere and do not just exist in 2-dimensional shapes. They can be part of a whole object or part of any quantity.

EXERCISE 4F

1 What fraction of each of the following different quantities has been circled?

a 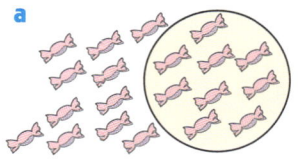   b    c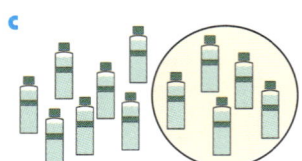

2 Use a full pack of 52 playing cards to work out the following questions. Calculate which fraction of the full pack are:

a   all the red cards, e.g.,    b   all the spades, e.g.,

c   all the aces, e.g.,   d   all the picture cards, e.g.,

e   all the odd numbered cards   f   all the even numbered black cards

3 3 is $\frac{1}{2}$ of 6.   What number is:

a $\frac{1}{2}$ of 10   b $\frac{1}{2}$ of 36   c $\frac{1}{3}$ of 12   d $\frac{1}{3}$ of 45

e $\frac{1}{4}$ of 20   f $\frac{1}{4}$ of 44   g $\frac{1}{5}$ of 30   h $\frac{1}{5}$ of 120

i $\frac{1}{6}$ of 30   j $\frac{1}{6}$ of 126   k $\frac{1}{8}$ of 48   l $\frac{1}{12}$ of 600 ?

When writing fractions that involve measurement it is important that we use the **same units** in the numerator and the denominator.

Example 3

What fraction of 1 metre is 37 cm?

$$37 \text{ cm as a fraction of 1 metre} = \frac{37 \text{ cm}}{1 \text{ metre}}$$
$$= \frac{37 \text{ cm}}{100 \text{ cm}} \quad \{\text{the same units}\}$$
$$= \frac{37}{100}$$

1 m = 100 cm

1 kg = 1000 g

A decade is 10 years.

4 In simplest form, state what fraction of:
- **a** 1 metre is 20 cm
- **b** 2 metres is 78 cm
- **c** 1 kg is 500 g
- **d** 3 kg is 750 g
- **e** 1 week is 1 day
- **f** 1 day is 5 hours
- **g** 1 hour is 23 minutes
- **h** November is two days
- **i** a decade is one year
- **j** 2 dollars is 27 cents

Fractions of time

5 What fraction of one hour is:
- **a** 30 minutes
- **b** 10 minutes
- **c** 45 minutes
- **d** 12 minutes?

6 What fraction of one day is:
- **a** 1 hour
- **b** 4 hours
- **c** 30 minutes
- **d** 1 minute?

7 What fraction of September is 10 days?

8 Winter is what fraction of a leap year?

For some of the following questions you could use a calculator to help.

9 What fraction of one week is:
- **a** 5 days
- **b** 12 hours
- **c** one minute
- **d** $\frac{1}{2}$ second?

10 In question **9**, as the fraction of the week got smaller, what happened to the denominator?
Although it may be fun to work out such big denominators, it is rare to refer to a second as a fraction of an hour or a day let alone a week!

Example 4

Matthew was given a box of chocolates. 5 had red wrappers, 4 had blue, 4 had gold and 2 had green.
- **a** What fraction of the chocolates had red wrappers?
- **b** What fraction of the chocolates did not have gold wrappers?

a Fraction with red wrappers $= \dfrac{\text{number with red wrappers}}{\text{total number of chocolates}}$

$= \dfrac{5}{15}$

$= \dfrac{1}{3}$

b 11 chocolates did not have gold wrappers.

Fraction without gold wrappers $= \dfrac{\text{number without gold wrappers}}{\text{total number of chocolates}}$

$= \dfrac{11}{15}$

11 Jenny scored 27 correct answers in her test of 40 questions. What fraction of her answers were incorrect?

12 Linda had a bag of apples. She ate 3 and 2 others were bad. If she had 9 apples to start with, what fraction of her apples remain?

13 James was travelling a journey of 420 km. His car broke down after 280 km. What fraction of his journey did he still have to travel?

14 Glen started his homework at 8.15 pm and completed it at 9.08 pm. If he had allowed one hour to do his homework, what fraction of that time did he use?

15 Gordon spent $3.25 on a drink and $3.15 on chocolates. What fraction of $10 did he spend?

16 Andrew cut 3 pieces of rope each 40 cm long from 1.5 m of rope. What fraction of the rope remained?

17 Fill in the missing fraction:

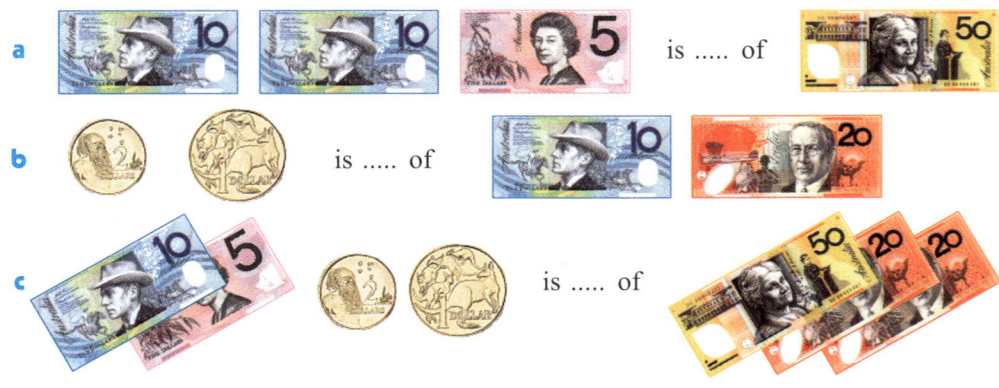

Example 5

On the first day of school this year, $\frac{1}{3}$ of the Year 7 class were aged 12 years or older. If there were 27 students in the class, how many were 12 years or older?

The full number is 27.

So, $\frac{1}{3}$ is $27 \div 3 = 9$ students

There were 9 students aged 12 years or older.

To find $\frac{1}{3}$ of 27 we need to divide 27 into 3 equal parts.

18 Find:

- **a** $\frac{1}{3}$ of 12
- **b** $\frac{1}{4}$ of 20
- **c** $\frac{1}{5}$ of 35
- **d** $\frac{1}{10}$ of 650 g
- **e** $\frac{1}{2}$ of $1.20
- **f** $\frac{1}{4}$ of 1 hour (in min)

19 Damien only won one third of the games of tennis that he played for his school team. If he played 15 games, how many did he win?

20 One fifth of the students at a school were absent because of colds. If there were 245 students in the school, how many were away?

21 One sixth of the cars from an assembly line were painted white. If 222 cars came from the assembly line, how many were painted white?

22 Lisa spent one third of her money on new jeans. If she had $117 before she bought the jeans, how much did the jeans cost?

23 While Evan was on holidays one eighth of the tomato plants in his greenhouse died. If he had 96 plants alive when he went away, how many were still alive when he came home?

24 Draw sketches of the amounts of money which represent $\frac{1}{4}$ of each of the following. Write their numerical value beneath your sketches.

a    **b**    **c**

d    **e**    **f**

25 There are $360°$ in 1 revolution (one full turn).

- **a** Find the number of degrees in:
  - **i** one quarter turn
  - **ii** a half turn
  - **iii** three quarters of a turn.
- **b** What fraction of a revolution is:
  - **i** $30°$
  - **ii** $60°$
  - **iii** $240°$?

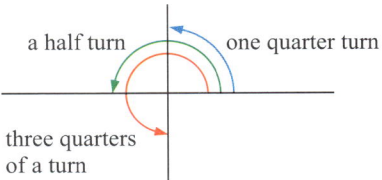

> **Example 6**
>
> $\frac{2}{5}$ of Freddy's money was $5260.
> How much money has Freddy in total?
>
> $\frac{2}{5}$ is $5260
> So, $\frac{1}{5}$ is $2630   {a half of $5260}
> ∴ $\frac{5}{5}$ is $2630 × 5
>   = $13 150
>
> ```
>   2 6 3 0
> ×       5
> ─────────
> 1 3 1 5 0
> ```

26 One morning two fifths of the passengers on my bus were school children. If there were 45 passengers, how many were school children?

27 Richard spent two thirds of his working day installing computers, and the remainder of the time travelling between jobs. If his working day was 8 hours, how much time did he spend travelling?

28 When Sasha played netball, she scored a goal with seven eighths of her shots for goal. If she shot for goal 16 times in a match, how many goals did she score?

29 A business hired a truck to transport boxes of equipment. The total weight of the equipment was 3 tonnes, but the truck could only carry $\frac{5}{8}$ of the boxes in one load.

  a What weight did the truck carry in the first load? Remember 1 tonne = 1000 kg.

  b If there were 80 boxes, how many did the truck carry in the first load?

G COMPARING FRACTION SIZES

It is not easy to compare a bowl of bananas with a bowl of apples. It is, however, easier to compare one bowl of fruit (containing bananas and apples) with another bowl of fruit (containing bananas and apples).

Two fractions are easily compared for size when they have the same denominator.

For example $\frac{3}{4} > \frac{2}{3}$ as $\frac{3}{4} = \frac{9}{12}$ and $\frac{2}{3} = \frac{8}{12}$ and $9 > 8$.

We convert the fractions to fractions with a common denominator which is the lowest common multiple of the original denominators.

This denominator is called the **lowest common denominator (LCD)**.

> **Example 7**
>
> Find the LCD of $\frac{1}{2}, \frac{1}{3}, \frac{1}{4}$ by first finding the lowest common multiple of 2, 3, and 4.
>
> Multiples of 2 are 2 4 6 8 10 **12** 14 16 18 20 22 **24**
> Multiples of 3 are 3 6 9 **12** 15 18 21 **24**
> Multiples of 4 are 4 8 **12** 16 20 **24**
> ∴ the common multiples of 2, 3 and 4 are: 12, 24, 36, etc.
> ∴ the lowest common multiple is 12.
> ∴ the LCD of $\frac{1}{2}, \frac{1}{3}$ and $\frac{1}{4}$ is 12.

LCD is the abbreviation for **L**owest **C**ommon **D**enominator.

EXERCISE 4G

1 Find the LCM of:
   a 7, 3   **b** 5, 3   **c** 3, 6   **d** 12, 18
   e 6, 8, 9   **f** 10, 5, 6 **g** 5, 6, 11   **h** 12, 4, 9

> **Example 8**
>
> Write the following fractions with the lowest common denominator (LCD) and hence write the original fractions in ascending order of size (smallest to largest): $\frac{2}{3}, \frac{3}{5}, \frac{3}{4}$.
>
> The lowest common multiple of 3, 5 and 4 is 60.
>
> So, the LCD of $\frac{2}{3}, \frac{3}{5}, \frac{3}{4}$ is 60.
>
> So $\frac{2}{3} = \frac{2 \times 20}{3 \times 20} = \frac{40}{60}$; $\frac{3}{5} = \frac{3 \times 12}{5 \times 12} = \frac{36}{60}$; $\frac{3}{4} = \frac{3 \times 15}{4 \times 15} = \frac{45}{60}$
>
> Now $\frac{36}{60} < \frac{40}{60} < \frac{45}{60}$,   so, $\frac{3}{5} < \frac{2}{3} < \frac{3}{4}$.

Ascending means *going up*.

Descending means *going down*.

2 Write each set of fractions with the lowest common denominator and hence write the original fractions in ascending order (smallest to largest):

   a $\frac{1}{2}, \frac{1}{4}$ **b** $\frac{2}{3}, \frac{3}{4}$ **c** $\frac{1}{2}, \frac{4}{7}$
   d $\frac{5}{8}, \frac{3}{4}$ **e** $\frac{7}{10}, \frac{5}{6}$ **f** $\frac{7}{9}, \frac{3}{4}$
   g $\frac{5}{8}, \frac{8}{10}$ **h** $\frac{8}{11}, \frac{5}{8}$ **i** $\frac{9}{25}, \frac{7}{20}, \frac{1}{4}$

3 By writing each fraction with a common denominator, arrange these fractions in descending order:

   a $\frac{1}{2}, \frac{2}{5}, \frac{7}{10}$ **b** $\frac{1}{2}, \frac{5}{8}, \frac{3}{4}$ **c** $\frac{1}{2}, \frac{7}{12}, \frac{4}{6}$

ACTIVITY — FRACTION STRIPS

What to do:

1. You need ten identical strips of paper 24 cm long.
2. Use a ruler to divide the first one into halves and name both pieces $\frac{1}{2}$.
   Divide another strip into thirds and name each piece $\frac{1}{3}$.

Use your ruler and your skills with division to divide the remaining strips into quarters, fifths, sixths, eighths, tenths, twelfths and sixteenths.

You should have one strip remaining as the whole ($\frac{1}{1}$).

3. Starting with the whole, arrange the strips in descending order of fraction size, one below the other. Use the strips to compare fractions.

For example, compare $\frac{3}{4}$ and $\frac{9}{10}$. Count across from the left of the arrangement for three $\frac{1}{4}$ pieces and for nine $\frac{1}{10}$ pieces. $\frac{9}{10}$ is further to the right than $\frac{3}{4}$ therefore $\frac{9}{10} > \frac{3}{4}$.

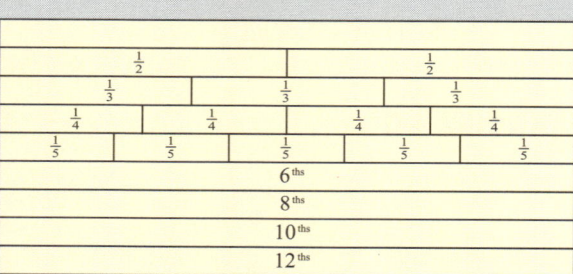

4. Use the fraction strips to answer these True or False questions:

   a $\frac{2}{5} < \frac{5}{12}$ **b** $\frac{5}{6} > \frac{13}{16}$ **c** $\frac{3}{5} < \frac{10}{16}$ **d** $\frac{3}{4} > \frac{12}{16}$

H IMPROPER FRACTIONS AND MIXED NUMBERS

IMPROPER FRACTIONS

All the fractions we have looked at so far have been less than one. These are proper fractions.

> A fraction which has a numerator **less** than its denominator is called a **proper fraction**.
>
> A fraction which has a numerator **greater** than its denominator is called an **improper fraction**.

For example, $\frac{2}{3}$ is a proper fraction      represents $\frac{2}{3}$

$\frac{5}{4}$ is an improper fraction   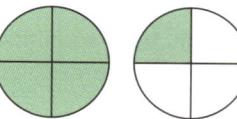   represents $\frac{5}{4}$

Note: To obtain five quarters ($\frac{5}{4}$) it is necessary to take two wholes, divide into quarters and shade 5 quarters. So, $\frac{5}{4}$ is the same as $1\frac{1}{4}$ (1 and $\frac{1}{4}$).

MIXED NUMBERS

> When an improper fraction is written as a whole number and a fraction, it is called a **mixed number**.

For example, $1\frac{1}{4}$ is a mixed number.

It is often necessary to change a number from an improper fraction to a mixed number and vice versa.

For example, $\quad \frac{8}{3} = 8 \div 3 = 2$ wholes and 2 equal parts (thirds) left over.

So, $\frac{8}{3} = 2\frac{2}{3}$.

Another way of doing this is
$$\frac{8}{3} = \frac{6}{3} + \frac{2}{3}$$
$$= 2 + \frac{2}{3}$$
$$= 2\frac{2}{3}$$

Example 9

Write as a whole number or a mixed number:

a $\frac{15}{5}$ b $\frac{21}{5}$

a $\quad \frac{15}{5}$
$= 15 \div 5$
$= 3$

b $\quad \frac{21}{5}$
$= \frac{20}{5} + \frac{1}{5}$
$= 4 + \frac{1}{5}$
$= 4\frac{1}{5}$

EXERCISE 4H

1 Write as a whole number:

a $\frac{16}{4}$ b $\frac{20}{5}$ c $\frac{18}{6}$ d $\frac{40}{8}$

e $\frac{30}{6}$ f $\frac{30}{3}$ g $\frac{30}{10}$ h $\frac{30}{1}$

i $\frac{30}{30}$ j $\frac{64}{8}$ k $\frac{125}{25}$ l $\frac{63}{7}$

2 Write as a mixed number:

a $\frac{5}{4}$ b $\frac{7}{6}$ c $\frac{18}{4}$ d $\frac{19}{6}$

e $\frac{15}{2}$ f $\frac{17}{3}$ g $\frac{16}{7}$ h $\frac{23}{8}$

i $\frac{22}{7}$ j $\frac{35}{9}$ k $\frac{41}{4}$ l $\frac{109}{12}$

Example 10

Write $2\tfrac{4}{5}$ as an improper fraction.

$2\tfrac{4}{5}$
$= 2 + \tfrac{4}{5}$ {Split the mixed number.}
$= \tfrac{10}{5} + \tfrac{4}{5}$ {Write with common denominator.}
$= \tfrac{14}{5}$

3 Write as an improper fraction:
- **a** $3\tfrac{1}{2}$
- **b** $4\tfrac{2}{3}$
- **c** $2\tfrac{3}{4}$
- **d** $1\tfrac{2}{3}$
- **e** $1\tfrac{1}{2}$
- **f** $3\tfrac{3}{4}$
- **g** $1\tfrac{4}{5}$
- **h** $6\tfrac{1}{2}$
- **i** $4\tfrac{5}{9}$
- **j** $5\tfrac{7}{8}$
- **k** $6\tfrac{6}{7}$
- **l** $1\tfrac{11}{12}$

4 Use 2 dice. Use one to roll the numerator and the other to roll the denominator. Find:
- **a** the smallest fraction it is possible to roll
- **b** the largest proper fraction it is possible to roll
- **c** the largest improper fraction (not a whole number) it is possible to roll
- **d** the number of different fractions it is possible to roll.
- **e** List the different combinations that can be simplified to a whole number.

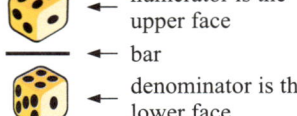
numerator is the upper face
bar
denominator is the lower face

I ADDING FRACTIONS

Using diagrams, find (1) $\tfrac{4}{6} + \tfrac{1}{6}$ (2) $\tfrac{7}{8} + \tfrac{3}{8}$

(1)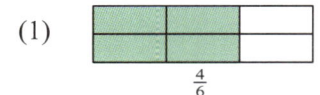

(2) 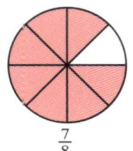 + 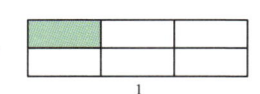 =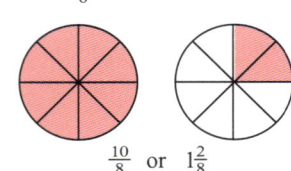

Notice that $\tfrac{4}{6} + \tfrac{1}{6} = \tfrac{4+1}{6}$ and $\tfrac{7}{8} + \tfrac{3}{8} = \tfrac{7+3}{8}$

So,

to add fractions with the same denominators, we add the numerators.

In symbols, this is: $\dfrac{a}{d} + \dfrac{b}{d} = \dfrac{a+b}{d}$

EXERCISE 4I

1 Without showing any working, add the following:

    a $\frac{1}{4} + \frac{2}{4}$ b $\frac{3}{10} + \frac{3}{10}$ c $\frac{1}{6} + \frac{4}{6}$

    d $\frac{4}{7} + \frac{2}{7}$ e $\frac{4}{9} + \frac{10}{9}$ f $\frac{3}{5} + \frac{4}{5}$

    g $3 + \frac{2}{3} + \frac{2}{3}$ h $2 + \frac{5}{8} + \frac{7}{8}$ i $1 + \frac{7}{10} + \frac{6}{10}$

ADDING FRACTIONS WITH DIFFERENT DENOMINATORS

If the denominators are different we need to convert each fraction to the same denominator. For example, $\frac{1}{4} + \frac{2}{5}$. As the denominators are 4 and 5 we draw a 5 by 4 grid the fractions.

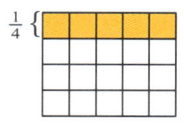
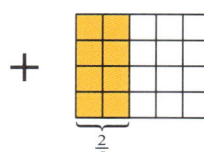
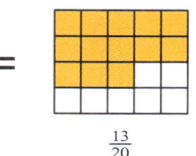

As we do not want to draw pictures each time to add fractions we use this method:

$$\frac{1}{4} + \frac{2}{5}$$
$$= \frac{1 \times 5}{4 \times 5} + \frac{2 \times 4}{5 \times 4} \quad \text{\{making the denominators 20\}}$$
$$= \frac{5}{20} + \frac{8}{20}$$
$$= \frac{13}{20}$$

Notice that 20 is the LCM of 4 and 5, and as we are dealing with denominators we say that 20 is the **Least Common Denominator** (LCD).

RULE FOR THE ADDITION OF FRACTIONS

> To add two or more fractions:
> - if necessary, change the fractions to fractions with a common denominator
> - add the new numerators whilst the denominator stays the same.

Example 11

Find: a $\frac{1}{2} + \frac{3}{5}$ b $\frac{3}{4} + \frac{5}{6}$

a $\frac{1}{2} + \frac{3}{5}$ has LCD of 10

$$= \frac{1 \times 5}{2 \times 5} + \frac{3 \times 2}{5 \times 2}$$
$$= \frac{5}{10} + \frac{6}{10}$$
$$= \frac{11}{10}$$
$$= 1\frac{1}{10}$$

b $\frac{3}{4} + \frac{5}{6}$ has LCD of 12

$$= \frac{3 \times 3}{4 \times 3} + \frac{5 \times 2}{6 \times 2}$$
$$= \frac{9}{12} + \frac{10}{12}$$
$$= \frac{19}{12}$$
$$= 1\frac{7}{12}$$

2 Find:

  a $\frac{1}{5} + \frac{3}{10}$ **b** $\frac{3}{5} + \frac{7}{10}$ **c** $\frac{1}{2} + \frac{1}{4}$ **d** $\frac{1}{2} + \frac{1}{10}$

  e $\frac{3}{4} + \frac{1}{3}$ **f** $\frac{7}{10} + \frac{1}{3}$ **g** $\frac{2}{3} + \frac{1}{2}$ **h** $\frac{5}{6} + \frac{5}{8}$

  i $\frac{3}{4} + \frac{1}{6}$ **j** $\frac{5}{9} + \frac{5}{6}$ **k** $\frac{3}{7} + \frac{3}{14}$ **l** $\frac{4}{9} + \frac{2}{5}$

Example 12

Find: $\frac{2}{3} + \frac{1}{4} + \frac{3}{8}$

$\frac{2}{3} + \frac{1}{4} + \frac{3}{8}$ has an LCD of 24

$= \frac{2 \times 8}{3 \times 8} + \frac{1 \times 6}{4 \times 6} + \frac{3 \times 3}{8 \times 3}$

$= \frac{16}{24} + \frac{6}{24} + \frac{9}{24}$

$= \frac{31}{24}$

$= 1\frac{7}{24}$

---

3 Find:

  a $\frac{1}{4} + \frac{1}{3} + \frac{1}{2}$ **b** $\frac{3}{5} + \frac{7}{10} + \frac{5}{20}$ **c** $\frac{5}{9} + \frac{5}{6} + \frac{1}{3}$ **d** $\frac{3}{4} + \frac{7}{8} + \frac{2}{3}$

Example 13

Find: **a** $1\frac{1}{3} + 2\frac{3}{4}$ **b** $4 + \frac{2}{3} + \frac{4}{5}$

a $1\frac{1}{3} + 2\frac{3}{4}$ {LCD of 12}

$= \frac{4}{3} + \frac{11}{4}$

$= \frac{4 \times 4}{3 \times 4} + \frac{11 \times 3}{4 \times 3}$

$= \frac{16}{12} + \frac{33}{12}$

$= \frac{49}{12}$

$= 4\frac{1}{12}$

b $4 + \frac{2}{3} + \frac{4}{5}$ {LCD of 15}

$= 4 + \frac{2 \times 5}{3 \times 5} + \frac{4 \times 3}{5 \times 3}$

$= 4 + \frac{10}{15} + \frac{12}{15}$

$= 4 + \frac{22}{15}$

$= 4 + 1\frac{7}{15}$

$= 5\frac{7}{15}$

---

4 Find:

  a $3\frac{1}{2} + 2\frac{1}{2}$ **b** $2\frac{2}{3} + 1\frac{1}{3}$ **c** $2\frac{2}{3} + 1\frac{1}{2}$ **d** $\frac{3}{4} + 1\frac{1}{5}$

  e $2\frac{1}{4} + \frac{1}{8}$ **f** $1\frac{7}{8} + 1\frac{1}{2}$ **g** $\frac{1}{2} + 1\frac{5}{6}$ **h** $2 + 1\frac{1}{3}$

  i $3\frac{3}{4} + \frac{1}{3}$ **j** $2 + \frac{1}{3} + 1\frac{1}{2}$ **k** $\frac{3}{4} + 1 + 1\frac{1}{3}$ **l** $\frac{3}{5} + 1\frac{1}{2} + 2$

J SUBTRACTING FRACTIONS

For fractions with the **same denominator**, just the numerators are subtracted.

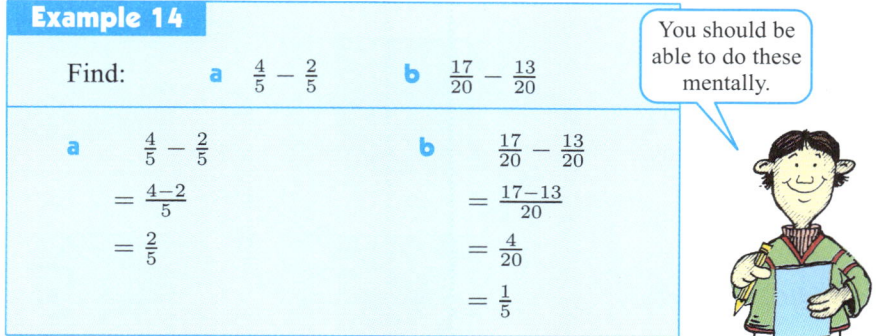

EXERCISE 4J

1 Find without showing any working:

a $\frac{3}{4} - \frac{1}{4}$ b $\frac{7}{9} - \frac{4}{9}$ c $\frac{7}{8} - \frac{5}{8}$ d $1 - \frac{5}{6}$

e $1 - \frac{11}{13}$ f $\frac{19}{20} - \frac{13}{20}$ g $5 - \frac{1}{2}$ h $2 - \frac{3}{5}$

i $3 - \frac{7}{10}$ j $4 - \frac{6}{7}$ k $1 - \frac{1}{7} - \frac{2}{7}$ l $1 - (\frac{1}{7} + \frac{2}{7})$

SUBTRACTING FRACTIONS WITH DIFFERENT DENOMINATORS

For fractions with **different denominators** we must first make the denominators equal using the **LCD**. Then we subtract the numerators.

Considering this example:

Grandma baked a large apple pie and gave half to her neighbour.

Her grandson Luke ate $\frac{3}{4}$ of what remained.

What fraction was left for Luke's sister Leanne?

Grandma has a good eye for the lowest common denominator (LCD). She also knows that smaller pieces of her pie are easier to eat.

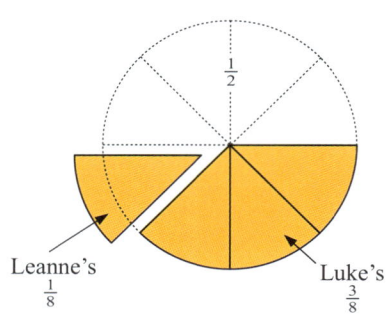

She originally cut the whole pie into 8 equal pieces.

One half ($\frac{1}{2}$ or $\frac{4}{8}$) had been given to Grandma's neighbour.

This left $\frac{4}{8}$ for Luke and Leanne.

Since 4 pieces remained and Luke ate $\frac{3}{4}$ of them, Luke ate three pieces.

So Luke ate three out of the original 8 pieces, that is, $\frac{3}{8}$ of the pie.

Leanne was left with one piece or $\frac{1}{8}$. So, $\frac{1}{2} - \frac{3}{8} = \frac{4}{8} - \frac{3}{8} = \frac{1}{8}$.

RULE FOR THE SUBTRACTION OF FRACTIONS

To subtract two fractions we change them to fractions with a common denominator and subtract the new numerators.

Visual demonstration for $\frac{4}{5} - \frac{3}{4}$

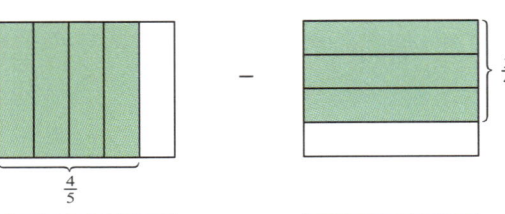

{subdividing into 20ths}

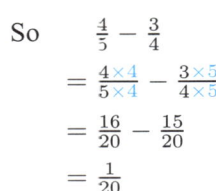
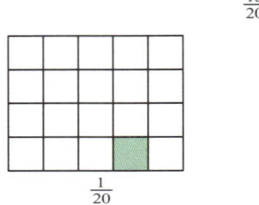

So $\frac{4}{5} - \frac{3}{4}$
$= \frac{4 \times 4}{5 \times 4} - \frac{3 \times 5}{4 \times 5}$
$= \frac{16}{20} - \frac{15}{20}$
$= \frac{1}{20}$

Example 15

Find: a $\frac{3}{4} - \frac{2}{3}$ b $\frac{4}{5} - \frac{3}{4}$

a $\frac{3}{4} - \frac{2}{3}$ has LCD 12
$= \frac{3 \times 3}{4 \times 3} - \frac{2 \times 4}{3 \times 4}$
$= \frac{9}{12} - \frac{8}{12}$
$= \frac{1}{12}$

b $\frac{4}{5} - \frac{3}{4}$ has LCD 20
$= \frac{4 \times 4}{5 \times 4} - \frac{3 \times 5}{4 \times 5}$
$= \frac{16}{20} - \frac{15}{20}$
$= \frac{1}{20}$

EXERCISE 4J (continued)

2 Find:

a $\frac{1}{3} - \frac{1}{4}$ b $\frac{5}{6} - \frac{1}{3}$ c $\frac{3}{4} - \frac{1}{5}$ d $\frac{1}{2} - \frac{3}{10}$

e $\frac{3}{4} - \frac{3}{8}$ f $\frac{5}{6} - \frac{1}{2}$ g $\frac{2}{3} - \frac{1}{6}$ h $\frac{4}{5} - \frac{1}{3}$

i $\frac{3}{8} - \frac{1}{4}$ j $\frac{7}{15} - \frac{1}{3}$ k $\frac{11}{12} - \frac{3}{4}$ l $\frac{7}{10} - \frac{3}{15}$

3 Find:

a $1 + \frac{2}{5} - \frac{3}{10}$ b $\frac{1}{6} + \frac{1}{4} - \frac{1}{8}$ c $\frac{5}{12} + \frac{5}{6} - \frac{2}{3}$ d $\frac{3}{4} + \frac{1}{8} - \frac{1}{6}$

Example 16

Find: **a** $4\frac{1}{2} - 1\frac{2}{3}$ **b** $3 - \frac{4}{7}$

When subtracting with mixed numbers, convert to an improper fraction first.

a $4\frac{1}{2} - 1\frac{2}{3}$
$= \frac{9}{2} - \frac{5}{3}$
$= \frac{9 \times 3}{2 \times 3} - \frac{5 \times 2}{3 \times 2}$
$= \frac{27}{6} - \frac{10}{6}$
$= \frac{17}{6}$
$= 2\frac{5}{6}$

b $3 - \frac{4}{7}$
$= \frac{21}{7} - \frac{4}{7}$
$= \frac{17}{7}$
$= 2\frac{3}{7}$

4 Find:

a $3\frac{1}{2} - 2\frac{1}{2}$ b $2\frac{2}{3} - 1\frac{1}{3}$ c $2\frac{2}{3} - 1\frac{1}{2}$ d $2\frac{3}{5} - 1\frac{2}{5}$

e $3\frac{7}{8} - 1\frac{1}{2}$ f $3\frac{1}{2} - 1\frac{5}{6}$ g $2\frac{1}{2} - \frac{4}{5}$ h $3\frac{3}{4} - 2\frac{1}{3}$

i $3\frac{5}{6} - 1\frac{2}{3}$ j $5\frac{4}{5} - 2\frac{1}{5}$ k $5\frac{7}{10} - 3\frac{4}{5}$ l $2\frac{11}{12} - 2\frac{1}{2}$

m $3\frac{1}{2} - 1\frac{4}{7}$ n $5 - 3\frac{4}{9}$ o $3 - \frac{7}{10}$ p $6\frac{3}{4} - 2\frac{7}{8}$

K MULTIPLYING FRACTIONS

During the basketball season, a player drinks $\frac{3}{4}$ of a litre of milk five days a week.

How much milk does the player drink each week?

We can show this diagrammatically.

We can get the answer by addition: $\frac{3}{4} + \frac{3}{4} + \frac{3}{4} + \frac{3}{4} + \frac{3}{4} = \frac{3+3+3+3+3}{4} = \frac{15}{4}$ litres

or we can use multiplication: $5 \times \frac{3}{4} = \frac{5 \times 3}{4} = \frac{15}{4}$ litres

Now consider the given diagram:

What fraction of the total is represented by the shading?

There are 12 eighths shaded and $4 \times \frac{3}{8} = \frac{4 \times 3}{8} = \frac{12}{8}$.

In both of the previous examples, whole numbers have been used to multiply the fraction $5 \times \frac{3}{4}$ and $4 \times \frac{3}{8}$.

If you consider that the number 5 can be written as $\frac{5}{1}$ and 4 can be written as $\frac{4}{1}$, the two examples could be written as $\frac{5}{1} \times \frac{3}{4}$ and $\frac{4}{1} \times \frac{3}{8}$.

This means that $\frac{5}{1} \times \frac{3}{4} = \frac{15}{4}$ and $\frac{4}{1} \times \frac{3}{8} = \frac{12}{8}$ from the milk and squares examples.

In the first example, when we multiply the numerators together we get the numerator 15.

When we multiply the denominators together we get the denominator 4.

This rule applies to any fraction which is multiplied by another fraction.

For example, $\frac{3}{4} \times \frac{2}{3} = \frac{3 \times 2}{4 \times 3} = \frac{6}{12}$.

DEMO

So, the rule for multiplying fractions is: $\boxed{\dfrac{a}{b} \times \dfrac{c}{d} = \dfrac{a \times c}{b \times d}}$

Note:
- Sometimes the fractions being multiplied will have **common factors** in the numerator of one fraction and the denominator of the other fraction.

  These common factors can be cancelled before multiplication as it keeps the numbers smaller and easier to handle.

- Mixed numbers must be converted to improper fractions before they can be multiplied or cancelled.

EXERCISE 4K

1 Find the missing number:

  a $5 \times \dfrac{2}{3} = \dfrac{\square}{3}$ **b** $6 \times \dfrac{3}{5} = \dfrac{\square}{5}$ **c** $3 \times \dfrac{7}{8} = \dfrac{\square}{8}$

2 Write as a mixed number:

  a $3 \times \frac{3}{5}$ **b** $6 \times \frac{4}{7}$ **c** $5 \times \frac{2}{3}$ **d** $9 \times \frac{3}{4}$

  e $6 \times \frac{1}{4}$ **f** $3 \times \frac{7}{8}$ **g** $8 \times \frac{1}{3}$ **h** $4 \times \frac{5}{6}$

  i $9 \times \frac{1}{2}$ **j** $7 \times \frac{4}{10}$ **k** $2 \times \frac{11}{12}$ **l** $4 \times \frac{4}{5}$

  m $3 \times \frac{5}{7}$ **n** $5 \times \frac{4}{9}$ **o** $9 \times \frac{4}{5}$ **p** $10 \times \frac{1}{3}$

3 Without showing any working, do the following:

  a $\frac{1}{3} \times \frac{2}{5}$ **b** $\frac{3}{4} \times \frac{2}{7}$ **c** $\frac{3}{5} \times \frac{6}{7}$ **d** $\frac{5}{8} \times \frac{5}{8}$

  e $\frac{5}{6} \times \frac{4}{7}$ **f** $\frac{3}{10} \times \frac{1}{3}$ **g** $\frac{9}{7} \times \frac{3}{4}$ **h** $\frac{8}{5} \times \frac{2}{9}$

  i $\frac{3}{4} \times \frac{7}{11}$ **j** $\frac{7}{6} \times \frac{2}{5}$ **k** $\frac{1}{2} \times \frac{1}{2} \times \frac{1}{2}$ **l** $\frac{2}{3} \times \frac{3}{2}$

  m $\frac{1}{2} \times \frac{2}{3} \times \frac{3}{4}$ **n** $\frac{1}{2} \times \frac{2}{3} \times \frac{3}{1}$ **o** $\frac{1}{3} \times \frac{1}{3} \times \frac{1}{3}$ **p** $\frac{3}{2} \times \frac{3}{2} \times \frac{3}{2}$

Example 17

Find:

a $\frac{3}{5} \times 10$

b $\frac{3}{4} \times 2\frac{2}{3}$

a $\frac{3}{5} \times 10$
$= \frac{3}{5} \times \frac{10}{1}$
$= \frac{3}{{}_1 5} \times \frac{{}^2 10}{1}$
$= \frac{6}{1}$
$= 6$

b $\frac{3}{4} \times 2\frac{2}{3}$
$= \frac{3}{4} \times \frac{8}{3}$
$= \frac{{}^1 3}{{}_1 4} \times \frac{{}^2 8}{3_1}$
$= \frac{2}{1}$
$= 2$

4 Find:

a $\frac{2}{3} \times \frac{4}{5}$
b $\frac{3}{8} \times \frac{4}{5}$
c $\frac{3}{4} \times \frac{5}{9}$
d $\frac{4}{7} \times \frac{7}{9}$

e $2\frac{2}{3} \times \frac{1}{7}$
f $2\frac{2}{3} \times \frac{6}{7}$
g $1\frac{1}{4} \times 1\frac{1}{15}$
h $\frac{4}{3} \times \frac{6}{7}$

i $2\frac{2}{5} \times 2\frac{1}{2}$
j $6\frac{3}{4} \times \frac{8}{9}$
k $1\frac{1}{4} \times \frac{9}{10} \times \frac{2}{3}$
l $\frac{3}{7} \times 3\frac{1}{2} \times 1\frac{1}{3}$

Example 18

Find: a $\frac{3}{8}$ of 16   b $\frac{2}{9}$ of 180

a $\frac{3}{8}$ of 16
$= \frac{3}{{}_1 8} \times \frac{{}^2 16}{1}$
$= \frac{6}{1}$
$= 6$

b $\frac{2}{9}$ of 180
$= \frac{2}{{}_1 9} \times \frac{{}^{20} 180}{1}$
$= \frac{40}{1}$
$= 40$

5 Find:

a $\frac{2}{3}$ of 12
b $\frac{3}{5}$ of 10
c $\frac{3}{4}$ of 4
d $\frac{2}{7}$ of 21

e $\frac{3}{10}$ of 20
f $\frac{3}{8}$ of 16
g $\frac{4}{5}$ of 60
h $1\frac{1}{3}$ of 9

i 49 of $\frac{3}{7}$
j $\frac{3}{4}$ of $\frac{3}{4}$
k $\frac{1}{4}$ of 6
l $\frac{1}{2}$ of $17\frac{1}{2}$

6 Find:

a $\frac{3}{4}$ of a kilometre
b $\frac{2}{3}$ of one day
c $\frac{3}{5}$ of a century

d $\frac{5}{6}$ of an hour
e $\frac{7}{10}$ of a litre
f $\frac{3}{20}$ of a tonne

7 The whole value of each of the following groups of shapes appears beneath them. What is the value of the coloured shapes in each group?

a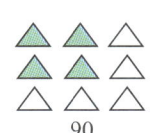
90

b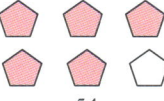
54

c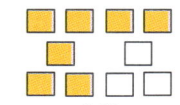
150

d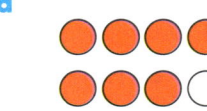
1000

L PROBLEM SOLVING

EXERCISE 4L

1 In a class of 28, four students were late handing in their project assignments. What fraction of the class were late?

2 Tom paid $2800 deposit on a car. He borrowed a further $8400 to pay for the car. What fraction of the car's total cost was Tom's deposit?

3 When Susan drove her car out of the yard the fuel tank was $\frac{1}{2}$ full.
She used $\frac{1}{3}$ of a tank to take her friends for a drive. How much fuel remained in the tank?

4 Alice has 42 birds in an aviary; 26 are canaries and the rest are budgerigars.
   a What fraction of the birds are budgerigars?
   b If half the budgerigars are female, what fraction of all the birds are male budgerigars?

5 Tony plays his computer games for an hour and a quarter each week night. On Saturday he plays for three and a half hours and he plays for four and three quarter hours on Sunday. At this rate how much time does Tony spend playing computer games during one year?

6 A swimmer swims $\frac{3}{7}$ of the way in the first hour and $\frac{2}{5}$ in the second hour.
What fraction has the swimmer left to swim?

7 To make a 20 kg blend of 5 different nuts, a wholesaler mixes 6 kg of peanuts, 4 kg of almonds, 3 kg of walnuts and 2 kg of cashews. The rest are macadamias. What fraction of the blend are the:
   a macadamias   **b** peanuts   **c** walnuts?

8 Wi filled one aquarium $\frac{3}{4}$ full of water. He filled an identical aquarium $\frac{11}{16}$ full of water. If the volume of one aquarium was 48 litres, how much water did he use altogether?

9 Zoe's development company plans to subdivide 60 hectares of land into a housing development. One tenth of the land must be used for parks and gardens and $\frac{1}{4}$ will be required for roads and walkways.

How many blocks with an area of $\frac{1}{5}$ hectare will she be able to create?

10 Which is the better score in a mathematics test:
   a 17 out of 20   **b** 21 out of 25?

11 An orchardist picked $\frac{1}{4}$ of his orange crop in July and $\frac{2}{3}$ of his crop in August.
   a How much of his crop remained to be picked in September?
   b If he picked 600 cases in September, how many cases did he pick that season?

FRACTIONS (CHAPTER 4) 147

12 Joe's Burger Shop makes 16 meat patties with every kilogram of minced beef. In his Double Pattie Delight, Joe uses 2 meat patties. The other varieties use only one pattie.

If Joe sells 600 burgers in one week and $\frac{1}{3}$ of them are his Double Pattie Delights, how much beef mince does Joe use in one week?

13 What fraction would 4 different pizzas need to be cut into if:
   a 12 people were to have one piece of each of the pizzas?
   b What fraction would these pizzas need to be cut into if each person was to have 2 pieces from each pizza?

REVIEW SET A   CHAPTER 4

1 What fraction is represented by the following?

   a 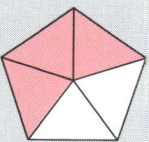   **b** 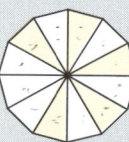   **c**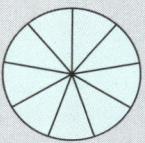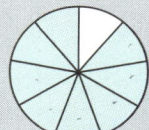

2 Complete the following patterns in lowest terms: $2, \ldots, 2\frac{1}{4}, \ldots, 2\frac{1}{2}, \ldots, \ldots, 2\frac{7}{8}, \ldots$

3 Find the lowest common multiple of:
   a 8 and 12   **b** 15, 6 and 5

4 Write T for true and F for false.
   a $\frac{3}{9} = \frac{15}{40}$ **b** $3\frac{4}{7} = \frac{24}{7}$ **c** $\frac{76}{8} = 9\frac{1}{2}$ **d** $\frac{375}{1000} = \frac{3}{8}$

5 Find:
   a $2\frac{1}{2} + 3\frac{4}{5}$ **b** $6\frac{1}{4} - 3\frac{2}{3}$ **c** $\frac{2}{3} \times 2\frac{1}{2}$

6 Find:
   a $\frac{3}{4}$ of \$28   **b** $\frac{5}{8}$ of 1 tonne

7 In lowest terms, state what fraction of:
   a one week is 3 days   **b** one metre is 35 cm

8 Solve the following problems:
   a There were 2728 paying spectators at a match. If three quarters supported the home team, how many supported the visiting team?
   b Three fifths of the students in a school order their lunch from the canteen. 142 do not. How many students are there in the school?
   c How many $1\frac{1}{5}$ metre long wall hangings can be cut from 60 metres of material?

9 Which is the greater, $\frac{3}{7}$ or $\frac{4}{9}$?

REVIEW SET B   CHAPTER 4

1. Draw and shade diagrams as follows:

   a a regular hexagon to represent $\frac{5}{6}$ **b** a rectangle to represent $\frac{7}{12}$

2. Find the fractions represented by the point on the number lines:

   a   **b**

   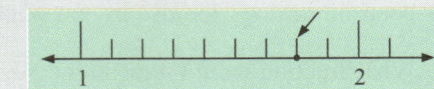

3. **a** Convert $\frac{39}{8}$ to a mixed number.

   b What fraction of $9.00 is $1.80?

   c What fraction of 1 km is 800 m?

4. Express $\frac{2}{5}$, $\frac{3}{4}$ and $\frac{13}{20}$ with a lowest common denominator.
   Then write the original fractions in order of size, the largest being first.

5. **a** If $\frac{3}{4}$ of a number is 21, find the number.

   b Find the values of $\square$ and $\triangle$ given that $\frac{3}{4} = \frac{\square}{20} = \frac{27}{\triangle}$.

6. Write T for true and F for false:

   a $\frac{3}{7} = \frac{6}{14} = \frac{15}{35}$ **b** $\frac{675}{1000} = \frac{5}{8}$ **c** $5\frac{6}{7} = \frac{41}{6}$

7. Find:

   a $2\frac{1}{9} - \frac{5}{6}$ **b** $3\frac{1}{2} + 2\frac{2}{5}$ **c** $4 \times \frac{4}{5}$

8. Solve the following problems:

   a A man who weighed 90 kg went on a diet and lost 10 kg. What fraction of his original weight did he lose?

   b $\frac{2}{5}$ of a flock of sheep numbered 240. Find the size of the whole flock.

   c $\frac{3}{7}$ of the students of a school attended a film night.
   If there were 840 students in the school, how many attended the film night?

9. Melissa works 2 nights a week after school.
   On the first night she works $2\frac{2}{3}$ hours and on the second $3\frac{1}{2}$ hours.
   What is her total time worked for the week?

Chapter 5
Decimals

Knowledge, skills and understandings

By the end of this chapter you should be able to

- round off decimals to 3 places
- divide decimals by a whole number
- use notation for recurring decimals such as $0.\dot{3}$ or $0.\overline{235}$
- multiply decimal numbers by decimal numbers to 2 places
  (e.g., $0.2 \times 0.3 = 0.06$)
- divide decimals using calculators (e.g., calculating averages)
- convert decimals to fractions
- use decimals in problem solving

A REPRESENTING DECIMALS

DECIMAL CURRENCY (MONEY)

Although one cent  and two cent  pieces are not used now, they were part of Australia's system of money or currency. The currency is called **decimal** because it uses a base 10 system. *Decima* in Latin means 'a tenth'.

is a tenth of  i.e., $\frac{1}{10}$ or 0.1 of 10 cents = 1 cent

 is a tenth of  i.e., $\frac{1}{10}$ or 0.1 of $1 or 100 cents = 10 cents

 is a tenth of  i.e., $\frac{1}{10}$ or 0.1 of $10.00 = $1.00

 is a tenth of  i.e., $\frac{1}{10}$ or 0.1 of $100.00 = $10.00

Similarly

 is $\frac{1}{10}$ or 0.1 of

 is $\frac{1}{10}$ or 0.1 of

 is $\frac{1}{10}$ or 0.1 of

 is $\frac{1}{10}$ or 0.1 of

and  is $\frac{1}{10}$ or 0.1 of

Australia's currency is one of the most practical and realistic ways to bring meaning to decimals. We use money and talk about money daily.

Talking about and using money means we are also talking about and using decimals.

The decimal point separates whole numbers from fractional numbers.

Example 1

Change these currency values to decimals of one dollar:

a     b

a Sum of amount shown is $5 and 95 cents

∴ decimal value is 5.95 dollars

b Sum of amount shown is zero dollars and 65 cents

∴ decimal value is 0.65 dollars.

EXERCISE 5A.1

1 Change these currency values to decimals of one dollar:

a

b

c

d

e

f

Example 2

Using one dollar as the unit, change to a decimal value:
a seven dollars, 45 cents   b 275 cents

a $7.45

b 275 cents
= 275 ÷ 100 dollars
= 275. ÷ 100 dollars
= $2.75

Sometimes the decimal point is called "point".

2 Write each amount as dollars using a decimal point:
- **a** 4 dollars 47 cents
- **b** 15 dollars 97 cents
- **c** seven dollars fifty five cents
- **d** 36 dollars
- **e** 150 dollars
- **f** thirty two dollars eighty cents
- **g** 85 dollars 5 cents
- **h** 30 dollars 3 cents

3 a Change these amounts to decimals using the dollar as the unit:
- **i** 35 cents
- **ii** 5 cents
- **iii** 405 cents
- **iv** 3000 cents
- **v** 487 cents
- **vi** 295 cents
- **vii** 3875 cents
- **viii** 638 475 cents

b Starting with the top row, what is the sum of each row above?

c Starting from the left, what is the sum of each column above?

Make sure each amount has its decimal point exactly below the other.

RESEARCH — DECIMAL CURRENCY

1 a i Find out what the denomination of Australia's currency was before decimal currency.
  ii What were the individual denominations?
  iii How many of any one denomination equalled one of the next denomination?
  iv How was this currency added, subtracted, multiplied or divided?

b Why, and when, was decimal currency introduced into Australia?

c What happened to all the pre-decimal currency?

d Find 10 countries who use decimal currency where the dollar is not that country's base unit.

e List any countries who do not use decimal currency.

f Why were the:
  i $1 and $2 notes replaced with coins
  ii 1 cent and 2 cent coins withdrawn?

g What were the advantages of changing our old decimal notes from paper to polymer?

2 Although our 1 cent and 2 cent coins are no longer in circulation, some values and prices still use cents.

In fact some values use decimals of a cent.

List a few of your own thoughts on why this is so.

3 From the television news, internet or newspaper, record the value of the Australian dollar.

  a Do this for one week. Record the value in terms of:
   i American dollars
   ii New Zealand dollars
   iii Japanese yen.
  b Find out why the value changes.

CURRENCIES
EXCHANGE RATES AS AT 8/09/03

Country	TT Buy	TT Sell
United States	0.6509	0.6433
Great Britain	0.4115	0.4020
New Zealand	1.1321	1.1071
Canada	0.8976	0.8742
Europe	0.5908	0.5737
Fiji	1.2451	1.2131
Hong Kong	5.1140	4.9800
Japan	76.560	74.540
Singapore	1.1520	1.1160
Switzerland	0.9060	0.8830
Denmark	4.3870	4.2730

4 Besides the value of shares, the cost of petrol and the value of the Australian dollar, what else uses decimals of a cent?

MULTI ATTRIBUTE BLOCKS

Multi Attribute Blocks (MA blocks) are another practical 3-dimensional way to represent decimals.

This time however

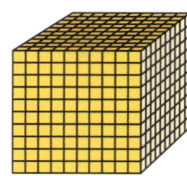 represents the unit or whole
i.e., 1 or $\frac{1}{1}$ or 1.0

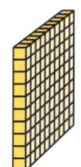 represents one tenth
i.e., $\frac{1}{10}$ or 0.1 of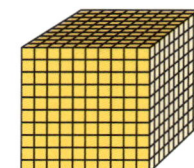

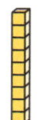 represents one hundredth
i.e., $\frac{1}{100}$ or 0.01 of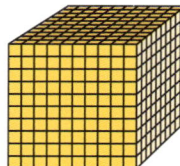

and ▫ represents one thousandth
i.e., $\frac{1}{1000}$ or 0.001 of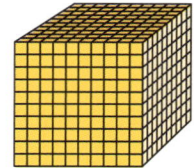

Notice how the smaller the decimal number, the more zeros there are after the decimal point.

DECIMALS (CHAPTER 5) 155

Example 3

Write the decimal value represented by the MA blocks if the larger block represents the unit.

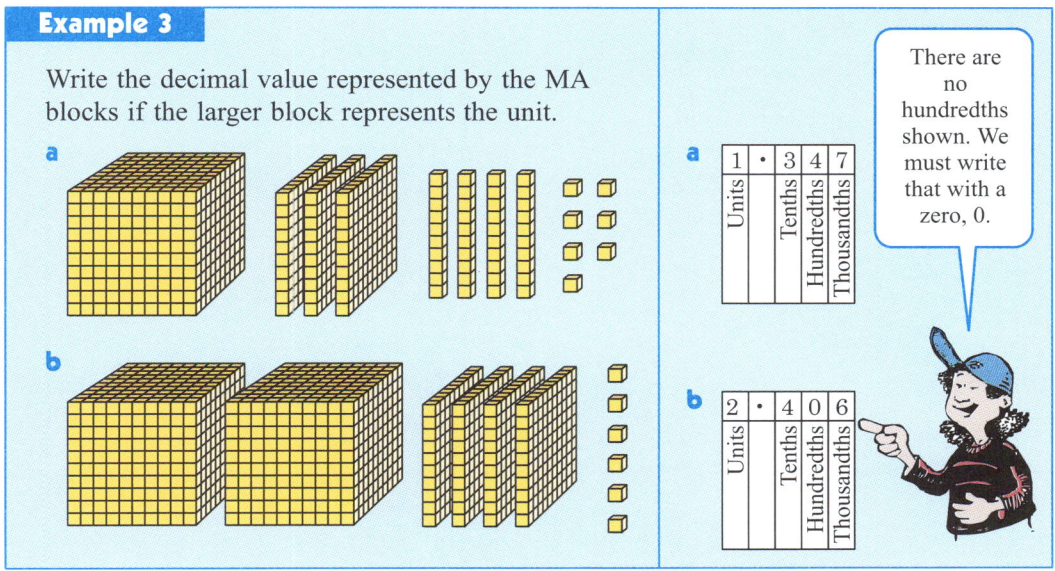

There are no hundredths shown. We must write that with a zero, 0.

a

Units	.	Tenths	Hundredths	Thousandths
1	.	3	4	7

b

Units	.	Tenths	Hundredths	Thousandths
2	.	4	0	6

EXERCISE 5A.2

1. Write the decimal value represented by the MA blocks if the largest block represents the unit:

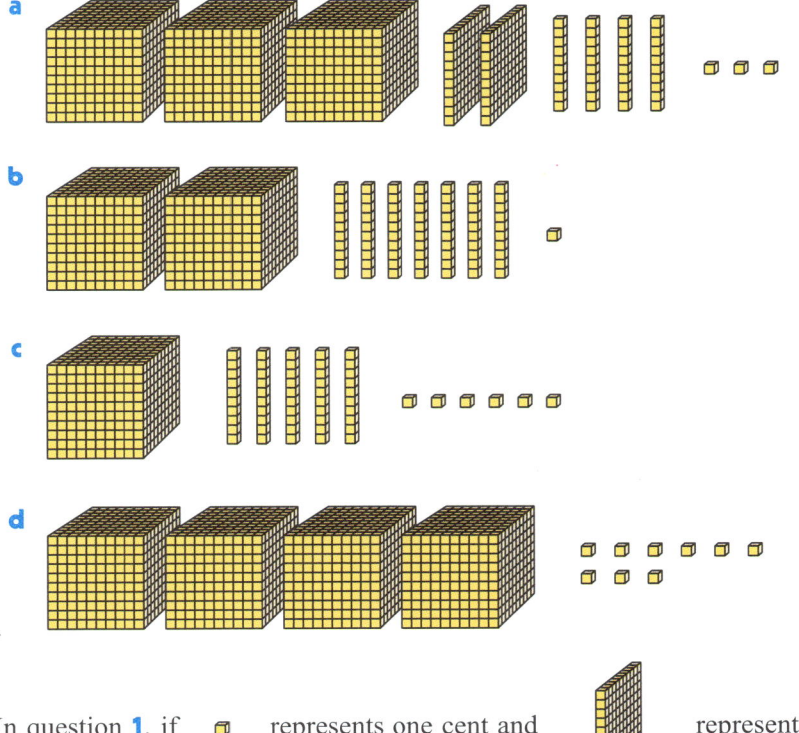

2. In question **1**, if ▫ represents one cent and ▨ represents one dollar:

   a what is the decimal currency value of each example
   b what is the total value?

DECIMAL GRIDS

Decimals can also be represented on 2 dimensional grids.

Let this square represent a whole unit.

1.0 is shaded

Here the unit has been divided into 10 equal parts representing tenths or 0.1

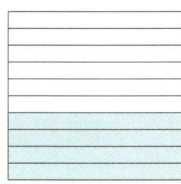

4 lots of $0.1 = 4 \times 0.1 = 0.4$ has been shaded.

Here the unit has been divided into 100 equal parts. Each part represents a hundredth or 0.01

27 lots of $0.01 = 27 \times 0.01 = 0.27$ has been shaded.

From a study of the unit and the three previous diagrams you can see that

$1 = \frac{10}{10} = \frac{100}{100}$ similarly $0.1 = \frac{1}{10} = \frac{10}{100}$ and so $0.3 = \frac{3}{10} = \frac{30}{100}$

Usually there is no need to write $\frac{30}{100}$ as 0.30

However, $\frac{301}{1000}$ must be written as 0.301 and $\frac{7}{1000}$ must be written as 0.007

EXERCISE 5A.3

1 Write the decimal that represents the shaded area:

   a   **b**   **c**   **d**

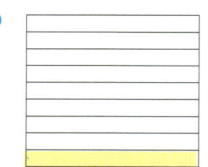 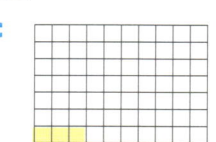 

2 **i** How many rectangles are shaded in each of the following diagrams?
    ii What decimal is represented by each of them?

   a   **b**

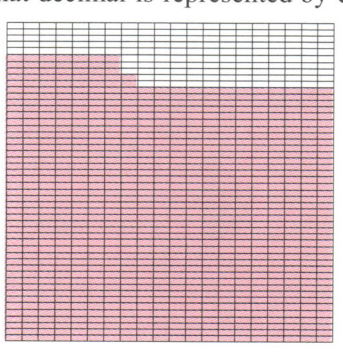 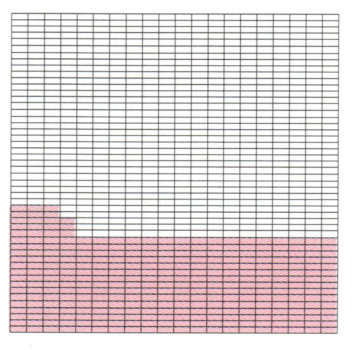

B PLACE VALUE

Just as whole numbers were grouped together according to their place value (**Chapter 1**) decimals are also grouped together.

There are however a few differences:

- The decimal point separates the whole numbers from the decimal numbers.
- "ths" is added to the pronunciation of the denominator.
- Numerals after the decimal point have a special way of being announced.

Grouping a small number of digits makes them easier to say.

Example 4

Express: **a** 0.9 **b** 3.407 in written or oral form.

a 0.9
0.9 is zero point nine

b 3.407
3.407 is three point four zero seven or three and four hundred and seven thousandths

"Oral form" means how you would say it.

Example 5

Express 0.000 032 in written or oral form.

If the decimal number has many zeros following the decimal point it is usually expressed as a fraction of a power of 10.

$$0.000\,032 = \frac{32}{10^6} = \text{thirty two millionths}$$

EXERCISE 5B

1 Express the following in 2 different written forms:

- **a** 0.6
- **b** 0.45
- **c** 0.908
- **d** 8.3
- **e** 6.08
- **f** 96.02
- **g** 5.864
- **h** 34.003
- **i** 7.581
- **j** 60.264

2 Convert the following to decimal form:
   a seventeen and four hundred and sixty five thousandths
   b two point nine eight three
   c thirty two point seven five two
   d twelve and ninety six thousandths
   e three and six hundred and ninety four thousandths
   f four and twenty two hundredths
   g forty point six five nine eight.

Example 6

Place the following into a place value table:
a 7 hundredths   **b** $23 + \frac{4}{10} + \frac{9}{1000}$

Number	Tens	Units	Dec. Point	Tenths	Hundredths	Thousandths	Written numeral
a 7 hundredths			.	0	7		0.07
b $23 + \frac{4}{10} + \frac{9}{1000}$	2	3	.	4	0	9	23.409

3 Draw up a place value table in your exercise book using the headings:

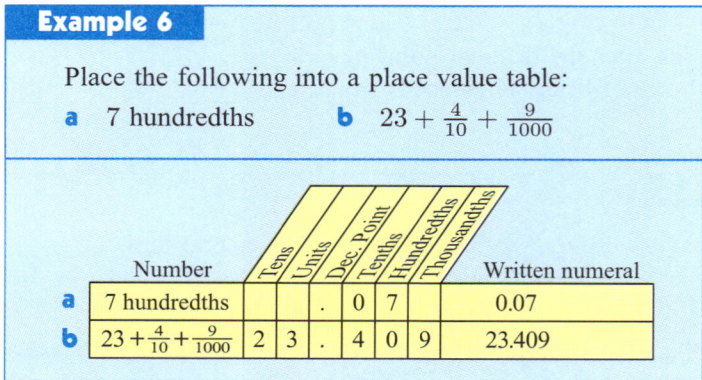

Place the following into the table:
   a 8 tenths
   b 3 thousandths
   c 7 tens and 8 tenths
   d 9 thousands and 2 thousandths
   e 2 hundreds, 9 units and 4 hundredths
   f 8 thousands, 4 tenths and 2 thousandths
   g 5 thousands, 20 units and 3 tenths
   h 6 tens, 8 tenths and 9 hundredths
   i 9 hundreds, 8 tens and 34 thousandths
   j 36 units and 42 hundredths

Example 7

Express 5.706 in expanded rational form (whole number and fractions).

$$5.706 = 5 + \frac{7}{10} + \frac{0}{100} + \frac{6}{1000}$$
$$= 5 + \frac{7}{10} + \frac{6}{1000}$$

4 Express the following in expanded rational form (whole number and fractions):

   a 5.4   **b** 14.9   **c** 2.03   **d** 32.86

   e 2.264   **f** 1.308   **g** 3.002   **h** 0.952

   i 4.024   **j** 2.973   **k** 20.816   **l** 7.777

   m 9.008   **n** 154.451   **o** 808.808   **p** 0.064

Example 8

In the decimal place value card game, what does this 'hand' represent in:

a oral and written decimal form

b expanded rational form?

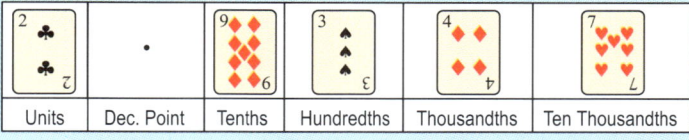

a Using only the numbered cards from 1 to 9 in each suit, this hand represents the number 2.9347, which is two point nine three four seven in written or oral form.

b It is $2 + \frac{9}{10} + \frac{3}{100} + \frac{4}{1000} + \frac{7}{10\,000}$ in expanded rational form.

5 In the decimal place value card game, what do the following hands represent in:

   i oral and written decimal form   **ii** expanded rational form?

a .

b 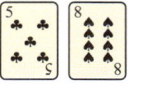 .

c  .

d .

6 a Express the value of the sum of all the above hands in question **5** in:

   i oral and written decimal form

   ii correctly as sketches (draw 3 different possible hands for your answer).

b Which of the above hands has the highest value in the:

   i thousandths place   **ii** tenths place

   iii ten thousandths place   **iv** hundredths place?

c Order these hands from lowest to highest value.

Example 9

Write $\frac{39}{1000}$ in decimal form.

$$\frac{39}{1000} = \frac{30}{1000} + \frac{9}{1000}$$
$$= \frac{3}{100} + \frac{9}{1000}$$
$$= 0.03 + 0.009$$
$$= 0.039$$

7 Write the following in decimal form:

a $\frac{6}{10}$
b $\frac{19}{100}$
c $\frac{4}{10} + \frac{3}{100}$
d $\frac{8}{10} + \frac{9}{1000}$
e $\frac{52}{1000}$
f $\frac{5}{100} + \frac{2}{1000}$
g $\frac{5}{10} + \frac{6}{100} + \frac{8}{1000}$
h $\frac{2}{1000} + \frac{3}{10\,000}$
i $\frac{9}{100} + \frac{4}{1000}$
j $\frac{1}{10} + \frac{1}{1000}$
k $4 + \frac{3}{10} + \frac{8}{100} + \frac{7}{1000}$
l $\frac{3}{100} + \frac{8}{10\,000}$

> **Example 10**
>
> State the value of the digit 6 in the following: 0.3964
>
> 0.3964
> $\frac{1}{10}$s $\frac{1}{1000}$s   ∴ the 6 stands for $\frac{6}{1000}$

8 State the value of the digit 3 in the following:

a 4325.9
b 6.374
c 32.098
d 150.953
e 43.4444
f 82.7384
g 24.8403
h 3874.941

9 State the value of the digit 5 in the following:

a 18.945
b 596.08
c 4.5972
d 94.8573
e 75 948.264
f 275.183
g 358 946.843
h 0.0005

10 State the value of the digit 2 in the following:

a $4\frac{324}{1000}$
b $62\frac{47}{100}$
c $946\frac{42}{100}$
d $24\frac{695}{1000}$
e $1\frac{3652}{10\,000}$
f $254\frac{8}{10}$
g $57\frac{2}{10}$
h $5\frac{652}{1000}$

C ROUNDING DECIMAL NUMBERS

Sometimes completely accurate answers are not required and so we **round off** to the required accuracy.

For example, we may be measuring the length of nails (in centimetres) to the nearest millimetre (i.e., tenth of a centimetre).

This is of course, *to one decimal place*.

Consider   5716
          ≑ 5720   (to the nearest 10)
          ≑ 5700   (to the nearest 100)
          ≑ 6000   (to the nearest 1000)

Likewise for   0.5864
              ≑ 0.586   (to 3 decimal places)
              ≑ 0.59   (to 2 decimal places)
              ≑ 0.6   (to 1 decimal place)

RULES FOR ROUNDING OFF DECIMAL NUMBERS

If, for example, an answer correct to 3 decimal places is required, we evaluate to 4 decimal places.

- If the number in the fourth decimal place is 0, 1, 2, 3 or 4, leave the first 3 digits after the decimal point unchanged.
- If the number in the fourth decimal place is 5, 6, 7, 8 or 9, increase the third digit after the decimal point by one.

Example 11

Find $\frac{2}{7}$ correct to 3 decimal places.

$$\begin{array}{r} 0.2\;8\;5\;7 \\ 7\,\overline{)\,2.0\,^60\,^40\,^50} \end{array} \qquad \therefore \quad \frac{2}{7} \doteq 0.286$$

If we want our answer to 3 decimal places, we divide to the fourth decimal place and then round to 3 decimal places.

ROUNDING

Example 12

Round: **a** 3.26 to 1 decimal place **b** 5.273 to 2 decimal places
  c 4.985 to 2 decimal places

a $3.26 \doteq 3.3$ {the 2nd decimal place is a 6, $\therefore$ increase 2 by 1}

b $5.273 \doteq 5.27$ {the 3rd decimal place is a 3, $\therefore$ 7 stays as is}

c $4.985 \doteq 4.99$ {the 3rd decimal place is a 5, $\therefore$ increase 8 by 1}

EXERCISE 5C

1 Write these numbers correct to 1 decimal place:
 a 2.43   **b** 3.57   **c** 4.92   **d** 6.38   **e** 4.275

2 Write these numbers correct to 2 decimal places:
 a 4.236   **b** 2.731   **c** 5.625   **d** 4.377   **e** 6.5237

3 Write 0.486 correct to:
 a 1 decimal place   **b** 2 decimal places

4 Write 3.789 correct to:
 a 1 decimal place   **b** 2 decimal places

5 Write 0.18375 correct to:
- **a** 1 decimal place
- **b** 2 decimal places
- **c** 3 decimal places
- **d** 4 decimal places

6 Find decimal approximations for:
- **a** 3.87 to the nearest tenth
- **b** 4.3 to the nearest integer
- **c** 6.09 to one decimal place
- **d** 0.4617 to 3 decimal places
- **e** 2.946 to 2 decimal places
- **f** 0.17561 to 4 decimal places

7 Evaluate correct to the number of decimal places shown in the square brackets:
- **a** $\frac{17}{4}$ [1]
- **b** $\frac{73}{8}$ [2]
- **c** 4.3×2.6 [1]
- **d** 0.12×0.4 [1]
- **e** $\frac{8}{11}$ [2]
- **f** 0.08×0.31 [3]
- **g** $(0.7)^2$ [1]
- **h** $\frac{37}{6}$ [2]
- **i** $\frac{17}{7}$ [3]

D LARGE DECIMAL NUMBERS

Very large numbers are often shortened using letters and decimals to represent them.

THOUSANDS

Older computers often have memory chips which hold thousands of bits or bytes of information.

The letter K is used to represent thousands.

For example, 512 K bytes is approximately 512000 bytes of information.

In the employment section of most newspapers you will find annual salaries offered in terms of thousands of dollars or K.

Some real estate advertisements show house prices in Ks.

Example 13

Explain $27.5 K - $29.6 K   in terms of salary.

When discussing salary K represents 1000   ∴ $27.5 K = $27500
and $29.6 K = $29600.

The dash, -, indicates a range of salaries between the lowest and highest.
∴ $27.5 K - $29.6 K means a salary between $27500 and $29600.

EXERCISE 5D

1 Explain these figures in terms of salary:
- **a** $38.7 K - $39.9 K
- **b** $43.2 K - $44.5 K
- **c** $95.5 K - $98.9 K

DECIMALS (CHAPTER 5) 163

2 Convert these salary ranges to 1 decimal place of a thousand dollars:
- **a** $56 345 - $61 840
- **b** $32 475 - $34 885
- **c** $23 159 - $24 386
- **d** $70 839 - $73 195
- **e** $158 650 - $165 749
- **f** $327 890 - $348 359

MILLIONS

The letter m is used to shorten amounts to decimals of a **million**.

Example 14

Round off $2 378 425 to 2 decimals of a million.

$$\$2\,378\,425 = \$\frac{2\,378\,425}{1\,000\,000}\text{ m}$$
$$= \$2.378\,425\text{ m}$$
$$= \$2.38\text{ m} \qquad \{\text{rounded to 2 decimal places}\}$$

3 Round these figures to 2 decimals of a million:
- **a** 3 179 486
- **b** 91 734 598
- **c** 23 456 654
- **d** 1 489 701
- **e** 30 081 896
- **f** 9 475 962

4 Expand these to whole numbers:
- **a** 21.65 m
- **b** 1.93 m
- **c** 16.03 m
- **d** 212.45 m
- **e** 0.97 m

BILLIONS

Australian and overseas companies often give their profits or losses in terms of decimals of billions of dollars.

Distances in space, world population, insect, animal and plague numbers, crops and human body cells are some of the large numbers that are presented in decimals of a **billion** (bn).

Example 15

Round 37 425 679 420 to 2 decimals of a billion.

$$37\,425\,679\,420 = \frac{37\,425\,679\,420}{1\,000\,000\,000}\text{ bn} \qquad \{1000\text{ million} = 1\text{ billion}\}$$
$$= 37.425\,679\,420\text{ bn}$$
$$= 37.43\text{ bn} \qquad \{\text{rounded to 2 decimal places}\}$$

5 Round these figures to 2 decimals of a billion:
- **a** 3 867 900 000
- **b** 2 713 964 784
- **c** 97 055 843 899
- **d** 2 019 438 421
- **e** 4 209 473 864 000
- **f** 549 000 000 000

6 Expand the following to whole numbers:
- **a** 3.86 bn
- **b** 375.09 bn
- **c** 21.95 bn
- **d** 4.13 bn

E FRACTION AND DECIMAL INTERCHANGE

In the earlier examples we used a decimal point to separate whole units (dollars, MA blocks and decimal grids) from those that are less than a whole. You will recall from **Chapter 1** that whole numbers are called **natural numbers**.

To compare certain quantities with whole amounts we use **fractions** (which are also called **rational numbers**).

Decimals numbers are really fractions in a different form. They always have a power of 10 (10, 100, 1000, 10 000, ...) as their denominators. This makes comparison between decimals much easier.

Example 16

Express $6.79 as a fraction of $1.

$6.79 as a fraction of $1.00 is $\dfrac{6.79}{1.00}$

$= \dfrac{679}{100}$

$= 6\dfrac{79}{100}$

EXERCISE 5E

1 Express the following amounts as a fraction of a dollar:

- **a** $1.75
- **b** $3.25
- **c** $52.40
- **d** 428 cents
- **e** $0.87
- **f** $5.90
- **g** $243.08
- **h** 958 cents
- **i** 64.9 cents
- **j** $31.13
- **k** 105 cents
- **l** 33.6 cents
- **m** $0.07
- **n** 3755 cents
- **o** 100 010 cents
- **p** 2.8 cents

Example 17

Convert **a** $4\tfrac{3}{10}$ **b** $2\tfrac{9}{1000}$ to decimals.

a $4\tfrac{3}{10}$

$= 4 + \tfrac{3}{10}$

$= 4.3 \quad \{0.3 = \tfrac{3}{10}\}$

b $2\tfrac{9}{1000}$

$= 2 + \tfrac{0}{10} + \tfrac{0}{100} + \tfrac{9}{1000}$

$= 2.009 \quad \{0.009 = \tfrac{9}{1000}\}$

2 Convert the following to a decimal number:

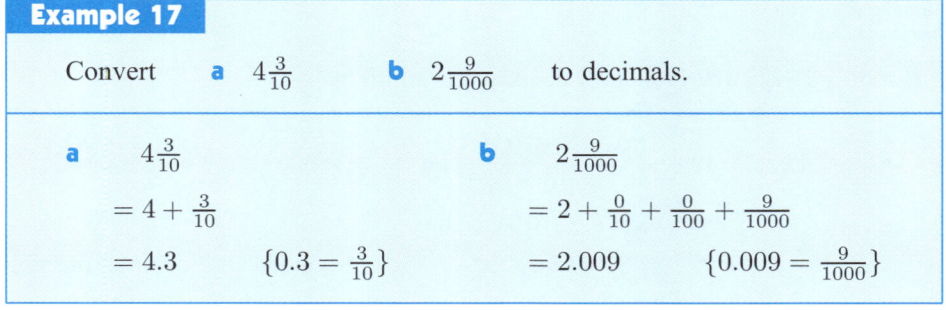

- **a** $\tfrac{8}{10}$
- **b** $\tfrac{17}{100}$
- **c** $14\tfrac{7}{10}$
- **d** $2\tfrac{38}{100}$
- **e** $6\tfrac{6}{100}$
- **f** $\tfrac{29}{10}$
- **g** $4\tfrac{3}{1000}$
- **h** $\tfrac{365}{100}$
- **i** $\tfrac{7344}{1000}$
- **j** $\tfrac{29}{1000}$
- **k** $\tfrac{2756}{100}$
- **l** $3\tfrac{56}{1000}$
- **m** $\tfrac{3846}{10}$
- **n** $56\tfrac{875}{1000}$
- **o** $21\tfrac{56}{100}$

Example 18

Convert **a** 0.8 **b** 6.209 into a fraction or mixed number.

a 0.8
$= \frac{8}{10}$

b 6.209
$= 6 + 0.209$
$= 6 + \frac{209}{1000}$
$= 6\frac{209}{1000}$

With practice, you should be able to do these mentally.

3 Write these decimals as fractions or mixed numbers:

a 0.6	**b** 0.59	**c** 3.8	**d** 5.04	**e** 37.46
f 0.06	**g** 9.58	**h** 4.827	**i** 8.305	**j** 14.02
k 0.006	**l** 3.003	**m** 7.6	**n** 84.879	**o** 947.749

Example 19

Convert to metres in decimal form: **a** 675 cm **b** 875 millimetres

a 675 cm $= \frac{675}{100}$ metres   {100 cm = 1 metre}

  $= 6.75$ metres   {2 places in decimals}

b 875 mm $= \frac{875}{1000}$ metres   {1000 mm = 1 metre}

  $= 0.875$ metres

4 Convert the following measurements in centimetres to metres in decimal form:

a 3872	**b** 8909	**c** 64 486	**d** 2005	**e** 987 654
f 400 004	**g** 32	**h** 7	**i** 945	**j** 1

5 Convert the following measurements in millimetres to metres in decimal form:

a 6858	**b** 3940	**c** 825	**d** 56	**e** 9009

Example 20

Convert to litres in decimal form: **a** 5980 mL **b** 75 mL

a 5980 mL $= \frac{5980}{1000}$ litres   {1000 mL = 1 L}

  $= 5.98$ litres   {3 zeros in the denominator is represented by 3 places in the decimal unless the last is a zero.}

b 75 mL $= \frac{75}{1000}$ litres   {3 zeros in the denominator}

  $= 0.075$ litres   {3 places in the decimals}

6 Convert the following to the units given:
   a 4975 m to km
   b 5685 g to kg
   c 3095 mm to cm
   d 9742 mg to g
   e 47 850 litres to kL
   f 2348 kg to tonnes
   g 634 000 cm to km
   h 75 400 cents to $s
   i 974 300 000 mm to km
   j 89 560 000 g to tonnes
   k 37 580 000 mL to kL
   l 342 mg to g
   m 368 metres to km
   n 795 g to kg
   o 987 mL to litres

7 Convert to smaller units:
   a 4.75 km to metres
   b 12.56 kL to litres
   c 3.86 cm to mm
   d 13.86 tonnes to kg
   e 9.847 m to mm
   f 2.08 kg to g
   g 6.95 litres to mL
   h 24.86 kg to mg
   i 8.94 km to cm

F   ORDERING DECIMALS

Just as whole numbers may be shown on a number line it is possible to do the same with decimals.
Consider the following number line:

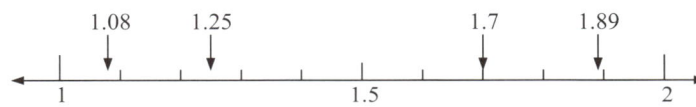

In the examples above the positions of 1.08, 1.25, and 1.89 are only approximate.

EXERCISE 5F

1 Write down the value of the number at A on the following number lines:

   a    **b**
   c    **d**
   e    **f**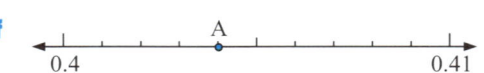

Example 21

Put the correct sign (>, < or =), in the box to make the statement true:
   a 0.305 □ 0.35
   b 0.88 □ 0.808

---

a 0.305 □ 0.35

b 0.88 □ 0.808

Place a zero digit so that each number has the same number of digits following the decimal point.

0.305 □ 0.350
∴ 0.305 is less than 0.350
i.e., 0.305 < 0.350

0.880 □ 0.808
∴ 0.880 is greater than 0.808
i.e., 0.880 > 0.808

2 Insert the correct sign {>, < or =} to make the statement true:

- **a** 0.7 □ 0.8
- **b** 0.06 □ 0.05
- **c** 0.2 □ 0.19
- **d** 4.01 □ 4.1
- **e** 0.81 □ 0.803
- **f** 2.5 □ 2.50
- **g** 0.304 □ 0.34
- **h** 0.03 □ 0.2
- **i** 6.05 □ 60.50
- **j** 0.29 □ 0.290
- **k** 5.01 □ 5.016
- **l** 1.15 □ 1.035
- **m** 21.021 □ 21.210
- **n** 8.09 □ 8.090
- **o** 0.904 □ 0.94

Example 22

Arrange these numbers in ascending (lowest to highest) order:
a 0.3, 0.9, 0.8   **b** 0.6, 0.06, 0.006

a 0.3, 0.9, 0.8 → 0.3, 0.8, 0.9

Since all the numbers are written to one decimal place we look at the digits to the right of the decimal point and write them from smallest to largest as 0.3, 0.8, 0.9.

b 0.6, 0.06, 0.006 → 0.006, 0.06, 0.6

Express all numbers to the same number of decimal places by adding zeros to the right of the last number.

∴ $0.6 = 0.600 = \frac{600}{1000}$ $0.06 = 0.060 = \frac{60}{1000}$

$0.006 = 0.006 = \frac{6}{1000}$

i.e., 0.006, 0.06, 0.6 from smallest to largest.

You can write zeros at the end of decimal fractions as this does not affect the place value of the other digits.

3 Arrange in ascending order (lowest to highest):

- **a** 0.8, 0.4, 0.6
- **b** 0.4, 0.1, 0.9
- **c** 0.14, 0.09, 0.06
- **d** 0.46, 0.5, 0.51
- **e** 1.06, 1.59, 1.61
- **f** 2.6, 2.06, 0.206
- **g** 0.095, 0.905, 0.0905
- **h** 15.5, 15.05, 15.55

Ascending means lowest to highest.

4 Arrange in descending order (highest to lowest):

- **a** 0.9, 0.4, 0.3, 0.8
- **b** 0.51, 0.49, 0.5, 0.47
- **c** 0.6, 0.596, 0.61, 0.609
- **d** 0.02, 0.04, 0.42, 0.24
- **e** 6.27, 6.271, 6.027, 6.277
- **f** 0.31, 0.031, 0.301, 0.311
- **g** 8.088, 8.008, 8.080, 8.880
- **h** 7.61, 7.061, 7.01, 7.06

Descending means highest to lowest.

5 Continue the number patterns by writing the next three terms:

- **a** 0.1, 0.2, 0.3, ...
- **b** 0.9, 0.8, 0.7, ...
- **c** 0.2, 0.4, 0.6, ...
- **d** 0.05, 0.07, 0.09, ...
- **e** 0.7, 0.65, 0.6, ...
- **f** 2.17, 2.13, 2.09, ...
- **g** 7.2, 6.4, 5.6, ...
- **h** 3.456, 3.567, 3.678, ...

RESEARCH

A library, the internet or encyclopaedias should be very useful to find the answers to the following questions.

1 What is the Dewey System and what is its relationship to the ordering and place value of decimals?

2 What system was used before the Dewey System was developed? How does it work?

G ADDING AND SUBTRACTING DECIMALS

When **adding or subtracting** decimal numbers we write the numbers under one another so that the decimal points lie vertically underneath each other. When this is done the digits for units, tenths, hundredths, etc. will also lie under one another. We then add or subtract as for whole numbers.

Example 23

Find $3.84 + 0.372$

$$\begin{array}{r} 3.840 \\ +\ 0.372 \\ \hline 4.212 \end{array}$$

Notice that the decimal points are vertically underneath each other.

EXERCISE 5G

1 Find:

a $0.4 + 0.5$
b $0.6 + 2.7$
c $0.9 + 0.23$
d $0.17 + 0.96$
e $23.04 + 4.78$
f $15.79 + 2.64$
g $0.4 + 0.8 + 4$
h $0.009 + 0.435$
i $0.95 + 1.23 + 8.74$
j $30 + 0.007 + 2.948$
k $0.0036 + 0.697$
l $0.071 + 0.677 + 4$

Example 24

Find: a $3.652 - 2.584$ b $6 - 0.637$

a
$$\begin{array}{r} {\scriptstyle 5\ 14\ 12} \\ 3.\cancel{6}\cancel{5}\cancel{2} \\ -2.584 \\ \hline 1.068 \end{array}$$

Place the decimal points vertically under one another and subtract as for whole numbers.

b
$$\begin{array}{r} {\scriptstyle 5\ 9\ 9\ 10} \\ \cancel{6}.\cancel{0}\cancel{0}\cancel{0} \\ -0.637 \\ \hline 5.363 \end{array}$$

We insert .000 (the same number of zeros as there are digits after the zero in the number that is being subtracted).

2 Find:
- **a** 1.7 − 0.9
- **b** 2.3 − 0.8
- **c** 4.2 − 3.8
- **d** 2 − 0.6
- **e** 4 − 1.7
- **f** 3 − 0.74
- **g** 4.5 − 1.83
- **h** 1 − 0.99
- **i** 10 − 0.98
- **j** 5.6 − 0.007
- **k** 1 − 0.999
- **l** 0.18 + 0.072 − 0.251

3
- **a** Add 2.094 to the following:
  - **i** 36.918
  - **ii** 0.04
  - **iii** 0.982
  - **iv** 5.906
- **b** Subtract 1.306 from the following:
  - **i** 2.407
  - **ii** 1.405
  - **iii** 13.06
  - **iv** 24

4 Add:
- **a** 31.704, 8.097, 24.2 and 0.891
- **b** 3.56, 4.575, 18.109 and 1.249
- **c** 1.001, 0.101, 0.011, 10.101 and 1
- **d** 3.0975, 1.904, 0.003 and 16.2874
- **e** 4, 4.004, 0.044 and 400.44
- **f** 0.76, 10.4, 198.4352 and 0.149

5 Subtract:
- **a** 29.712 from 35.693
- **b** 6.089 from 7.1
- **c** 19 from 23.481
- **d** 3.7 from 171.048
- **e** 9.674 from 68.3
- **f** 8.0096 from 11.11
- **g** 3.333 from 22.2
- **h** 38.018 + 17.2 from 63
- **i** (47.64 − 18.79) from 33.108
- **j** $109.75 from $115.05
- **k** $24.13 from $30.10
- **l** $38.45 and $16.95 from $60

6 Add:
- **a** three point seven nine four two, eleven point zero five zero nine, thirty six point eight five nine four and three point four one three eight
- **b** seventeen and four hundred and twenty five thousandths, twelve and eighty five hundredths, three and nine hundred and seven thousandths and eight and eighty four thousandths
- **c** thirteen hundredths and twenty seven thousandths and one and four hundredths
- **d** fourteen dollars seventy eight, three dollars forty, six dollars eighty seven and ninety three dollars and five cents.

7
- **a** By how much is forty three point nine five four greater than twenty eight point zero eight seven?
- **b** How much less than five and thirty eight hundredths is two and six hundred and forty nine thousandths?
- **c** What is the difference between nine and seventy two hundredths and nine and thirty nine thousandths?
- **d** How much have I got remaining from my sixty four dollars seventy five if I spend fifty seven dollars ninety?

8 John gets $5.40 pocket money, Pat gets $3.85 and Jill $7.85. How much pocket money do they get altogether?

9 Helena is 1.75 m tall and Fred is 1.38 m tall. How much taller is Helena than Fred?

10 Out of interest I weighed myself weekly. In the first week I put on 1.2 kg while in the second week I lost 1.6 kg. Unfortunately I put on another 1.4 kg in the third week. If at the beginning I weighed 68.4 kg, how much did I weigh after the three weeks?

11 At a golf tournament two players hit the same ball, one after the other. First Jeff hit the ball 132.6 m. Janet then hit the ball a further 204.8 m. How far did the ball travel altogether?

12 Shin needed to save $62.50 for a computer game. He had $16.40 in his bank to start with and earned the following amounts doing odd jobs: $2.45, $6.35, $19.50, $14.35. Does he have enough money? If he does not, how much more does he need to earn?

13 Our class went trout fishing and caught five fish weighing the following amounts: 10.6 kg, 3.45 kg, 6.23 kg, 1.83 kg and 5.84 kg. What was the total weight of all five fish?

14 In a fish shop, four large fish weigh 4.72, 3.96, 3.09 and 4.85 kg. What must the minimum mass of the fifth fish be if the customer wants a minimum of 20 kg of fish?

15 What is the total length of these three pieces of timber: 2.755 m, 3.084 m and 7.240 m?

16 How much change from $100 is left after I buy items for $10.85, $37.65, $19.05 and $24.35?

H MULTIPLYING / DIVIDING BY POWERS OF 10

MULTIPLICATION

Consider multiplying 3.57 by **a** 100 and by **b** 1000.

a $3.57 \times 100 = \frac{357}{100} \times \frac{100}{1}$ and
$ = 357$

b $3.57 \times 1000 = \frac{357}{100} \times \frac{1000}{1}$
$ = 357 \times 10$
$ = 3570$

We observe that the decimal point of 3.57 has shifted 2 places to the right in **a** and 3 places to the right in **b**,

i.e., in **a** 3.57 to become 357
and in **b** 3.570 to become 3570

RULE FOR MULTIPLYING BY 10^n

> When multiplying by 10^n we simply shift the decimal point n places to the **right**. The number becomes 10^n times **larger** than it was originally.

Remember $10^1 = 10$
$10^2 = 100$
$10^3 = 1000$
$10^4 = 10\,000$ etc.

The index or power number indicates the number of zeros.

Example 25

Find: **a** 8.3×10 **b** 0.0932×100 **c** $4.32 \times 10\,000$

a 8.3×10
$= 8.3 \times 10^1$ {$10 = 10^1$, so shift decimal point 1 place right}
$= 83$

b 0.0932×100
$= 0.0932 \times 10^2$ {$100 = 10^2$, so shift decimal point 2 places right}
$= 9.32$

c $4.32 \times 10\,000$
$= 4.3200 \times 10^4$ {$10\,000 = 10^4$, so shift decimal point 4 places right}
$= 43\,200$

EXERCISE 5H.1

1 Multiply the numbers to complete the table:

	Number	×10	×100	×1000	×10^4	×10^6
a	0.0943					
b	4.0837					
c	0.0008					
d	24.6801					
e	$57.85					

2 Find:

- **a** 43×10
- **b** 8×1000
- **c** 5×10^6
- **d** 0.6×10
- **e** 4.6×10
- **f** 0.58×100
- **g** 3.09×100
- **h** 2.5×100
- **i** 0.8×100
- **j** 3.24×100
- **k** 0.9×1000
- **l** 0.845×1000
- **m** 0.24×1000
- **n** 2.085×10^2
- **o** 8.94×10^3
- **p** 0.053×1000
- **q** 0.0094×10^1
- **r** $0.718 \times 100\,000$

DIVISION

Consider dividing by 10, 100, 1000 etc.

For example, consider dividing 5.2 by **a** 100 and **b** 1000.

a $5.2 \div 100 = \frac{52}{10} \div \frac{100}{1}$ and **b** $5.2 \div 1000 = \frac{52}{10} \times \frac{1}{1000}$

$= \frac{52}{10} \times \frac{1}{100}$ $= \frac{52}{10\,000}$

$= \frac{52}{1000}$ $= 0.0052$

$= 0.052$

We can see from these examples that the decimal point of 5.2 has moved two places left in **a** and three places left in **b**,

i.e., in **a** 005.2 to become 0.052

and in **b** 0005.2 to become 0.0052

RULE FOR DIVIDING BY 10^n

> When dividing by 10^n we simply shift the decimal point n places to the **left**.
> The number becomes 10^n times **smaller** than it was originally.

Example 26

Find: **a** $0.6 \div 10$ **b** $0.37 \div 1000$

a $0.6 \div 10$

$= 0.6 \div 10^1$ {$10 = 10^1$, so shift the decimal point 1 place left}

$= 0.06$

b $0.37 \div 1000$

$= 000.37 \div 10^3$ {$1000 = 10^3$, so shift the decimal point 3 places left}

$= 0.000\,37$

DEMO

EXERCISE 5H.2

1 Divide the numbers to complete the table:

	Number	÷10	÷100	÷1000	÷10^5
a	647.352				
b	93 082.6				
c	42 870				
d	10.94				

2 Find:

a $2.3 \div 10$
b $3.6 \div 100$
c $42.6 \div 100$
d $3 \div 10$
e $58 \div 10$
f $58 \div 100$
g $394 \div 10$
h $7 \div 100$
i $45.8 \div 100$
j $8.007 \div 10$
k $24.05 \div 1000$
l $632 \div 10\,000$
m $579 \div 100$
n $579 \div 1000$
o $579 \div 10\,000$
p $0.03 \div 10$
q $0.03 \div 100$
r $0.046 \div 1000$

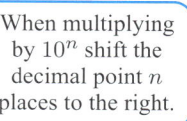

When multiplying by 10^n shift the decimal point n places to the right.

When dividing by 10^n shift the decimal point n places to the left.

3 Write the divisor to complete the equation:

a $9.6 \div \square = 0.96$
b $38.96 \div \square = 0.3896$
c $6.3 \div \square = 0.063$
d $5.8 \div \square = 0.0058$
e $15.95 \div \square = 1.595$
f $386 \div \square = 0.0386$
g $3016.4 \div \square = 30.164$
h $874.86 \div \square = 0.847\,86$

4 Write the multiplier to complete the equation:

a $5.3 \times \square = 530$
b $0.89 \times \square = 890$
c $0.04 \times \square = 400$
d $38.094 \times \square = 3809.4$
e $70.4 \times \square = 704$
f $38.69 \times \square = 386.9$
g $65.871 \times \square^2 = 6587.1$
h $0.0006 \times \square = 600$
i $0.003\,934 \times \square^3 = 3.934$

I MULTIPLYING DECIMAL NUMBERS

When two whole numbers greater than 1 are multiplied the product is larger than both of them. For example, $4 \times 2 = 8$.

When two decimal numbers which are less than 1 are multiplied the answer is smaller than both of them. For example, $0.4 \times 0.2 = 0.08$. Below is an explanation of why this is so.

Study the following examples:

▶ 3×0.6 looks like 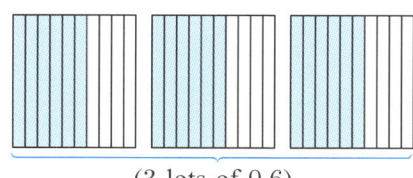 i.e., 18 shaded tenths

(3 lots of 0.6)

which is 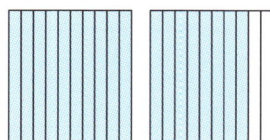 which is a whole plus 8 tenths, or 1.8   So, $3 \times 0.6 = 1.8$

▶ 0.3×0.6 looks like 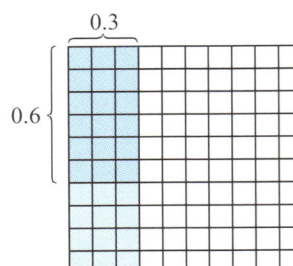 which is 18 hundredths of the whole shaded, or 0.18

So, $0.3 \times 0.6 = 0.18$

▶ 1.3×0.5 looks like 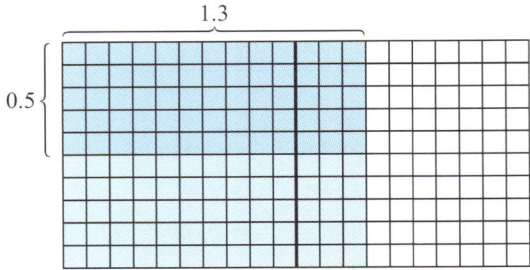 which is 65 hundredths of the whole amount, or 0.65

So, $1.3 \times 0.5 = 0.65$

INVESTIGATION — DECIMAL PLACES IN THE PRODUCT

 In this investigation we will look at the number of decimal places in a question like "0.67×0.8" and the number of decimal places in the final answer.

0.8 is a one decimal place number.

0.67 is a two decimal place number.

What to do:

1. Write the number of decimal places in each of the following:
   a 36.42 **b** 12.8 **c** 0.095 **d** 1.805 **e** 29.0908

2. Copy and complete the table:

	Question	Number of decimal places in question	Estimate of product	Calculator answer	Number of decimal places in product
a	2.91×3.04				
b	42.8×2.16				
c	5.072×1.9				
d	69.1×20.05				
e	0.87×0.96				
f	9.84×3.092				
g	6.094×2.837				

3 Write the number of decimal places you would expect in the products of the following:
   a 0.8×0.9
   b 2.07×1.93
   c 0.3×0.04
   d 9×0.45
   e 0.6×0.06
   f 0.857×3
   g 2.5×4.03
   h $2 \times 0.2 \times 0.02$
   i $0.5 \times 0.05 \times 0.005$

   Find the actual answer with a calculator.

RULE FOR DECIMAL MULTIPLICATION

From the **Investigation** we notice that:

> When **multiplying by decimals**, the number of decimal places in the question equals the number of decimal places in the answer.

We will now look at a method for multiplying decimal numbers.

Example 27

Find: **a** 3×0.6 **b** 0.4×0.03

a 3×0.6 *Step 1:* Delete the decimal point
   $= 18.$ *Step 2:* Find $3 \times 6 = 18$
   $= 1.8$ *Step 3:* Replace decimal point after counting the number of decimal places in the question

b 0.4×0.03 *Step 1:* Delete decimal points, i.e., $\times 10^3$
   $= 0012.$ *Step 2:* Find $4 \times 3 = 12$
   $= 0.012$ *Step 3:* Replace decimal point after counting the number of decimal places in the question

EXERCISE 51

1 Find the value of:
   a 2.4×3
   b 6.5×4
   c 2.7×5
   d 0.8×7
   e 9×0.04
   f 0.4×0.6
   g 0.3×0.02
   h 0.04×0.004
   i 7×0.005
   j 1.2×0.12
   k 0.12×11
   l 5.05×0.09
   m 30×0.003
   n $(0.6)^2$
   o 0.08×80
   p 700×1.2
   q $(0.09)^2$
   r $0.4 \times 0.3 \times 0.2$

2 Given that $34 \times 28 = 952$, find the value of the following:
   a 34×2.8
   b 3.4×2.8
   c 34×0.028
   d 0.34×2.8
   e 0.034×28
   f 0.34×0.28
   g 0.034×2.8
   h 0.034×0.028
   i 340×0.0028

3 Given that $57 \times 235 = 13\,395$, find the value of the following:
- **a** 5.7×235
- **b** 5.7×23.5
- **c** 5.7×2.35
- **d** 5.7×0.235
- **e** 57×0.235
- **f** 0.57×2.35
- **g** 0.57×0.235
- **h** $5.7 \times 0.000\,235$
- **i** 570×0.235

4 Find the value of:
- **a** 0.4×6
- **b** 0.11×8
- **c** 0.5×5.0
- **d** 0.03×9
- **e** 0.03×90
- **f** 3.8×4
- **g** 0.9×0.8
- **h** 0.007×0.9
- **i** 0.04×0.04
- **j** 0.16×0.5
- **k** $(0.2)^2$
- **l** $(0.03)^2$
- **m** 1.2×0.06
- **n** $(1.1)^2$
- **o** 2.5×0.004

5 Find the perimeter of the following regular polygons:

a 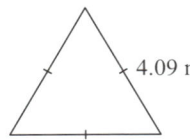 4.09 m

b 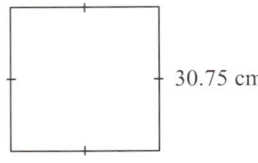 30.75 cm

c 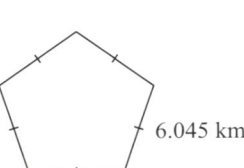 6.045 km

d 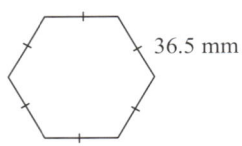 36.5 mm

6
- **a** Find the cost of 45 litres of petrol at 87.8 cents per litre.
- **b** Find the cost of 9.6 metres of pipe at $3.85 a metre.
- **c** Find the capacity of 6 dozen 1.25 litre bottles.

7 Jennifer bought 6 iceblocks each costing 55 cents. How much did she pay for them in total?

8 A stone weighed 5.6 kg. If Duncan was able to lift 8 of these stones, how much weight did he lift in total?

9 Matthew was concreting a small fish pond. He needed 0.4 m³ of concrete which cost $72.50 per m³. How much would the concrete for the pond cost Matthew?

10 I need 4.5 m of hose to water my garden. If hose costs me $3.40 per metre, how much will it cost me to buy my hose?

11 Fred needed at least 25 metres of timber. He found 6 pieces of timber in a shed each 3.9 m long. Did he have enough altogether? How much timber did he have over or did he still need to find?

12 A caterer orders 5700 pies and 3600 pasties to sell at a football match. The pies and pasties each have a mass of 0.16 kg. What is the total mass of the:

    a pies   **b** pasties   **c** pies and pasties?

    d How many heated vans ($\frac{1}{2}$ tonne capacity) are needed to deliver the pies and pasties?

    e If the caterer has a profit margin of 29.7 cents on each pie or pasty, what is her total profit if she sells the lot?

ACTIVITY   ESTIMATING DECIMAL PRODUCTS

When multiplying decimal numbers it is best to first try to get an approximate idea of what the answer should be. Making an estimate is very important when you use calculators or if you are making mental calculations. An estimate can warn you of any error you may have made with the calculator. An estimate also helps you check your mental or written computations.

For example, $8.19 \times 4.87 \doteqdot 8 \times 5$ i.e., $\doteqdot 40$ and so, we expect the actual answer to be somewhere near 40.

What to do:

1 Choose the correct answer and then **check** using your calculator:

    a 4.387×6 **i** 263.22   **ii** 26.322   **iii** 2.6322   **iv** 2632.2

    b 59.48×9 **i** 5.3532   **ii** 5353.2   **iii** 535.32   **iv** 53.532

    c 18.71×19 **i** 355.49   **ii** 35.549   **iii** 35 549   **iv** 3554.9

    d 0.028×11 **i** 3.080   **ii** 0.0308   **iii** 0.308   **iv** 30.800

2 Estimate the following using 1 figure approximations:

For example, $19.8 \times 41.89 \doteqdot 20 \times 40 \doteqdot 800$

    a 8.6×5.1 **b** 9.8×13.2 **c** 12.2×11.9

    d 1.96×3.09 **e** 15.39×8.109 **f** 39.04×2.08

    g 0.976×92.8 **h** 109.4×21.84 **i** 1446×49.2

Find the actual answers using your calculator.

DIVIDING DECIMALS BY WHOLE NUMBERS

Follow these steps to divide decimal numbers by whole numbers:

Step 1:   Put a decimal point in the answer directly above the decimal point of the question.

Step 2:   Carry out normal division ignoring the decimal point.

Example 28

Find: **a** $4.64 \div 4$ **b** $5.28 \div 8$

a
$$4 \overline{)4.6^24} = 1.16$$
$\therefore \; 4.64 \div 4 = 1.16$

b
$$8 \overline{)5.2^48} = 0.66$$
$\therefore \; 5.28 \div 8 = 0.66$

EXERCISE 5J

1 Find:

- **a** $3.2 \div 4$
- **b** $7.5 \div 5$
- **c** $1.26 \div 3$
- **d** $3.57 \div 7$
- **e** $24.16 \div 8$
- **f** $2.46 \div 6$
- **g** $0.72 \div 9$
- **h** $81.6 \div 4$

Example 29

Divide a 6.4 m length of timber into four equal lengths. How long will each piece be?

$$4 \overline{)6.^24} = 1.6$$

$\therefore$ each piece is 1.6 m long.

2
- **a** How much money would each person get if $76.50 is divided equally among 9 people?
- **b** A 10.75 kg tub of icecream is divided equally among 5 people. How much ice-cream does each receive?
- **c** One 3.5 m length of timber is cut into five equal pieces. How long is each piece?
- **d** How many full 7 kg bags of potatoes can be filled from a bag of potatoes weighing 88.2 kg?
- **e** If $96.48 is divided equally among six people, how much does each person get?

Sometimes when we divide with decimals we do not get an exact answer. When this is the case we add zeros onto the end of the number we are dividing into and continue to divide until we get an **exact answer** or a **recurring pattern**.

Example 30

Find: **a** $6.3 \div 5$ **b** $3.5 \div 4$

a
$$5 \overline{)6.^13\,^30} = 1.26$$
$\therefore \; 6.3 \div 5 = 1.26$

b
$$4 \overline{)3.5\,^30\,^20} = 0.875$$
$\therefore \; 3.5 \div 4 = 0.875$

DECIMALS (CHAPTER 5) 179

3 Find:

a $5.3 \div 2$
b $6.1 \div 5$
c $3.4 \div 4$
d $3.4 \div 8$
e $6.5 \div 2$
f $5.9 \div 4$
g $2.41 \div 2$
h $6.32 \div 5$

Example 31

Find: $4.1 \div 3$

$$\begin{array}{r} 1\,.\,3\;6\;6\;6\;6.... \\ 3\,\overline{)\,4\,.\,^11 2\,0\;^2 0\;^2 0\;^2 0} \end{array}$$

$\therefore\;\; 4.1 \div 3 = 1.3\overline{6}$

$1.3\overline{6}$ is called one point three six recurring.

4 Find:

a $3.1 \div 3$
b $3.5 \div 3$
c $4.1 \div 9$
d $2.47 \div 3$
e $8.15 \div 3$
f $13.6 \div 9$
g $2.6 \div 7$
h $6.15 \div 7$

K TERMINATING AND RECURRING DECIMALS

Every fraction can be written as either a **terminating** or a **recurring** decimal.

Terminate, like terminus and terminal, means that something has or will reach an end. Recurring is the opposite and means that something continues endlessly with a repeating pattern.

Terminating decimals result when the rational number has a denominator which has no prime factors other than 2 or 5.

For example: $\frac{3}{4} = 0.75$ and the only prime factor of 4 is 2

$\frac{14}{25} = 0.56$ and the only prime factor of 25 is 5

$\frac{13}{40} = 0.325$ as the prime factors of 40 are 2 and 5.

USING MULTIPLICATION

Some fractions can be converted to decimals using multiplication.

Example 32

Write the following in decimal form, without carrying out a division: a $\frac{4}{5}$ b $\frac{9}{25}$ c $\frac{7}{8}$

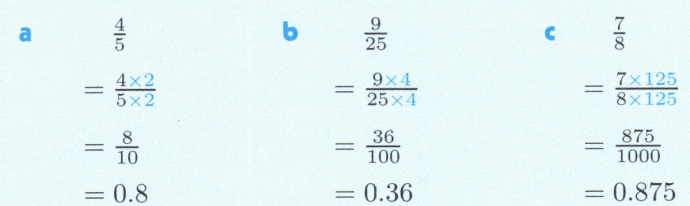

We have to get 10, 100, 1000 etc. for the denominator.

EXERCISE 5K

1 Write as decimals using the method of **Example 32**:

- **a** $\frac{7}{10}$
- **b** $\frac{1}{2}$
- **c** $\frac{2}{5}$
- **d** $\frac{3}{10}$
- **e** $\frac{4}{5}$
- **f** $\frac{1}{4}$
- **g** $\frac{4}{25}$
- **h** $\frac{3}{4}$
- **i** $\frac{1}{8}$
- **j** $\frac{5}{8}$
- **k** $\frac{7}{20}$
- **l** $\frac{6}{25}$
- **m** $\frac{13}{20}$
- **n** $\frac{11}{25}$
- **o** $4\frac{1}{4}$
- **p** $2\frac{1}{5}$
- **q** $5\frac{3}{5}$
- **r** $2\frac{9}{20}$
- **s** $1\frac{7}{25}$
- **t** $3\frac{7}{8}$

USING DIVISION

> **Example 33**
>
> Use division to write the following rational numbers as decimals: **a** $\frac{2}{5}$ **b** $\frac{5}{8}$
>
> **a** $\quad 5 \overline{)2.0}^{\,0.4}$ So, $\frac{2}{5} = 0.4$
>
> **b** $\quad 8 \overline{)5.0\,^20\,^40}^{\,0.6\,2\,5}$ So, $\frac{5}{8} = 0.625$

2 Use division to write as a decimal:

- **a** $\frac{3}{5}$
- **b** $\frac{9}{5}$
- **c** $\frac{3}{8}$
- **d** $\frac{9}{8}$
- **e** $2\frac{3}{4}$
- **f** $5\frac{4}{5}$
- **g** $4\frac{7}{8}$
- **h** $5\frac{3}{8}$

RECURRING DECIMALS

In year 6 we wrote $\frac{1}{3}$ and $\frac{2}{3}$ as recurring decimals.

By division $\quad \frac{1}{3} = 0.333\,333\,33.....$ which we wrote as $0.\overline{3}$

$\quad\quad\quad\quad\quad \frac{2}{3} = 0.666\,666\,66.....$ which we wrote as $0.\overline{6}$

Recurring decimals repeat the same sequence of numbers without stopping. Recurring decimals result when the denominator of a rational number has one or more prime factors other than 2 or 5.

For example, $\quad \frac{3}{14} = 0.214\,285\,714\,285\,714\,285\,7....$

We indicate a recurring decimal by writing the full sequence once with a line over the repeated section.

For example, $\quad \frac{1}{3} = 0.\overline{3}$ and $\frac{3}{14} = 0.2\overline{14\,285\,7}$

Some decimals take a long time to recur. For example, $\frac{1}{17} = 0.0\overline{588\,235\,294\,117\,647}$

In some books dots are used, for example $\frac{1}{3} = 0.\dot{3}$
and 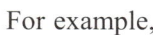 $\frac{3}{14} = 0.2\dot{1}4\,285\,\dot{7}$.

Example 34

Write as decimals: a $\frac{4}{9}$ b $\frac{7}{11}$

a $\frac{4}{9}$
 $= 0.4444....$
 $= 0.\overline{4}$

$$9 \overline{\smash{)}4.0\,^40\,^40\,^40....}$$
 $0.\ 4\ \ 4\ \ 4\ \ 4$

{The bar over the 4 indicates that 4 recurs endlessly.}

b $\frac{7}{11}$
 $= 0.636\,363....$
 $= 0.\overline{63}$

$$11 \overline{\smash{)}7.0\,^40\,^70\,^40....}$$
 $0.\ 6\ \ 3\ \ 6\ \ 3$

{The 63 recurs endlessly.}

3 Convert the following fractions to decimals. Use a bar to show the repeating pattern of digits.

a $\frac{1}{3}$ b $\frac{2}{3}$ c $\frac{1}{6}$ d $\frac{1}{7}$ e $\frac{2}{7}$

f $\frac{1}{12}$ g $\frac{2}{9}$ h $\frac{5}{6}$ i $\frac{3}{11}$ j $\frac{7}{12}$

4 Copy and complete the following pattern:

Fraction:	$\frac{1}{9}$	$\frac{2}{9}$	$\frac{3}{9}$	$\frac{4}{9}$	$\frac{5}{9}$	$\frac{6}{9}$	$\frac{7}{9}$	$\frac{8}{9}$	$\frac{9}{9}$
Decimal:	$0.\overline{1}$	$0.\overline{2}$							

5 Write as decimals:

a $\frac{23}{32}$ b $\frac{11}{16}$ c $\frac{17}{80}$ d $\frac{11}{25}$ e $1\frac{3}{16}$

f $\frac{3}{14}$ g $\frac{2}{15}$ h $\frac{9}{11}$ i $2\frac{7}{30}$ j $\frac{97}{50}$

k $\frac{6}{13}$ l $\frac{49}{160}$ m $3\frac{5}{12}$ n $\frac{31}{123}$ o $\frac{23}{45}$

6 The following table contains commonly used **rational numbers**.

Copy and complete the table by calculating the decimal form.

Try to remember these conversions.

$\frac{1}{2} =$ $\frac{1}{4} =$ $\frac{3}{4} =$ $\frac{1}{5} =$ $\frac{2}{5} =$ $\frac{3}{5} =$ $\frac{4}{5} =$

$\frac{1}{8} =$ $\frac{3}{8} =$ $\frac{5}{8} =$ $\frac{7}{8} =$ $\frac{1}{20} =$ $\frac{1}{40} =$ $\frac{1}{25} =$

$\frac{1}{3} =$ $\frac{2}{3} =$ $\frac{1}{6} =$ $\frac{5}{6} =$ $\frac{1}{9} =$ $\frac{1}{11} =$ $\frac{1}{99} =$

L CONVERTING DECIMALS TO FRACTIONS

Every decimal number which terminates can be written as a fraction involving integers, i.e., as a rational number.

Some fractions can be cancelled down to their **simplest form** (lowest terms) by dividing both the numerator and denominator by their **highest common factor (HCF)**.

For example, $0.48 = \frac{48}{100} = \frac{12}{25}$ when all common factors have been cancelled.

Even recurring decimals can be written as rational numbers.

Example 35

Write the following in simplest rational form:
  a 0.6   b 6.44   c 0.625

a $\quad 0.6$
$= \frac{6}{10}$
$= \frac{3}{5}$

b $\quad 6.44$
$= 6 + \frac{44}{100}$
$= 6\frac{11}{25}$

c $\quad 0.625$
$= \frac{625}{1000}$
$= \frac{5}{8}$

EXERCISE 5L

1 Write the following in simplest rational form:

a 0.1   b 0.7   c 1.5   d 2.2
e 3.9   f 4.6   g 0.19   h 1.25
i 0.18   j 0.65   k 0.05   l 0.07
m 2.75   n 1.025   o 0.04   p 2.375

2 Write the following as fractions in their simplest form:

a 0.8   b 0.88   c 0.888   d 3.5
e 0.49   f 0.25   g 5.06   h 3.32
i 0.085   j 3.72   k 1.096   l 4.56
m 0.064   n 0.625   o $0.\overline{3}$ p $0.\overline{6}$

M USING A CALCULATOR FOR DECIMAL NUMBERS

Suppose you were asked to write $\frac{2}{3}, \frac{3}{4}, \frac{13}{16}, \frac{7}{10}, \frac{8}{11}$ and $\frac{9}{13}$ in ascending order.

Converting to a common denominator would be long and tedious.

It would be better to convert each fraction to a decimal and use the decimals to write the fractions in order.

$\frac{2}{3} \doteq 0.666,$ $\frac{3}{4} = 0.750,$ $\frac{13}{16} \doteq 0.813,$

$\frac{7}{10} = 0.700,$ $\frac{8}{11} \doteq 0.727,$ $\frac{9}{13} \doteq 0.692$

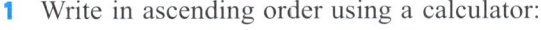

So, the ascending order is: $\frac{2}{3}, \frac{9}{13}, \frac{7}{10}, \frac{8}{11}, \frac{3}{4}, \frac{13}{16}$

EXERCISE 5M

1 Write in ascending order using a calculator:

  a $\frac{3}{10}, \frac{7}{22}, \frac{7}{20}, \frac{5}{17}, \frac{1}{3}$ **b** $\frac{4}{7}, \frac{3}{8}, \frac{5}{9}, \frac{5}{12}, \frac{7}{16}$

  c $\frac{8}{9}, \frac{7}{8}, \frac{9}{11}, \frac{10}{13}, \frac{11}{12}$ **d** $\frac{11}{20}, \frac{12}{23}, \frac{10}{19}, \frac{6}{11}, \frac{8}{15}$

2 Write in descending order using a calculator:

  a $\frac{2}{3}, \frac{5}{8}, \frac{7}{11}, \frac{11}{17}, \frac{15}{23}$ **b** $\frac{8}{21}, \frac{3}{8}, \frac{5}{13}, \frac{6}{17}, \frac{4}{11}$

  c $\frac{7}{20}, \frac{1}{3}, \frac{5}{16}, \frac{8}{23}, \frac{9}{25}$ **d** $\frac{14}{17}, \frac{16}{19}, \frac{17}{20}, \frac{20}{23}, \frac{3}{4}$

3 The widths of snail shells were measured in centimetres:

    1.3, 1.1, 1.0, 1.1, 1.4, 0.9, 0.8, 0.9, 1.0, 1.1, 1.2, 0.9, 1.0

Find the average width of a snail shell.

4 The heights of the girls in the Primary School Basketball team were measured in metres and the results were:

1.56, 1.43, 1.51, 1.36, 1.32, 1.45, 1.39, 1.38

Find the mean height.

5 Janine's weekly earnings for 6 weeks were: $272.25, $301.50, $260.40, $278.85, $284.70 and $288.30. Find the average amount Janine earned per week.

6 A square has a perimeter of 12.66 metres. Find the length of each side of the square.

7 A piece of wood is 6.4 m long and must be cut into short lengths of 0.36 m.

  a How many full lengths can be cut?
  b What length is left over?

8 How many 2.4 metre lengths of piping are needed to make a drain 360 metres long?

9 21 DVDs cost $389.55. How much does one DVD cost?

REVIEW SET A — CHAPTER 5

1 Given that the boundary of the square represents one unit, what decimals are represented in the following grids?

a 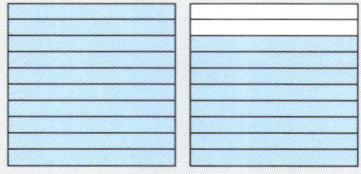 b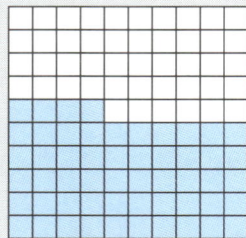

2 **a** Write 9.4357 correct to 2 decimal places.
  b Find the value of $(0.5)^2$.
  c Express 2.049 in expanded fractional form.
  d State the value of the 2 digit in 51.932
  e Convert 53.6 cm to metres.

3 Given that $58 \times 47 = 2726$, evaluate:
  a 5.8×47 **b** 5.8×0.47 **c** 5.8×4.7

4 Find:
  a 6.2×10 **b** 2.158×100 **c** $5.6 \div 10$ **d** $4.2 \div 100$

5 Round off correct to 1 decimal place:
  a $29\,762$ to $K
  b $3\,472\,613\,250$ to bn

6 **a** Find the difference between 246 and 239.84
  b What is the product of 4.8 and 0.2?
  c Find 0.03×0.5
  d A square has sides of length 3.7 m. What is its perimeter?
  e How much would each person get if $82.40 was divided equally between four people?

7 Write the following decimal numbers in ascending order:
    0.216,   0.621,   0.062,   0.206,   0.026

8 In 3 seasons a vineyard produces the following tonnage of grapes: 638.17, 582.35 and 717.36.
  a What was the total tonnage for the 3 years?
  b Find the average tonnage for the 3 years.

9 A marathon runner stops for a drink $\frac{1}{3}$ of the way at the 14.1 km mark. How far has she still to run?

REVIEW SET B   CHAPTER 5

1 If ▫ represents one thousandth, what are the decimal values of the following?

  a 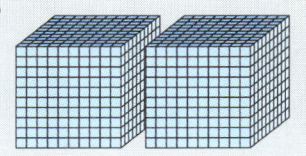   **b**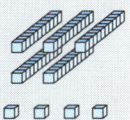

  c What is the sum of **a** and **b**?

2 Convert the following:

  a $352.76 to cents   **b** 8.94 kL to litres   **c** 8.763 metres to cm
  d 15.0924 tonne to kg   **e** 36 475 mm to m   **f** 375 mL to litres

3 **a** Convert $8 + \frac{7}{10} + \frac{9}{1000}$ to decimal form.

  b Convert $\frac{13}{8}$ to decimal form.

  c State the value of the 6 digit in 9.016

  d Write $\frac{7}{9}$ in recurring decimal form.

4 A golf shop buys 10 000 golf balls from a manufacturer at $1.15 each and sells them all for $2.40 each.

  a What is the total amount that the manufacturer gets?
  b How much total profit does the golf shop make?

5 Given that $26 \times 53 = 1378$, evaluate:

  a 2.6×5.3 **b** 2.6×0.053

6 Write the following decimal numbers in descending order:

  0.444, 4.04, 4.44, 4.044, 4.404

7 Evaluate:

  a $31.426 - 29.527$ **b** 28.6×0.09 **c** $4.4 + 4.04 + 0.444$

8 The first horse in a 1000 metre sprint finished in 56.98 seconds. The second and third horses were 0.07 seconds and 0.23 seconds behind the winner. What were the times of the:

  a second horse   **b** third horse?

9 A marathon runner stops for a drink $\frac{1}{3}$ of the way on his 42.2 km race. How far has he

  a run (correct to 2 decimal places)
  b still got to run (correct to 2 decimal places)?

REVIEW SET C   CHAPTER 5

1 Convert the following to decimal form:
   a 57 906 cents to dollars   **b** 7408 cm to metres   **c** 426 mL to litres
   d 45 831 gm to kg   **e** 750 kg to tonnes   **f** 978 mm to metres

2 If the dollar represents the unit, what are the decimal values of the following?
   a
   b

   c What is the sum of **a** and **b**?

3 Round off correct to 1 decimal place:
   a 0.465   **b** $35 650 to $K   **c** 8 094 387 to m

4 **a** Express 18.346 in expanded fractional form.
   b State the value of the 3 digit in 41.039
   c Write $\frac{3}{8}$ in decimal form.
   d Convert 0.45 to a fraction in simplest form.

5 Evaluate:
   a $3.018 + 20.9 + 4.836$ **b** $423.54 - 276.49$
   c 4.2×1.2 **d** $0.96 \div 0.08$

6 Continue the number pattern by writing the next three terms: 0.3, 0.7, 1.1, ...

7 Solve the following problems:
   a Determine the total cost of 14 show bags costing $7.85 each.
   b Share $5885.25 equally amongst 5 people. How much does each get?
   c Find the number of 3.2 metre lengths of pipe necessary for a 6.4 kilometre pipeline.
   d How much change from $100.00 would you receive if items costing $27.55, $18.30, $22.05 and $3.75 were bought?

Chapter 6
Percentage

Knowledge, skills and understandings

By the end of this chapter you should be able to

- convert fractions to frequently used decimals and percentages (e.g., $\frac{2}{5}$, $\frac{5}{8}$, $\frac{2}{3}$)
- convert percentages to fractions and decimals
- convert fractions and decimals to percentages
- express fractions of quantities as percentages (e.g., 20 out of 25 is $\frac{4}{5}$ is 80%)
- find simple percentages of quantities (e.g., 20% of $80) using both pen and paper, and calculator
- find discount as a percentage, especially money
- solve practical problems involving percentage (e.g., simple interest, banking problems)

PERCENTAGES

Rather than just saying that something is better or stronger or faster or dearer or sweeter or brighter than something else, percentage allows us to compare one thing with another using numbers.

For instance, we could compare the strength of a 12 year old with a 30 year old by seeing who could lift the heavier weight.

A better way would be to work out each person's strength by calculating the mass they lifted as a percentage of their body mass. Then we would compare the percentages for the two people.

As consumers of goods and services we constantly make comparisons. Money, costs, quality, quantity, accuracy and reliability can all be compared using percentage.

REPRESENTING PERCENTAGES

Pie charts and bar graphs are often used to represent percentage. We do this in **Chapter 9**. Here are some examples of eye-catching graphs using percentages which create an impact.

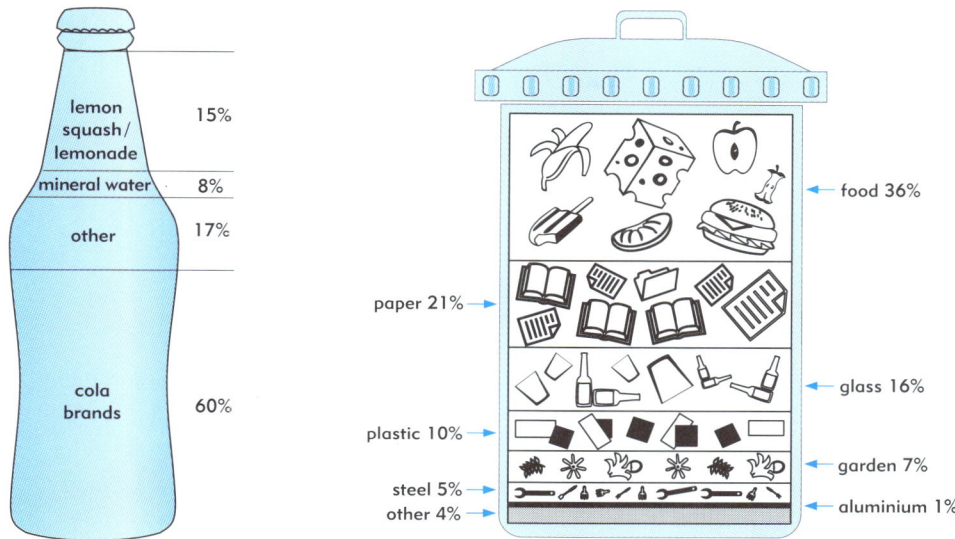

Sales of all carbonated softdrinks

Contents of a garbage can

ACTIVITY CATCHING ATTENTION WITH PERCENTAGE

What to do:

Think of some eye-catching ways you could present different types of information in percentage form. Remember when representing a percentage that a symbol or statement showing the whole quantity must be given.

A PERCENTAGE

EXERCISE 6A

1 In each of the following patterns there are 100 tiles. For each pattern write the number of coloured tiles (numerator) as a fracton of 100 (denominator).

a 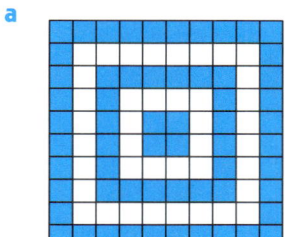   b 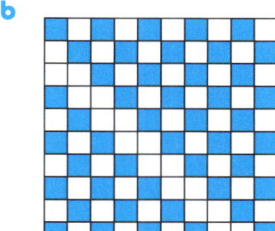   c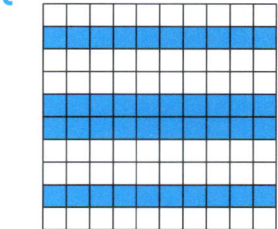

2 In this circle there are 100 symbols. Count each type then write the number of each type of symbol as a fraction of 100.

a   M =
b   C =
c   L =
d   X =
e   V =

Check to see that your numerators total 100.

3 Using the numerals from 1 to 100 inclusive and using 100 as the denominator, write the fraction which represents the numbers that:

a   are odd
b   are divisible exactly by 5
c   are multiples of 4
d   can be divided by 10 exactly
e   contain the digit 1
f   have only 1 digit
g   are prime numbers
h   are even
i   are composite

PERCENTAGES

From the chapter on fractions you would remember the difficulty of comparing some fractions.

Fractions with the same denominators like $\frac{1}{5}, \frac{3}{5}, \frac{4}{5}$ or $\frac{8}{5}$ were easy enough but fractions with different denominators like $\frac{1}{4}, \frac{3}{10}, \frac{7}{25}$ or $\frac{37}{20}$ needed to be converted to fractions with the same denominator before they could be compared.

Percentages are special kinds of fractions because their denominator is always 100. If you look carefully at the percentage symbol, you can see the individual numerals for 100. It possibly evolved like this:

$\frac{12}{100}$ became 12/100 which became 12/00 which became 12 0/0 which became 12%.

> **Percentages** are comparisons with the whole amount which is 100%.

The word **percent** comes from the Latin meaning out of every hundred.

| ACTIVITY | EVERYDAY USE OF PERCENTAGE |

What to do:

1 Read the following examples of everyday percentage use:

- In my street 25% of the homes have roses growing in the front garden.
- Sixty five percent of students at a school voted for a greater variety of lollies in the school canteen.
- Twenty seven percent of primary school age children do not eat fruit and vegetables.
- The netball goal shooter had a 68% accuracy rate for the whole season.
- Sarah improved by 10% in her times table tests.
- Australia's unemployment rate dropped to 8.1%.
- Last year, over 52% of 5-14 year old children living in Australia played sport outside school hours.
- House prices in the Henley Beach area increased by 15% in the last year.
- Nearly 27% of Australians visited a museum in 2002-2003.
- The number of children attending the local cinema during the school holidays has dropped 12% on last year's attendance.
- The humidity at 9 am was 46% and at 3 pm it was 88%.
- After the weekend rainfalls the Myponga Dam was at 75% capacity.

2 In all the above examples, write suggestions on how and why these percentages may have been worked out.

3 Find out about The Australian Bureau of Statistics.

4 What is a census? How is it conducted? Why is it conducted? What types of questions may be asked?

5 What census do schools conduct? Why?

B FRACTIONS TO PERCENTAGES

If an object is divided into 100 equal parts then each single part is called 1 percent and is written as 1%.

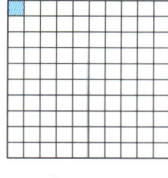
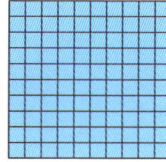

Thus $\frac{1}{100} = 1\%$ and $\frac{100}{100} = 100\%$

Percent means 'out of one hundred'.

Most common fractions and decimal fractions can be changed into percentage form by first converting into common fractions with a denominator of 100.

For example:

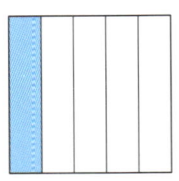   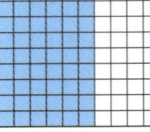

$\frac{1}{5}$ = 0.2 = $\frac{20}{100}$ = 20%

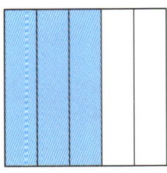

$\frac{3}{5}$ = 0.6 = $\frac{60}{100}$ = 60%

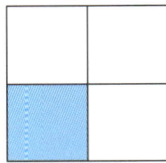

$\frac{1}{4}$ = 0.25 = $\frac{25}{100}$ = 25%

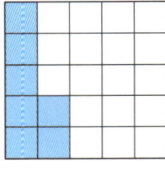   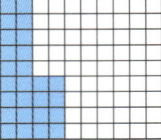

$\frac{7}{25}$ = 0.28 = $\frac{28}{100}$ = 28%

EXERCISE 6B

1 What percentage is represented by the following shaded diagrams?

a 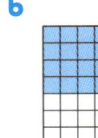 **b** 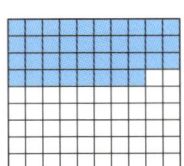 **c** 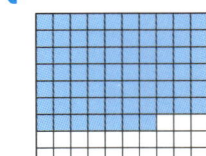 **d**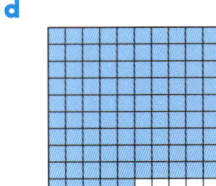

2 Estimate the percentage shaded:

a 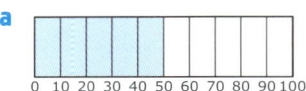 **b** 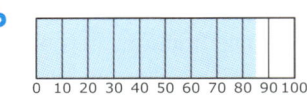 **c**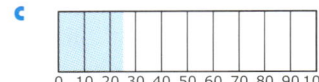

PERCENTAGE (CHAPTER 6)   193

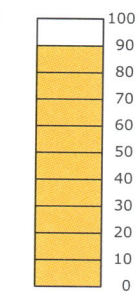 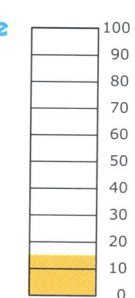 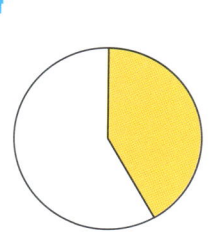 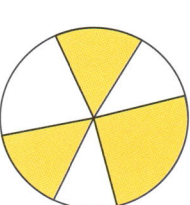

Example 1

Write as percentages:

a $\frac{19}{100}$ b $\frac{76.8}{100}$ c $\frac{557}{1000}$

a $\frac{19}{100}$
$= 19\%$

b $\frac{76.8}{100}$
$= 76.8\%$

c $\frac{557}{1000}$
$= \frac{557 \div 10}{1000 \div 10}$
$= \frac{55.7}{100}$
$= 55.7\%$

3 Write the following fractions as percentages:

a $\frac{19}{100}$ b $\frac{3}{100}$ c $\frac{37}{100}$ d $\frac{54}{100}$
e $\frac{79}{100}$ f $\frac{50}{100}$ g $\frac{100}{100}$ h $\frac{85}{100}$
i $\frac{6.6}{100}$ j $\frac{34.5}{100}$ k $\frac{75}{1000}$ l $\frac{356}{1000}$

Example 2

Write as percentages:

a $\frac{2}{5}$ b $\frac{13}{25}$

a $\frac{2}{5}$
$= \frac{2 \times 20}{5 \times 20}$
$= \frac{40}{100}$
$= 40\%$

b $\frac{13}{25}$
$= \frac{13 \times 4}{25 \times 4}$
$= \frac{52}{100}$
$= 52\%$

4 Write the following as fractions with denominator 100, and then convert to percentages:

a $\frac{7}{10}$ b $\frac{1}{10}$ c $\frac{9}{10}$ d $\frac{1}{2}$ e $\frac{1}{4}$
f $\frac{3}{4}$ g $\frac{2}{5}$ h $\frac{4}{5}$ i $\frac{7}{20}$ j $\frac{11}{20}$
k $\frac{7}{25}$ l $\frac{19}{25}$ m $\frac{23}{50}$ n $\frac{47}{50}$ o 1

5 Write these statements in full:

   a Fourteen percent means fourteen out of every ....

   b If 53% of the students in a school are girls, 53% means the fraction $\frac{.......}{.......}$.

6 Refer to the illustration given and then complete the table which follows:

	Students	Number	Fraction	Fraction with denominator of 100	Percentage
a	wearing shorts				
b	with a ball				
c	wearing a dress or a skirt				
d	wearing shorts and with a ball				
e	wearing track pants, baseball cap and striped top				
f	wearing shorts or track pants				
g	every student in the picture				

> **Example 3**
>
> In a class of 25 students, 6 have black hair. What percentage of the class have black hair?
>
> The fraction with black hair $= \frac{6}{25}$
>
> $ = \frac{6 \times 4}{25 \times 4}$
>
> $ = \frac{24}{100}$
>
> So the percentage is 24%.

7 In a class of 25 students, 13 have blue eyes. What percentage of the class have blue eyes?

8 There are 35 Nindi netballers. 14 of them are boys. What percentage are girls?

9

A pack of 52 playing cards has been shuffled and 25 cards have been dealt as shown.

- **a** What percentage of the cards shown are:
  - **i** hearts
  - **ii** black
  - **iii** picture cards
  - **iv** spades?
- **b** If an ace is 1 and picture cards are higher than 10, what percentage of the cards shown are:
  - **i** 10 or higher
  - **ii** 5 or lower
  - **iii** higher than 5 and less than 10?
- **c** From a full pack what percentage are:
  - **i** red
  - **ii** picture cards
  - **iii** diamonds
  - **iv** spades and clubs?

(J, Q and K are picture cards.)

C PERCENTAGES TO FRACTIONS

Percentages are easily changed into fractions.

First write the percentage as a fraction with a denominator of 100.

The fraction can then be expressed in its lowest terms.

Example 4

Express as fractions in lowest terms:

a 70% **b** 85%

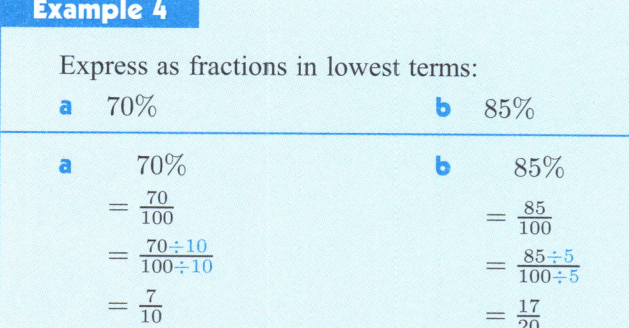

First convert to a fraction with denominator 100, then write in simplest form.

EXERCISE 6C

1 Write as a fraction in lowest terms:

a 43%	**b** 37%	**c** 50%	**d** 70%
e 90%	**f** 20%	**g** 40%	**h** 25%
i 75%	**j** 95%	**k** 100%	**l** 3%
m 5%	**n** 44%	**o** 200%	**p** 350%

Example 5

Express 2.5% as a fraction in lowest terms.

$$2.5\%$$
$$= \frac{2.5}{100}$$
$$= \frac{2.5 \times 10}{100 \times 10} \quad \text{\{to remove the decimal\}}$$
$$= \frac{25}{1000}$$
$$= \frac{25 \div 25}{1000 \div 25}$$
$$= \frac{1}{40}$$

2 Write as a fraction in lowest terms:

- **a** 12.5%
- **b** 7.5%
- **c** 0.5%
- **d** 17.3%
- **e** 97.5%
- **f** 0.2%
- **g** 0.05%
- **h** 0.02%

D CONVERTING DECIMALS TO PERCENTAGES

To write a decimal number as a percentage we **multiply it by 100%**.

Since $100\% = \frac{100}{100} = 1$, when you multiply by 100%, you are really multiplying by 1, and therefore you have not changed the value of the number.

Example 6

Change to percentages by multiplying by 100%:
- **a** 0.27
- **b** 0.055

a $\quad 0.27$
$= 0.27 \times 100\%$
$= 27\%$

b $\quad 0.055$
$= 0.055 \times 100\%$
$= 5.5\%$

Remember that 100% = 1

EXERCISE 6D

1 Change the following into percentage form by multiplying by 100%:

- **a** 0.37
- **b** 0.89
- **c** 0.15
- **d** 0.49
- **e** 0.73
- **f** 0.05
- **g** 1.02
- **h** 1.17

2 Change the following into percentage form by multiplying by 100%:

- **a** 0.2
- **b** 0.7
- **c** 0.9
- **d** 0.4
- **e** 0.074
- **f** 0.739
- **g** 0.0067
- **h** 0.0018

E CONVERTING PERCENTAGES INTO DECIMALS

Percentages are also readily converted into decimal fraction form by first writing the percentage as a common fraction with a denominator of 100.

Example 7

Write as a decimal:
a 21%   **b** $12\frac{1}{2}\%$

a 21%
$= \frac{21}{100}$
$= \frac{21.}{100}$
$= 0.21$

b $12\frac{1}{2}\%$
$= 12.5\%$
$= \frac{12.5}{100}$
$= \frac{12.5}{100}$
$= 0.125$

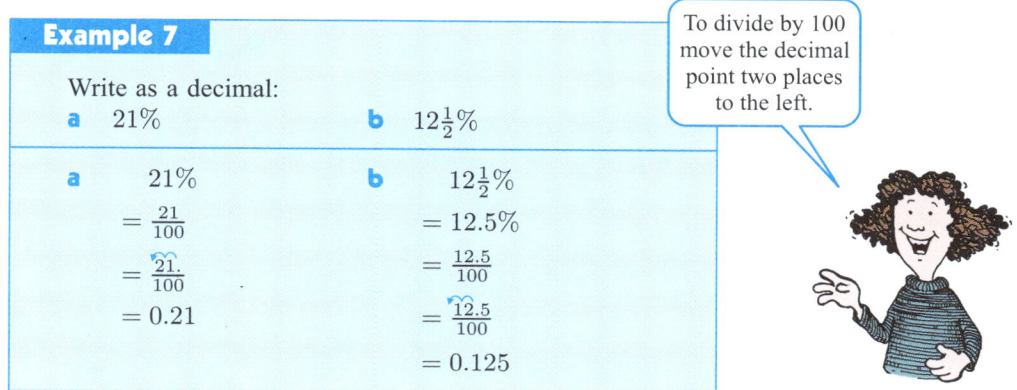

To divide by 100 move the decimal point two places to the left.

EXERCISE 6E

1 Write as a decimal:
  a 50%   **b** 30%   **c** 25%   **d** 60%
  e 85%   **f** 5%   **g** 45%   **h** 42%
  i 15%   **j** 100%   **k** 67%   **l** 125%

2 Write as a decimal:
  a 7.5%   **b** 18.3%   **c** 17.2%   **d** 106.7%
  e 0.15%   **f** 8.63%   **g** $37\frac{1}{2}\%$ **h** $6\frac{1}{2}\%$
  i $\frac{1}{2}\%$ **j** $1\frac{1}{2}\%$ **k** $\frac{3}{4}\%$ **l** $4\frac{1}{4}\%$

Another way of converting a **fraction to a percentage** is to first convert it to a decimal,

i.e.,   fraction → decimal → percentage

Example 8

Change to percentages by multiplying by 100%:
a $\frac{4}{5}$ **b** $\frac{3}{4}$

a $\frac{4}{5}$
$= 0.8$
$= 0.8 \times 100\%$
$= 80\%$

b $\frac{3}{4}$
$= 0.75$
$= 0.75 \times 100\%$
$= 75\%$

3 Change to percentages by writing as a decimal first:

- **a** $\frac{1}{10}$
- **b** $\frac{8}{10}$
- **c** $\frac{4}{10}$
- **d** $\frac{3}{5}$
- **e** $\frac{2}{5}$
- **f** $\frac{1}{2}$
- **g** $\frac{3}{20}$
- **h** $\frac{1}{4}$
- **i** $\frac{19}{20}$
- **j** $\frac{3}{50}$
- **k** $\frac{39}{50}$
- **l** $\frac{17}{25}$
- **m** $\frac{3}{8}$
- **n** 1
- **o** $\frac{11}{100}$
- **p** $\frac{3}{8}$
- **q** $\frac{1}{3}$
- **r** $\frac{2}{3}$

4 Copy and complete these patterns:

- **a** 1 is 100%
  $\frac{1}{2}$ is 50%
  $\frac{1}{4}$ is ......
  $\frac{1}{8}$ is ......
  $\frac{1}{16}$ is ......
- **b** $\frac{1}{5} = 20\%$
  $\frac{2}{5} = $ ......
  $\frac{3}{5} = $ ......
  $\frac{4}{5} = $ ......
  $\frac{5}{5} = $ ......
- **c** $\frac{1}{3}$ is $33\frac{1}{3}\%$
  $\frac{2}{3}$ is ......
  $\frac{3}{3}$ is ......
- **d** $\frac{1}{4}$ is ......
  $\frac{2}{4} = \frac{1}{2}$ is ......
  $\frac{3}{4} = $ ......
  $\frac{4}{4} = $ ......

5 Copy and complete the table below:

	Percent	Fraction	Decimal			Percent	Fraction	Decimal
a	20%		0.2		g			0.35
b	40%	$\frac{2}{5}$			h	12.5%		
c			0.5		i		$\frac{5}{8}$	
d		$\frac{3}{4}$			j	100%		
e			0.85		k		$\frac{3}{20}$	
f		$\frac{2}{25}$			l			0.375

SUMMARY

Some percentages occur frequently in business calculations and advertisements, so it is worthwhile to become familiar with their conversions to fractions.

A **table of common conversions** follows. Copy this table and add others if you wish.

Percentage	Common Fraction	Decimal Fraction	Percentage	Common Fraction	Decimal Fraction
100%	1	1.0	5%	$\frac{1}{20}$	0.05
75%	$\frac{3}{4}$	0.75	$33\frac{1}{3}\%$	$\frac{1}{3}$	$0.\overline{3}$
50%	$\frac{1}{2}$	0.5	$66\frac{2}{3}\%$	$\frac{2}{3}$	$0.\overline{6}$
25%	$\frac{1}{4}$	0.25	$12\frac{1}{2}\%$	$\frac{1}{8}$	0.125
20%	$\frac{1}{5}$	0.2	$6\frac{1}{4}\%$	$\frac{1}{16}$	0.0625
10%	$\frac{1}{10}$	0.1	$\frac{1}{2}\%$	$\frac{1}{200}$	0.005

F PLOTTING NUMBERS ON A NUMBER LINE

Plotting numbers on a number line can be difficult, especially when the numbers are given as fractions, decimals and percentages. We convert all fractions and decimals to percentages to make the comparison easier.

Example 9

Convert $\{\frac{1}{4}, 0.42, 33\%\}$ to percentages and plot them on a number line.

Convert each to a percentage.

	Answer:	Order:
• $\frac{1}{4} \times 100\%$	25%	1
• $0.42 \times 100\%$	42%	3
• 33% (already a percent)	33%	2

Use the percentages to arrange the numbers in order from lowest to highest.

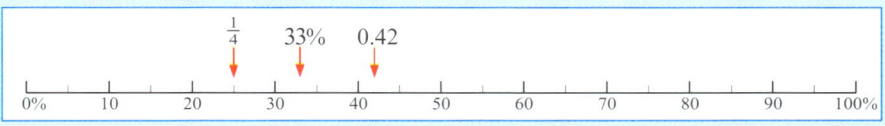

EXERCISE 6F

1 Convert each set of numbers to percentages and plot them on a number line:

    a $\{\frac{3}{5}, 70\%, 0.65\}$ **b** $\{55\%, \frac{9}{20}, 0.83\}$ **c** $\{0.93, 79\%, \frac{17}{20}\}$

    d $\{0.85, \frac{3}{4}, 92\%\}$ **e** $\{\frac{27}{50}, 67\%, 0.59\}$ **f** $\{47\%, 0.74, \frac{18}{30}\}$

    g $\{\frac{3}{4}, 0.65, 42\%\}$ **h** $\{0.39, 58\%, \frac{7}{20}, \frac{2}{5}\}$ **i** $\{\frac{5}{8}, 73\%, \frac{13}{20}, 0.47\}$

2 Write each of the following number line positions in fraction notation with 100 as the denominator, as decimals and using % notation:

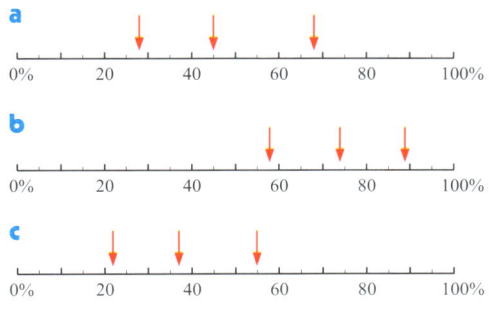

G PERCENTAGES ARE ALL AROUND US

Information about things that affect us directly is often presented as percentages. Even in countries where the metric system does not exist, information that is important to the people is presented in percentages. We could say that the use of percentage is universal.

Examples:

Food

Look at the labels on any collection of packaged food. Find the percentage (%) symbols. Here are some we found:

Vitaweat   "more than 80% cooked whole wheat, less than 28% energy from fat ..."

Natural muesli   "for diabetics, 100% of the sugar content of this product is derived naturally from added fruit"

Juice   "99.9% fresh natural unsweetened orange juice, 0.03% potassium sorbate"

On some labels, energy, protein, fat, carbohydrate, dietary fibre, sodium and potassium may be shown as % or as parts per 100 gm.

Clothing

Look at the labels on some of your clothing.
- 100% polyester
- 100% pure silk
- 60% wool, 30% cotton, 10% rayon
- 45% linen, 55% cotton

PERCENTAGE   (CHAPTER 6)   201

WHAT DOES A PERCENTAGE OF SOMETHING LOOK LIKE?

When a pizza is cut into quarters, the pieces are 25% of the whole pizza, and the 25% sizes are obvious.

However, a pizza with 25% ham, 25% pineapple, 25% mushroom and 25% pepperoni would not look like the diagram.

Because the toppings are mixed the percentages of the different toppings are not so obvious.

It is important to the consumer to know the percentages of the different contents making up the whole product. But there are many reasons why the different contents do not stand out.

Working through the following activity should help you understand why this is so.

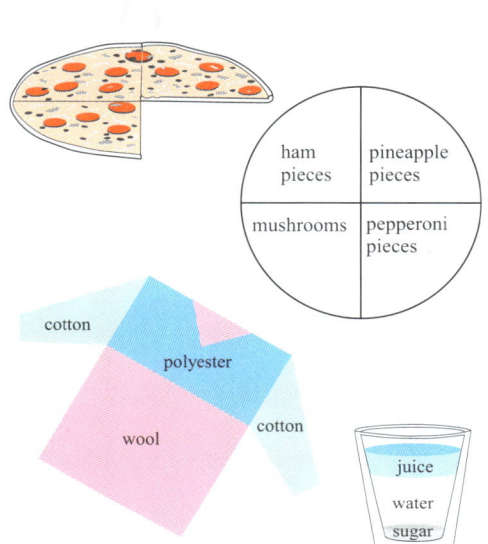

ACTIVITY LOOKING CLOSELY AT THE PERCENTAGES WHICH SURROUND US

What to do:

1. Find out why and how it is important to the buyer and the maker to say:
   a. what is in the product
   b. how much there is of it in the product.

2. Look at labels, newspapers, journals, catalogues, magazines and brochures, watch or listen to the news or current event programs or browse the internet to find different examples of the use of percentage. Where possible, mark copies or record the examples you find to share with your classmates.

3. Use the following headings, for example, to focus on your search for percentages:
      Sport, Medication, Weather, Education, Government and Gender differences.
   Who would want to know these percentages? In each example, give different reasons why they would want to know.

4. List 10 different products and suggest ways that the percentage of their different parts could sensibly make up the completed item.

GRAPHICAL REPRESENTATION

We often see percentages marked on pie charts and other statistical graphs.

On pie charts the sector angle must accurately show the actual percentage.

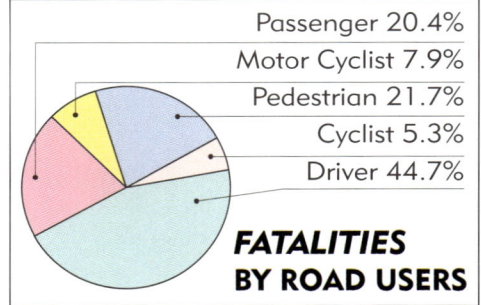

INVESTIGATION — MATCHING THE SECTOR

What to do:

1. The following sectors of a pie chart of percentages represent 3 age groups of people living in Australia in 1996. Match your prediction with the graph and give reasons for your choice.

   a Under 15 **b** 15 - 64 **c** 65 and over.

   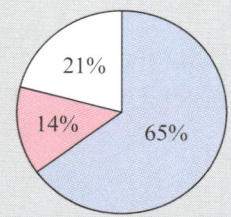

2.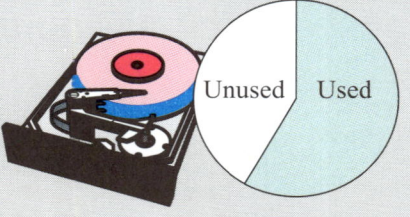

   On this computer disk space indicator, estimate the percentage of unused space.

3. **a** Name the states and territories whose percentage of Australia's total area is represented by the figures shown on the graph. You may find it helpful to study a map of Australia to compare the areas with the percentages shown on the graph.

   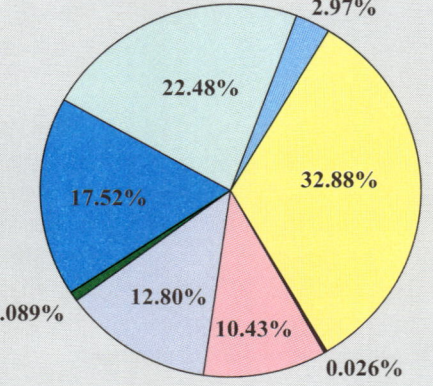

   b Suggest several reasons why the percentages have not been rounded to the nearest whole number.

   c Which part of this graph may not be accurate?

   d What could be done to make a pie graph, using these figures, much more accurate?

GEOMETRIC REPRESENTATION

Example 10

For the given figure:
a what fraction of the figure is unshaded
b what percentage of the figure is unshaded?

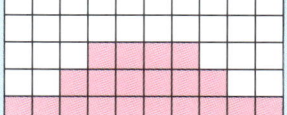

a There are 50 squares
30 squares are unshaded
∴ $\frac{30}{50} = \frac{3}{5}$ is unshaded.

b $\frac{3}{5} \times 100$ is unshaded
∴ 60% is unshaded

EXERCISE 6G

1 Copy and complete the following table, filling in the shading where necessary:

	Figure	Fraction shaded	Percentage shaded	Percentage unshaded
a				
b		$\frac{3}{4}$		
c				
d		$\frac{1}{6}$		
e			25%	
f				30%

MORE PRACTICE

Click on the icon for a worksheet which gives more practice questions like those in question **1**.

2 Construct a square with 10 cm sides. Divide it into 1 cm squares.

   a How many squares must you shade to leave 65% unshaded?

   b In lowest terms, what fraction of the largest square is unshaded?

3 Construct a rectangle 10 cm by 5 cm. Divide it into 1 cm squares. Shade 7 squares blue, 9 squares red and 20 squares yellow. What percentage of the rectangle is:

   a red   **b** blue   **c** not shaded   **d** either red or blue?

4 Use a compass to draw a circle.
Colour 50% of your circle red, 25% blue, 10% orange, 5% green, 5% purple, 5% yellow.

$$\begin{array}{ll} \textbf{Hint:} & 100\% \text{ of a circle} = 360° \\ & 1\% \text{ of a circle } = \frac{360°}{100} = 3.6° \\ & 20\% \text{ of a circle } = \frac{360°}{100} \times 20 = 72° \end{array}$$

What fraction of the whole circle is:

   a blue   **b** red   **c** orange

   d orange or blue   **e** red or purple or yellow   **f** coloured?

5 Divide a circle into 5 equal sectors of 20%. Colour $\frac{1}{5}$ of the circle red, 40% yellow, $\frac{1}{5}$ blue and 20% green. If you drew 4 such identical circles:

   a what percentage of *all* the circles would be   **i** blue   **ii** red?

   b What fraction of the 4 circles would be yellow?

ACTIVITY   MATCHING PERCENTAGES WITH GEOMETRIC REPRESENTATIONS

What to do:

1 Match these statements with the appropriate section on the graphs. Of the total number of people attending an AFL final between the Power and the Crows:

   a 55% were Power supporters
   b 45% were passengers in a car
   c 38% were Crows supporters
   d 25% travelled by bus
   e 18% drove their own cars
   f 7% caught a taxi
   g 6% didn't mind which team won
   h 5% walked to the stadium
   i 1% were employed at the game.

2 How might this information have been collected?

3 Why would this information be important to collect?

4
  a If there were 45 500 people at the game, work out the number of people in categories **a** to **i** in question **1**.
  b Sixty percent of the people who drove their cars paid $5 to park. What was the total collected for car parking?
  c Eighty five percent of the Power supporters had season tickets. How many Power supporters got their tickets some other way?
  d At half time 10 010 cups of soft drink were sold. If each cup was drunk by only one person, what percentage of the attendance drank soft drink at half time?
  e Twenty percent of the people who didn't mind which team won were male. How many females did not mind which team won?

H ONE QUANTITY AS A PERCENTAGE OF ANOTHER

Because percentages are often used to compare quantities it is useful to be able to express one quantity as a percentage of a second quantity.

We may only compare "like with like", so we must take care that both quantities are in the same units.

For example, if we are asked to express "35 cm as a percentage of 7 m" we would normally convert the larger unit to the smaller one   i.e., "35 cm as a percentage of 700 cm".

We must also be careful to read the question. For example,

expressing 3 apples as a percentage of 7 bananas  is not possible,

but, 3 apples as a percentage of 10 apples  is possible,

and 7 bananas as a percentage of 10 bananas 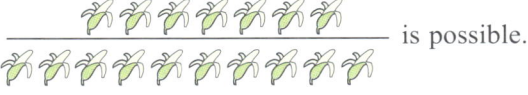 is possible.

Once again, expressing "5 bicycles as a percentage of 45 cars" is not possible but expressing "5 bicycles as a percentage of 50 vehicles" does make sense as bicycles are a type of vehicle.

ACTIVITY — CHOOSING A COMMON NAME OR SAME UNIT

What to do:

1 Choose a common name (denominator) which could be sensibly used to express either unit as a percentage of any other unit in that same example.

- **a** coffee, tea
- **b** hamburgers, pizza
- **c** Virgin Blue, Qantas
- **d** fins, wetsuit, goggles
- **e** train, bus, tram
- **f** e-mail, letters, fax, telephone
- **g** saxophone, clarinet, recorder, trumpet
- **h** museum, art gallery
- **i** Holden, Ford, Mitsubishi, Toyota
- **j** hydrogen, helium, oxygen, nitrogen
- **k** zloty, euro, pound, dollar
- **l** canola, rice, barley, wheat, oats
- **m** cedar, pinus, kauri, eucalyptus
- **n** locusts, termites, millipedes, mice

2 For each of the above examples above, prepare a statement and a question which uses the common name you have chosen.

For example, "Of all the people who had breakfast in the hotel dining room, 12 ordered coffee and 28 ordered tea. What percentage of the people who ordered a hot drink ordered tea?"

ONE QUANTITY AS A PERCENTAGE OF ANOTHER

To express one quantity as a percentage of another, we first write them as a fraction then convert the fraction to a percentage.

Example 11

Express the first quantity as a percentage of the second:
a 12 hours, 5 days   **b** 800 m, 2 km

a
$$\frac{12 \text{ hours}}{5 \text{ days}}$$
$$= \frac{\cancel{12}^1 \text{ h}}{5 \times \cancel{24}_2 \text{ h}}$$
$$= \frac{1}{10}$$
$$= 10\%$$

b
$$\frac{800 \text{ m}}{2 \text{ km}}$$
$$= \frac{800 \text{ m}}{2000 \text{ m}}$$
$$= \frac{800 \div 400}{2000 \div 400}$$
$$= \frac{2}{5}$$
$$= 40\%$$

EXERCISE 6H

1 Express the first quantity as a percentage of the second:

- **a** 10 km, 50 km
- **b** $2, $8
- **c** 3 m, 4 m
- **d** 120°, 360°
- **e** 60 cents, $2
- **f** 90°, 360°
- **g** 400 mL, 2 L
- **h** 6 months, 4 years
- **i** 50 g, 1 kg
- **j** 48 kg, 1 tonne
- **k** 36 cents, $2
- **l** 5 mm, 8 cm
- **m** 25 cm, 0.5 m
- **n** 48 min, 2 hours
- **o** 180 cm, 3 m
- **p** 90 cents, $45
- **q** 5 mg, 2 g
- **r** 6 hours, 2 days

Example 12

Express as a percentage:
a A test mark of 17 out of a possible 25.
b Out of 1250 cars sold in one month, 250 were made by Ford.

a $\dfrac{17 \text{ marks}}{25 \text{ marks}}$

$= \dfrac{17 \times 4}{25 \times 4}$

$= \dfrac{68}{100}$

$= 68\%$

b $\dfrac{250 \text{ cars}}{1250 \text{ cars}}$

$= \dfrac{250 \div 250}{1250 \div 250}$

$= \dfrac{1}{5} \times 100\%$

$= 0.2 \times 100\%$

$= 20\%$

2 Express as a percentage:
  a 13 marks out of a possible 25
  b 72 marks out of a possible 80
  c 427 books sold out of a total 500 printed
  d 650 square metres of lawn in a 2000 square metre garden
  e 27 400 spectators in a 40 000 seat stadium
  f An archer scores 95 points out of a possible 125 points.

3 What percentage is:
  a 42 of 60
  b 34 of 40
  c 48 seconds of 2 min
  d 3 minutes of one hour
  e 175 g of 1 kg
  f 440 mL of 2 L
  g 420 kg of 1 tonne
  h 16 hours of 1 day
  i 174 cm of 1 m?

I FINDING PERCENTAGES OF QUANTITIES

To find the quantity which is given as a percentage of another quantity we could first convert the percentage to a fraction. Then we find the required fraction of the given quantity.

For example, 50% of 40 is $\frac{1}{2}$ of 40, which is 20.

However, by converting the percentage to a decimal we can also get the same result, as 50% of 40 = 0.5 × 40 = 20.

Example 13

Find: **a** 10% of 7 m (in cm) **b** 35% of 5000 people

a 10% of 7 m
$= 0.1$ of 700 cm
$= 0.1 \times 700$
$= 70$ cm

b 35% of 5000 people
$= 0.35$ of 5000
$= 0.35 \times 5000$
$= 1750$ people

EXERCISE 61

1 Find:

- **a** 20% of 360 hectares
- **b** 25% of 4200 square metres
- **c** 5% of 9 m (in cm)
- **d** 40% of 400 tonnes
- **e** 10% of 3 hours (in min)
- **f** 8% of 80 metres (in cm)
- **g** 30% of 2 tonnes (in kg)
- **h** 4% of 12 m (in mm)
- **i** 15% of 12 hours (in min)
- **j** 75% of 250 kilolitres (in litres)

2 A school with 485 students enrolled takes 20% of them for an excursion to the museum. How many are left at school?

3 An orchardist picks 2400 kg of apricots for drying. If 85% of the weight is lost in the drying process, how many kilograms of dried apricots are produced?

4 A council collects 4500 tonnes of rubbish each year from its ratepayers. If 27% is recycled how many tonnes is that?

5 A marathon runner improves her best time of 3 hours by 5%. What is her new best time?

6 Damian was 1.5 metres tall at the beginning of the school year. At the end of the year his height had increased by 5.6%. What was his new height?

7 A fruit drink made at a packaging plant consists of 65% water blended with pure juice. If the plant produced 25.5 kL of fruit drink last season, how many litres of this was pure juice?

8 Which is the larger amount?

- **a** 40% of a litre or $\frac{1}{3}$ of a litre
- **b** 20% of one metre or $\frac{1}{4}$ of a metre
- **c** 8% of $100 or 85 cents
- **d** 5% of a kilolitre or 5000 millilitres
- **e** 33% of 1000 or $\frac{1}{3}$ of 1000
- **f** 30% of a kg or 315 g

J PERCENTAGES AND MONEY

In societies where money is the most common way of trading goods and services, examples of the use of percentages occur frequently. For countries like ours which use decimal currency, percentage is easily calculated.

Look at the following examples:

20% of one dollar could look like = $\frac{20 \text{ cents}}{100 \text{ cents}}$ or $\frac{20}{100}$

represents 15 cents out of every one hundred cents   or $\frac{15}{100}$ or   15%

is $12\frac{1}{2}$ dollars for every 100 dollars   or $\frac{12\frac{1}{2}}{100}$ or $\frac{12.5}{100}$

   or $12\frac{1}{2}\%$ or   12.5%

Not all examples of percentage involve $1, $100 or $1000 amounts or multiples of these amounts.

So the denominator is not always a power of 10 or a multiple of 10.

Percentages of any amounts of money can be calculated.

Example 14

Find: **a**   15% of $200   **b**   20% of $3500

a   15% of $200
= 0.15 of $200
= 0.15 × $200
= $30

b   20% of $3500
= 0.2 of $3500
= 0.2 × $3500
= $700

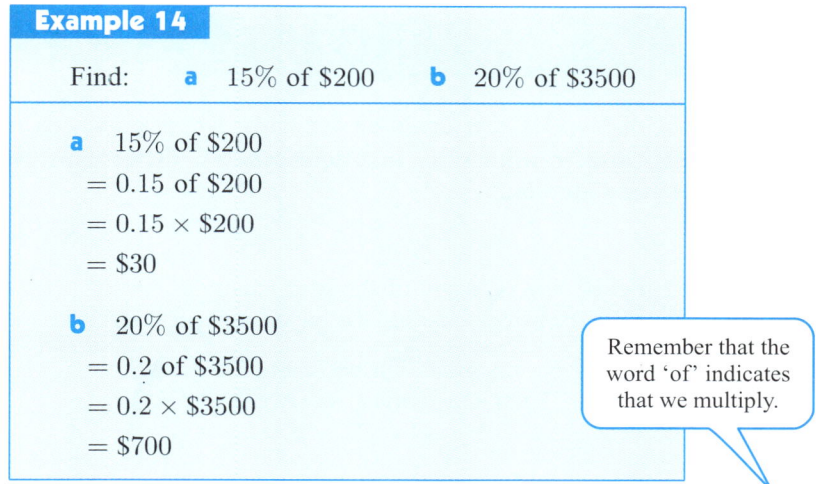

Remember that the word 'of' indicates that we multiply.

EXERCISE 6J

1 Find:

- **a**   10% of $47
- **b**   30% of $180
- **c**   70% of $21
- **d**   11% of $20
- **e**   27% of $150
- **f**   45% of $9700
- **g**   83% of $720
- **h**   36% of $4.50
- **i**   8% of $48.50
- **j**   12% of $2950
- **k**   37% of $700
- **l**   54% of $2500
- **m**   17.5% of $4000
- **n**   6.8% of $40
- **o**   10.9% of $50 000

Example 15

Express:
- **a** $4 as a percentage of $40
- **b** $16 as a percentage of $80

a $4 as a percentage of $40
$= \frac{4}{40} \times 100\%$
$= 0.1 \times 100\%$
$= 10\%$

b $16 as a percentage of $80
$= \frac{16}{80} \times 100\%$
$= \frac{16 \div 8}{80 \div 8} \times 100\%$
$= \frac{2}{10} \times 100\%$
$= 0.2 \times 100\%$
$= 20\%$

A as a percentage of B is $\frac{A}{B} \times 100\%$

2 Express:
- **a** $5 as % of $20
- **b** $15 as % of $150
- **c** $3 as % of $20
- **d** $20 as % of $80
- **e** $25 as % of $125
- **f** $6 as % of $120
- **g** $1.50 as % of $30
- **h** 35 cents as % of $1.40
- **i** $8 as % of $24
- **j** $40 as % of $60
- **k** $334 as % of $33 400
- **l** $9.95 as % of $99.50

K WHO USES PERCENTAGES?

These are some of the words that are used regularly where money is being considered: **discount, interest, rates, commission, taxation, rebates, deposit, profit, loss, increase, decrease, gross, nett, deduction**.

Examples:

- If there is a 10% discount on a pair of shoes originally priced at $90, $9 is taken **off** the price, meaning the buyer only pays $81.

- When the Australian Taxation Office takes 17% **off** a fortnightly salary of $1000 the worker receives $830 for the fortnight.

- When a bank charges 8.59% simple **interest** on a $10 000 loan for one year you must pay the bank $10 859 back at the end of that year. You pay them $859 **more** than you borrowed.

- When a real estate agent sells your home for $150 000 and charges you $4\frac{1}{2}\%$ **commission** he receives $6750 and you receive $143 250. You receive **less** than the house was sold for.

- If you buy a mountain bike for $500 and sell it a few days later for $400 you have made a **loss** of $100 or 20%.

- To buy a block of land for $60 000 you may be asked to put down a **deposit** of 20%. By paying the $12 000 you can then arrange a loan to borrow the remaining 80% **balance**. Most lenders will not provide a loan for the full 100% value of the land.

- If your doctor charged you $36 for a visit, Medicare would **return** to you a **rebate** of say $21 which is about 58%. This means you really only paid $15 of your own for the visit.

- If a car dealer buys a second hand car for $3800 and spends a further $400 fixing the engine and putting better tyres on it and then sells it for $5040, he makes a **profit** of 20% or $840 **more** on his costs.

- When you start working you may be on a salary of $500 per week.
  This is your **gross** salary and represents 100% of what your employer pays you. However, you will be expected to pay about 17% in **taxation** and you may choose to make a 5% contribution to superannuation. This would mean that 22% is **taken off** in **deductions** leaving you with a **nett** salary of 78% or $390.00.

INVESTIGATION

PERCENTAGES IN YOUR HOME, CLASSROOM OR SCHOOL

What to do:

What methods will you use to work out the following?

Write down an estimate before you use your method to work it out.

Draw pie graphs to show your answers.

1 What percentage of all the floor area in your home is either carpeted or tiled?

2 What percentage of all the internal wall space in your home is taken up by:
  a doors
  b windows?

3 What percentage of the electrical items in your home are used every day?

4 Look at the labels of the groceries in your home. What percentage were made in Australia?

5 What percentage of your body is covered up when you are:
  a at school in winter
  b on the beach in summer?

There may be a simple way of finding this out.

6 Of all the students in your school, what percentage regularly buy their lunch from the school canteen?

7 From the Resource Centre, find out the percentage of:
  a non-fiction books
  b books that are replaced each year
  c books that are borrowed by your class compared to the whole school
  d borrowing that the most popular author has.

8 What percentage of **a** your classmates **b** the students in the school have parents born overseas?

9 From a normal school week, work out the percentage of lesson time spent on each subject.

10 In a normal week during a school term, work out the percentage of time you spend:

   a at school
   b asleep
   c watching television
   d playing sport (outside school hours)
   e using the computer or playing electronic games
   f talking to adults
   g reading.

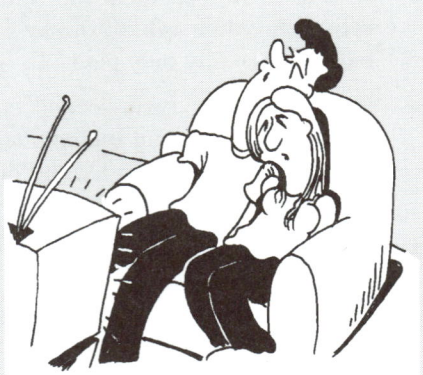

11 Using the White Pages of this year's telephone book as your information source (data) answer the following questions:

   a What percentage of the listings in the White Pages begin with

   i E **ii** I **iii** P **iv** R **v** S **vi** Z?

   b What percentage of all the 'S' listings are represented by the name 'Smith'?

   c What percentage of all the listings are represented by the name 'Smith'?

   d What percentage of all the R listings are represented by the name 'Robinson'?

   e What percentage of all the listings are represented by the name 'Nguyen'?

Study the hints before you start counting.

Hints:
   - Do not count all the individual names. Use the number of full columns as your data.
   - The first listing does not start on page 1 and the last listing is not on the last page of the telephone book.
   - Work out the total number of listings A to Z before you attempt any of the questions.
   - So that you do not forget it, record each bit of information as you go.

12 Choose either a short story from a newspaper or a page from a novel you are reading. Calculate the percentage of vowels. Compare your first sample with other stories or pages.

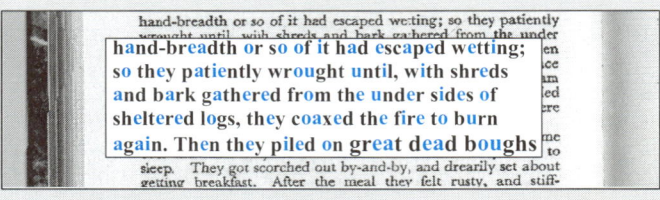

L PROBLEM SOLVING WITH PERCENTAGES

EXERCISE 6L

1 Write these scores as percentages. Arrange them in descending order.

   a Jan threw 18 goals from 25 shots, Jill 30 from 40, Jessie 38 from 50 and Jenny 20 from 32.

   b Jeff threw 21 from 30, Jake 40 from 60, Joel 34 from 50 and Juan 50 from 80.

2 In the same matches, Kim scored 5 goals from 9 shots, 7 from 11 and 4 from 5 and Kathy scored 15 from 20, 7 from 14 and 9 from 16.

   a Who was the more accurate scorer overall?

   b By what percentage was one girl better than the other?

3 Each of the following students saved a percentage of their allowance. Arrange the names of the students and their percentage saved in descending order.

   a Tom saved $6 from a $10 per week allowance, Tina $35 from $70 per month, Tao $13 from $25 a fortnight and Toni $11 from $20 a week.

   If each student was promised an extra 10% on the amount they saved over one year, how much more would be received by:

   b Tao   c Toni?

4 Nicholas pitched 9 strikeouts and 4 walks against the 36 batters who faced him. What was Nicholas's percentage of:

   a strikeouts   b walks?

5 A goal kicker had 80 kicks for goal during the football season. He kicked 56 goals. What percentage of his scoring attempts were:

   a goals   b not goals?

6 Sarah gets paid 30% of $1200 and Jack gets paid 45% of $1200. Peter is paid the remainder. How much does each person receive?

7 45% of an energy food drink is sugars. How many grams of sugars would there be in a 450 g can of this drink?

8 Simon used 20% of a 4 L can of paint. How much paint was left? Answer in millilitres.

9 30% of a farmer's crop was barley, and the rest was wheat. If he planted 2400 acres in total, how many acres were planted with wheat?

10 a Column A represents the students of room 16 who are driven to school.
  i What percentage are driven to school?
  ii What percentage find some other way to get to school?

b Column B represents the students of room 16 who play a musical instrument.
  i What percentage play a musical instrument?
  ii In lowest terms, what fraction play a musical instrument?

c Column C represents the students of room 16 who play sport for the school teams.
  i What percentage play sport for the school teams?
  ii In lowest terms what fraction does not play sport for the school teams?

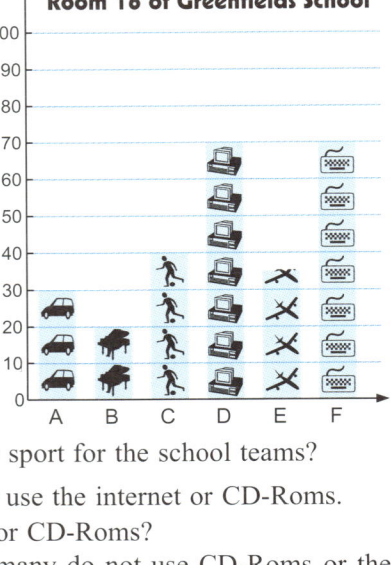

d Column D represents the students who regularly use the internet or CD-Roms.
  i What percentage regularly use the internet or CD-Roms?
  ii If there are 30 students in this class, how many do not use CD-Roms or the internet regularly?

e Column E represents the students who have been overseas.
  i What percentage have not been overseas?
  ii What fraction of the students is still to go overseas? (lowest terms)

f Column F represents the students who can type more than 20 words a minute. If there are an equal number of boys and girls in this class of 30 and 3 more girls than boys can type more than 20 words a minute, what percentage of the girls can type over 20 words a minute?

ACTIVITY — SURVEYING YOUR CLASSMATES

What to do:

1 With your class teacher's permission, collect information from the students in your class and construct your own percentage graphs.

2 Compare your sample with the class of Greenfields students' sample. Discuss.

3 Collect information from other classes in the school. How do their percentages compare with yours or the one above?

4 Organise ways to collect information from the whole school about, for example, canteen use, favourite sporting teams, TV programs, family cars, heroes, icecream and so on.

Remember to give your graph a title.

What is the best size sample of people to use?

M DISCOUNT

In order to attract customers, or to get rid of old stock or stock which is not selling very well, many businesses reduce the prices of items from those shown on the price tags (called the marked price or ticket price).

The amount of money by which the marked price of an item is reduced is called the **discount**. Discounts are often stated as a percentage of the marked price or recommended retail price (original selling price).

Therefore discount % is a percentage decrease.

All prices following include GST.

Example 16

If the marked price of a wetsuit is $200 and 15% discount is offered, find the actual selling price.

15% of marked price
= 15% of $200
= 15% × $200
= 0.15 × $200
= $30   discount

Normal price	$200
Less 15% discount	$30
Selling price	$170

EXERCISE 6M

1 **a** If the marked price of a DVD player is $320 and 15% discount is offered, find the actual selling price.

  b A camera's normal price is $460. By buying it duty free a 25% discount is offered. What is the actual selling price?

  c A supermarket is offering 2% discount on the total of your shopping docket. How much will you pay if your docket is $130?

  d If the marked price of a computer is $2600 and 12% discount is offered, what is the new selling price?

2 Find the selling price after the following discounts have been made:

  a    **b**    **c**

216   PERCENTAGE   (CHAPTER 6)

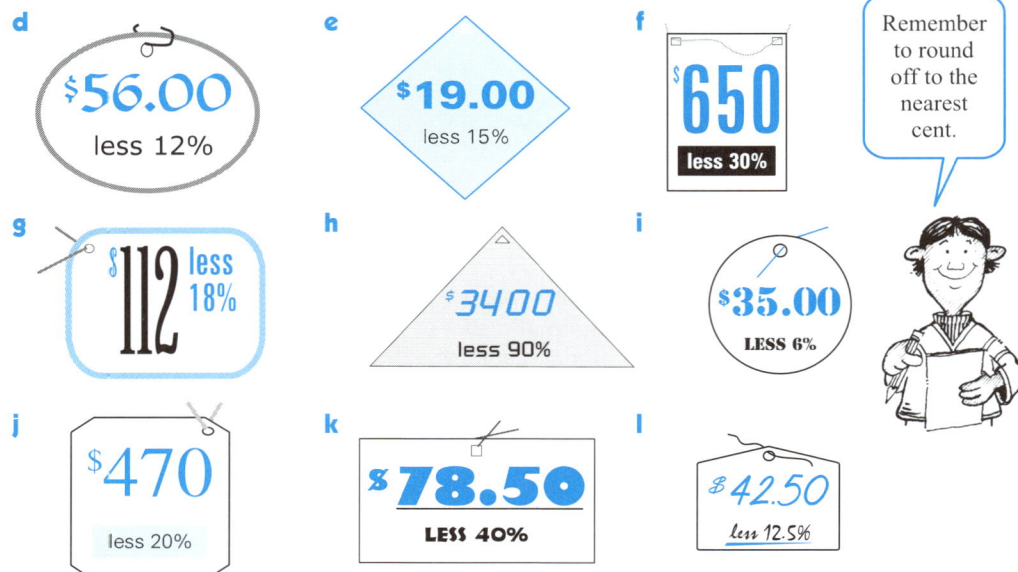

d $56.00 less 12%
e $19.00 less 15%
f $650 less 30%
g $112 less 18%
h $3400 less 90%
i $35.00 LESS 6%
j $470 less 20%
k $78.50 LESS 40%
l $42.50 less 12.5%

Remember to round off to the nearest cent.

N GOODS AND SERVICES TAX (GST)

Many goods and services sold in Australia include a **goods and services tax (GST)**.

In 2004 the GST rate was 10%. This means that the final purchaser of goods (shopping items) or services (such as an electrician) must pay an extra 10% for the item. GST is not payable on some items such as fresh foods.

Example 17

In order to make a profit a shop must sell an item for $80 and the GST must be added to this price.
  a What is the GST amount?   **b** What price should the item be sold for?

  a The GST is   10% of $80   **b**   The shop sells the item for
                    $= 0.1 \times \$80$ $\$80 + \$8$
                    $= \$8$ $= \$88$

EXERCISE 6N

1 What is the GST which must be added to the following items?

a
Selling price = $20 + GST

b
Selling price = $800 + GST

c
Selling price = $56 + GST

2 What is the GST on an item which would otherwise sell for:
  a $100   **b** $10   **c** $16   **d** $320?

3 What is the price, GST included, on a service which would otherwise cost:
  a $100   **b** $48   **c** $2000   **d** $640?

4 A shopkeeper needs to sell a pair of shoes for $160 to make the profit she wants and GST must be added.
  a What is the GST she must add on?
  b What must she sell the shoes for?

5 A bicycle shop sells bicycles for $250 and GST is to be added to this price.
  a What is the GST amount?
  b How much will the customers have to pay for a bicycle?

O SIMPLE INTEREST

When a person borrows money from a bank or a finance company, the borrower must repay the loan in full, and pay an additional charge which is called **interest**.

If the charge is calculated each year, or per annum, as a fixed percentage of the original amount of money borrowed, then the charge is called **simple interest**.

For example, if $8000 is borrowed for 4 years at 10% per annum simple interest, then the simple interest charged for 1 year is

  10% of $8000
  $= 0.1 \times \$8000$
  $= \$800$

So the simple interest for 4 years is $800 \times 4 = \$3200$.

The borrower must repay $8000 + \$3200 = \$11\,200$.

Mortgage rates lowest in 27 years
5.99% p.a. fixed

Example 18

Simple interest is often called flat rate interest and is not used as often as compound interest.

Find the simple interest payable on a loan of $5000 for $3\frac{1}{2}$ years at 8% p.a.

The simple interest charge for 1 year $= 8\%$ of $5000
$= 0.08 \times \$5000$
$= \$400$

∴ simple interest for $3\frac{1}{2}$ years $= \$400 \times 3.5$
$= \$1400$

EXERCISE 6O

1 Find the simple interest when:
   a $1000 is borrowed for 1 year at 15% per annum simple interest
   b $3500 is borrowed for 2 years at 10% per annum simple interest
   c $5000 is borrowed for 4 years at 8% per annum simple interest
   d $20 000 is borrowed for $1\frac{1}{2}$ years at 12% per annum simple interest
   e $140 000 is borrowed for $\frac{1}{2}$ year at 20% per annum simple interest.

2 Find the total amount to repay on a loan of:
   a $2000 for 5 years at 8% p.a. simple interest
   b $6500 for 3 years at 10% p.a. simple interest
   c $8000 for $4\frac{1}{2}$ years at 12% p.a. simple interest
   d $10 000 for 10 years at 10% p.a. simple interest.

DEMO

REVIEW SET A — CHAPTER 6

1 a Write $\frac{3}{4}$ as a percentage.   **b** Write 66% as a fraction in lowest terms.
   c Convert 0.125 into a percentage.   **d** Write 82% as a decimal.

2 What percentage is the first quantity of the second?
   a 4 hours, 25 hours   **b** $6, $15   **c** 8 months, 1 year

3 Write $\{\frac{3}{4}, 0.78, 72\%\}$ as percentages and then plot them on a number line.

4 An airline offers a special 30% off normal prices during its off-peak time flights to Melbourne. If its normal price is $324 return, what is the special price?

5 About 8% of all students are left-handed. In a school of 375 how many left-handed students would you expect to find?

6 A small country town had 280 households. 45% used a wood burning fire to warm their homes, 30% used electricity, 15% gas and the rest used oil or kerosene. How many households used gas, oil or kerosene?

7 What GST is paid on a shirt which would otherwise sell for $30?

8 A survey of 500 year 8 students showed that 55% always started their homework as soon as they arrived home from school, and 30% always started after tea. The rest had no regular pattern as to when they did their homework. How many students:
   a had no regular pattern   **b** started as soon as they arrived home?

9 In a town of 7200 people, 1800 were over 60 years of age and 3600 were under 40. Find the percentage of people aged from 40 to 60.

10 As a result of dieting a weight watcher reduced his 90 kg mass by 10%. What was his reduced weight?

11 Maryanne received 12% p.a. simple interest on her $3500 investment.
   a How much interest did she earn after 2 years?
   b What was her new balance?

12 A salesman offered 20% discount on a holiday package costing $2100.
   a Find the amount of discount.
   b Find the new price of the holiday.

REVIEW SET B — CHAPTER 6

1 a Write 0.47 as a percentage. **b** Write 40% as a fraction in lowest terms.
   c Write $\frac{2}{3}$ as a percentage. **d** Write $12\frac{1}{2}\%$ as a decimal.

2 Convert to percentages and plot on a number line: $\{\frac{2}{5}, 0.75, 56\%\}$

3 Express the first quantity as a percentage of the second.
   a 13 goals from 25 shots **b** 58 cm from 2 m **c** 500 mL from 5 L

4 Anthony lost 6 marks in a test out of 25. What percentage did he score for the test?

5 What percentage is 650 kilometres of a 2000 km journey?

6 One hundred students agree to come to a fund raising school disco. What price should the committee charge each student if the DJ costs $180, balloons and streamers cost a further $20 and they want to make a 50% profit on their costs?

7 A fridge has a selling price of $840 but a discount of 15% is given.
   a Find the discount.
   b What is the actual price paid for the fridge?

8 A telemarketing company offers a "100% Money Back Guarantee". If I return my $189 exercise machine, how much will I get back?

9 a Find the interest on a loan of $7000 for 5 years at 8% p.a. simple interest.
   b Find the total amount of money that must be repaid.

10 A survey of 250 primary school students found that 63% usually had the TV on when they were doing their homework, 36% never had the TV on and 1% gave no response. How many:
   a gave no response **b** never had the TV on?

11 Klaus spent $15 from the $50 he was given for his birthday. What percentage of his money did he spend?

12 A dentist charges $270 for dental treatment and GST must be added to this amount.
   a What is the GST amount?
   b How much will the customer have to pay?

REVIEW SET C   CHAPTER 6

1 a Write $\frac{7}{25}$ with a denominator of 100.
   b Change $\frac{1}{3}$ to a percentage.
   c Convert 0.45 to a percentage.
   d Express 6 minutes as a percentage of one hour.
   e Find 30% of $600.
   f Find 140% of 2 kilometres (in metres).

2 What percentage of the diagram is unshaded?

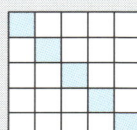

3 Convert to percentages and plot on a number line: $\{\frac{1}{8}, 52\%, 0.8\}$

4 Samantha had a budget of $200 to spend on clothes. She paid $58 for jeans and $82 for shoes. She spent 24% of her budget on a jacket and the balance on a baseball cap.
   a How much was the baseball cap?
   b What percentage of her budget did she spend on the baseball cap and shoes?

5 Write the first quantity as a percentage of the second:
   a 45°, 360°   **b** 2 mm, 5 cm

6 The deposit on a new car was 20% of its cost. If the car cost $16 800 how much was the deposit?

7 A variety store is having a "20% off the ticket price" sale. If I bought a $38.90 toaster, a $79.90 sleeping bag, 2 bath towels at $12.90 each and a $5.40 blank video tape, how much would I save?

8 A plumber charges $940 for supplying and installing a new hot water service.
   a How much GST must be added?
   b What amount is the customer charged?

9 Joshua bought $690 of goods at the hardware store. He was allowed 5% discount for paying cash. How much did he pay to the hardware store?

10 Find the simple interest when $2400 is borrowed for 2 years at 12% p.a.

Chapter 7

Measurement (length and mass)

Knowledge, skills and understandings

By the end of this chapter you should be able to

- convert between millimetres, centimetres, metres and kilometres
  (e.g., 25 mm = 0.025 m)
- use scale in ratio form to calculate either original size or drawing size
- choose the appropriate units and tools to measure weight of a variety of objects
- identify the relationships between milligrams, grams, kilograms and tonnes
  (e.g., 1 kg = 1000 g, 1 t = 1000 kg, 1 g = 1000 mg)
- apply the knowledge of mass to practical problem-solving situations (e.g., mass of 1 litre of water to 1 kilogram)

In our everyday life we **measure** many things, but what do we actually mean by measurement? If we measure something we are trying to determine its size or how much of it there is.

The more common types of measurement are:

Measurement	Example
Distance or length	How far we have travelled.
Mass or weight	How heavy we are.
Time	How long a tennis match will last.
Temperature	How hot it is going to be tomorrow.
Area	The size of the block of land I need to buy.
Volume	How much concrete I need for the driveway.
Speed	How fast I travel if I get there in 2 hours.

However, in everyday life, people measure a whole range of different things and different characteristics. For instance there are measures for energy, sound, diamonds, power, elasticity, gravity, colour, smell, typing rate and pollen count.

Some things like art, beauty, taste, desire, ambition, success, attitude and intelligence are much harder to measure.

ACTIVITY — MEASURING INSTRUMENTS

What do these instruments measure? Match the instrument to its name.

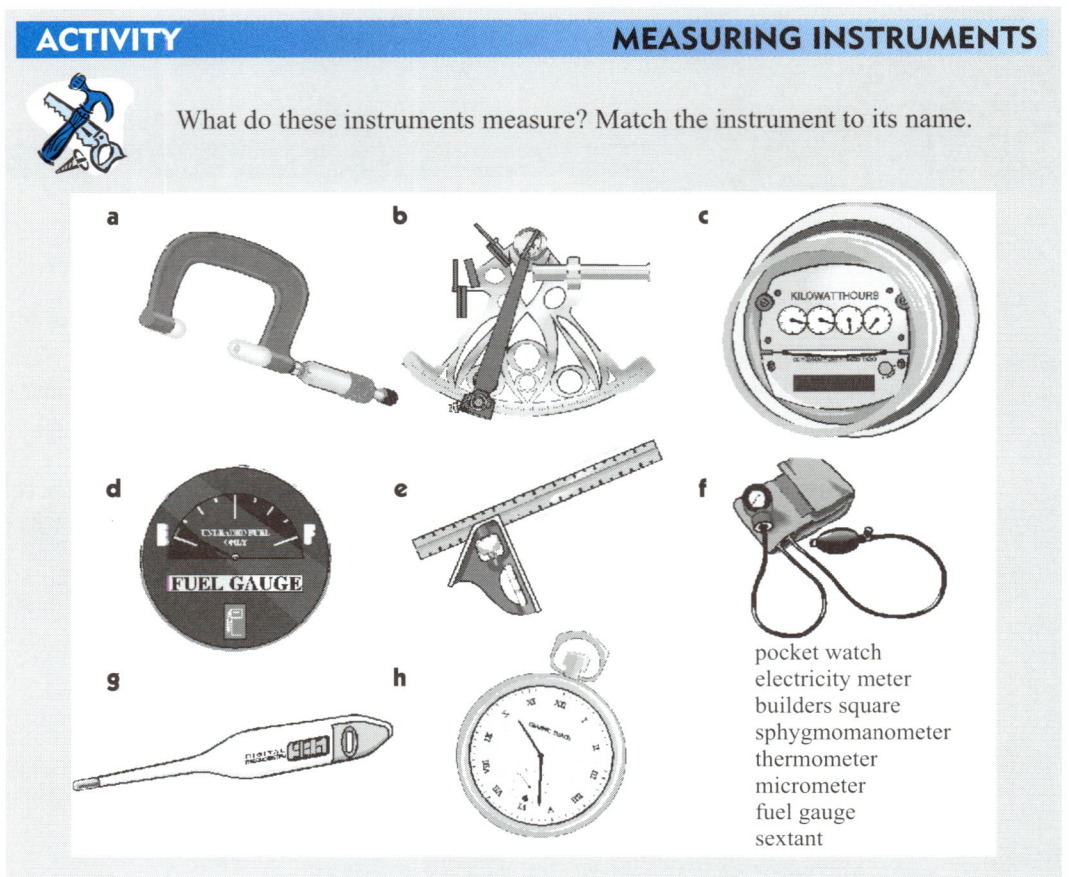

pocket watch
electricity meter
builders square
sphygmomanometer
thermometer
micrometer
fuel gauge
sextant

In this chapter we will consider mainly the measurement of length and mass.

MEASUREMENT (LENGTH AND MASS)   (CHAPTER 7)

ACTIVITY — MEASURES AND WHO USES THEM

What to do:

1. Find out what is measured by the following instruments and what caused their development.
   - Geiger counter
   - Callipers
   - Calorimeter
   - Theodolite
   - Seismometer
   - Altimeter
   - Micrometer
   - Barometer
   - Sphygmomanometer
   - Hydrometer
   - Dynamometer
   - Tachometer

2. Find what sort of measuring tools would be used by:
   - Architects
   - Scientists
   - Farmers
   - Weather Forecasters
   - Doctors
   - Pilots
   - Computer Engineers
   - Mechanics
   - Builders
   - Surveyors
   - Sports Officials
   - Teachers

3. How would you measure the following?
   - angles
   - density
   - electricity
   - location
   - tides
   - reading
   - audience
   - humidity

4. Without using any units of measurement (for example, metres or hours) write sentences which measure or compare attributes of the following pairs of words. Try not to repeat any terms.

   For example, bottle - can.   This bottle holds more water than that can.

   a car - motorbike   b glass - plastic   c tree - building
   d brick - tile   e greyhound - cheetah   f today - yesterday
   g golfball - softball   h Melanie - Melissa   i sugar - saccharin

   Suggest other pairs of words which your class mates could compare using different measurement descriptors. What items are impossible to measure?

5. If skill is a very important part of AFL football, why are tables of heights and weights comparing individual team members often printed before important matches? Why aren't the players' and coaches' skills measured and compared? Discuss.

A   UNITS OF MEASUREMENT

The earliest units of measurement used were of lengths related to parts of the body. Two of these are illustrated below – the **span** and the **cubit**. Two others in common use were the **yard** (the distance from your nose to your fingertip) and the **pace** (1000 paces to a Roman mile).

All of these measurements were inaccurate because people are different sizes.

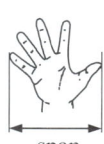
span

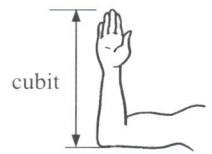
cubit

pace

INTERNATIONAL SYSTEM OF UNITS

In order to standardise these lengths, King Henry VIII of England said that the distance from his nose to the fingertips of his hand would be the standard unit of length. This finally led to the British Imperial System of units which uses inches, feet, yards and miles for length and ounces, pounds and tons for mass.

This system is still used in a few countries but the Metric System, developed in France in 1789, is now used in Australia. The advantage of this system is that it uses powers of ten for different sizes. The basic unit for length is the **metre** and for mass it is the **kilogram**. Other smaller (or larger) units are named by using prefixes. This system of units is now known as the **International System of Units**.

LENGTH UNITS

$$1 \text{ millimetre (mm)} = \tfrac{1}{1000} \text{ metre} = 0.001 \text{ metre}$$
$$1 \text{ centimetre (cm)} = \tfrac{1}{100} \text{ metre} = 0.01 \text{ metre}$$
$$1 \text{ kilometre (km)} = 1000 \text{ metres}$$

MASS UNITS

The **mass** of an object is a measure of the amount of matter it contains.

$$1 \text{ milligram (mg)} = \tfrac{1}{1000} \text{ g} = 0.001 \text{ g}$$
$$1 \text{ gram (g)} = \tfrac{1}{1000} \text{ kg} = 0.001 \text{ kg}$$
$$1 \text{ tonne (t)} = 1000 \text{ kg}$$

EXERCISE 7A

1 State what units you would use to measure the following:
  a the mass of a person
  b the distance between two towns
  c the length of a sporting field
  d the mass of a tablet

  e the length of a bus
  f the mass of a car
  g the width of this book
  h the mass of a truck

B   READING SCALES

There are many instruments which are used for measuring. These instruments have a scale marked on them. The one with which students are most familiar is the ruler and rulers have a scale marked in both millimetres and centimetres. In this exercise we will look at reading from the scale of some measuring instruments.

Example 1

Read the following ruler measurements:

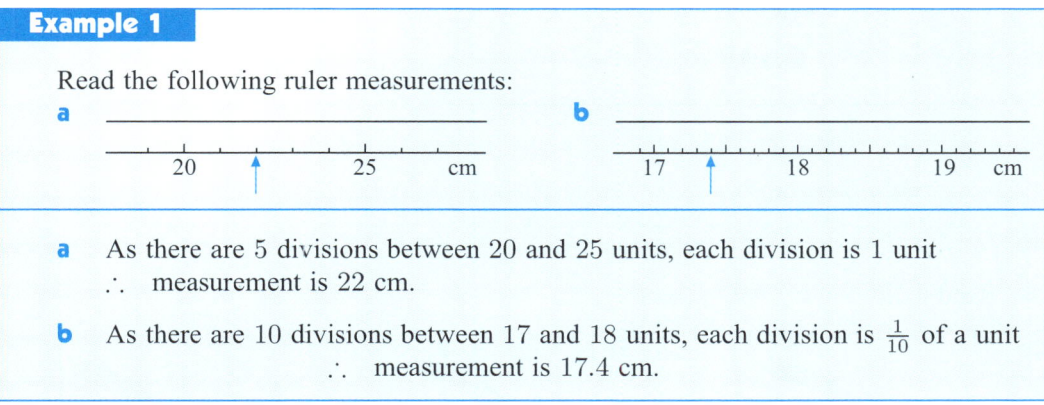

a   As there are 5 divisions between 20 and 25 units, each division is 1 unit
    ∴ measurement is 22 cm.

b   As there are 10 divisions between 17 and 18 units, each division is $\frac{1}{10}$ of a unit
    ∴ measurement is 17.4 cm.

EXERCISE 7B

1 Read the following ruler measurements (in cm):

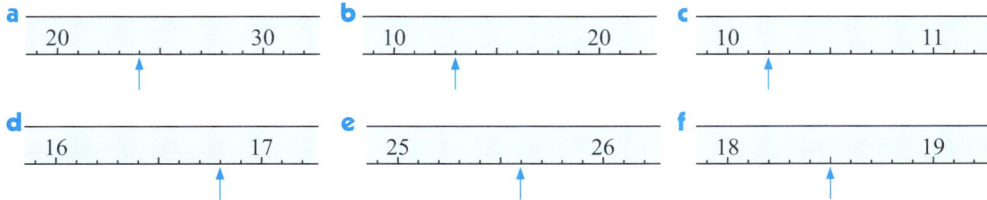

Example 2

Read the temperature on the following centigrade thermometer:

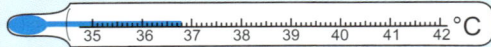

As there are 10 divisions between 36°C and 37°C, each division is 0.1°C
∴ temperature is 36.8°C.

2 Read the temperature (in °C) for the following thermometers:

a 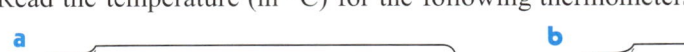   **b**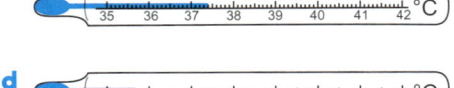

c 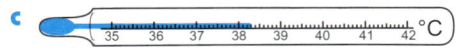   **d**

Example 3

Read as accurately as possible the measurement for:
a the fuel gauge   **b** the speedometer

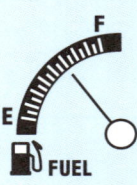   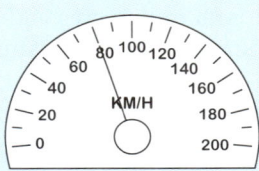

a There are eight main divisions from empty to full ∴ $\tfrac{5}{8}$ full.
b Speed is 80 km/h.

3 Read the following fuel gauges:

a    **b**    **c**

4 Find as accurately as possible the speeds for the following:

a 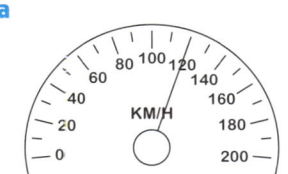   **b** 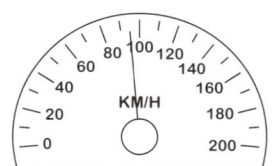   **c**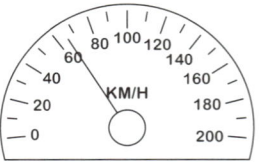

5 Find the weights, in kilograms, shown by the following bathroom scales:

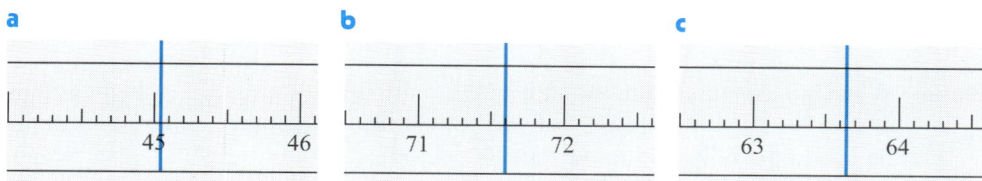

Example 4

Find the quantity of electricity (in kilowatt hours, kWh) used as shown by the meter:

If the meter reads between the numbers, use the smaller number.

The quantity of electricity used is 26 593 kWh.

6 Find the quantity of electricity used as shown by the following meters:

7 Find the mass (in grams) on the following scales:

8 Find the quantity of fluid (in mL) in the following jugs:

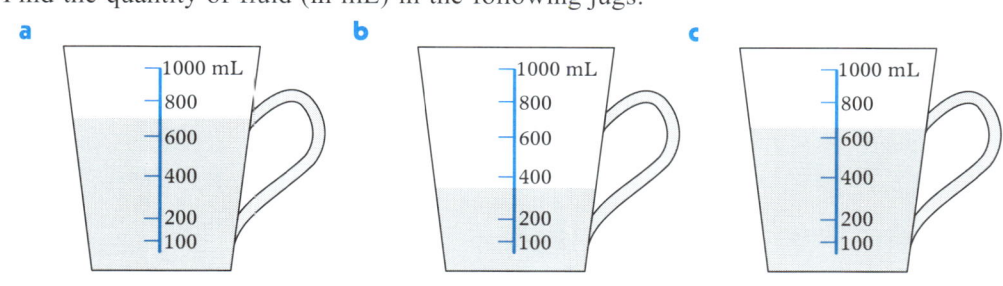

C LENGTH CONVERSIONS

Note: When we convert from one unit to a smaller unit, there will be more smaller units and so we must multiply. When we convert from one unit to a larger unit, there will be less larger units and so we must divide.

CONVERSION DIAGRAM

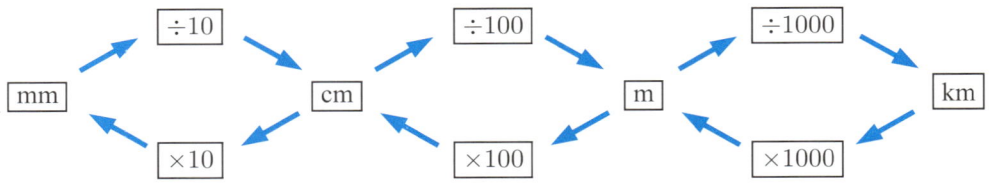

Example 5

Write the following in metres:
- **a** 640 cm
- **b** 3.8 km
- **c** 7560 mm

a 640 cm to m
smaller unit to larger
∴ divide

640 cm
= 640 ÷ 100 m
= 6.4 m

b 3.8 km to m
larger unit to smaller
∴ multiply

3.8 km
= 3.8 × 1000 m
= 3800 m

c 7560 mm to m
smaller unit to larger
∴ divide

7560 mm
= 7560 ÷ 1000 m
= 7.56 m

EXERCISE 7C

1 Convert these metres into centimetres:
- **a** 4
- **b** 34
- **c** 2.5
- **d** 15.6
- **e** 2.45
- **f** 0.46

2 Convert these metres into millimetres:
- **a** 3
- **b** 45
- **c** 3.6
- **d** 16.2
- **e** 5.46
- **f** 0.09

3 Convert these centimetres into millimetres:
- **a** 5
- **b** 23
- **c** 2.7
- **d** 12.5
- **e** 5.78
- **f** 0.25

4 Convert these centimetres into metres:
- **a** 200
- **b** 3000
- **c** 35
- **d** 950.5
- **e** 28 492
- **f** 0.4

5 Convert these millimetres into centimetres:
- **a** 20
- **b** 400
- **c** 450
- **d** 45.6
- **e** 7500
- **f** 0.3

6 Convert these kilometres into metres:
- **a** 3
- **b** 75
- **c** 6.5
- **d** 2000
- **e** 78.2
- **f** 0.2

7 Convert these metres into kilometres:
   a 2000   **b** 35 000   **c** 234.5   **d** 34 567   **e** 3900   **f** 2.4

8 Write the following in metres:
   a 920 cm   **b** 643 cm   **c** 4753 cm   **d** 5000 mm
   e 9743 mm   **f** 13 500 mm   **g** 6.2 km   **h** 13.5 km

9 Write the following in centimetres:
   a 720 m   **b** 13.8 m   **c** 6.3 m   **d** 134 mm
   e 85 mm   **f** 1328 mm   **g** 5.2 km   **h** 0.43 km

10 Write the following in millimetres:
   a 7 m   **b** 3.4 cm   **c** 78 cm   **d** 0.46 m

11 Write the following in kilometres:
   a 4562 m   **b** 17 458 m   **c** 653 000 cm   **d** 16 400 cm

12 For the following lines:
   i estimate the length
   ii using a ruler, measure the length to the nearest mm.
   iii What was the error in your estimation?

13 Convert all lengths to metres and then add:
- **a** 3 km + 110 m + 32 cm
- **b** 72 km + 43 m + 47 cm + 16 mm
- **c** 153 m + 217 cm + 48 mm
- **d** 15 km + 348 m + 63 cm + 97 mm
- **e** 23 m + 47 cm + 338 mm
- **f** 23 km + 76 m + 318 cm + 726 mm

14 Write the following in the same units and then put in ascending order:
- **a** 37 mm, 4 cm
- **b** 750 cm, 8 m, 7800 mm
- **c** 1250 m, 1.3 km
- **d** 0.005 km, 485 cm, 5.2 m
- **e** 3500 mm, 347 cm, 3.6 m
- **f** 0.134 km, 128 m, 13 000 cm
- **g** 4.82 m, 512 cm, 4900 mm
- **h** 72 m, 7150 cm, 71 800 mm

ACTIVITY YOU AND YOUR SHADOW

What to do:

1 Over a long period of time (ideally 3 to 4 months) measure the length of your shadow on the same day, once a week, at the same place and the same time. For example: at midday on Wednesday outside your classroom, with a partner to help you, would be ideal. Use a ruler or a tape measure.

2 Each shadow length that is measured should be plotted on a graph or made into a bar graph.

3 **a** What was the length of the shadow at its:
   i longest   **ii** shortest?
  b When did the shadows begin to:
   i lengthen   **ii** shorten?
   Why did this happen?
  c What difficulties did you come across with your measurements?
  d What did you notice about the position of your shadow?

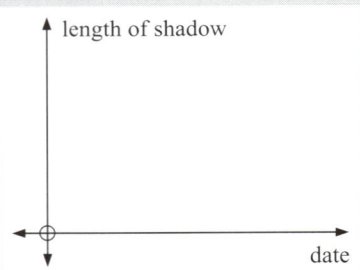

ACTIVITY HEIGHT OF STUDENTS

What to do:

1 At the beginning of the year draw up separate tables for the height of each student in the class.
2 Each term measure and record each student's height.
3 Compare the growth over a term and the whole year.
4 Draw graphs comparing individual and class growth.
5 Calculate the average heights and compare them.
6 Calculate the percentage growth for the term, for the year, for individuals or for the class.

7 Compare the percentage growth between boys and girls.

8 Discuss these results as part of Growth and Development or Health lessons.

D PERIMETER

The **perimeter** of a closed figure is a measurement of the distance around the boundary of the figure.

*The word **perimeter** is also used to describe the boundary of a closed figure.*

If the figure has straight sides, it is a **polygon** and the perimeter is found by adding the lengths of the sides.

The rules for very common simple shapes are as follows:

In figures, sides having the same markings show equal lengths.

Triangle

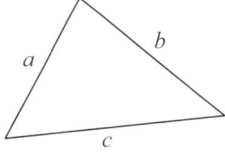

$P = a + b + c$

Square

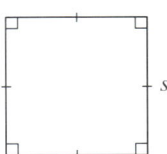

$P = 4 \times s$
$[P = 4 \times \text{side length}]$

Rectangle

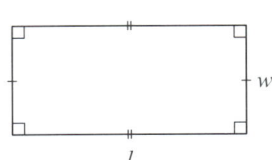

$P = (l + w) \times 2$
$[P = (\text{length} + \text{width}) \times 2]$

Example 6

Find the perimeter of:

a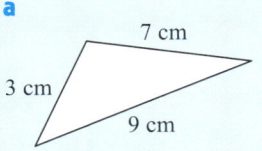

b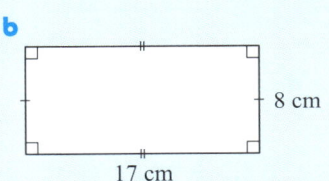

a Perimeter $= 3 + 7 + 9$ cm
$= 19$ cm

b $P = (8 + 17) \times 2$ cm
$= 25 \times 2$ cm
$= 50$ cm

EXERCISE 7D

1   **i**   Estimate the perimeter of each figure.
     ii   Check your estimate with a ruler.

a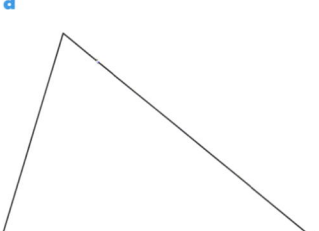

b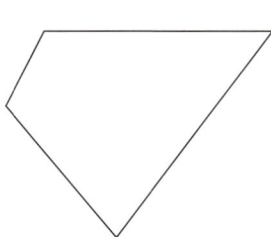

c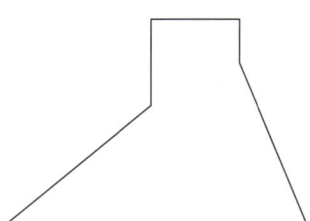

2 Find the perimeter of each of the following triangles:

a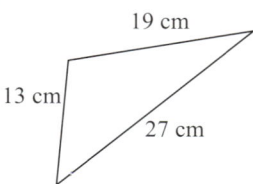

b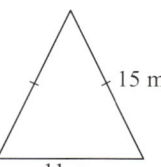

c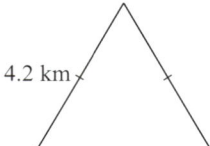

3 Find the perimeter of:

a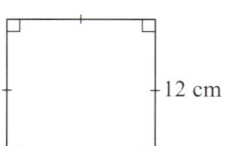

b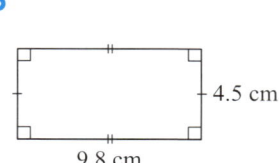

c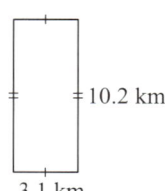

4 Find the perimeter of:

a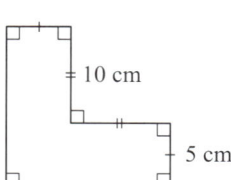

b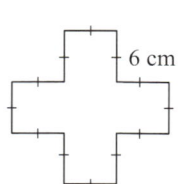

c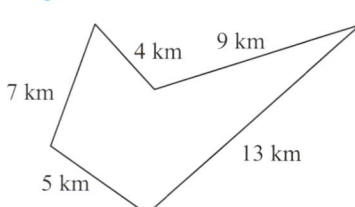

d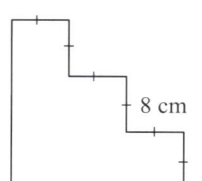

e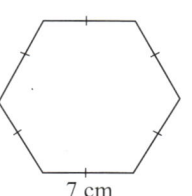

f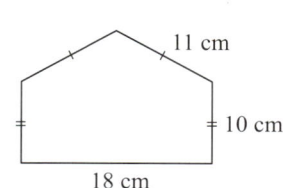

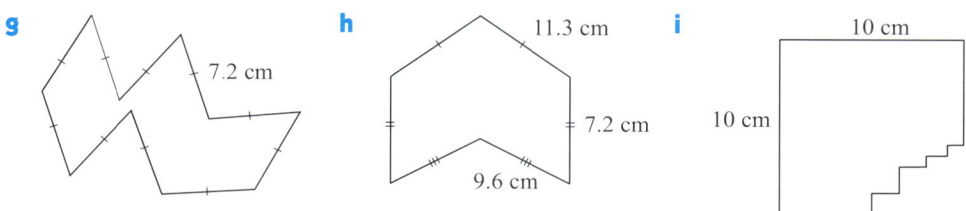

5 Use a piece of string to find the perimeter of the following:

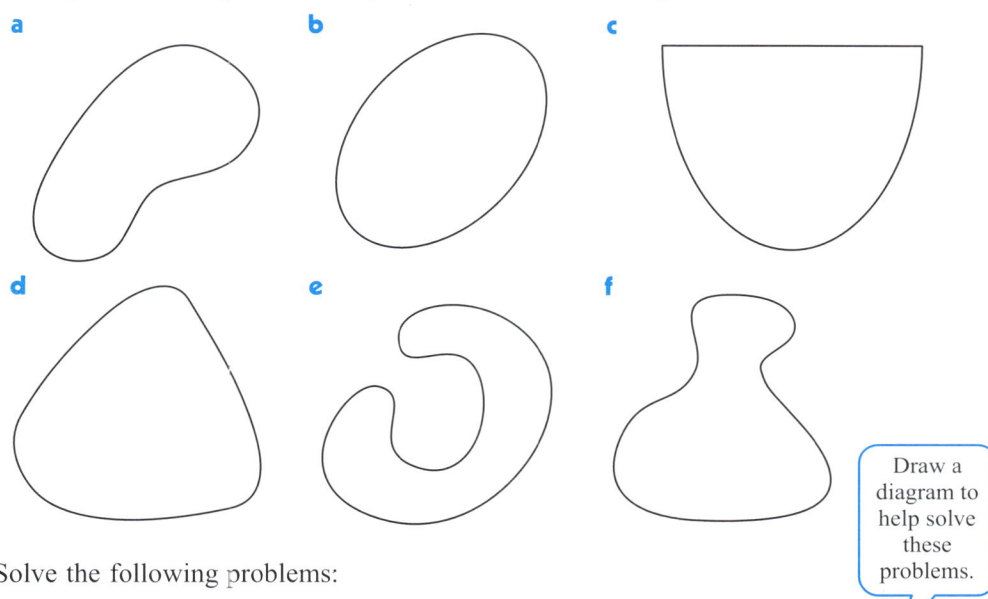

6 Solve the following problems:

a A rectangular paddock 120 m by 260 m is to be fenced. Find the length of the fence.

b How far will a runner travel if he runs 5 times around a triangular block with sides 320 m, 480 m and 610 m?

c Find the cost of fencing a square block of land with side length 75 m if the fence costs $14.50 per metre.

Draw a diagram to help solve these problems.

7 **a** What is the perimeter of an equilateral triangle with 35.5 mm sides?

b If the perimeter of a regular pentagon is 1.35 metres, what is the length of one side?

c One half of the perimeter of a regular hexagon is 57 metres. What is the length of one of its sides?

d One third of the sum of the lengths of sides of a regular dodecagon is 39 centimetres. What is its perimeter?

e The perimeter of 2 identical regular octagons joined equally along one side is 98 cm. What is their combined perimeter when they are separated?

8 **a** Find the length of the sides of a square with perimeter 56 cm.

b Find the length of the sides of a rhombus which has a perimeter of 72 metres.

9 A rectangle has a length of 18 cm and a perimeter of 66 cm. What is the rectangle's width?

ACTIVITY — FUN WITH PERIMETERS

What to do:

1. Use your shoe length or 'paces' to calculate the perimeter of your school hall, netball or tennis courts.

2. Combine with 3 classmates to form a chain by joining your arms. Use chain lengths to measure perimeter. Add extra class mates to your chain. What happens to your measurement when you add another 2, 4 or 6 classmates?

What determines the maximum chain length you can create with your class? Try it.

SPREADSHEET — PERIMETERS OF RECTANGLES

Below is an exercise using a spreadsheet to calculate the perimeter of a rectangle.

What to do:

1. Open a new spreadsheet and type in the following:

	A	B
1	Length	10
2	Width	6
3	Perimeter	=2*(B1+B2)

This formula calculates the perimeter given the length and width.

2. Try different values of the length and width and observe the changing value of the perimeter.

3. Set the length as 11.39 and experiment with the width until the perimeter is 32.

4.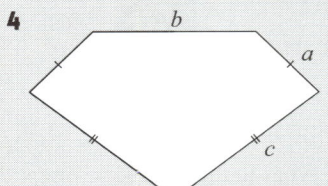

Jani makes thousands of satin pieces of the given shape. She sews lace around the edge of each piece.

Construct a spreadsheet for the perimeter of this shape, so that when the values of a, b and c are changed, the length of the lace edging required will be immediately calculated.

ACTIVITY — TRUNDLE WHEEL

A trundle wheel is an instrument used for measuring distances. It consists of a wheel on a handle and a "clicker" which counts the number of revolutions of the wheel.

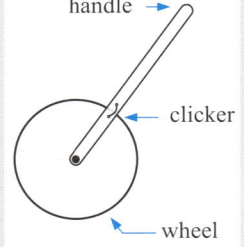

What to do:

1. Make a trundle wheel of circumference 1 metre. You will need to work out the radius of the wheel using the formula

radius = circumference ÷ 6.283   and a calculator.

2 Use your trundle wheel to measure objects around your school, for example, distance around the oval, length of a school building, length of a tennis court, perimeter of a tennis court, length of fence of the school.

3 How much error would there be in your measurement of a kilometre if your trundle wheel had a radius which was:
   a 5 cm too small   **b** 5 cm too large?

Extension:

4 For each centimetre error in the radius of the trundle wheel, what error occurs in the circumference of the wheel?

THE CIRCLE

Click on the icon for printable pages on the circumference of a circle and how it is measured from knowing its diameter or radius.

PRINTABLE MATERIAL

E   SCALE DIAGRAMS

A **scale diagram** is a drawing or plan which shows the original either smaller or larger while keeping the proportions the same.

The best examples of scale diagrams are architects' plans and maps.

For consistency, we say the scale is the ratio
scale length : actual length.

This ratio is used to avoid confusion as, for example, 5 : 3 is not the same as 3 : 5.

Example 7

If the scale is 1 : 20, find the:
a actual length if the scale length is 3.4 cm
b scale length if the actual length is 1.2 m.

a scale is 1 : 20   ∴ actual length = 20 × scale length
                                         = 20 × 3.4 cm
                                         = 68 cm

b scale is 1 : 20   ∴ scale length = actual length ÷ 20
                                        = 1.2 m ÷ 20
                                        = 120 ÷ 20 cm
                                        = 6 cm

MAP SCALE

Map scales are often given by diagrams.

For example:

From this diagram we can write the scale in ratio form. As the length of the line segment is 10 cm, we can write:

$$\begin{aligned}\text{scale} &= 10 \text{ cm} : 25 \text{ km} \\ &= 10 \text{ cm} : 25 \times 1000 \times 100 \text{ cm} \\ &= 10 : 2\,500\,000 \\ &= 1 : 250\,000 \end{aligned}$$

EXERCISE 7E

1 For the following scales, find if the drawing or the actual object is larger:
  a 1 : 500   **b** 3 : 1   **c** 2 : 5   **d** 1 : 4   **e** 1 : 10 000

2 Find the scale if:
  a an aeroplane has wingspan 50 m and the diagram is 50 cm
  b a truck is 15 m long and the diagram has length 12 cm
  c a bacterium has body length 0.5 mm and the diagram has length 10 cm.

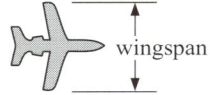

3 Find the actual length for a scale length of 5 cm if the scale is:
  a 1 : 50   **b** 1 : 2000   **c** 1 : 10 000   **d** 1 : 5 000 000

4 If the scale is 1 : 5000, find:
  a the actual length if the scale length is
    i 4 cm   **ii** 5.8 cm   **iii** 2.4 cm   **iv** 12.6 cm
  b the scale length if the actual length is
    i 500 m   **ii** 175 m   **iii** 20 m   **iv** 108 m

5 If the scale is 1 : 200, find:
  a the actual length if the scale length is
    i 3 cm   **ii** 4.5 cm   **iii** 8.2 cm   **iv** 0.8 cm
  b the scale length if the actual length is
    i 200 m   **ii** 18 m   **iii** 5.6 m   **iv** 12.2 m

6 The drawing of a gate alongside has a scale of 1 : 100. Find:
  a the width of the gate
  b the height of the gate
  c the length of the diagonal support.

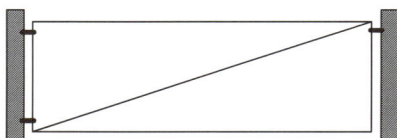

7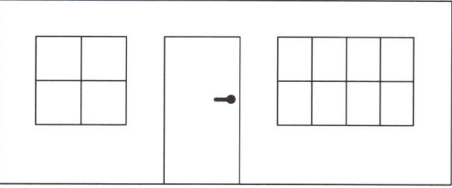

If the plan of a house wall alongside has been drawn with a scale of 1 : 200, find:
- **a** the length of the wall
- **b** the height of the wall
- **c** the measurements of the door
- **d** the measurements of the windows.

8 For the truck alongside, find:
- **a** the actual length of the truck
- **b** the maximum height of the truck.

(Scale 1 : 100)

9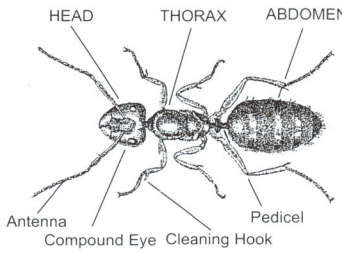

Real length = 5 mm

- **a** Measure the length of the body of the ant and determine the scale for the diagram.
- **b** Using the scale calculated in **a**, find the length of:
  - **i** the antenna
  - **ii** the abdomen
  - **iii** the thorax
  - **iv** the head.

10
- **a** Measure the length of the body of the dragonfly and find the scale for the diagram.
- **b** Using the scale in **a**, find:
  - **i** the length of the head
  - **ii** the wingspan
  - **iii** the greatest width of the rear wing.

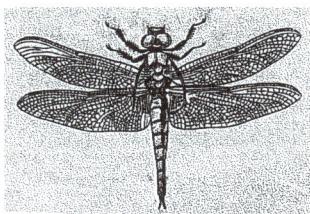

(Real length = 50 mm)

11 Using the scale shown on the map, find:
- **a** the actual distance shown by 1 cm
- **b** the map distance required for an actual distance of 200 km
- **c** the distance from
  - **i** A to B
  - **ii** D to E
  - **iii** C to F.

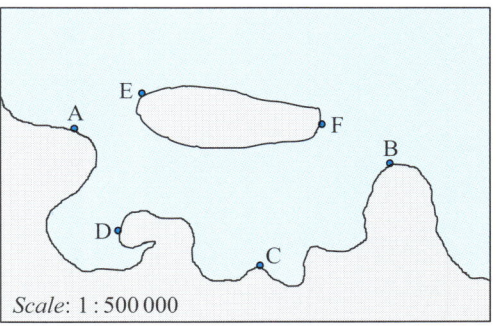

Scale: 1 : 500 000

12 You have to draw an accurate scale diagram of an 85 m × 73 m × 58 m triangular building block to fit within a 10 cm by 10 cm square.
  a What scale would you choose?
  b How would you draw the diagram accurately?

13 Using the measurements on the given rough sketch and a scale of 1 cm represents 2 m, draw an accurate scale diagram.

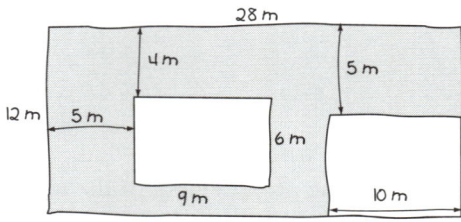

14

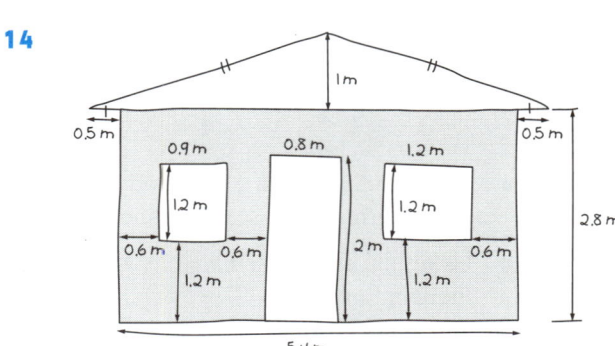

One view of a house is seen on the given rough sketch. Using a scale of 1 : 100 draw an accurate scale diagram of this view.

15 The scale diagram given is of a new house and the scale is 1 : 250.

  a Find the internal measurements of bedroom 2.
  b Find the actual dimensions of the porch.
  c Find the dimensions of the rumpus room and on a larger sketch mark your measurements.
  d Determine the area of the rumpus room floor in m^2.
  e Determine the cost of tiling the rumpus room floor at $47.50 per square metre.

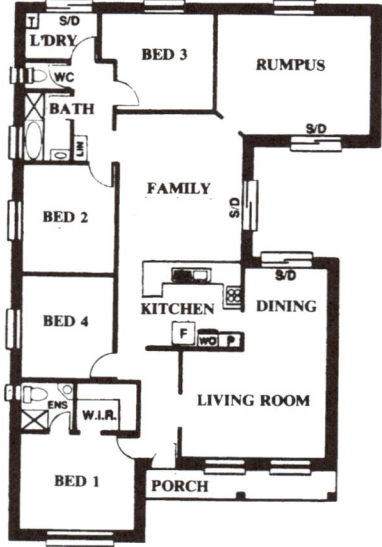

MASS

The **mass** of an object is the amount of matter it contains.

In everyday use the terms mass and weight are interchanged. In fact, they have different meaning. The mass of an object is constant, i.e., it is the same no matter where the object is, whilst the weight varies as the force due to gravity exerted on the object. For example, an object will have less weight on the moon than on the earth although the mass remains the same.

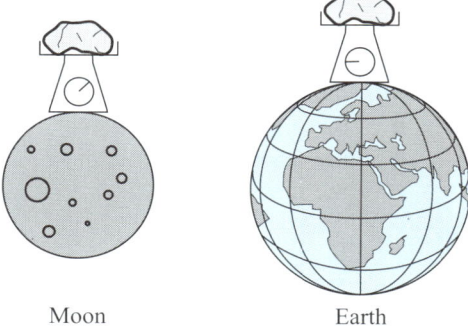

Moon   Earth

The **kilogram** (kg) is the base unit of mass in the metric system. Other units of mass which are commonly used are the milligram (mg), gram (g) and tonne (t).

$$1 \text{ g} = 1000 \text{ mg}$$
$$1 \text{ kg} = 1000 \text{ g}$$
$$1 \text{ t} = 1000 \text{ kg}$$

CONVERSION DIAGRAM FOR MASS:

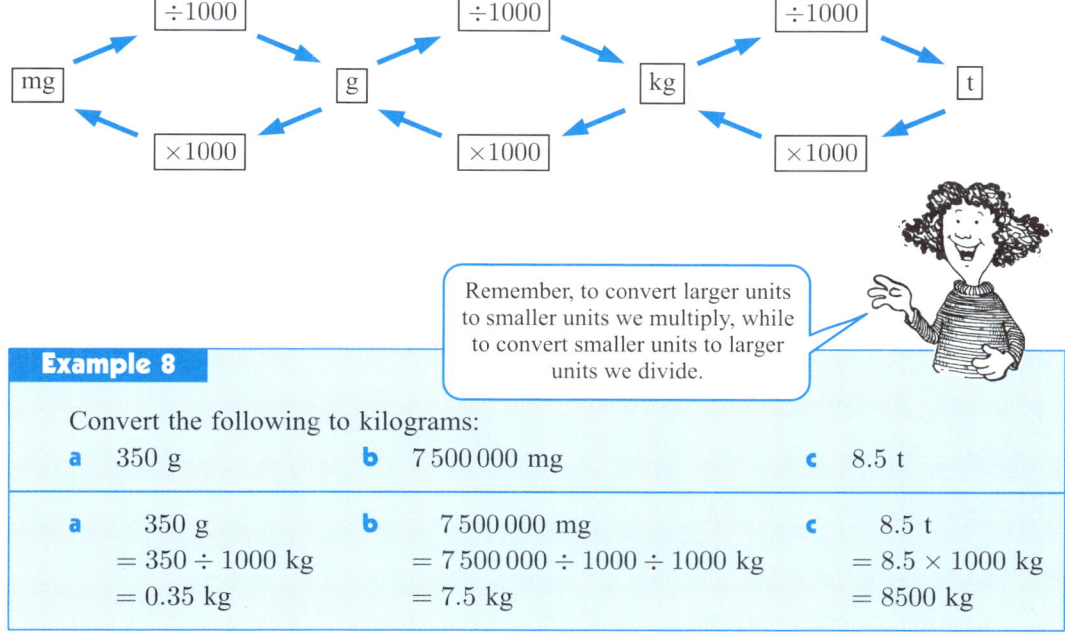

Remember, to convert larger units to smaller units we multiply, while to convert smaller units to larger units we divide.

Example 8

Convert the following to kilograms:
a 350 g
b 7 500 000 mg
c 8.5 t

a 350 g
= 350 ÷ 1000 kg
= 0.35 kg

b 7 500 000 mg
= 7 500 000 ÷ 1000 ÷ 1000 kg
= 7.5 kg

c 8.5 t
= 8.5 × 1000 kg
= 8500 kg

EXERCISE 7F

1 Give the units you would use to measure:
- **a** a person's mass
- **b** the mass of a ship
- **c** the mass of a tablet
- **d** the mass of a book
- **e** the mass of an orange
- **f** the mass of a lounge suite
- **g** the mass of a raindrop
- **h** the mass of a boulder
- **i** the mass of your school lunch
- **j** the mass of a cricket bat
- **k** the mass of a refrigerator
- **l** the mass of a dinner plate
- **m** the mass of a school ruler
- **n** the mass of a slab of concrete
- **o** the mass of a bulldozer
- **p** the mass of a leaf
- **q** the mass of a calculator
- **r** the mass of a computer
- **s** the mass of an ant
- **t** the mass of a horse

2

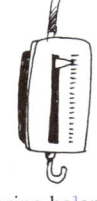

spring balance   kitchen scales   bathroom scale   weigh bridge

Which of the above devices should be used to measure the items in question **1**?

3 Convert these grams into milligrams:
- **a** 2
- **b** 34
- **c** 350
- **d** 4.5
- **e** 0.3

4 Convert these tonnes into kilograms:
- **a** 4
- **b** 25
- **c** 3.6
- **d** 294
- **e** 0.4

5 Convert these kilograms to grams:
- **a** 6
- **b** 34
- **c** 2.5
- **d** 256
- **e** 0.6

6 Convert these milligrams to grams:
- **a** 3000
- **b** 2500
- **c** 45 000
- **d** 67.5
- **e** 9.5

7 Convert these kilograms to tonnes:
- **a** 4000
- **b** 95 000
- **c** 4534
- **d** 45.6
- **e** 0.8

8 Write the following in grams:
- **a** 8 kg
- **b** 3.2 kg
- **c** 14.2 kg
- **d** 380 mg
- **e** 4250 mg
- **f** 75 420 mg
- **g** 6.8 t
- **h** 0.56 t

9 Convert the following to kilograms:
- **a** 13 870 g
- **b** 3.4 t
- **c** 786 g
- **d** 3496 mg

10 Solve the following problems:
- **a** Find the total mass, in kilograms, of 200 blocks of chocolate each 120 grams.
- **b** If a nail has mass 25 g, find the number of nails in a 5 kg packet.
- **c** Find the mass in tonnes of 15 000 bricks if each brick has a mass of 2.2 kg.

G QUALITATIVE DATA

Qualitative data is data that we cannot measure or quantify using ordinary units of measurement. It includes, for example, people's attitudes and feelings. We can record this data on a graph.

For example:

The graph alongside records how much a person enjoys playing sport and the amount of TV he/she watches.

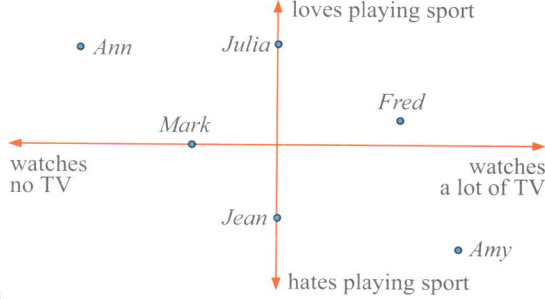

Notice that there are no numbers on the axes. However, each axis is a scale.

In this graph we can see that:

- Ann watches no TV and loves playing sport.
- Amy watches a lot of TV and hates playing sport.
- Mark watches a little TV and likes playing sport about an average amount.
- Julia and Jean both watch an average amount of TV but Julia loves playing sport while Jean dislikes it.

The problem for a person constructing this graph is to decide where a person is to be placed on it. For example, how do we decide on 'attitude to sport'? This cannot be measured or counted in the same way as a person's height or beans in a jar.

Before each person gives their two pieces of information tests might have to be made up so that they can place themselves on scales with reasonable accuracy and consistency.

EXERCISE 7G

1. The given graph shows data on people's age plotted against their attitude to Australia accepting refugees. Write a statement about:
   - **a** Ali
   - **b** Ben
   - **c** Dean
   - **d** Erica
   - **e** Rewi

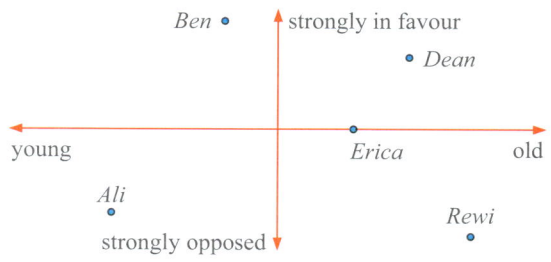

2. Six people were asked whether they were concerned about the Greenhouse Effect and how often they used public transport instead of driving their car. Write a statement about:
   - **a** Ravi
   - **b** Sally
   - **c** Tom
   - **d** Sam
   - **e** Jill
   - **f** Peter

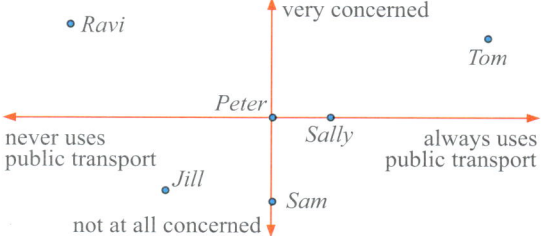

ACTIVITY   COLLECTING AND GRAPHING QUALITATIVE DATA

What to do:

1 Collect some information from your classmates on the following topic: "How good are you at mathematics and do you like mathematics?"

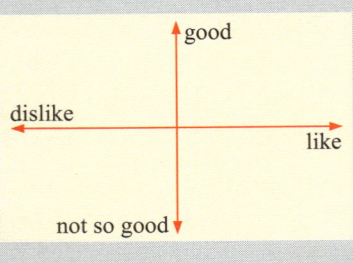

You will need to create a scale and then put your results on the graph. You might like to see if a clear pattern forms from the results.

Note: You do not have to put names on the graph; an X will do.

2 Collect information from your class on the following: "Do people who use computers a lot like sport?"

Plot a graph of your results.

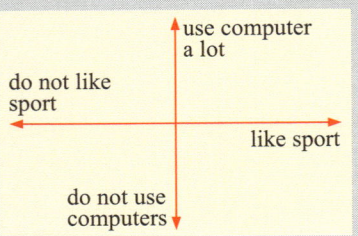

H PROBLEM SOLVING WITH LENGTH AND MASS

Example 9

A cattle run is to be built in the shape shown. The run has 4 wooden rails and a post every 2 m.
- **a** Find the total length of wooden rails required.
- **b** Find the number of posts required.
- **c** If the rails cost $3.80 per metre and each post costs $12, find the total cost of building the run.

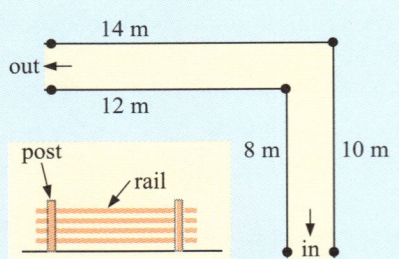

a Total length of rails $= 4 \times (14 + 10 + 12 + 8)$ m
$= 176$ m

b Number of posts for longer fence $= (14 + 10) \div 2$
$= 12$
One post needed at start and finish $\therefore$ need 13 posts.

Number of posts for shorter fence $= (12 + 8) \div 2 = 10$
One post needed at start and finish $\therefore$ need 11 posts.
$\therefore$ $13 + 11 = 24$ posts are needed.

c Total cost $=$ cost of rails $+$ cost of posts
$= 176 \times \$3.80 + 24 \times \$12$
$= \$956.80$

When trying to solve a problem given to you in words the following series of steps are advisable:

Step 1: Draw a reasonably large diagram (or diagrams) of the described situation.
Step 2: Make sure all dimensions and other key features are marked on your diagrams.
Step 3: Think about what the question is asking and the units you will have to work in.
Step 4: Set out your answer in a clear and logical fashion.
Step 5: Write your final answer in a sentence.

EXERCISE 7H

1. A farmer fences a 250 m by 400 m rectangular paddock with a 3 strand wire fence.
   a Find the total length of wire needed.
   b Find the cost of the wire if wire costs $2.40 per metre.

   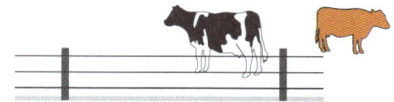

2. a A house owner has a block of land 30 m by 75 m (30 m across the back). If he wishes to fence two sides and the back of the block, what is the total length of the fence needed?

   b If the fence is to be made of "Good Neighbour" panelling which comes in sheets 2 m wide costing $18.50, what will be the cost of the fence?

3.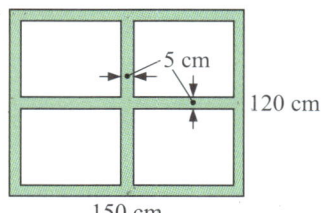

   A carpenter has to make a window frame with the dimensions shown. What is the total length of timber he requires?

4. A bowling club is to have a brush fence placed around the outside of its property.

   a If the property has dimensions as shown, find the total length of the fence.
   b If the brush costs $13.50 for a metre of the fence, find the total cost.

   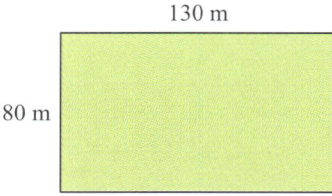

5. A supermarket buys cartons of canned peaches. Each carton contains 12 cans and each can weighs 825 g. Find the mass in kilograms of a carton of peaches.

6. A bale of lucerne hay weighs approximately 21 kg.
   a Find the approximate mass carried by a truck which is loaded with 36 bales of lucerne.
   b Is it carrying more or less than half a tonne? Show your working.

Example 10

A vineyard owner wishes to fence his 700 m by 350 m property. He needs a post every 5 metres.
- **a** Find the number of posts required.
- **b** If each post has a mass of 25 kg, find the total mass of the posts.
- **c** If the farmer has a trailer which can carry at most 2.5 tonnes, how many trailer loads of posts will he need?

a Total length of fence $= 2 \times (700 + 350)$
$= 2100$ m

$\therefore$ number of posts $= \dfrac{2100}{5}$
$= 420$

b Total mass of posts $= 420 \times 25$ kg
$= 10\,500$ kg
$= 10.5$ tonnes

c Number of trailer loads $= \dfrac{10.5}{2.5} = 4.2$

$\therefore$ needs 5 trailer loads of posts.

---

7 a Henry edges his garden with railway sleepers. If his garden has two plots as shown, find the total length of sleepers required.

b If each sleeper is 2 m long and weighs 40 kg, find:
  - **i** the total number of sleepers needed
  - **ii** the total mass of sleepers.

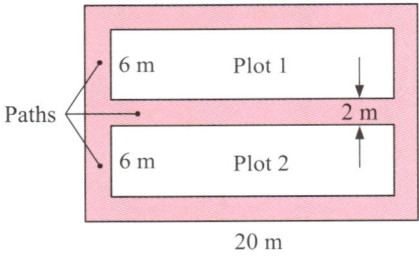

8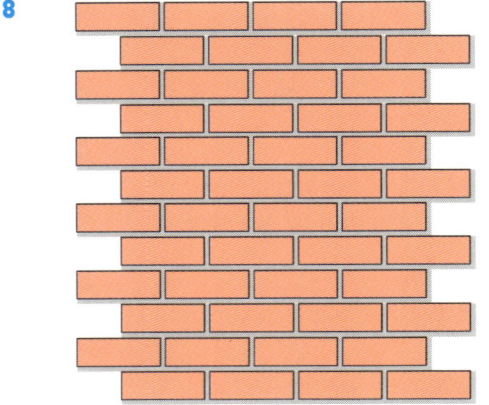

a A house-proud couple wish to build a brick fence along the 60 m front of their block of land. If they want 12 rows of bricks and each brick is 20 cm long, find the number of bricks required.

b If each brick weighs 2.5 kg, find the total mass in tonnes of the bricks needed.

9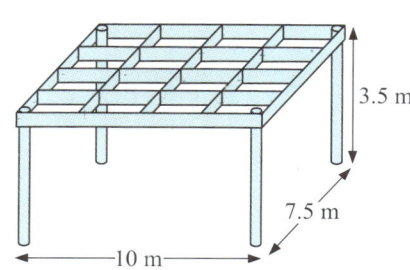

A builder needs to construct a pergola with the dimensions as shown. The support posts cost $15 per metre and the timber for the top costs $4.50 per metre.

a   Find the total length of timber for the top and hence the cost of this timber.

b   Find the cost of the posts.

c   Find the total cost of building the frame for the pergola if nails etc. cost $27.

10 A fish tank weighs 25 kg when empty and 253 kg when full of water. How many litres of water have been added to the tank? (1 litre of water has a mass of 1 kilogram.)

11 A type of paving brick weighs 4.4 kg.

a   Katy needs 900 of them to pave her courtyard. What is their total mass in   i   kg   ii   tonnes?

b   If Katy's trailer can carry at most 1 tonne, how many trips does she need to get the bricks home?

12 A tree trunk weighs 3.2 tonnes and can be cut into 80 planks. What is the mass of each plank?

13 A 30 m picket fence, as shown, is to be built. There is a 2 m post every 2 m, to which the rails are attached. If the timber for the pickets costs $1.80 per metre, for the rails costs $2.50 per metre and for the posts costs $4.50 per metre, find:

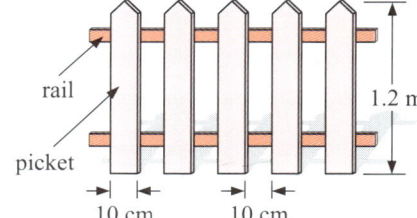

a   the number of posts and hence the total length of timber required for the posts

b   the total length of rails needed

c   the number of pickets needed and the length of timber needed to make these pickets

d   the total cost of the fence.

14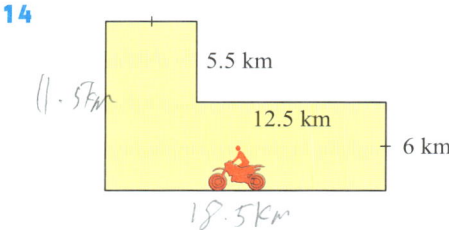

A grazier has a property with the dimensions illustrated. One of the farmhands is asked to check the fence on his motorbike. If he can travel at 15 km/h, how long will it take him to check the whole fence?

15 a   Using the scale diagram alongside, find the total length of timber required to make the gate frame shown.

b   If the timber costs $4.50 per metre, find the total cost of the timber used.

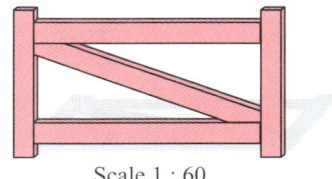

Scale 1 : 60

16 **a** Allowing 20 cm for a bow, what is the least amount of ribbon needed to tie around a cube shaped box like this?

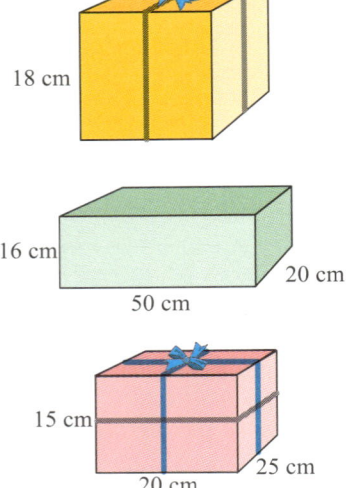

b If you need 10 cm to tie a knot, what is the least amount of string you would need to tie round both the length and width of this rectangular box?

c If you allow 20 cm for a bow, what is the least amount of ribbon you would need to tie around this rectangular box as shown?

ACTIVITY — MEASUREMENT MESSAGE

For each metric measurement given in the first column, match it with the item in the second column which would best be measured in that unit. Transfer the letter to the table below to find the message.

PRINTABLE WORKSHEET

1	mm
2	cm
3	m
4	km
5	mm²
6	cm²
7	m²
8	hectare
9	mm³
10	cm³
11	m³
12	mL
13	L
14	ML
15	second
16	minute
17	hour
18	day
19	year
20	g
21	kg
22	t

N	your age
C	how long between meals
U	how long until the weekend
S	the volume of a small teaspoon of sand
R	the time to spell your name
I	the volume of a block of chocolate
M	the capacity of a can of softdrink
M	the area of a small toenail
F	the length of an ant
S	the mass of a train
N	the volume of a truckload of soil
K	the area of a paddock
I	the mass of your pencil
E	the capacity of a bucket
R	the area of your driveway
T	the capacity of a lake
T	your own mass
A	the area of a handkerchief
L	the distance from home to school
I	the time to swim 1500 m
U	the length of a pencil
L	the width of your house

1	2	3	4	5	6	7	8	9	10	11	12	13	14	15	16	17	18	19	20	21	22

ACTIVITY   MATHEMATICS EXHIBITION

A maker of mathematical games wants to exhibit his products using the theme of **regular polygons**. He plans to hire some parkland space near a shopping centre.

Within a circle of 50 metre radius, he plans to measure out an equilateral triangle, a square, a pentagon and a hexagon with 5 metre long sides. At the vertices of each of these shapes he plans to hammer an upright 1.4 m long wooden stake. He also plans to set out an octagon, a decagon and a dodecagon with 4 metre long sides and again hammer in stakes in each of the vertices. Each of his regular polygons will be separated from one another. Around the boundary of the circle he plans to place stakes every 5 metres. To make each of the shapes stand out he plans to hang bunting along the boundaries of the shapes. He also plans to have bunting around the circle.

What to do: Answer the following questions.

1. How much bunting will he need for the exhibition?
2. How many stakes will he need?
3. If the stakes were laid end to end in a straight line, how far would they stretch?
4. If bunting is $1.80 a metre and stakes are $1.30 each, how much will he need to spend to set up his exhibition?
5. What is the total mass of the stakes if one weighs 450 g?

REVIEW SET A   CHAPTER 7

1. Convert:
   - **a** 356 cm to mm
   - **b** 3200 g to kg
   - **c** 450 m to km
   - **d** 83 000 kg to t
   - **e** 7.63 m to mm
   - **f** 630 cm to m

2. Find the perimeter of:

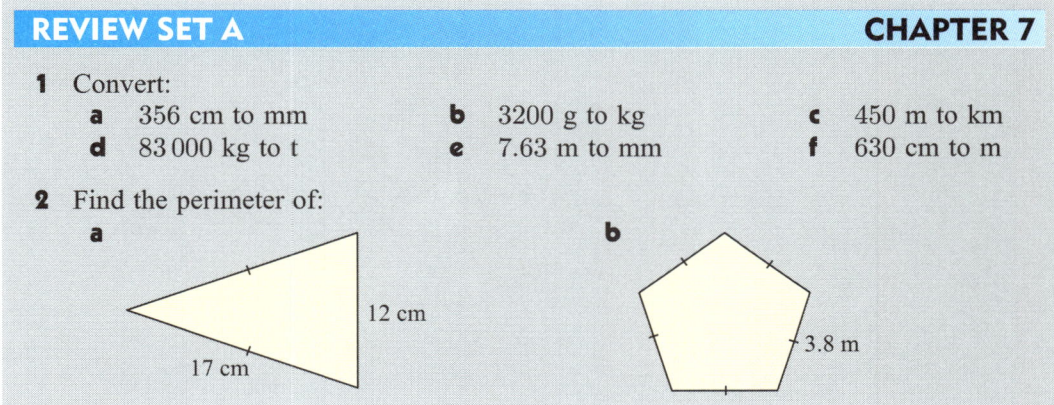

3 Read the following scales:

a 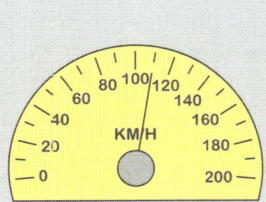   b 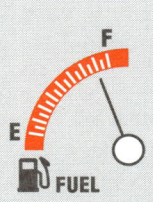   c (measuring jug showing 2000 mL and 1000 mL markings)

4 If the scale is $1 : 500\,000$ determine:
   a the actual length if the scale length is
      i 3.8 cm   **ii** 6.4 cm   **iii** 12.2 cm
   b the scale length if the actual length is
      i 50 km   **ii** 22 km   **iii** 130 km

5 Kym competes in the 200 metre, 400 metre, 800 metre, 1500 metre and 5000 metre running events on sports day. How many kilometres does she run?

6 a Find the total mass in kg of 1500 oranges if the average mass of an orange is 180 g.

b If a truck can carry 1400 kg of soil, how many truckloads will be needed to remove 42 tonnes of soil?

REVIEW SET B   CHAPTER 7

1 Convert:
   a 3480 g to kg   **b** 8623 mm to m   **c** 4.6 g to mg
   d 5.4 m to cm   **e** 13.2 t to kg   **f** 13.3 km to m

2 Find the perimeter of:

a 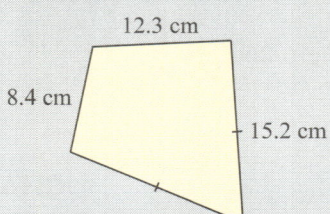   b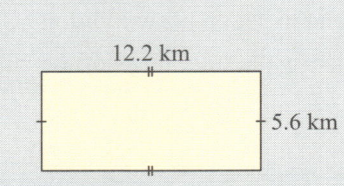

3 Read the following gauge for the amount of electricity used:

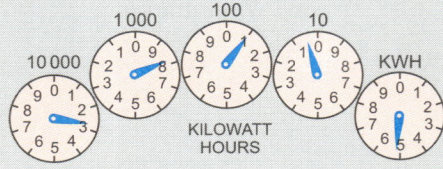

4 If a bag of nails contains 50 nails and each nail weighs 45 g, find the total weight of 100 bags of nails.

5 Read the following scales:

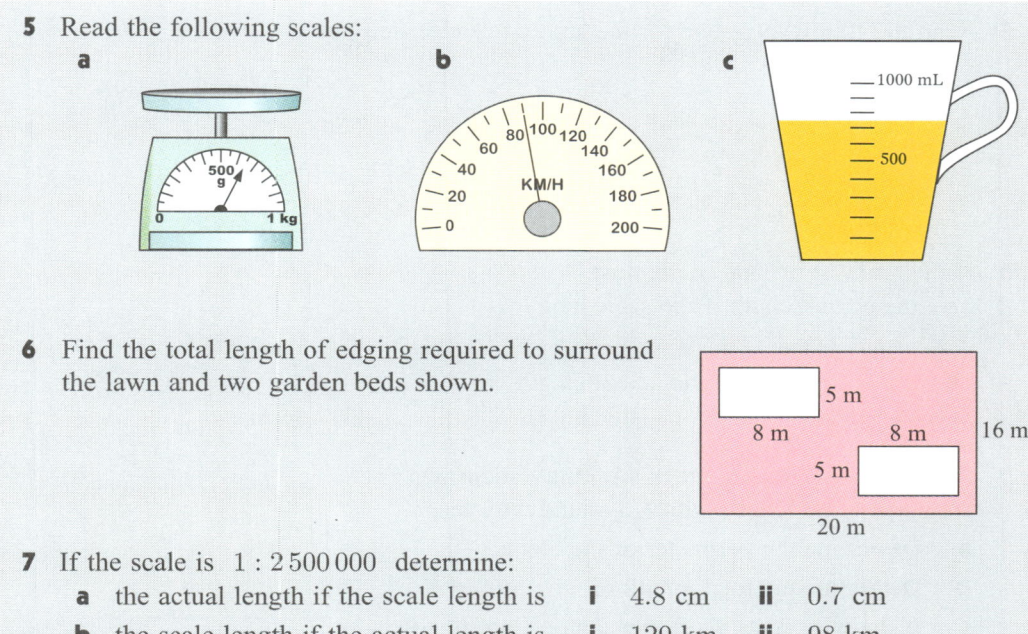

6 Find the total length of edging required to surround the lawn and two garden beds shown.

7 If the scale is $1 : 2\,500\,000$ determine:
  a the actual length if the scale length is **i** 4.8 cm **ii** 0.7 cm
  b the scale length if the actual length is **i** 120 km **ii** 98 km

REVIEW SET C   CHAPTER 7

1 Convert:
  a 324.5 cm to m   **b** 6400 mm to m   **c** 4.5 kg to g

2 Find the perimeter of:

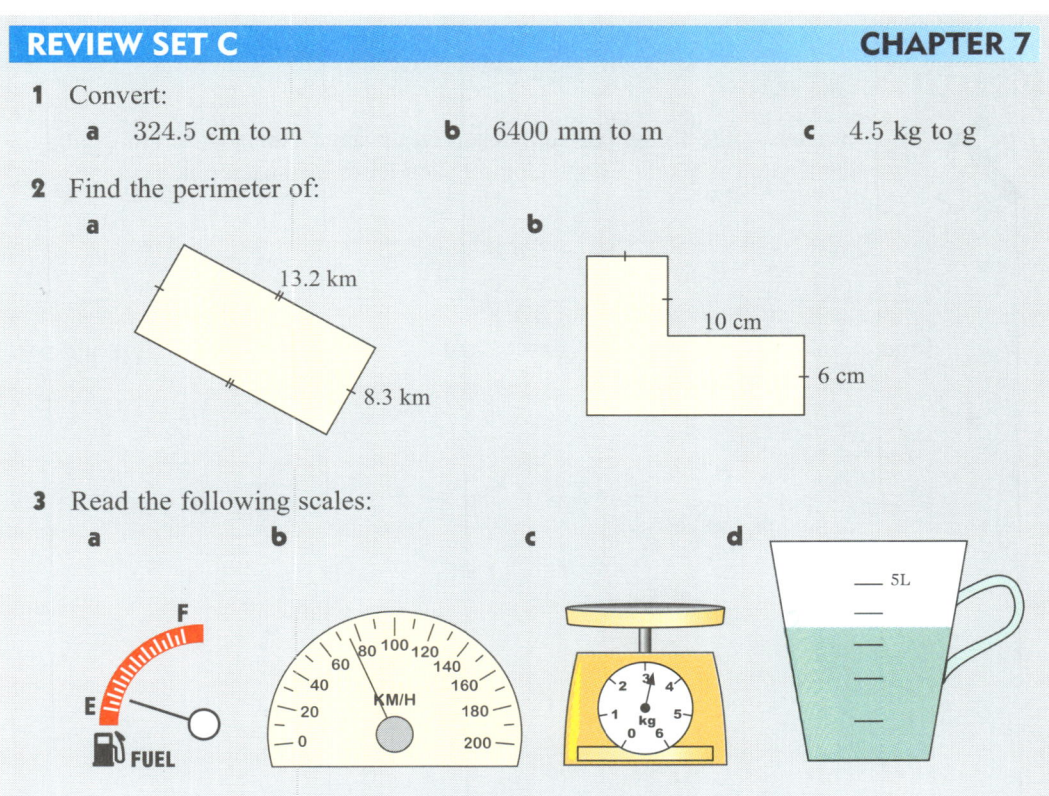

3 Read the following scales:

4 How many 1.8 kg bricks can be carried by a truck which has a maximum allowable carrying mass of 3.6 tonne?

5 Read the following gauge for the amount of electricity used:

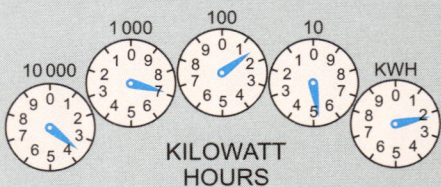

KILOWATT HOURS

6 If the scale is 1 : 500 determine:
  a the actual length if the scale length is
    i 4 cm   **ii** 3.8 cm   **iii** 1.5 cm
  b the scale length if the actual length is
    i 15 m   **ii** 8.6 m   **iii** 64 m

7 A rectangular farming block with the dimensions as shown is to be fenced with a 3-strand wire fence.
  a Determine the perimeter of the block.
  b Determine the total length of wire required.
  c If the wire costs $1.75 per metre, find the total cost of the wire.

180 m

320 m

ACTIVITY

In each of the following sums each letter stands for a different digit. See if you can work out which digit each letter is in each case.

a
```
   2 a 4
 − 1 3 c
 ───────
   1 3 8
```
Find a and c.

b
```
     d 3
   ×   e
 ───────
   3 1 8
```
Find d and e.

c
```
   2 f 4 g
 ×       9
 ─────────
   1 9 2 h 7
```
Find f, g and h.

d
```
     r r
 +   p p
 ───────
   q p q
```
Find p, q and r.

Chapter 8

Measurement (area and volume)

Knowledge, skills and understandings

By the end of this chapter you should be able to

- develop and use the formula for the area of a triangle (e.g., $A = \frac{1}{2}B \times H = B \times H \div 2$)
- use the appropriate units of measurement (e.g., km², cm², m², mm², ha)
- use appropriate strategies and devices to estimate and accurately measure the area of a shape (e.g., using an overlay grid)
- calculate the area of irregular shapes by separating them into simple parts (i.e., rectangles and triangles as below)

- demonstrate understanding of the relationship between perimeter and area through practical problem-solving activities (e.g., investigating floor plans of the classroom or sports fields)
- use scale in ratio form to calculate either original size or drawing size
- convert mL to L and L to kL
- use the symbols cm³, m³, mL, L and kL
- demonstrate understanding of volume through practical problem-solving activities
- develop and use formula for volume of rectangular prisms: $V = L \times W \times H$ or $V = L \times B \times H$
- demonstrate awareness that capacity is related to volume (e.g., through displacement activities where 1 mL = 1 cm³)

A AREA UNITS

In your school there are certain areas where you are allowed to be and others where you are not. Around the home, surfaces such as driveways, carpets, ceilings, walls and shelves are seen. All these surfaces have boundaries, that is, they are enclosed within a two-dimensional (2-D) shape.

Area is the amount of surface inside a two-dimensional shape.

Descriptions on cans of paint, insect surface spray and bags of fertiliser refer to the area they can cover. Garden sprinklers are designed to spray water over a particular surface area.

Weather forecasts refer to the 'metropolitan and southern settled areas'.

Television, radio and mobile phones have good and poor reception areas. Some spaces are 'security areas' or 'prohibited areas' or 'no parking areas'.

There are many other examples.

People need to compare or measure areas. When the same unit is used, we can measure area by comparing or counting the number of units.

EXERCISE 8A

1 Compare the area of these shapes. Which has the bigger area from each pair?

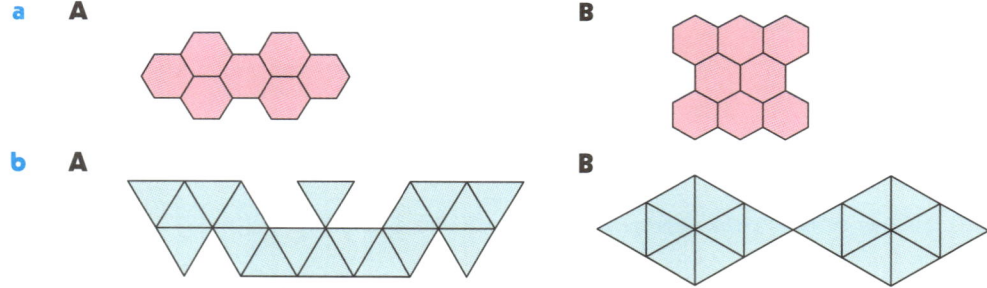

However, not all shapes have clearly outlined units of area within their boundaries. The following activities will highlight this.

ACTIVITY — TRIALLING DIFFERENT UNITS OF AREA

What to do:

1 Using each of these units of area estimate and record how many times you think each unit will fit into the shapes below.

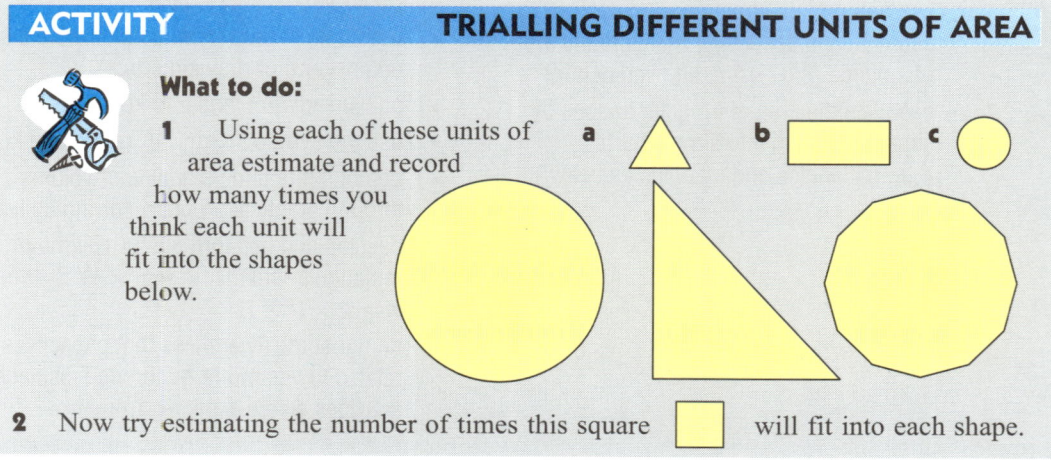

2 Now try estimating the number of times this square ▢ will fit into each shape.

3 Make several exact copies of the △ and place them side by side inside the circle.

   Carefully move the copies around inside the circle so that you can tally how many can fit. Repeat this process for the other two shapes.

4 Follow the steps in **3** and repeat them using ▭ ○ and ▢.

5 Compare your tallies with your estimates. How close were you?

6 What were the advantages or disadvantages of using each of these units to measure the area? Discuss.

EXERCISE 8A (continued)

2 Use the △ unit of area to measure the area of each of the shapes:

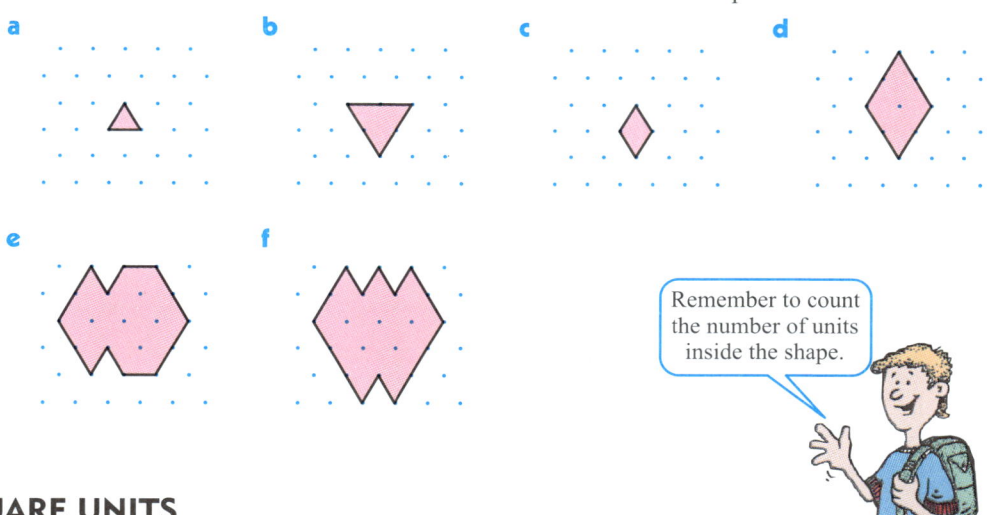

Remember to count the number of units inside the shape.

SQUARE UNITS

What made these shapes easier to measure than those in the previous activity?

As you have seen it is possible to compare area using a variety of shapes. Some shapes have advantages over others.

In the world around us, particularly in the things humans have made, the shape of the rectangle occurs almost everywhere.

To be able to compare shapes, a standard unit is required.

- The rectangle ▭ needs two measurements, its length and its width.
- The square ▢, however, has the advantage of having only one measurement.
  It has the same measurement on all 4 sides.

The square is the universal unit used to measure area.

> The **area** of a closed figure, no matter what shape, is the number of square units (unit^2 or u^2) it encloses.

3 Find the area in square units of each of the following shapes:

a 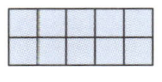 b  c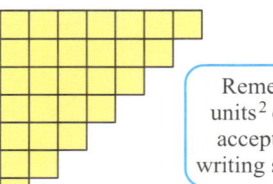

d 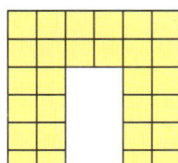 e 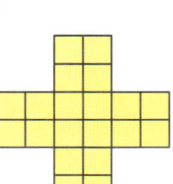 f

Remember that units² or u² is the accepted way of writing square units.

METRIC AREA UNITS

In the metric system, the units of measurement used for area are related to the units we use for length.

> 1 **square millimetre** (mm²) is the area enclosed by a square of side length 1 mm.
>
> 1 **square centimetre** (cm²) is the area enclosed by a square of side length 1 cm.
>
> 1 **square metre** (m²) is the area enclosed by a square of side length 1 m.
>
> 1 **hectare** (ha) is the area enclosed by a square of side length 100 m.
>
> 1 **square kilometre** (km²) is the area enclosed by a square of side length 1 km.

EXERCISE 8A (continued)

4 What units of area would most sensibly be used to measure the area of the following?

a the floor space in a house
b a dog's paw
c wheat grown on a farm
d carpet for a doll's house
e a freckle on your skin
f Tasmania
g micro chip for a computer
h bathroom mirror
i postage stamp
j your school grounds
k sheep station
l suburban railway station
m fingernail
n your pupil

5 a Check to see that the following shapes all have the same area.
b What is the perimeter of each?

i 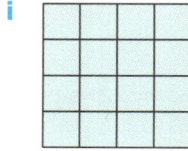 ii 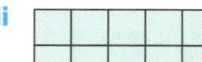 iii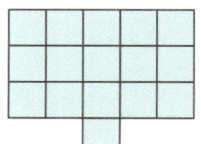

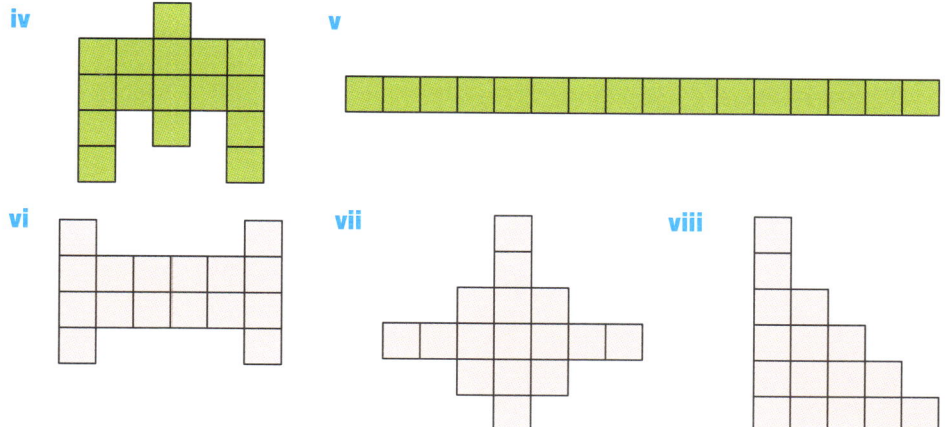

c What does this exercise tell you about the area and the perimeter of a shape?

6 In the given sketch:

  a how many tiles have been used for

    i the floor   **ii** the walls?

  (Do not forget tiles behind and under the sink cabinet and in the shower.)

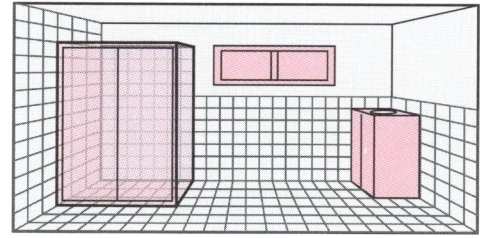

These tiles are only sold in square metre lots. There are 25 tiles for each square metre.

  b How many square metres need to be bought?

  c The tiles cost $36.90 per square metre and the tiler charges $18.00 per square metre to glue them. What is the total cost of tiling?

7 **a** In the given picture, how many pavers were used for:

    i the driveway   **ii** the patio?

  b The pavers in the patio are the same as the pavers in the driveway. If there are 50 pavers for every square metre, how many square metres of paving were laid?

  c If the cost of the pavers is $16.90 per m², and the cost of laying them is $14 per m², what is the total cost of the paving?

10 rows of 28 bricks

30 rows of 18 bricks

  d One paver is 20 cm long and 10 cm wide. How far would all the pavers used in this example stretch if they were placed:

    i end to end in a straight line   **ii** side by side in a straight line?

  e What do you notice about the answers to **d i** and **d ii**?

INVESTIGATION — AREAS OF IRREGULAR SHAPES

Have you ever thought how you could determine the area of a shape which is not regular? For example:

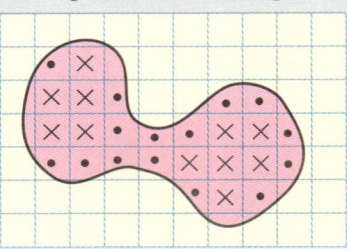
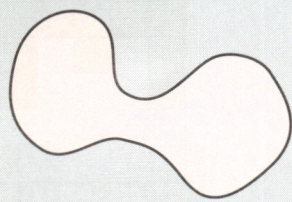

At best we can only estimate the answer, and one method of doing this is to draw grid lines across the figure.

Then we count all the full squares and, as we do so, cross them out.

Now we have to make a decision about the other part squares inside the shape.

For a good approximate answer, one possibility is to count squares which are more than half a square unit as 1, and those less than half a square unit as 0.

We hope that errors will cancel each other out when we add all of these together.

Thus our estimate for the total area is 26 square units.

Estimate the areas of:

a
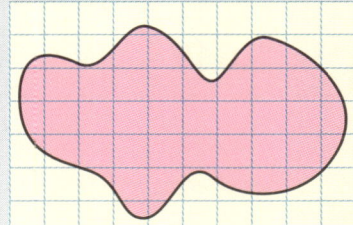

b
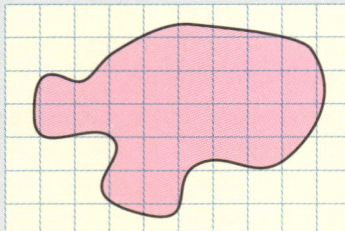

Draw some irregular shapes of your own and draw 5 mm grid lines on your shape. Estimate the area of each shape giving your answer in square centimetres.

ACTIVITY — MEASURING AREA

PRINTABLE GRID PAPER

What to do:

1. Use cm^2 graph paper to measure the surface area of:
   - **a** the front cover of this book
   - **b** your chair's seat
   - **c** the top of your desk
   - **d** the base of your drawer

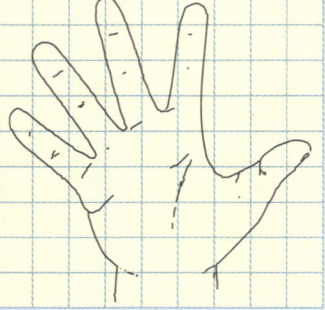

2. Place your hand on cm^2 grid paper and trace around the outside. Use the method described in the previous **Investigation** to work out the area of your hand. What is the difference in area between your hand with its fingers together and when the fingers are apart? Why is this?

3 **a** Try the above technique with the sole of your shoe.
   b Try it again barefoot.

What is the difference in area between:
   i your bare foot and the sole of your shoe
   ii your bare foot and your hand?

Can you calculate the percentage difference?

Will one outline be enough to measure all of the skin?

UNIT CONVERSION

We can convert from one unit of area to another using length relationships.

For example, $1 \text{ cm} = 10 \text{ mm}$
 and $1 \text{ cm}^2 = 1 \text{ cm} \times 1 \text{ cm}$
        $= 10 \text{ mm} \times 10 \text{ mm}$
        $= 100 \text{ mm}^2$

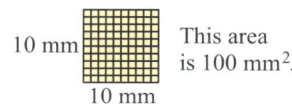

This area is 100 mm².

This process can be repeated for other area units to obtain

$1 \text{ cm}^2 = 100 \text{ mm}^2$ $\qquad$ $1 \text{ ha} = 10\,000 \text{ m}^2$
$1 \text{ m}^2 = 100 \times 100 \text{ cm}^2 = 10\,000 \text{ cm}^2$ $\qquad$ $1 \text{ km}^2 = 100 \text{ ha}$

and hence we can summarise in a **conversion table**.

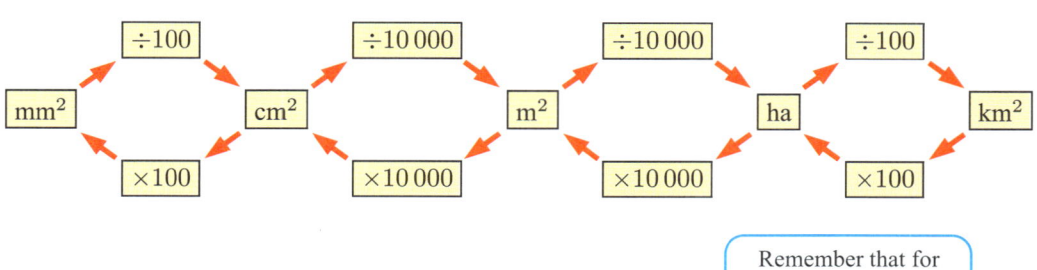

Remember that for larger units to smaller units, multiply, while for smaller units to larger units, divide.

Example 1

Convert: **a** 0.56 m^2 to cm^2 **b** $350\,000 \text{ m}^2$ to ha

a 0.56 m^2
    $= 0.56 \times 10\,000 \text{ cm}^2$
    $= 5600 \text{ cm}^2$

b $350\,000 \text{ m}^2$ to ha
    $= 350\,000 \div 10\,000 \text{ ha}$
    $= 35 \text{ ha}$

EXERCISE 8A (continued)

8 Convert:

- **a** 452 mm² to cm²
- **b** 7.5 m² to cm²
- **c** 5.8 ha to m²
- **d** 3579 cm² to m²
- **e** 6.3 km² to ha
- **f** 36.5 m² to mm²
- **g** 550 000 mm² to m²
- **h** 5.2 cm² to mm²
- **i** 6800 m² to ha
- **j** 4400 mm² to cm²
- **k** 0.6 ha to m²
- **l** 200 ha to km²
- **m** 0.7 cm² to mm²
- **n** 480 ha to km²
- **o** 25 cm² to mm²
- **p** 0.8 m² to cm²
- **q** 8800 mm² to cm²
- **r** 6600 cm² to m²
- **s** 0.5 km² to ha
- **t** 550 ha to km²
- **u** 10 cm² to m²

B   AREA OF A RECTANGLE

Consider a rectangle 5 units long and 3 units wide.

Clearly the number of square units that this rectangle contains is 15 but $15 = 5 \times 3$.

This leads to the general rule

Area of rectangle = length × width
$$A = l \times w$$

Since a **square** is a rectangle with equal length and width,

$A = $ length $\times$ length
$\therefore \ A = l \times l$
$\therefore \ A = l^2$

Example 2

Find the area of the following rectangles:

a 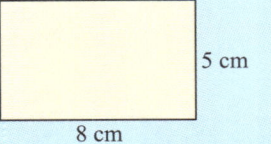 8 cm by 5 cm

b 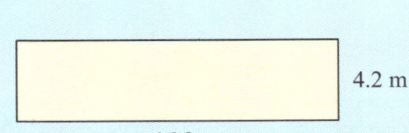 16.3 m by 4.2 m

a Area = length × width
= 8×5 cm²
= 40 cm²

b Area = length × width
= 16.3×4.2 m²
= 68.46 m²

EXERCISE 8B

1 Find the area of the following rectangles:

a 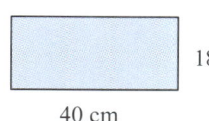   b 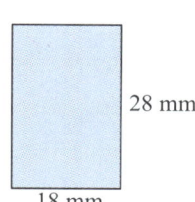   c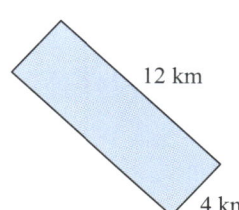

2 Find the area of the following squares:

a 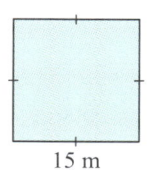   b 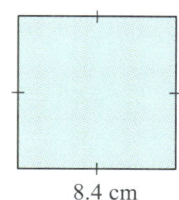   c 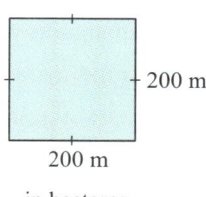 in hectares

---

Example 3

Find the yellow shaded area of:

a 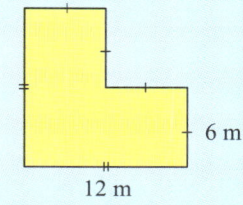   b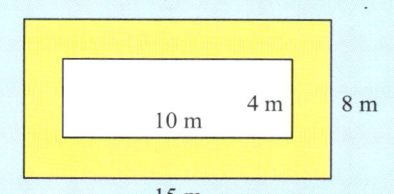

a The shape can be split into two rectangles.

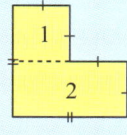

Shaded area = Area 1 + Area 2
= 6 × 6 + 12 × 6 m²
= 36 + 72 m²
= 108 m²

b Shaded area
= area large rectangle
  − area small rectangle
= 15 × 8 − 10 × 4 m²
= 120 − 40 m²
= 80 m²

---

3 Find the shaded areas:

a 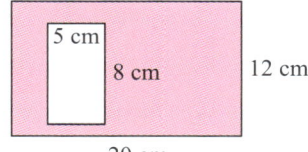   b 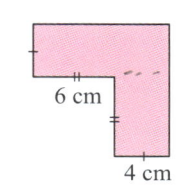   c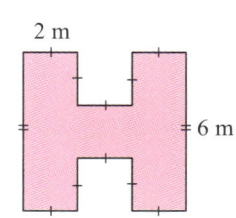

d 15 m, 12 m, 2 m (inner rectangle cutout)

e 3 m, 10 m, 4 m, 3m, 3 m, 3m, 5 m, 3 m

f 20 cm, 20 cm, 10 cm, 30 cm

4 A rectangular garden bed 3 m by 5 m is cut into a lawn 10 m by 8 m. Find the area of lawn remaining.

5 A rectangular wheat field is 450 m by 600 m.
  a Find the area of the field in hectares.
  b Find the cost of planting the field if planting costs $180 per hectare.

6 A floor 3.5 m by 5 m is to be covered with floor tiles which are 25 cm by 25 cm.
  a Find the number of tiles required.
  b Find the total cost of the tiles if each tile costs $3.50.

Example 4

Using only whole units of measurement, write all the possible lengths L, widths W and perimeters P of a rectangle of area 20 units^2. Use scale drawings to represent your answer.

Area = length × width,   Perimeter = $2L + 2W$
The possible factors of 20 are: 20×1, 10×2, 5×4.

20 units × 1 unit
$P = 2 \times 20 + 2 \times 1$
$= 42$ units   (or 42 u)

10 units × 2 units
$P = 2 \times 10 + 2 \times 2$
$= 24$ units   (or 24 u)

5 units × 4 units
$P = 2 \times 5 + 2 \times 4$
$= 18$ units   (or 18 u)

7 Using only whole units, write all the possible lengths, widths and perimeters of the following rectangular areas. For each question, use a scale drawing to represent one of the answers:
  a 12 m^2 **b** 18 cm^2 **c** 36 km^2
  d 48 mm^2 **e** 64 u^2 **f** 144 mm^2

8 Using only whole numbers for sides, write all possible areas which can be found from rectangles or squares with perimeters of:
  a 12 m   **b** 20 m   **c** 36 km

Illustrate the possible answers for **a**.

| ACTIVITY | ESTIMATING AREA |

What to do

1 **a** Get permission to use an overhead projector (OHP) and an overhead grid which has square units.

  b Prepare a number of rectangular shapes.

  c In turn, place one of the shapes on the OHP. Switch the light on for a number of seconds and have your class mates attempt to estimate the number of square units which are silhouetted by the shape.

  d Turn the light off. Check the estimates. Your classmates must give their estimate and say "square units" before you can accept their answer.

  e Repeat this for the other rectangles. You will find that the estimates improve as more examples are shown and checked.

2 Use some irregular shapes and repeat the activity.

3 Try using overheads which have:

  i equilateral triangles   **ii** hexagons   **iii** octagons

joined together to form a grid instead of squares.

This time each estimate must be followed by a statement like:

"...... 54 equilateral triangle units"   or

"...... 38 hexagonal units"   or

"...... 49 octagonal units".

| ACTIVITY | WORKING WITH AREA |

What to do:

1 Construct or cut out a square metre. You could use material, strong plastic, cardboard or pieces of dowling or 20 mm diameter plastic pipe. Measure and record areas within your classroom. Outside the classroom you could measure areas like the tennis court, netball courts, cricket pitch, activity hall, paved areas, undercover areas and so on.

  a Estimate how many of your classmates can stand inside a square metre.

  b Estimate how many students from the junior classes can stand inside a square metre.

  c How could you check your estimates?

2 South Australia's population density is $1\frac{1}{2}$ people per square kilometre.

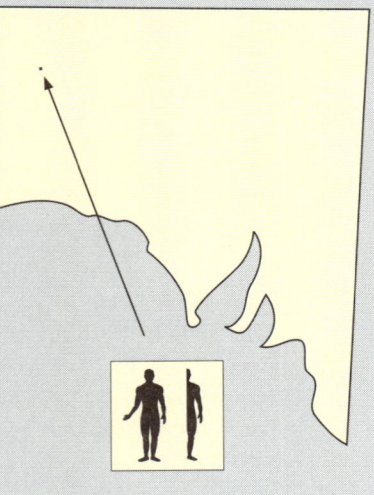

  a Explain:
  - **i** what this means
  - **ii** how it is measured
  - **iii** why it is measured.

  b Find out the population density of:
  - **i** Victoria
  - **ii** New South Wales
  - **iii** England
  - **iv** India
  - **v** United States
  - **vi** Antarctica

  c What would you need to know to be able to compare the population density of the city of Adelaide with the city of Sydney?

3 Design a car park for a new school. You are to:

  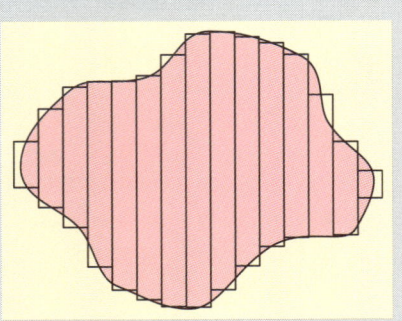

  a use the least amount of area to park up to 50 cars
  b use the least amount of area and yet still make parking easy and practical.
  c Record all the things you need to consider.
  d Use graph paper and a scale to show your finished design.

4 Collect 2 identical pages of a newspaper, scissors and a tape measure.

  a Find out what part of the page is taken up with:
  - **i** pictures of the news
  - **ii** advertisements.

  b Present your answers as:
  - **i** a fraction of all the pages of the newspaper
  - **ii** a percentage of all the pages of the newspaper
  - **iii** $\dfrac{\text{area of pictures (or advertisements) in m}^2}{\text{area of whole newspaper in m}^2}$

INVESTIGATION AREAS BY "STRIPS"

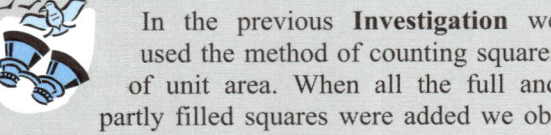

In the previous **Investigation** we used the method of counting squares of unit area. When all the full and partly filled squares were added we obtained an approximate figure for the area of the irregular shape.

In this investigation we look at a different method, using rectangles of unit width. In the example, rectangles that are one unit wide have been drawn over the shape.

The area of each rectangle is simply worked out by measuring its height. The total area is the sum of the area of all the rectangles.

Using the method above, determine the approximate area for each of the following shapes:

a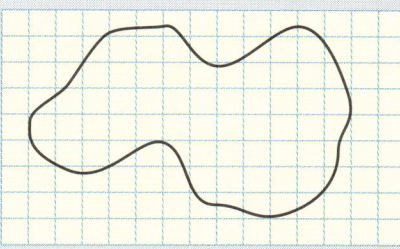

b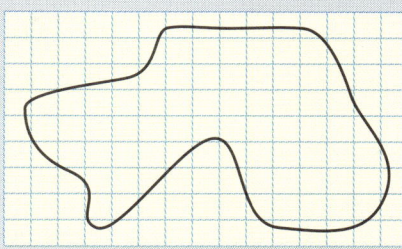

Compare the answer that you obtained with those obtained by other members of your class.

C   AREA OF A TRIANGLE

ACTIVITY   FINDING THE RULE FOR THE AREA OF A TRIANGLE

You will need:

scissors, ruler, pencil and square centimetre graph paper.

What to do:

1 On the graph paper draw three separate 20 cm by 10 cm rectangles. Cut them out. Fold the first rectangle vertically and the second rectangle horizontally through the middle.

Count the area in each new section. Did you get 100 cm^2?

Now fold the third rectangle diagonally and cut it. Place one piece of paper over the top of the other.

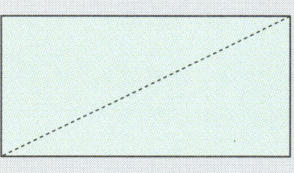 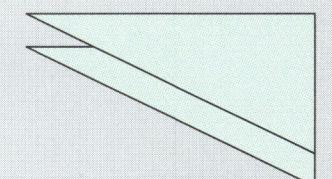

What is the area of each of the triangles?

What fraction of the rectangle is each triangle,

i.e., $\dfrac{\text{area of triangle}}{\text{area of rectangle}}$ or $\dfrac{\text{number of cm}^2 \text{ of triangle}}{\text{number of cm}^2 \text{ of rectangle}}$?

2 On the graph paper draw rectangles like the ones shown. Within the boundaries of the rectangles draw triangles like the ones shown. Use the rule **area = length × width** to determine the area of each rectangle. Write down the result. Use the counting method to check your calculations.

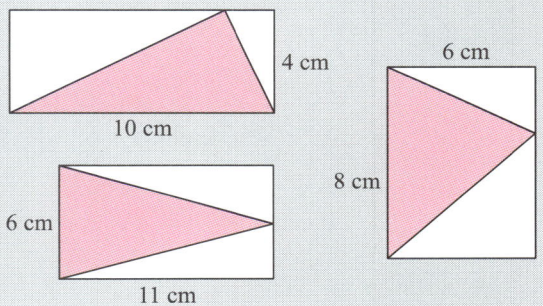

> **a** From the first rectangle, cut out the shaded triangle.
> **b** Use the counting method to determine the area of the shaded triangle. What do you observe?
> **c** Determine the total area of the remaining pieces. What do you observe?
> **d** Place the remaining pieces to cover the shaded triangle exactly.
>
> Repeat steps **a** to **d** for the other two rectangles.

You will have found from the activity above that the area of a triangle is half the area of a rectangle which has the *same base and height* as the triangle.

This finding can be easily verified by drawing rectangles around the triangle as shown below:

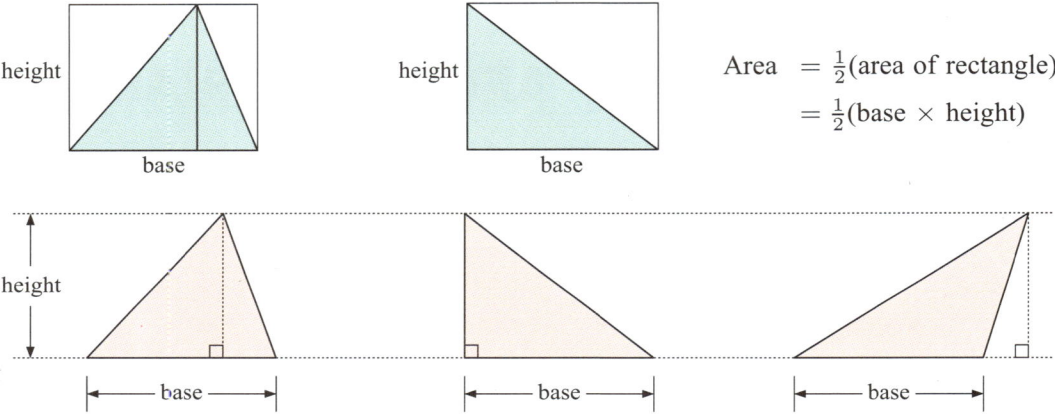

Area $= \frac{1}{2}$(area of rectangle)
     $= \frac{1}{2}$(base $\times$ height)

If the base and height of a triangle are known then a very simple rule is

> **Area of triangle $= \frac{1}{2} \times$ base $\times$ height** or $\dfrac{\text{base} \times \text{height}}{2}$.

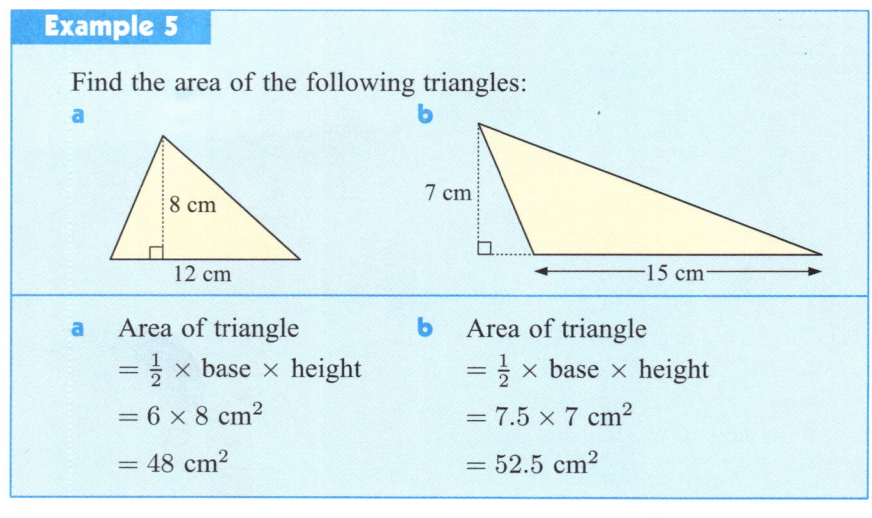

Example 5

Find the area of the following triangles:

a (triangle with height 8 cm, base 12 cm)

b (triangle with height 7 cm, base 15 cm)

a Area of triangle
$= \frac{1}{2} \times$ base $\times$ height
$= 6 \times 8$ cm^2
$= 48$ cm^2

b Area of triangle
$= \frac{1}{2} \times$ base $\times$ height
$= 7.5 \times 7$ cm^2
$= 52.5$ cm^2

EXERCISE 8C

1 Find the area of the following triangles:

a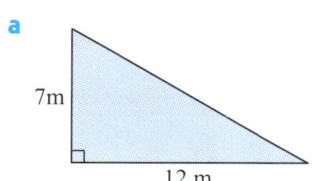
b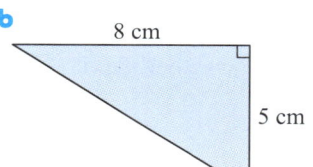
c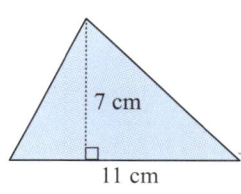
d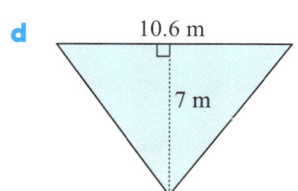
e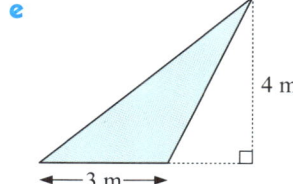
f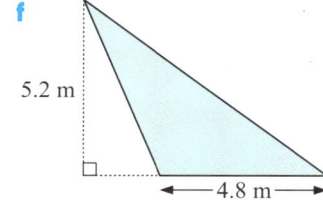

Example 6

Find the shaded area:

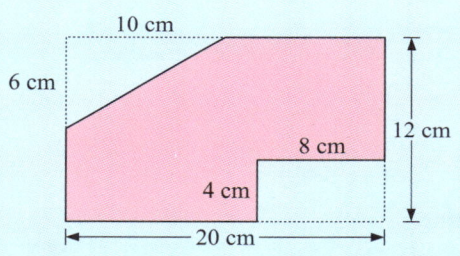

Shaded area = area large rectangle − area triangle − area small rectangle
= $20 \times 12 - 3 \times 10 - 8 \times 4$ cm^2
= $240 - 30 - 32$ cm^2
= 178 cm^2

2 Find the shaded area:

a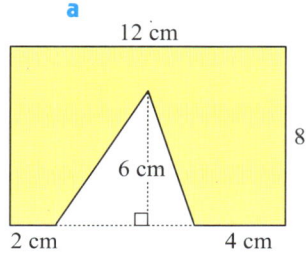
b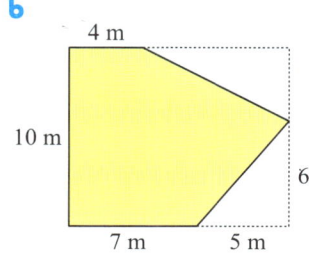
c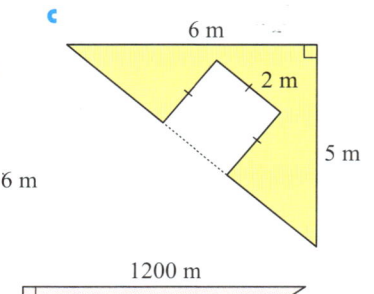

3 **a** Find the area in hectares of the triangular paddock shown.

b How much would it cost to plant the paddock with wheat if planting costs $150 per hectare?

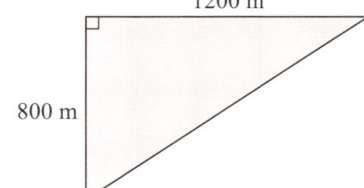

4 Above the bricks on both sides of this house the walls have been topped to the roof with weatherboard.

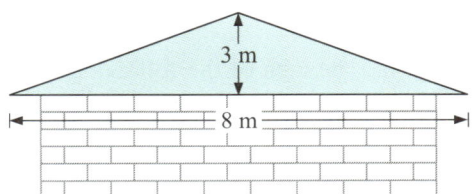

  a How much weatherboard was used?
  b What was the total cost if weatherboard costs $13.90 per m²?

5 Find the shaded area:

  a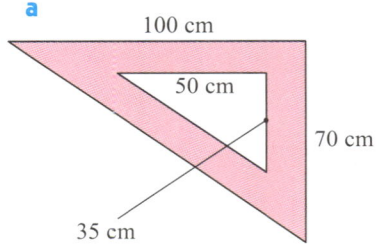
  b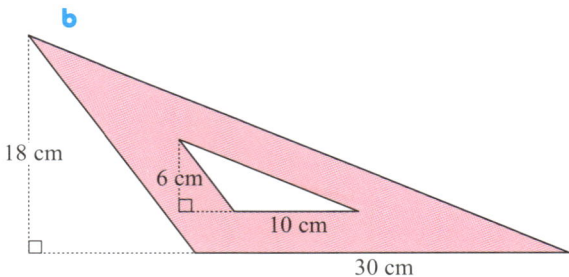

INVESTIGATION — AREAS WITH A SPREADSHEET

The spreadsheet below is used to calculate the area of a rectangle and a triangle given the dimensions of each figure.

What to do:

1 Open a new spreadsheet and type into the cells the labels and formulae as shown.

	A	B	C	D	E
1	Rectangle	Length	Width		Area
2		10	6		=B2*C2
3	Triangle	Base	Height		Area
4		12	7		=(B4*C4)/2

2 Change the dimensions of the shapes and check that your spreadsheet gives you the correct answers in each case.

EXTENSION

INVESTIGATION — PICK'S RULE

Alongside is a diagram of a polygon whose **vertices** (corner points) lie on **lattice points**. Lattice points which lie on the figure are called **boundary points**. Lattice points which lie inside the figure are called **interior points**. The figure has 14 boundary points and 3 interior points.

Suppose
  B = the number of boundary points,
  and I = the number of interior points.

For the figures below, copy and complete the table which follows:

a b 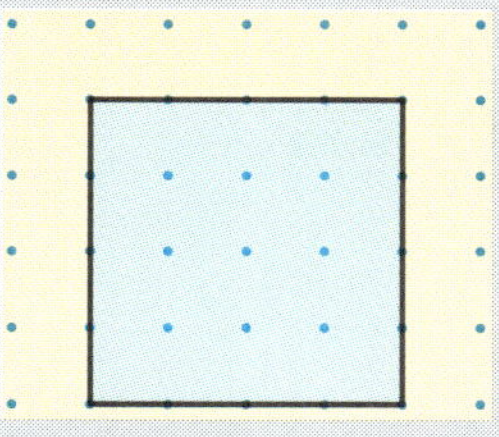 c

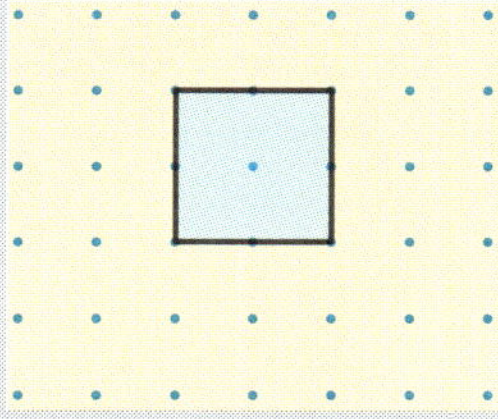

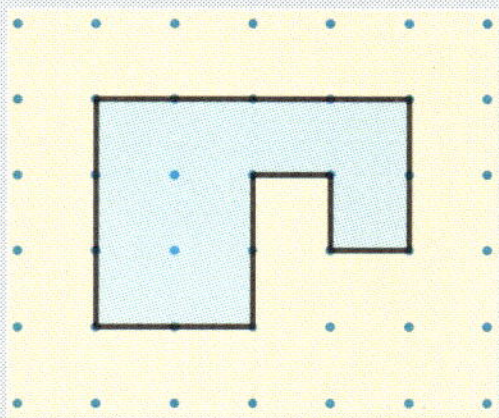

d 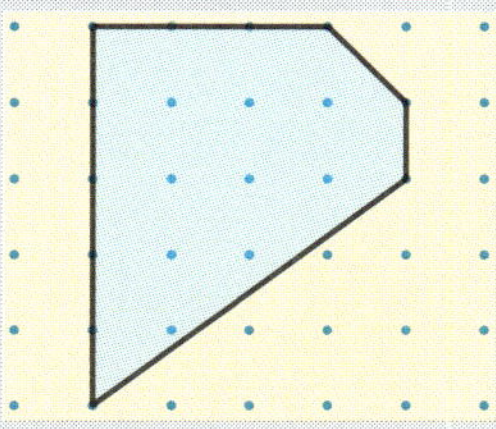 e 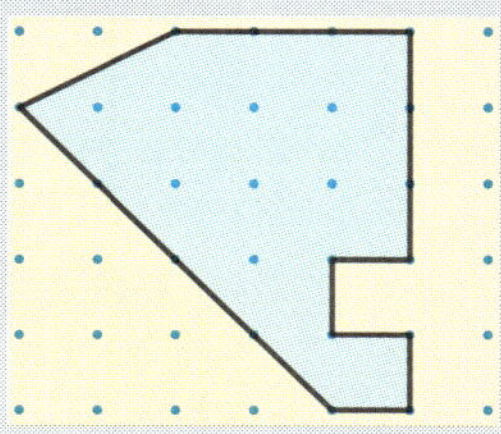 f

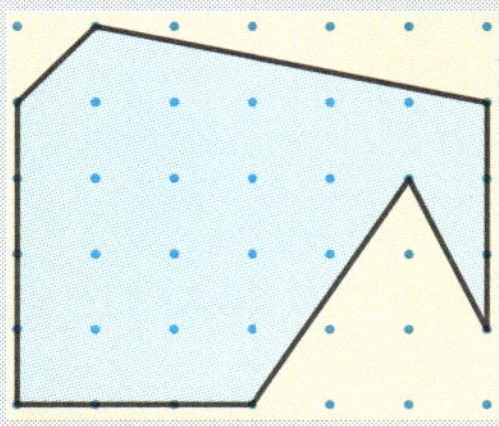

Figure	B	$\frac{B}{2}$	I	$\frac{B}{2}+I$	Area, A
a					
b					
c					
d					
e					
f					

Look at the last two columns of your table. What is your guess for a law connecting A, B and I?

Draw several polygons of your own on dotty paper (or grid paper) and check that your deduction about areas from above is correct.

This result is called **Pick's Rule**.

D VOLUME AND CAPACITY

INVESTIGATION CHOOSING A SUITABLE UNIT OF MEASURE

You will need:
- marbles, bottle caps, dried broadbeans, steel nuts
- a small rectangular takeaway food container (A)
- a small cylindrical empty soup can (B)
- a 250 mL rectangular milk or fruit juice container (C)
- a liquid measuring device.

What to do:

1. Work in small groups and draw up a table like the one given:

Container	Number of units of measure needed to fill the container											
	marbles			bottle caps			dried beans			steel nuts		
	estimate	carefully arranged	volume of water	estimate	carefully arranged	volume of water	estimate	carefully arranged	volume of water	estimate	carefully arranged	volume of water
A												
B												
C												

2. First, estimate how many marbles will fill container A. Marbles are our first units of measure. Record your estimate. Count each marble as you carefully fill container A to the top. Record the number of marbles used to fill the container.

3. Using a liquid measuring device, accurately find how much water is needed to fill the gaps between the marbles.

4. Repeat steps **2** and **3** with other units of measure, and the other two containers, completing a table of results.

5. Dry everything after use.

6. Answer the following questions:
   a For each container, which unit gave the most accurate estimate of capacity? Give reasons for your answers.
   b For each container, give several reasons why the other three units may not be used universally.
   c With which unit were you closest with your estimates?
   d With which container were you closest with your estimates?
   e What does this investigation tell you about the different units of measure?

GROUP ACTIVITY — REVISITING VOLUME AND CAPACITY

Part 1:
You will need:
- cylindrical cans of various capacities, rectangular plastic or foil takeaway food containers, soup bowls, drink bottles and lengths of clear plastic tube with different diameters
- a measure containing 300 mL of dyed water
- a marker.

What to do:

a Block one end of one of the plastic tubes.

b On the tube, mark where you think the water level will be if 300 mL of coloured water is added to it.

c Carefully pour the coloured water into the tube. Give yourself a rating for the accuracy of your estimate.

d Make sure all the water is poured back into the measure before you attempt your estimate with the next container.

e Repeat the above procedure using each container in turn.

f Answer the following questions:
   i With which container was your estimate the least accurate?
   ii Why do you think this was the least accurate for measuring liquid volumes?

Part 2:

You will need: a piece of plasticine, a centicube and a scientific pipette or graduated eye dropper.

What to do:

a Work the plasticine into a lump. Carefully push the centicube into the plasticine so that it leaves a full and firm impression. Remove the centicube.

b Measure the volume of water needed to fill the impression.

c Answer the following questions:
   i How much water filled the impression?
   ii What does this tell you about the capacity of a centicube?

ACTIVITY — MEASURING VOLUME BY WATER DISPLACEMENT

Part 1:

You will need: a small rectangular aquarium, water, masking tape, a liquid measuring device, a 1000 MA block, a can of soft drink and a tennis ball.

What to do:

1 Make sure that there is enough water in the aquarium to fully submerge the MA block.

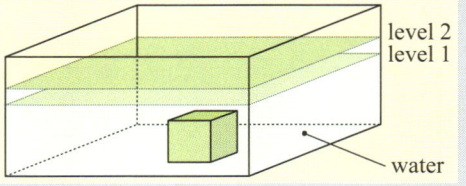

2 Use masking tape to accurately mark the level of the water once it becomes still. Call this level 1.

3 Fully submerge the MA block.

4 Mark the new water level and call it level 2.

5 Remove the block and allow the water to drip back into the aquarium. The water level should return to its original position (level 1).

6 Carefully measure the volume of water you add to the aquarium so that the water reaches level 2 again. This must be the volume of the MA block.

7 Repeat this activity with the can of soft drink and also with a tennis ball. Keep the ball still and avoid displacing water with your fingers.

8 Answer the following questions.
   a How much water was displaced by:
      i the MA block   **ii** the can of soft drink   **iii** the tennis ball?
   b What conclusions can you make about volume from your experiments?

Part 2:

You will need: a softened and stretched balloon, a rectangular aquarium, water and a liquid measuring device.

What to do:

1 Take a large breath and in one single blow, empty the air from your lungs into the balloon. Tie the balloon off.

2 Use the method described in **Part 1** to measure the volume of air in your lungs. This measurement is an indicator of your lung capacity.

3 What are the problems with this method?

Part 3:

You will need: a large measuring cylinder, water, a rectangular aquarium and a plastic tube.

What to do:

1 Submerge the measuring cylinder in the water of the partly filled aquarium, then invert it as shown in the diagram, making sure that no water escapes.

2 Place one end of a plastic tube inside the measuring cylinder.

3 Take a large breath and slowly blow through the other end of the tube until all your breath is gone. The volume of air you blow out forces the same volume of water out of the measuring cylinder.

4 Measure your lung capacity. It is the volume of air in the cylinder.

5 Compare and discuss the results of this method with those of **Part 2**.

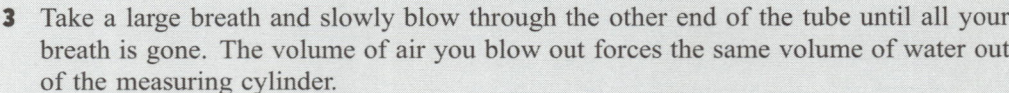

AREAS OF PARALLELOGRAMS, TRAPEZIA, CIRCLES

This **extension** material is found by clicking on the icon and printing off the pages required.

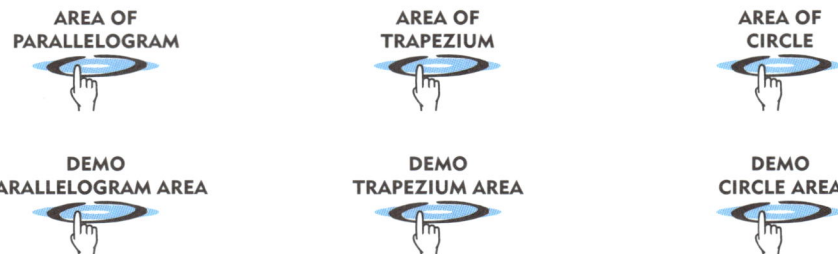

Click on any demo icon to see how the formulae are made up.

HOME RESEARCH

In and around your home look for clues which tell you the capacity of the:
- fridge
- washing machine
- watering can
- freezer compartment
- bath tub
- cistern flush
- engine of the family car
- garbage bin
- fuel tank of the family car.

If you cannot find the clues, describe ways that you could measure the capacity.

E   VOLUME

CLASS DISCUSSION

In groups, see if you can answer the following questions:
- What is volume?
- What is the difference between volume and capacity?
- Why do we need to measure volume?
- What units do we use to measure volume?

When the groups have had an opportunity to discuss these questions, come together as a class and see what you have discovered or know about volume.

The **volume** of a solid is the amount of space it occupies.
This space is measured in **cubic units**.

Remember that volume is not just a measure for water or fluids like drinks, petrol, paint, medicine, blood or sewage. Volume is also a measure for soil, concrete, bark chips, rubble, gases, recyclable material and waste.

As with area, the units used for the measurement of volume are related to the units used for the measurement of length.

1 cubic millimetre (mm^3) is the volume of a cube with a side of length 1 mm.
1 cubic centimetre (cm^3) is the volume of a cube with a side of length 1 cm.
1 cubic metre (m^3) is the volume of a cube with a side of length 1 m.

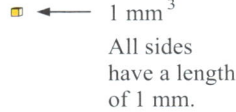

1 mm^3
All sides have a length of 1 mm.

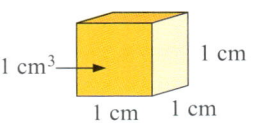

CONVERSIONS:

Converting from one unit of volume to another unit of volume can be done by considering a cube of side unit length.

For example, 1 cm = 10 mm,

$\therefore$ 1 cm^3 = 1 cm × 1 cm × 1 cm
= 10 mm × 10 mm × 10 mm
= 1000 mm^3

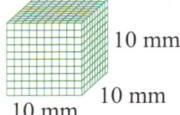

A similar conversion can be performed for other volume units.

1 m^3 = 100 cm × 100 cm × 100 cm
= 1 000 000 cm^3

This can be summarised in a conversion diagram:

The little ^{3} in mm^3, cm^3, and m^3 indicates that the shape has 3 dimensions $L \times W \times H$

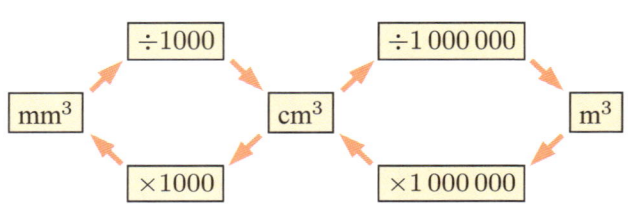

Example 7

Convert:
a   0.163 m^3 to cm^3 b   7953 mm^3 to cm^3

a   0.163 m^3
= 0.163 × 1 000 000 cm^3
= 163 000 cm^3

b   7953 mm^3
= 7953 ÷ 1000 cm^3
= 7.953 cm^3

To change larger units to smaller units we multiply.

To change smaller units to larger units we divide.

EXERCISE 8E

1 Perform the following conversions:
   a   8 mm^3 to cm^3 b   0.06 m^3 to cm^3 c   11.8 cm^3 to mm^3
   d   0.64 cm^3 to mm^3 e   3 m^3 to mm^3 f   0.0075 m^3 to mm^3

2 Perform the following conversions:
   a   500 mm^3 to cm^3 b   7000 mm^3 to cm^3
   c   5 000 000 cm^3 to m^3 d   450 000 cm^3 to m^3
   e   2 000 000 mm^3 to m^3 f   5 400 000 000 mm^3 to m^3

RECTANGULAR PRISMS

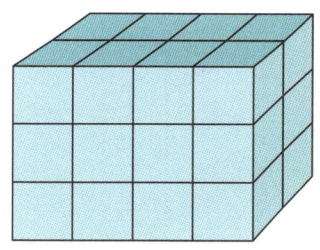

A **rectangular prism** is a 3 dimensional solid which has the same size (cross-section) for its whole length.

For example, a $4 \times 2 \times 3$ prism is shown alongside.

Clearly there are 3 layers and each of these layers contains 8 cubes (4×2).

Hence, there are 24 (8×3) cubes altogether.

i.e., the volume is 24 $(4 \times 2 \times 3)$ units^3.

This leads to the following rule for volume:

Volume of a rectangular prism = length × width × height

This can be written as the formula: $V = l \times w \times h$

but as $l \times w =$ area of base, we can write

Volume of rectangular prism = area of base × height

SOLIDS OF UNIFORM CROSS-SECTION

The above can be extended to the volume of any solid of uniform cross-section.

For example:

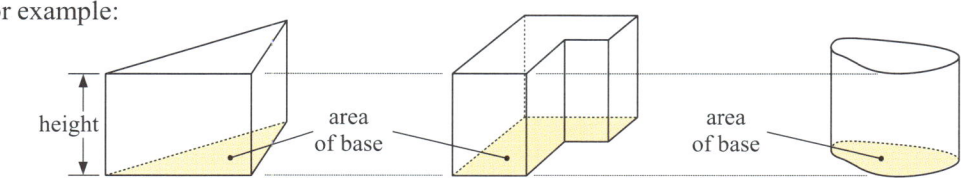

The volume can be found by multiplying base area and height.

Volume of solid of uniform cross-section = area of base × height

EXERCISE 8E (continued)

3 Find the number of cubic units in each of the following solids:

   a   **b**   **c**

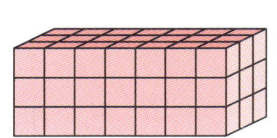 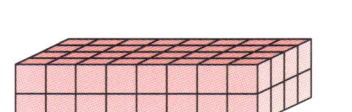 

d 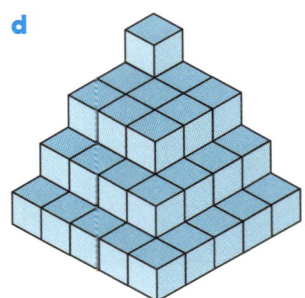   e   f

Example 8

Find the volume of the following prisms:

a 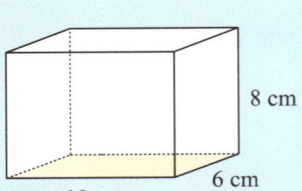   b 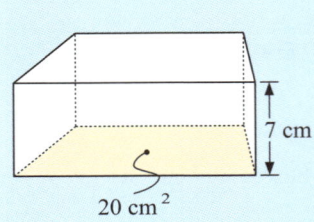   c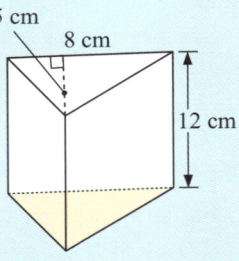

a   Volume
= area of base × height
= 10 cm × 6 cm × 8 cm
= 480 cm³

b   Volume
= area of base × height
= 20 cm² × 7 cm
= 140 cm³

c   Volume = area of base × height   = $\frac{1}{2}(8 \times 5)$ cm² × 12 cm
= 20 × 12 cm³
= 240 cm³

4 Find the volume of the following rectangular prisms:

a 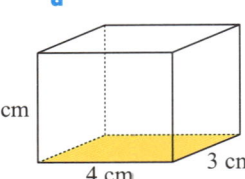   b 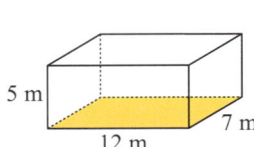   c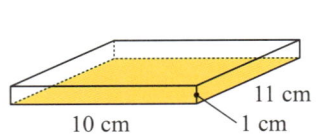

5 Find the volume of the following solids of uniform cross-section:

a 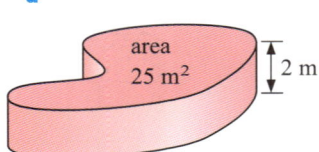   b 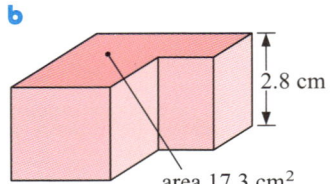   c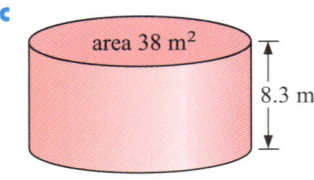

MEASUREMENT (AREA AND VOLUME) (CHAPTER 8) 275

d 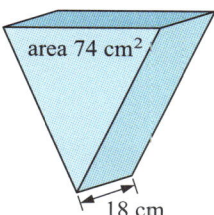 area 74 cm² , 18 cm

e 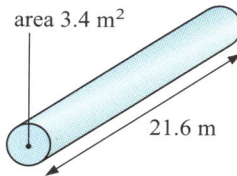 area 3.4 m² , 21.6 m

f 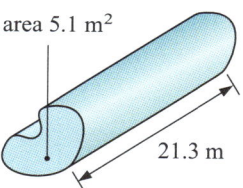 area 5.1 m² , 21.3 m

6 Find the volume of the illustrated prisms:

a 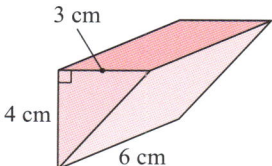 3 cm, 4 cm, 6 cm

b 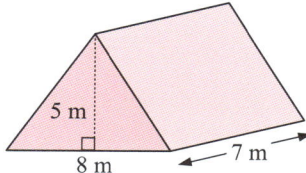 5 m, 8 m, 7 m

c 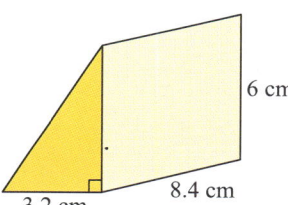 6 cm, 3.2 cm, 8.4 cm

d 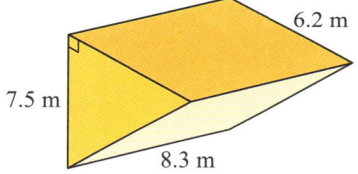 6.2 m, 7.5 m, 8.3 m

---

Example 9

Using only whole units, how many other prisms can be constructed using the same number of cubic units as are shown in the diagram?

Show their dimensions. Give one scale drawing to illustrate your answer.

Count the cubic units to find the volume of the prism.

$V = 72$ cubic units
$\therefore V = $ area of base $\times$ height
$\therefore V = $ length $\times$ width $\times$ height
$72 \text{ u}^3 = 6 \text{ u} \times 4 \text{ u} \times 3 \text{ u}$

Also $72 \text{ u}^3 = 72 \text{ u} \times 1 \text{ u} \times 1 \text{ u}$
$= 36 \text{ u} \times 2 \text{ u} \times 1 \text{ u}$
$= 18 \text{ u} \times 4 \text{ u} \times 1 \text{ u}$
$= 18 \text{ u} \times 2 \text{ u} \times 2 \text{ u}$
$= 9 \text{ u} \times 4 \text{ u} \times 2 \text{ u}$
$= 24 \text{ u} \times 3 \text{ u} \times 1 \text{ u}$
$= 12 \text{ u} \times 6 \text{ u} \times 1 \text{ u}$
$= 12 \text{ u} \times 3 \text{ u} \times 2 \text{ u}$
$= 8 \text{ u} \times 3 \text{ u} \times 3 \text{ u}$
$= 8 \text{ u} \times 9 \text{ u} \times 1 \text{ u}$

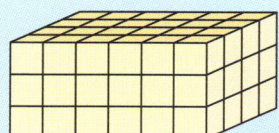 this one

7 List all the possible dimensions (side lengths) for all the rectangular prisms which can be made using the same number of cubic units as these shown. Use only whole units.

   a   **b**   **c**

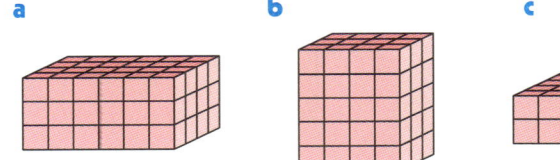

8 Using only whole units, list all the possible dimensions for the rectangular prisms with volumes:

   a 30 m³   **b** 100 cm³   **c** 144 cm³

9 Using only whole units, draw scale drawings of all the rectangular prisms it is possible to construct with volumes:

   a 24 cm³   **b** 40 m³   **c** 64 mm³

10 Arrange the rectangular prisms with dimensions as given, in ascending order of volumes, from the lowest number of cubic units to the highest:

   a   **b**   **c**   **d**

11 Find the volume of this book.

ACTIVITY   PACKAGING

 **You will need:**   scissors, thin cardboard, stickytape, ruler and centicubes.

What to do:

1 Use the dimensions of the following nets to make packages. Tape the sides together to make open boxes. Estimate the number of centicubes needed to fill each box. Check your estimate by:

   a filling the box and counting the centicubes
   b using the formula to determine the number.

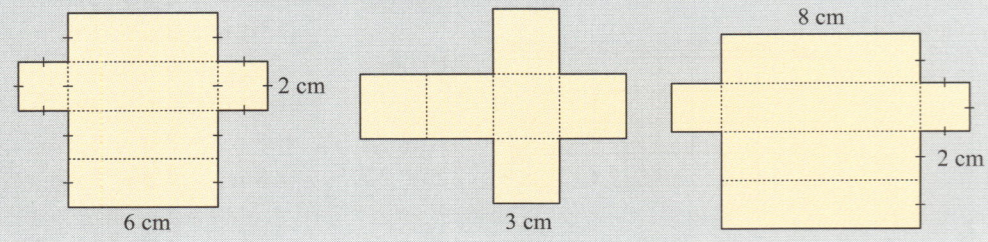

2 Work in groups. Collect thin cardboard, scissors, stickytape and ruler. Make nets for 21 identical rectangular prisms 4 cm × 6 cm × 12 cm. Use tape to make the nets into prisms. Design a larger rectangular prism which will allow you to neatly and efficiently stack the smaller ones inside.

Leave the lid of your larger prism unstuck whilst you try packing the smaller ones.

a What are the dimensions of your larger prism?

b Is there more than one way to stack the prisms?

F CAPACITY

Volume and capacity are very similar terms.

The word capacity is usually used when referring to either a liquid or gas (fluid).

> The **capacity** of a container is a measure of the amount of fluid it can contain.

The units for capacity are very closely related to those of volume.

The most commonly used units of capacity are litre (L) and millilitre (mL) while for larger capacities (for example, reservoirs, swimming pools, etc.) the units of kilolitre (kL) and megalitre (ML) are used.

$$1 \text{ L} = 1000 \text{ mL}$$
$$1 \text{ kL} = 1000 \text{ L}$$
$$1 \text{ ML} = 1\,000\,000 \text{ L}$$

The relationship between capacity units and volume units is:

$$1 \text{ mL} = 1 \text{ cm}^3$$
$$1 \text{ L} = 1000 \text{ cm}^3$$
$$1 \text{ kL} = 1\,000\,000 \text{ cm}^3$$
$$= 1 \text{ m}^3$$

EXERCISE 8F

1 What units of capacity are most suitable to measure the following?

- **a** perfume bottle
- **b** thermos flask
- **c** Olympic pool
- **d** 6 cylinder car engine
- **e** drinking glass
- **f** teardrop
- **g** household water use
- **h** roll-on deodorant
- **i** service station petrol tank
- **j** model aeroplane engine
- **k** oil refinery
- **l** ocean tanker
- **m** reservoirs
- **n** domestic gas use
- **o** ocean
- **p** pipeline
- **q** baby's bottle
- **r** beads of perspiration

Example 10

Convert:
a   8 L to mL
b   12.4 kL to L
c   3400 cm³ to L

a   8 L
    = 8 × 1000 mL
    = 8000 mL

b   12.4 kL
    = 12.4 × 1000 L
    = 12 400 L

c   3400 cm³
    = 3400 ÷ 1000 L
    = 3.4 L

2 Convert:
a   5.6 kL to L
b   3540 mL to L
c   760 000 L to ML
d   7200 cm³ to L
e   6.3 kL to m³
f   12.4 kL to mL
g   0.0625 L to mL
h   400 cm³ to mL
i   3.5 ML to kL

3 Find the capacity in mL of:

a   b   c

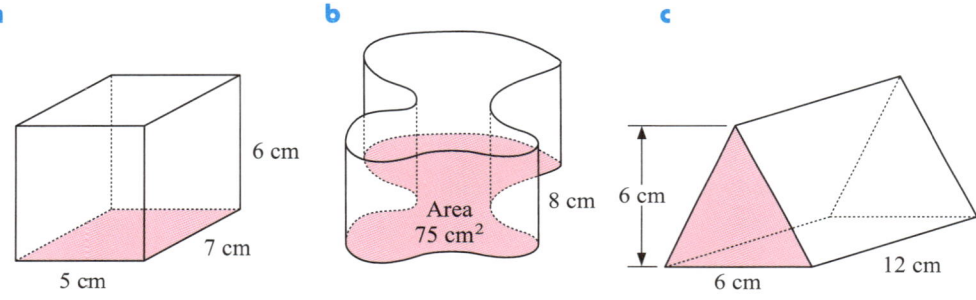

4 What is the capacity in litres of a rectangular fuel tank 80 cm by 60 cm by 15 cm?

5 How many times could a water container 15 cm by 8 cm by 5 cm be filled from a 40 L container?

6 How many 30 cm by 20 cm by 90 cm fuel tanks can a car manufacturer fill from its 27.54 kL storage tank?

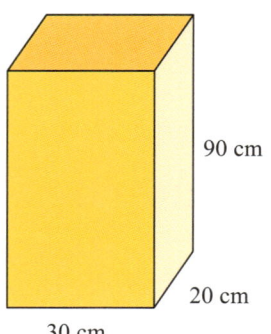

7

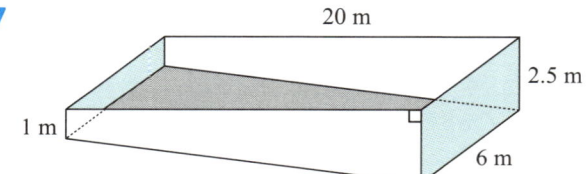

Find the amount of water (in kL) required to fill the swimming pool shown alongside.

Hint: Draw a line on the trapezium side of the swimming pool to divide it into a rectangle and a triangle.

ACTIVITY — CALIBRATING A CONTAINER

You will need: three different containers like the ones shown.

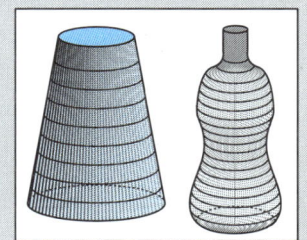

What to do:

1 Find out what 'calibrate' means.

2 Clearly describe the experiment, the methods and the equipment you intend to use to calibrate each of the containers.

3 Answer the following questions:

   a How did you check the accuracy of your calibration?

   b What did you notice about the spacing of the calibration marks on the different containers?

G PROBLEM SOLVING

Example 11

A concrete path, 1.5 m wide, is to be laid around a 20 m by 8 m swimming pool. Concrete of the required depth costs $41 per square metre.

a Find the area to be concreted.

b Find the cost of the concrete.

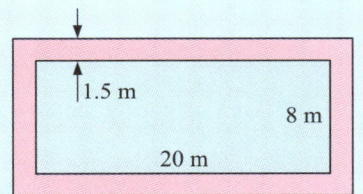

a Area of path = area of large rectangle − area of small rectangle
$$= (20 + 1.5 + 1.5) \times (8 + 1.5 + 1.5) \; - \; 20 \times 8 \text{ m}^2$$
$$= 23 \times 11 \; - \; 20 \times 8$$
$$= 253 - 160 \text{ m}^2$$
$$= 93 \text{ m}^2$$

b ∴ cost of path = 93 × $41
                    = $3813

The required area is found by subtracting areas.

EXERCISE 8G

1 A room 5 m by 6 m by 3 m high is to have its walls timber panelled.

   a Find the area of timber panelling required.

   b If the timber panelling costs $12.50 per square metre, find the total cost of the panelling.

2 A rectangular playing field 120 m by 80 m is to be surrounded by a 10 m wide strip of bitumen.

   a Find the area of bitumen.

   b If each truckload of bitumen covers 50 m², how many truckloads of bitumen will be required?

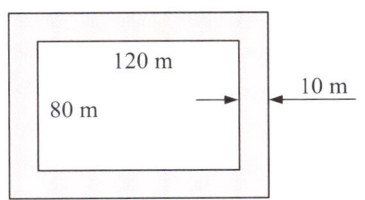

3 If each page of a book is 25 cm by 15 cm, find the total area (in m²) of paper used in a book of 420 pages.

4 A roll of toilet tissue contains 1000, individually perforated, 110 mm × 100 mm sheets.
  a Find the area of each roll when unrolled.
  b Find how many such rolls would be needed to cover a 50 metre by 66 metre paved area.

5 The area of a rectangle is 1 hectare. Find the width of the rectangle if it has a length of:
  a 100 m   **b** 1 kilometre   **c** 250 metres   **d** 2000 metres
  e 800 metres   **f** 1.25 km   **g** 500 metres   **h** 12.5 metres

Example 12

If a gardener orders 30 cubic metres of top soil, to what depth can this be spread over a triangular garden with dimensions shown?

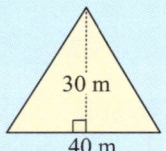

Area of garden bed = $\frac{1}{2}$ base × height
     = 20 × 30
     = 600 m²

Volume of soil = area × depth
∴ 30 m³ = 600 m² × depth
∴ depth = $\frac{30}{600}$ = 0.05 m
     = 0.05 × 100 cm
     = 5 cm

∴ top soil can be spread to a depth of 5 cm.

'Depth' here would mean 'average depth'.

6 To celebrate her 3 years in business a baker bakes this large cake with the dimensions shown. How much icing must she make if she covers the top of the cake to a depth of 5 mm with icing?

view from above

7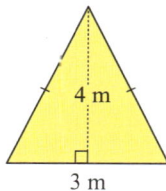

How much canvas is needed for a tent which has three identical sides like this?

Example 13

How many 80 mL oil bottles can be filled from a rectangular container 20 cm by 16 cm by 40 cm?

Volume of container = $20 \times 16 \times 40$ cm^3
= 12 800 cm^3

∴ number of bottles = $\dfrac{\text{volume container}}{\text{volume bottle}}$

= $\dfrac{12\,800 \text{ cm}^3}{80 \text{ mL}}$

= 160

∴ 160 bottles can be filled.

Remember that 1 mL = 1 cm^3

8 How many 300 mL spring water bottles can be filled from a rectangular container $3 \text{ m} \times 2 \text{ m} \times 1.5 \text{ m}$?

9 Engineers dug a 150 metre × 80 metre × 17 metre deep hole to dump the town's rubbish. How much compacted rubbish can be dumped if the engineers need a depth of 2 metres of soil on top once the hole is full of rubbish?

10 a How much water is in this rainwater tank if it is $\frac{3}{4}$ full?

b How many 8 litre buckets full would it take to empty it?

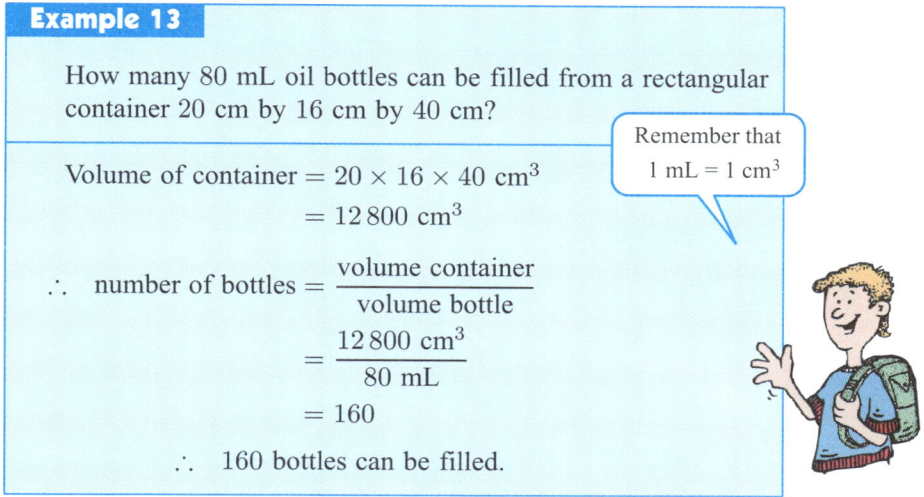

11 Draw a sketch to show the best way to pack the maximum number of the smaller prisms into the larger box. How many can be packed?

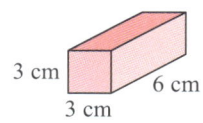

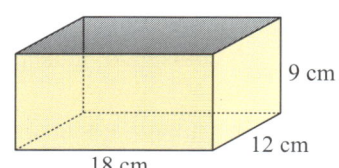

12  Vertical blinds are to be fitted to a 1430 mm wide by 1200 mm high window. Each slat in the blind is 13 cm wide and is cut to the full height of the window. When they are hanging and the blinds are closed, each slat overlaps another by 2 cm.

a How many slats are needed for this window?

b How much reflective sheeting is needed to cover the glass?

13 The blind company (in question **12**) also fitted two identical 2200 mm wide by 1300 mm high windows with the same vertical blinds and reflective sheeting for the neighbour's house.

a How many slats did they use?

b If the sheeting is sold by the square metre and costs $26.50 per m^2, what was the cost for this house?

REVIEW SET A — CHAPTER 8

1 Convert:
   a 3.56 ha to m^2
   b 357 000 mm^2 to m^2
   c 7.2 cm^3 to mm^3

2 Find the shaded area:
   a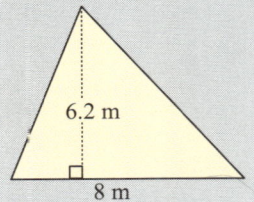
   b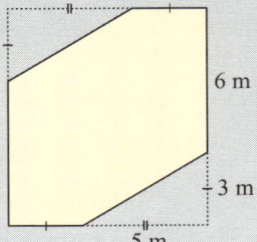

3 Find the volume of:
   a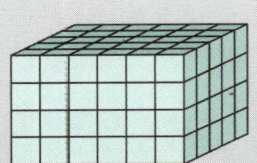
   b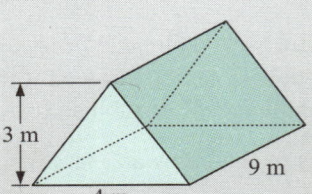
   c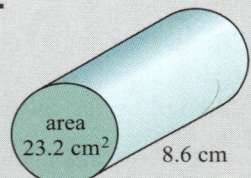

4 Convert the following:
   a 380 mL to L
   b 5.4 kL to m^3
   c 7528 cm^3 to L

5 The outside of a shed with the dimensions shown is to be painted.
   a Find the total area to be painted (including the roof).
   b If a litre of paint covers 15 m^2, what quantity of paint will be required if two coats of paint are used?

6 **a** How many posters 120 cm long by 90 cm high can Lotus stick on her 3.6 m by 3 m high bedroom wall?
   b She wants the space between the posters equal. What is the area of each space if the top row of posters is level with the ceiling and the bottom row is level with the floor?

7 **a** How many 2 cm by 3 cm stamps can fit on a sheet 200 mm by 300 mm?
   b If each stamp costs 45 cents, what is the cost of half a sheet?

8 Determine the number of kilolitres that will be held in a rectangular rainwater tank 5 m by 3 m by 4.5 m.

REVIEW SET B CHAPTER 8

1 Convert:
   a 3400 m² to ha
   b 3.2 cm² to mm²
   c 7.2 m² to mm²

2 Find the yellow coloured area:
   a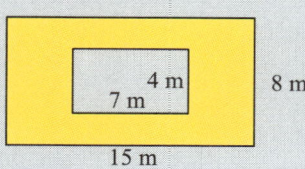
   b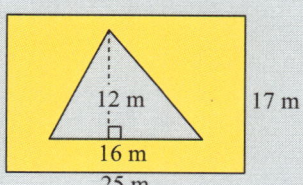

3 Convert the following:
   a 45 000 L to kL
   b 8900 mm³ to cm³
   c 4.6 kL to L

4 Find the volume of:
   a
   b, c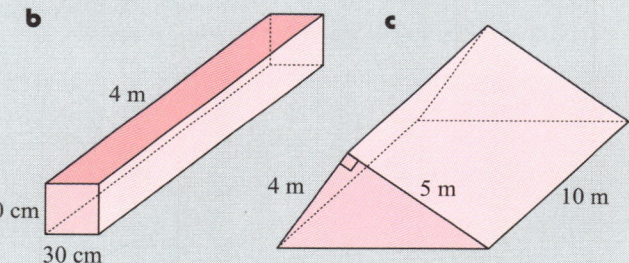

5 How many 10 cm × 5 cm × 10 cm containers can be filled from a container with dimensions 1 m × 1 m × $\frac{1}{2}$ m?

6 Using only whole units, how many different rectangular prisms can be made from 63 cm³?

7 How many kilolitres of sea water are needed to fill this seal's enclosure at the zoo?

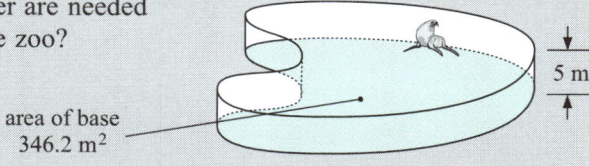

area of base 346.2 m²

8 A wall of a house has two windows and a door with the dimensions illustrated. If the wall is wallpapered and the wallpaper costs $3.75 per square metre, find the cost of papering the wall.

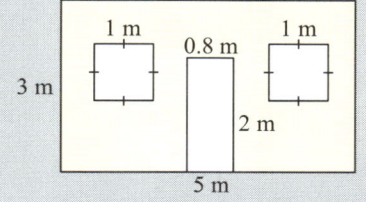

9 Find the area of floorboards showing if a 5 m by 3 m carpet is placed on the floor of a 6.5 m by 8 m room.

TRY THESE

1. Shane sold raffle tickets for the local football club. The tickets cost $1 each, or 3 for $2. If Shane sold 50 tickets for a total of $41, how many tickets at $1 were sold?

2. Kiri has a 2 litre and a 5 litre container. Explain how she can use the containers to measure exactly 1 litre.

3. **a** 3, 4, 5 and 6 are four consecutive whole numbers.
   Find *four* consecutive whole numbers which add up to 50.

   b Find *three* consecutive *odd* numbers which add up to 45.

4. There were gold, black and spotted fish swimming in a pond. There were less than 30 fish, and there was a prime number of each type. Find how many spotted fish were in the pond if the product of the number of gold fish and black fish was twenty more than the number of spotted fish?

5. Copy and complete the given magic square:

$1\frac{1}{3}$	1	$2\frac{2}{3}$
3		
		2

Chapter 9

Data collection and representation

Knowledge, skills and understandings

By the end of this chapter you should be able to

- understand the purpose of taking a sample from a population
- explain the difference between a random sample and a biased sample
- plan a range of ways to collect data (e.g., surveys, interviews)
- record data using spreadsheets, and use simple formulae to create graphs using graphing software
- construct and interpret pie graphs using graphing software
- find the mean, median and mode from given data
- interpret information from data, graphs and tables

Statistics is about collection, organisation, display, analysis and interpretation of data.

Many groups such as schools, businesses and government departments collect information. The information is used to determine whether changes are needed, or whether changes that have been made have been successful.

One major data collection time is called the Census, when the government collects information about the nation's population. This information is used to help make decisions which will affect us all in the future.

For example, the government must consider how much money may need to go into health care in the years ahead because the number of elderly people in Australia is increasing.

Results of the collection and interpretation of data are displayed using graphs, tables and diagrams.

As you work through this chapter you should gain the skills which will allow you to complete your own statistical survey and present your findings.

SAMPLES AND POPULATIONS

SOME WORDS WE NEED TO UNDERSTAND

Population: The whole group of objects or people about whom we want to make truthful statements.

Sample: The group chosen to take part in a survey or to be measured or tested in some way.

Random sample: A sample selected in such a way that any person or object has as much chance as any other of being selected.

Inferences: Conclusions you make based on your survey or investigation. For example, after completing a survey on the chocolate eating habits of students, you might *infer* (conclude) that most year 7 students eat chocolate once a week.

When the government carries out a Census it wants all Australian householders to take part and it spends many millions of dollars trying to make sure that this happens. However, for most projects we cannot afford the time or the money to survey all of the **population** so we select a smaller group of people to survey and hope that the result gained is true for the whole population.

To try and make our result as true as possible for us all we select people **randomly**. One way of doing this would be to, say, take every tenth person on some list such as the electoral roll. We must select as large a **sample** (group) from the population as we can to try and make the result as accurate as we can.

Many surveys used by television to show trends have a sample of 1000 people.

If you were going to make a statement about the height of Year 7 students at your school a sample of 5 students may produce a result which is inaccurate. A sample of 20 randomly chosen Year 7 students will improve the accuracy of your **inferences** (conclusions). We should always try to have a sample *as large as possible*.

DISCUSSION

1. Discuss why:
   a. clothing manufacturers would like to know the body measurements of people in all age groups
   b. the manager of your school tuckshop would be interested in the types and quantities of food you eat
   c. your school keeps records of what is bought by the school population throughout the year
   d. transport services gather information on passenger movement on regular services and on special occasions
   e. meteorology departments are interested in temperature, rainfall and atmospheric pressure measurements throughout the country and throughout the world.

2. For each of the 5 situations listed in question **1**, discuss how the information could be collected.

3. Discuss how you would gather data in each of the following situations:
   a. You wish to manufacture shoes and want to know how many of each size to make.
   b. As a private citizen you wish to make a case for pedestrian lights near the local school.
   c. You own a chain of fast food outlets and are wanting to expand to a new area.
   d. You are the manager of a school tuckshop and are thinking of introducing a new line of food.
   e. You are an employer and you need to choose one person from 50 applicants.

ACTIVITY — WAYS OF COLLECTING DATA

Organisations and marketing researchers have many clever ways of gathering information by tempting us with offers. Brainstorm some of the clever ways information is collected from you. Collect samples from newspapers, magazines, packaging and letter box deliveries which invite you to provide data.

ACTIVITY — RATINGS

1 Use the internet, encyclopaedias or library to find out:
   a what a 'ratings survey' is
   b why radio and television stations want to know the results of ratings surveys
   c how ratings surveys are conducted.

2 Contact a radio or television station or the agency which conducts surveys in your area and ask for a copy of their survey questions.

3 Find out what other methods radio and television stations use to gather information about their audiences.

EXERCISE 9A

1 Explain why the following surveys may provide biased data:
   a asking farmers if the government needs to give financial assistance to farmers in times of drought
   b asking 16 year olds if it should be easier for 16 year olds to get a licence to drive a car
   c asking girls if they spend too much money on clothes
   d asking boys if girls spend too much money on clothes
   e asking a football team if they like ballet
   f asking people in an expensive restaurant whether taxes are too high.

2 Suggest how to select a random sample of:
   a 400 adults
   b bottles of soft drink at a factory
   c 30 students at a school
   d words from the English language

   Mention the advantages and disadvantages of the method you suggested.

3 How would you randomly select:
   a one ticket out of 5 tickets
   b one of the letters A or B
   c one of the numbers 1, 2, 3, 4, 5 or 6
   d a card from a pack of 52 playing cards?

Example 1

From a school of 400 students, a random sample of 60 students was selected. 13 were found to have blue eyes.

a How many are in the population?
b How many are in the sample?
c What fraction of the sample has blue eyes?
d Estimate how many in the population have blue eyes.

---

a There are 400 students in the population.

b There are 60 students in the sample.

c 13 out of 60 students in the sample have blue eyes

∴ the fraction of the sample with blue eyes is $\frac{13}{60}$.

d $\frac{13}{60}$ of 400   {$\frac{13}{60}$ of the population have blue eyes}

$= \frac{13}{60} \times 400$

≈ 87 13 ÷ 60 × 400 =

So, approximately 87 students in the school have blue eyes.

You must know the difference between a population and a sample.

4 From a colony of 10 000 ants, 300 are collected to examine for red eye colour. 36 were found to have red eyes.
  a How many ants form the population?
  b How large was the sample taken?
  c What percentage of the sample had red eyes?
  d Estimate the total number of red-eyed ants.

5 50 people are randomly selected from the 750 who attended the opening night of a new play. Of the 50 people, 33 said that they liked the play.
  a How many people attended the play (the population)?
  b How large was the sample?
  c What percentage of the sample did *not* like the play?
  d Estimate the total number of people who did not like the play.

B ORGANISING CATEGORICAL DATA

Categorical data is data which can be placed in categories.

Consider the example of observing car colours at a given street intersection.

We might use a code such as   R = red,   B = blue,   G = green,   W = white,
O = other colours.

The following results were observed in a sample of 50 cars:

BGWWR   OGWRW   OOBBG   OGRWR   WWWGB
BBGGW   WWWOG   WOBWW   RWWRB   OOBWR

Once categorical information or data has been collected, it is usual to organise it in groups before it is displayed.

Categorical data may be organised using either
- a **dot plot**   or
- a **tally / frequency table**

THE MODE

The **mode** is the most frequently occurring category.

DOT PLOTS

A **dot plot** is a graph which displays data, where each dot represents one data value.

Dot plots are often used to record data initially and may be **horizontal** or **vertical**.

For the car colour data:

If the graph is set up prior to the data collection it could look like this:

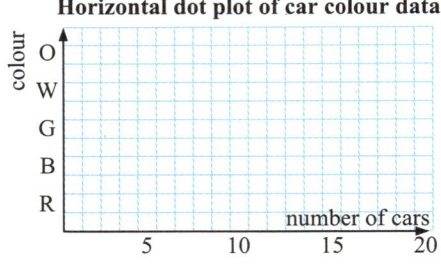

This is how the graph looks, after filling it in with data.

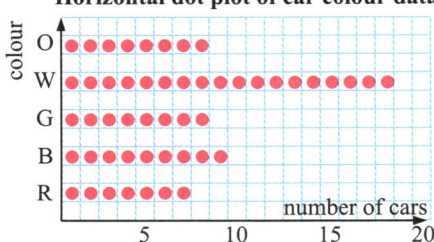

The mode is 'white' as W is the most frequently occurring category.

Example 2

At recess time the sales of drinks over a 3-minute period were recorded, with
O = orange juice, S = soft drink, C = chocolate milk, I = iced coffee.

The data was: OSSCI OCISO IOCSO OOOSC SOCOS SOOCO OIOIS

a Draw a dot plot of the data **b** What is the mode?

a
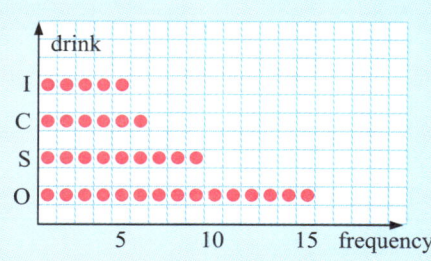

b The mode is 'orange juice'.

EXERCISE 9B.1

1 The given vertical dot plot shows shoe sizes for students in year 8.

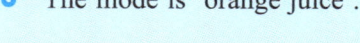

  a How many students are in year 8 at the school?
  b How many have shoe sizes 9 or more?
  c What percentage have shoe sizes of 8 or more?

2 The given vertical dot plot shows the numbers of students playing various instruments in the school orchestra.

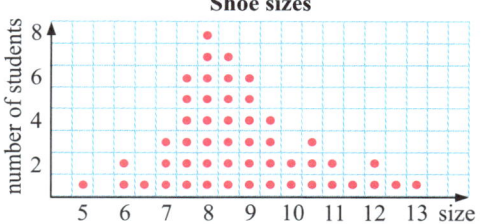

  a How many play stringed instruments?
  b How many students are in the orchestra?
  c Find the mode of the data.

3 Students in a class were asked which summer sport they wanted to play. The choices were: T = tennis, S = swimming, C = cricket, B = basketball and G = golf.

The data was: SSCTC CSSST TTBGS GGCSS TGTBC

  a Draw a horizontal dot plot of the data.
  b Find the mode of the data.

4 Students voted the most popular attractions at the Royal Adelaide show to be the side shows (S), the farm animals (F), the ring events (R), the dogs and cats (D) and the wood chopping (W). The students in a class were then asked to name their favourite.

The data was: SRWSS WFDDS RRFWS RSRWS SRRRF

  a Draw a vertical dot plot of the data.
  b Find the mode of the data.

TALLY / FREQUENCY TABLES

Another convenient method for collating information is a table containing **tally** (the counting method) and **frequency** (the number of times a particular result occurs) columns.

Such a table is called a **tally / frequency table**, a **frequency distribution table** or simply a **frequency table**.

For the car colour data the tally / frequency table is:

Colour	Tally	Frequency
Other	‖‖‖ ‖‖	8
White	‖‖‖ ‖‖‖ ‖‖‖ ‖‖‖	18
Green	‖‖‖ ‖‖	8
Blue	‖‖‖ ‖‖‖	9
Red	‖‖‖ ‖‖	7

The tally is a way of recording using strokes.

The **frequency** of a category is the number of items in that category.

Example 3

Following is data on how students in a class travel to school on a particular day. The code is W = walk, Bi = bicycle, Bu = bus, C = car, T = train

The data is:
 W Bi Bu T C Bi C W Bi Bu Bi C C Bi Bu W Bu Bu T C
 Bi Bi Bu T C C Bi C C C   W W Bu T C

a Draw a tally / frequency table to organise the data.
b What is the mode of the data?

a

Method of Travelling	Tally	Frequency
Walk	‖‖‖	5
Bicycle	‖‖‖ ‖‖‖	8
Bus	‖‖‖ ‖‖	7
Car	‖‖‖ ‖‖‖ ‖	11
Train	‖‖‖	4
	Total	35

b The mode is 'Car'.

It is the category that occurs most frequently.

EXERCISE 9B.2

1 A survey of eye colour in a class of 28 year 7 students was carried out and the results were: Br Bl Gn Bl Gn   Br Br Bl Gn Gr   Br Gr Br Br Bl   Br Bl Br Gr Gn
Br Bl Br Gn Gr   Br Bl Gn

where   Br = brown,   Bl = blue,   Gn = green,   Gr = grey

a Complete a tally / frequency table for the data.
b What is the mode of the data?

2 Students in a science class obtained the following levels of achievement:

D C C A A C C D C B C C C D B C C C C E B A C C B C B C

  a Complete a frequency distribution table for the data above.

  b Use your table to find the:

   i number of students who obtained a C

   ii fraction of students who obtained a B.

  c What is the mode of the data?

3 Tourists staying in a city hotel were surveyed to find out what they thought about the service by the hotel staff. They were asked to choose E = excellent, G = good, S = satisfactory or U = unsatisfactory. The results were:

EGGSE   USSGG   SGUGG   ESGUG   SSEGG

  a Complete a tally / frequency table for the data.

  b What is the mode of the data?

  c Suggest a reason why this survey would be carried out.

C GRAPHING CATEGORICAL DATA WITH TECHNOLOGY

Graph types for categorical data are usually
- column graphs
- pie graphs

STATISTICS PACKAGE

USING HAESE & HARRIS SOFTWARE

Click on the icon to bring up an easy to use statistical package.
It can be used to draw a variety of statistical graphs.
Change to a different graph by clicking on a different icon.
See how easy it is to change the labels on the axes and the title of the graph.

What to do:

Colour	Frequency
white	38
red	27
blue	19
green	18
other	11

Type into the correct cells the information given on car colour.

Print off the graphs of the data as a pie chart, a column graph or a strip graph.

USING A SPREADSHEET

Suppose you want to draw a frequency column graph of the car colour data given above. Perhaps you may wish to compare two sets of data from different locations.

The following steps using **MS Excel** enable you to do this quickly and easily:

Step 1: Start a new spreadsheet and type in the table as shown and then highlight the area shown.

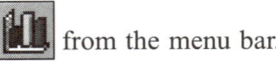

Step 2: Click on from the menu bar.

Step 3: Choose 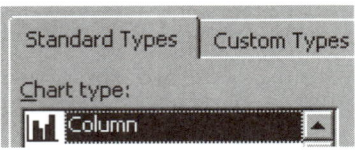 This is probably already hightlighted. Click Finish

You should get: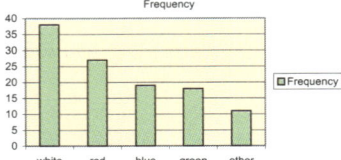

Suppose now you wish to compare two distributions:

Colour	white	red	blue	green	other
Frequency 1	38	27	19	18	11
Frequency 2	15	13	8	11	4

Step 4: Into the C column type the *Frequency 2* data and highlight the three columns as shown.

Step 5: Click on , then Column then Finish

Step 6: Choose then Finish

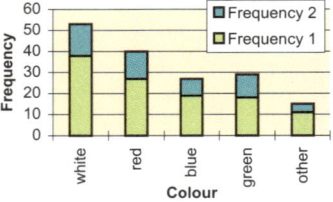

Step 7: Experiment with other types of graphs and data.

What to do:

1. Gather statistics of your own or use data from questions in the previous exercise and use the spreadsheet to draw an appropriate statistical graph of the data.

2. Find out how to adjust labels, scales, etc.

EXERCISE 9C

Use the Haese & Harris software and/or a spreadsheet to reproduce some of the statistical graphs that follow in the remaining part of this chapter.

You should also use this software in any statistical project you may be required to do.

D INTERPRETING GRAPHS OF CATEGORICAL DATA

COLUMN GRAPHS

Column graphs consist of rectangular columns of equal width which may vary in height.

The variation in height represents the difference in the number of objects in each group.

Example 4

The given graph shows the type of drink purchased by students at recess time.
- **a** What is the least popular drink?
- **b** What is the mode of the data?
- **c** How many students drink orange juice?
- **d** What percentage of students drink chocolate milk?

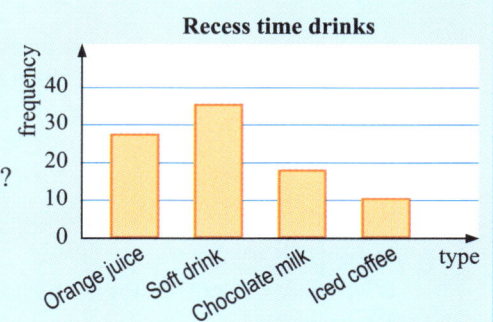

- **a** Iced coffee   {shortest column}
- **b** 'Soft drink' is the mode.
- **c** 27 drink orange juice.
- **d** The total number of students purchasing drinks $= 27 + 35 + 18 + 10 = 90$

  $\therefore$ % drinking chocolate milk $= \frac{18}{90} \times 100\% = 20\%$

EXERCISE 9D.1

1 A survey of eye colour in a class of 28 year 8 students was given and the results were:

Eye colour	Brown	Blue	Green	Grey
Frequency	11	7	6	4

- **a** Illustrate these results using a hand drawn column graph.
- **b** What is the most frequently occurring eye colour (the mode)?
- **c** What percentage of the students have blue eyes?

2 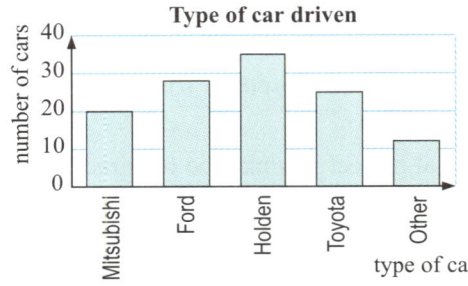 Given is a column graph of the type of vehicle driven by 120 randomly selected people.

   a Use the graph to estimate the frequency of each type of car.

   b Which make of car is most popular?

   c What percentage of the surveyed people drive Fords?

3 Yearly profit and loss figures for a business can be easily illustrated on a column graph as shown.

   a In what years was a profit made?

   b What happened in 1996?

   c What was the overall profit (or loss) over the 6-year period?

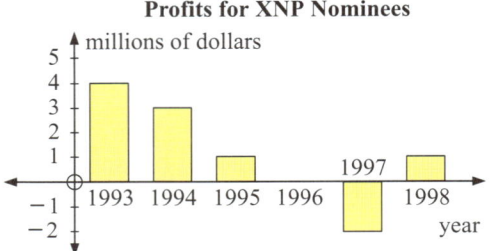

4 **Back-to-back bar graphs** are often used to compare two sets of data.

The graph alongside compares the profits of two pizza shops from the same chain of stores over several months. Shop A undertook extensive advertising during this period.

   a In what month were the highest profits for each shop?

   b What were the profits for each shop during May?

   c What feature(s) of the graph indicate the effectiveness of the advertising?

   d Find the total profit for each shop over the 6 month period.

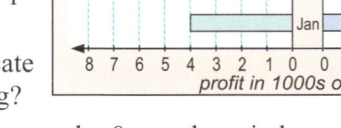

PIE GRAPHS (PIE CHARTS)

A **pie chart** is a useful way of displaying data when we want to show how things are divided up.

A full circle represents all of the data and we divide the circle into **sectors** (pie shaped wedges) to show each type or category.

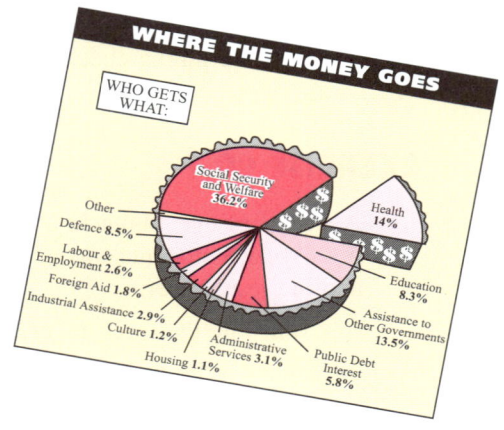

Alongside is an example of a pie graph.

Consider the following data which is the result of a survey where year 8 students were asked 'What is your favourite fruit?'.

Fruit	Frequency
Orange	13
Apple	21
Banana	10
Pineapple	7
Pear	9
Total	60

Since there are 60 people in the sample, each person is entitled to $\frac{1}{60}$th of the pie chart and $\frac{1}{60}$th of $360°$ is $6°$.

So, the sector angles for the pie chart are:

$13 \times 6° = 78°$ for the orange sector
$21 \times 6° = 126°$ for the apple sector
$10 \times 6° = 60°$ for the banana sector
$7 \times 6° = 42°$ for the pineapple sector
$9 \times 6° = 54°$ for the pear sector.

The completed pie chart is shown alongside.

We will use a spreadsheet later to put data on a pie chart.

In the following exercise we will interpret data from given pie charts.

Favourite fruit chart

Example 5

The pie chart shows the results of a survey of 120 Year 8 students. All students were asked the question:

"What is your favourite sport?"

Use the chart to determine:

a the most popular sport
b the least popular sport
c the number of students whose favourite sport is basketball
d the number of students whose favourite sport is cricket.

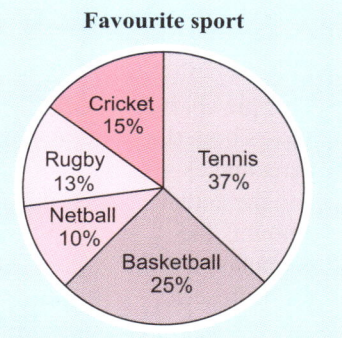

Favourite sport

a The largest sector angle indicates the most popular sport, and this is *tennis*.

b *Netball* is the least popular sport (smallest sector angle).

c 25% of students said basketball is their favourite sport.
So, the number of students whose favourite sport is basketball is

    25% of 120   {120 students altogether}
$= 0.25 \times 120$ {'%' means per hundred; "of" means $\times$}
$= 30$ *Calculator:* 25 ÷ 100 × 120

d Number of students whose favourite sport is cricket is

    15% of 120
$= 0.15 \times 120$
$= 18$

EXERCISE 9D.2

1. The pie chart alongside illustrates the proportion of water for various household uses.

   a For what purpose is the most water used?

   b For what purpose is the least amount of water used?

   c If the household used 400 kilolitres of water during a particular period, estimate the quantity of water used in:

   i showering   **ii** cleaning.

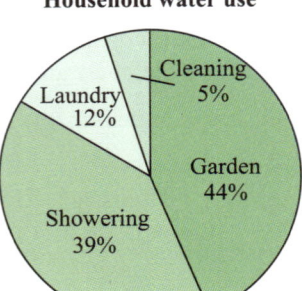

2.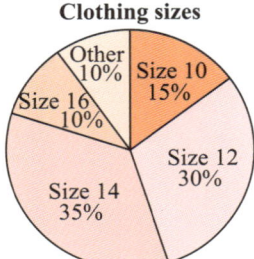

   The pie chart alongside shows the percentages of women who wear certain sizes of clothing.

   a Find what size is least commonly worn.

   b A group of 200 women attends a fashion parade. Estimate how many would wear size 14 clothing.

3. This pie chart shows both the percentages and the actual amounts the council spent for each sector.

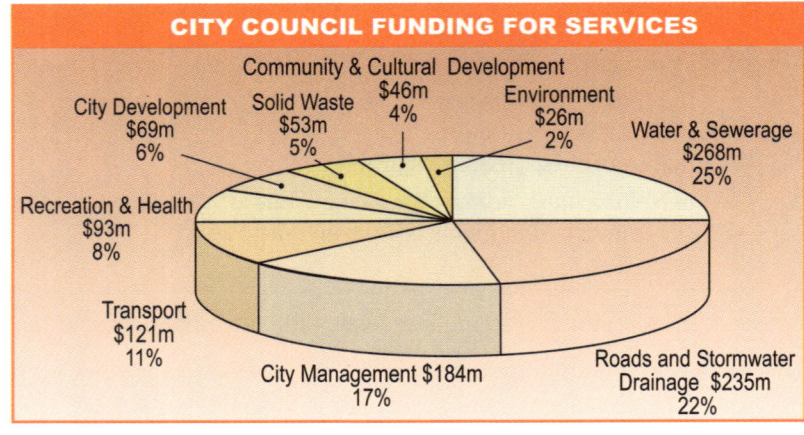

   a Briefly describe what the graph is about.

   b Comment on the usefulness of having both percentages and amounts shown.

   c What percentage of total funding is spent on:

   i Recreation and Health   **ii** Community and Cultural Development?

   d How much money is spent on:

   i Environment   **ii** City Development?

   e On what service is the largest amount spent?

   f How much is spent in total?

E NUMERICAL DATA

Numerical data is data which is in number form.

Numerical data is *organised* using a **stem-and-leaf plot** or a **tally / frequency table**.

Numerical data is usually **represented graphically** by a column graph.

STEM-AND-LEAF PLOTS

When data has been grouped and displayed as a frequency column graph the original individual scores may be lost.

To avoid this loss of original data a **stem-and-leaf plot** is often drawn instead of the column graph. This plot shows the original data. The stem and leaves are clearly shown in the following example.

The weights (in kg) of army recruits are: 101, 91, 83, 84, 72, 93, 67, 85, 79, 87, 78, 89, 68, 80, 107, 70, 85, 64, 95, 76, 87, 74, 68, 59, 82, 77

Stem-and-leaf display of weight data

unit = 1
the scale or key

```
 5 | 9
 6 | 4 7 8 8          ← a stem
 7 | 0 2 4 6 7 8 9
 8 | 0 2 3 4 5 5 7 7 9  ← a leaf
 9 | 1 3 5
10 | 1 7
```

a stem label → 9

Notice that:

- 6 | 4 7 8 8   represents the 4 scores 64, 67, 68 and 68.
- The leaves are placed in ascending order.
- The **scale** (unit = 1) tells us the place value of each leaf. If the scale was 'unit = 0.1' then   6 | 4 7 8 8   would represent   6.4, 6.7, 6.8, 6.8
- Rotating the diagram through 90° we see the "shape" of a column graph.

```
 5 | 9
 6 | 4 7 8 8
 7 | 0 2 4 6 7 8 9
 8 | 0 2 3 4 5 5 7 7 9
 9 | 1 3 5
10 | 1 7
```

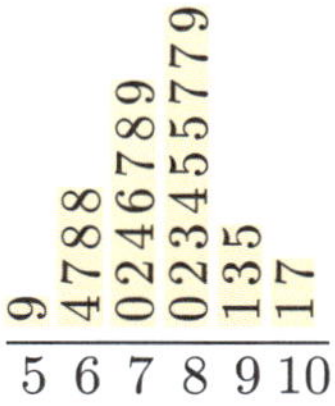

Example 6

A fisherman recorded the total weight of all schnapper caught each day. Construct a stem-and-leaf plot for the data shown below (in kg):

11, 16, 07, 25, 39, 26, 14, 17, 18, 31
31, 25, 43, 32, 25, 19, 16, 08, 34, 21

Stem-and-leaf display for schnapper catch (in kg).

```
0 | 7 8
1 | 1 4 6 6 7 8 9
2 | 1 5 5 5 6
3 | 1 1 2 4 9
4 | 3
```

unit = 1

Example 7

A greengrocer recorded the weights of all rockmelons sold on a particular day. Construct a stem-and-leaf plot for the data shown below (in kg):

1.1, 1.6, 0.7, 2.5, 3.9, 2.6, 1.4, 1.7, 1.8, 3.1
3.1, 2.5, 4.3, 3.2, 2.5, 1.9, 1.6, 0.8, 3.4, 2.1

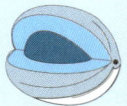

Stem-and-leaf display for rockmelons sold (in kg).

unit = 0.1

0	7 8
1	1 4 6 6 7 8 9
2	1 5 5 5 6
3	1 1 2 4 9
4	3

EXERCISE 9E.1

1 The weights of 24 soccer players were recorded to the nearest kg and the following data was obtained:

72 63 90 70 67 71 89 64 93 86
66 78 75 89 80 91 81 72 87 72
86 84 84 87

Construct a stem-and-leaf display of this data.

2 The weights of 30 fifteen week old piglets were obtained to the nearest kg. The weights were:

18 20 30 30 25 19 30 34 28 36 32 33 38 13 37
29 43 50 20 44 23 27 27 47 37 17 38 51 29 39

Construct a stem-and-leaf display of this data.

3 The time (in hours) taken by farmers to plough, fertilise and seed each paddock is given below:

7   24   9 12 41 30 36
28 18 27 32 24 13 25

Construct a stem-and-leaf display of the data.

4 The time (in hours) taken by farmers to travel to their nearest town centre is given below:

1.0 2.4 0.9 1.2 3.6 3.0 0.7
0.8 1.8 2.7 0.2 2.4 1.3 0.5

Construct a stem-and-leaf display of the data stating the scale used.

WORKING WITH NUMERICAL DATA

Example 8

An exceptional hockey player scores the following number of goals each match for 25 matches: 4 3 6 1 5   8 4 2 2 4   6 0 5 1 9   3 7 2 6 6   8 3 6 2 10

a Organise the data in a tally / frequency table.
b Graph the data on a column graph.
c On how many occasions did the player score 5 or more goals in a match?
d On what percentage of occasions did the player score 4 or more goals in a match?

a
Goals	Tally	Frequency
0	|	1
1	||	2
2	||||	4
3	|||	3
4	|||	3
5	||	2
6						5
7	|	1
8	||	2
9	|	1
10	|	1

b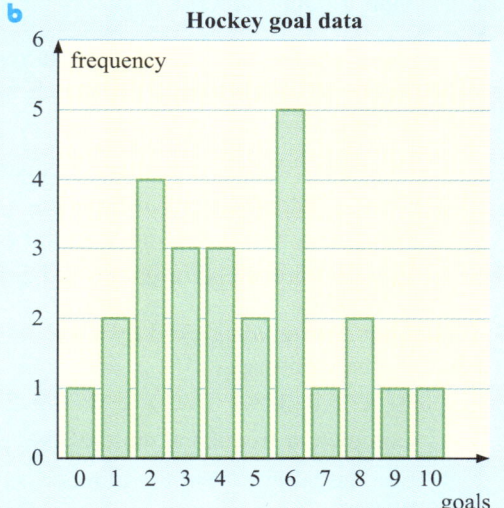

c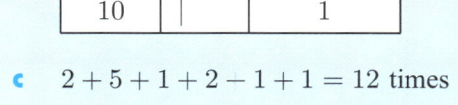

d scored 4 or more goals on 15 occasions

$$\therefore \text{ percentage } = \frac{15}{25} \times 100\%$$
$$= 0.6 \times 100\%$$
$$= 60\%$$

EXERCISE 9E.2

1 a Complete a frequency distribution table (tally / frequency) for the number of children in 30 families:
    0, 4, 6, 2, 1, 3, 2, 4, 0, 2, 1, 2, 5, 0, 2, 3, 1, 4, 2, 1, 2, 4, 3, 3, 0, 4, 5, 2, 2, 4
  b Use your table to find the:
    i   number of families with two children
    ii fraction of families with three children.

2 Following are the ages of children at a party:
    12, 11, 17, 12, 14, 13, 11, 12, 15, 13, 12, 14, 11, 14, 12, 10, 12, 11, 13, 14
  a Organise the data in a tally / frequency table.
  b How many attended the party?

c How many were aged 12 or 13?
d What percentage were 13 or more years old?
e Display the data on a column graph.

3 The given graph shows the number of points scored by a basketballer over a 60-match period.

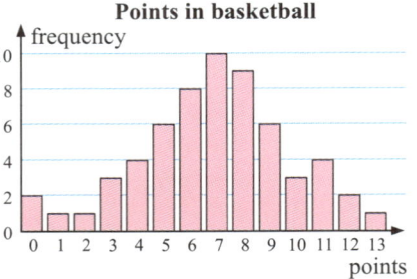

  a What point score occurred most frequently?
  b On how many occasions were 10 or more points scored?
  c In what percentage of matches were fewer than 5 points scored?

4 Following are the number of goals thrown by a netballer during a 23 match season. The number of goals scored per match were:

17 22 18 23 20 20 19 20 21 26 23 22 20 24 20 19 19 23 22 17 19 21 21

  a Organise the data in a tally / frequency table.
  b Draw a column graph of the data.
  c How many times did she score 20 or more goals?
  d In what percentage of games did she score 22 or more goals?

5 The number of goals kicked by a soccer player each match for the 2002 season was:

3 0 4 2 0 3 3 1 2 1 1 2 3 3 2 2 5 0 2 1 4 3

  a Complete a frequency table of the given data.
  b Use the table to find the number of games where the player kicked:
    i exactly 3 goals   **ii** at least 3 goals.

6 A record was kept of the number of goals scored by a goal shooter in netball games during the season. The number of goals was:

10, 7, 8, 5, 8, 7, 10, 10, 6, 11, 5, 7, 7, 12, 7, 11, 6, 5, 8, 8, 7

  a Complete a frequency table for the data above.
  b Use your table to find the number of games in which the shooter scored:
    i exactly 8 goals   **ii** at least 8 goals.

7 It is stated on match-boxes that the average contents is 50. When 40 boxes were sampled, the following numbers of matches were counted:

48, 51, 49, 50, 51, 52, 50, 48, 49, 51, 50, 53, 48, 49, 51, 50, 52, 49, 50, 52,
51, 48, 50, 49, 50, 51, 52, 50, 49, 48, 52, 50, 51, 49, 50, 50, 48, 53, 52, 49

  a Prepare a frequency distribution table for this data.
  b How many boxes had exactly 50 matches?
  c How many boxes had 50 or more matches?
  d What fraction of boxes had less than 50 matches?
  e Should the manufacturer be prosecuted for false advertising?

F   MEAN AND MEDIAN

The mean and median are measures of the 'middle' of a set of numerical data.

THE MEAN

The **mean** (or **average**) of a set of numbers is a measure of the middle of the distribution. Performances in various sports are often measured by using means (or averages).

For example, in cricket, batting performances are compared using averages. The higher the average, the better the performance.

> The **mean** (or **average**) is the total of all scores divided by the number of scores.

For example,

the mean of   2, 3, 3, 5, 6 and 11   is

$$\frac{2+3+3+5+6+11}{6}$$
$$=\frac{30}{6}$$
$$=5$$

Often $\bar{x}$ is the symbol used to represent the mean of a set of numbers.

DISCUSSION

1. In cricket, why is the batting average a better measure of performance than the total number of runs scored?
2. In football, why are heights and weights of individuals in grand final teams published?
3. Why are the skill levels of individuals in sporting teams not published?

Example 9

Find the mean of   7, 11, 15, 6, 11, 19, 23, 0 and 7.

$$\bar{x} = \frac{7+11+15+6+11+19+23+0+7}{9}$$
$$\therefore \quad \bar{x} = \frac{99}{9}$$
$$\therefore \quad \bar{x} = 11$$

Remember that the mean is a measure of the middle of a set of scores.

EXERCISE 9F.1

1 Find the mean of   1, 2, 3, 4, 5, 6 and 7.

2 Calculate the mean of the scores   7, 8, 0, 3, 0, 6, 0, 11 and 1.

3 In basketballer Michael Jordan's last 12 games of a season he scored 23, 18, 36, 29, 38, 44, 18, 52, 47, 20, 50 and 42 points. What was his mean point score over this period?

4 Compare the performance of two groups of students in the same mental arithmetic test out of 10 marks.

    Group X: 7, 6, 6, 8, 6, 9, 7, 5, 4, 7   *Group Y:* 9, 6, 7, 6, 8, 10, 3, 9, 9, 8, 9

  a Calculate the mean of each group.

  b There are 10 students in *group X* and 11 in *group Y*. Because of unequal numbers in each group it is unfair to compare their means. True or false?

  c Which group performed better at the test?

5 A cricketer has scored   23, 34, 2, 17, 83, 0, 19 and 28. At 23 he is given not out when the TV replay clearly shows he was caught behind. He then continues and is eventually out at 131. Find:

  a the actual mean score

  b what his mean score would have been if he was given out at 23.

6 The given data shows the goals scored by girls in the local netball association.

  a Find the mean number of goals for each goal shooter.

  b Which goal shooter has the best average performance?

Name	Goals	Games
Sally Brown	238	9
Jan Simmons	235	10
Jane Haren	228	9
Peta Piper	219	7
Lee Wong	207	8
Polly Lynch	199	7
Sam Crawley	197	6

THE MEDIAN

> The **median** of a set of scores is found by placing the scores in order of size and then choosing the middle score (or average of the two middle scores).

Example 10

Find the median of the scores:

  a 7, 9, 8, 6, 7, 10, 8, 7, 9   **b** 2, 1, 3, 4, 4, 2, 3, 2

  a In order of size the scores are: 6, 7, 7, 7, $\underbrace{8}_{\text{middle score}}$, 8, 9, 9, 10

    ∴ the median is 8.

  b In order of size the scores are: 1, 2, 2, $\underbrace{2, 3}_{\text{two middle scores}}$, 3, 4, 4

    ∴ the median is $2\tfrac{1}{2}$.   {the average of 2 and 3 $= \dfrac{2+3}{2} = 2\tfrac{1}{2}$}

EXERCISE 9F.2

1 Find the median of:
  a 3, 2, 2, 5, 4, 4, 3, 2, 6, 4, 5, 4, 1
  b 7, 11, 4, 8, 6, 9, 8, 8, 1, 3
  c 2, 5, 3, 3, 6, 3, 5, 4, 5, 1, 7

MEDIAN DEMO

2 Which is the better measure of the 'middle' for the following data; the mean or median?
    1, 2, 1, 1, 3, 1, 4, 1, 2, 1, 9, 11   (Find each of these measures first.)

3 A cricketer has scores of 3, 8, 42, 11, 0, 0, 12, 113, 7 and 17.
  a Find the cricketer's median score.
  b Find the cricketer's mean score.
  c Which of the measures (median or mean) best describes the cricketers batting performance?

4 For the dot plot of shoe sizes, determine the median size.

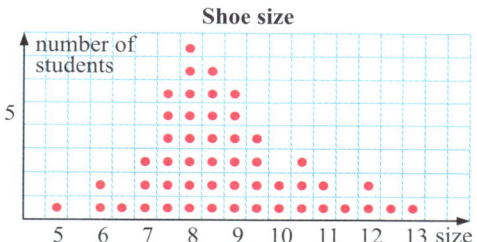

Example 11

For the given schnapper catch stem-and-leaf plot, find the median weight.

Weight in kg

0	7 8
1	1 4 6 6 7 8 9
2	1 5 5 5 6
3	1 1 2 4 9
4	3

unit = 1

0	~~7 8~~
1	~~1 4~~ 6 6 ~~7 8 9~~
2	1 5 5 5 6
3	~~1 1 2 4 9~~
4	3

Crossing off in pairs from top and bottom, 21 and 25 remain

∴ median = 23 kg

{the average of these two scores}

5 For each of the following stem-and-leaf plots, find the median.

a

2	2 5
3	0 1 3 7
4	2 2 4 5 9
5	0 4 8
6	1

unit = 1

b

4	0 6
5	1 2 3 3 3 9
6	4 4 5 6 7 7 8
7	1 2 5

unit = 1

c

1	2 3 7
2	0 0 2 1 6
3	2 4 4 5 5 5 8
4	0 1 7 7
5	6

unit = 1

6 The ages of the employees of International Sports Coaching Clinics are given below:

23, 18, 29, 31, 25, 24, 17, 33, 22, 20, 21, 25, 16, 34
21, 23, 22, 27, 28, 30, 28, 19, 20, 22, 22, 21, 27, 26

- **a** Draw a stem-and-leaf plot of the data.
- **b** Find the:
    - **i** median age
    - **ii** mean age.

7 Two year 7 mathematics classes sat for the same mathematics test out of 20 marks. Their results were:

Class 7P: 19 20 11 15 16 17 17 14 16 17 20 18 17 16 15 15 16 16 17 16
Class 7Q: 14 13 16 17 20 13 16 15 18 12 13 14 17 14 12 13 13 14 10

- **a** State the highest and lowest marks for each class.
- **b** Find the mean and median of results for each class.
- **c** Which class performed better at the test?

| ACTIVITY | A SURVEY |

What to do:

1. Brainstorm a list of ways information is gathered.

2. Organise the list into categories such as questionnaires, face to face interviews, opinion polls, telephone surveys etc.
3. Organise a way of recording the data including the person who provided it, i.e., adult male/female, child male/female.
4. Prepare a set of questions which every student in the class will use. Your aim is to find out:
    - **a** which members of the households have been involved in providing data in the last 12 months
    - **b** what methods were used to collect this data.
5. Have every student in your class use the prepared questions to interview every member of their household.
6. Decide on a time you want all the information collected by.
7. Collect all the information gathered by each student.
8. Organise and present the information in tables and graphs.
9. For one set of data draw a column graph and a pie chart.
10. Put titles and keys on all graphs and tables.
11. Discuss:
    - **a** the results
    - **b** how you could have improved the accuracy of the data gathering.

G   LINE GRAPHS AND TIME SERIES

Line graphs are obtained by joining data points with lines.

The lines help us to see the **changing nature** of the graph and possible **trends**.

When we have time on the horizontal axis, the graph is often called a **time series**.

Example 12

The given graph shows the weight of a girl as recorded on her birthday each year. It is her birthday today. Estimate:
- **a** her weight at birth
- **b** her weight at age 10
- **c** her weight today
- **d** her weight increase from age 8 to 12.
- **e** What is the meaning of the graph between years 6 and 8?

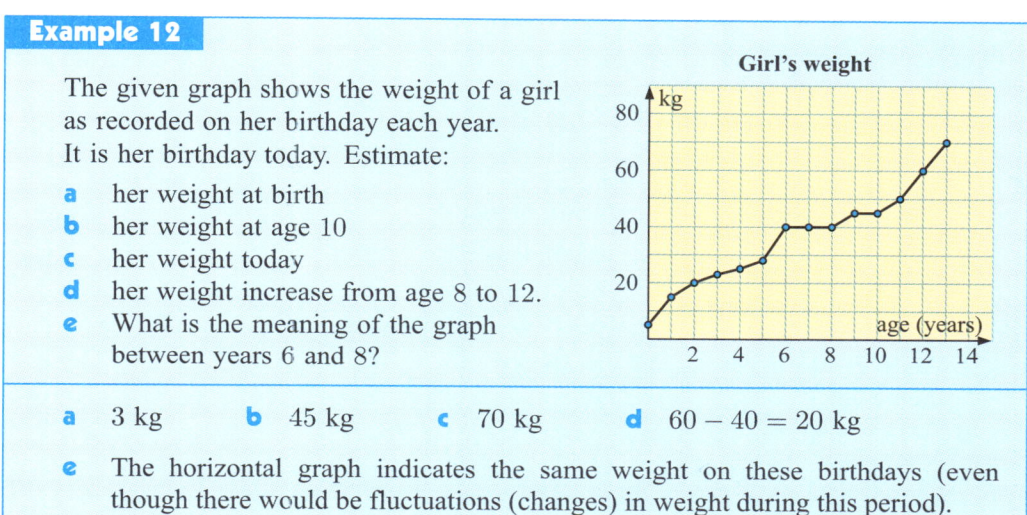

- **a** 3 kg
- **b** 45 kg
- **c** 70 kg
- **d** 60 − 40 = 20 kg
- **e** The horizontal graph indicates the same weight on these birthdays (even though there would be fluctuations (changes) in weight during this period).

EXERCISE 9G

1 Kiri rides her bicycle to the shop. She has hooked up a device which measures her pulse rate. The data is later graphed over 1 minute time intervals.

- **a** Find her pulse rate after 2 minutes.
- **b** Find her pulse rate after 7 minutes.
- **c** During what time intervals did her pulse rate increase?
- **d** Find the change in her pulse rate during the interval from 4 to 9 minutes.
- **e** What was her highest recorded pulse rate?
- **f** Is this a time series graph?

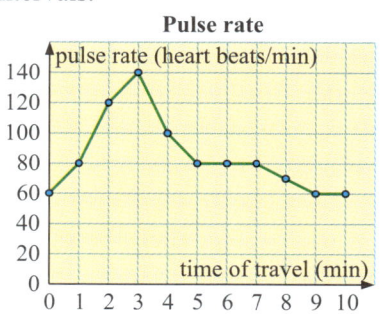

2 The rainfall for various months of the year is given in the following table:

Month	Ja	Fe	Ma	Ap	Ma	Ju	Ju	Au	Se	Oc	No	De
Rainfall (mm)	50	80	50	100	200	350	270	160	100	80	40	70

- **a** Plot the data using a line graph with months on the horizontal axis.
- **b** During which period of 4 months did most rain fall?
- **c** What was the driest month?
- **d** What percentage of the year's rainfall fell in winter (June to August)?

3 The following graph gives the average maximum daily temperature for all months of the year for a country town.

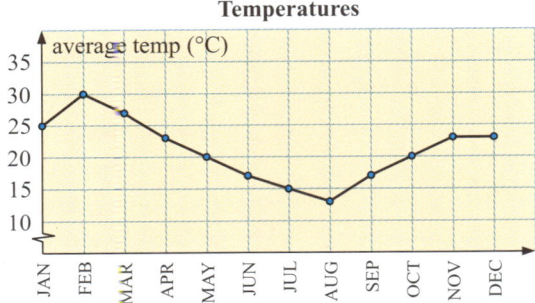

a What is the meaning of ⌇ on the temperature axis?

b Which month was the hottest?

c Which 4 month period was coldest?

d Why is the graph decreasing from February to August?

e Find the average of the monthly temperatures.

4 The following graph shows the income and costs of a small business over a 13 week period.

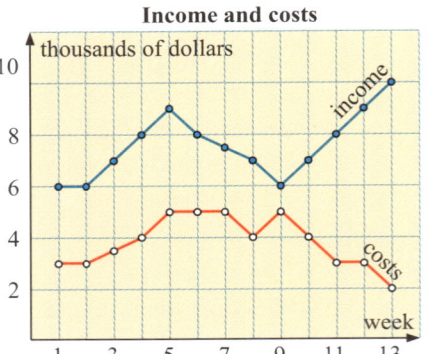

  a What were the income and costs figures for week 5?

  b What was the profit during week 5?

  c During which period did the weekly income fall?

  d Which week had the greatest profit:
  i in the first 6 weeks
  ii in the entire 13 weeks?

ACTIVITY — A POSSIBLE STATISTICAL EXPERIMENT

Aim: To grow wheat over a 21 day period in a controlled experiment using 6 grains of wheat per plot.

You will need: 4 saucers or coffee jar lids, cotton wool, 24 grains of wheat, measure, eye dropper, diluted liquid fertiliser.

What to do:

1 Layer the cotton wool three quartars of the way up each lid.
  Place 6 grains of wheat at equal distances apart in each lid.

2 Label the lids as plot 1, 2, 3 and 4. Saturate each plot with 15 mL of water.

3 In plot 1 squeeze 2 drops of water onto each grain of wheat every week day.

4 In plot 2 squeeze 2 drops of water onto each grain of wheat every Monday, Wednesday and Friday.

5 In plot 3 squeeze 2 drops of water and one drop of diluted fertiliser every Monday, Wednesday and Friday.

6 In plot 4 squeeze 2 drops of water and 1 drop of diluted fertiliser onto each grain of wheat every weekday.

7 Place all the plots in the same safe, sheltered and sunny place.

8 Every Monday, Wednesday and Friday, record the mean height in of any germinating seeds for each plot in table form. Avoid handling any shoots.

9 Use graphs and the language of statistics to comment on your results. (You could use a spreadsheet.) Variations on this experiment:
   a use other seeds like broad beans instead of wheat
   b keep the plots inside a cupboard away from natural light
   c use potting mix or soil instead of cotton wool.

REVIEW SET A — CHAPTER 9

1 The data below represents birth months in a year 7 class. January is represented by the number 1, February by the number 2 and so on up to December which is 12. Boys are shown in black and girls in blue.

6	7	3	9	5	5	9	12	10	4	1	12	6	3	5
7	7	4	10	3	7	1	9	5	9	4	8	7	11	4

   a Prepare a tally / frequency table to show this data.
   b Answer the following questions:
      i How many students were in the class?
      ii How many girls were in the class?
      iii In which month were the most boys born?
      iv What fraction of the class was born in April?
      v In which month were the least number of students born?
      vi What percentage of the class was born in March?
      vii In which months were the least number of girls born?

2 Write T(true) or F(false) for the following statements:
   a Investigating what Australian students like to eat by asking every student in a school is a sample survey.
   b Asking every tenth person at a netball match whether they liked sport would be a random survey.
   c Asking 100 people in a shopping centre who they would vote for in a state election is too small a sample for a poll.

3 At netball Sally threw the following number of goals in 15 matches:
8 11 5 17 13 16 15 16 6 16 11 11 20 7 8
Find Sally's
   a median number of goals
   b mean number of goals.

4 Use the line graph to answer the following questions:

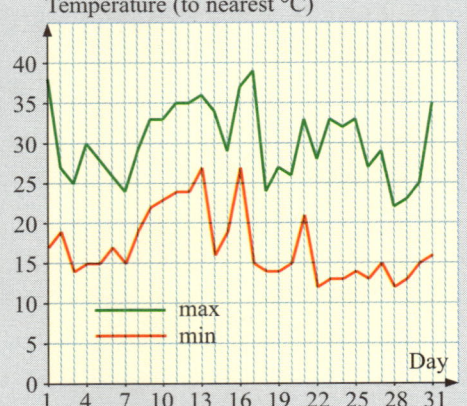

  a On how many days was the minimum temperature
     i below 15°C   **ii** above 20°C?
  b On what day was the
     i highest maximum
     ii lowest maximum
     iii greatest difference between maximum and minimum
     iv smallest difference between maximum and minimum?
  c How many times did a daily minimum temperature exceed the lowest maximum for the month?

5 Use the circle graph alongside to answer the following questions:

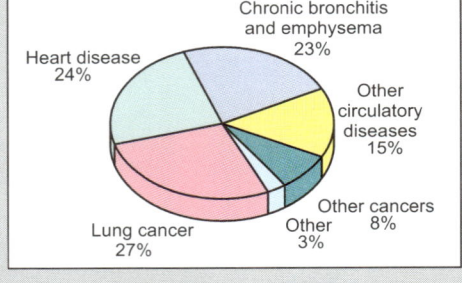

  a What was the major disease caused by smoking?
  b What 2 groups of diseases made up 50% of all smoking related deaths?
  c If 20 000 people died in one year as a result of smoking, how many died from
     i heart disease   **ii** lung cancer
     iii other cancers?

REVIEW SET B   CHAPTER 9

1 A medal is awarded to the best and fairest player in a national sporting competition. Umpires award 3 votes to the player they feel was the best and fairest in each game. 2 votes are awarded for second best and 1 vote for the third best.

Listed below are the votes awarded to a recent winner. The first vote from the left was for the first game, the second vote was for the second game etc.

    0   2   0   3   1   0   3   2   3   1   1   3   2   0   3   2   1   0   3   2

  a Use the tally method to prepare a frequency chart to show the votes awarded to the winner for each game.
  b Draw a column graph to show the frequency of the votes.
  c Draw a line graph to show the progressive vote total at the end of each game. Your horizontal axis should show each week in the season.
  d In how many games did the winner not receive votes?
  e What was the winner's total vote?
  f In what percentage of games did the winner receive votes?
  g What was the **i** mean   **ii** median of the winner's votes?

2 Write T(true) or F(false) for the following statements:
  a Collecting data from your own customers about the quality of the food in your restaurants would be an example of a biased survey.
  b When the Australian Bureau of Statistics carries out its National Census of Housing and Population it is using a random sample.
  c Voting in a national election is an example of a population survey.

3 The given pie chart represents the sale of $100 000 worth of goods by a sports store during its February sale.
  a Gear from which two sports sold best?
  b What value of goods (in dollars) from watersports and tennis was sold?
  c If the same percentage of goods was sold in the sports store's $\frac{1}{2}$ million dollar 'End of Financial Year Sale':
    i how much fitness gear was sold
    ii what was the total amount of tennis and water sports sales?

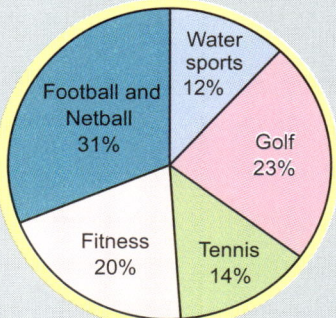

4 For the given stem-and-leaf plot find the median.

```
5 | 1 3 5
6 | 2 3 3 4 6 8 8 8 9
7 | 0 1 3 4 5 5 7 8
8 | 1 1 2 5 6 7
9 | 2 7        unit = 1
```

5 Bill's Bakery advertises a new variety in its range of pies. The daily sales of the new variety are: 23, 25, 18, 21, 17, 14, 15, 19, 18, 11, 15, 12, 6, 9
  a Find:
    i the median number of pies sold   **ii** the mean number of pies sold
  b Comment on the trend of the sales.

REVIEW SET C   CHAPTER 9

1 a In a pie chart a full circle is divided into .... to show each type or category.
  b The number of times a particular result occurs in a table of information is called the ....
  c In a column graph the difference in .... represents the difference in the number of objects in each group.

2 a Draw a column graph for the following number of pars scored by a golfer in consecutive rounds of 18 holes:
    3, 5, 2, 7, 5, 8, 1, 9, 3, 5, 7, 4, 6, 5, 2, 5, 8, 6, 3, 5, 4, 7, 5, 8, 3.
  b Use your column graph to find the:
    i median **ii** mean number of pars per round.

3 The heights of 10 of the tallest hockey players in centimetres are:
175, 183, 176, 179, 177, 188, 176, 177, 178, 181.
What is the   **a** median height   **b** mean height?

4 The following are the ages of teachers in a school:
56 37 44 51 49 23 40 47 43 38 61 52 21 54 37
43 48 53 45 51 23 58 50 63 45 31 42 39 46 51

a From this data make   **i** a stem-and-leaf plot   **ii** a column graph
b Find the   **i** modal age   **ii** median age   **iii** mean age

5 The column graph represents the value of one month's sales at Stan's Super Savings Store.

a **i** What goods represent the highest value of electrical items sold?
   ii Give two reasons why this may have happened.
b What was the total value of entertainment items?
c What was the total value of goods sold?
d If 200 small kitchen appliances like kettles, toasters, irons etc. were sold, what was their average price?

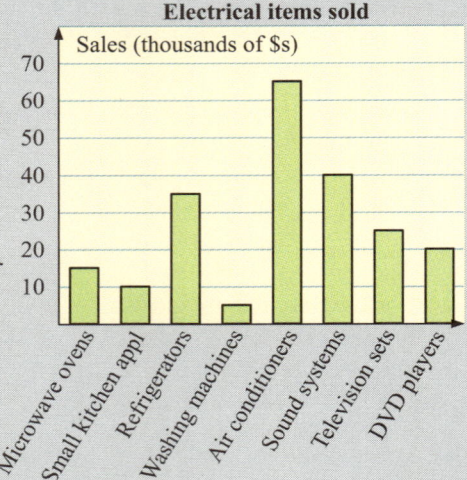

6 A travel club offers discount on travel and accommodation to its members. The more members it has, the bigger discounts it can offer. The pie chart shows membership categories.

a Which category (**A**, **B**, **C** or **D**) has most members?
b If the club has 5400 members, how many have been members for more than 10 years?
c Can you say whether the number of members is increasing? Give reasons for your answer.

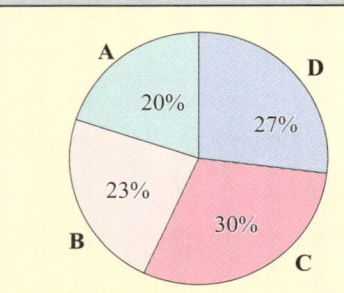

A members for more than 10 years
B members for 5 years but less than 10 years
C members for 1 year but less than 5 years
D members for less than 1 year

Chapter 10

Time and temperature

Knowledge, skills and understandings

By the end of this chapter you should be able to

- make comparisons between time zones in Australia and calculate changes incorporating daylight saving
- read and use a variety of timetables
- construct and interpret timelines using an appropriate scale
- explain ways in which time is measured in other cultures (e.g., calendars which are calculated by moon cycles)
- use Speed = $\dfrac{\text{Distance}}{\text{Time}}$ to answer problems
- use formula Distance = Speed × Time to solve problems
- interpret the terminology Fahrenheit, °F
- use online resources to compare current temperatures in different parts of the world

For most of us, time seems to control our lives. Questions like the following all involve time:

How long until the bus leaves?
What time do you have to be at school?
When did the Second World War finish?
For how long did Elizabeth I reign in England?
What time does the netball grand final start?
How long will it take us to travel to Tokyo?

ACTIVITY   TIME OUT

What to do:

Work in small groups.
Read through the following activities then choose any two.

1 Brainstorm 20 different things that indicate a particular time for you. For example:
   a You feel that your hair is getting too long .... it's time for a haircut.
   b The UV reading is increasing .... it's time to put on sunscreen and protective clothing.
   c Heavy clouds are approaching .... it's time to take the washing off the line.
   Share your list with the rest of the class.

2 List ways that the following would be aware of time changes:
   a animals in the wild   b domestic animals   c human infants
   d farmers   e sailors at sea 300 years ago

3 Imagine you are in an age before watches were invented. Suggest 20 different ways that people in that era may have observed or measured time.

4 a Outline some of the problems people may have had in measuring time using:
      i   candles   ii water clocks   iii shadow sticks
      iv sundials   v   sand-glasses   vi   pendulum clocks
      vii mechanical clocks
   b Describe how the makers of each of the above may have **calibrated** and controlled their measures to make them more accurate.

5 Before the development of modern time measuring equipment, imagine what it may have been like comparing record performances between athletes around the world. For example:

   "Sally Jones swam the 1500 metre freestyle in 4.753 beeswax candles"
   or "Carl Lewis ran the 100 metres in $12\frac{1}{2}$ drips from the water clock".

   Use examples other than sport to create a few of your own timing situations.

6 List 20 occupations where time or timing is very important, for example, musicians, restaurant chefs, race starters, etc. For each of the occupations listed, write 2 consequences for wrong timing.

A TIME LINES

Time lines are simple graphs which display time, often in the form of dates, underneath the line and key events which have happened (or ones we want to happen) above the line.

Example 1

The following time line shows some of the important dates in Sarah's life:

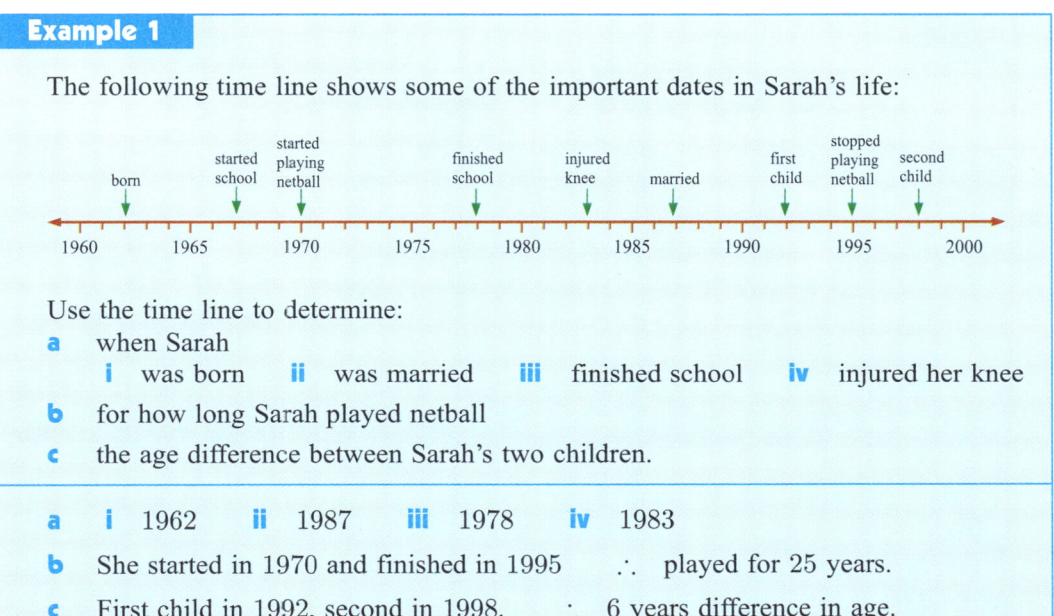

Use the time line to determine:
a when Sarah
  i was born   **ii** was married   **iii** finished school   **iv** injured her knee
b for how long Sarah played netball
c the age difference between Sarah's two children.

a i 1962   **ii** 1987   **iii** 1978   **iv** 1983
b She started in 1970 and finished in 1995   ∴ played for 25 years.
c First child in 1992, second in 1998.   ∴ 6 years difference in age.

EXERCISE 10A

1 The following time line shows when various methods of writing first appeared:

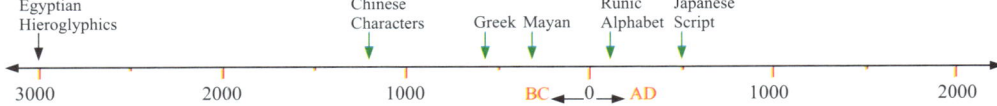

a What does BC stand for on the time line above?
b Estimate when the Runic Alphabet first appeared.
c How long was there between the appearance of Egyptian Hieroglyphics and Chinese Characters?

AD stands for Anno Domini and means 'In the Year of Our Lord'.

2 The given time line shows the monarchs of England during the 20th century:

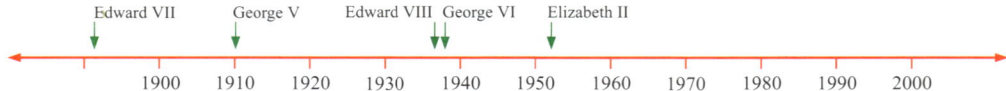

    a Which monarch reigned longest in the 20th century?
    b How long did the reign of George VI last?
    c How much longer was the reign of Edward VII than Edward VIII?

3 The following time line shows the period of various Chinese civilizations:

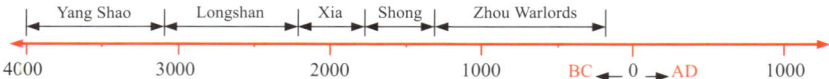

Use the time line and a ruler to:

    a find the Chinese civilization which lasted longest
    b determine the period for which the Xia dynasty lasted
    c find how much longer the Longshan civilization lasted compared with the Shong civilization.

ACTIVITY — DEVELOPING TIME LINES

The purpose of this activity is to draw at least one time line based on your research of relevant information.

What to do:

1. Decide on a suitable topic to research. Below is a list of possible topics, but you should consider researching a topic which interests you and not necessarily one of these:
   - Prime Ministers of Australia
   - Wars of the 20th century
   - Significant dates in your family's history (birthdays, marriages, special holidays, etc).
2. Choose a suitable scale for your time line and complete it with all relevant information.
3. Write down 4 questions based on your time line which a fellow class member can try to answer.

Swap your time line with a fellow student and answer the questions asked.

ACTIVITY — ESTIMATING A MINUTE

In small groups or as a whole class arrange a competition to find who is best at estimating one minute.

One student (or teacher) has a watch and others try to estimate a minute without seeing a watch or clock.

B UNITS OF TIME

We are all familiar with the concept of time and the measurement of time in years, months, weeks, days, hours, minutes and seconds.

RELATIONSHIP BETWEEN TIME UNITS

1 year	1 week = 7 days
= 12 months	1 day = 24 hours
= 52 weeks	1 hour = 60 minutes
= 365 days (or 366 in a leap year)	1 minute = 60 seconds

The number of days in the month varies:

January	31		July	31
February	28	(29 in a leap year)	August	31
March	31		September	30
April	30		October	31
May	31		November	30
June	30		December	31

These are easily remembered using:

Note: A **leap year** occurs if the year is divisible by 4 but not by 100 except if the year is divisible by 400.

For example, 1996 is a leap year
2000 is a leap year
1800 and 2100 are not leap years.

Thirty days have September, April, June and November. All the rest have thirty one except February which has twenty eight and twenty nine in a leap year.

SPECIAL NAMES

1 decade = 10 years
1 century = 100 years
1 millennium = 1000 years

With the introduction of high speed computers which are performing calculations in shorter and shorter times we often speak in units which are less than one second. Some small time units are:

1 millisecond = $\frac{1}{1000}$ of a second
1 microsecond = $\frac{1}{1\,000\,000}$ of a second
1 nanosecond = $\frac{1}{1\,000\,000\,000}$ of a second

Example 2

Convert 3 days, 9 hours and 42 minutes to minutes.

3 days	9 hours	∴ 3 days	4320
= 3 × 24 hours	= 9 × 60 min	9 hours	540
= 3 × 24 × 60 min	= 540 min	42 mins	42
= 4320 min		Total	4902 min

EXERCISE 10B (Calculators can be used here)

1 Convert to minutes:
  a 7 hours 24 min
  b 3 days 5 hours 43 min
  c 12 days 15 hours 36 min
  d 2 weeks 3 days 8 hours 17 min

2 Convert to seconds:
  a 40 min 38 sec
  b 3 hours 35 min 27 sec
  c 14 hours 12 min 43 sec
  d 22 hours 52 min 11 sec

3 Find the number of minutes in:
  a one day
  b one week
  c one 365 day year

4 Find the number of seconds in:
  a one day
  b one fortnight
  c one 365 day year

5 Consider a four year period which includes a leap year. Find the number of:
  a days
  b hours
  c minutes

6 Find the following:
  a 3 h 7 min + 5 h 23 min
  b 5 h 17 min + 3 h 25 min + 4 h 35 min
  c 11 h 43 min + 2 h 24 min + 5 h 16 min
  d 7 h 53 min − 3 h 36 min
  e 17 h 42 min − 12 h 53 min
  f 10 h 32 min + 5 h 47 min − 7 h 57 min

Example 3

Convert 1635 hours to days and hours.

$$\frac{1635}{24} = 68.125 \quad \{\text{using a calculator}\}$$

∴ there are 68 days and 0.125 of a day remaining

i.e., 68 days, 3 hours $\{0.125 \times 24 = 3\}$

7 Convert:
  a 124 hours to days
  b 552 hours to days

TIME AND TEMPERATURE (CHAPTER 10) 319

    c   873 hours to days   **d**   2167 hours to days

Extension:

8 Convert:

    a   67 680 minutes to days   **b**   31 717 minutes to days, hours and minutes

---

RESEARCH — MEASURING TIME IN DIFFERENT CULTURES

What to do:

1 Research the development of the current Western calendar.

2 Find out what the Gregorian calendar is.

3 Compare the calendars of Christian, Orthodox, Muslim, Jewish, and Chinese people.

4 List the days of great importance to these people and place these dates on your calendar.

RESEARCH — IT TAKES TIME

The following words are all linked with time:

chronometer	punctuality	metronome	astronomy
millennium bug	solstice	curfew	chronological
real time	longitude	duration	time signature
rhythm	synchronise	equinox	sesquicentenary
pendulum	geological time	meridian	almanac

What to do:

1 Find out what they mean.

2 Add others to the list.

3 Prepare a detailed talk or demonstration on any two of the listed words.

C   DIFFERENCES IN TIME

Time difference calculations are frequently made by travellers, credit card owners and businesses.

In Australia, a date is often represented using three numbers. For example, 13/6/99 is the shorthand way of writing "the thirteenth day of the sixth month (June) of the year 1999".

Example 4

Sally will turn 17 on 23/4/05. What does this mean?

Sally's 17th birthday is on the 23rd of April 2005.

EXERCISE 10C

1 Write out in sentence form the meaning of:
    a Wei joined the club on 17/12/99
    b Jon arrived on 13/3/00
    c Piri is departing for Malaysia on 30/7/04
    d Sam will turn 21 on 28/5/09

Example 5

How many days is it from April 24th to July 17th?

April has 30 days   ∴   6 days remain   (30 − 24 = 6)

So,   April   6
       May   31
       June   30
       July   17
       Total   84 days

In questions like this, we assume full days.

---

2 Find the number of days from:
    a March 11th to April 7th
    b May 11th to June 23rd
    c July 12th to November 6th
    d September 19th to January 8th
    e January 7th to March 16th in a non-leap year
    f February 6th to August 3rd in a leap year
    g 6/7/02 to 2/11/02
    h 7/2/03 to 17/5/03

3 Lou Wong needs to save money to buy a bicycle costing $279. Today is the 23rd of March and the shop will hold the bicycle until May 7th at this price.
    a How many days does Lou have to save for the bicycle?
    b How much needs to be saved each day to reach the $279 target?

4 Sean can save $18 a day. Today is May 9th and on November 20th he wishes to travel to Fiji on a package deal costing $5449. If he does not reach the target of $5449 he will have to borrow the remainder from a bank.
    a How many days has he for saving?
    b What is the total he will save?
    c Does he need to borrow money? If so, how much?

5 On 17th July 1999 Sung Kim proudly announced that he had been in Australia for 1000 days. On what day did he arrive in Australia?

Example 6

If it is now 10:15 am and the plane departs at 3:20 pm, how long is it before departure?

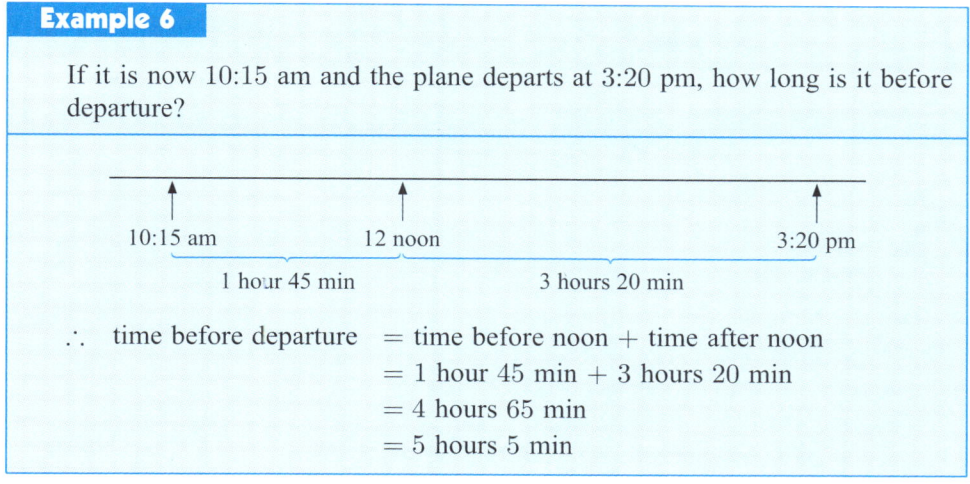

$\therefore$ time before departure = time before noon + time after noon
= 1 hour 45 min + 3 hours 20 min
= 4 hours 65 min
= 5 hours 5 min

6 What is the time:
   a 4 hours after 3:00 am
   b 5 hours after 8:00 pm
   c 34 minutes after 6:15 am
   d 45 minutes after 7:21 pm
   e 2 hours 13 min after 8:19 pm
   f 3 hours 27 min after 12:42 pm
   g 2 hours 55 min before 2 pm
   h 5 hours 18 minutes before noon
   i 1 hour 47 mins before 1:30 pm
   j 3 hours 16 minutes before 2 am Monday?

7 What is the time difference from:
   a 3:24 am to 11:43 am
   b 7:36 pm to 10:55 pm
   c 8:29 am to 3:46 pm
   d 5:32 am to 6:24 pm
   e 3:18 pm to 11:27 am next day
   f 4:29 pm to 2:06 am next day
   g 2:23 pm Sunday to 5:11 pm Monday
   h 3:42 am Tuesday to 7:36 pm Friday?

8 If a courier travelling between two cities takes $2\frac{1}{4}$ hrs for a one way trip, how many trips can she do in an 8 hour working day?

9 Herbert was born in 1895. How old was he when he had his birthday in 1920?

10 It takes Jill 10 seconds to put each can into her supermarket display. If there are 120 cans to be displayed how long will it take Jill to complete the job?

11 Mary's watch loses 3 seconds every hour. If it is correct at 8 am on Wednesday, how slow will it be when the real time is 5 pm on Friday of the same week?

12 If a high tide happens every 6 hours and 20 minutes after the last, and the next is at 0125 hrs on Monday, list the times for the next 8 high tides after that one.

13 How many times will a second hand of a clock pass 12 in a full day starting at 11 pm?

D   READING CLOCKS AND WATCHES

ACTIVITY — HOW LONG DOES IT TAKE?

You will need: A stopwatch or digital watch with similar functions and a partner to work with.

What to do:
1. Become familiar with what the watch can do and how you should operate it.
2. Read through the list of activities.
3. Organise how and when you can do them together.
4. Prepare your own copy of the chart.
5. Write down both estimates before you start the activity.
6. Take it in turns to do the activity or operate the watch.

Activity	Estimated Time (A)	Actual Time (B)	Difference between A and B
Count to 200 by ones			
Accurately write down your 3-11 times tables			
Carefully read aloud one page from a novel			
Carefully read aloud the same page backwards			
Walk one kilometre			
Throw 10 goals			
Record the total commercial time in 1 hour of TV			
Make a cup of coffee			

How many times each day do you look at a clock, watch or timetable? There are many occasions each day when we need to determine 'the time'.

For example:
- the time that lesson 2 starts today
- the time when the next bus or train departs
- the time dinner will be served tonight.

ACTIVITY — TIME–ESTIMATION ACTIVITIES

You will need: A couple of partners, a stopwatch and a netball.

Before starting draw up a record chart like this.

Activity	Estimate	Actual	Difference
100 m			
10 second run	10 sec.		
⋮			

What to do:
1. The men's world record for the 100 m sprint is under 10 seconds. Run a timed 100 m and estimate the time you took. Your partner will tell you your actual time when you have recorded your estimate.

b Now run the 100 m again but this time stop when you estimate you have been running for 10 seconds. Your partner will tell you the actual time. Record the results.

c Use a netball to shoot as many goals as you can in your estimate of 2 minutes. Your partner will tell you the actual time when you stop. Record your results.

d Write as many examples as possible of where being able to estimate time accurately could be very important.

2 If the average walking pace is 6 kmph and you have 58 km to walk, what is your estimate of the time it will take?

3 If you read at the rate of one page every 5 minutes and your book has 345 pages, what is your estimate of how long it will take to read it? Now work out the actual time.

4 Find the electricity cost for the family if their electricity account is as follows:

    Usage: Standard rate   405 kWh   @ 9.10 cents per kWh

                Economy rate   100 kWh   @ 9.06 cents per kWh

    Daily charge: 29 days   @ 98.96 cents per day

5 **a** Draw a pie graph to show the daily usage of a sports stadium if it is used as follows:
    Bowling 2 hrs   Tennis 4 hrs   Badminton 3 hrs
    Basketball 4 hrs   Fitness class 2 hrs

   b How many hours per day is the stadium not in use?

   c If the owners charge $50 per hour of use, how much does the stadium earn in a day, week, year?

6 A cell phone company charges a flat rate of 40 cents per minute for calls. If you pre-pay $50.00, what length of time can you spend on calls?

12-HOUR CLOCKS

Traditional analogue clocks give us 12-hour time.

For example,

    reads 3 o'clock and could   reads 20 minutes past 8 o'clock and
    be 3:00 am or 3:00 pm   could be either 8:20 am or 8:20 pm.

> **am** stands for *ante meridiem* which means 'before the middle of the day'.
> **pm** stands for *post meridiem* which means 'after the middle of the day'.

Some digital clocks are also 12-hour clocks, i.e., they go through two cycles per day.

These usually have a small **am** or **pm** somewhere on the display.

For example,  is 8:15 in the evening.

24-HOUR CLOCKS

Most digital clocks today display 24-hour time.

Since for example **8:15** could mean 8:15 am or 8:15 pm for a 12-hour clock and we do not know which, a 24-hour clock overcomes this problem by displaying **8:15** for the morning (am) and **20:15** for the afternoon (pm).

The 20:15 means 20 hours 15 minutes since midnight, which is 8 hours 15 minutes since midday, that is, 8:15 pm.

FOUR DIGIT NOTATION

7:15 am appears as **7:15** and is written as 0715 hours.

8:15 pm appears as **20:15** and is written as 2015 hours.

Following are some examples which compare 12-hour time and 24-hour time.

12-hour time	Digital display	24-hour time
midnight	0:00	0000 hours
7:42 am	7:42	0742 hours
midday (noon)	12:00	1200 hours
11:29 pm	23:29	2329 hours

Remember that 24-hour time always uses 4 digits.

Example 7

a Convert 7:38 am into 24-hour time.

b Convert the digital display **17:38** into 12-hour time.

a 7:38 am is 0738 hours

b 17:38 is 5:38 pm   {as 17 − 12 = 5}

EXERCISE 10D

1 Write as 24-hour time:

    a 3:13 am   **b** 11:17 am   **c** midnight   **d** 12:47 pm

    e 5:41 pm   **f** noon   **g** 8:19 pm   **h** 11:59 pm

2 Write the following 24-hour times as 12-hour times:

    a 0300 hours   **b** 0630 hours   **c** 1800 hours   **d** 1200 hours

    e 0615 hours   **f** 1545 hours   **g** 2017 hours   **h** 2348 hours

3 Write the following analogue times as 24-hour times:

    a  morning   **b**  afternoon   **c**  evening

4 What, if anything, is wrong with the following 24-hour times:

    a 0862 hours   **b** 0713 hours   **c** 2541 hours?

5 The following arrivals appear on a TV monitor at Sydney International Airport:

    a Convert each 24-hour arrival time to 12-hour time.

    b At what time is the Singapore Airlines flight from Bali arriving?

    c At what time is the Qantas flight from Brisbane arriving?

    d If fog delays all arrivals by 7 hours, what time will:

        i the QANTAS flight from Brisbane arrive

        ii the Singapore Airlines flight from London arrive?

QF is Qantas
SQ is Singapore Airlines
NZ is Air New Zealand

ARRIVALS		
Flight	*From*	*Arr. Time*
QF62	Adelaide	10:35
QF67	Melbourne	11:45
SQ34	Singapore	12:50
SQ42	London	13:50
SQ71	Bali	14:25
SQ82	Japan	14:45
NZ97	USA	15:15
QF83	Brisbane	16:10

E   TIMETABLES

Timetables are tables of information which tell us when events are to occur.

The timetable alongside provides information on phases of the moon and the rising and setting of the planets of our solar system. From such a table we can observe, for example:

- the next full moon is on October the 6th
- Mercury rises at 5:59 am tomorrow
- Saturn sets at 8:23 pm tomorrow.

The Moon			
New	First $\frac{1}{4}$	Full	Last $\frac{1}{4}$
Sep 21	Sep 29	Oct 6	Oct 12

The Sun and Planets		
Tomorrow	Rise	Set
Sun	6 : 15 am	6 : 07 pm
Moon	2 : 29 am	1 : 00 pm
Mercury	5 : 59 am	5 : 20 pm
Venus	5 : 51 am	5 : 09 pm
Mars	4 : 43 am	3 : 11 pm
Jupiter	6 : 01 am	6 : 34 pm
Saturn	9 : 10 am	8 : 23 pm

EXERCISE 10E

1 The tide timetable below is for a particular day in 2003.

a When is the tide highest in the morning at Port Xenon?

b When is the tide lowest in the afternoon at Paradise Point?

c What is the lowest tide at Joseph's Bay in the morning and at what time does it occur?

d What is the highest tide at Port Dowell in the afternoon and at what time does it occur?

Tide times				
Port Xenon	12:55 AM	0.8 m	7:21 AM	2.5 m
	1:56 PM	1.2 m	7:13 PM	1.8 m
Port Dowell	5:15 AM	1.4 m	11:45 AM	1.1 m
	1:46 PM	1.2 m	9:22 PM	0.6 m
Windcok	2:47 AM	0.9 m	9:53 AM	2.4 m
	5:12 PM	1.2 m	8:41 PM	1.3 m
Joseph's Bay	3:20 AM	0.9 m	10:22 AM	2.6 m
	5:24 PM	1.3 m	9:13 PM	1.5 m
Paradise Point	3:22 AM	1.4 m	7:57 AM	0.9 m
	12:19 PM	1.3 m	9:08 PM	0.6 m
Sunny Inlet	12:29 AM	0.5 m	9:03 AM	1.3 m
	11:29 PM	0.4 m		

2 Below is a timetable for a tourist bus service in Adelaide SA for the summer season:

Departure Times	Bus A	Bus B	Bus C	Bus D	Bus E	Bus F
City depot	7:30	7:45	8:00	8:15	8:30	8:45
Adelaide Oval	7:40	7:55	8:10	8:25	8:40	8:55
Adelaide Zoo	8:20	8:35	8:50	9:05	9:20	9:35
Stonyfell Winery	10:15	10:30	10:45	11:00	11:15	11:30
Hahndorf	11:20	11:35	11:50	12:05	12:20	12:35
Murray Mouth	1:00	1:15	1:30	1:45	2:00	2:15
Victor Harbor	1:40	1:55	2:10	2:25	2:40	2:55
Port Adelaide	3:15	3:30	3:45	4:00	4:15	4:30
Museum	4:00	4:15	4:30	4:45	5:00	5:15
Arrive at City depot	5:00	5:15	5:30	5:45	6:00	6:15

a How many bus services are available?

b What is the latest departure time?

c What is the earliest arrival time back at the depot?

d How long does it take between arrivals at
  i the Adelaide Zoo and the Stonyfell Winery
  ii the Murray Mouth and Victor Harbor?

e How long does a complete trip last?

f If you wanted to be at Victor Harbor no later than 3:15, what bus should you take?

g If a friend is meeting the bus at Port Adelaide at 3:30, what bus is it best to travel on?

3 I am visiting Sydney and have obtained this Carlingford to Wynyard train timetable:

CARLINGFORD-WYNYARD TRAIN TIMETABLE

	p.m.	p.m.	p.m.	p.m.	p.m.	p.m.	p.m.
Carlingford	3.32	4.11	4.45	5.23	5.55	6.26	6.52
Telopea	3.34	4.13	4.47	5.25	5.57	6.28	6.54
Dundas	3.36	4.15	4.49	5.27	5.59	6.30	6.56
Rydalmere	3.38	4.17	4.51	5.29	6.01	6.32	6.58
Camellia	3.40	4.19	4.53	5.31	6.03	6.34	7.00
Rosehill UA	3.42	4.21	4.55	5.33	6.05	6.36	7.02
Clyde........arr	3.45X	4.24X	4.58X	5.36X	6.08X	6.39X	7.05
dep	3.51	4.26	5.00	5.48	6.18	6.48	7.06
Lidcombe.....arr							
dep	3.57	4.31	5.06	5.54	6.24	6.54	7.12
Strathfield....arr	4.02	4.36	5.11	5.59	6.29	6.59	7.18X
dep	4.03	4.37	5.12	6.00	6.30	7.00	7.23
Central........arr	4.17	4.50	5.26	6.14	6.44	7.14	7.36
dep	4.18	4.51	5.27	6.15	6.45	7.15	7.37
Townhall	4.21	4.54	5.30	6.18	6.48	7.18	7.40
Wynyard	4.24	4.57	5.33	6.20	6.50	7.20	7.42

   a What do the following mean:
      i arr   **ii** dep?

   b If I catch the 4:17 pm train at Rydalmere, what time will I arrive at Central?

   c At what time will I have to catch the train from Dundas in order to arrive at Lidcombe by 6:00 pm?

   d If I miss the 5:00 pm train from Clyde, what would be the earliest time that I could arrive at Wynyard?

   e   **i** If I come out of the cinema at 3:45 pm at Carlingford, what is the time of the first train that I can catch to Strathfield?

      ii At what time will this train reach Strathfield?

      iii If I have an errand at Strathfield that will take no more than half an hour, what is the shortest time that I will have to wait for the next train that I can catch to Townhall?

   f Calculate the time it takes for the **i** 3:32 pm **ii** 5:23 pm **iii** 6:52 pm   trains from Carlingford to reach Central. Can you suggest a reason for the differences in times?

ACTIVITY   MAKING TIMETABLES

What to do:

1 a Make a timetable like the one given to show events in your day yesterday.

Activity	12-hour time	24-hour time
got up	7:30 am	0730 hours
⋮		

   b Share your timetable with a partner and discuss any similarities and differences.

2 Now try making a timetable for your class for one week at school.

3 You are about to start a new airline flying between Adelaide and Mt Gambier using three jet aircraft. Construct a timetable showing prospective travellers departure and arrival times for both cities.

For this exercise your planes travel at an average 400 kmph. Do not forget to allow turnaround time for refuelling, disembarking, cleaning and unloading.

TIME ZONES (EXTENSION)

The Earth rotates from West to East about its axis. This rotation causes day and night.

As the sun rises in Adelaide, Perth is still in darkness. So it is earlier in the day in Perth than in Adelaide.

As the sun rises in Perth, Adelaide has already experienced about two hours of daylight. So it is later in the day in Adelaide than in Perth.

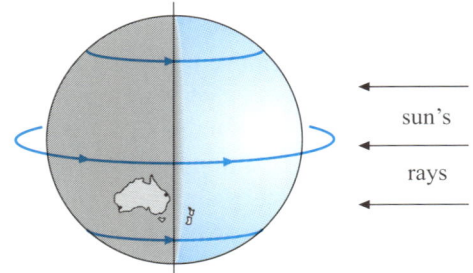

TRUE LOCAL TIME

The Earth rotates a full $360°$ every day.

That is $360°$ in 24 hours
or $15°$ in 1 hour ($360 \div 24 = 15$)
or $1°$ in 4 minutes. ($\frac{1}{15}$ of 60 min $=$ 4 min)

Places on the same line of longitude share the same **true local time**.

However using true local time would cause many problems.

For example, as each degree of longitude represents a difference of 4 minutes you could have different times in the same room of your home.

Some states stretch across almost $15°$ of longitude. This would mean time differences of up to one hour in the same state. The solution to these problems was to create **Time Zones**.

STANDARD TIME ZONES

The map following shows lines of longitude between the North and South Poles. These lines then follow the borders of countries, states or regions or natural boundaries such as rivers and mountains.

The first line of longitude, $0°$, passes through Greenwich near London. This first or **prime meridian (line)** is the starting point for 12 time zones west of Greenwich and 12 time zones east of Greenwich.

Places which lie within a time zone share the same **standard time**. Standard Time Zones are mostly measured in $\frac{1}{2}$ or 1 hour units.

Time along the prime meridian is called **Greenwich Mean Time (GMT)**.

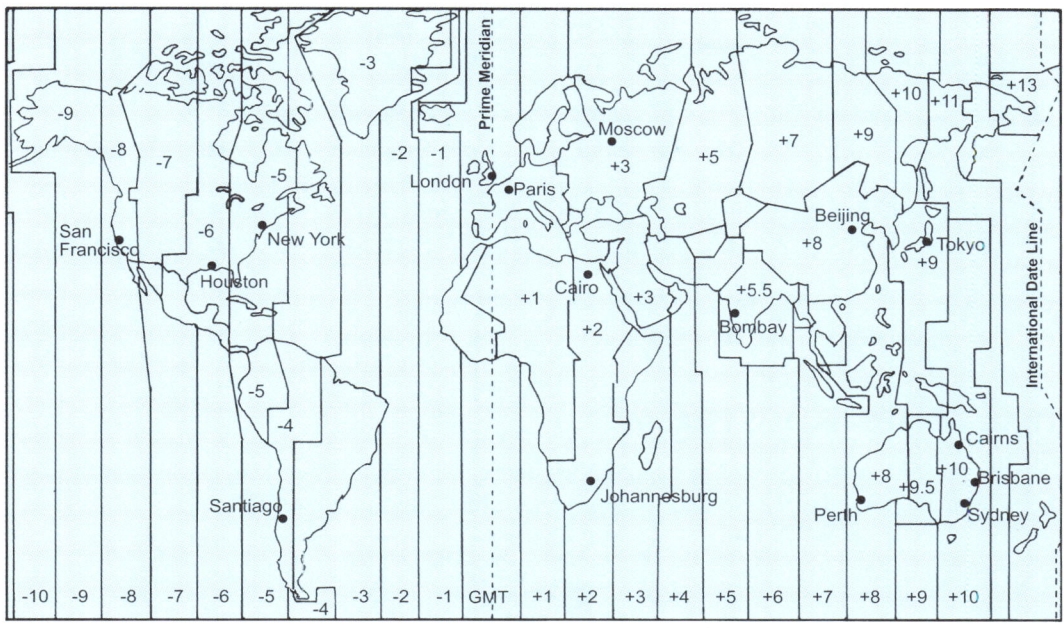

Places to the East of the prime meridian are **ahead** of GMT.

Places to the West of the prime meridian are **behind** GMT.

The numbers in the zones show how many hours have to be added or subtracted from Greenwich Mean Time to work out the **standard time** for that zone.

Some cultures believe a new day begins at sunrise. Most countries use midnight as the beginning of a day.

Example 8

If it is 12 noon in Greenwich, what is the standard time in:
  a Sydney   **b** San Francisco?

a Sydney is in a zone marked +10

∴ standard time in Sydney is 10 hours ahead of GMT

∴ standard time in Sydney is 10 pm.

b San Francisco is in a zone marked −8

∴ standard time in San Francisco is 8 hours behind GMT

∴ standard time in San Francisco is 4 am.

EXERCISE 10F

Use the Standard Time Zone map to answer these questions.

1 If it is 12 noon in Greenwich, what is the standard time in:

  a Moscow   **b** Beijing   **c** Sydney   **d** Santiago?

2 If it is 12 midnight Monday in Greenwich, what is the standard time in:
    a Cairo   **b** Bombay   **c** Tokyo   **d** London?

3 If it is 10 pm on Tuesday in Greenwich, what is the standard time in:
    a New York   **b** San Francisco   **c** Brisbane   **d** Johannesburg?

4 If it is 2:45 am on Sunday in Greenwich, what is the standard time in:
    a Adelaide   **b** Bombay   **c** Santiago   **d** Houston?

5 If it is 3 pm in Moscow on Friday, what is the standard time in:
    a Adelaide   **b** Beijing   **c** London   **d** San Francisco?

TIME ZONES IN AUSTRALIA

Despite the fact that Australia is one country, there are three different time zones because of the size of the country. These zones are given on the diagram which follows:

During summer, Australia uses **Daylight Saving Time** in the ACT, NSW, SA, Tasmania and Victoria.

This is done by putting forward (advancing) the time by 1 hour in these states and the ACT and results in Australia having 5 different time zones in summer.

EXERCISE 10F (continued)

6 It is 3:30 pm normal time in Adelaide. What is the time in:
    a Darwin   **b** Canberra   **c** Brisbane   **d** Hobart?

7 If it is 4:20 am normal time in Brisbane, what is the time in:
    a Mt Gambier   **b** Alice Springs   **c** Kalgoorlie   **d** Sydney?

8 It is summer and daylight saving is in operation. Draw a sketch of Australia and mark on it the five different time zones. If it is 3 pm in SA, what is the time in:
  a WA   **b** NT   **c** QLD   **d** NSW   **e** Tasmania?

9 If it is 7:40 am normal time in SA, what will be the normal time in:
  a Melbourne   **b** Perth   **c** Darwin   **d** Canberra?

10 Determine the arrival times for the following:

  a a $4\frac{1}{2}$ hour flight from Melbourne to Perth departing Melbourne at 6:00 am normal time

  b a $10\frac{1}{2}$ hour drive from Sydney to Brisbane during daylight saving leaving Sydney at 8:20 am

  c a $2\frac{1}{2}$ hour flight from Adelaide to Alice Springs leaving Adelaide at 4 pm central summer time

  d a 2 hour flight from Adelaide to Sydney, followed by a $2\frac{1}{2}$ hour flight from Sydney to Townsville departing Adelaide at 2:15 pm normal time with a delay of 45 minutes in Sydney.

G AVERAGE SPEED

People think of speed as a measure of how fast something is travelling.

In fact, average speed is the distance travelled in a unit of time and can be found using the rule:

$$\text{speed} = \frac{\text{distance}}{\text{time}}$$

For example, if a car travels a distance of 180 km in two hours then its average speed is 90 kmph (or 90 km/h).

So, each hour it travels, on average, 90 km.

Notice that $\dfrac{180 \text{ km}}{2 \text{ hours}} = 90 \text{ km/h}$ This sloping line reads as 'per'.

Speeds are measured in km/h or $\dfrac{\text{km}}{\text{h}}$ which is $\dfrac{\text{distance}}{\text{time}}$

Example 9

Find the average speed of a car which travels 720 km in 9 hours.

$$\begin{aligned}\text{Average speed} &= \frac{\text{distance}}{\text{time}} \\ &= \frac{720 \text{ km}}{9 \text{ hour}} \\ &= 80 \text{ km/h}\end{aligned}$$

EXERCISE 10G

1 Find the average speed travelled by a vehicle if it covers:
  a 540 km in 6 hours
  b 840 km in 12 hours
  c 664 km in 8 hours
  d 846 km in 9 hours

> If you find it difficult to remember this formula, think of a simple example like the one given alongside.

FINDING DISTANCES TRAVELLED

If we travel at 60 kmph for 3 hours we will travel a distance of 180 km.

Notice that we worked out $60 \times 3 = 180$
                                          speed   time   distance

So,   **distance = average speed × time**

Example 10

How far would you travel in 5 hours at an average speed of 96 kmph?

Using   distance = speed × time   ∴   distance = 96×5
                                                 = 96×5
                                                 = 480 km

2 If a vehicle is travelling at 90 km/h, find how far it will travel in:
  a 7 hours
  b 5 hours
  c 10 hours
  d 3.5 hours
  e 11 hours 24 mins   (**Hint:** 24 min = $\frac{24}{60}$ hours)

3 How far would you travel in:
  a 3 hours at an average speed of 85 km/h
  b 8 hours at an average speed of 110 km/h
  c $4\frac{1}{2}$ hours at an average speed of 98 km/h
  d 2 hours 15 mins at an average speed of 76 km/h?

FINDING TIME TAKEN

If we travel 200 km at 100 km/h it would take us 2 hours. Notice that $\frac{200}{100} = 2$

This example shows us that   **time = $\frac{\text{distance}}{\text{average speed}}$**

Example 11

How long would it take to travel 300 km at 75 km/h?

Using   time = $\frac{\text{distance}}{\text{speed}}$ ∴   time = $\frac{300}{75}$ = 4 hours

4 Find how long it will take to travel:
- **a** 90 km at 30 km/h
- **b** 720 km at 120 km/h
- **c** 440 km at 80 km/h
- **d** 750 km at 90 km/h
- **e** 208 km at 64 km/h

 # TEMPERATURE

In most of the world temperatures are measured in **degrees Celsius** (°C).

　　0°C is the temperature at which pure water freezes.

　　100°C is the temperature at which pure water boils.

In a few countries, including the USA, the old **Fahrenheit scale** (°F) is still used.

　　32°F is the temperature at which pure water freezes.

　　212°F is the temperature at which pure water boils.

The following graph allows us to convert from °C to °F or from °F to °C.

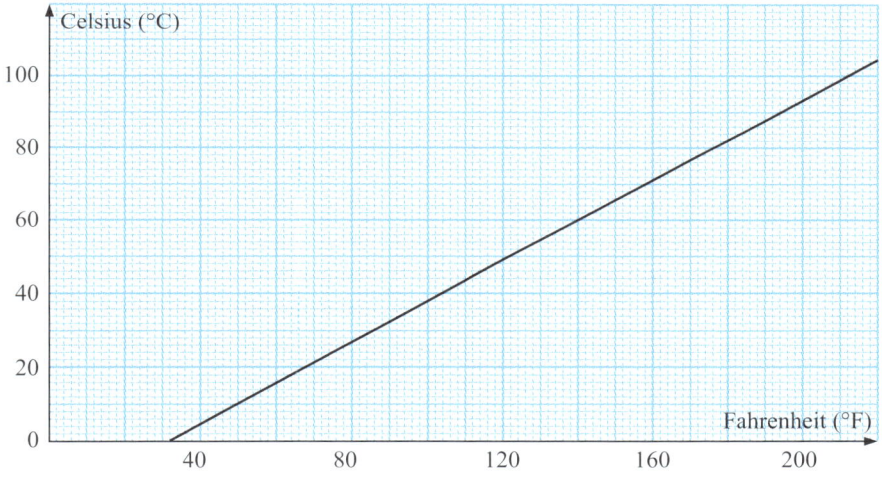
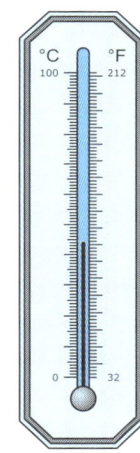

EXERCISE 10H

1 Convert these °C temperatures into °F temperatures:
- **a** 50°C
- **b** 80°C
- **c** 20°C

2 Convert these °F temperatures into °C temperatures:
- **a** 100°F
- **b** 50°F
- **c** 80°F

3 The formula for converting °C temperatures into °F temperatures is $F = 1.8 \times C + 32$. Use this formula to check your answers to question **1**.

4 The formula for converting °F temperatures into °C temperatures is $C = 5 \times (F - 32) \div 9$.
- **a** Use the formula to check your answers to question **2**.
- **b** If you were in New York where the temperature was 90°F, what would the °C temperature be?

ACTIVITY — TEMPERATURES ONLINE

Visit a world temperatures internet site to compare temperatures in three different world cities.

On the same graph plot the daily maximum temperatures over a fortnightly period.

REVIEW SET A — CHAPTER 10

1 What is the best unit of time measurement for the following?
   a a plane flight from Adelaide to New York
   b the length of an average lesson
   c the calculating speed of a modern computer
   d the life cycle of a human being
   e the age of buildings in ancient Rome
   f the time for an Olympic sprinter running 100 metres

2 Copy and complete:
   a 7 weeks = □ days
   b 12 minutes = □ seconds
   c $9\frac{1}{4}$ hours = □ minutes
   d 1 millenium = □ years

3 Write the following in   **i** 12-hour time   **ii** 24-hour time:
   a quarter to seven in the morning
   b quarter past midnight
   c half past nine at night

4 Find the following:
   a 9 hours 38 mins + 6 hours 45 mins + 4 hours 18 mins
   b 7 hours 27 min − 3 hours 49 mins

5 Josh began saving 15 dollars a day from the 4th April. He needs $3000 to have his teeth straightened on September 27th.
   a How many days does he have to save?
   b What is the total he will save?
   c How much will he still owe the orthodontist?

6 To reach her goal of running 1000 km before the season starts, a netballer plans to run 10 km each day. If the season starts on the 8th September, when should she start her running?

7 Use the Standard Time Zone map to answer the following questions.
   a If it is 11 am on Saturday in Greenwich, what is the Standard Time in:
      i Moscow   **ii** Adelaide?
   b If it is 8 pm on Tuesday in Greenwich, what is the standard time in:
      i Cairo   **ii** Bombay?

8 How far would I ride in 3 hours if I can travel at 18 km/h on my bicycle?

9 If I can walk at 5 km/h, how far would I walk in 36 minutes?

REVIEW SET B — CHAPTER 10

1 How many days from:
   a 15th January to 4th April in a leap year
   b 1st January 2003 to 31st December 2004
   c 1st January 1995 to 31st December 2004?

2 How many Thursdays were there in 2004 if January 1st was a Thursday?

3 On the day 7/12/99, what was the present:
   a decade   **b** century   **c** millenium?

4 How many years are there from the start of the first year to the end of the second year in the following:
   a 1004, 2004   **b** AD54, AD86   **c** 174BC, 23BC?

5 Will a 180 minute video tape be long enough to record programs from:
   a 11:50 pm to 2:45 am   **b** 10:35 am to 1:50 pm?

6 Write the following 24-hour times as 12-hour times:
   a 0415 hours   **b** 1300 hours   **c** 2335 hours

7 Convert:
   a 19 hours 54 minutes to minutes   **b** 475 hours to days

8 What distance is travelled by a car in 4 hours if it is travelling at 87 km/h?

9 How long would it take me to travel 25 km if I can ride at 20 km/h on my bicycle?

10 a The first placed swimmer's time was 14 min 58.29 seconds. Second place was 2.78 seconds slower with third place a further 4.35 seconds behind. What are the second and third placed swimmers' times?

   b A marathon runner finished 2 minutes 13 seconds slower than his personal best time of 2 hours 58 minutes and 48 seconds. What was his finishing time?

   c If the sun rose at 5:24 am and set at 7:43 pm, how many hours and minutes of daylight were there?

REVIEW SET C — CHAPTER 10

1 How many:
   a days from 7th July to 22nd October
   b hours from 11 pm Monday to noon the following Thursday
   c minutes from 9:47 am to 11:08 am
   d seconds from 11:59 pm to 12:04 am?

2 In what **a** decade **b** century **c** millennium was the year 1786?

3 How many years are there from the start of the first year to the end of the second?
    a 1908 to 1974   **b** 1545 to 1695   **c** 14BC to 25AD

4 **a** Write the twenty first of November nineteen sixty three in numerals.
    b Zoe was born on the seventeenth of October nineteen eighty nine. In numerals write the date for Zoe's 21st birthday.

5 Write this **pm** time as:
    a an analogue time in words
    b 12-hour digital time
    c 24-hour time

 afternoon

6 Find the following:
    a 4 hour 8 min + 5 hour 35 min + 3 hour 47 min
    b 2 days 9 hours 18 min + 3 days 15 hours 45 min
    c 3 hours 15 min − 1 hour 57 min

7 Find the speed of a car which travels 752 km in 8 hours.

8 How long would it take you to travel 440 km at 80 km/h?

9

| A DECADE OF MANNED SPACE FLIGHTS (MODIFIED) ||||
Spacecraft	Launch date	Duration (h:min)	Remarks
Vostok 1	12/04/61	1:48	first manned flight
Vostok 2	06/08/61	25:18	first flight exceeding 24 hours
Merc. - Atlas 6	20/02/62	4:55	first American to orbit
Vostok 6	06/06/63	70:50	first woman in space
Voskhod 1	12/10/64	24:17	first 3-man crew
Gemini 8	16/03/66	10:41	first docking of 2 orbiting spacecraft
Gemini 11	12/09/66	71:17	highest Earth orbit altitude (1372 km)
Soyuz 1	23/04/67	26:37	cosmonaut killed in re-entry accident
Apollo 8	21/12/68	147:01	first manned orbit(s) of moon
Soyuz 4	14/01/69	71:23	Soyuz 4 and 5 docked and transferred
Soyuz 5	15/01/69	72:56	2 cosmonauts from Soyuz 5 to Soyuz 4
Apollo 11	16/07/69	195:19	first landing of human on the moon
Apollo 12	14/11/69	244:36	second manned lunar landing

    a For how many days did Apollo 11 fly?
    b On what space craft did the first woman in space travel?
    c How much longer was Apollo 12's flight than Apollo 8's?
    d How soon after the first manned orbit of the moon was the first human on the moon?
    e To the nearest month, determine how long it was from the first manned flight in space to the first landing of humans on the moon.

Chapter 11
Algebra

Knowledge, skills and understandings

By the end of this chapter you should be able to

- extend and describe the rule for numerical and geometric patterns (e.g., 7, 36, 181, 906)
- investigate pattern rules in solving problems (e.g., rates charged by tradespeople 1 hr - $35, 2 hrs - $60, 3 hrs - $95 = $n \times 35 - 10$ for various hours worked)
- investigate and analyse graphs showing the relationship between variables (e.g., analysing winter rainfall patterns and making comparisons and predicting future trends)
- predict future trends from linear graphs
- construct a number sentence to match a problem that is presented in words and that requires finding an unknown
- use inverse operations to solve a number sentence (e.g., $2x = 8$, $x = 8 \div 2$)

PATTERNS

Patterns with numbers and shapes that are easy to recognise are often seen in geometry and arithmetic.

These patterns have rules which describe them. They can be used to predict further shapes or numbers in the patterns.

These rules can be written in a shorthand form using **algebra**.

It is said that algebra is the language of mathematics. Algebra is used by engineers, architects, scientists and in many other professions and businesses.

A GEOMETRIC PATTERNS

 ..... and  ..... are examples of **geometric patterns**.

Like number patterns these can continue indefinitely. We often call these patterns **matchstick patterns** as we can construct the first few members of them using matchsticks.

INVESTIGATION — THE TRIANGLES PATTERN

Consider the pattern , 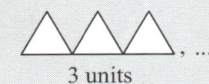, ...
1 unit, 2 units, 3 units

What to do:

1. Copy the given pattern and draw the next 4 members as well.

2. Copy and complete the table showing the number of matches required to make each member.

Unit number	1	2	3	4	5	6	7
Matches needed	3	6					

3. Without drawing them, write down the number of matches needed to make the members with unit numbers 8, 9, 10 and 11.

4. Predict the number of matchsticks needed to make the member for:
   a 30 units b 50 units c 200 units d 1 000 000 units.

5. **Extension:** Can you predict the number of matchsticks required to make n units?

From the **Investigation** you may have discovered the following:

Unit number	1	2	3	4	5	6	7
Matches needed	3	6	9	12	15	18	21

+3 +3 +3 +3 +3 +3

Notice that to get the next member we add 3 to the previous one.

Notice also

Unit number	Figure	Matches needed	Pattern
1	△	3	1 × 3
2	△△	6	2 × 3
3	△△△	9	3 × 3
4	△△△△	12	4 × 3

So, for the 100-unit figure, the number of matches needed is 100×3.

Consequently, for the n-unit figure, where n could be any positive whole number, the number of matches (which we shall call M), is given by the **rule** (or **equation**) $M = n \times 3$.

> A rule or equation in mathematics is a sentence in algebra which contains an equals sign.

Example 1

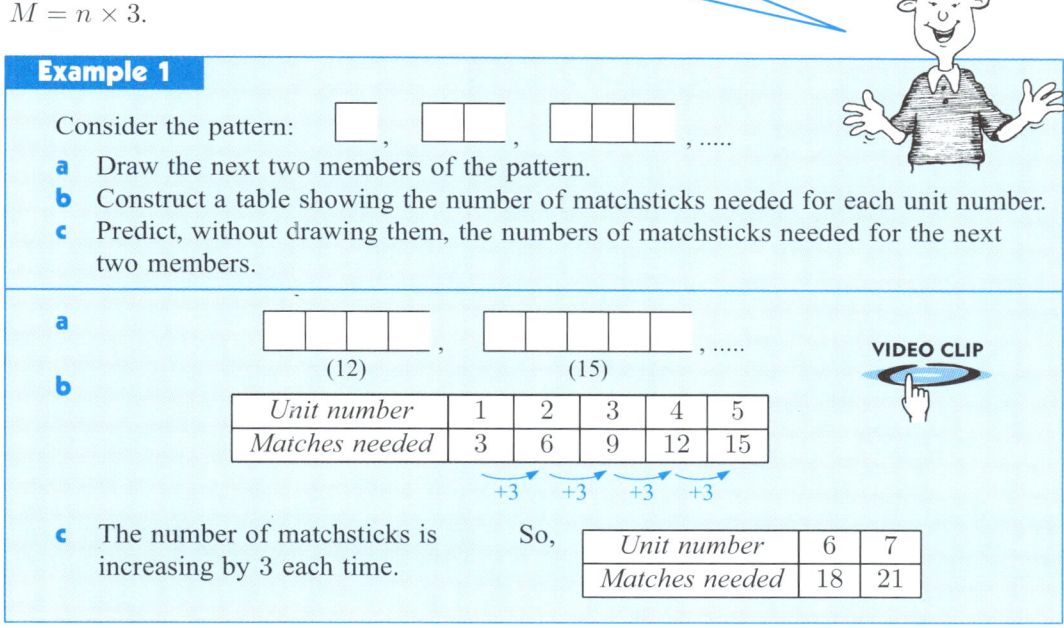

EXERCISE 11A

1 For each of the following matchstick patterns:
   i   draw the next two members
   ii construct a table of 'matches needed' for the first 5 members
   iii without drawing them, predict the number of matchsticks needed to make the next two members.

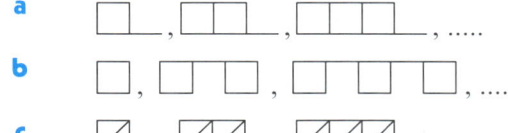

Example 2

Consider the number pattern: $1 \times 3 + 2$, $2 \times 3 + 2$, $3 \times 3 + 2$, $4 \times 3 + 2$, ...

a Find the value of the first 4 members of the pattern.
b Find the value of the 100th member of the pattern.
c Draw a matchstick pattern which fits the number pattern.

a
$1 \times 3 + 2 = 5$
$2 \times 3 + 2 = 8$
$3 \times 3 + 2 = 11$
$4 \times 3 + 2 = 14$

b The 100th member is
$100 \times 3 + 2$
$= 300 + 2$
$= 302$

c  , ...

Reason: [3 + 2]   [3 + 3 + 2]   [3 + 3 + 3 + 2]   etc.

---

2 Consider the following number pattern, then:
   i find the value of its first 4 members
   ii find the value of its 100th member
   iii draw a matchstick pattern which fits the number pattern.

a $1 \times 3 + 1$, $2 \times 3 + 1$, $3 \times 3 + 1$, $4 \times 3 + 1$, ...
b $1 \times 3 - 1$, $2 \times 3 - 1$, $3 \times 3 - 1$, $4 \times 3 - 1$, ...
c $1 \times 4 + 2$, $2 \times 4 + 2$, $3 \times 4 + 2$, $4 \times 4 + 2$, ...
d $1 \times 4 - 3$, $2 \times 4 - 3$, $3 \times 4 - 3$, $4 \times 4 - 3$, ...

B NUMBER PATTERNS

Examine the number sequence 3, 7, 11, 15, 19, ...

These dots indicate that the sequence continues indefinitely.

Have you noticed that to get the next member from the previous one we simply add 4, that is

$7 = 3 + 4$
$11 = 7 + 4$
$15 = 11 + 4$
$19 = 15 + 4$, etc?

With number patterns like this one we should be able to continue the number sequence as far as we like.

A possible rule could be given in words as

"the next number is equal to the previous number plus 4".

> **Example 3**
>
> Find the next 3 members of the following number patterns and in each case write down the *rule* used to find the next member:
> **a** 1, 7, 13, 19, 25, ...　　**b** 50, 47, 44, 41, 38, ...　　**c** 2, 10, 50, 250, ...
>
> **a** To get the next member we *add* 6,
> ∴ the next 3 members are: 31, 37 and 43.
> *Rule:* "The next member is equal to the previous one, plus 6."
>
> **b** To get the next member we *take* 3,
> ∴ the next 3 members are: 35, 32 and 29.
> *Rule:* "The next member is equal to the previous one, minus 3."
>
> **c** To get the next member we *multiply by* 5,
> ∴ the next 3 members are: 1250, 6250, 31 250.
> *Rule:* "The next member is equal to the previous one multiplied by 5."

EXERCISE 11B

1 Find the next 3 members of the following number patterns and in each case write down the *rule* for finding the next member:

  a 1, 4, 7, 10, 13, ...　　　　　　**b** 11, 15, 19, 23, 27, ...
  c 2, 9, 16, 23, 30, ...　　　　　　**d** 6, 12, 18, 24, ...
  e 13, 22, 31, 40, ...　　　　　　**f** 7, 20, 33, 46, ...

2 Find the next 3 members of the following number patterns and in each case write down the rule for finding the next member:

  a 38, 36, 34, 32, 30, ...　　　　**b** 29, 26, 23, 20, ...
  c 57, 51, 45, 39, ...　　　　　　**d** 100, 97, 94, 91, ...
  e 250, 242, 234, 226, ...　　　　**f** 65, 61, 57, 53, 49, ...
  g 1, 2, 4, 8, 16, ...　　　　　　**h** 2, 6, 18, 54, ...
  i 2, 8, 32, 128, ...　　　　　　**j** 64, 32, 16, 8, 4, ...
  k 80, 40, 20, 10, ...　　　　　　**l** 243, 81, 27, 9, ...
  m 250, 25, 2.5, 0.25, ...　　　　**n** 2, 3, 5, 8, 12, 17, ...
  o 1, 1, 2, 3, 5, 8, 13, ...

3 Using the first number and the rule given, write down the next three numbers in each pattern:

  a 7;　'add 6'　　　　　　　　　　**b** 3;　'add 9'
  c 4;　'add $1\frac{1}{2}$'　　　　　　　　　**d** 56;　'take 11'
  e 150;　'subtract 25'　　　　　　**f** 3.8;　'reduce by 0.5'
  g 4;　'multiply by 2 add 3'　　　**h** 3;　'times by 10 subtract 4'
  i 97;　'add one then divide by two'　**j** 2;　'multiply number by itself'

4 Write down the missing number from each pattern:

   a 3, 9, □, 21, 27
   b 12, □, 36, 48, 60
   c 75, 60, □, 30, 15
   d 3, 6, □, 24, 48
   e 6, 10, □, 21, 28, 36
   f 3, 9, 27, □, 243
   g 0.08, 0.8, □, 80, 800
   h 10, □, 32, 43
   i 2, 6, 24, □, 720
   j 100, 50, □, 12.5
   k 2, 5, 11, □, 47
   l 96, □, 6, 1.5

C FORMULAE AND VARIABLES

INVESTIGATION — THE SQUARES PATTERN

 Consider the matchstick pattern

What to do:

1 Copy and draw the pattern to 6 units.

2 How many matchsticks are needed to make the 1 unit, 2 unit, 3 unit, 4 unit, 5 unit and 6 unit figures?

   Copy and complete:

Unit number	1	2	3	4	5	6
Matchsticks needed						

3 Without drawing them, find the number of matchsticks needed to make the next 3 members of the pattern.

4 Predict the number of matchsticks needed to make:
   a 7 units
   b 10 units.

5 **Extension:** Predict the number of matchsticks needed to make the n-unit member.

From the **Investigation** you may have noticed:

Unit number	1	2	3	4	5	6
Matches needed	4	7	10	13	16	19

+3 +3 +3 +3 +3

where once again the number of matchsticks needed for the next pattern is 3 more than the one before it.

Examine the following table for an explanation:

Unit number	Figure	Matchsticks needed	Pattern	Explanation
1	□	4	$1 \times 3 + 1$	□∣
2	□□	7	$2 \times 3 + 1$	□□∣
3	□□□	10	$3 \times 3 + 1$	□□□∣
4	□□□□	13	$4 \times 3 + 1$	□□□□∣

Notice the groups of 3 here ⟶

So, for the 300-unit figure there are $300 \times 3 + 1$ matches needed
and for the n-unit figure there are $n \times 3 + 1$ matches needed,

and if M represents the total number of matches needed then $M = n \times 3 + 1$.

$M = n \times 3 + 1$ is the **rule** or **formula** for the pattern.

The formula is simply a shorthand way of writing down a mathematical sentence:

$$\underbrace{\text{the number of matchsticks}}_{M} \quad \underbrace{\text{is}}_{=} \quad \underbrace{\text{three times the number of units}}_{3 \times n} \quad \underbrace{\text{plus}}_{+} \quad \underbrace{\text{one}}_{1}.$$

VARIABLES (OR PRONUMERALS)

The symbols M and n are called **variables**. They are used in place of numbers which may vary.

However, when a symbol such as k or $\triangle$ is used to take the place of a number which does not vary, it is called a **constant**.

A rule or formula can be written in words or in symbols and we must be able to convert from one form to the other.

Example 4

You are given the rule: "the number of matchsticks is three times the unit number plus three".

a Rewrite the rule using variables and state what each symbol means.
b Make up a matchstick pattern which shows the rule.

a $M = 3 \times n + 3$ where M is the number of matchsticks and n is the unit number.

b  is one of many such patterns. Can you find another?

EXERCISE 11C

1 For the following rules:
  i Rewrite using variables, explaining what each variable represents.
  ii Make up a matchstick pattern which fits the rule.

  a The number of matchsticks is two times the unit number plus one.
  b The number of matchsticks is three times the unit number plus two.
  c The number of matchsticks is three times the unit number minus one.
  d The number of matchsticks is four times the unit number plus three.

Example 5

For the following matchstick rule $M = 2 \times n - 1$:

a find the value of M for $n = 1, 2, 3$ and 4 and table your results
b write out the formula in words
c draw the first four diagrams of a pattern that fits the rule.

a

n	1	2	3	4
M	1	3	5	7

b The number of matchsticks equals the unit number times two and then one is subtracted.

c , ...

---

2 For the following rules:

  i Write down the value of M for $n = 1, 2, 3$ and 4. Put your answers in table form.
  ii If M represents the number of matchsticks and n the unit number, write out the formula in words.
  iii Draw the first four diagrams of a matchstick pattern that fits the rule.

  a $M = 2 \times n$ **b** $M = n + 3$ **c** $M = 3 \times n - 2$ **d** $M = 4 \times n - 3$

INVESTIGATION — THE CUBES PATTERN (PART 1)

Consider the pattern , 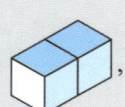, 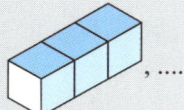, ...

What to do:

1 Collect a container of multilink blocks.
2 Arrange them in the pattern as shown.
3 Count the number of cube faces not joined.
4 Copy and complete the table:

Number of cubes	1	2	3	4	5	6
Number of cube faces not joined	6	10				

5 Predict the number of cube faces not joined for the next 3 members of this pattern.
6 Check your prediction by arranging and counting.
7 Without using the unit cubes predict the number of cube faces not joined for:

  a 10 cubes **b** 20 cubes **c** 100 cubes **d** 1 000 000 cubes.

8 Can you predict the number of cube faces not joined using n units?

INVESTIGATION   THE CUBES PATTERN (PART 2)

Consider the pattern 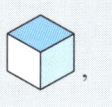, 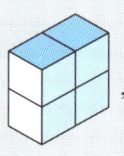, 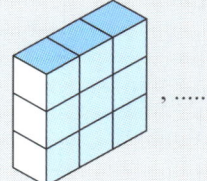, ...

What to do:

1. Arrange cubes in the pattern as shown.
2. Count the number of cubes used.
3. Copy and complete the table:

Number of cubes along each side	1	2	3	4	5	6
Number of cubes used	1	4	9			
Number of cube faces not joined	6	16	30			

4. Predict the number of cubes needed for the next 3 members of this pattern.
5. Predict the number of cube faces not joined for the next 3 members of this pattern.
6. Predict the number of cubes needed for sides of:
      a   10 cubes   **b**   12 cubes   **c**   15 cubes   **d**   30 cubes.
7. Can you predict the number of cubes needed for sides of n cubes?

INVESTIGATION   THE CUBES PATTERN (PART 3)

Consider the pattern 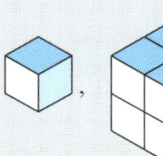, 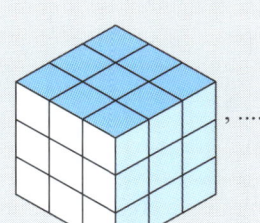, ...

What to do:

1. Arrange the cubes in the pattern as shown.
2. Count the number of cubes used.
3. Copy and complete the table:

Number of cubes on each dimension (LWD)	1	2	3	4	5	6
Number of cubes used	1	8				

4. Predict the number of cubes needed for the next 3 members of this pattern.
5. Predict the number of cubes needed if each dimension has:
      a   10 cubes   **b**   20 cubes   **c**   40 cubes   **d**   100 cubes.
6. Predict the number of cubes needed if each dimension has n cubes.

D DISCOVERING FORMULAE

☐, ☐☐, ☐☐☐, ☐☐☐☐, ... is a geometric pattern.

Diagram	1	2	3	4
Matches	4	7	10	13

The formula which makes numbers in this pattern is

$$M = 3 \times d + 1 \quad \text{where} \quad \begin{cases} M \text{ is the number of matches} \\ d \text{ is the diagram number} \end{cases}$$

How can you discover a formula like this one, by yourself?

You could notice that "the number of matches is 3 times the diagram number, plus one more".

However, some pattern formulae are too hard to guess. So, we need a method for finding them.

Example 6

Examine the matchstick pattern:  , ...

a Draw the next two members of the pattern.
b Copy and complete:

Unit number (n)	1	2	3	4	5
Matchsticks needed (M)	2				

c Find the rule connecting M and n.
d Find the number of matchsticks needed to make the 17th member.

a  ,  , ...

b

n	1	2	3	4	5
M	2	5	8	11	14

+3 +3 +3 +3

If the increases were +4 instead of +3, the form of the rule would be $M = 4 \times n + \square$.

c As the n values increase by 1, the M values increase by 3,

∴ the rule has form $M = 3 \times n + \square$.

If the rule was $M = 3 \times n$

the M values would be 3 6 9 12 15
but they are 2 5 8 11 14

(one less, i.e., $\square = -1$)

So, the rule is $M = 3 \times n - 1$.

d When $n = 17$, $M = 3 \times 17 - 1 = 50$

∴ 50 matchsticks are needed.

EXERCISE 11D

1 Examine the matchstick pattern: 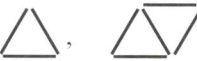, , ...

    a Copy the pattern and add to it the next 3 members.

    b Copy and complete:

Unit number (n)	1	2	3	4	5	6
Matchsticks needed (M)						

    c Find the rule connecting M and n.

    d Find the number of matchsticks needed to make the 23rd member.

2 Examine the matchstick pattern: , ...

    a Copy the pattern and add to it the next 3 members.

    b Copy and complete:

Unit number (n)	1	2	3	4	5	6
Matchsticks needed (M)						

    c Find the rule connecting M and n.

    d Find the number of matchsticks needed to make the 43rd member.

3 Look at the following pattern: , ...

    a Draw the next two members of the pattern.

    b Copy and complete:

Unit number (n)	1	2	3	4	5
Matchsticks needed (M)					

    c Find the rule connecting M and n.

    d Find the number of matchsticks needed to make the 57th member.

4 Look at the following pattern:

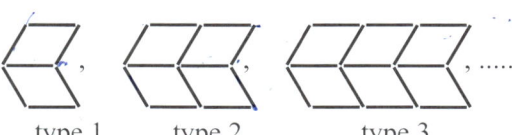

type 1   type 2   type 3

    a Draw the figures for type 4 and type 5 and count the number of matchsticks to make each of them.

    b Copy and complete:

Type number (t)	1	2	3	4	5
Matchsticks needed (M)					

    c Find the rule connecting M and t.

    d Find the number of matchsticks needed to make type 32.

5 Examine the following matchstick pattern:

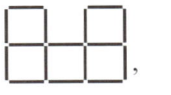, 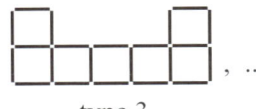, ...

type 1   type 2   type 3

a Draw type 4 and type 5 diagrams and count the number of matchsticks needed to construct type 1 to type 5.

b Copy and complete:

Type number (t)	1	2	3	4	5
Matchsticks needed (M)					

c Find the rule connecting M and t.

d Find the number of matchsticks needed to make type 19.

E PRACTICAL PROBLEMS USING FORMULAE

Useful formulae can be set up and used in many practical situations.

Below is an example of a situation where a rule can be established from a pattern.

Joe Smith hires small trucks for moving furniture.

His terms are:

an initial fee of $10 plus $2 per kilometre travelled.

He could form a table such as the one shown.

Distance travelled	Hire fee
0 km	$10
1 km	$12
2 km	$14
3 km	$16
⋮ etc	

However, a **rule** or **formula** is useful to describe this situation. Can you see what this rule is?

Actually the rule is: Hire fee = distance travelled × $2 + $10

or $H = d \times 2 + 10$ dollars

if we let H replace 'hire fee' and d replace 'distance travelled'.

We will develop a method for finding rules such as this one as we proceed through this chapter.

Example 7

A taxi company charges $3 'flag fall' and $2 for each kilometre travelled. If the total charge is C for travelling n kilometres, find:

a tabled values of C for $n = 0, 1, 2, 3$ and 4

b the formula connecting C and n

c the total charge for travelling 21 km.

a

n	0	1	2	3	4
C	3	5	7	9	11

+2 +2 +2 +2

b As the n values increase by 1, the C values increase by 2.

This suggests that $C = 2 \times n + \square$.

If the rule was $C = 2 \times n$

we would have C values of   0   2   4   6   8

But they are   3   5   7   9   11

which are 3 more, so $\square = 3$

So, the rule is $C = 2 \times n + 3$.

c For travelling 21 km, $n = 21$ $\therefore$ $C = 2 \times 21 + 3$
$= 42 + 3$
$= 45$

So, it would cost $45.

EXERCISE 11E

1 A mechanic charges $40 callout plus $20 for every hour attending a weekend breakdown. So, for a breakdown taking two hours to fix, the total cost would be $40 + 2 \times $20 = 80.

The formula the mechanic uses is $C = $40 + h \times 20 where C is the total charge for a callout of h hours. Find the total charge for callouts of:

  a 1 hour   **b** 3 hours   **c** 5 hours

2 A bean plant grows 5 cm in the first hour of sunlight each day and then 3 cm each hour afterwards. There are 10 hours of sunlight today and the plant starts at 8 cm tall.

  a Copy and complete the chart showing the height of the bean plant for each hour during the day.

Hours of sunlight	0	1	2	3	4	5	6	7	8	9	10
Height (cm)	8										

  b Write a rule that connects the hours of sunlight to the height of the bean plant.

3 A satellite TV company charges $75 installation and $42.00 per month from then on. What would it cost to install the service and then use it for:

  a 7 months   **b** 1 year
  c 18 months   **d** 5 years?

Show how you get your answer.

4 On a rainy day the flow of a river increases by 2 cumecs each hour. When the rain starts the river flow is 8 cumecs.
  a Calculate the flow after 9 hours of rain.
  b Write a formula to show how you got your answer.
  c Construct a table to show the flow each hour for 9 hours.

HARDER

5 Below is a table of labour charges used by an electrician for various hours worked on a job.

Number of hours (h)	1	2	3	4	5
Cost of job (C)	$70	$110	$150	$190	$230

  a Find the rule connecting C and h.
  b Find the cost of a job taking: **i** 23 hours **ii** $17\frac{1}{2}$ hours.

6 A runner in a 14 km road-race starts quickly but then slows. She runs the first kilometre in 7 minutes but then takes an extra 12 seconds for each kilometre afterwards.

  a Write a formula and make a table showing the elapsed time for each kilometre of the race.
  b The winner of the race took 7 minutes for the first kilometre. She then increased her pace by an average 12 seconds for each remaining kilometre.

  How long did she take to run the race? Write the formula to solve the problem and show your answer in the form of a table.

INVESTIGATION — RULES USING SPREADSHEETS

Suppose you wish to use a spreadsheet to find the values of M in the formula $M = 3 \times n + 7$ for values of n from 1 to 50.

What to do:

1 Open a new spreadsheet.
  In cell A1 type n
  In cell B1 type M
  In cell A2 type 1
  In cell A3 type = A2+1
  and **fill down** to cell A51.
  In cell B2 type =3*A2+7
  and **fill down** to cell B51.
  You should now see:

	A	B
1		
2		
3		

	A	B
1	n	M
2	1	10
3	2	13
4	3	16
5	4	19

SPREADSHEET

VIDEO CLIP

See the video clip for an another method of filling down.

2 Go back to cell B2 and replace the formula =3*A2+7 with =3*A2+11 and observe what happens.

3 Repeat **2** with =5*A2−2 and try other formula replacements.

LINEAR GRAPHS

In **Example 7**, the taxi charges formula was $C = 2 \times n + 3$ where
C is the cost in dollars and
n is the number of kilometres travelled.

This formula was found using a table of values.

n	0	1	2	3	4
C	3	5	7	9	11

Rather than use a formula, sometimes a graph is easier to use and find information from. The graph in this case is a **linear graph** as all points lie on a straight line.

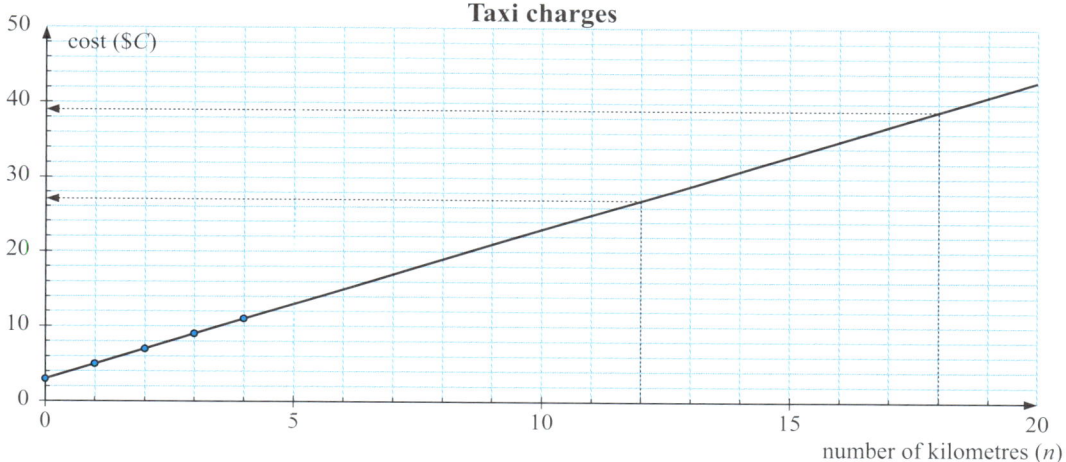

It can easily be read from the graph that when $n = 12$, $C = 27$ and when $n = 18$, $C = 39$.

EXERCISE 11F

1 a Use only the graph above to find the cost of a taxi ride which is:
   i 7 km   **ii** 14 km   **iii** 17 km

   b Why is it easier to use the formula $C = 2 \times n + 3$ for trips of more than 20 km?

2 On grid paper draw the graph of P against n from the table which follows.

n	0	1	2	3	4	5	6
P	7	10	13	16	19	22	25

P is the profit in dollars for selling n spanner sets. Make sure that your graph can be extended to $n = 25$.

   a Find the profit in selling:
      i 10 spanner sets   **ii** 18 spanner sets   **iii** 22 spanner sets

   b Tania found the formula for calculating the profit. Her formula was $P = 3 \times n + 7$.
      i Check that this formula fits the tabled values.
      ii Check your answers to **a**.
      iii Find the profit when selling 35 spanner sets.

3 The following graph shows the growth of a seedling over a period of weeks.

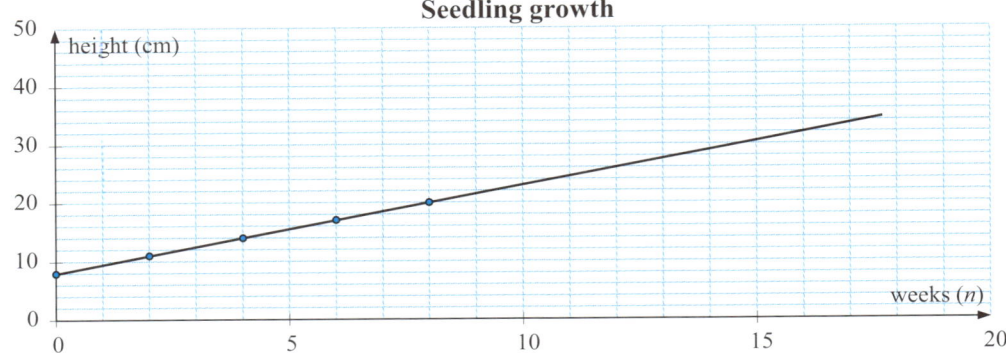

  a Find the height of the seedlings:
    i when planted   **ii** after 4 weeks   **iii** after 16 weeks
  b If the linear trend continues, how long will it take for the seedlings to reach a height of:
    i 20 cm   **ii** 26 cm   **iii** 33.5 cm?

G SOLVING EQUATIONS

In **Example 7**, the taxi charges formula was $C = 2 \times n + 3$. C is the cost in dollars, n is the number of kilometres travelled.

The question may arise: "How far could you travel for \$37?"

Since $C = 37$, we have $2 \times n + 3 = 37$
so, $2 \times n = 34$ {as $34 + 3 = 37$}
and $n = 17$ {as $2 \times 17 = 34$}

We can travel for 17 km.

The method given above is one way of **solving the equation**.

Example 8

Solve the equation:
  a $2 \times p = 10$ **b** $q - 3 = 10$

  a $2 \times p = 10$ **b** $q - 3 = 10$
    $\therefore p = 5$ {as $2 \times 5 = 10$} $\therefore q = 13$ {as $13 - 3 = 10$}

EXERCISE 11G

1 Use the method above to solve the equations:
  a $a + 6 = 9$ **b** $12 + b = 17$ **c** $x + 11 = 32$
  d $a - 6 = 9$ **e** $12 - b = 3$ **f** $x - 20 = 1$
  g $a \times 9 = 45$ **h** $6 \times b = 54$ **i** $3 \times x = 60$
  j $a \div 5 = 5$ **k** $b \div 6 = 4$ **l** $49 \div x = 7$

Example 9

Solve the equation: $2 \times r + 4 = 10$

$2 \times r + 4 = 10$
$\therefore \quad 2 \times r = 6 \quad$ {as $6 + 4 = 10$}
$\therefore \quad r = 3 \quad$ {as $2 \times 3 = 6$}

2 Use the method above to solve the equations:

- **a** $2 \times a + 3 = 27$
- **b** $3 \times a - 1 = 14$
- **c** $4 \times a + 5 = 13$
- **d** $2 \times x + 10 = 30$
- **e** $5 \times x - 11 = 9$
- **f** $7 \times x - 12 = 23$
- **g** $9 \times y + 2 = 29$
- **h** $6 \times y - 5 = 67$
- **i** $3 \times y + 6 = 6$

INVERSE OPERATIONS

$10 + 7 - 7 = 10$ and
$15 - 7 + 7 = 15$ show that $+7$ and -7 are *inverse* operations.

$6 \times 3 \div 3 = 18 \div 3 = 6$ and
$6 \div 3 \times 3 = 2 \times 3 = 6$ show that $\times 3$ and $\div 3$ are *inverse* operations.

Adding 11 to both sides removes the +11 on the left of the = sign.

The operations are called inverse as one undoes what the other does.
We can use inverse operations to help us solve equations.

For example, if we have to solve $3 \times x + 11 = 50$

we first take 11 from both sides of the equation

So $\quad 3 \times x + 11 - 11 = 50 - 11$
$\therefore \quad 3 \times x = 39$

We now divide both sides by 3 to leave $x = 13$.

Example 10

Solve for x: **a** $2 \times x + 11 = 43$ **b** $7 \times x - 5 = 58$

a
$2 \times x + 11 = 43$
$\therefore \quad 2 \times x + 11 - 11 = 43 - 11 \quad$ {the inverse of $+11$ is -11}
$\therefore \quad 2 \times x = 32$
$\therefore \quad x = 16 \quad$ {dividing both sides by 2 as $\div 2$ is the inverse of $\times 2$}

b
$7 \times x - 5 = 58$
$\therefore \quad 7 \times x - 5 + 5 = 58 + 5 \quad$ {the inverse of -5 is $+5$}
$\therefore \quad 7 \times x = 63$
$\therefore \quad x = 9 \quad$ {dividing both sides by 7}

3 Solve for x:

- **a** $2 \times x + 5 = 19$
- **b** $2 \times x + 3 = 27$
- **c** $5 \times x + 2 = 22$
- **d** $4 \times x + 7 = 15$
- **e** $3 \times x + 9 = 30$
- **f** $3 \times x + 11 = 35$
- **g** $6 \times x + 1 = 55$
- **h** $7 \times x + 8 = 8$
- **i** $7 \times x + 21 = 42$

4 Solve for x:

- **a** $2 \times x - 1 = 11$
- **b** $2 \times x - 7 = 15$
- **c** $3 \times x - 5 = 25$
- **d** $7 \times x - 8 = 41$
- **e** $6 \times x - 2 = 40$
- **f** $9 \times x - 7 = 83$
- **g** $4 \times x - 3 = 45$
- **h** $5 \times x - 4 = 41$
- **i** $2 \times x - 8 = 18$

PROBLEM SOLVING WITH EQUATIONS

One of the hardest things to do in using equations is to write the equation in the language of algebra. We know what the problem says, but how do we *start* solving it?

Example 11

If we multiply a number by 3 and then add 5, the result is 23.
Write this as an algebraic equation.

Suppose we represent the number with the letter, n (for number).

Start with a number	n
multiply it by 3	$3 \times n$
add 5	$3 \times n + 5$
the result is 23	$3 \times n + 5 = 23$

So, the algebraic equation which represents the problem is $3 \times n + 5 = 23$.

5 Starting with the number n, rewrite each of these sentences as an equation in algebra.

- **a** I think of a number and subtract 5 from it, getting an answer of 16.
- **b** I think of a number and subtract 8 from it, giving an answer of 30.
- **c** I think of a number and add 3 to it, giving an answer of 31.
- **d** The sum of a number and 8 is 11.
- **e** The product of a number and 7 is 35.
- **f** A number is doubled, and the result is 26.
- **g** I think of a number and divide it by 5, getting an answer of 7.
- **h** A number is divided by 3 and the result is 9.
- **i** I think of a number, multiply it by 7, and subtract 6, giving a result of 64.
- **j** A number is multiplied by 8 then 5 is subtracted to give a result of 27.
- **k** I find the product of a number and 3, then add 2 to give a result of 38.
- **l** I think of a number, multiply it by 5 then add 12, giving a result of 72.

6 Construct an equation from the sentence(s) given and then use it to solve the problem.

- **a** I think of a number and subtract 10 from it, giving an answer of 11.

b I think of a number and add 3 to it. The answer is 17.

c When I multiply a number by 9 the result is 63.

d When I divide a number by 9 the result is 6.

e I think of a number, multiply it by 8, then subtract 6. The result is 50.

f A number is multiplied by 4 then 3 is added. The result is 23.

g A number is trebled then 1 is added. The answer is 64.

h A number is multiplied by 5 then 11 is subtracted. The result is 54.

7 An electrician charges $45 an hour plus a callout fee of $60. A large job costs $465. For how many hours did the electrician work?

  a Set up an equation where x is the number of hours worked.

  b Solve the problem.

8 At the start of the school year Craig has $800 in his bank account. Each week while Craig is studying he withdraws $15 for pocket money. At the mid-year break Craig has $500 left in his account. How many weeks has he been studying?

  a Set up an equation where w is the number of weeks that Craig has been studying.

  b Solve the problem.

9 A plant was 6 cm high when I bought it from the nursery. It grew 3 cm a day. After how many days was it 21 cm high?

  a Set up an equation where d is the number of days after the plant was bought.

  b Solve the problem.

10 The depth of water in a lake was 360 m on January 1. For the rest of the year it decreased in depth by 4 m a month. On what date was the depth of the lake 320 m?

  a Set up an equation where x is the number of months after January 1.

  b Solve the problem.

H GRAPHS OF REAL LIFE SITUATIONS

A graph is often called a "picture" of what is happening.

Example 12

This graph shows the water level of a spa bath. Write a story explaining the graph.

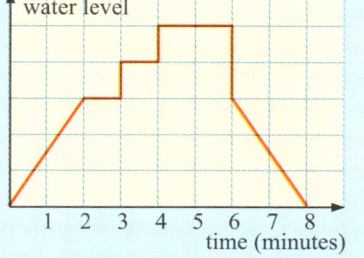

The spa bath is filling for 2 minutes. After one minute a person gets in and one minute later someone else gets in. After 2 minutes they both get out. The water is then let out of the spa bath.

EXERCISE 11H

1 Write a story for each of the following graphs showing the water level in a spa bath:

a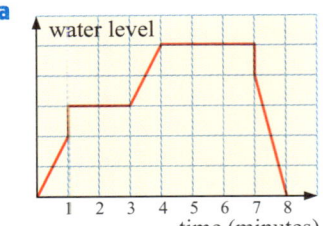

b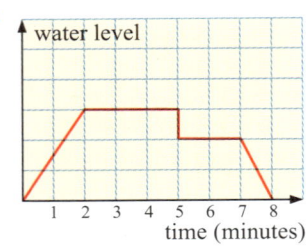

2 Draw graphs to illustrate the following stories:

   a A spa bath is run for 3 minutes. A person gets in and stays in for 2 minutes, then his brother gets in and they both get out after a further 3 minutes. The spa bath is emptied and this takes 2 minutes.

   b A spa bath is run for 2 minutes. Two people get in and after 3 minutes one gets out. After 2 minutes the other person gets out and the spa bath is emptied taking 2 minutes.

3 This graph shows the depth of water in a lake used to store water for irrigation at certain times throughout the year. Write a story for this graph. (Think at what times of the year irrigation is needed on farms and what times of the year water would be filling the lake.)

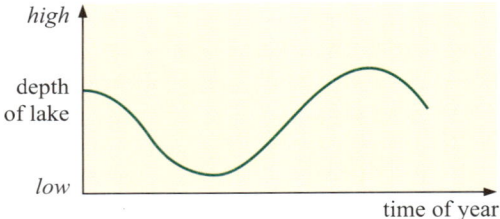

4 Now it is your turn to draw some graphs of real life situations. Draw a graph that could fit each of the following situations.

   a Brett runs a 1500 m race. He starts off very fast but soon gets tired so slows down. After a short distance he has recovered his breath so he speeds up a little bit. Janice comes up fast behind Brett and nearly overtakes him so Brett decides to sprint to stay in front. Unfortunately he trips up and has to stop for a minute. He is brave so he decides to get up and struggle to the finish.

   b The amount of soft drink in a bottle as Rose takes her time to drink the whole lot!

   Hint:

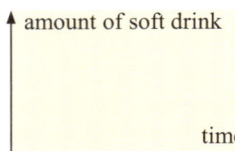

REVIEW SET A   CHAPTER 11

1. Give the next three members of the following number patterns:
   a 2, 11, 20, ..., ..., ...
   b 20, 40, 80, ..., ..., ...
   c $1\frac{1}{2}, 3\frac{1}{2}, 5\frac{1}{2}$, ..., ..., ...
   d 40, 20, 10, ..., ..., ...

2. The following pattern is built out of matchsticks: □, □□, □□□, ...

   a Draw the next 2 members of the pattern.
   b Copy and complete:

Unit number (n)	1	2	3	4	5
Matchsticks needed (M)					

   c Find the rule connecting M and n.
   d How many matchsticks are needed to build:
      i 7 squares   ii 101 squares?

3. TLC Carpet Cleaning Company charges $35 for the first room it cleans and $15 for every other room. Copy and complete the table of values for the charge C dollars for cleaning n rooms:

n	1	2	3	4	5	6
C						

   a What is TLC's fee formula?
   b Find how much TLC would charge for cleaning a mansion with 27 rooms.

4. VideoOz charges $3 for the first video it hires out and $2 for each video hired out thereafter. The table of charges for video hire is:

Number of videos (n)	1	2	3	4	5
Charge ($C)	3	5	7	9	11

   a On grid paper plot the graph of C against n from the table of values.
   b Determine the VideoOz hire formula for hiring out n videos.
   c Calculate the hire charge for the following number of videos:
      i 9   ii 17

5. I think of a number, multiply it by 6 and subtract 1. The answer is 47. Construct an equation and use it to find the number.

6. Solve the following equations:
   a $f - 12 = 23$ b $n \div 7 = 6$ c $8 \times b - 7 = 49$

REVIEW SET B — CHAPTER 11

1 Give the next three members of the following number patterns:
   a 39, 52, 65, 78, ..., ..., ...
   b 4, 8, 16, 32, ..., ..., ...
   c 1.8, 3.6, 5.4, ..., ..., ...
   d 55, 49, 43, 37, ..., ..., ...

2 The following patterns are made with matchsticks: □, □□, □□□, ...

   a Copy and complete the table of values:

Number of rectangles (r)	1	2	3	4	5
Number of matchsticks (M)					

   b Find the rule connecting M and r.
   c Write down the rule in sentence form.
   d Use the rule to find the number of matches needed for 30 rectangles.

3 How much would Joe collect from his customers if the hire fee for his vans was:
$H = $ distance (in km) $\times \$1.50 + \$10$ and the distances travelled were:
   a 32 km
   b 100 km?

4 Joe sells television sets. He is paid $400 per week plus $80 for every television set he sells.

   a Copy and complete the table of values showing the amount Joe earns (E dollars) for selling n television sets:

n	0	1	2	3	4	5
E						

   b Write a formula for the amount that Joe earns.
   c How much would Joe earn if he sold 8 television sets in a week?

5 Solve the following equations:
   a $p + 4 = 10$
   b $r \div 8 = 4$
   c $3 \times f - 2 = 25$

6 Sketch the graph of the following situation:

"Jenny is swimming in a 4×50 m medley race. She swims the first lap breaststroke which is her third best stroke, the second length backstroke which is her second fastest stroke, the third length butterfly which is her slowest stroke and finishes with freestyle which is her fastest stroke."

Sketch Jenny's *distance from the starting end of the pool* at any time during her swim.

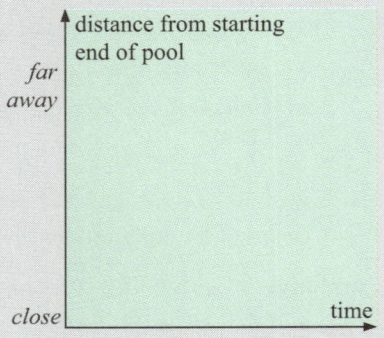

REVIEW SET C — CHAPTER 11

1 The rule is "the next number is equal to the previous one multiplied by 2, minus 3". What are the values for the next 3 numbers in the following sets?
   a 5, 7, ..., ..., ...
   b 10, 17, 31, ..., ..., ...

2 The following pattern is built out of matchsticks:

   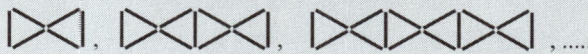

   a Copy and complete the table of values:

Number of units (n)	1	2	3	4	5	6
Number of matchsticks (M)						

   b Find the rule connecting M and n.
   c Write down the rule in sentence form.
   d Use the rule to write the number of matchsticks needed for 80 units.

3 A disc jockey charges $150 to set up the equipment and $40 for each $\frac{1}{2}$ hour to provide entertainment for school discos.

   a Complete the table of values:

Number of $\frac{1}{2}$ hours (n)	0	1	2	3	4
Charge ($C)	150				

   b What is the disc jockey's fee formula?
   c How much would the disc jockey charge for:
      i a lunch hour disco
      ii $2\frac{1}{2}$ hours
      iii 3 hours?

4 A baby sitter charges $12 for the first hour and $8 for each hour after that.

   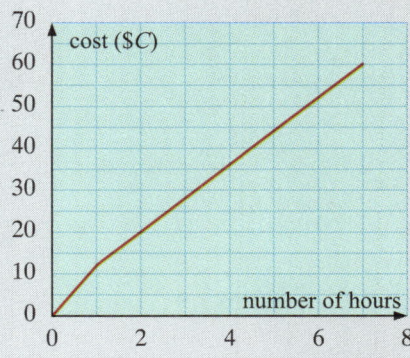

   a Use the graph to find how much the babysitter would charge for:
      i 3 hours
      ii 6 hours.
   b Write down a formula for the babysitter's fee.
   c Use the formula to find how much the babysitter would charge if she worked from 8 am until 10 pm.

5 Kathy earns $532 a week plus $21 an hour for working overtime. Last week she earned $637 in total. How many hours overtime did she work?
   a Set up an equation where x is the number of hours of overtime worked.
   b Solve the problem.

6 Solve the following equations:
   a $k - 11 = 24$
   b $m \times 8 = 24$
   c $4 \times d + 5 = 65$

TRY THESE

1 a How many children are in a family if each boy has one brother and one sister?

  b Find the ages of the three children in a family if the product of their ages is 100 and there are no twins.

  c How many children are in a family if each girl has the same number of sisters as brothers, but each boy has twice as many sisters as brothers.

2 In the arrangement of matches shown, describe how to
  a remove two matches to leave two squares
  b move two matches to make three squares.

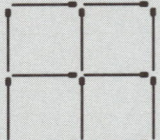

3 The six cakes shown were marked to sell at $2.20, $2.50, $2.70, $2.90, $3.10 and $3.40.

Five of the cakes were sold to two customers, with one customer paying twice as much as the other. Which cake remained?

4 Copy and complete the given magic square.

Remember that the numbers in each row, column and main diagonal add to the same number.

1		2
	$1\frac{3}{4}$	
		$2\frac{1}{2}$

5 Replace each letter with a different digit so that the given sum gives the correct answer.

```
       A
   MERRY
 + XMAS
 -------
  TURKEY
```

Chapter 12

Transformation and Location

Knowledge, skills and understandings

By the end of this chapter you should be able to

- rotate a shape about a point (e.g., rotate 90° clockwise)
- reflect a complex shape or design on a line
- translate shapes over a given distance (e.g., translate the shape 5 squares horizontally to the left on grid paper)
- enlarge and reduce shapes using a scale
- create a simple tessellation using rotation, translation and reflection (e.g., using software)
- compare quantities using ratio in problem solving
- draw environmental and geometric objects from different perspectives
- describe and draw what is seen and not seen from different views of 3-D shapes (e.g., pyramids and prisms)
- draw 3-D shapes using solid lines for visible edges and dotted lines for invisible edges
- recognise that a location can be represented on maps or plans using different scales
- use a scale to calculate the distance between two points on a map
- read, write and use scales in words, ratios and diagrams
- produce scaled plans (e.g., classroom, bedroom)
- evaluate maps and plans in terms of appropriateness of scale, use of symbols, appropriateness for task, clarity of purpose, accuracy, etc.
- use coordinate grids to make more complex 2-D shapes
- explain a pathway to a location on models, maps or plans using distance, direction, angle multiples of 45°, compass points and coordinates
- find alternative routes using a scale (e.g., to find the shortest route between two points)
- follow simple directions to move from point to point on a given path, using maps, a magnetic compass, and written and oral instructions
- use understanding of angles to determine compass bearings and true bearings
- develop a simple orienteering course

DISCUSSION

LOCATION

 Archeologists use a grid to mark the positions of buildings and artefacts discovered at a site where they are digging. Consider the following questions:

1. Mr Bone has used pegs and ropes to form a grid over his archeological 'dig'. What else does he need to do so that he can identify the positions of his discoveries?

2. How could Mr Bone improve his accuracy in identifying positions? Discuss your ideas.

3. Mr Bone wants to record the position of an object in his grid and the depth at which it is found. Suggest a way in which he could do this.

4. What books enable us to locate:
   - countries and states
   - roadways between capital cities
   - streets, public places and suburbs?

5. Which of the following are important features of atlases, road maps and street directories? Give reasons.
   - They show the direction of north.
   - They have a scale.
   - They show the direction of prevailing winds.
   - They have clearly marked grid systems.
   - The writing on them is large enough to read easily.

Following is a typical part page from a road map.

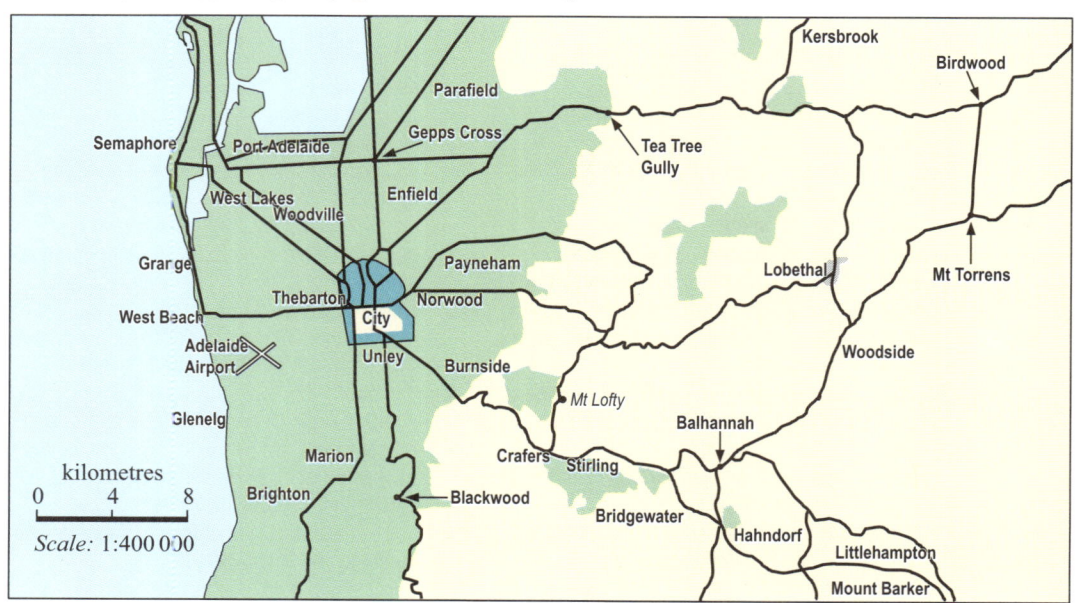

Can you locate • Adelaide Airport • Lobethal • Littlehampton • Parafield?

A NUMBER PLANES

Number planes help to make maps, street directories and graphs easier to read. When two number lines or axes (one axis, two axes) join at right angles they form a **number plane**.

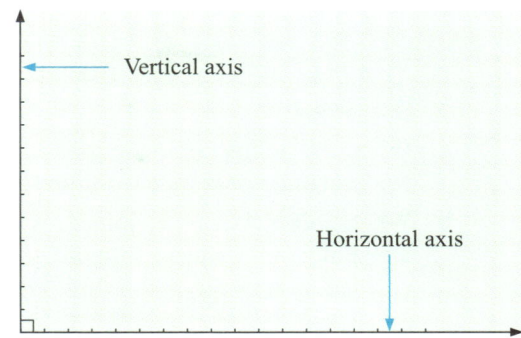

Vertical lines can be drawn or imagined to be drawn from the equally spaced points along the **horizontal axis**. Similarly, horizontal lines can be drawn from the equally spaced points along the **vertical axis**.

A grid is formed.

Each line from each axis is itself a number line.

Labelling both sets of lines allows points on the number plane to be located.

The point where 2 lines intersect can be identified by the numbers of the two lines. These are the **coordinates** of a point or an **ordered pair**.

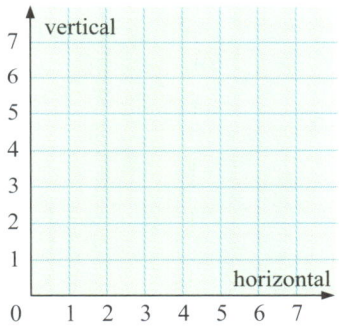

The horizontal number line is called the **horizontal axis**. The vertical number line is called the **vertical axis**.

Example 1

Write the coordinates or ordered pairs for the following points:
a A **b** B **c** C **d** D **e** E

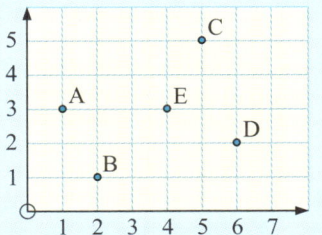

a Go to the right 1 and up 3, A is (1, 3).
b Go to the right 2 and up 1, B is (2, 1).
c Go to the right 5 and up 5, C is (5, 5).
d Go to the right 6 and up 2, D is (6, 2).
e Go to the right 4 and up 3, E is (4, 3).

The horizontal coordinate is always named and located first.

EXERCISE 12A.1

1 Copy and draw the given grid.

Locate the following points:

A(1, 2)   B(3, 6)   C(3, 1)   D(5, 5)
E(2, 4)   F(4, 3)   G(1, 6)   H(5, 1)
I(1, 1)   J(5, 6)

  a When the points GIHJ are joined, is a rectangle or a square formed?
  b When points ACFE are joined, is a rectangle or a square formed?
  c Is triangle AGJ right angled?

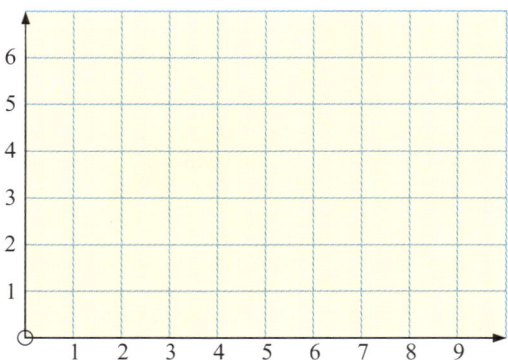

2 Use the following ordered pairs of numbers to locate the letters on the number plane:

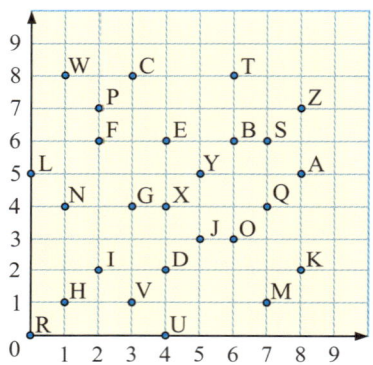

a (6, 6)	**b** (1, 8)	**c** (7, 4)	**d** (2, 7)
e (5, 5)	**f** (6, 8)	**g** (1, 1)	**h** (8, 5)
i (3, 4)	**j** (6, 3)	**k** (0, 0)	**l** (4, 0)
m (7, 6)	**n** (0, 5)	**o** (2, 2)	
p (8, 2)	**q** (4, 6)	**r** (4, 2)	
s (7, 1)	**t** (1, 4)	**u** (4, 4)	
v (3, 8)	**w** (5, 3)	**x** (3, 1)	

ABCD is a short way of saying the figure with vertices A, B, C and D.

3 Plot the points with coordinates A(3, 2), B(7, 2), C(7, 5) and D(3, 5). What type of quadrilateral is ABCD?

4 Plot the points with coordinates P(1, 1), Q(5, 1), R(7, 4) and S(3, 4). What type of quadrilateral is PQRS?

5 A(2, 3) and B(6, 3) form one side of square ABCD. What are the coordinates of C and D?

6 P(3, 0) and Q(5, 1) form one side of square PQRS. What are the coordinates of R and S?

7 Using this map find:
  a the grid coordinates for
     i Gnometown
     ii Magic Cave
     iii Ferry Landing
     iv where the roads cross Dawson's River
  b the places located at
     i (9.2, 3.7)   **ii** (5.3, 2.7)
     iii (1.6, 3.5)   **iv** (1.4, 5)

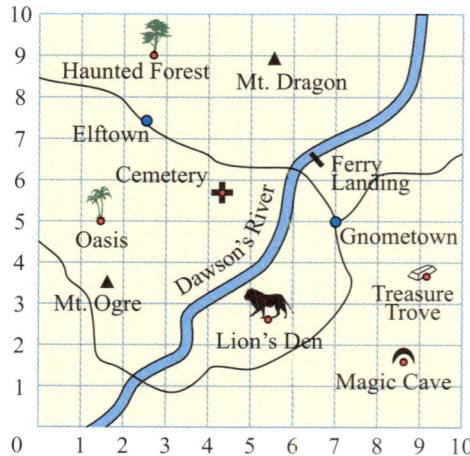

8 Use the map of Australia to determine:
  a the grid coordinates for
   i Perth   **ii** Hobart   **iii** Cairns   **iv** Adelaide
  b the city/town located at
   i (3, 4.6)   **ii** (6.8, 7.4)   **iii** (8.7, 8.7)   **iv** (13, 5.7)

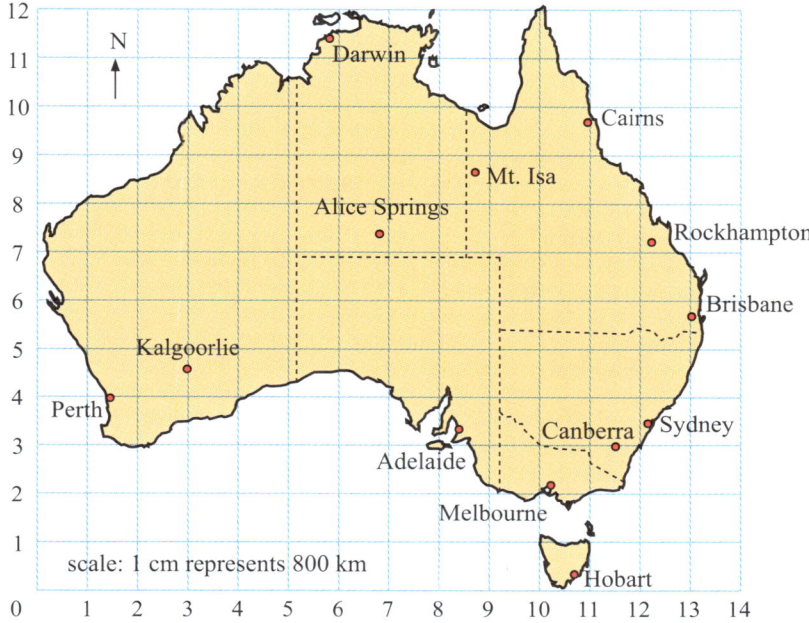

ANOTHER USEFUL MAP

As we hinted earlier not all number planes have lines intersecting across them.
There are good reasons for this.

- Lines across a map or street directory can cover important information or take one's attention from it.
- Not all places on a map or directory are located exactly where the number lines intersect.
- The area between the lines forms grid squares. Coordinates can also be used to locate a particular grid square.

To avoid confusion and to be consistent, many atlases, street directories and maps name the points on the horizontal axis alphabetically.

Many cities and major towns have a Show and the organisers produce a map to help people locate exhibits, sideshows and facilities.

Following is one of these.

SHOWGROUNDS MAP

EXERCISE 12A.2

1. Write the closest coordinates for each of the following:
   - **a** dogs
   - **b** beef cattle
   - **c** showbags
   - **d** Duncan Hall
   - **e** woodcutting
   - **f** Ferris Wheel
   - **g** Blockbuster Stage
   - **h** poultry/pigeons
   - **i** Jubilee Pavilion
   - **j** Pet Centre

2. What could I find at:
   - **a** D2
   - **b** G9
   - **c** H5
   - **d** E2
   - **e** D6
   - **f** G3?

3. Which entrance is closest to:
   - **a** F8
   - **b** Wayville Pavilion?

B TRANSFORMATIONS

Translations, reflections, rotations and enlargements are all examples of **transformations**. Here are some examples of the four transformations:

a **translation** (or **shift**)

shift to a new position in a particular direction

a **reflection**

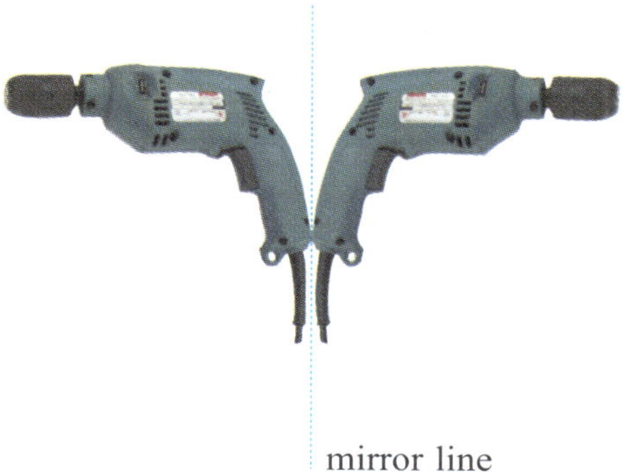

mirror line

a **rotation** about O

an **enlargement**

The original shape is called the **object**, and the shape produced as a result of the transformation is called the **image**.

REFLECTION AND LINE SYMMETRY

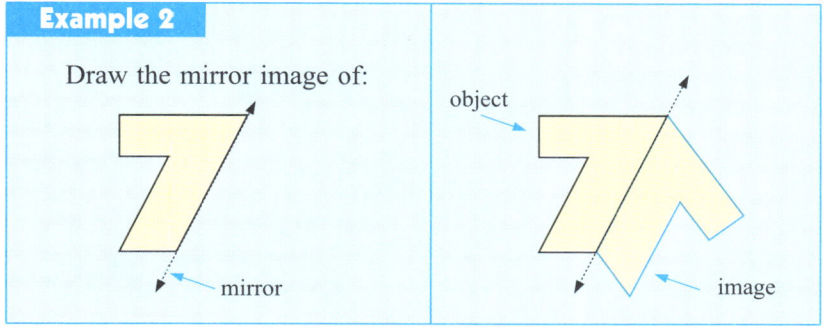

Example 2

Draw the mirror image of:

mirror

object

image

ACTIVITY — LINES OF SYMMETRY

Recall that a **line of symmetry** is a line a shape may be folded on so that both parts of the shape will match.

For example:

— fold line

line of symmetry also called a 'mirror line'

What to do:

1 Copy the following figures and draw on them any lines of symmetry:

   a A   b O   c S   d +   e ↕

2 Check **1** using a mirror.

3 From a magazine or newspaper cut out a picture which seems to have line symmetry. Fold along the line of symmetry and then cut along this line with scissors. Glue half the picture onto a sheet of paper and then draw the other half to make it symmetrical. Display your work on the wall of your room.

4 Click on the **icon** which enables you to check the symmetry of people's faces. Write down your observations.

EXERCISE 12B.1

1 Place your mirror on the mirror line, shown using dashes, and observe the mirror image. Then draw the object and its mirror image in your work book.

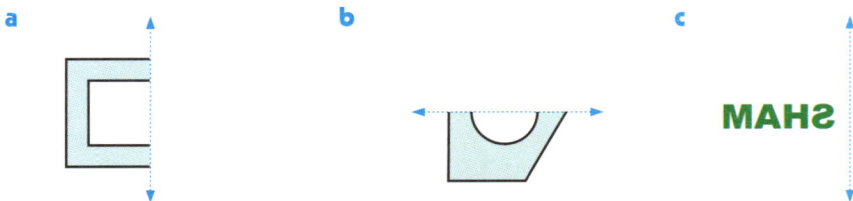

2 a Predict and draw the image of the following if a mirror was placed on the mirror line:

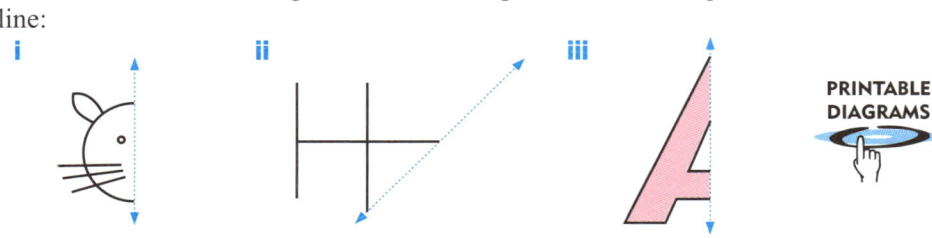

   b Check your answers to **a** using a mirror.

3 On grid paper reflect the geometrical shape in the mirror line shown:

a 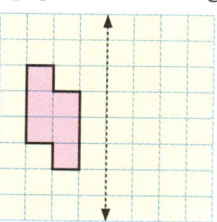 b 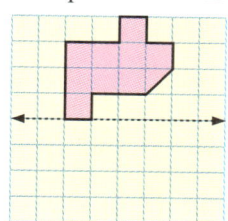 c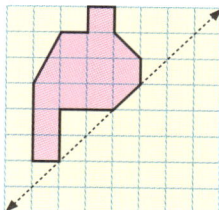

ROTATIONS AND ROTATIONAL SYMMETRY

We rotate an object by turning it around a fixed point through a certain number of degrees.

For example:

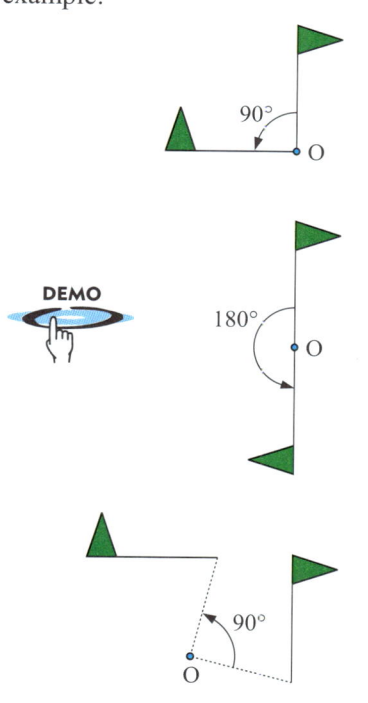

This flag has been rotated anticlockwise through $90°$ about O. O is the fixed point and is called the **centre of rotation**.

This flag has been rotated anticlockwise through $180°$ about O.

This flag has been rotated anticlockwise through $90°$ about O.

You will notice that under a rotation the flag does not change in size or shape.

In mathematics we rotate in an anticlockwise direction unless we are told otherwise.

(**Note:** $90°$ is a $\frac{1}{4}$-turn, $180°$ is a $\frac{1}{2}$-turn, $270°$ is a $\frac{3}{4}$-turn and $360°$ is a full turn.)

| ACTIVITY | ROTATIONAL SYMMETRY |

 **You will need:** a dressmakers pin, scissors.

What to do:

1 Click on the icon and print a page containing the regular polygons. Each regular polygon has its centre of symmetry marked.

2 With scissors cut out each shape.

3 Starting with the equilateral triangle, place the pin through its centre and hold it to your page by putting your finger on top of it.

Draw around the shape to make your starting figure. Now rotate the shape anticlockwise and count the number of times in the first revolution that the cut out fits onto the original figure. Record your results.

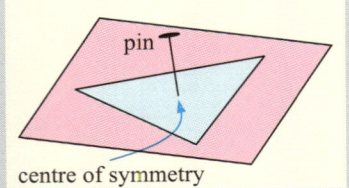

4 Repeat for the square, pentagon, hexagon, heptagon and octagon.

5 Copy and complete:

The number of symmetries is the number of positions where a 'match' occurs. $360°$ is to be included, $0°$ is not included.

Regular polygon	Number of sides	Number of symmetries
triangle		
square		
pentagon		
hexagon		
heptagon		
octagon		

6 What do you observe from **5**? Write your answer in words.

ROTATIONAL SYMMETRY

The **order of rotational symmetry** is the number of times a shape looks exactly the same and is in the same position during one complete turn about the centre.

For example:

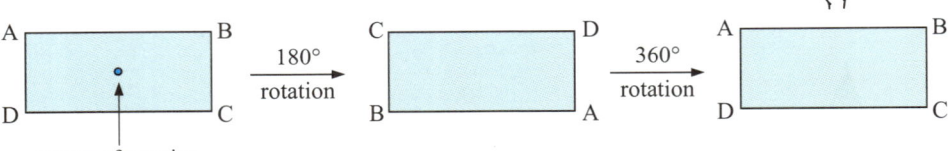

The rectangle has order of rotational symmetry of 2 since it moves back top its original postion under rotations of $180°$ and $360°$.

Click on the icon to find the order of rotational symmetry for an equilateral triangle.

EXERCISE 12B.2

1 We could rotate the object ⊢ to obtain:

A ⊔⊔   B ⊐   C ⊓   D ⊢

Which of **A**, **B**, **C**, or **D** is a rotation of the object through:

a $180°$ **b** $360°$ **c** $90°$ **d** $270°$?

2 Copy and rotate each of the following shapes about the centre of rotation O, for the number of degrees shown. Tracing paper can be used.

a 90°
b 180°
c 270°
d 360°
e 90°
f 270°
g 180°
h 90°
i 90°

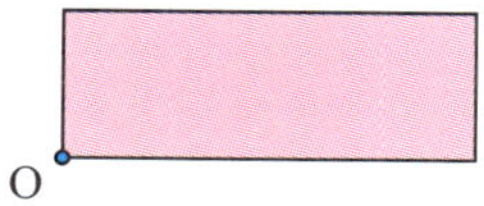

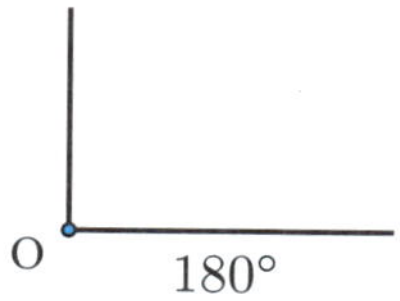

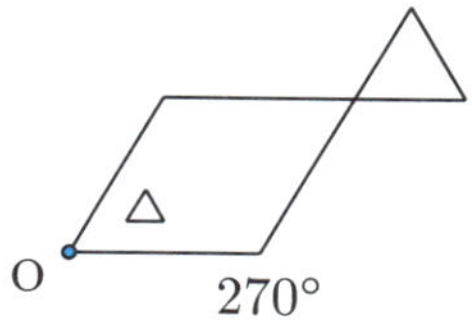

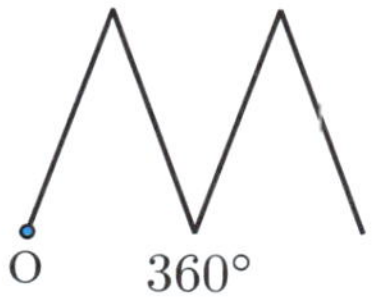

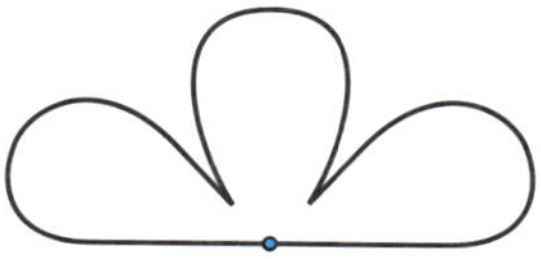

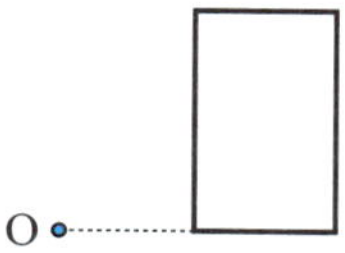

PRINTABLE WORKSHEET

3 Rotate about O through the angle given:

a 90°
b 180°
c 270°
d 180°
e 90°
f 270°

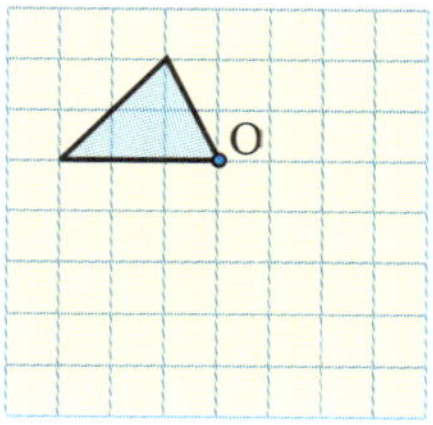

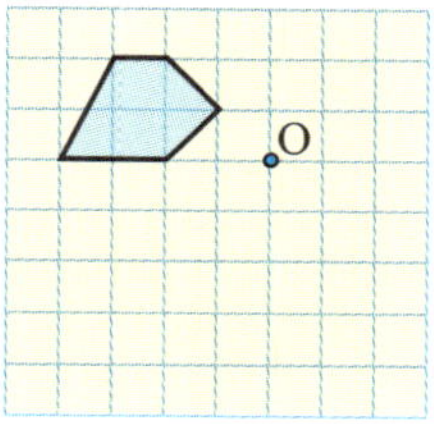

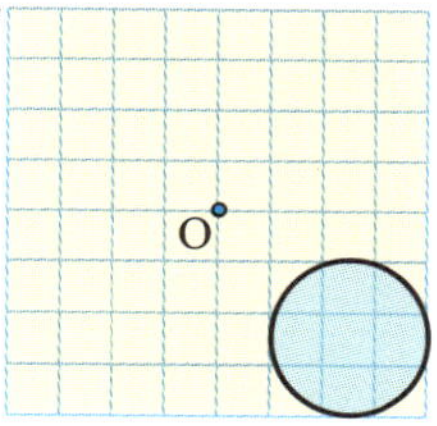

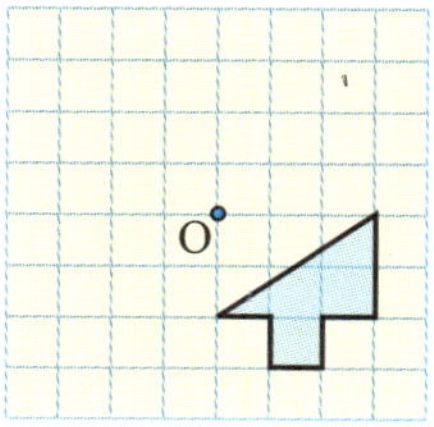

DEMO

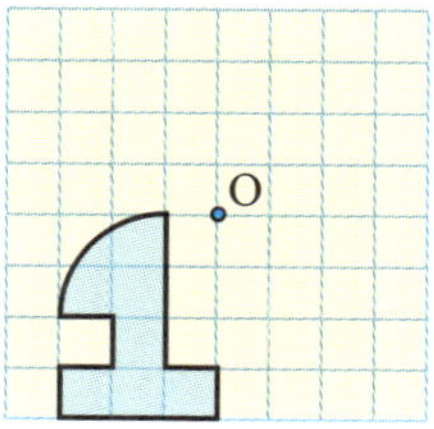

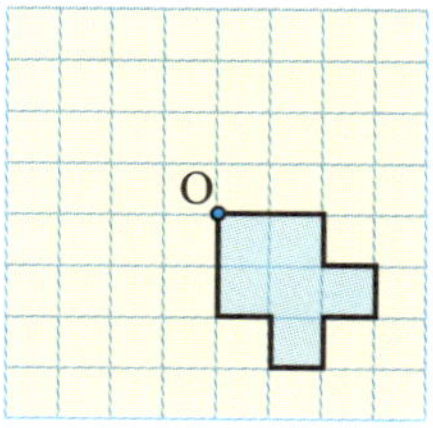

4 For each of the following shapes find the *order* of rotational symmetry (tracing paper may help):

a   b   c   d

e   f   g   h

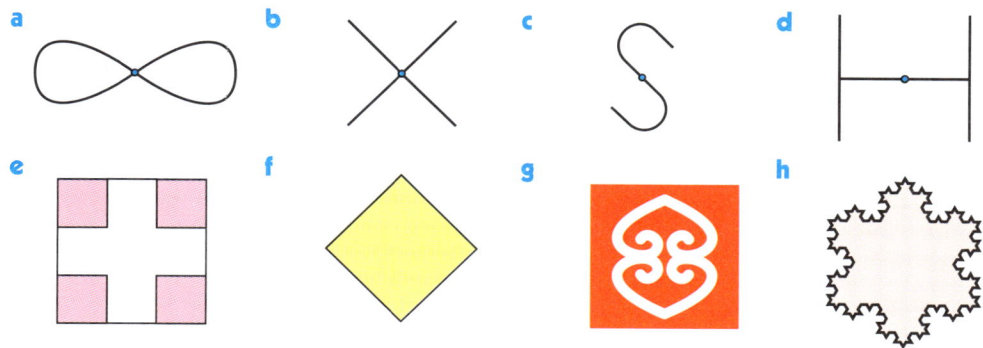

5 Design your own shape which has order of symmetry of:
  a 2   **b** 3   **c** 1   **d** 4   **e** 6

TRANSLATIONS

A **translation** occurs when every point on a figure is moved the same distance in the same direction.

Under translations the original figure (the object) and the image are **congruent**.

Example:

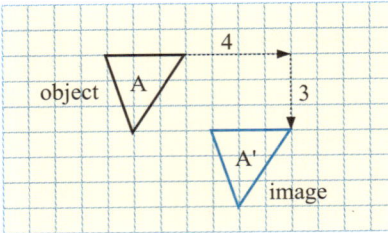

We say that the original figure A, has been translated 4 units right and 3 units down to the position of the image A′.

(We say 'A dashed' when we see A′.)

EXERCISE 12B.3

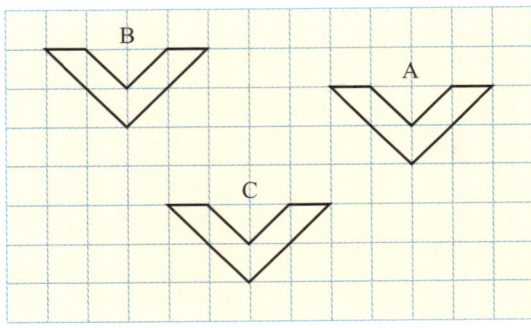

1 For the given figures, describe the translation from:
  a A to B   **b** B to A
  c B to C   **d** C to B
  e A to C   **f** C to A

2 Copy onto grid paper and translate in the directions shown:
  a 3 right, 4 down   **b** 6 left, 4 up   **c** 2 right, 5 up

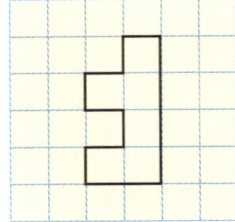
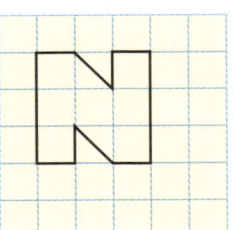

ENLARGEMENTS AND REDUCTIONS

When you take a photo of a scenic view the photo is a smaller version of the real view. You will notice that every object has been shrunk (**reduced**) by the same amount.

Under a microscope, everything is enlarged by the same amount.

The amount of enlargement or reduction is called the **scale factor**.

When enlarging an object using a scale factor of 2, all lengths on the image figure are twice as long as on the object.

Example 3

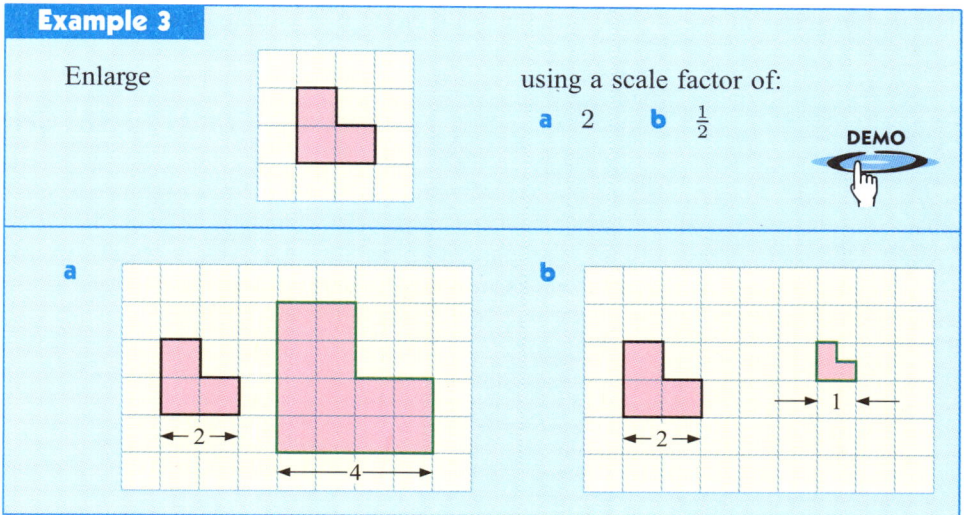

Enlarge [figure] using a scale factor of:
a 2 **b** $\frac{1}{2}$

EXERCISE 12B.4

1 Enlarge each of the following objects by the scale factor given:

a scale factor 2

b scale factor 3

c scale factor $\frac{1}{2}$

d scale factor $\frac{1}{3}$

e scale factor 4

f scale factor 2

2 Find the scale factor when A is transformed to B:

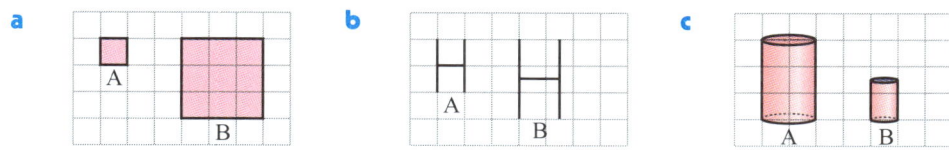

3 The following are *not drawn accurately*. Find the scale factor if A is transformed to B:

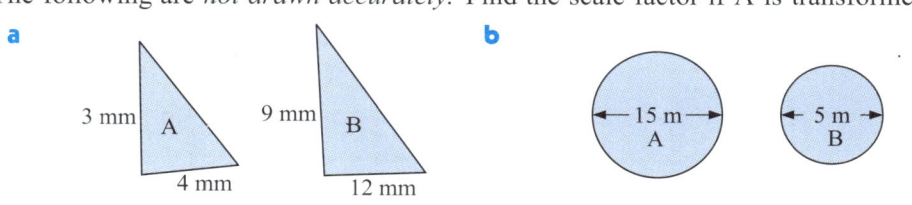

4 For the diagrams in question **3**, find the scale factor if B is transformed to A.

ACTIVITY — ENLARGEMENT SKETCHES

If the sides of a shape are not straight lines or the picture is complex you can enlarge it with reasonable accuracy by drawing a grid over the original diagram. A second grid is prepared to place the enlargement on. For example, on the original the grid distances might be 5 mm. So, on the enlarged grid the distances would be 10 mm for scale factor 2, or 15 mm for scale factor 3.

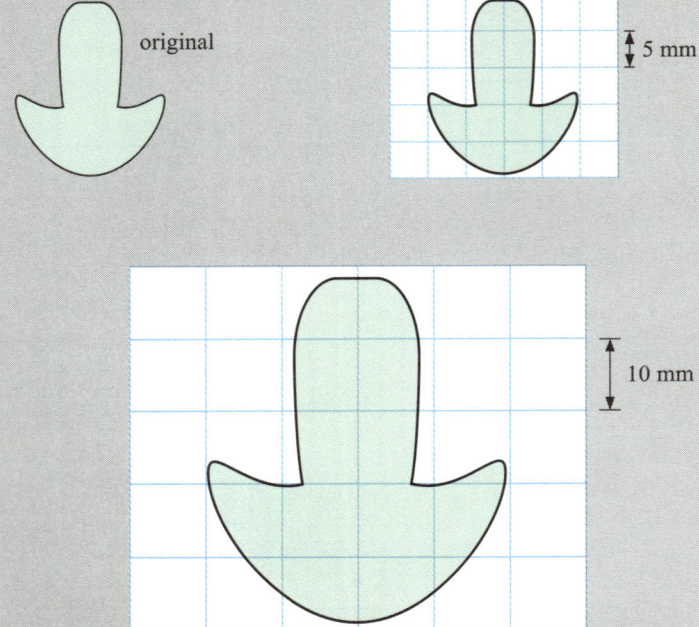

What to do:

Make a drawing of your own choosing and then enlarge it by using a scale factor of:
  a 2 **b** $\frac{1}{2}$.

INVESTIGATION — ENLARGEMENT AND AREA

When an object is enlarged by scale factor 2, what happens to its area?
Investigate this question by drawing a rectangle and a triangle on grid paper. Enlarge by scale factor 2 and calculate the areas of both objects and images.

Continue the investigation to see what happens if the scale factor is **a** 3 and **b** $\frac{1}{2}$.

Write a short report on your findings.

TESSELLATIONS

Following are some brick paving patterns.

Can you draw any other paving patterns for these 2 by 1 shaped bricks?

> A **tessellation** is a pattern made by using 'tiles' of the same shape and size which cover an area without leaving any gaps.

Which of the above brick paving patterns are tessellations? Why/why not?

Example 4

Tessellate: a △   b ✚

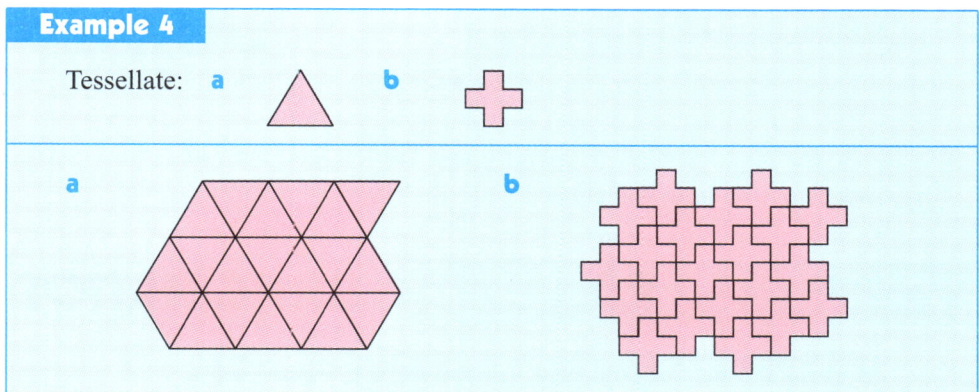

Tessellations can look spectacular, especially with added colour or designs on each individual tile.

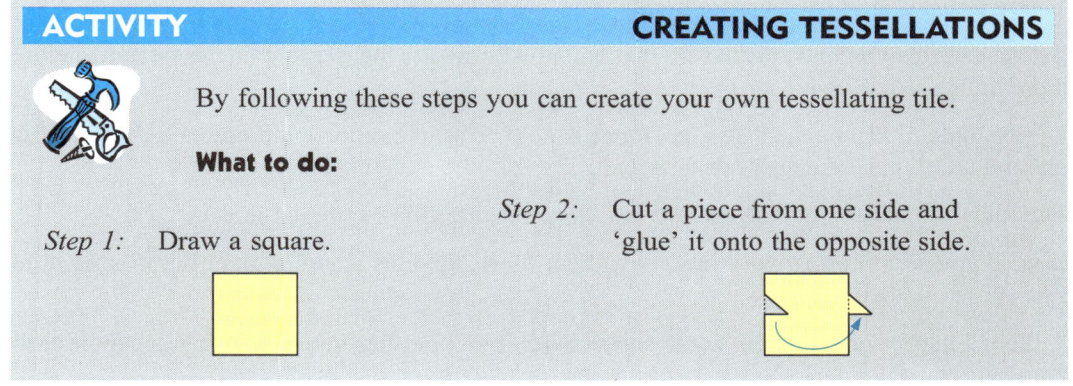

ACTIVITY — CREATING TESSELLATIONS

By following these steps you can create your own tessellating tile.

What to do:

Step 1: Draw a square.

Step 2: Cut a piece from one side and 'glue' it onto the opposite side.

Step 3: Rub out any unwanted lines and add features.

Step 4: Photocopy this several times and cut out each face. Combine them.

Now it is your turn. Make your own tessellation pattern and produce a full page pattern with 3 cm by 3 cm tiles. Be creative and colourful. You could use a computer drawing package to do this activity.

EXERCISE 12B.5

1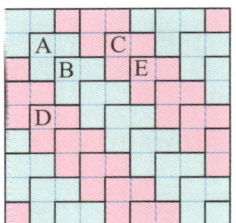

Give the translation that moves:

a A to B
b A to C
c A to D
d C to E

2 a Make a tile out of card which you can use to create a tessellation using translations only.

b Construct your own tessellation, colour it and display it on the wall.

c Give instructions on how you created your tile pattern.

C USING RATIOS

A **ratio** is a way of comparing quantities of the same kind.

For example, if Damian has $3 and Donna has $7, then the ratio of Damian's money to Donna's money is 3 : 7. We read this as "3 is to 7."

Note that the **order** is important. The ratio of Donna's money to Damian's money is 7 : 3.

The ratio itself is written **without** units i.e., 3 : 7 not $3 : $7.

Because of this you must make sure that both quantities are measured in the same units before these units are omitted.

For example, if Damian had $3 and Donna had 96 cents, the ratio would **not** be 3 : 96 because the units (dollars and cents) are different.

The ratio would be 300 : 96 where both amounts are first expressed in cents.

If we converted to dollars our ratio would be 3 : 0.96. This is still correct but it is usual to use whole numbers in ratios.

Although most ratios you will come across involve 2 quantities, ratios may involve more than 2 quantities.

Example 5

In a gymnastics class there are three times as many girls as boys. Write this fact as a ratio of **a** girls to boys   **b** boys to girls.

a Since there are three times as many girls as boys,
girls : boys = 3 : 1   {three parts girls to one part boys}

b So, boys : girls = 1 : 3

Note:
- Ratios have no units.
- Order of numbers in a ratio is important, e.g., 1 : 3 is not the same as 3 : 1.
- The terms of a ratio must be expressed in the same units.

EXERCISE 12C

1 Express as a ratio without simplifying your answer:
- **a** $9 is to $7
- **b** 5 kg is to 3 kg
- **c** 14 cm is to 5 cm
- **d** 8 km is to 7 km
- **e** 2 tonne is to 11 tonne
- **f** 3 years is to 4 years
- **g** 95 cents is to $1
- **h** 7 months is to 2 years
- **i** $5 is to 78 cents
- **j** 500 metres is to 2 km
- **k** 300 kg is to 1 tonne
- **l** 1 cm is to 20 metres

2 From this set of shapes, find the ratio of:
- **a** **i** blue to grey   **ii** blue to white
  iii blue to grey to white
- **b** **i** triangles to squares   **ii** circles to triangles
  iii squares to triangles to circles
- **c** **i** blue triangles to white triangles
  ii grey circles to white circles
  iii white squares to white triangles to white circles
- **d** If this set of shapes was multiplied in exactly the same ratio so that there were now 6 blue squares, how many of each of the following would there be?
  i white triangles   **ii** blue circles
  iii grey squares

Example 6

The sides of a rectangular field are 1.2 km and 500 m. Find the ratio of the sides.

500 m
1.2 km

Ratio of sides is 1.2 km to 500 m = 1200 m to 500 m
= 1200 : 500
= 12 : 5   {dividing each by 100}

Multiplying or dividing both numbers in a ratio by the same number produces an equal ratio.

3 Write as a simplified ratio or write the ratio in simplest form:

   a Tom caught 8 fish and Tamara caught 13.
   b At a disco there are 3 girls to every boy.
   c In my class there are three blue-eyed students for every five hazel-eyed students.
   d There are 30 cars on the road for every 2 motor bikes.
   e A library spent $15 on books for every $5 on computer software.
   f There are 35 Power supporters for every 40 Crows supporters.
   g William weighs 60 kg and Thomas weighs 75 kg.

> **Example 7**
>
> The ratio of sales of lemonade to cola in a supermarket is $2:5$.
> If 60 litres of lemonade are sold, determine how much cola is sold.
>
> With a ratio of $2:5$,
> for every 2 litres of lemonade sold, 5 litres of cola are sold.
>
>   ↓ ×30   ↓ ×30
>
> So for 60 litres of lemonade,   150 litres of cola are sold.

4 **a** The ratio of sales of chocolate biscuits to plain biscuits is $4:7$. Given that 120 packets of chocolate biscuits are sold, how many packets of plain biscuits are sold?

   b A sports store sells 9 pairs of Ekin shoes for every 5 pairs of Amup shoes. If 300 pairs of Amup were sold, how many pairs of Ekin were sold?

   c The ratio of girls to boys passing a maths test was $5:4$. Given that 100 boys passed, how many girls passed?

   d In a school the ratio of students who bring lunch from home to those why buy it at the canteen is $5:2$. If 70 buy their lunch, how many bring it from home?

   e The ratio of the sides of a rectangular field is $7:3$. Given that the shorter side is 75 metres, determine:

      i the length of the longer side   **ii** the perimeter of the field.

D   BEARINGS AND DIRECTIONS

One of the most important applications of angles is in **navigation**. When flying an aeroplane, sailing a ship or hiking across land, you need to know in which direction to travel.

COMPASS POINTS

The method of giving directions which is most familiar to us is based on the four main compass points:

North, South, East and West as shown.

These 4 main points are often called the **cardinal points**.

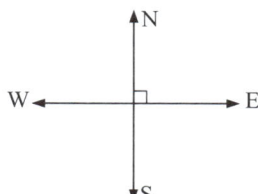

Using these 4 directions which are 90° apart we can divide each 90° into 45° angles to create 'half way' directions, NE, SE, SW and NW.

So, for example, South-West (SW) is half way between South and West.

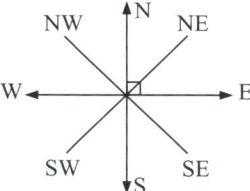

Further subdivisions into directions which are $22\frac{1}{2}^{o}$ apart are possible.

For example, North-North-East is halfway between N and NE and is written NNE.

The subdivisions between the cardinal points are called **intermediate points**. Altogether there are 16 compass points represented by letters.

However, in order to navigate a ship more accurately, there are two main methods used.

These are:

COMPASS BEARINGS

This method uses only **acute angles** (i.e., between 0° and 90°) where angles are measured either clockwise or anticlockwise from either **North** or **South**.

For example, we say that:

the bearing of B from A is N35°E

this means the observer is at A looking towards B

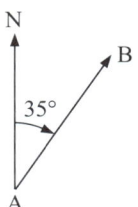

The observer at A, facing North, needs to turn 35° towards the East to face B.

Remember that you must start facing North or South and turn towards the East or West.

Example 8

Find the compass bearing of B from A:

a

b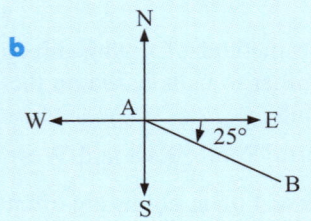

a Bearing of B from A is N60°E.

b $90° - 25° = 65°$
∴ the bearing of B from A is S65°E.

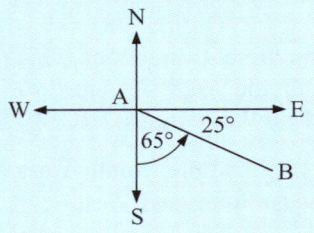

TRUE BEARINGS

This method uses **clockwise** rotations from the **true north** direction and so angles between $0°$ and $360°$ are used.

Examples:

For 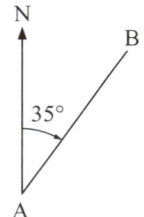 the **true bearing of B from A** is $35°T$ or $035°$.

3 digit representation

For 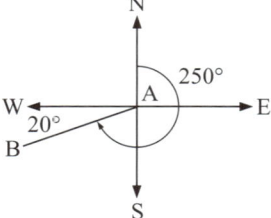 the **true bearing of B from A** is $250°T$ or $250°$.

For 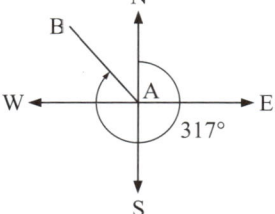 the **true bearing of B from A** is $317°T$ or $317°$.

Example 9

Find the true bearing of B from A for:

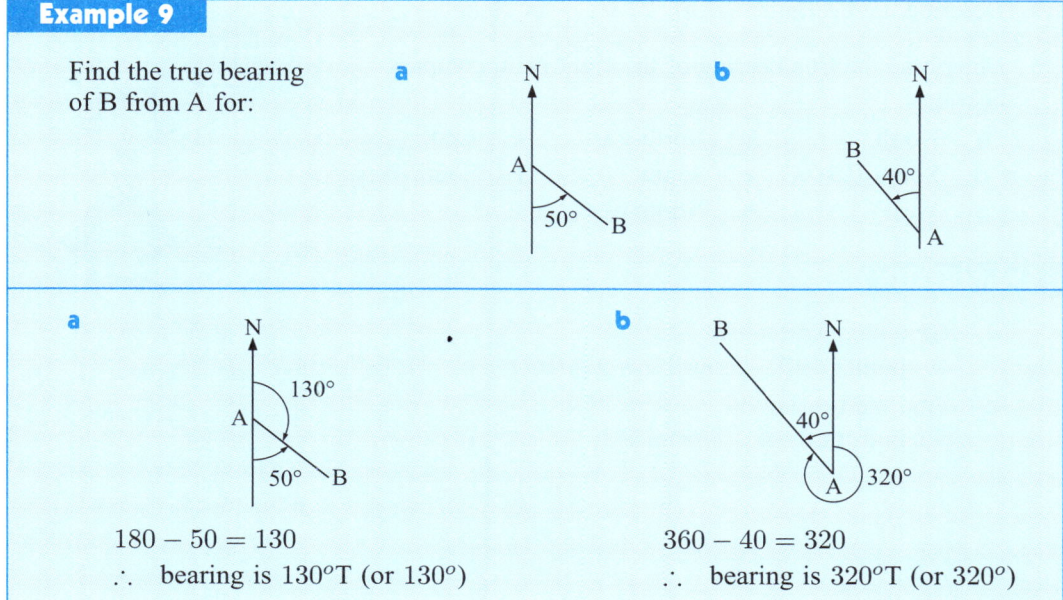

$180 - 50 = 130$
∴ bearing is 130°T (or 130°)

$360 - 40 = 320$
∴ bearing is 320°T (or 320°)

EXERCISE 12D

1 Give the compass bearing of B from A in each of the following:

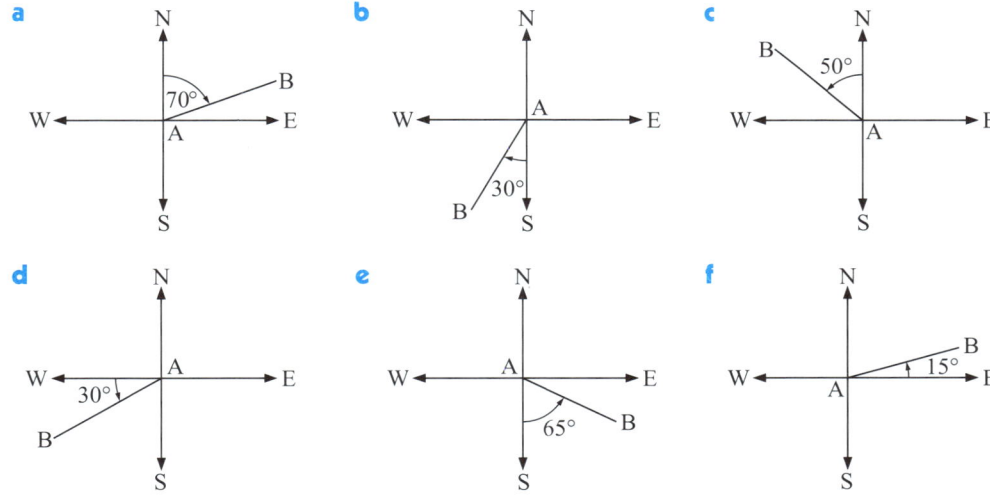

2 Use a protractor to draw fully labelled diagrams to show the compass bearing for:
   a B from A is N40°E   **b** A from B is S50°W   **c** C from D is S45°E
   d P from Q is N65°W   **e** X from Y is S80°E   **f** M from N is N84°E

3 Give true bearings for B from A for each of the diagrams in **1**.

4 Use a protractor to draw fully labelled diagrams showing true bearings of:
   a 070°T   **b** 160°T   **c** 213°   **d** 312°   **e** 096°

(**Note:** The T is not necessary.)

5 Describe the bearings: **a** 270° **b** 000°

A diagram could be useful here.

6 Determine the true bearing of the eight main compass bearings:
- **a** North
- **b** North-East
- **c** East
- **d** South-East
- **e** South
- **f** South-West
- **g** West
- **h** North-West

Example 10

a Give the grid references of:
  i point R   **ii** point S   **iii** point T

b Find the bearing of:
  i R from S   **ii** T from S

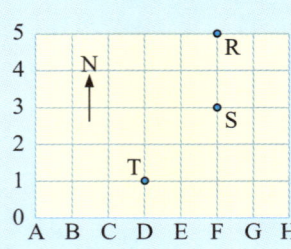

a
  i R has grid reference (F, 5)
  ii S has grid reference (F, 3)
  iii T has grid reference (D, 1)

b
  i R is North of S
  ii T is South-West of S

7

A person who is orienteering must travel from the Start to P, then to Q, then to R and finally to the Finish point.

a The Start is given by the grid reference C7. Find the grid references for:
  i P   **ii** Q   **iii** R   **iv** Finish.

b Use a protractor to find the true bearing of:
  i P from the Start
  ii R from Q
  iii Q from R
  iv the Start from the Finish.

PRINTABLE PAGE

8 P, Q and N are landmarks on the given map and S is a ship at sea. The position of S is given by (7, 10). 7 is the horizontal shift from the origin and 10 is the vertical shift.

a What is at the point given by (3, 1)?

b What is the compass bearing of N from P?

c What is the true compass bearing of:
  i the ship from P
  ii the ship from Q
  iii Q from P?

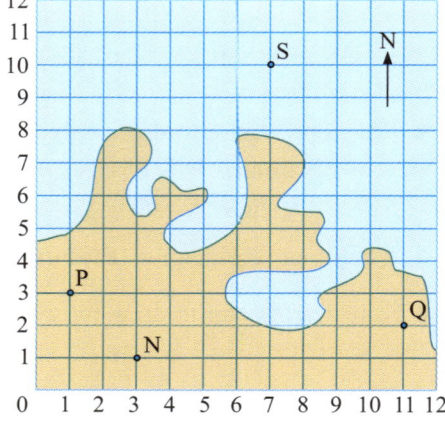

Example 11

Use the given scale diagram to find the distance and true bearing of A from B.

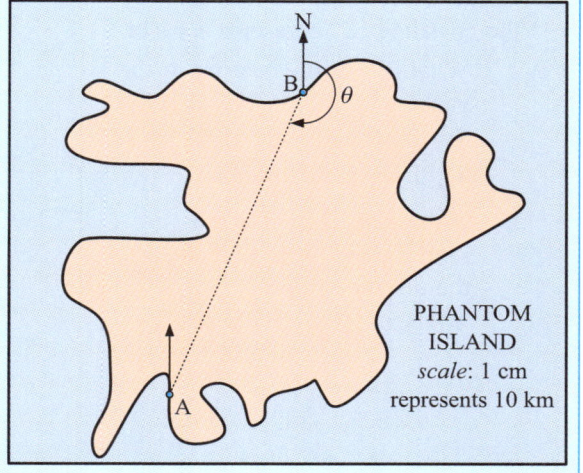

PHANTOM ISLAND
scale: 1 cm represents 10 km

Using a ruler, $AB = 4.5$ cm
$\therefore$ actual AB $= 4.5 \times 10$ km
$= 45$ km

Using a protractor $\theta = 203°$
$\therefore$ A is $203°$T from B

9

scale: 1 cm represents 350 km

a Use the map of Australia to estimate (using the scale) the distances from:
  i Adelaide to Brisbane
  ii Sydney to Perth
  iii Melbourne to Darwin

b From the map find the bearing of:
  i Cairns from Adelaide
  ii Kalgoorlie from Hobart
  iii Canberra from Alice Springs

10 X and Y are radar stations on the coastline. Z represents a yacht.

   a What is the true bearing of the yacht:

   i from radar station X

   ii from radar station Y?

   b If the map scale is 1 cm represents 20 km, find the distance from:

   i X to Z **ii** Y to Z

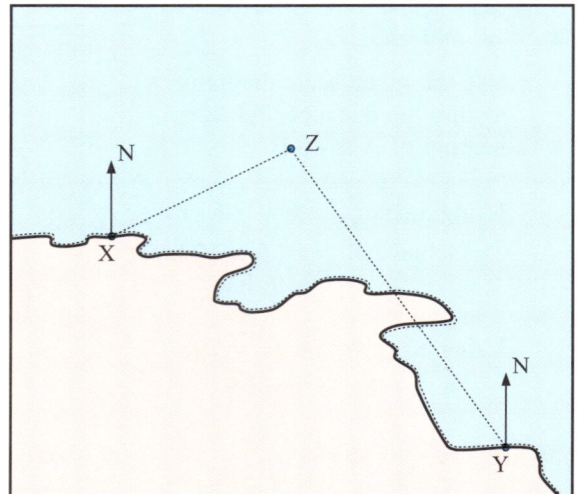

E   ACTIVITIES

ACTIVITY — ORIENTEERING IN THE SCHOOL YARD

You will need: A direction compass, a trundle wheel (or tape measure)

What to do:

1 Find 4 or 5 major objects in the school grounds that are easily accessible and where you have a clear line of sight from one to the next.

2 Draw a rough sketch of the situation showing the objects you have selected. For example, flag pole, goal post, corner of building, etc.

3 From a starting point measure distances and directions from one point to the next on a selected pathway. Record all distances and bearings on your rough sketch.

4 Accurately draw your pathway on clean paper, showing all distances and bearings.

5 Give the detailed map to another student and see if he/she can follow your directions accurately.

ACTIVITY — SCALE DIAGRAMS – DISTANCES IN AUSTRALIA

You will need: some string, a ruler marked in mm, and an atlas or map showing major highways of Australia.

What to do:

1. Use your ruler and the scale given on the map to estimate the "straight line" or "as the crow flies" distance from:
   - **a** Sydney to Townsville
   - **b** Adelaide to Brisbane
   - **c** Mt Isa to Perth
   - **d** Melbourne to Cairns

2. Hold one end of your string on Perth and carefully lay your string along the main highway to Adelaide.

   Mark the string at this point.

   Now pull the string straight and measure with your ruler.

   Use the scale to find the distance by car from Perth to Adelaide.

   Use this method to find the shortest distance by car (along the major highways marked on the map) from:
   - **a** Adelaide to Melbourne
   - **b** Melbourne to Sydney
   - **c** Perth to Darwin

ACTIVITY — STREET DIRECTORY

What to do:

1. In a street directory for your local area, find the page which shows the street where you live.

2. Find the map references for where you live, where friends live, where the shops are, where any other special features are.

3. Write down *two* alternative routes, by road, from your house to another place X several streets away.

4. Find the "as the crow flies" compass bearing from your place to X.

5. Using the scale given, find estimates of the distance from your place to X by both the routes that you chose earlier.

6. Find the shortest route by road between the two places.

REVIEW SET A — CHAPTER 12

1. Write the coordinates or ordered pairs for the following points:
   - **a** A
   - **b** B
   - **c** C
   - **d** D
   - **e** E

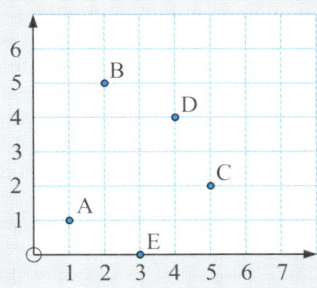

2 Plot the points with coordinates P(4, 0), Q(4, 4) and R(0, 4).
What type of quadrilateral is OPQR?

3 a Draw the mirror image of:

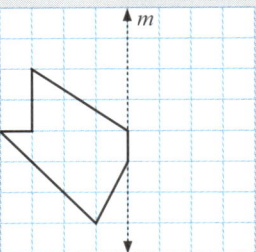

b Draw the axes of symmetry (if they exist) for:

4 a Rotate the given figure through 90° clockwise.

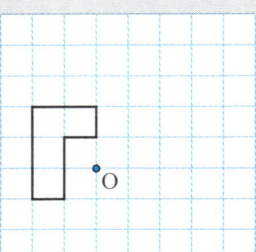

b Translate the given figure one unit to the right and 3 units down.

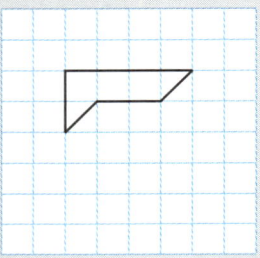

5 In an office, the ratio of staff who supported football to those who supported soccer was 5 : 2. If 21 staff gave their opinions, how many supported soccer?

6 X and Y are radar stations on the coastline. Z represents a yacht.

  a What is the true bearing of the radar station X:
    i from the yacht Z
    ii from radar station Y?

  b If the map scale is 1 cm represents 20 km, find the distance from X to Y.

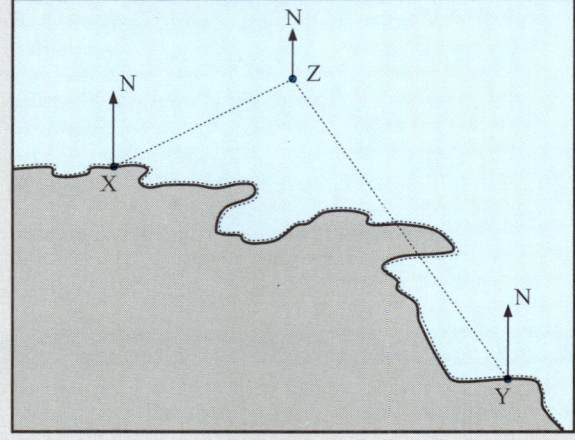

7 For a scale of 1 : 500, find the length drawn on a map if the actual distance is 26.5 m.

8

Using the measurements given on the rough sketch and a scale of 1 cm represents 5 m, draw an accurate scale diagram.

REVIEW SET B CHAPTER 12

1 Plot the points with coordinates A(1, 1), B(2, 4), C(6, 6) and D(5, 3). What type of quadrilateral is ABCD?

2 a Draw the image if a mirror was placed on the mirror line.

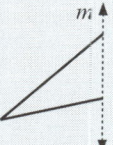

b Draw the axes of symmetry for:

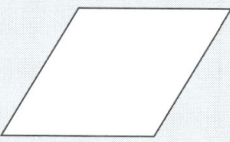

3 a Find the order of rotational symmetry for:

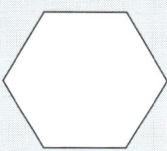

b Rotate the given figure 180° anticlockwise about O.

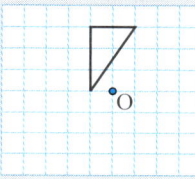

4 a Translate the figure three units left and one unit up.

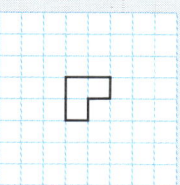

b Enlarge the figure with scale factor 2.

5 At a barbeque, the ratio of chops to sausages eaten was 4 : 7. If 56 sausages were eaten, how many pieces of meat in total were eaten?

6 R and Q are two landmarks on the given map and S is a ship at sea.

a Find the true compass bearing of:
  i the ship from R
  ii the ship from Q
  iii R from Q

b If the scale is 1 cm represents 50 km, find the distance from:
  i R to Q
  ii S to Q

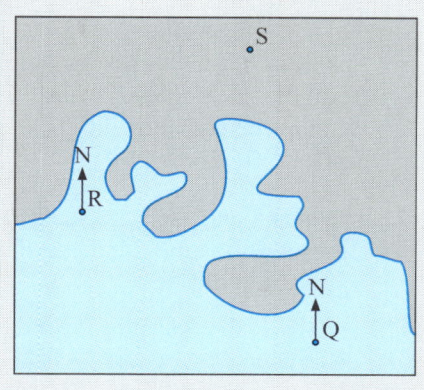

7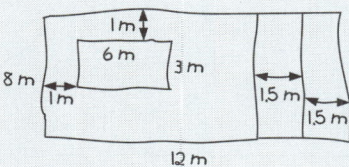

Using the measurements shown on the rough sketch and a scale of 1 cm represents 2 m, draw an accurate scale diagram.

REVIEW SET C   CHAPTER 12

1 Write the coordinates or ordered pairs for the following points:

   a P **b** Q **c** R **d** S **e** T

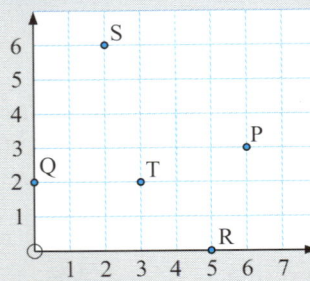

2 Plot 3 vertices A(4, 2), B(7, 2) and C(7, 5) of a rectangle on grid paper and find the coordinates of D, the fourth vertex.

3 Draw the mirror image of:

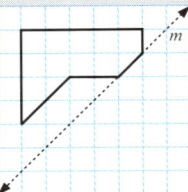

4 **a** Draw the axes of symmetry of:

   b What is the order of rotational symmetry for this shape?

5 **a** Rotate the figure shown through 90° anticlockwise about O.

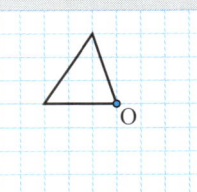

  b Enlarge the figure with scale factor $\frac{1}{3}$.

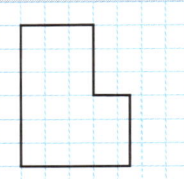

6 The ratio of pies to pasties purchased from the local bakery was 9 : 5. If 63 pies were bought, how many pasties were bought?

7 The map alongside has a scale of 1 cm represents 10 km. Find the distance and bearing of:

  a the Fishing Centre from the Surf Shop

  b the ship from the Hilltop

  c the Lighthouse from the Hilltop.

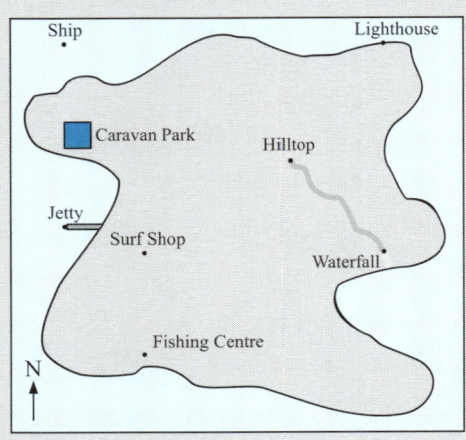

8 If a scale is written as 1 : 5000, explain what 1 cm would represent.

Chapter 13
Chance

Knowledge, skills and understandings

By the end of this chapter you should be able to

- identify risks and consequences of taking chances
- demonstrate an understanding of what constitutes gambling (e.g., lotto, raffles, poker machines)
- identify some of the social consequences of gambling (e.g., implications for families adversely affected by problem gambling)
- assign numbers and percentage to chance (i.e., if it has no chance of occurring it is assigned 0 or 0%; if it is certain to occur it is assigned 1 or 100%)
- make your own probability generator (e.g., a spinner or a die to show Pr(red) = $\frac{2}{5}$)
- assign probabilities for given situations (e.g., 'Five discs are placed in a bag, two are blue and three are black. What is the probability of drawing a blue disc?')
- test predictions (e.g., coin tossing)

INTRODUCTION

Statements like
"It is very likely that snow will fall today"
"I probably won't go to watch the football on Saturday"
"I am almost certain that I saw Lap Mun in the city yesterday"
"It is most unlikely that Jacqui will attend the meeting tonight"

all have a message dealing with the likelihood or chance of a particular event happening or not happening.

Notice that the key words in the above statements are: very likely, probably won't, almost certain, most unlikely.

A DESCRIBING CHANCE

Chance is to do with the likelihood or probability of events occurring (or happening).

Words are used to describe chance, and these include

possible, likely, impossible, unlikely, maybe, certain, uncertain, no chance, little chance, good chance, highly probable, probable, improbable, doubtful, often, rarely.

Example 1

a How likely is it for a man to be playing for an AFL team at the age of 50?

b What is the chance that Lisa, now 12, will have a birthday next year?

a Very few men would play AFL on a regular basis beyond 35, let alone 50. So we would say "highly unlikely".

b We cannot say "certain" as there is a small chance that Lisa may not be alive next year. She could, for example, die in a car accident. So we would say "highly likely" or "almost certain".

EXERCISE 13A

1 Describe by using a word or phrase the chance of the following happening:
   a A person will live to the age of 140 years.
   b There will be a public holiday on the 25th day of December.
   c A gigantic meteorite will strike the earth in your lifetime.
   d You will win a major lottery in your lifetime.
   e Your birthday in three years' time will fall on a weekend day.
   f You will get homework in at least one subject tonight.
   g You will be struck by lightning next January.
   h The sun will rise tomorrow.
   i You could do 1000 laps around the school ground in 24 hours.

2   Below is a number line. Copy it and add the following words to it using arrows where necessary.

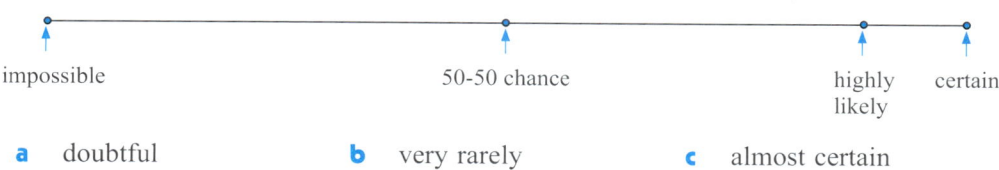

   a   doubtful   b   very rarely   c   almost certain
   d   a little more than even chance

> **Example 2**
>
> A bag contains 200 discs, of which 199 are red and one is blue. If a disc is randomly chosen from the bag, what are the chances that it is blue?
>
> This is a very unlikely event as only 1 in 200 are blue.

3   A bag contains 50 marbles, of which 49 are black and one is white. A marble is randomly chosen from the bag.
   a   How likely is the marble to be black?
   b   Is it certain that the marble is going to be black?
   c   True or false? "There is a 1 in 50 chance it will be white."

4   A tin contains 10 red and 11 green discs and one disc is randomly selected from the tin.
   a   Is it more likely that the disc is red than it is green? Explain.
   b   What colour is more likely to be selected?
   c   True or false? "There is a 10 in 21 chance that the disc is green."

5   Describe the following events as either *certain*, *possible* or *impossible*:
   a   When tossing a coin, a tail faces upwards.
   b   When tossing a coin, it falls on its edge.
   c   When tossing a coin ten times, it falls heads every time.
   d   When rolling a die, a 3 results.
   e   When rolling a die, a 7 results.
   f   When rolling a pair of dice a sum of 1 results.
   g   When twirling a square spinner a 4 results.
        i   ii

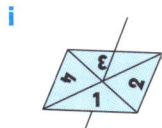 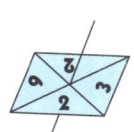 

THE CONSEQUENCES (RISKS) OF CHANCE

Chance is the likelihood or probability of events happening.

Chance can also mean **risk**. With every risk there is a **consequence**.

If you take a chance at breaking a rule you risk facing the consequence.

For example, a student breaks a school rule by running around the corner of a school building.

The risks range from nothing happening, to getting caught and being disciplined, to colliding with another person and causing serious or even fatal injury.

The risk or consequence when playing a computer or board game is usually minor. Possibly the worst consequence will be that you lose the game.

The risks and consequences of any chance event depend on the situation.

In groups, discuss the following:

1 What are the risks and possible consequences of taking a chance at:
   a being out in the sun without proper protection
   b speeding in a car
   c playing the pokies
   d not doing your homework
   e "putting all your eggs in one basket"?

2 What are the possible consequences of:
   a rolling a 'double' in a board game where two dice are used
   b planting grain which has an 81% probability of germinating
   c continuing with a manned space flight which has a slight risk of failing
   d lending money to someone you have only recently met
   e giving a cancer patient a new drug which is 100% successful on mice before it has been developed for humans?

CHANCE IS A RISKY BUSINESS

Gambling is one industry or occupation which obviously has risks and consequences. However, there are others. Banking, insurance, stockmarket, sport and farming are just some of the many industries where risks are taken. How successful these industries and occupations become often depends on how well they have prepared for all probabilities.

People in these industries use mathematics to work out the possibility of particular outcomes and the costs or risks of any consequences.

CHANCE (CHAPTER 13)

DISCUSSION — TO GAMBLE OR NOT TO GAMBLE

Discuss some of these ideas to do with gambling.

1. If you play enough games you must have a 'big' win.
2. If you have a win on a poker machine then that machine will not have another win for a long time, so you swap to another machine.
3. You only gamble if you have better than average chance of winning.
4. You should have control of the result that you are gambling on.
5. If you have a win you should continue to play to win more.
6. It is all a matter of luck.
7. It is better to gamble on poker machines than horses.
8. In the long term you will lose more money than you win.
10. The organisation controlling the gambling must make a profit, so winnings must be less than the amount people pay to play gambling games.
11. Money from gambling goes to the government to support charities, so you should gamble.
12. If you are betting on, for example, coin tossing, always wait for three heads in a row before betting on tails because you have a greater chance of winning 'by the law of averages'.
13. Buying raffle tickets is not really gambling.
14. If you have a big loss you will make up the money with a big win another day.

From the discussion you should understand that gambling is taking a risk with your money and you cannot control the outcome.

B ASSIGNING NUMBERS TO CHANCE

There are two extreme possibilities.

> If an event **cannot occur**, i.e., it has no chance of occurring, we give it the number 0.
> If an event is **certain to occur** we give it the number 1.

Because of this, we give numbers between 0 and 1 (inclusive) to any event.

Events which may or may not happen with equal chance are given the probability number 0.5 or $\frac{1}{2}$. This is because they happen, on average, once every two times.

> **Example 3**
>
> Give the probabilities 0, 0.5 or 1 to best describe:
> **a** the chance of a new born baby being a girl
> **b** the chance of it snowing in January in Darwin next year
> **c** the chance that the Sun emits light tomorrow.
>
> **a** Girls and boys occur equally often (roughly so anyway).
>   ∴ the chance of a girl is 0.5.
>
> **b** It does not snow in January in Darwin.
>   ∴ the chance of snow is 0.
>
> **c** The Sun will emit light tomorrow.
>   ∴ the chance of light from the Sun is 1.

EXERCISE 13B

1 A container has 5 green and 5 blue balls and one ball is randomly selected from it.
   a What is the probability of selecting a green ball?
   b If all blue balls are now removed, what is the probability of selecting:
      i a green ball   **ii** a blue ball?

2 Here is a probability number line:

Draw your own probability line and mark on it the approximate probabilities of:
   a the Sun rising tomorrow   **b** a holiday on January 1st
   c winning Lotto   **d** being born on a Monday
   e rain falling tomorrow   **f** being born on any week day.

> **Example 4**
>
> Which of the following outcomes are equally likely to occur?
> **a** Getting a head or a tail with a single toss of a coin.
> **b** Winning a 100 m sprint contested by 8 athletes.
>
> **a** Because of the symmetry of a coin, a head or a tail is equally likely to occur.
>
> **b** The athletes are certain to have different running abilities.
>   Each one does not have the same chance of winning.
>   ∴ the possible outcomes are not equally likely.

3 a Is it equally likely that:
   i any team in a 10-team netball competition can win the competition
   ii any of the results 1, 2, 3, 4, 5 or a 6 could occur when a die is rolled
   iii two people selecting a card from two separate full decks get the Queen of Hearts
   iv either of two people in a raffle with 100 tickets could win it?

CHANCE (CHAPTER 13)   395

b Discuss the difference between events in which outcomes are equally likely and those events in which outcomes are not equally likely. Did you notice that you began your answer to this question with "It depends ...."?

C DEFINING PROBABILITY

Probability can be worked out by counting the total number of outcomes and the number of outcomes you want.

Example 5

Two blue and three white discs are placed in a bag and one disc is randomly selected from it. What is the probability of selecting:
a a blue disc   **b** a white disc?

For a truly random selection, each disc has the same chance of being selected.

There are 5 discs which could be selected with equal chance.
a Since two are blue there is a 2 in 5 chance of selecting a blue, ∴ the probability of a blue is $\frac{2}{5}$.

b Since three are white there is a 3 in 5 chance of selecting a white, ∴ the probability of a white is $\frac{3}{5}$.

EXERCISE 13C

1 Blue and white discs are placed in a bag and one disc is randomly selected from it. For the following bags of discs given, answer the following questions:
  i How many of each disc are there in the bag?
  ii What is the probability of selecting a blue disc?
  iii What is the probability of selecting a white disc?

a 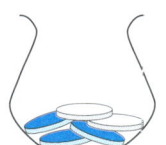   **b** 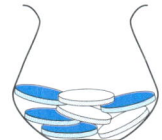   **c**

We can now make the following statement:

If outcomes are equally likely to occur,

$$\Pr[\text{an event}] = \frac{\text{number of outcomes in that event}}{\text{total number of possible outcomes}}$$

An outcome is a result or happening.

Note: Pr[............]   is read   "the probability of .... occurring".

For example,
- when flipping a coin,
  Pr[a H]   is read   *the probability of a 'head' occurring.*

- when rolling a die,
  Pr[a 6]   is read   *the probability of a 6 occurring.*

- when rolling a pair of dice,
  Pr[a sum of 7]   is read   *the probability of a sum of 7 occurring.*

Example 6

A die has 4 faces painted blue and 2 faces painted grey. When the die is rolled, what is the chance of getting the uppermost face:
a   a blue   b   a grey?

4 faces are blue, 2 faces are grey, 6 faces in all.

a $\therefore$ Pr[a blue] $= \frac{4}{6}$ ← total blue faces
                                              ← total outcomes possible

b   Pr[a grey] $= \frac{2}{6}$

2 Find the probability that the spinning needle will finish on blue in:

a 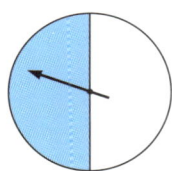   b 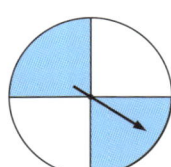   c 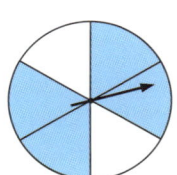   d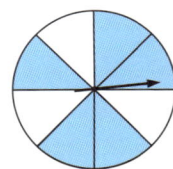

3 A 10-cent coin is tossed. Find the probability that it will finish with the uppermost face:
   a   a head (queen)   b   a tail (other side).

DEMO

4 The given spinner has sector angles of $120°$, $90°$, $50°$, $60°$ and $40°$.

   a   After a spin, are the outcomes equally likely?
   b   What outcome do you expect to occur:
      i   most often   ii   least often?
   c   What is the probability of getting a dark blue?
   d   If you spin the spinner 40 times, how often would you expect it to finish on the dark blue?

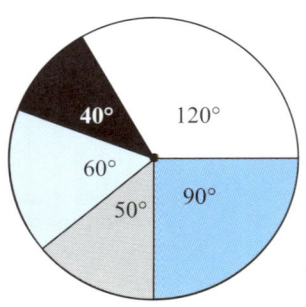

Example 7

A die is rolled. What is the probability of getting:
a a 3   b a 3 or a 4?

The equally likely outcomes are:

a The 3 is one of the 6 possibilities ∴ Pr[3] = $\frac{1}{6}$

b 'a 3 or a 4' are two of the 6 possibilities
    ∴ Pr[a 3 or a 4] = $\frac{2}{6} = \frac{1}{3}$

---

5 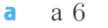 A square spinner has A, B, C or D on its equal sides. After one spin, what is the probability of getting:
  a a B   b a B or a C   c an E
  d an A, B, C or D?

6 Consider the illustrated spinner (a regular octagon).

If the spinner is spun once, find the probability of getting:
  a a 6   b a 3 or a 4   c a 1, 2 or 3
  d a result less than 6   e a result more than 8?

Example 8

 A hat contains three blue, three white and one grey ticket. One ticket is selected at random from the hat. Find the chance of getting:
a a blue ticket   b a grey ticket   c a grey or a white ticket.

There are $3 + 3 + 1 = 7$ tickets, all equally likely to be selected.

a Pr[a blue] = $\frac{3}{7}$ {three blues out of 7 possible}

b Pr[a grey] = $\frac{1}{7}$ {one grey out of 7 possible}

c Pr[grey or white] = $\frac{4}{7}$ {4 are either grey or white}

---

7 A hat contains 4 red, 3 white and 2 grey discs and one disc is randomly selected from it. Find the likelihood that it is:
  a red   b white   c grey
  d green   e not red   f not white
  g not grey   h not red or grey   i red, white or grey

8 This illustration shows a full pack of playing cards. For this exercise, the pack is well shuffled and placed face down. For our pack of cards hearts and diamonds are blue. Spades and clubs are black. Jacks, Queens and Kings are called picture cards.

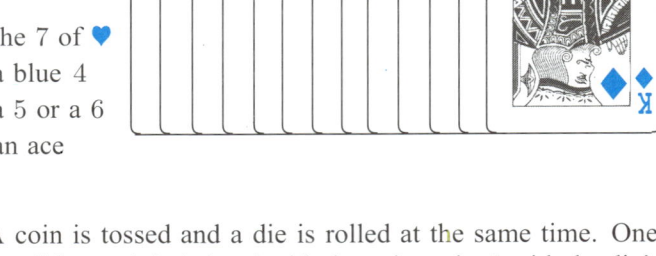

Jason picks one card at random from the shuffled pack.

Find the chance of getting:

- **a** a heart ♥
- **b** the 7 of ♥
- **c** a club ♣
- **d** a blue 4
- **e** a black ace
- **f** a 5 or a 6
- **g** a green card
- **h** an ace
- **i** a picture card

9   A coin is tossed and a die is rolled at the same time. One possible result is 'a head with the coin and a 5 with the die', and this result could be represented by H5.

- **a** Using this shorthand notation, list the possible results from this experiment.
- **b** How many different results are possible from one performance of this experiment?
- **c** Find the probability of getting:
  - **i** H6
  - **ii** a tail and an even number
  - **iii** a head and a prime number
  - **iv** T5 or T6

10 The two illustrated spinners are twirled together. One possible result is **A3**, 'an **A** with the first spinner and a **3** with the second'. This result is shown.

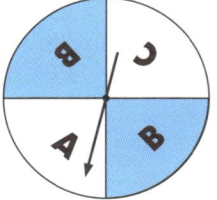 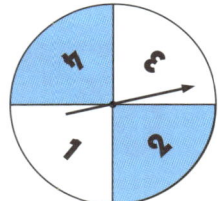

- **a** Using this shorthand notation, list the possible results from this experiment.
- **b** Find the probability of getting:
  - **i** a **C** and a **4**
  - **ii** a **B** and a **2** or **3**
  - **iii** a **B**
  - **iv** an **A** or **B** and a **1**

Probability can also be worked out from experimenting. Do the following activity to see how this works.

ACTIVITY

In a bag place ten counters (three red, five blue and two green). If you do not have these colours use your own colours.

Without looking, take out one counter and record its colour. Then put the counter back in the bag. Repeat this 100 times.

Count the total number of each colour counter that you have taken out of the bag.

Now find the probability of each counter being selected in your experiment by completing the following (example for red counter):

$$\text{Probability of red counter} = \frac{\text{number of red counters selected}}{\text{total number of counters selected}} = \frac{\text{number of reds}}{100}$$

Repeat the experiment and calculate the probability for each colour counter again.

Now find the probability of each colour counter being selected without doing the experiment. Were your experimental results the same as your expected results? Explain any differences.

D   TREE DIAGRAMS

Tree diagrams are a good method of systematically finding all the possible outcomes of an experiment.

Example 9

Draw a tree diagram to show all possible outcomes when a coin is tossed two times.

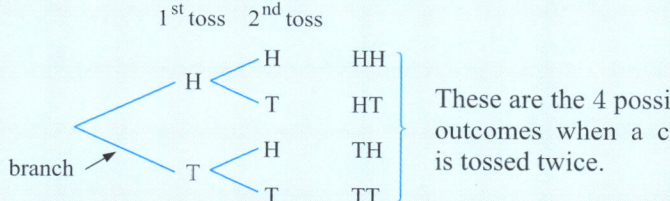

These are the 4 possible outcomes when a coin is tossed twice.

You read this tree diagram as follows. Start at the left. The number of 'branches' equals the number of outcomes possible. In this case there are only two (heads or tails). If you get a head on the first toss you have a further two possibilities on the second toss - therefore there are two 'branches' after the first H. The same is true if you get a tail on the first toss.

EXERCISE 13D

1 Draw a tree diagram to show each of the following situations and list all possible outcomes.

   a A coin is tossed and a die is rolled at the same time.

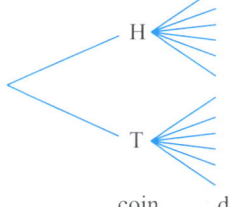

   b Three coins are tossed at the same time.

   c A bag contains some red, blue and green counters. One counter is selected, replaced and another counter is selected.

d 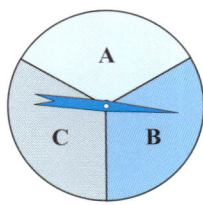 The given disc is spun two times with the letter recorded each time.

Now we can use the tree diagrams to work out the probability of an outcome happening.

Example 10

Consider the coin tossed twice. From the tree diagram alongside, find the probability of getting:
a   two heads
b   a head and a tail
c   at least one head

	1st toss	2nd toss	outcome
	H	H	HH
		T	HT
	T	H	TH
		T	TT

There are 4 equally likely outcomes.
a   The probability of getting two heads is 1 out of 4   i.e.,   one outcome has two heads and there are four possible outcomes.
b   The probability of getting a head and a tail is two out of four as two outcomes have a head and a tail in them.
c   The probability of getting at least one head is three out of four.

2   Draw a tree diagram for each of the following. Use the tree diagram to work out the probabilities. (You may use your diagram from question **1**.)

a   This spinner is twirled twice. Find the probability that:
  i   you get an **A** followed by a **B**
  ii   you get a **C** followed by a **C**
  iii   you have at least one **C** in your outcomes
  iv   you have a **B** and a **C**

b   A family has three children in it (assume a boy and a girl are equally likely to happen). Find the probability the family has:
  i   three boys   ii   two girls   iii   at least 1 girl
  iv   no boys   v   no more than 2 girls

c   A bag contains the same number of red, blue, pink and green counters. One counter is selected, replaced and another counter selected. Find the probability that:
  i   two green counters are selected
  ii   one red counter is selected
  iii   at least 1 blue counter is selected
  iv   no pink counters are selected
  v   a red and a pink counter are selected

E. MAKING YOUR OWN PROBABILITY GENERATORS

Suppose you wish to make a device which generates probabilities of $\frac{2}{3}$ and $\frac{1}{3}$, that is, one outcome has a $\frac{2}{3}$ chance of occurring and the alternative outcome has $\frac{1}{3}$ chance of occurring.

For example, Pr[blue] $= \frac{2}{3}$ and Pr[grey] $= \frac{1}{3}$.

We could use a **spinner** or a **die**.

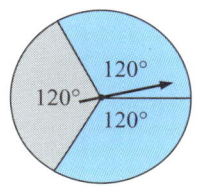

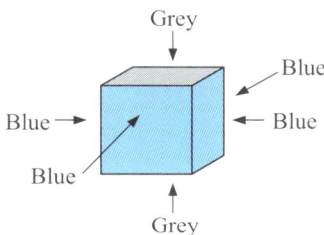

$120°$ is $\frac{1}{3}$ of $360°$

$240°$ is $\frac{2}{3}$ of $360°$

4 faces are blue and
2 faces are grey

EXERCISE 13E

1 Design *two* devices which generate Pr[A] $= \frac{1}{2}$ and Pr[B] $= \frac{1}{2}$.

2 Design a device which generates Pr[red] $= \frac{2}{5}$ and Pr[blue] $= \frac{3}{5}$.
   (**Hint:** $\frac{1}{5}$ of $360° = 72°$.)

3 Design *two* devices which generate Pr[A] $= \frac{1}{6}$, Pr[B] $= \frac{2}{6}$ and Pr[C] $= \frac{3}{6}$.

4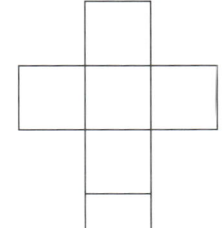

   a What can this net be used to make?
   b What would you do to the squares to make a device which generates Pr[A] $= \frac{1}{6}$, Pr[B] $= \frac{2}{6}$ and Pr[C] $= \frac{1}{2}$?

5 Suppose you want to develop a way of generating probabilities in the ratio $1:2:4$ and do not wish to make a spinner.
   a What simple way could you do this?
   b If the outcomes that are required are X, Y and Z in the ratio $1:2:4$, what are:
      i Pr[X]   **ii** Pr[Y]   **iii** Pr[Z]?

F EXPECTATION

When a single coin is tossed 10 times, will you always get 5 heads and 5 tails resulting?

INVESTIGATION   COIN TOSSING EXPERIMENTS

When a single coin is tossed our theoretical probabilities for the chances of getting a head or a tail are based on the symmetry of the coin. We have observed that $\Pr[H] = \Pr[T] = \frac{1}{2}$.

But does this mean that when we toss a coin a large number of times we will get 50% of heads and 50% of tails?

TOSSING ONE COIN

What to do:

1. Toss a coin 20 times and record the number of heads (H) and tails (T) resulting.

2. Repeat this a second time and a third time.

	Expect to get		Actual result	
Experiment	H	T	H	T
First 20 tosses				
Second 20 tosses				
Third 20 tosses				

3. Did you always get 10 heads and 10 tails?

4. How many heads did you expect to get for the 60 tosses?
   How many heads did you actually get for the 60 tosses?

5. How accurate were your expectations against the actual result?

6. Rather than toss coins you could use the computer simulation. Click on the icon to bring up a one coin toss simulation. Use the software to simulate tossing a coin
   - 1000 times and repeat 4 times.
   - 10 000 times and repeat 4 times.

   Record all the results in a table.

TOSSING ONE COIN

7. Write a sentence or two about your discoveries.

TOSSING TWO COINS

What to do:

1. From **Example 10** where we tossed two coins, what are Pr [two heads], Pr [a head and a tail], Pr [two tails]?

2. Click on the icon for simulating tossing two coins. Use the software to toss two coins:
   - 100 times and repeat 4 times
   - 1000 times and repeat 4 times
   - 10 000 times and repeat 4 times.

   Record all results in a table.

TOSSING TWO COINS

3. Write a sentence or two about your discoveries.

From the previous **Investigation** you should have discovered that you do not always get equal numbers of heads and tails. However, after tossing the coin a large number of times we expect about 50% of each.

> The **expectation** of an event occurring is found by multiplying the probability of the event occurring by the number of observations.

For example, if we toss a coin 100 times, we expect $\frac{1}{2} \times 100 = 50$ heads as $\Pr[H] = \frac{1}{2}$.

Example 11

a If a die is rolled 120 times, how many 5s would you expect?
b In July, the probability of rain on any particular day is 0.68
   On how many days would you expect rain?

a When rolling a die, $\Pr[a\ 5] = \frac{1}{6}$.
   $\therefore$ in 120 rolls we expect $\frac{1}{6} \times 120 = 20$ of them to be 5s.

b July has 31 days. $\therefore$ we expect $0.68 \times 31 \doteqdot 21$ rainy days.

EXERCISE 13F

1 A coin is tossed 50 times.
   a How many heads do you expect to get?
   b If 31 are heads and 19 are tails, which of the following is the most likely explanation?
      A the coin is biased
      B the result is due to chance
      C your counting is not accurate
      D the person doing the coin tossing tricked you

2 A die has 3 green, 2 red and 1 blue faces. If the die is rolled 30 times, what is your expectation for a:
   a green result   b red result   c blue result?

3 The chance of hail on any one day is 1.5%. On how many days in a year would you expect hail to fall?

4 The chance of rain falling on a September day in Melbourne is 0.28. On how many September days do you expect rain in Melbourne?

5 Only 83% of wheat grains germinate, and Rohan planted 250 grains.
   a What is $\Pr[\text{a wheat grain germinates}]$?
   b How many wheat grains should Rohan expect to germinate?

6  The given spinner is spun 400 times.
   a Determine:
      i $\Pr[1]$ ii $\Pr[2]$ iii $\Pr[3]$ iv $\Pr[4]$
   b How many of each result do you expect?

ACTIVITY

PROBABILITY OF RAINFALL

The Bureau of Meterology has been collecting information about the weather for almost 100 years. It gathers and analyses data on a daily, even hourly, basis.

From this huge collection of data it is able to draw probability charts, tables and graphs.

Frequency charts, tables and graphs help the Bureau to make fairly accurate predictions about the chance of a particular event with the weather.

	FEBRUARY				JULY		
Day	% freq of rain	% freq of rain ≥ 2 mm	% freq of rain ≥ 10 mm	Day	% freq of rain	% freq of rain ≥ 2 mm	% freq of rain ≥ 10 mm
1	13	6	3	1	51	28	1
2	13	3	1	2	51	29	6
3	6	3	1	3	54	30	9
4	9	3	1	4	51	30	6
5	9	5	2	5	54	36	8
6	9	5	1	6	59	35	8
7	13	5	2	7	57	34	6
8	20	7	2	8	52	28	6
9	15	7	2	9	54	34	4
10	11	3	1	10	54	30	4
11	10	3	1	11	51	29	6
12	10	5	1	12	53	33	8
13	18	6	0	13	54	23	4
14	16	8	3	14	55	35	6
15	17	8	3	15	58	34	6
16	14	6	1	16	53	33	8
17	17	10	3	17	57	31	4
18	15	7	3	18	49	27	6
19	18	8	2	19	47	27	6
20	17	7	5	20	57	33	4
21	15	5	1	21	51	32	6
22	13	6	2	22	56	30	4
23	17	10	2	23	50	27	6
24	17	8	1	24	54	30	6
25	11	5	1	25	46	23	1
26	9	5	1	26	51	27	4
27	12	6	1	27	52	32	8
28	15	8	3	28	54	25	6
29	21	9	0	29	53	30	5
				30	51	24	4
				31	58	35	4

(Information courtesy Bureau of Meterology)

What to do:

1. From these tables answer the following:
   a. In which month is the chance of more than 10 mm of rain greatest?
   b. On which day and month is the chance of any rain most likely?
   c. On which day and month is the chance of any rain least likely?
   d. Which day in July is most likely to have more than 10 mm of rain?
   e. On February 29th:
      i. what is the frequency of more than 10 mm of rain falling?
      ii. Give two reasons for your answer.

2. You will need to refer to the rainfall chart to answer the following questions.

   A concert organiser staged an outdoor event in February. It cost him $87 470 to hire the acts, the ground, stage, seating and lighting. He spent a further $11 310 on advertising. He charged $10 per person admission.

   The organiser has taken some risks. Here are some possible consequences.

   a. i. 23 500 people attended and he made ..... profit.
      ii. 8750 people attended and he made ..... loss.
      iii. It rained. The concert was cancelled and he made a total loss of .....

   b. The organiser insured against more than 2 mm of rain falling in the 3 hours before the concert. For a $10 000 charge he would get $55 000 if more than 2 mm of rain fell. Find the consequences as a profit or loss if the following happened:
      i. 18 300 people attended and it did not rain.
      ii. 1.9 mm of rain fell $3\frac{1}{2}$ hours before the concert and only 3850 people attended.
      iii. 12 450 people attended even though a sudden storm dropped 10 mm of rain 2 hours before the concert started.

   c. Given that weekends are the best days for concerts and that February 1st was a Tuesday, use the chart to find the best day with the least likelihood of more than 10 mm of rain falling.

GROUP ACTIVITY

In groups discuss

- the importance of knowing the probability of rain falling on a given day
- which groups of people would benefit most from knowing about the likelihood of rain
- what major family events could be influenced by information about the chance of it raining.

G GAMBLING SYSTEMS

Mathematicians keep telling us that *there is no such thing as an effective gambling system*, and yet every year gambling systems are advertised in newspapers and magazines.

Do they work?

Can a person successfully use a gambling system to make money over a period of time?

Following is a gambling game and a system to win money.

THE GAME OF HEADS AND TAILS

A coin is tossed. You can play the game for a $1 entry fee. If you bet on a 'head' and it comes up, you win and get your $1 back plus an extra 90 cents. If a 'tail' results you lose your $1.

> *Jack's foolproof gambling system*
>
> Wait until 3 tails come up in a row and then place your bet for a 'head' on the next throw as 4 tails in a row is very unlikely.

To examine this system we investigate results of many coin tosses.

INVESTIGATION — THE GAME OF HEADS AND TAILS

Consider the following results of tossing a coin

H T T H H H T H T T T H T T T H T T T H H T H T .....

We look for 3 consecutive tails and the result following them.

So far the result is

Fourth Toss	
H	T
2	0

What to do:

1 Use a coin tossing simulation with at least 1000 results printed out to test whether Jack's Foolproof Gambling System is valid or not.

2 Also test Jack's modified system which tells you to bet on a head after 4 tails have come up in a row.

3 Do you think that this is a successful gambling system? If so, why? If not, why not?

| INVESTIGATION | THE 'DOUBLING-UP' GAMBLING SYSTEM |

 Gamblers have used many different *gambling systems* that they have created, hoping that the system will make them certain winners. One such system for betting on coin tossing is given below.

Suppose that getting a head constitutes a win and getting a tail is a loss, and you are betting an amount of $1 per game. The system is:

- When you win a toss, bet $1 on the next game.
- When you lose a toss, double your bet in the next game.

This system has been named the *doubling-up system* by some people; others know it as *the gambler's ruin*.

The strategy is clearly seen in the given *flow chart*.

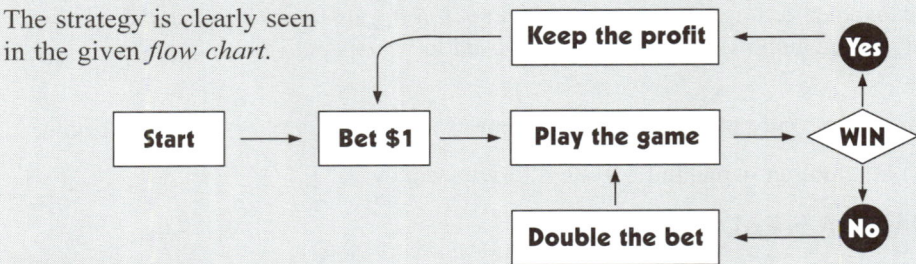

What to do:

1. Perform this game using the 'doubling-up' system and record your results over 100 games.

   Note: You have a maximum of $25 to play with.

   Here is a possible start to the game:

Game	Bet	Result	Win/Lose	Amount in pocket
1	$1	H	$1	$26 (you started with $25)
2	$1	H	$1	$27
3	$1	T	−$1	$26
4	$2	H	+$2	$28
5	$1	T	−$1	$27
6	$2	T	−$2	$25
7	$4	H	+$4	$29
8	$1	T	−$1	$28
9	$2	T	−$2	$26
10	$4	T	−$4	$22
11	$8	H	+$8	$30

   Notice a slow gain of $1 over time.

2. Can the method fail? What, if any, are the problems with the system?
3. Now click on the icon and play the game many times. Record your observations.
4. Do you think it is possible to construct a fail-proof gambling system?

SOMETHING TO THINK ABOUT

- It costs hundreds of millions of dollars to build and run casinos. Where do you think the money comes from?
- For every winning $1 ticket in a million dollar lottery, there will be more than one million losing tickets.
- If poker machines allowed every player to win, where would the prize money come from?

REVIEW SET A — CHAPTER 13

1 Use the words no chance, little chance, some chance, good chance or certain to describe the likelihood of the following events occurring:
   a A manned space ship from Earth will land on another planet before 2010.
   b A $5 coin will replace the $5 note.
   c Your Mathematics teacher will not set any homework this week.
   d A blue moon will occur twice this year.

2 a The chance of rain falling on a January day in Darwin is 0.77. On how many days would you expect rain during January?
   b In a scientific trial of 500 people with coughs, 79% of the people who took a cough mixture found that their cough cleared.
   i What was Pr[cough clears]?
   ii How many people found their cough cleared?

3 The given spinner is spun 40 times.
   a Determine
   i Pr[blue]   **ii** Pr[odd number]
   iii Pr[even blue number]   **iv** Pr[even black number]
   v Pr[odd black number]
   b How many of each result do you expect?

4 In each of the following examples there are two possible outcomes.
   For each example write the   **i** ratio of one result to the other
   ii possible result of the 11th outcome.

   a (Heads or Tails) - HTHTHHHHHH
   b (Odds or Evens) - OEEOOOEEOE
   c (Red or Black) - RRRBRRBBBR

5 a List these spinners in the order from where **A** is most likely to occur to **A** being least likely to occur.

P

Q

R

S

   b In the spinners above, what is the probability of **C** occurring in example:
   i P   **ii** Q   **iii** R   **iv** S?

REVIEW SET B   CHAPTER 13

1. Assign the probabilities 0, 0.5 or 1 to best describe the chance that:
   a school will be cancelled for the rest of the term
   b the next person entering your classroom will be a male
   c you will have a drink today
   d tomorrow's date is an odd number.

2. There are 8 blue, 5 red and 3 green discs in a bag. One disc is taken at random from the bag.
   a How many different outcomes are possible?
   b What is the probability that a blue disc is taken?
   c What is the probability that a red disc is taken?
   d What is the probability that a non-blue disc is taken?

3. Complete the following for the spinners shown:
   a Spinner A, Pr[dark blue] = ...   Spinner B, Pr[light blue] = ...
     Spinner C, Pr[black] = ...
   b From 60 spins, with which spinner would you expect to get:
     i 30 whites   ii 20 whites   iii 15 whites?
   c From 120 spins, with which spinner are you most likely to get:
     i 20 whites   ii 50 dark blues
     iii 30 dark blues, 30 whites, 30 light blues and 30 greys?
   d Use the words *likely*, *highly likely*, *unlikely* or *impossible* to describe the probability of spinning:
     (Assume likely means somewhere between $\frac{1}{3}$ and $\frac{2}{3}$.)
     i dark blue with spinners C, D or E
     ii grey with spinners B, C or D
     iii black with spinners C, D or E

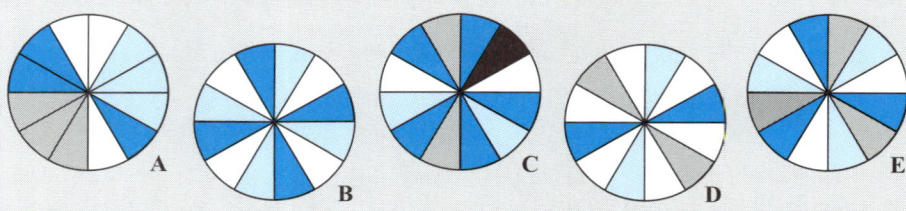

4. a A gambler bets $1 and loses then 'doubles up' to bet $2 and loses then 'doubles up' to bet $4 and loses again etc. Which of the following amounts represent his total loss if he has 6 losses in a row?
     i $6   ii $32   iii $33   iv $63   v $64
   b What would be the gambler's total loss if he doubled up:
     i one more time and lost   ii two more times and lost?

5. When rolling two six-sided dice, rank in order from the highest probability to the lowest probability the following totals which could occur: 3, 5, 7, 8, 12

Answers

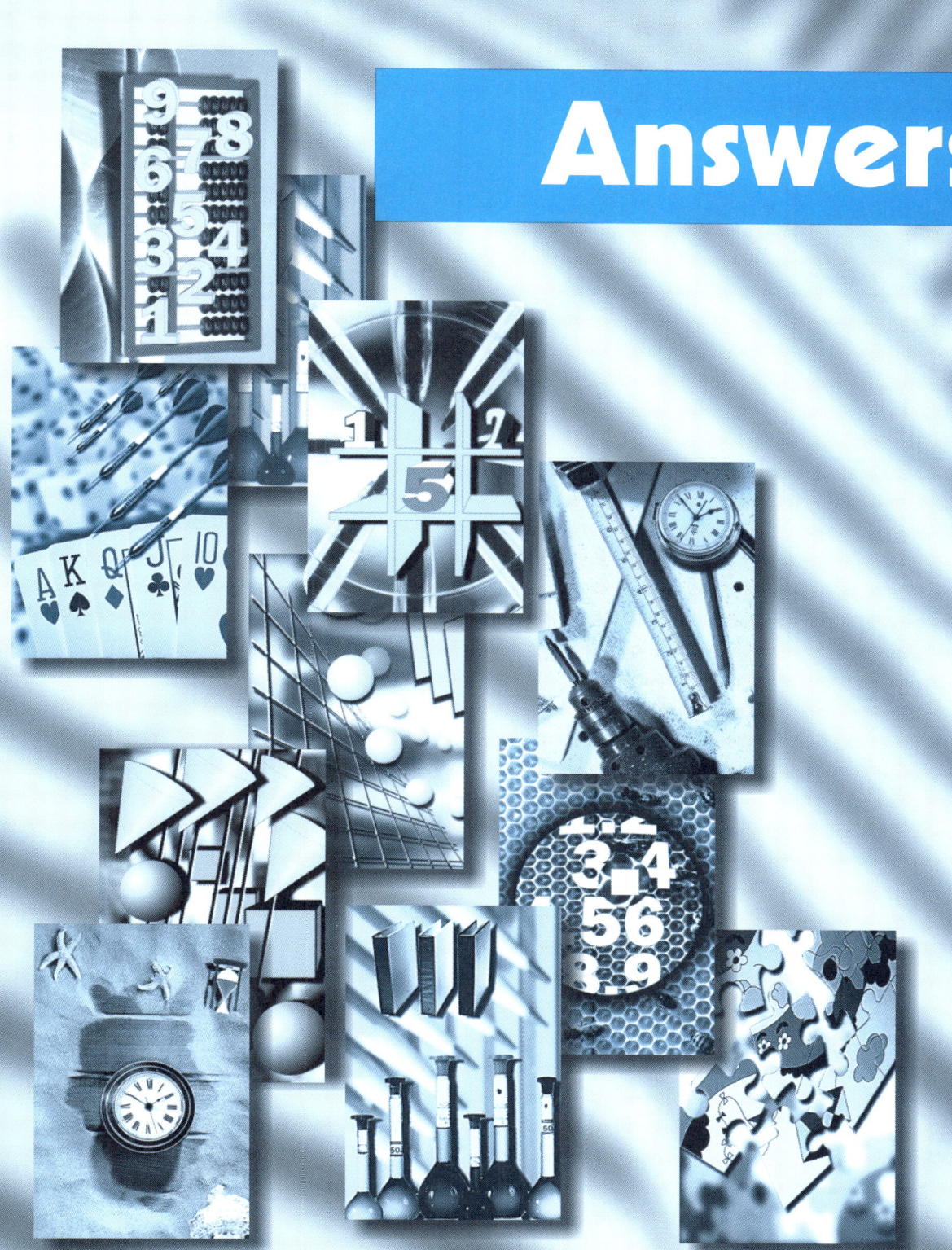

ANSWERS

EXERCISE 1A.1
1. **a** 27 **b** (hieroglyphic numerals)
2. **a** 31 427 **b** 21 123 423

EXERCISE 1A.2
1. **a** 768 **b** 429 **c** 2716 **d** 26 350 **e** 555 555 **f** 2 300 000
2. **a** LXXXIX **b** CCCXLVII **c** DCLIV **d** V̄DCL **e** L̄X̄X̄V̄CMXLII **f** C̄M̄L̄M̄V̄
3. 888

EXERCISE 1A.3
1. **a** . / ... **b** .. / = **c** .... / ..../ =
   d — **e** = / .. **f** ≡ / ...
2. **a** 14 **b** 120 **c** 218 **d** 168 **e** 313 **f** 380

EXERCISE 1A.4
1. **a** 765 **b** 3248 **c** 9999
2. **a** 四百九十七 **b** 八千四百 **c** 千百十一

3.

	words	Hind.-Arab.	Roman	Egypt.
a	thirty seven	37	XXXVII	(hieroglyph)
b	one hundred and four	104	CIV	(hieroglyph)
c	one hundred and fifty nine	159	CLIX	(hieroglyph)
d	eighty	80	LXXX	(hieroglyph)

	words	Mayan	Chinese Japanese
a	thirty seven	(mayan)	三十七
b	one hundred and four	(mayan)	一百四
c	one hundred and fifty nine	(mayan)	一百五十九
d	eighty	(mayan)	八十

EXERCISE 1B
1. **a** 8 **b** 80 **c** 8 **d** 800 **e** 80 **f** 8000 **g** 800 **h** 8000 **i** 8 **j** 80 000 **k** 8000 **l** 80 000
2. **a** 7 units **b** 7 thousands **c** 7 hundreds **d** 7 hundred thousands
3. **a** 3 thousands, 5 ten thousands, 8 tens
   b 3 thousands, 5 hundreds, 8 tens
   c 3 units, 5 ten thousands, 8 tens
   d 3 hundreds, 5 thousands, 8 hundred thousands
4. **a** 864 **b** 974 210 **c** 997 722
   d 345, 354, 435, 453, 534, 543 (6 numbers)
5. **a** 8, 16, 19, 54, 57, 75 **b** 6, 60, 600, 606, 660
   c 1008, 1080, 1800, 1808, 1880
   d 40 561, 45 061, 46 051, 46 501, 46 510
   e 207 653, 227 635, 236 705, 265 703
   f 545 922, 554 922, 594 522, 595 242
6. **a** 631, 613, 361, 316, 163, 136
   b 9877, 9787, 8977, 8779, 7987, 7897, 7789
   c 498 321, 498 231, 492 813, 428 931, 428 391
   d 675 034, 673 540, 607 543, 576 304, 563 074
7. **a** 86 **b** 674 **c** 9638 **d** 50 240
   e 27 003 **f** 73 298 **g** 500 375 **h** 809 302
8. **a** $9 \times 100 + 7 \times 10 + 5 \times 1$ **b** $6 \times 100 + 8 \times 10$
   c $3 \times 1000 + 8 \times 100 + 7 \times 10 + 4 \times 1$
   d $9 \times 1000 + 8 \times 10 + 3 \times 1$
   e $5 \times 10\,000 + 6 \times 1000 + 7 \times 100 + 4 \times 10 + 2 \times 1$
   f $7 \times 10\,000 + 5 \times 1000 + 7 \times 1$
   g $6 \times 100\,000 + 8 \times 100 + 2 \times 10 + 9 \times 1$
   h $3 \times 100\,000 + 5 \times 10\,000 + 4 \times 1000 + 7 \times 100 + 1 \times 10 + 8 \times 1$
9. **a** 27 **b** 80 **c** 608 **d** 1016 **e** 8200 **f** 19 538 **g** 75 403 **h** 602 818
10. **a** 7 **b** 13 **c** 21 **d** 299 **e** 4007 **f** 9997 **g** 400 004 **h** 209 026
11. **a** $375 + 836 \neq 1200$ **b** $79 \times 8 \neq 640$
    c $978 - 463 = 515$ **d** $7980 \div 2 \neq 400$
    e $455 + 544 = 999$ **f** $50 \times 400 = 20\,000$
    g $2000 - 1010 = 990$ **h** $3000 \div 300 = 10$
12. **a** $5268 - 3179 < 4169$ **b** $29 \times 30 < 900$
    c $672 + 762 < 1444$ **d** $720 \div 80 > 8$
    e $20 \times 80 > 160$ **f** $700 \times 80 > 54\,000$
    g $5649 + 7205 > 12\,844$
    h $6060 - 606 > 5444$

EXERCISE 1C
1. **a** 80 **b** 80 **c** 300 **d** 2380 **e** 3990 **f** 1650 **g** 9800 **h** 61 020 **i** 49 570 **j** 30 940 **k** 999 570 **l** 128 670
2. **a** 100 **b** 500 **c** 1000 **d** 3000 **e** 25 400 **f** 14 800 **g** 130 000 **h** 44 000
3. **a** 1000 **b** 6000 **c** 10 000 **d** 44 000 **e** 65 000 **f** 123 000 **g** 435 000 **h** 571 000

ANSWERS 411

4 a $45 000 **b** 330 kg **c** $500 **d** 4800 km
e 362 kL or 362 000 L **f** $490 000 **g** 37 000
h 600 000 **i** 36 000 000 **j** $2 000 000 000

EXERCISE 1D

1 a 807 **b** 1330 **c** 3995 **d** 1644 **e** 1597 **f** 13 059
2 a 79 **b** 107 **c** 748 **d** 696 **e** 2155
f 6565 **g** 814 **h** 4955 **i** 4619
3 a 82 **b** 44 **c** 109 **d** 453 **e** 665 **f** 3656
4 a 34 **b** 48 **c** 6 **d** 22 **e** 182 **f** 476
g 376 **h** 3767
5 a 22 m **b** $432 **c** 6 kg **d** $41 **e** 22
f 3923 km **g** 1178 cm

EXERCISE 1E

1 a 500 **b** 5000 **c** 50 000 **d** 6900
e 69 000 **f** 690 000 **g** 12 300 **h** 246 000
i 96 000 **j** 490 000 **k** 49 000 **l** 490 000
2 a 200 **b** 20 **c** 2 **d** 57 **e** 5.7 **f** 0.57
g 24.3 **h** 2.43 **i** 0.243 **j** 450 **k** 45 **l** 4.5
m 7.2 **n** 0.72 **o** 0.072 **p** 0.6 **q** 0.06 **r** 0.006
3 a 120 **b** 148 **c** 496 **d** 1272 **e** 405
f 2744 **g** 14 580 **h** 23 112 **i** 5754
j 45 026 **k** 10 413 **l** 26 864
4 a 14 **b** 54 **c** 21 **d** 75 **e** 901 **f** 619
5 a 6 **b** 25 **c** 52 **d** 48 **e** 208 **f** 817
6 a 22.5 **b** 15.75 **c** 16.2 **d** 12.125 **e** 71.5
f 68.75 **g** 87.8 **h** 82.625 **i** 477.5
j 258.25 **k** 240.2 **l** 587.375 **m** 3674.5
n 2115.75 **o** 1599.8
7 a 90 **b** $80 **c** 82 min **d** 2450 mm
e 672 km **f** 81 min **g** $1.44

EXERCISE 1F

1 a $200 **b** $60 **c** $60 **d** $30 **e** $50 **f** $28 000
2 a $280 **b** $120 **c** No **d** $40
3 a 320 **b** 400 **c** 420 **d** 540 **e** 180 **f** 200
4 a 413 **b** 747 **c** 375
5 a 900 **b** 4200 **c** 3600 **d** 3000 **e** 6400
f 14 000
6 a 4753 **b** 3560 **c** 33 831
7 a 2400 **b** 4200 **c** 9000 **d** 15 000 **e** 28 000
f 150 000 **g** 90 000 **h** 360 000 **i** 720 000
8 a 100 **b** 1000 **c** 10 000 **d** 300 **e** 2000
f 200 **g** 10 **h** 100 **i** 200 **j** 75 **k** 250
l 2000
9 a 9291 **b** 56 382 **c** 347 723 **d** 36
10 a 400 books **b** 12 000 words **c** 16 000 bricks
d 80 min **e** 10 000 vines **f** 5 000 000 bottles
g 50 km/h **h** 400 meters
11 a 500 **b** 800

EXERCISE 1G

1 20 000 hours **2** 83 days 8 hours
3 10 000 hours **4 a** 135 km **b** 27 hours
5 125 hours
6 a 370 **b** CN Tower, 205 000 coins;
Sears Tower, 165 000 coins;
Empire State, 141 000 coins;
Sky Tower, 121 000 coins;
Centrepoint, 113 000 coins;
Eiffel Tower, 111 000 coins
7 a 20 000 **b** 4000 **c** 2500 **d** 500 **e** 10 000
f 12 500 **g** 8000 **h** 25 000 **i** 6250 **j** 125 000
8 a 1 000 000s $\doteqdot$ 16 666.7 min $\doteqdot$ 277.8 h $\doteqdot$ 11.6 d
b 1 000 000 min $\doteqdot$ 16 666.7 h $\doteqdot$ 694.4 days
$\doteqdot$ 99.2 weeks
c 1 000 000 h $\doteqdot$ 41 666.7 days $\doteqdot$ 5952.4 weeks
$\doteqdot$ 114.5 years
d 1 000 000 days $\doteqdot$ 2739.7 years
e 1 000 000 years = 10 000 cent = 1000 millennia

EXERCISE 1H

1 a 80 **b** 50 000 000 **c** 600 **d** 400 000
e 70 000 **f** 2
2 a 3 000 000, 600 000, 40 000, 8000, 500, 90, 7
b 30 000 000, 4 000 000, 800 000, 60 000,
5000, 200, 70, 1
3 a 37 000 000 **b** 200 000 000, 17 000 000
c 150 000 000 **d** $111 240 463.10
e 21 240 657 **f** 415 000 000 **g** 1 048 576 bytes
4 Mercury, Venus, Earth, Mars, Jupiter, Saturn,
Uranus, Neptune, Pluto
5 a Asia **b** Africa, Asia, North America
c Antarctica, Australia
6 a 3.97 times **b** 2.58 times **c** 4.23 times
d 63.73 times **e** 39.44 times

EXERCISE 1I

1 $26 **2** $201 **3** 11 oranges **4** 54 **5** $11
6 $30 **7** a goal **8** $1860 **9** $743 **10** $550
11 48 km **12** 600 g

EXERCISE 1J

1

	Statement	Directed number	Opposite to statement	Directed number
a	20 m above sea level	+20	20 m below sea level	−20
b	45 km south of the city	−45	45 km north of the city	+45
c	a loss of 2 kg in weight	−2	a gain of 2 kg in weight	+2
d	a clock is 2 minutes fast	+2	a clock is 2 minutes slow	−2

	Statement	Directed number	Opposite to statement	Directed number
e	she arrives 5 minutes early	−5	she arrives 5 minutes late	+5
f	a profit of $4000	+4000	a loss of $4000	−4000
g	2 floors above ground level	+2	2 floors below ground level	−2
h	10°C below zero	−10	10°C above zero	+10
i	an increase of $400	+400	a decrease of $400	−400
j	winning by 34 points	+34	losing by 34 points	−34

2 lift +1, car −3, parking attendant −2, rubbish skip −5

3 A −2, B −6, C +5, D +3, E 0

4 a +11 **b** −6 **c** −8 **d** +29 **e** −14

5 a −30 **b** +200 **c** −431 **d** −751 **e** +809

6 a +7 **b** −15 **c** −115 **d** +362 **e** −19.6

7 a A 35°C, B 5°C, C −10°C, D 25°C, E 10°C, F −5°C
  b i 15°C **ii** 20°C **iii** 30°C **iv** 35°C
  c i 45°C **ii** 20°C **iii** 5°C **iv** 15°C
  d i 30°C **ii** 15°C **iii** 20°C **iv** 5°C
    v 10°C **vi** 30°C

8 a 11 **b** −1 **c** 9 **d** −5 **e** −4 **f** 8 **g** 1
  h −3 **i** −1 **j** 1 **k** −5 **l** −1 **m** 6
  n 2 **o** −2 **p** 2 **q** −6 **r** 4 **s** −4 **t** 4

REVIEW SET 1A

1 a F **b** T **c** F **d** T **e** F

2 654 662, 673 502, 674 551, 750 467, 765 442

3 4 126 350 **4** 0 **5** 88 **6** 140 000 **7** 1098

8 $2688 **9** 1200 **10 a** $39 800 **b** 600 000

11 $29 **12 a** a deposit of $30 **b i** −3 **ii** −7

13 a 16 000 000 **b** 5 times

REVIEW SET 1B

1 a F **b** F **c** F **d** T

2 1000 times **3** 40 000 **4** 40 000

5 6 080 699, 968 099, 698 096, 680 969, 608 699

6 1585 **7** $184.80 **8** $728

9 a a fall in temperature of 5°C **b** 5°C

10 ÷ 2.9 times **11** $475

REVIEW SET 1C

1 a $60 \times 1000 > 59\,000$ **b** $499\,994 > 499\,949$

2 874 310

3 a 8 hundreds **b** 8 thousands
  c 8 hundred thousands **d** 8 millions

4 a 40 **b** 4000 **c** 500 000

5 a 194 257 **b** 19 355 **c** 0

6 187.5 g **7** No ($1 short)

8 79 562, 96 572, 569 207, 652 097, 795 602

9 a winning by 2 goals **b i** 26°C **ii** 4°C

EXERCISE 2A

1 a 60 **b** 19 **c** 392 **d** 22 **e** 100
  f 3840 **g** 100

2 a 1534 m **b** $97 196 **c** 23 124 **d** $3457
  e $357 **f** 5600 people **g** 51 840 cans **h** $16 280
  i $3000 **j** 358 **k** 27 840 plants
  l 2717 passengers **m** 114 cartons **n** 15 kg
  o 12 kg **p** 9513 people

EXERCISE 2B

1 a 8 **b** 46 **c** 45 **d** 15 **e** 49 **f** 11
  g 11 **h** 16 **i** 24 **j** 3 **k** 21 **l** 10
  m 29 **n** 36 **o** 16

2 a 30 **b** 32 **c** 2 **d** 48 **e** 18 **f** 96
  g 0 **h** 35 **i** 88 **j** 30 **k** 5 **l** 23

3 a $(6+3) \times 2 = 18$ **b** $21 - 7 \times 3 = 0$
  c $8 + 4 - 3 \times 2 = 6$ **d** $50 \div (5+5) = 5$
  e $5 \times (3-1) + 7 = 17$ **f** $(4+4) \times 4 \div 16 = 2$
  g $50 \div 5 + 5 = 15$ **h** $9 \times (7+5) + 2 = 110$
  i $9 \times 7 + 5 - 2 = 66$

4 a $96 \div (4+8) \times 10 - 9 = 71$
  b $96 \div 4 + 8 \times (10-9) = 32$
  c $96 \div 4 + 8 \times 10 - 9 = 95$
  d $96 \div (4+8) \times (10-9) = 8$

5 a true **b** false **c** true **d** false **e** false
  f true **g** false **h** true **i** false

6 a 4 **b** 6 **c** 6 **d** 27 **e** 10 **f** 9
  g 28 **h** 1

EXERCISE 2C

1 a 1, 3, 5, 15 **b** 1, 2, 4, 8, 16 **c** $16 = 2 \times 8$
  d 1×16, 2×8, 4×4

2 a 1, 2, 4, 8 **b** 1, 2, 3, 4, 6, 9, 12, 18, 36
  c 1, 2, 4, 5, 8, 10, 20, 40
  d 1, 2, 3, 6, 7, 14, 21, 42
  e 1, 2, 3, 4, 6, 8, 12, 16, 24, 48
  f 1, 3, 7, 9, 21, 63 **g** 1, 2, 3, 5, 6, 10, 15, 30
  h 1, 2, 3, 4, 6, 7, 12, 14, 21, 28, 42, 84
  i 1, 3, 13, 39 **j** 1, 5, 7, 35
  k 1, 2, 3, 4, 5, 6, 10, 12, 15, 20, 30, 60
  l 1, 3, 9, 27, 81

3 a $33 = 3 \times 11$ **b** $55 = 5 \times 11$ **c** $28 = 4 \times 7$
  d $50 = 10 \times 5$ **e** $27 = 9 \times 3$ **f** $42 = 2 \times 21$
  g $35 = 5 \times 7$ **h** $72 = 8 \times 9$ **i** $99 = 11 \times 9$

ANSWERS 413

   j $49 = 7 \times 7$ **k** $121 = 11 \times 11$ **l** $48 = 6 \times 8$
   m $64 = 16 \times 4$ **n** $108 = 12 \times 9$
   o $88 = 2 \times 44$

4 **a** 6 **b** 9 **c** 9 **d** 24 **e** 22 **f** 25
   g 45 **h** 13

5 2, 3, 5, 7, 11, 13, 17, 19, 23, 29, 31, 37, 41, 43, 47, 53, 59, 61, 67, 71, 73, 79, 83, 89, 97

6

Set of Numbers	No of primes
0 - 9	4
10 - 19	4
20 - 29	2
30 - 39	2
40 - 49	3
50 - 59	2
60 - 69	2

no pattern

7 **a** factor tree for 28 **b** factor tree for 80 **c** factor tree for 75

8 **a** $2 \times 2 \times 2 \times 2$ **b** $2 \times 2 \times 3 \times 3$ **c** $2 \times 2 \times 7$
   d $2 \times 2 \times 2 \times 7$ **e** $3 \times 3 \times 7$ **f** $3 \times 5 \times 5$
   g $2 \times 2 \times 2 \times 3 \times 7$ **h** $2 \times 2 \times 3 \times 3 \times 7$
   i 5×61 **j** $2 \times 2 \times 2 \times 7 \times 7$

9 **a** 3 **b** 7 **c** 6 **d** 7 **e** 9 **f** 25
   g 40 **h** 27 **i** 12

10 **a** 14, 16, 18 **b** 35, 37, 39, 41, 43 **c** 2, 8

11 **a** even **b** even **c** even **d** odd **e** odd
    f odd **g** odd **h** odd **i** even

EXERCISE 2D

1 **a, b** 1 2 ③ 4 5 ⑥ 7 ⑧ ⑨ 10 11 ⑫ 13 14 ⑮ ⑯ 17 ⑱ 19 ⑳ ㉑ 22 23 ㉔ 25 26 ㉗ ㉘ 29 ㉚
   c 12, 24

2 **a** 30, 60, 90, 120, 150 **b** 45, 90, 135
   c 60, 120 **d** 60, 120

3 **a** 6 **b** 12 **c** 40 **d** 60 **e** 24 **f** 12
   g 60 **h** 60

4 36 m **5** 18 seconds **6** 20 tokens **7** 30 km

8 60th bar

EXERCISE 2E

1 **a** T **b** F **c** F **d** T **e** T **f** F **g** T
   h T

2 a, b, c, f, g, h, i, j, k, l

3 **a** □ = 0, 3, 6, 9 **b** □ = 0, 3, 6, 9
   c □ = 1, 4, 7 **d** □ = 2, 5, 8 **e** □ = 1, 4, 7
   f □ = 2, 5, 8 **g** □ = 1, 4, 7
   h □ = 2, 5, 8

4 **a** and **b** are divisible by 4

5 **c** and **d** are divisible by 9

EXERCISE 2F

1 **a** 6^4 **b** 4^6 **c** 13^5 **d** $3^2 \times 5^3$ **e** $2^4 \times 9^2$
   f $3^3 \times 8^3$ **g** $2^2 \times 4^3 \times 5^2$ **h** $3^2 \times 6 \times 11^3$
   i $3^3 \times 5^2 \times 9^2$

2 **a** 30 **b** 12 **c** 54 **d** 90 **e** 396
   f 2200 **g** 480 **h** 2880 **i** 648

3 **a** 7 **b** 17 **c** 513 **d** 63 **e** 228 **f** 3584
   g 924 **h** 110 **i** 0

4 **a** $5 \times 5 \times 5 \times 5 = 625$ **b** $7 \times 7 \times 7 = 343$
   c $3 \times 3 \times 3 \times 3 \times 3 \times 3 \times 3 = 2187$
   d $12 \times 12 \times 12 \times 12 \times 12 = 248\,832$
   e $100 \times 100 \times 100 = 1\,000\,000$
   f $14 \times 14 \times 14 \times 14 \times 14 = 537\,824$

5 **a** $2^{10}, 8^4, 3^8, 6^5, 10^4, 5^7$
   b $1^{27}, 27^3, 9^5, 5^8, 1000^2$

6 $1^2 = 1$
   $11^2 = 121$
   $111^2 = 12\,321$
   $1111^2 = 1\,234\,321$
   $11\,111^2 = 123\,454\,321$
   $111\,111^2 = 12\,345\,654\,321$
   $1\,111\,111^2 = 1\,234\,567\,654\,321$

EXERCISE 2G

1 **a** 862 953 **b** 6 987 096 **c** 3 050 709
   d 4 892 260 **e** 20 369 068 **f** 1 011 190
   g 9836 **h** 890 637 **i** 50 875 000

2 **a** $(9 \times 1000) + (7 \times 100) + (3 \times 10) + (8 \times 1)$
   b $(2 \times 10\,000) + (9 \times 1000) + (7 \times 100) + (8 \times 10) + (2 \times 1)$
   c $(4 \times 10\,000) + (4 \times 100) + (4 \times 1)$
   d $(6 \times 100\,000) + (5 \times 10\,000) + (7 \times 1000) + (9 \times 100) + (3 \times 10) + (1 \times 1)$
   e $(8 \times 100\,000) + (8 \times 100) + (8 \times 10) + (8 \times 1)$
   f $(1 \times 1\,000\,000) + (2 \times 100\,000) + (4 \times 10\,000) + (7 \times 1000) + (9 \times 10) + (1 \times 1)$
   g $(4 \times 10\,000\,000) + (9 \times 1\,000\,000) + (7 \times 100\,000) + (5 \times 10\,000) + (5 \times 1000) + (4 \times 100)$
   h $(6 \times 1\,000\,000) + (7 \times 100\,000) + (7 \times 10\,000) + (7 \times 1000) + (7 \times 100) + (7 \times 10) + (7 \times 1)$

3 **a** $(6 \times 10^2) + (5 \times 10^1) + (8 \times 1)$
   b $(3 \times 10^3) + (8 \times 10^2) + (7 \times 10^1) + (4 \times 1)$
   c $(9 \times 10^4) + (5 \times 10^3) + (6 \times 10^2) + (3 \times 10^1) + (6 \times 1)$
   d $(1 \times 10^5) + (1 \times 10^2)$

e $(5 \times 10^5) + (5 \times 10^3) + (7 \times 10^2) + (5 \times 10^1)$
f $(1 \times 10^6) + (2 \times 10^5) + (7 \times 10^4) + (4 \times 10^3) + (9 \times 10^2) + (4 \times 10^1) + (7 \times 1)$
g $(3 \times 10^7) + (6 \times 10^6) + (6 \times 10^5)$
h $(4 \times 10^6) + (2 \times 10^5) + (9 \times 10^4) + (3 \times 10^3) + (3 \times 10^2) + (7 \times 10^1) + (5 \times 1)$
i $(4 \times 10^5) + (6 \times 10^2) + (8 \times 10^1) + (7 \times 1)$
j $(2 \times 10^7) + (3 \times 10^6) + (6 \times 10^5) + (9 \times 10^4) + (7 \times 10^3) + (5 \times 10^2)$

EXERCISE 2H

1 a 16 **b** 25 **c** 49 **d** 100 **e** 1024 **f** 5184 **g** 21 **h** 9 **i** 20 **j** 36
2 a 18 496 **b** 166 464 **c** 1 361 889 **d** 5 313 025
3 a 0, 1, 4, 5, 6, 9 **b** no
4 a 1 **b** 4 **c** 6 **d** 9 **e** 12
5 a 7 **b** 8 **c** 10 **d** 0 **e** 20
6 1, 8, 27, 64, 125, 216, 343, 512, 729, 1000
7 a 4 **b** 120 **c** 72 **d** 294
8 a

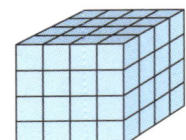

b Each block is
n units long $\times$ n units wide $\times$ n units high
$= n \times n \times n$
$= n^3$

9 a $2^3 - 1^3 - 1 = 6$ $3^3 - 2^3 - 1 = 18$
$4^3 - 3^3 - 1 = 36$ $5^3 - 4^3 - 1 = 60$
b i $10^3 - 9^3 - 1 = 270$
ii $53^3 - 52^3 - 1 = 8268$
All of the answers in **a** and **b** are divisible by 6.

EXERCISE 21.1

1 25 and 26 *or* 16, 17, 18 *or* 6, 7, 8, 9, 10, 11
2 4 spiders and 9 beetles
3 36 **4** $2 + 3 \times 4 - 5$ **5** 23
6 Increase the 8 to 9 or the 2 to 3 *or* decrease the 2 in the answer by 1
7 11 **8** $a = 6, b = 4, c = 3$
9 6 boys and 3 girls
10 Fred is 11, Karen is 13 and Jill is 17

EXERCISE 21.2

1 128 **2** 12 **3** 105 **4** 108
5 54, dodecagon **6** 56

EXERCISE 21.3

1 6 **2** 9.42 am **3** 43 **4** Row 9 **5** Stephen

EXERCISE 21.4

1 4 months before the end of last month
2 12 **3** 15 **4** 9.25 am **5** 27 cm

REVIEW SET 2A

1 a 8 **b** 8 **c** 5 **d** 100
2 a 14 **b** 24 **c** 23 **3** 41
4 a 1, 2, 4, 7, 8, 14, 28, 56 **b** 20 **c** 6
5 a no **b** yes **c** yes **d** yes
6 a 360 **b** 3200 **c** 1 000 000
7 a 50 730 **b** 4 020 305
8 a 9 **b** 8 **c** 7 **9** $1800

REVIEW SET 2B

1 a 4 each **b** 15 **c** 36 **d** 12
2 a 17 **b** 14 **c** 13
3 a 1, 2, 5, 10, 11, 22, 55, 110 **b** 8
4 a 32, 40, 48, 56 **b** 36, 49
c 31, 37, 41, 43, 47, 53, 59
5 60 000 km **6 a** 11 **b** 2
7 a 40 830 960 **b** 930 647
8 1000, 10 000, 100 000, 1 000 000
9 $22 140

REVIEW SET 2C

1 a 7 **b** 29 **c** 13 **d** 18
2 65 more attended than were expected.
3 a 1, 2, 4, 8, 16, 32, 64 **b** 11, 13, 17, 19
c 105 **d** $2 \times 2 \times 2 \times 3 \times 5$ **e** 9
4 36 cm
5 a $49 = 7^2$ **b** $121 = 11^2$ **c** $\sqrt{81} = 9$
d $27 = 3^3$ **e** $\sqrt{400} = 20$
6 a 2000 **b** 63 000 **c** 1 000 000 **d** 37 012
e 6 504 308
7 $358.20

EXERCISE 3A

1 a (1) a speck of dust
(2) corner where two walls and the floor meet
b (1) where two walls meet
(2) bottom of blackboard
2 a A vertex is a corner point of figure A, B and C are all vertices

b A point of intersection is the point where two lines meet.

c Two lines which are always the same distance apart.

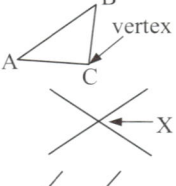

ANSWERS 415

3 a $\overleftrightarrow{LM}$ or $\overleftrightarrow{ML}$ b $\overleftrightarrow{CD}$, $\overleftrightarrow{CE}$, $\overleftrightarrow{DE}$, $\overleftrightarrow{DC}$, $\overleftrightarrow{EC}$, $\overleftrightarrow{ED}$
4 a B b C 5 a B b $\overline{AB}$
6 a $\overrightarrow{PQ}$ b Q c $\overrightarrow{QR}$ d $\overrightarrow{QR}$
7 a $\overline{KL}, \overline{LM}, \overline{MN}, \overline{NK}$ b $\overline{LM}, \overline{MN}$
8 a $\overline{AB}, \overline{BC}, \overline{CD}, \overline{DE}, \overline{EA}$ b $\overline{AB}, \overline{BC}$
   c $\overline{AC}, \overline{BC}, \overline{DC}, \overline{EC}$

EXERCISE 3B.1

1 a b 120° c

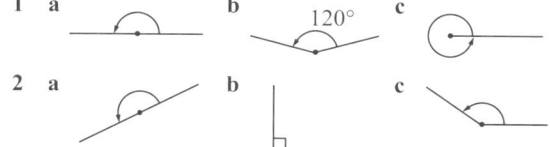

2 a b c

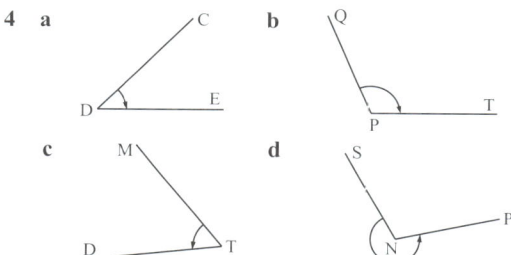

3 a ∠ABC, acute angle b ∠PQR, obtuse angle
   c ∠KLM, reflex angle
4 a, b, c, d (diagrams)

5 ∠ABC, ∠BCD, ∠ADC, ∠BAD, ∠BAC,
   ∠BCA, ∠CAD, ∠ACD

6
Number of lines	2	3	4	5	8
Number of angles	1	3	6	10	28

EXERCISE 3B.2

1 a 32° b 71° c 123° d 156°
2 a ∠BAC = 83°, ∠ACB = 31°, ∠ABC = 66°
   b ∠FDE = 119°, ∠DEF = 32°, ∠DFE = 29°
   c ∠MKL = 90°, ∠KLM = 50°, ∠LMK = 40°
   d ∠XYZ = 10°, ∠YZX = 140°, ∠ZXY = 30°
3 a ∠ABC = 94°, ∠BCD = 78°, ∠CDA = 78°,
      ∠DAB = 110°
   b ∠PQR = 54°, ∠QRS = 127°, ∠RST = 127°,
      ∠STP = 91°, ∠TPQ = 141°
   c ∠OKL = 130°, ∠KLM = 110°, ∠LMN = 80°,
      ∠MNO = 150°, ∠NOK = 70°
   d ∠JEF = 120°, ∠EFG = 120°, ∠FGI = 70°,
      ∠GIJ = 160°, ∠IJE = 70°
4 Your answer might look like this:

	Estimate	Actual
a	50°	53°
b	90°	92°
c	20°	17°

EXERCISE 3C

1 a $a = 85$ b $b = 25$ c $c = 46$ d $d = 53$
   e $e = 37$ f $f = 46$ g $g = 22.8$
   h $h = 117$ i $i = 42, j = 48, k = 63$
2 a $p + q + r = 180$ b $a + b = 90$ c $a + b = 140$
   d $r + s = 90$ e $m + n = 75$ f $p + m = 90$

EXERCISE 3D

1 a $x = 110$ b $x = 90$ c $x = 40$
   d $x = 80$ e $x = 90$ f $x = 90$
2 a $a + b + c + d = 360$ b $m + n = 170$
   c $x + y = 180$

EXERCISE 3E

1 a not closed b not all straight sides
   c some sides cross each other
2 a no, as all angles are not equal
   b yes, is regular c no, angles not equal
3 a regular quadrilateral b quadrilateral
   c triangle d quadrilateral e heptagon
   f decagon g dodecagon h quadrilateral
   i dodecagon j decagon k quadrilateral
   l quadrilateral
4 a, b, c, d, e, f (shapes)

5 a, b, c

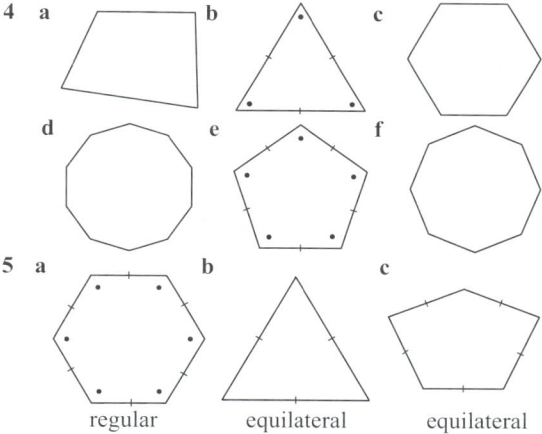

regular hexagon — equilateral triangle — equilateral non-regular pentagon

6 a I b I c R d R e R f I

EXERCISE 3F.1

1 a scalene b isosceles c scalene
   d equilateral
2 a, b, c (shapes)

3 rectangle, rhombus, square
4 a square b rectangle c parallelogram
   d rhombus e kite f trapezium
5 a True b True c True d True e True f True
6 a RQ ⊥ QP b AB ∥ DC
   c HI ∥ KJ, HI ⊥ IJ, IJ ⊥ KJ d KM ⊥ LN

e PQ ∥ SR, PQ ⊥ SP, SP ⊥ RS
f WX ∥ ZY, WZ ∥ XY, WX ⊥ XY, XY ⊥ YZ, YZ ⊥ ZW, ZW ⊥ WX

7 a

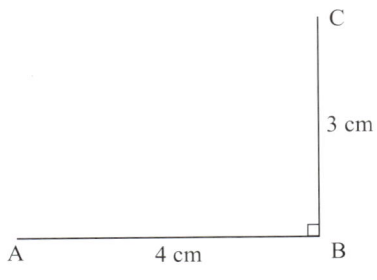

b

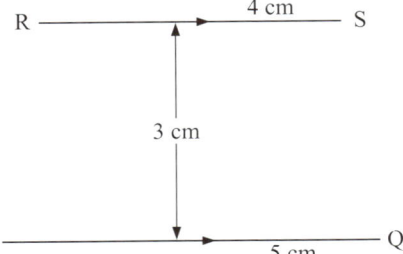

c

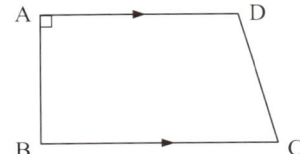

d

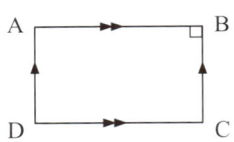

EXERCISE 3F.2

1 a 6 **b** 7 **c** 4

2 a   **b**   **c**

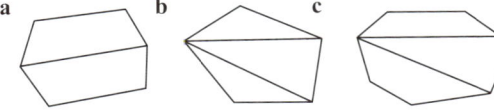

3 $E = 7, V = 5, R = 4$

(1)   **(2)**

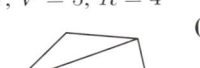 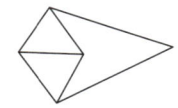

EXERCISE 3G

2 a equilateral triangle **b** all angles measure $60°$
  c All angles of an equilateral triangle measure $60°$.
3 a isosceles **b** ∠ABC = ∠ACB
  c In an isosceles triangle the angles opposite the equal sides are equal.

4 a Triangle has two sides of equal length (the cut line).
  b The cut line makes equal angles with the bottom of the paper.
6 a $x = 46$ **b** $x = 66$ **c** $x = 4$ **d** $x = 40$
  e $x = 70, y = 4$ **f** $p = 90$

EXERCISE 3H

2 The arcs are all the same length so triangle WXZ is is equilateral. Therefore all angles are $60°$.
4 Hint: Construct a $60°$ angle and then bisect it.
6 The angle bisectors of any triangle appear to meet at a point.
7 Hint: Join QR, PS, OQ, OR, OS, OP.
8 Hint: Join all adjacent sides of the hexagon and draw all lines from O to the vertices.

EXERCISE 3I

1 a 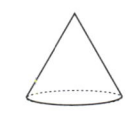 **b**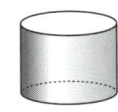

c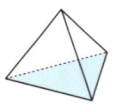

d 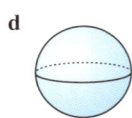 **e**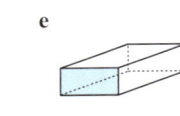

f

2 a sphere **b** cone **c** cylinder **d** cube
  e rectangular prism **f** cylinder

3 a 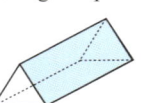 **b**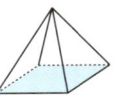

c 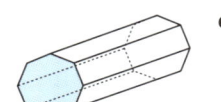 **d**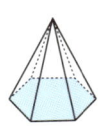

4 a A, B, C, D, E, F, G, H
  b ABCD, BCFE, CDGF, ADGH, ABEH, EFGH
  c AB, DC, GF, HE, BC, AD, EF, HG, AH, BE, CF, DG
5 a rectangles **b** triangles
6 a 4 **b** 6 **c** 4

EXERCISE 3J

1 a C, (2) **b** A, (3) **c** B, (4) **d** D, (1)
3 Yes! Make it!

EXERCISE 3K

1

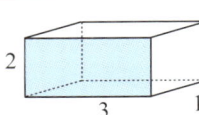

2 a   b   c

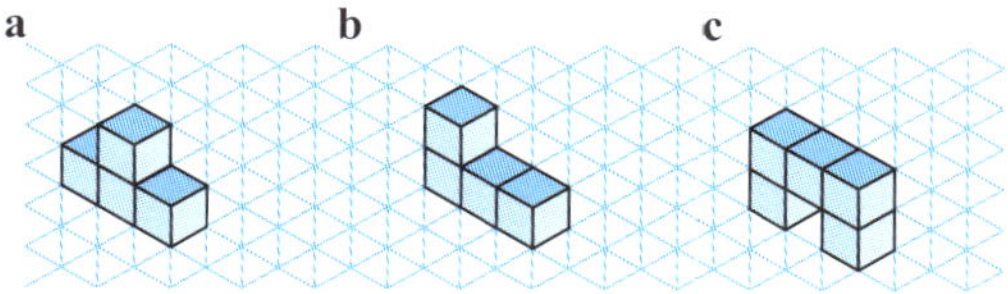

3 a   b   c

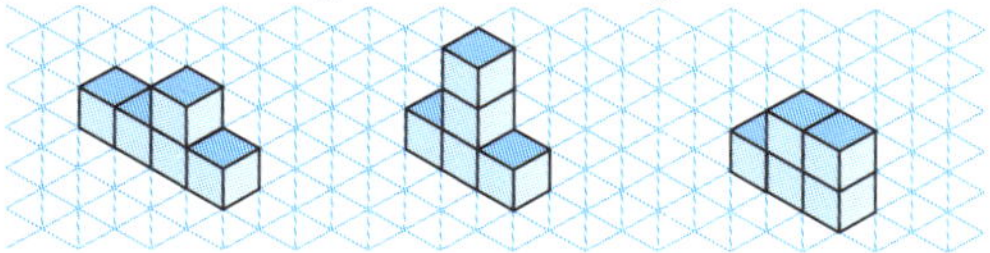

4

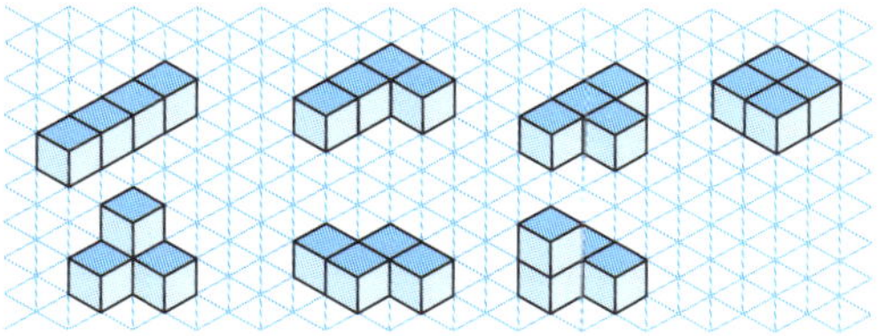

EXERCISE 3L

1 a

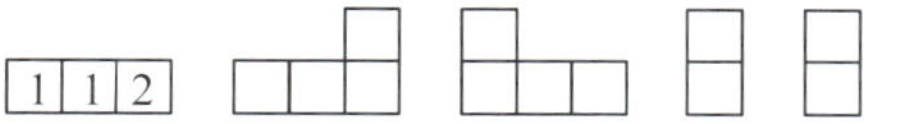

| 1 | 1 | 2 |

top front back left right

b

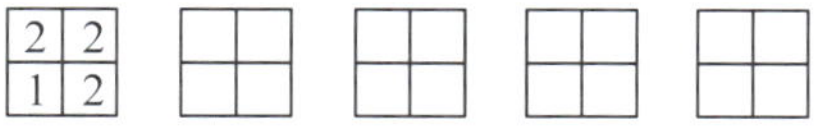

| 2 | 2 |
| 1 | 2 |

top front back left right

c

| 1 | 2 | 1 |

top front back left right

2 a   b

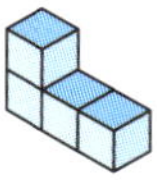

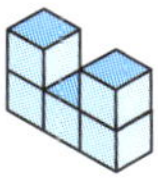

3 Any 5 of these:

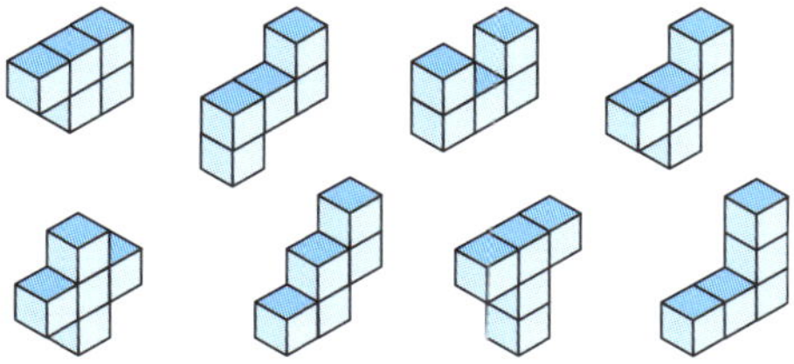

EXERCISE 3M

1 a 2 units, 1 unit, 1 unit   b 2 units, 1 unit, 1 unit

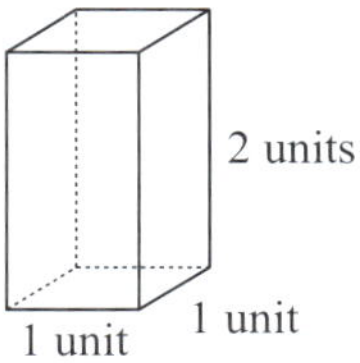

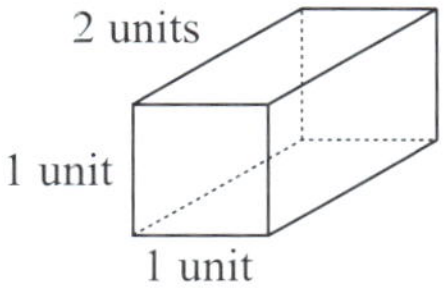

c 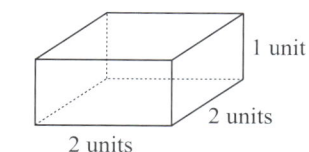 1 unit, 2 units, 2 units

2 a 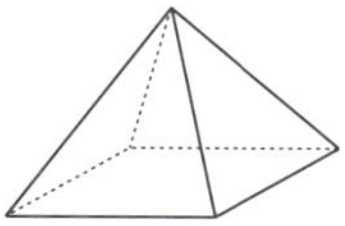   b 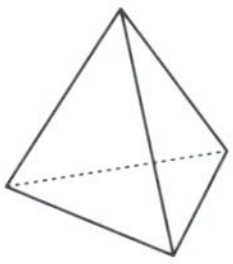   c 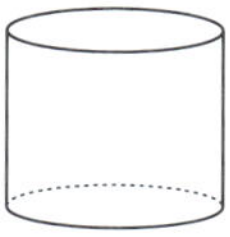   d 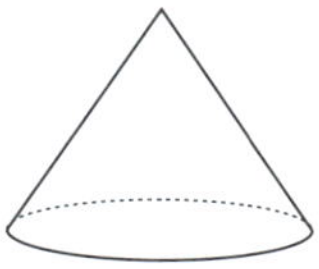   e 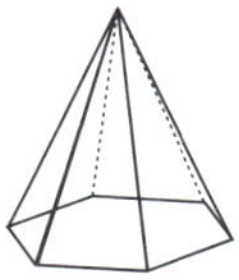   f

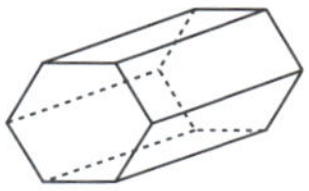

REVIEW SET 3A

1 a $\overline{BC}$ b $\overline{BC}$
2 a parallel lines   b equal angles   c equal sides
3 a $90°$ b $180°$ **4** a $a = 60$ b $b = 27$
5 a 9 vertices   b 6 regions
6 a   b 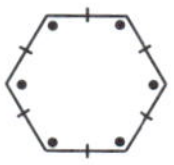   c

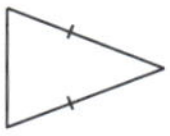

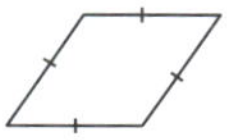

7 Any 5 of these: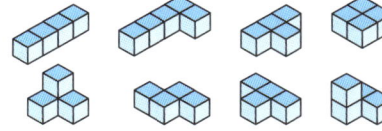

8 a 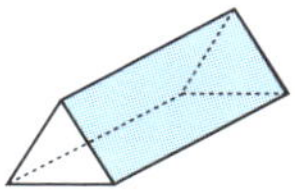 triangular prism   b pentagonal-based pyramid

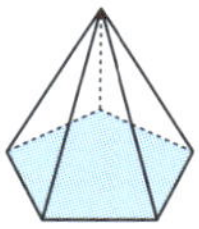

9 a A, B, C, D, E, F
   b $\overline{AB}$, $\overline{AC}$, $\overline{BC}$, $\overline{AE}$, $\overline{BF}$, $\overline{CD}$, $\overline{DF}$, $\overline{DE}$, $\overline{EF}$
   c ABC, EFD, ABFE, ACDE, BCDF

REVIEW SET 3B

1 a Lines continue indefinitely in both directions.
   b $\overline{AB}$ is the line segment joining A to B.
   c $\overleftrightarrow{CD}$ is the line passing through C and D.
   d X is the point of intersection of $\overleftrightarrow{AB}$ and $\overleftrightarrow{CD}$.

2 **a** pentagon **b** quadrilateral **c** octagon

3 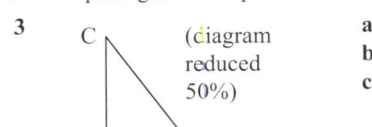 **a** BC = 10 cm
  b ∠ABC = 53°
  c ∠ACB = 37°

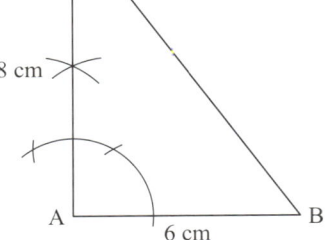

(diagram reduced 50%)

4 a   **b**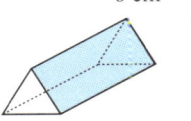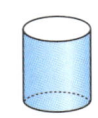

5 a   **b**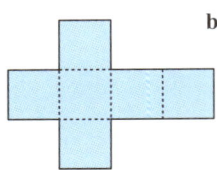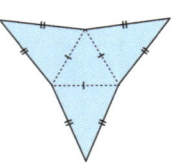

6 a $a = 94$ **b** $c = 112$

7 To draw the bisector (NR) of ∠MNO.

8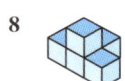

9 a 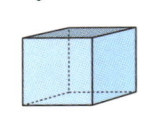 **b**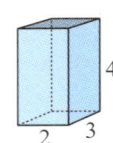

REVIEW SET 3C

1 a scalene **b** equilateral **c** isosceles
2 a $a = 90$ {angles on a line}
  b $a = 145$ {angles about a point}
  c $a = 35$ {angles on a line}
  d $a = 14$ {angle sum of triangle}
3 a $x = 33$ {angle sum of triangle}
  b $x = 68$ {isosceles triangle, angle sum of triangle}
  c $x = 16$ {angle sum of triangle}
4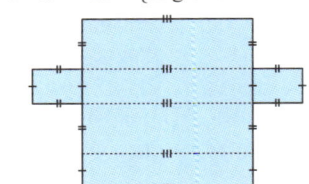
5 a 14 **b** 10
6 a 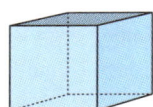 **b**

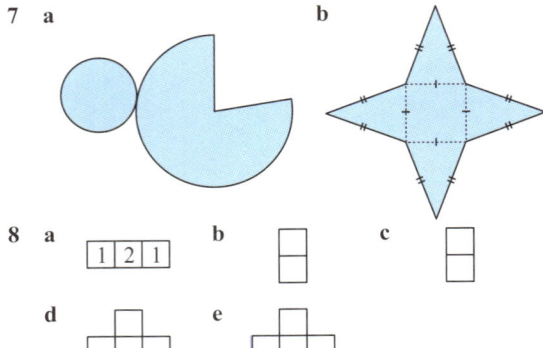

7 a **b**

8 a | 1 | 2 | 1 | **b**   **c**

  d   **e**

EXERCISE 4B

1

	Symbol	Words	Num.	Denom.
a	$\frac{1}{2}$	one half	1	2
b	$\frac{3}{4}$	three quarters	3	4
c	$\frac{2}{3}$	two thirds	2	3
d	$\frac{2}{7}$	two sevenths	2	7
e	$\frac{7}{9}$	seven ninths	7	9
f	$\frac{5}{8}$	five eighths	5	8
g	$\frac{7}{11}$	seven elevenths	7	11

	Meaning	Number line
a	One whole divided into two equal parts and one is being considered.	one half
b	One whole divided into four equal parts and three are being considered.	three quarters
c	One whole divided into three equal parts and two are being considered.	two thirds
d	One whole divided into seven equal parts and two are being considered.	two sevenths
e	One whole divided into nine equal parts and seven are being considered.	seven ninths
f	One whole divided into eight equal parts and five are being considered.	five eights
g	One whole divided into eleven equal parts and seven are being considered.	seven elevenths

EXERCISE 4C.1

1 C, D, E, H

EXERCISE 4C.2

1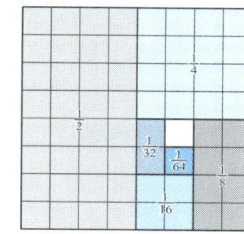

   a $\frac{63}{64}$ **b** shaded square is one square out of 64
   c 64   **d** $\frac{1}{2}$ **e** $\frac{8}{64} = \frac{1}{8}$ **f** $\frac{4}{64} = \frac{1}{16}$

2 **a** 4   **b** $\frac{1}{4}$ **c** $\frac{1}{4}$
   d piece 1 is $\frac{1}{4}$, piece 2 is $\frac{1}{4}$, piece 3 is $\frac{1}{16}$,
   piece 4 is $\frac{1}{8}$, piece 5 is $\frac{1}{16}$, piece 6 is $\frac{1}{8}$,
   piece 7 is $\frac{1}{8}$

EXERCISE 4D

1 **a** $\frac{2}{8}$ **b** $\frac{4}{8}$ **c** $\frac{6}{8}$ **d** $\frac{8}{8}$

2 **a** $\frac{15}{30}$ **b** $\frac{24}{30}$ **c** $\frac{25}{30}$ **d** $\frac{9}{30}$ **e** $\frac{6}{30}$ **f** $\frac{20}{30}$
   g $\frac{30}{30}$ **h** $\frac{18}{30}$

3 **a** $\frac{2}{16}$ **b** $\frac{4}{16}$ **c** $\frac{16}{16}$ **d** $\frac{0}{16}$ **e** $\frac{14}{16}$ **f** $\frac{12}{16}$
   g $\frac{10}{16}$ **h** $\frac{32}{16}$

4 **a** $\frac{50}{100}$ **b** $\frac{25}{100}$ **c** $\frac{80}{100}$ **d** $\frac{90}{100}$ **e** $\frac{28}{100}$
   f $\frac{26}{100}$ **g** $\frac{100}{100}$ **h** $\frac{85}{100}$

5 **a** $\frac{5\times 2}{6\times 2} = \frac{10}{12}$ **b** $\frac{8\times 3}{9\times 3} = \frac{24}{27}$ **c** $\frac{5\times 5}{7\times 5} = \frac{25}{35}$
   d $\frac{3\times 8}{4\times 8} = \frac{24}{32}$ **e** $\frac{4\times 10}{5\times 10} = \frac{40}{50}$ **f** $\frac{7\times 4}{8\times 4} = \frac{28}{32}$

6 **a** $\frac{6\div 2}{8\div 2} = \frac{3}{4}$ **b** $\frac{8\div 2}{10\div 2} = \frac{4}{5}$ **c** $\frac{10\div 5}{15\div 5} = \frac{2}{3}$
   d $\frac{18\div 3}{21\div 3} = \frac{6}{7}$ **e** $\frac{15\div 5}{25\div 5} = \frac{3}{5}$ **f** $\frac{18\div 2}{20\div 2} = \frac{9}{10}$

7 **a** $\square = 1$ **b** $\square = 4$ **c** $\square = 8$ **d** $\square = 3$
   e $\square = 3$ **f** $\square = 1$ **g** $\square = 3$ **h** $\square = 8$

8 **a** $\triangle = 20$ **b** $\triangle = 120$ **c** $\triangle = 8$
   d $\triangle = 25$ **e** $\triangle = 40$ **f** $\triangle = 81$
   g $\triangle = 69$ **h** $\triangle = 66$

EXERCISE 4E

1 **a** $\frac{4}{5}$ **b** $\frac{1}{4}$ **c** $\frac{3}{4}$ **d** $\frac{3}{7}$ **e** $\frac{4}{7}$ **f** $\frac{5}{7}$
   g $\frac{4}{7}$ **h** $\frac{1}{5}$ **i** $\frac{41}{100}$ **j** $\frac{5}{8}$

2 **a** $\frac{4}{5}$ **b** $\frac{9}{10}$ **c** $\frac{3}{4}$ **d** $\frac{5}{7}$ **e** $\frac{7}{13}$ **f** $\frac{3}{4}$
   g $\frac{3}{4}$ **h** $\frac{3}{11}$ **i** $\frac{41}{100}$ **j** $\frac{7}{8}$

3 **a** $\frac{8}{11}$ **b** $\frac{9}{16}$ **c** $\frac{3}{5}$ **d** $\frac{1}{3}$ **e** $\frac{1}{4}$ **f** $\frac{1}{17}$
   g $\frac{8}{27}$ **h** $\frac{1}{4}$ **i** $\frac{1}{15}$ **j** $\frac{3}{8}$

4 b, c, h, j, k

EXERCISE 4F

1 **a** $\frac{9}{20}$ **b** $\frac{8}{15}$ **c** $\frac{5}{12}$

2 **a** $\frac{1}{2}$ **b** $\frac{1}{4}$ **c** $\frac{1}{13}$ **d** $\frac{3}{13}$ **e** $\frac{4}{13}$ **f** $\frac{5}{26}$

3 **a** 5   **b** 18   **c** 4   **d** 15   **e** 5   **f** 11
   g 6   **h** 24   **i** 5   **j** 21   **k** 6   **l** 50

4 **a** $\frac{1}{5}$ **b** $\frac{39}{100}$ **c** $\frac{1}{2}$ **d** $\frac{1}{4}$ **e** $\frac{1}{7}$ **f** $\frac{5}{24}$
   g $\frac{23}{60}$ **h** $\frac{1}{15}$ **i** $\frac{1}{10}$ **j** $\frac{27}{200}$

5 **a** $\frac{1}{2}$ **b** $\frac{1}{6}$ **c** $\frac{3}{4}$ **d** $\frac{1}{5}$

6 **a** $\frac{1}{24}$ **b** $\frac{1}{6}$ **c** $\frac{1}{48}$ **d** $\frac{1}{1440}$

7 $\frac{1}{3}$ 8 $\frac{46}{183}$

9 **a** $\frac{5}{7}$ **b** $\frac{1}{14}$ **c** $\frac{1}{10\,080}$ **d** $\frac{1}{1\,209\,600}$

10 The denominator became larger.

11 $\frac{13}{40}$ 12 $\frac{4}{9}$ 13 $\frac{1}{3}$ 14 $\frac{53}{60}$ 15 $\frac{16}{25}$

16 $\frac{1}{5}$ 17 **a** $\frac{1}{2}$ **b** $\frac{1}{10}$ **c** $\frac{1}{5}$

18 **a** 4   **b** 5   **c** 7   **d** 65 g   **e** 60 cents
   f 15 min

19 5 games   20 49 students   21 37 cars

22 $39   23 84 plants

24 **a** $25   **b** $5

   c $12.50   **d** $2.50

   e 25 cents   **f** 15 cents

25 **a** **i** $90°$ **ii** $180°$ **iii** $270°$
   b **i** $\frac{1}{12}$ **ii** $\frac{1}{6}$ **iii** $\frac{2}{3}$

26 18 children   27 2 h 40 min   28 14 goals

29 **a** 1875 kg   **b** 50 boxes

EXERCISE 4G

1 **a** 21   **b** 15   **c** 6   **d** 36   **e** 72   **f** 30
   g 330   **h** 36

2 **a** $\frac{1}{4}, \frac{1}{2} = \frac{2}{4}$ **b** $\frac{2}{3} = \frac{8}{12}, \frac{3}{4} = \frac{9}{12}$
   c $\frac{1}{2} = \frac{7}{14}, \frac{4}{7} = \frac{8}{14}$ **d** $\frac{5}{8}, \frac{3}{8} = \frac{6}{8}$
   e $\frac{7}{10} = \frac{21}{30}, \frac{5}{6} = \frac{25}{30}$ **f** $\frac{3}{4} = \frac{27}{36}, \frac{7}{9} = \frac{28}{36}$
   g $\frac{5}{8} = \frac{25}{40}, \frac{8}{10} = \frac{32}{40}$ **h** $\frac{5}{8} = \frac{55}{88}, \frac{8}{11} = \frac{64}{88}$
   i $\frac{1}{4} = \frac{25}{100}, \frac{7}{20} = \frac{35}{100}, \frac{9}{25} = \frac{36}{100}$

3 **a** $\frac{7}{10}, \frac{1}{2} = \frac{5}{10}, \frac{2}{5} = \frac{4}{10}$ **b** $\frac{3}{4} = \frac{6}{8}, \frac{5}{8}, \frac{1}{2} = \frac{4}{8}$
   c $\frac{4}{6} = \frac{8}{12}, \frac{7}{12}, \frac{1}{2} = \frac{6}{12}$

EXERCISE 4H

1 **a** 4   **b** 4   **c** 3   **d** 5   **e** 5   **f** 10   **g** 3
   h 30   **i** 1   **j** 8   **k** 5   **l** 9

2 **a** $1\frac{1}{4}$ **b** $1\frac{1}{6}$ **c** $4\frac{1}{2}$ **d** $3\frac{1}{6}$ **e** $7\frac{1}{2}$ **f** $5\frac{2}{3}$
   g $2\frac{2}{7}$ **h** $2\frac{7}{8}$ **i** $3\frac{1}{7}$ **j** $3\frac{8}{9}$ **k** $10\frac{1}{4}$ **l** $9\frac{1}{12}$

3 a $\frac{7}{2}$ b $\frac{14}{3}$ c $\frac{11}{4}$ d $\frac{5}{3}$ e $\frac{3}{2}$ f $\frac{15}{4}$
  g $\frac{9}{5}$ h $\frac{13}{2}$ i $\frac{41}{9}$ j $\frac{47}{8}$ k $\frac{48}{7}$ l $\frac{23}{12}$

4 a $\frac{1}{6}$ b $\frac{5}{6}$ c $\frac{5}{2}$ d 36
  e $\frac{1}{1} = \frac{2}{2} = \frac{3}{3} = \frac{4}{4} = \frac{5}{5} = \frac{6}{6}$, $\frac{2}{1} = \frac{4}{2} = \frac{6}{3}$,
  $\frac{3}{1} = \frac{6}{2}$, $\frac{4}{1}$, $\frac{5}{1}$, $\frac{6}{1}$

EXERCISE 4I

1 a $\frac{3}{4}$ b $\frac{6}{10} = \frac{3}{5}$ c $\frac{5}{6}$ d $\frac{6}{7}$ e $1\frac{5}{9}$ f $1\frac{2}{5}$
  g $4\frac{1}{3}$ h $3\frac{1}{2}$ i $2\frac{3}{10}$

2 a $\frac{1}{2}$ b $1\frac{3}{10}$ c $\frac{3}{4}$ d $\frac{3}{5}$ e $1\frac{1}{12}$ f $1\frac{1}{30}$
  g $1\frac{1}{6}$ h $1\frac{11}{24}$ i $\frac{11}{12}$ j $1\frac{7}{18}$ k $\frac{9}{14}$ l $\frac{38}{45}$

3 a $1\frac{1}{12}$ b $1\frac{1}{20}$ c $1\frac{13}{18}$ d $2\frac{7}{24}$

4 a 6 b 4 c $4\frac{1}{6}$ d $1\frac{19}{20}$ e $2\frac{3}{8}$ f $3\frac{3}{8}$
  g $2\frac{1}{3}$ h $3\frac{1}{3}$ i $4\frac{1}{12}$ j $3\frac{5}{6}$ k $3\frac{1}{12}$ l $4\frac{1}{10}$

EXERCISE 4J

1 a $\frac{1}{2}$ b $\frac{1}{3}$ c $\frac{1}{4}$ d $\frac{1}{6}$ e $\frac{2}{13}$ f $\frac{3}{10}$
  g $4\frac{1}{2}$ h $1\frac{2}{5}$ i $2\frac{3}{10}$ j $3\frac{1}{7}$ k $\frac{4}{7}$ l $\frac{4}{7}$

2 a $\frac{1}{12}$ b $\frac{1}{2}$ c $\frac{11}{20}$ d $\frac{1}{5}$ e $\frac{3}{8}$ f $\frac{1}{3}$
  g $\frac{1}{2}$ h $\frac{7}{15}$ i $\frac{1}{8}$ j $\frac{2}{15}$ k $\frac{1}{6}$ l $\frac{1}{2}$

3 a $1\frac{1}{10}$ b $\frac{7}{24}$ c $\frac{7}{12}$ d $\frac{17}{24}$

4 a 1 b $1\frac{1}{3}$ c $1\frac{1}{6}$ d $1\frac{1}{5}$ e $2\frac{3}{8}$ f $1\frac{2}{3}$
  g $1\frac{7}{10}$ h $1\frac{5}{12}$ i $2\frac{1}{6}$ j $3\frac{3}{5}$ k $1\frac{9}{10}$
  l $\frac{5}{12}$ m $1\frac{13}{14}$ n $1\frac{5}{9}$ o $2\frac{3}{10}$ p $3\frac{7}{8}$

EXERCISE 4K

1 a $\square = 10$ b $\square = 18$ c $\square = 21$

2 a $1\frac{4}{5}$ b $3\frac{3}{7}$ c $3\frac{1}{8}$ d $6\frac{3}{4}$ e $1\frac{1}{2}$ f $2\frac{5}{8}$
  g $2\frac{2}{3}$ h $3\frac{1}{3}$ i $4\frac{1}{2}$ j $2\frac{4}{5}$ k $1\frac{5}{6}$ l $3\frac{1}{5}$
  m $2\frac{1}{7}$ n $2\frac{2}{9}$ o $7\frac{1}{5}$ p $3\frac{1}{3}$

3 a $\frac{2}{15}$ b $\frac{3}{14}$ c $\frac{18}{35}$ d $\frac{25}{64}$ e $\frac{10}{21}$ f $\frac{1}{10}$
  g $\frac{27}{28}$ h $\frac{16}{45}$ i $\frac{21}{44}$ j $\frac{7}{15}$ k $\frac{1}{8}$ l 1
  m $\frac{1}{4}$ n 1 o $\frac{1}{27}$ p $3\frac{3}{8}$

4 a $\frac{8}{15}$ b $\frac{3}{10}$ c $\frac{5}{12}$ d $\frac{4}{9}$ e $\frac{8}{21}$ f $2\frac{2}{7}$
  g $1\frac{1}{3}$ h $1\frac{1}{7}$ i 6 j 6 k $\frac{3}{4}$ l 2

5 a 8 b 6 c 3 d 6 e 6 f 6 g 48
  h 12 i 21 j $\frac{9}{16}$ k $1\frac{1}{2}$ l $\frac{35}{4} = 8\frac{3}{4}$

6 a 750 m b 16 hours c 60 years
  d 50 minutes e 700 mL f 150 kg

7 a 40 b 45 c 105 d 875

EXERCISE 4L

1 $\frac{1}{7}$ **2** $\frac{1}{4}$ **3** $\frac{1}{6}$ of a tank **4** a $\frac{8}{21}$ b $\frac{4}{21}$

5 754 hours **6** $\frac{6}{35}$ **7** a $\frac{1}{4}$ b $\frac{3}{10}$ c $\frac{3}{20}$

8 69 litres **9** 195 blocks **10** 17 out of 20

11 a $\frac{1}{12}$ b 7200 cases **12** 50 kg

13 a twelfths b twenty fourths

REVIEW SET 4A

1 a $\frac{3}{5}$ b $\frac{5}{12}$ c $1\frac{8}{9}$ or $\frac{17}{9}$

2 2, $2\frac{1}{8}$, $2\frac{1}{4}$, $2\frac{3}{8}$, $2\frac{1}{2}$, $2\frac{5}{8}$, $2\frac{3}{4}$, $2\frac{7}{8}$, 3

3 a 24 b 30 **4** a F b F c T d T

5 a $6\frac{3}{10}$ b $2\frac{7}{12}$ c $1\frac{2}{3}$

6 a $21 b 625 kg **7** a $\frac{3}{7}$ b $\frac{7}{20}$

8 a 682 spectators b 355 students c 50

9 $\frac{4}{9}$

REVIEW SET 4B

1 a 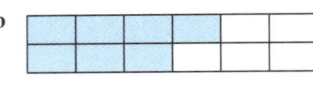 b

2 a $2\frac{1}{6}$ b $1\frac{7}{9}$ **3** a $4\frac{7}{8}$ b $\frac{1}{5}$ c $\frac{4}{5}$

4 $\frac{3}{4} = \frac{15}{20}$, $\frac{13}{20}$, $\frac{2}{5} = \frac{8}{20}$

5 a 28 b $\square = 15$, $\triangle = 36$

6 a T b F c F

7 a $1\frac{5}{18}$ b $5\frac{9}{10}$ c $3\frac{1}{5}$

8 a $\frac{1}{9}$ b 600 sheep c 360 students

9 $6\frac{1}{6}$ hours (6 h 10 min)

EXERCISE 5A.1

1 a $7.25 b $24.50 c $61.10 d $205.05
  e $12.70 f $120.65

2 a $4.47 b $15.97 c $7.55 d $36.00
  e $150.00 f $32.80 g $85.05 h $30.03

3 a i $0.35 ii $0.05 iii $4.05 iv $30.00
     v $4.87 vi $2.95 vii $38.75 viii $6384.75
  b $0.40, $34.05, $7.82, $6423.50
  c $48.02, $6417.75

EXERCISE 5A.2

1 a 3.243 b 2.071 c 1.056 d 4.009

2 a $32.43, $20.71, $10.56, $40.09 b $103.79

EXERCISE 5A.3

1 a 0.7 b 0.2 c 0.33 d 0.46

2 a i 837 ii 0.837 b i 318 ii 0.318

EXERCISE 5B

1 a zero point six, six tenths
  b zero point four five, forty five hundredths
  c zero point nine zero eight,
     nine hundred and eight thousandths

ANSWERS

    d eight point three, eight and three tenths
    e six point zero eight, six and eight hundredths
    f nine six point zero two,
       ninety six and two hundredths
    g five point eight six four,
       five and eight hundred and sixty four thousandths
    h three four point zero zero three,
       thirty four and three thousandths
    i seven point five eight one, seven and
       five hundred and eighty one thousandths
    j six zero point two six four, sixty and two
       hundred and sixty four thousandths

2 a 17.465 **b** 2.983 **c** 32.752
   d 12.096 **e** 3.694 **f** 4.22 **g** 40.6598

3 Final written numeral is
   a 0.8 **b** 0.003 **c** 70.8 **d** 9000.002
   e 209.04 **f** 8000.402 **g** 5020.3
   h 60.89 **i** 980.034 **j** 36.42

4 a $5+\frac{4}{10}$ **b** $10+4+\frac{9}{10}$ **c** $2+\frac{3}{100}$
   d $30+2+\frac{8}{10}+\frac{6}{100}$ **e** $2+\frac{2}{10}+\frac{6}{100}+\frac{4}{1000}$
   f $1+\frac{3}{10}+\frac{8}{1000}$ **g** $3+\frac{2}{1000}$
   h $\frac{9}{10}+\frac{5}{100}+\frac{2}{1000}$ **i** $4+\frac{2}{100}+\frac{4}{1000}$
   j $2+\frac{9}{10}+\frac{7}{100}+\frac{3}{1000}$ **k** $20+\frac{8}{10}+\frac{1}{100}+\frac{6}{1000}$
   l $7+\frac{7}{10}+\frac{7}{100}+\frac{7}{1000}$ **m** $9+\frac{8}{1000}$
   n $100+50+4+\frac{4}{10}+\frac{5}{100}+\frac{1}{1000}$
   o $800+8+\frac{8}{10}+\frac{8}{1000}$ **p** $\frac{6}{100}+\frac{4}{1000}$

5 a i 1.6558 or one point six five five eight
    ii $1+\frac{6}{10}+\frac{5}{100}+\frac{5}{1000}+\frac{8}{10000}$
  b i 1.6459 or one point six four five nine
    ii $1+\frac{6}{10}+\frac{4}{100}+\frac{5}{1000}+\frac{9}{10000}$
  c i 1.7332 or one point seven three three two
    ii $1+\frac{7}{10}+\frac{3}{100}+\frac{3}{1000}+\frac{2}{10000}$
  d i 1.5884 or one point five eight eight four
    ii $1+\frac{5}{10}+\frac{8}{100}+\frac{8}{1000}+\frac{4}{10000}$

6 a i 6.6233 or six point six two three three
   ii for example
  b i d **ii** c **iii** b **iv** d
  c d, b, a, c

7 a 0.6 **b** 0.19 **c** 0.43 **d** 0.809 **e** 0.052
   f 0.052 **g** 0.568 **h** 0.0023 **i** 0.094
   j 0.101 **k** 4.387 **l** 0.0308

8 a 300 **b** $\frac{3}{10}$ **c** 30 **d** $\frac{3}{1000}$ **e** 3 **f** $\frac{3}{100}$
   g $\frac{3}{10000}$ **h** 3000

9 a $\frac{5}{1000}$ **b** 500 **c** $\frac{5}{10}$ **d** $\frac{5}{100}$ **e** 5000
   f 5 **g** 50 000 **h** $\frac{5}{10000}$

10 a $\frac{2}{100}$ **b** 2 **c** $\frac{2}{100}$ **d** 20 **e** $\frac{2}{10000}$
    f 200 **g** $\frac{2}{10}$ **h** $\frac{2}{1000}$

EXERCISE 5C

1 a 2.4 **b** 3.6 **c** 4.9 **d** 6.4 **e** 4.3
2 a 4.24 **b** 2.73 **c** 5.63 **d** 4.38 **e** 6.52
3 a 0.5 **b** 0.49 **4 a** 3.8 **b** 3.79
5 a 0.2 **b** 0.18 **c** 0.184 **d** 0.1838
6 a 3.9 **b** 4 **c** 6.1 **d** 0.462 **e** 2.95
   f 0.1756
7 a 4.3 **b** 9.13 **c** 11.2 **d** 0.0 **e** 0.73
   f 0.025 **g** 0.5 **h** 6.17 **i** 2.429

EXERCISE 5D

1 a Salary between $38 700 and $39 900
  b Salary between $43 200 and $44 500
  c Salary between $95 500 and $98 900
2 a $56.3K - $61.8K **b** $32.5K - $34.9K
  c $23.2K - $24.4K **d** $70.8K - $73.2K
  e $158.7K - $165.7K **f** $327.9K - $348.4K
3 a 3.18 m **b** 91.73 m **c** 23.46 m
  d 1.49 m **e** 30.08 m **f** 9.48 m
4 a 21 650 000 **b** 1 930 000 **c** 16 030 000
  d 212 450 000 **e** 970 000
5 a 3.87 bn **b** 2.71 bn **c** 97.06 bn
  d 2.02 bn **e** 4209.47 bn **f** 549.00 bn
6 a 3 860 000 000 **b** 375 090 000 000
  c 21 950 000 000 **d** 4 130 000 000

EXERCISE 5E

1 a $1\frac{3}{4}$ **b** $3\frac{1}{4}$ **c** $52\frac{2}{5}$ **d** $4\frac{7}{25}$ **e** $\frac{87}{100}$
   f $5\frac{9}{10}$ **g** $243\frac{2}{25}$ **h** $9\frac{29}{50}$ **i** $\frac{649}{1000}$
   j $31\frac{13}{100}$ **k** $1\frac{1}{20}$ **l** $\frac{42}{125}$ **m** $\frac{7}{100}$
   n $37\frac{11}{20}$ **o** $1000\frac{1}{10}$ **p** $\frac{7}{250}$

2 a 0.8 **b** 0.17 **c** 14.7 **d** 2.38 **e** 6.06
   f 2.9 **g** 4.003 **h** 3.65 **i** 7.344 **j** 0.029
   k 27.56 **l** 3.056 **m** 384.6 **n** 56.875
   o 21.56

3 a $\frac{3}{5}$ **b** $\frac{59}{100}$ **c** $3\frac{4}{5}$ **d** $5\frac{1}{25}$ **e** $37\frac{23}{50}$ **f** $\frac{3}{50}$
   g $9\frac{29}{50}$ **h** $4\frac{827}{1000}$ **i** $8\frac{61}{100}$ **j** $14\frac{1}{50}$ **k** $\frac{3}{500}$
   l $3\frac{3}{1000}$ **m** $7\frac{3}{5}$ **n** $84\frac{879}{1000}$ **o** $947\frac{749}{1000}$

4 a 38.72 m **b** 89.09 m **c** 644.86 m
   d 20.05 m **e** 9876.54 m **f** 4000.04 m
   g 0.32 m **h** 0.07 m **i** 9.45 m **j** 0.01 m

5 a 6.858 m **b** 3.94 m **c** 0.825 m
   d 0.056 m **e** 9.009 m

6 a 4.975 km **b** 5.685 kg **c** 309.5 cm
   d 9.742 g **e** 47.85 kL **f** 2.348 tonnes
   g 6.34 km **h** $754.00 **i** 974.3 km
   j 89.56 tonnes **k** 37.58 kL **l** 0.342 g

m 0.368 km **n** 0.795 kg **o** 0.987 L

7 a 4750 m **b** 12 560 L **c** 38.6 mm
d 13 860 kg **e** 9847 mm **f** 2080 g
g 6950 mL **h** 24 860 000 mg **i** 894 000 cm

EXERCISE 5F

1 a 6.7 **b** 47.8 **c** 3.77 **d** 1.953 **e** 0.042
f 0.404

2 a $0.7 < 0.8$ **b** $0.06 > 0.05$ **c** $0.2 > 0.19$
d $4.01 < 4.1$ **e** $0.81 > 0.803$ **f** $2.5 = 2.50$
g $0.304 < 0.34$ **h** $0.03 < 0.2$
i $6.05 < 60.50$ **j** $0.29 = 0.290$
k $5.01 < 5.016$ **l** $1.15 > 1.035$
m $21.021 < 21.210$ **n** $8.09 = 8.090$
o $0.904 < 0.94$

3 a 0.4, 0.6, 0.8 **b** 0.1, 0.4, 0.9
c 0.06, 0.09, 0.14 **d** 0.46, 0.5, 0.51
e 1.06, 1.59, 1.61 **f** 0.206, 2.06, 2.6
g 0.0905, 0.095, 0.905 **h** 15.05, 15.5, 15.55

4 a 0.9, 0.8, 0.4, 0.3 **b** 0.51, 0.5, 0.49, 0.47
c 0.61, 0.609, 0.6, 0.596
d 0.42, 0.24, 0.04, 0.02
e 6.277, 6.271, 6.27, 6.027
f 0.311, 0.31, 0.301, 0.031
g 8.880, 8.088, 8.080, 8.008
h 7.61, 7.061, 7.06, 7.01

5 a 0.4, 0.5, 0.6 **b** 0.6, 0.5, 0.4
c 0.8, 1.0, 1.2 **d** 0.11, 0.13, 0.15
e 0.55, 0.5, 0.45 **f** 2.05, 2.01, 1.97
g 4.8, 4.0, 3.2 **h** 3.789, 3.9, 4.011

EXERCISE 5G

1 a 0.9 **b** 3.3 **c** 1.13 **d** 1.13 **e** 27.82
f 18.43 **g** 5.2 **h** 0.444 **i** 10.92
j 32.955 **k** 0.7006 **l** 4.748

2 a 0.8 **b** 1.5 **c** 0.4 **d** 1.4 **e** 2.3
f 2.26 **g** 2.67 **h** 0.01 **i** 9.02 **j** 5.593
k 0.001 **l** 0.001

3 a i 39.012 **ii** 2.134 **iii** 3.076 **iv** 8
b i 1.101 **ii** 0.099 **iii** 11.754
iv 22.694

4 a 64.892 **b** 27.493 **c** 12.214 **d** 21.2919
e 408.488 **f** 209.7442

5 a 5.981 **b** 1.011 **c** 4.481 **d** 167.348
e 58.626 **f** 3.1004 **g** 18.867 **h** 7.782
i 4.258 **j** $5.30 **k** $5.97 **l** $4.60

6 a 55.1183 **b** 42.266 **c** 1.197 **d** $118.10

7 a 15.867 **b** 2.731 **c** 0.681 **d** $6.85

8 $17.10 **9** 0.37 m **10** 69.4 kg **11** 337.4 m

12 No, he has only $59.05 and needs another $3.45.

13 27.95 kg **14** 3.38 kg **15** 13.079 m **16** $8.10

EXERCISE 5H.1

1

	Number	×10	×100
a	0.0943	0.943	9.43
b	4.0837	40.837	408.37
c	0.0008	0.008	0.08
d	24.6801	246.801	2468.01
e	$57.85	$578.50	$5785
	×1000	×10^4	×10^6
a	94.3	943	94 300
b	4083.7	40 837	4 083 700
c	0.8	8	800
d	24 680.1	246 801	24 680 100
e	$57 850	$578 500	$57 850 000

2 a 430 **b** 8000 **c** 5 000 000 **d** 6 **e** 46
f 58 **g** 309 **h** 250 **i** 80 **j** 324 **k** 900
l 845 **m** 240 **n** 208.5 **o** 8940 **p** 53
q 0.094 **r** 71 800

EXERCISE 5H.2

1

	a	b	c	d
Num.	647.352	93 082.6	42 870	10.94
÷10	64.7352	9308.26	4287	1.094
÷100	6.473 52	930.826	428.7	0.1094
÷1000	0.647 352	93.0826	42.87	0.010 94
÷10^5	0.006 473 52	0.930 826	0.4287	0.000 109 4

2 a 0.23 **b** 0.036 **c** 0.426 **d** 0.3 **e** 5.8
f 0.58 **g** 39.4 **h** 0.07 **i** 0.458 **j** 0.8007
k 0.024 05 **l** 0.0632 **m** 5.79 **n** 0.579
o 0.0579 **p** 0.003 **q** 0.0003 **r** 0.000 046

3 a 10 **b** 100 **c** 100 **d** 1000 **e** 10
f 10 000 **g** 100 **h** 1000

4 a 100 **b** 1000 **c** 10 000 **d** 100 **e** 10
f 10 **g** 10 **h** 1 000 000 **i** 10

EXERCISE 5I

1 a 7.2 **b** 26.0 **c** 13.5 **d** 5.6 **e** 0.36
f 0.24 **g** 0.006 **h** 0.000 16 **i** 0.035
j 0.144 **k** 1.32 **l** 0.4545 **m** 0.09
n 0.36 **o** 6.4 **p** 840 **q** 0.0081 **r** 0.024

2 a 95.2 **b** 9.52 **c** 0.952 **d** 0.952 **e** 0.952
f 0.0952 **g** 0.0952 **h** 0.000 952 **i** 0.952

3 a 1339.5 **b** 133.95 **c** 13.395 **d** 1.3395
e 13.395 **f** 1.3395 **g** 0.133 95
h 0.001 339 5 **i** 133.95

4 a 2.4 **b** 0.88 **c** 2.5 **d** 0.27 **e** 2.7
f 15.2 **g** 0.72 **h** 0.0063 **i** 0.0016
j 0.08 **k** 0.04 **l** 0.0009 **m** 0.072
n 1.21 **o** 0.01

5 a 12.27 m **b** 123 cm **c** 30.225 km **d** 219 mm

6 a $39.51 **b** $36.96 **c** 90 L

ANSWERS 423

7 $3.30 **8** 44.8 kg **9** $29 **10** $15.30
11 $6 \times 3.9 = 23.4$,
so Fred needs to find another 1.6 m.
12 a 912 kg **b** 576 kg **c** 1488 kg
  d 3 vans **e** $2762.10

EXERCISE 5J

1 a 0.8 **b** 1.5 **c** 0.42 **d** 0.51 **e** 3.02
  f 0.41 **g** 0.08 **h** 20.4
2 a $8.50 **b** 2.15 kg **c** 0.7 m **d** 12 bags
  e $16.08
3 a 2.65 **b** 1.22 **c** 0.85 **d** 0.425 **e** 3.25
  f 1.475 **g** 1.205 **h** 1.264
4 a $1.0\overline{3}$ **b** $1.1\overline{6}$ **c** $0.4\overline{5}$ **d** $0.8\overline{23}$ **e** $2.71\overline{6}$
  f $1.5\overline{1}$ **g** $0.3\overline{714285}$ **h** $0.87\overline{857142}$

EXERCISE 5K

1 a 0.7 **b** 0.5 **c** 0.4 **d** 0.3 **e** 0.8
  f 0.25 **g** 0.16 **h** 0.75 **i** 0.125 **j** 0.625
  k 0.35 **l** 0.24 **m** 0.65 **n** 0.44 **o** 4.25
  p 2.2 **q** 5.6 **r** 2.45 **s** 1.28 **t** 3.875
2 a 0.6 **b** 1.8 **c** 0.375 **d** 1.125 **e** 2.75
  f 5.8 **g** 4.875 **h** 5.375
3 a $0.\overline{3}$ **b** $0.\overline{6}$ **c** $0.1\overline{6}$ **d** $0.\overline{142857}$
  e $0.\overline{285714}$ **f** $0.08\overline{3}$ **g** $0.\overline{2}$ **h** $0.8\overline{3}$
  i $0.\overline{27}$ **j** $0.58\overline{3}$
4 $0.\overline{1}, 0.\overline{2}, 0.\overline{3}, 0.\overline{4}, 0.\overline{5}, 0.\overline{6}, 0.\overline{7}, 0.\overline{8}, 0.\overline{9} = 1$
5 a 0.71875 **b** 0.6875 **c** 0.2125 **d** 0.44
  e 1.1875 **f** $\doteqdot 0.2\overline{142857}$ **g** $0.1\overline{3}$
  h $0.\overline{81}$ **i** $2.2\overline{3}$ **j** 1.94 **k** $0.\overline{461538}$
  l 0.30625 **m** $3.41\overline{6}$ **n** $0.\overline{25203}$ **o** $0.5\overline{1}$
6 $\frac{1}{2}=0.5$ $\frac{1}{4}=0.25$ $\frac{3}{4}=0.75$ $\frac{1}{5}=0.2$
  $\frac{2}{5}=0.4$ $\frac{3}{5}=0.6$ $\frac{4}{5}=0.8$ $\frac{1}{8}=0.125$
  $\frac{3}{8}=0.375$ $\frac{5}{8}=0.625$ $\frac{7}{8}=0.875$
  $\frac{1}{20}=0.05$ $\frac{1}{40}=0.025$ $\frac{1}{25}=0.04$
  $\frac{1}{3}=0.\overline{3}$ $\frac{2}{3}=0.\overline{6}$ $\frac{1}{6}=0.1\overline{6}$ $\frac{5}{6}=0.8\overline{3}$
  $\frac{1}{9}=0.\overline{1}$ $\frac{1}{11}=0.\overline{09}$ $\frac{1}{99}=0.\overline{01}$

EXERCISE 5L

1 a $\frac{1}{10}$ **b** $\frac{7}{10}$ **c** $1\frac{1}{2}$ **d** $2\frac{1}{5}$ **e** $3\frac{9}{10}$
  f $4\frac{3}{5}$ **g** $\frac{19}{100}$ **h** $1\frac{1}{4}$ **i** $\frac{9}{50}$ **j** $\frac{13}{20}$ **k** $\frac{1}{20}$
  l $\frac{7}{100}$ **m** $2\frac{3}{4}$ **n** $1\frac{1}{40}$ **o** $\frac{1}{25}$ **p** $2\frac{3}{8}$
2 a $\frac{4}{5}$ **b** $\frac{22}{25}$ **c** $\frac{111}{125}$ **d** $3\frac{1}{2}$ **e** $\frac{49}{100}$ **f** $\frac{1}{4}$
  g $5\frac{3}{50}$ **h** $3\frac{8}{25}$ **i** $\frac{17}{200}$ **j** $3\frac{18}{25}$ **k** $1\frac{12}{125}$
  l $4\frac{14}{25}$ **m** $\frac{8}{125}$ **n** $\frac{5}{8}$ **o** $\frac{1}{3}$ **p** $\frac{2}{3}$

EXERCISE 5M

1 a $\frac{5}{17}, \frac{3}{10}, \frac{7}{22}, \frac{1}{3}, \frac{7}{20}$ **b** $\frac{3}{8}, \frac{5}{12}, \frac{7}{16}, \frac{5}{9}, \frac{4}{7}$

  c $\frac{10}{13}, \frac{9}{11}, \frac{7}{8}, \frac{8}{9}, \frac{11}{12}$ **d** $\frac{12}{23}, \frac{10}{19}, \frac{8}{15}, \frac{6}{11}, \frac{11}{20}$
2 a $\frac{2}{3}, \frac{15}{23}, \frac{11}{17}, \frac{7}{11}, \frac{5}{8}$ **b** $\frac{5}{13}, \frac{8}{21}, \frac{4}{11}, \frac{6}{17}, \frac{3}{8}$
  c $\frac{9}{25}, \frac{7}{20}, \frac{8}{23}, \frac{1}{3}, \frac{5}{16}$ **d** $\frac{20}{23}, \frac{17}{20}, \frac{16}{19}, \frac{14}{17}, \frac{3}{4}$
3 $\doteqdot 1.05$ cm **4** 1.425 m **5** $281 **6** 3.165 m
7 a 17 **b** 0.28 m **8** 150 **9** $18.55

REVIEW SET 5A

1 a 1.8 **b** 0.54
2 a 9.44 **b** 0.25 **c** $2 + \frac{4}{100} + \frac{9}{1000}$ **d** $\frac{2}{1000}$
  e 0.536 m
3 a 272.6 **b** 2.726 **c** 27.26
4 a 62 **b** 215.8 **c** 0.56 **d** 0.042
5 a $29.8 K **b** 3.5 bn
6 a 6.16 **b** 0.96 **c** 0.015 **d** 14.8 m **e** $20.60
7 0.026, 0.062, 0.206, 0.216, 0.621
8 a 1937.88 t **b** 645.96 t **9** 28.2 km

REVIEW SET 5B

1 a 1.493 **b** 2.058 **c** 3.551
2 a 35 276 cents **b** 8940 L **c** 876.3 cm
  d 15 092.4 kg **e** 36.475 m **f** 0.375 L
3 a 8.709 **b** 1.625 **c** $\frac{6}{1000}$ **d** $0.\overline{7}$
4 a $11 500 **b** $12 500 **5 a** 13.78 **b** 0.1378
6 0.444, 4.04, 4.044, 4.404, 4.44
7 a 1.899 **b** 2.574 **c** 8.884
8 a 57.05 seconds **b** 57.21 seconds
9 a 14.07 km **b** 28.13 km

REVIEW SET 5C

1 a $579.06 **b** 74.08 m **c** 0.426 L
  d 45.831 kg **e** 0.75 t **f** 0.978 m
2 a $16.95 **b** $302.35 **c** $319.30
3 a 0.5 **b** $35.7 K **c** 8.1 m
4 a $10 + 8 + \frac{3}{10} + \frac{4}{100} + \frac{6}{1000}$ **b** $\frac{3}{100}$
  c 0.375 **d** $\frac{9}{20}$
5 a 28.754 **b** 147.05 **c** 5.04 **d** 12
6 1.5, 1.9, 2.3
7 a $109.90 **b** $1177.05 **c** 2000 **d** $28.35

EXERCISE 6A

1 a $\frac{60}{100}$ **b** $\frac{46}{100}$ **c** $\frac{40}{100}$
2 a $M = \frac{11}{100}$ **b** $C = \frac{17}{100}$ **c** $L = \frac{10}{100}$
  d $X = \frac{35}{100}$ **e** $V = \frac{27}{100}$
3 a $\frac{50}{100}$ **b** $\frac{20}{100}$ **c** $\frac{25}{100}$ **d** $\frac{10}{100}$ **e** $\frac{20}{100}$
  f $\frac{9}{100}$ **g** $\frac{25}{100}$ **h** $\frac{50}{100}$ **i** $\frac{74}{100}$

EXERCISE 6B

1 a 14%   b 38%   c 67%   d 95%
2 a 50%   b 86%   c 25%   d 90%
   e 15%   f 40%   g 55%
3 a 19%   b 3%   c 37%   d 54%
   e 79%   f 50%   g 100% h 85%
   i 6.6% j 34.5% k 7.5% l 35.6%
4 a 70%   b 10%   c 90%   d 50%
   e 25%   f 75%   g 40%   h 80%
   i 35%   j 55%   k 28%   l 76%
   m 46%   n 94%   o 100%
5 a Fourteen percent means fourteen out of every hundred.
   b If 53% of the students in a school are girls, 53% means the fraction $\frac{53}{100}$.

6

	Number	Fraction	Denom. of 100	%
a	5	$\frac{5}{20}$	$\frac{25}{100}$	25%
b	9	$\frac{9}{20}$	$\frac{45}{100}$	45%
c	8	$\frac{8}{20}$	$\frac{40}{100}$	40%
d	3	$\frac{3}{20}$	$\frac{15}{100}$	15%
e	2	$\frac{2}{20}$	$\frac{10}{100}$	10%
f	10	$\frac{10}{20}$	$\frac{50}{100}$	50%
g	20	$\frac{20}{20}$	$\frac{100}{100}$	100%

7 52%   8 60%
9 a i 24%   ii 52%   iii 24%   iv 32%
   b i 28%   ii 36%   iii 36%
   c i 50%   ii ≑ 23% iii 25%   iv 50%

EXERCISE 6C

1 a $\frac{43}{100}$ b $\frac{37}{100}$ c $\frac{1}{2}$ d $\frac{7}{10}$ e $\frac{9}{10}$ f $\frac{1}{5}$
   g $\frac{2}{5}$ h $\frac{1}{4}$ i $\frac{3}{4}$ j $\frac{19}{20}$ k 1 l $\frac{3}{100}$
   m $\frac{1}{20}$ n $\frac{11}{25}$ o 2 p $\frac{7}{2}$
2 a $\frac{1}{8}$ b $\frac{3}{40}$ c $\frac{1}{200}$ d $\frac{173}{1000}$ e $\frac{39}{40}$
   f $\frac{1}{500}$ g $\frac{1}{2000}$ h $\frac{1}{5000}$

EXERCISE 6D

1 a 37%   b 89%   c 15%   d 49%
   e 73%   f 5%   g 102% h 117%
2 a 20%   b 70%   c 90%   d 40%
   e 7.4% f 73.9% g 0.67% h 0.18%

EXERCISE 6E

1 a 0.5   b 0.3   c 0.25 d 0.6   e 0.85
   f 0.05 g 0.45 h 0.42 i 0.15 j 1
   k 0.67 l 1.25
2 a 0.075 b 0.183 c 0.172 d 1.067
   e 0.0015 f 0.0863 g 0.375 h 0.065
   i 0.005 j 0.015 k 0.0075 l 0.0425
3 a 10%   b 80%   c 40%   d 60%   e 40%
   f 50%   g 15%   h 25%   i 95%   j 6%
   k 78%   l 68%   m $37\frac{1}{2}$%   n 100%
   o 11%   p 37.5% q $33\frac{1}{3}$%   r $66\frac{2}{3}$%
4 a $\frac{1}{4}$ is 25%, $\frac{1}{8}$ is $12\frac{1}{2}$%, $\frac{1}{16}$ is $6\frac{1}{4}$%
   b $\frac{2}{5}$ is 40%, $\frac{3}{5}$ is 60%, $\frac{4}{5}$ is 80%, $\frac{5}{5}$ is 100%
   c $\frac{2}{3}$ is $66\frac{2}{3}$%, $\frac{3}{3}$ is 100%
   d $\frac{1}{4}$ is 25%, $\frac{1}{2}$ is 50%, $\frac{3}{4}$ is 75%, $\frac{4}{4}$ is 100%

5

	%	Fraction	Decimal
a	20%	$\frac{1}{5}$	0.2
b	40%	$\frac{2}{5}$	0.4
c	50%	$\frac{1}{2}$	0.5
d	75%	$\frac{3}{4}$	0.75
e	85%	$\frac{17}{20}$	0.85
f	8%	$\frac{2}{25}$	0.08
g	35%	$\frac{7}{20}$	0.35
h	12.5%	$\frac{1}{8}$	0.125
i	62.5%	$\frac{5}{8}$	0.625
j	100%	1	1.00
k	15%	$\frac{3}{20}$	0.15
l	37.5%	$\frac{3}{8}$	0.375

EXERCISE 6F

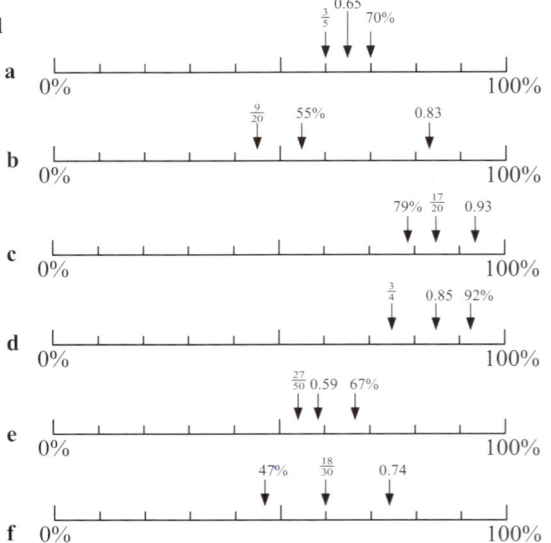

ANSWERS 425

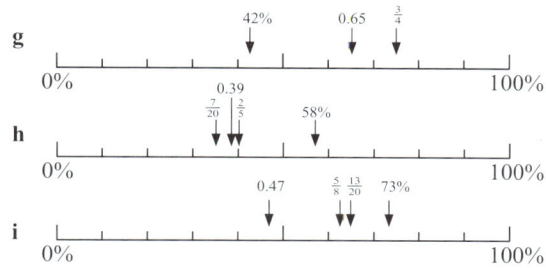

2. a $\frac{28}{100} = 0.28 = 28\%$, $\frac{45}{100} = 0.45 = 45\%$,
      $\frac{68}{100} = 0.68 = 68\%$
   b $\frac{58}{100} = 0.58 = 58\%$, $\frac{74}{100} = 0.74 = 74\%$,
      $\frac{89}{100} = 0.89 = 89\%$
   c $\frac{22}{100} = 0.22 = 22\%$, $\frac{37}{100} = 0.37 = 37\%$,
      $\frac{55}{100} = 0.55 = 55\%$

EXERCISE 6G

1.

	Figure	Frac.	% shaded	% unshad.
a		$\frac{1}{2}$	50%	50%
b		$\frac{3}{4}$	75%	25%
c		$\frac{1}{4}$	25%	75%
d		$\frac{1}{6}$	$16\frac{2}{3}\%$	$83\frac{1}{3}\%$
e		$\frac{1}{4}$	25%	75%
f		$\frac{7}{10}$	70%	30%

2. a 35 squares   b $\frac{13}{20}$
3. a 18%   b 14%   c 28%   d 32%
4. a $\frac{1}{4}$ b $\frac{1}{2}$ c $\frac{1}{10}$ d $\frac{7}{20}$ e $\frac{3}{5}$ f 1
5. a i 20%   ii 20%   b $\frac{2}{5}$

EXERCISE 6H

1. a 20%   b 25%   c 75%   d $33\frac{1}{3}\%$ e 30%
   f 25%   g 20%   h 12.5%   i 5%   j 4.8%
   k 18%   l 6.25%   m 50%   n 40%
   o 60%   p 2%   q 0.25%   r 12.5%

2. a 52%   b 90%   c 85.4%   d 32.5%
   e 68.5%   f 76%
3. a 70%   b 85%   c 40%   d 5%   e 17.5%
   f 22%   g 42%   h $66\frac{2}{3}\%$ i 174%

EXERCISE 6I

1. a 72 ha   b 1050 m²   c 45 cm   d 160 t
   e 18 min   f 640 cm   g 600 kg   h 480 mm
   i 108 min   j 187 500 L
2. 388 students   3 360 kg   4 1215 tonnes
5. 2 h 51 min   6 1.584 m   7 8.925 kL
8. a 40% of a litre   b $\frac{1}{4}$ of a metre
   c 8% of $100   d 5% of a kilolitre
   e $\frac{1}{3}$ of 1000   f 315 g

EXERCISE 6J

1. a $4.70   b $54   c $14.70   d $2.20
   e $40.50   f $4365   g $597.60   h $1.62
   i $3.88   j $354   k $259   l $1350
   m $700   n $2.72   o $5450
2. a 25%   b 10%   c 15%   d 25%
   e 20%   f 5%   g 5%   h 25%
   i $33\frac{1}{3}\%$ j $66\frac{2}{3}\%$ k 1%   l 10%

EXERCISE 6L

1. a Jessie (76%), Jill (75%), Jan (72%),
      Jenny ($62\frac{1}{2}\%$)
   b Jeff (70%), Joel (68%), Jake ($66\frac{2}{3}\%$),
      Juan ($62\frac{1}{2}\%$)
2. a Kim   b 2%
3. a Tom (60%), Toni (55%), Tao (52%), Tina (50%)
   b $33.80   c $57.20
4. a 25%   b $11\frac{1}{9}\%$ 5 a 70%   b 30%
6. Sarah $360, Jack $540, Peter $300
7. 202.5 g   8 3200 mL   9 1680 ha
10. a i 30%   ii 70%   b i 20%   ii $\frac{1}{5}$
    c i 40%   ii $\frac{3}{5}$ d i 70%   ii 9
    e i 65%   ii $\frac{13}{20}$ f 80%

EXERCISE 6M

1. a $272   b $345   c $127.40   d $2288
2. a $5.60   b $27   c $128.80   d $49.28
   e $16.15   f $455   g $91.84   h $340
   i $32.90   j $376   k $47.10   l $37.19

EXERCISE 6N

1. a $2   b $80   c $5.60
2. a $10   b $1   c $1.60   d $32
3. a $110   b $52.80   c $2200   d $704
4. a $16   b $176   5 a $25   b $275

EXERCISE 6O

1 a $150 b $700 c $1600 d $3600
   e $14 000
2 a $2800 b $8450 c $12 320 d $20 000

REVIEW SET 6A

1 a 75% b $\frac{33}{50}$ c 12.5% d 0.82
2 a 16% b 40% c $66\frac{2}{3}$%
3 $\frac{3}{4}$ = 75%, 0.78 = 78%, 72%

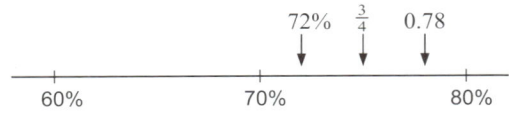

4 $226.80 5 30 students 6 70 households
7 $3 8 a 75 students b 275 students
9 25% 10 81 kg 11 a $840 b $4340
12 a $420 b $1680

REVIEW SET 6B

1 a 47% b $\frac{2}{5}$ c $66\frac{2}{3}$% d 0.125
2 $\frac{2}{5}$ = 40%, 0.75 = 75%, 56%

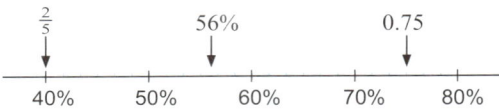

3 a 52% b 29% c 10% 4 76%
5 32.5% 6 $3 7 a $126 b $714
8 $189 9 a $2800 b $9800
10 a 2 or 3 students b 90 students
11 30% 12 a $27 b $297

REVIEW SET 6C

1 a $\frac{28}{100}$ b $33\frac{1}{3}$% c 45% d 10%
   e $180 f 2800 m 2 80%
3 $\frac{1}{8}$ = 12.5%, 52%, 0.8 = 80%

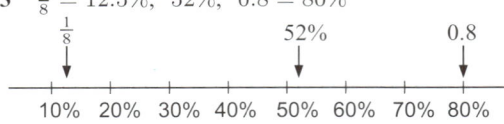

4 a $12 b 47% 5 a $12\frac{1}{2}$% b 4%
6 $3360 7 $30 8 a $94 b $1034
9 $655.50 10 $576

EXERCISE 7A

1 a kilograms b kilometres c metres
   d milligrams e metres f kilograms
   g centimetres h tonnes

EXERCISE 7B

1 a 24 cm b 13 cm c 10.2 cm d 16.8 cm
   e 25.6 cm f 18.5 cm

2 a 35°C b 37.4°C c 38.3°C d 35.7°C
3 a $\frac{3}{4}$ full b $\frac{1}{4}$ full c $\frac{9}{16}$ full
4 a 120 km/h b 95 km/h c 65 km/h
5 a 45.05 kg b 71.6 kg c 63.63 kg
6 a 50 381 kWh b 16 443 kWh
7 a 700 g b 250 g c 850 g
8 a 700 mL b 350 mL c 650 mL

EXERCISE 7C

1 a 400 b 3400 c 250 d 1560 e 245 f 46
2 a 3000 b 45 000 c 3600 d 16 200
   e 5460 f 90
3 a 50 b 230 c 27 d 125 e 57.8 f 2.5
4 a 2 b 30 c 0.35 d 9.505 e 284.92
   f 0.004
5 a 2 b 40 c 45 d 4.56 e 750 f 0.03
6 a 3000 b 75 000 c 6500 d 2 000 000
   e 78 200 f 200
7 a 2 b 35 c 0.2345 d 34.567 e 3.9
   f 0.0024
8 a 9.2 b 6.43 c 47.53 d 5
   e 9.743 f 13.5 g 6200 h 13 500
9 a 72 000 b 1380 c 630 d 13.4
   e 8.5 f 132.8 g 520 000 h 43 000
10 a 7000 b 34 c 780 d 460
11 a 4.562 b 17.458 c 6.53 d 0.164
12 a 49 mm b 63 mm c 132 mm
    d 81.5 mm e 151 mm f 235.5 mm
    g 116 mm h 205 mm i 102 mm
    j 101 mm k 146 mm l 230 mm
13 a 3110.32 b 72 043.486 c 155.218
    d 15 348.727 e 23.808 f 23 079.906
14 a 37 mm, 40 mm b 750 cm, 780 cm, 800 cm
    c 1.25 km, 1.3 km d 4.85 m, 5 m, 5.2 m
    e 3.47 m, 3.5 m, 3.6 m
    f 128 m, 130 m, 134 m
    g 4.82 m, 4.9 m, 5.12 m
    h 71.5 m, 71.8 m, 72 m

EXERCISE 7D

1 a 11.5 cm b 10.0 cm c 11.9 cm
2 a 59 cm b 41 m c 12.6 km
3 a 48 cm b 28.6 cm c 26.6 km
4 a 60 cm b 72 cm c 38 km d 96 cm
   e 42 cm f 60 cm g 72 cm h 56.2 cm
   i 40 cm
5 a 10.3 cm b 10.1 cm c 12.2 cm
   d 11.5 cm e 15.5 cm f 12.4 cm
6 a 760 m b 7.05 km c $4350
7 a 106.5 mm b 27 cm c 19 m d 117 cm

ANSWERS

e 112 cm

8 a 14 cm **b** 18 m   **9** 15 cm

EXERCISE 7E

1 **a** actual object **b** drawing **c** actual object
    d actual object **e** actual object
2 **a** 1 : 100 **b** 1 : 125 **c** 200 : 1
3 **a** 2.5 m **b** 100 m **c** 500 m **d** 250 km
4 **a** **i** 200 m **ii** 290 m **iii** 120 m **iv** 630 m
    b **i** 10 cm **ii** 35 mm **iii** 4 mm **iv** 2.16 cm
5 **a** **i** 6 m **ii** 9 m **iii** 16.4 m **iv** 1.6 m
    b **i** 1 m **ii** 9 cm **iii** 2.8 cm **iv** 6.1 cm
6 **a** 4.5 m **b** 1.5 m **c** 4.7 m
7 **a** 12 m **b** 5 m **c** 2 m by 4 m
    d 2.4 m by 2.4 m and 3.6 m by 2.4 m
8 **a** 5.3 m **b** 2.3 m
9 **a** 30 mm, ∴ scale is 6 : 1
    b **i** 2.5 mm **ii** 2.2 mm **iii** 1.5 mm **iv** 1 mm
10 **a** 1 : 2
    b **i** 6 mm **ii** 7.6 cm **iii** 1.1 cm
11 **a** 5 km **b** 40 cm
    c **i** 21 km **ii** 9.5 km **iii** 10.5 km
12 **a** 1 : 1000 **b** use a compass

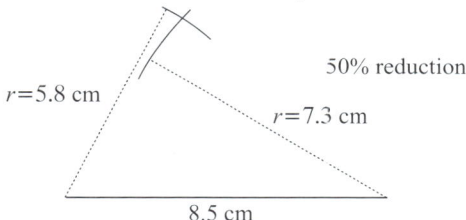

13

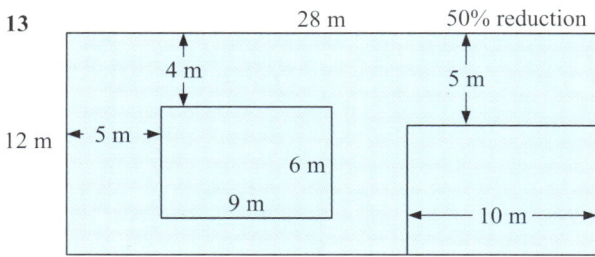

14

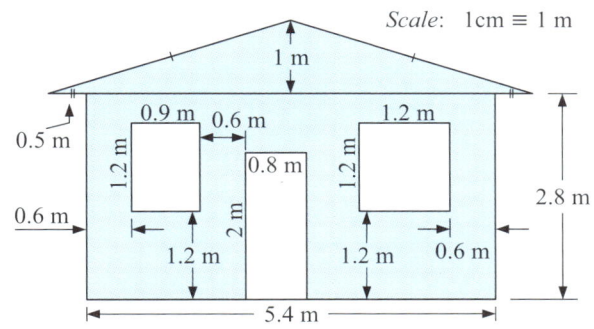

15 a 3.75 m by 3.0 m **b** 6.25 m by 1 m
    c   **d** 20 m² **e** $950

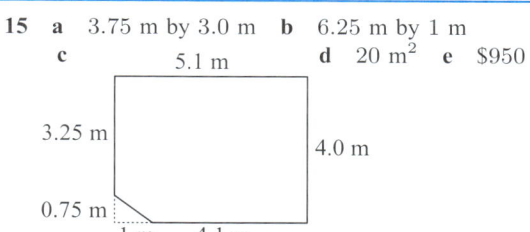

EXERCISE 7F

1 **a** kg **b** tonnes **c** mg **d** g **e** g **f** kg
    g mg **h** tonnes **i** g **j** kg **k** kg **l** g
    m g **n** tonnes **o** tonnes **p** g **q** g **r** kg
    s mg **t** kg
2 **a** C **b** None of these devices is suitable.
    c A **d** B **e** B **f** D **g** A **h** D
    i B **j** B **k** D **l** B **m** A **n** D
    o D **p** A **q** B **r** C **s** A **t** D
3 **a** 2000 **b** 34 000 **c** 350 000 **d** 4500 **e** 300
4 **a** 4000 **b** 25 000 **c** 3600 **d** 294 000 **e** 400
5 **a** 6000 **b** 34 000 **c** 2500 **d** 256 000 **e** 600
6 **a** 3 **b** 2.5 **c** 45 **d** 0.0675 **e** 0.0095
7 **a** 4 **b** 95 **c** 4.534 **d** 0.0456 **e** 0.0008
8 **a** 8000 **b** 3200 **c** 14 200 **d** 0.38
    e 4.25 **f** 75.42 **g** 6 800 000 **h** 560 000
9 **a** 13.87 **b** 3400 **c** 0.786 **d** 0.003 496
10 **a** 24 kg **b** 200 nails **c** 33 tonnes

EXERCISE 7G

1 **a** Ali is quite young and quite strongly opposed to Australia accepting refugees.
    b Ben is a little younger than average and strongly in favour of Australia accepting refugees.
    c Dean is quite old and quite strongly in favour of Australia accepting refugees.
    d Erica is somewhat older than average and she is neutral regarding Australia accepting refugees.
    e Rewi is very old and strongly opposed to Australia accepting refugees.
2 **a** Ravi is very concerned about the Greenhouse Effect but hardly ever uses public transport.
    b Sally is neutral, neither particularly concerned nor unconcerned, about the Greenhouse Effect. She uses public transport somewhat more than average.
    c Tom is very concerned about the Greenhouse Effect and almost always uses public transport.
    d Sam is not concerned about the Greenhouse Effect and uses public transport an average amount.
    e Jill is concerned somewhat less than average about the Greenhouse Effect and uses public transport less than average.

428 ANSWERS

  f Peter is concerned to an average degree by the Greenhouse Effect and uses public transport an average amount.

EXERCISE 7H

1 a 3900 m   b $9360   2 a 180 m   b $1665
3 7.65 m   4 a 420 m   b $5670   5 9.9 kg
6 a 756 kg   b more, as half a tonne is 500 kg
7 a 88 m   b i 44 sleepers   ii 1760 kg
8 a 3600 bricks   b 9 t
9 a 87.5 m, $393.75   b $210   c $630.75
10 228 L   11 a i 3960 kg   ii 3.96 t   b 4 trips
12 40 kg
13 a 16 posts, 32 m   b 60 m
     c 150 pickets, 180 m   d $618
14 4 hours   15 a 7.92 m   b $35.64
16 a 164 cm   b 214 cm   c 260 cm

REVIEW SET 7A

1 a 3560 mm   b 3.2 kg   c 0.45 km   d 83 t
   e 7630 mm   f 6.3 m
2 a 46 cm   b 19 m
3 a 110 km/h   b $\frac{7}{8}$ full   c 600 mL
4 a i 19 km   ii 32 km   iii 61 km
   b i 10 cm   ii 4.4 cm   iii 26 cm
5 7.9 km   6 a 270 kg   b 30 truckloads

REVIEW SET 7B

1 a 3.48 kg   b 8.623 m   c 4600 mg
   d 540 cm   e 13 200 kg   f 13 300 m
2 a 51.1 cm   b 35.6 km   3 28 105 kWh
4 225 kg   5 a 650 g   b 90 km/h   c 750 mL
6 124 m   7 a i 120 km   ii 17.5 km
               b i 4.8 cm   ii 3.92 cm

REVIEW SET 7C

1 a 3.245 m   b 6.4 m   c 4500 g
2 a 43 km   b 56 cm
3 a $\frac{1}{8}$ full   b 75 km/h   c 3.2 kg   d 3.5 L
4 2000 bricks   5 37 152 kWh
6 a i 20 m   ii 19 m   iii 7.5 m
   b i 3 cm   ii 1.72 cm   iii 12.8 cm
7 a 1000 m   b 3000 m   c $5250

EXERCISE 8A

1 a B   b A
2 a 1 △   b 4 △s   c 2 △s   d 8 △s
   e 22 △s   f 24 △s
3 a 10 units^2 b 20 units^2 c 40 units^2
   d 28 units^2 e 20 units^2 f 28 units^2

4 a m^2 b cm^2 c ha   d cm^2 e mm^2
   f km^2 g mm^2 or cm^2 h m^2 i cm^2
   j ha   k km^2 l m^2 m mm^2 n mm^2
5 a yes
   b i 16 units   ii 20 units   iii 18 units
      iv 26 units   v 34 units   vi 24 units
      vii 26 units   viii 22 units
   c For different shapes of the same area, the perimeter varies.
6 a i 132   ii 302   b 18 m^2 c $988.20
7 a i 540   ii 280   b 16.4 m^2 c $506.76
   d i 164 m   ii 82 m   e d i is double d ii
8 a 4.52 cm^2 b 75 000 cm^2 c 58 000 cm^2
   d 0.3579 m^2 e 630 ha   f 36 500 000 mm^2
   g 0.55 m^2 h 520 mm^2 i 0.68 ha
   j 44 cm^2 k 6000 m^2 l 2 km^2
   m 70 mm^2 n 4.8 km^2 o 2500 mm^2
   p 8000 cm^2 q 88 cm^2 r 0.66 m^2
   s 50 ha   t 5.5 km^2 u 0.001 m^2

EXERCISE 8B

1 a 720 cm^2 b 504 mm^2 c 48 km^2
2 a 225 m^2 b 70.56 cm^2 c 4 ha
3 a 200 cm^2 b 64 cm^2 c 28 m^2 d 92 m^2
   e 198 m^2 f 400 cm^2
4 65 m^2 5 a 27 ha   b $4860
6 a 280 tiles   b $980
7 a 12 m by 1 m, 26 m; 6 m by 2 m, 16 m;
      4 m by 3 m, 14 m
   b 18 cm by 1 cm, 38 cm;
      9 cm by 2 cm, 22 cm;
      6 cm by 3 cm, 18 cm
   c 36 km by 1 km, 74 km;
      18 km by 2 km, 40 km;
      12 km by 3 km, 30 km;
      9 km by 4 km, 26 km;
      6 km by 6 km, 24 km
   d 48 mm by 1 mm, 98 mm;
      24 mm by 2 mm, 52 mm;
      16 mm by 3 mm, 38 mm;
      12 mm by 4 mm, 32 mm;
      8 mm by 6 mm, 28 mm
   e 64 u by 1 u, 130 u; 32 u by 2 u, 68 u;
      16 u by 4 u, 40 u;   8 u by 8 u, 32 u
   f 144 mm × 1 mm, 290 mm;
      72 mm × 2 mm, 148 mm;
      48 mm × 3 mm, 102 mm;
      36 mm × 4 mm, 80 mm;
      24 mm × 6 mm, 60 mm;
      18 mm × 8 mm, 52 mm;
      16 mm × 9 mm, 50 mm;
      12 mm × 12 mm, 48 mm

ANSWERS

8 a

A = 5 m², 1 m, 5 m

A = 8 m², 2 m, 4 m

A = 9 m², 3 m, 3 m

b 9 m², 16 m², 21 m², 24 m², 25 m²

c 17 km², 32 km², 45 km², 56 km², 65 km², 72 km², 77 km², 80 km², 81 km²

EXERCISE 8C

1 a 42 m² **b** 20 cm² **c** 38.5 cm²
 d 37.1 m² **e** 6 m² **f** 12.48 m²

2 a 78 cm² **b** 89 m² **c** 11 m²

3 a 48 ha **b** $7200

4 a 24 m² **b** $333.60

5 a 2625 cm² **b** 240 cm²

EXERCISE 8E

1 a 0.008 cm³ **b** 60 000 cm³ **c** 11 800 mm³
 d 640 mm³ **e** 3 000 000 000 mm³
 f 7 500 000 mm³

2 a 0.5 cm³ **b** 7 cm³ **c** 5 m³ **d** 0.45 m³
 e 0.002 m³ **f** 5.4 m³

3 a 63 units³ **b** 64 units³ **c** 96 units³
 d 51 units³ **e** 40 units³ **f** 61 units³

4 a 60 cm³ **b** 420 m³ **c** 110 cm³

5 a 50 m³ **b** 48.44 cm³ **c** 315.4 m³
 d 1332 cm³ **e** 73.44 m³ **f** 108.63 m³

6 a 36 cm³ **b** 140 m³ **c** 80.64 cm³
 d 192.975 m³

7 a 36 × 1 × 1   **b** 48 × 1 × 1   **c** 162 × 1 × 1
   18 × 2 × 1   24 × 2 × 1   81 × 2 × 1
   12 × 3 × 1   16 × 3 × 1   54 × 3 × 1
   9 × 4 × 1   12 × 4 × 1   27 × 6 × 1
   6 × 6 × 1   8 × 6 × 1   18 × 9 × 1
   9 × 2 × 2   12 × 2 × 2   27 × 3 × 2
   6 × 3 × 2   8 × 3 × 2   9 × 9 × 2
   4 × 3 × 3   6 × 4 × 2   18 × 3 × 3
                   4 × 4 × 3   9 × 6 × 3

8 a 30 × 1 × 1   **b** 100 × 1 × 1   **c** 144 × 1 × 1   24 × 3 × 2
   15 × 2 × 1   50 × 2 × 1   72 × 2 × 1   18 × 4 × 2
   10 × 3 × 1   25 × 4 × 1   48 × 3 × 1   12 × 6 × 2
   6 × 5 × 1   20 × 5 × 1   36 × 4 × 1   9 × 8 × 2
   5 × 3 × 2   10 × 10 × 1   24 × 6 × 1   16 × 3 × 3
                   25 × 2 × 2   18 × 8 × 1   12 × 4 × 3
                   10 × 5 × 2   16 × 9 × 1   8 × 6 × 3
                   5 × 5 × 4   12 × 12 × 1   9 × 4 × 4
                                      36 × 2 × 2   6 × 6 × 4

9 Your prisms should have dimensions
 a 24 × 1 × 1   **b** 40 × 1 × 1   **c** 64 × 1 × 1
   12 × 2 × 1   20 × 2 × 1   32 × 2 × 1
   8 × 3 × 1   10 × 4 × 1   16 × 4 × 1
   6 × 4 × 1   8 × 5 × 1   8 × 8 × 1
   6 × 2 × 2   10 × 2 × 2   16 × 2 × 2
   4 × 3 × 2   5 × 4 × 2   8 × 4 × 2
                                    4 × 4 × 4

10 **b, c, a, d** **11** ≑ 1100 cm³

EXERCISE 8F

1 a mL **b** mL or L **c** kL **d** L **e** mL
 f mL **g** kL **h** mL **i** kL **j** mL
 k ML **l** ML **m** ML **n** kL **o** ML
 p ML **q** mL **r** mL

2 a 5600 L **b** 3.54 L **c** 0.76 ML
 d 7.2 L **e** 6.3 m³ **f** 12 400 000 mL
 g 62.5 mL **h** 400 mL **i** 3500 kL

3 a 210 mL **b** 600 mL **c** 216 mL

4 72 L **5** $66\frac{2}{3}$ ∴ 66 times

6 510 fuel tanks **7** 210 kL

EXERCISE 8G

1 a 66 m² **b** $825

2 a 4400 m² **b** 88 truck loads

3 7.875 m² **4 a** 11 m² **b** 300 rolls

5 a 100 m **b** 10 m **c** 40 m **d** 5 m
 e 12.5 m **f** 8 m **g** 20 m **h** 800 m

6 1350 cm³ or 1.35 L **7** 18 m²

8 30 000 bottles **9** 180 000 m³

10 a 630 L **b** $78\frac{3}{4}$ buckets

11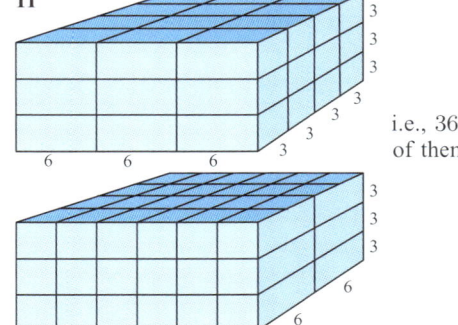

i.e., 36 of them.

or

12 a 13 slats b 1.716 m^2
13 a 40 slats b $151.58

REVIEW SET 8A

1 a 35 600 m^2 b 0.357 m^2 c 7200 mm^3
2 a 24.8 m^2 b 57 m^2
3 a 120 units^3 b 54 m^3 c 199.52 cm^3
4 a 0.38 L b 5.4 m^3 c 7.528 L
5 a 47 m^2 b 6.27 L ∴ 7L needed
6 a 9 b 5400 cm^2 (or 0.54 m^2)
7 a 100 stamps b $22.50   **8** 67.5 kL

REVIEW SET 8B

1 a 0.34 ha b 320 mm^2 c 7 200 000 mm^2
2 a 92 m^2 b 329 m^2
3 a 45 kL b 8.9 cm^3 c 4600 L
4 a 36 units^3 b 0.36 m^3 c 100 m^3
5 1000 containers   **6** 4 prisms   **7** 1731 kL
8 $42.75   **9** 37 m^2

EXERCISE 9A

1 a-f All of these samples are unrepresentative as they are not randomly selected. The sample groups named may be likely to share a particular view on the subject under consideration. For example, farmers may be more likely than the population as a whole to believe that the government should give drought assistance to farmers.

2 a Pick a page at random from the Electoral Roll and then pick a name at random. Repeat until 400 names have been obtained.
 b Remove a bottle every 2 or 3 minutes from the assembly line.
 c Use the school's enrolment list numbers. Place the numbers in a hat and randomly select 30 of them.
 d Use a dictionary. Randomly select a page and then randomly select a word on it. Repeat this process.

3 a Mix the tickets in a hat and take out one before identifying it.
 b Place A on one side of a coin and B on the other. Flip the coin.
 c Use a die. Roll it.
 d Shuffle a pack of cards, select one at random before identifying it.

4 a 10 000 b 300 c 12% d 1200
5 a 750 b 50 c 34% d 255

EXERCISE 9B.1

1 a 50 b 22 c 74%
2 a 12 b 28 c violin
3 a

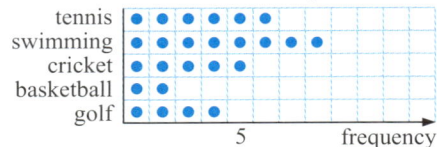

 b swimming

4 a

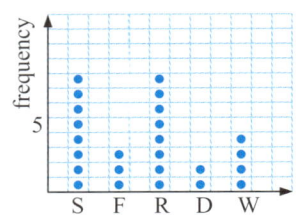

 b Side shows and ring events are both modes.

EXERCISE 9B.2

1 a

Eye Colour	Tally	Frequency
Brown	|||| ||||		11
Blue	|||| ||	7
Green	||||		6
Grey	||||	4
	Total	28

 b brown

2 a

Grade	Tally	Frequency
A	|||	3
B	||||	5
C	|||| |||| ||||		16
D	|||	3
E			1
	Total	28

 b i 16   ii $\frac{5}{28}$ c C

3 a

Grade	Tally	Frequency
excellent	||||	4
good	|||| ||||		11
satisfactory	|||| ||	7
unsatisfactory	|||	3
	Total	25

 b good
 c To see if improvement in service is needed.

ANSWERS

EXERCISE 9D.1

1 a

frequency bar chart: brown 11, blue 7, green 6, grey 4 (eye colour)

b brown **c** 25%

2 a Mitsubishi 20, Ford 28, Holden 35, Toyota 25, Other 12
b Holden **c** 23%

3 a 1993, 1994, 1995, 1998
b The business broke even. **c** $7 million profit

4 a shop A, June; shop B, January;
b shop A, $6000; shop B, $5000
c Increase in length of bars from February to June for shop A
d Shop A, $28 000; shop B, $27 000

EXERCISE 9D.2

1 a garden **b** cleaning
c i 156 kL **ii** 20 kL

2 a size 14 **b** 70

3 a The ways (and percentages) in which 'City Council' spends its money.
b Saves reader having to do the calculations.
c i 8% **ii** 4% **d i** $26 m **ii** $69 m
e Water and Sewerage **f** $1095 m

EXERCISE 9E.1

1
```
6 | 3 4 6 7
7 | 0 1 2 2 2 5 8
8 | 0 1 4 4 6 6 7 7 9 9
9 | 0 1 3           unit = 1
```

2
```
1 | 3 7 8 9
2 | 0 0 3 5 7 7 8 9 9
3 | 0 0 0 2 3 4 6 7 7 8 8 9
4 | 3 4 7
5 | 0 1           unit = 1
```

3
```
0 | 7 9
1 | 2 3 8
2 | 4 4 5 7 8
3 | 0 2 6
4 | 1
        unit = 1
```

4
```
0 | 2 5 7 8 9
1 | 0 2 3 8
2 | 4 4 7
3 | 0 6
        unit = 0.1
```

EXERCISE 9E.2

1 a

No. of children	Tally	Frequency
0	||||	4
1	||||	4
2										9
3	||||	4
4	|||| |	6
5	||	2
6	|	1
	Total	30

b i 9 **ii** $\frac{2}{15}$

2 a

Ages of children	Tally	Frequency
10	|	1
11	||||	4
12	|||| |	6
13	|||	3
14	||||	4
15	|	1
16		0
17	|	1
	Total	20

b 20 **c** 9 **d** 45%

e

Ages of children at party — bar chart: 10→1, 11→4, 12→6, 13→3, 14→4, 15→1, 16→0, 17→1

3 a 7 points **b** 10 **c** ≑ 18.3%

4 a

No. of goals	Tally	Frequency
17	||	2
18	|	1
19	||||	4
20						5
21	|||	3
22	|||	3
23	|||	3
24	|	1
25		0
26	|	1
	Total	23

b Netball goals

(frequency bar chart: 17→2, 18→1, 19→4, 20→5, 21→3, 22→3, 23→3, 24→1, 25→0, 26→1; x-axis: no. of goals)

c 16   **d** ≑ 34.8%

5 a

No. of goals	Tally	Frequency
0	III	3
1	IIII	4
2	HH I	6
3	HH I	6
4	II	2
5	I	1
	Total	22

b i 6   **ii** 9

6 a

No. of goals	Tally	Frequency
5	III	3
6	II	2
7	HH I	6
8	IIII	4
9		0
10	III	3
11	II	2
12	I	1
	Total	21

b i 4   **ii** 10

7 a

No. of matches	Tally	Frequency
48	HH I	6
49	HH III	8
50	HH HH I	11
51	HH II	7
52	HH I	6
53	II	2
	Total	40

b 11   **c** 26   **d** $\frac{7}{20}$ **e** no

EXERCISE 9F.1

1 4   **2** 4   **3** 34.75

4 a X, 6.5; Y, ≑ 7.64   **b** false   **c** Y

5 a 37.4   **b** 25.4

6 a Sally, 26.4; Jan, 23.5; Jane, 25.3; Peta, 31.3; Lee, 25.9; Polly, 28.4; Sam, 32.8
  b Sam

EXERCISE 9F.2

1 a 4   **b** $7\frac{1}{2}$ **c** 4

2 mean ≑ 3.1,   median $1\frac{1}{2}$
  The mean is the better measure.

3 a $9\frac{1}{2}$ runs   **b** 21.3 runs   **c** median   **4** size $8\frac{1}{2}$

5 a 42   **b** 64   **c** 34

6 a
  1 | 6 7 8 9
  2 | 0 0 1 1 1 2 2 2 2 3 3 4 5 5 6 7 7 8 8 9
  3 | 0 1 3 4   unit = 1

b i 23 years   **ii** ≑ 24.1 years

7 a 7P, 20 and 11;   7Q, 20 and 10
  b 7P, mean 16.4 marks, median 16 marks
    7Q, mean ≑ 14.4 marks, median 14 marks
  c 7P

EXERCISE 9G

1 a 120 beats/min   **b** 80 beats/min
  c from 0 to 3 minutes   **d** 40 beats/min decrease
  e 140 beats/min   **f** yes

2 a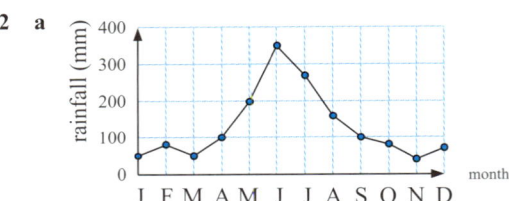

b May to August   **c** November   **d** ≑ 50%

3 a A break in the scale at that place. Scale does not start at 0.
  b February   **c** June to September
  d Temperature is getting colder from end of summer to end of winter.   **e** ≑ 21.1°C

4 a Income $9000, costs $5000   **b** $4000
  c from week 5 to week 9
  d i weeks 4 & 5   **ii** week 13

REVIEW SET 9A

1 a

Month	Tally G	Tally B	Frequency G	Frequency B	Total
1	I	I	1	1	2
2			0	0	0
3	II	I	2	1	3
4	III	I	3	1	4
5	II	II	2	2	4
6	II		2	0	2
7	III	II	3	2	5
8	I		1	0	1
9	I	III	1	3	4
10		II	0	2	2
11		I	0	1	1
12	I	I	1	1	2
	Total		16	14	30

   b **i** 30 **ii** 16 **iii** September **iv** $\frac{2}{15}$
     v February **vi** 10%
     vii February, October, November

2 **a** True **b** False **c** True

3 **a** 11 goals **b** 12 goals

4 **a** **i** 10 days **ii** 7 days
   b **i** day 17 **ii** day 28 **iii** day 17
     iv day 2 **c** 5 days

5 **a** lung cancer
   b lung cancer and chronic bronchitis/emphysema
   c **i** 4800 **ii** 5400 **iii** 1600

REVIEW SET 9B

1 **a**

No. of votes	Tally	Frequency
0						5
1						4
2						5
3							6
	Total	20

b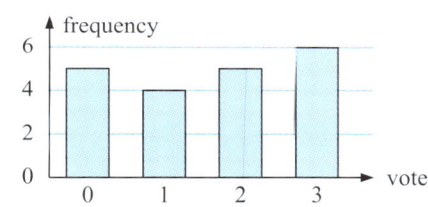

c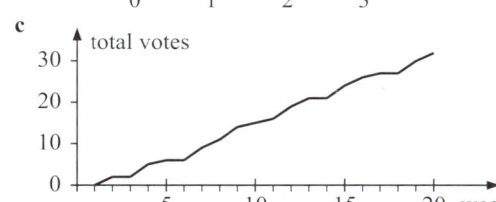

   d 5 **e** 32 **f** 75% **g** **i** 1.6 votes **ii** 2 votes

2 **a** False **b** False **c** True (in theory). Why?

3 **a** Football and netball **b** $26 000
   c **i** $100 000 **ii** $130 000

4 72   **5** **a** **i** 16 pies **ii** $\doteqdot$ 15.9 pies
            b The sales are gradually decreasing.

REVIEW SET 9C

1 **a** .... sectors .... **b** .... frequency
   c .... height of columns ....

2 **a**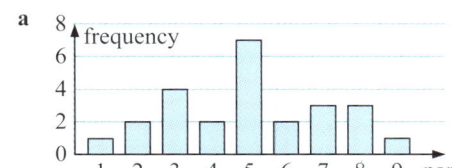

b **i** 5 pars per round **ii** 5.04 pars per round

3 **a** $177\frac{1}{2}$ cm **b** 179 cm

4 **a** **i**
```
2 | 1 3 3
3 | 1 7 7 8 9
4 | 0 2 3 3 4 5 5 6 7 8 9
5 | 0 1 1 1 2 3 4 6 8
6 | 1 3
        Unit = 1
```
   ii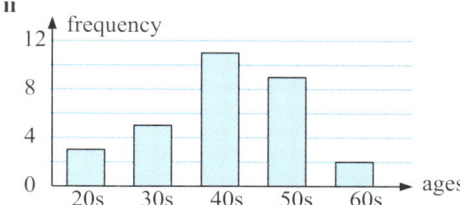

   b **i** 51 **ii** $45\frac{1}{2}$ **iii** 44.7

5 **a** **i** air conditioners
     ii hot summer, or cold winter
   b $85 000 **c** $215 000 **d** $50

6 **a** D **b** 1080
   c You can't say. You don't know how many people join for a year only.

EXERCISE 10A

1 **a** Before Christ **b** 125AD **c** 1800 years

2 **a** Elizabeth II **b** 14 years **c** 18 years

3 **a** Zhou Warlords **b** 450 years **c** 450 years

EXERCISE 10B

1 **a** 444 min **b** 4663 min **c** 18 216 min
   d 24 977 min

2 **a** 2438 sec **b** 12 927 sec **c** 51 163 sec
   d 82 331 sec

3 **a** 1440 min **b** 10 080 min **c** 525 600 min

4 **a** 86 400 sec **b** 1 209 600 sec
   c 31 536 000 sec

5 **a** 1461 days **b** 35 064 h **c** 2 103 840 min

6 **a** 8 h 30 min **b** 13 h 17 min **c** 19 h 23 min
   d 4 h 17 min **e** 4 h 49 min **f** 8 h 22 min

7 **a** 5 days 4 h **b** 23 days **c** 36 days 9 h
   d 90 days 7 h

8 **a** 47 days **b** 22 days 37 min

EXERCISE 10C

1 **a** Wei joined the club on the 17th Dec. 1999.
   b Jon arrived on the 13th March 2000.
   c Piri is departing for Malaysia on the 30th July 2004.
   d Sam will turn 21 on the 28th May 2009.

2 **a** 27 days **b** 43 days **c** 117 days
   d 111 days **e** 68 days **f** 179 days
   g 119 days **h** 99 days

3 a 45 days b $6.20
4 a 195 days b $3510 c Yes, $1939
5 19th October 1996
6 a 7:00 am b 1:00 am c 6:49 am
    d 8:06 pm e 10:32 pm f 4:09 pm
    g 11:05 am h 6:42 am i 11:43 am
    j 10:44 pm Sunday
7 a 8 h 19 min b 3 h 19 min c 7 h 17 min
    d 12 h 52 min e 20 h 9 min f 9 h 37 min
    g 26 h 48 min h 87 h 54 min
8 3 one way trips **9** 25 **10** 1200 s = 20 min
11 171 sec **12** 0745, 1405, 2025 (Mon)
                0245, 0905, 1525, 2145 (Tue)
13 1440 times   0405 (Wed)

EXERCISE 10D

1 a 0313 h b 1117 h c 0000 h d 1247 h
    e 1741 h f 1200 h g 2019 h h 2359 h
2 a 3:00 am b 6:30 am c 6:00 pm
    d 12:00 noon e 6:15 am f 3:45 pm
    g 8:17 pm h 11:48 pm
3 a 0930 h b 1240 h c 1915 h
4 a More than 60 minutes is not possible.
    b 0713 h is correct.
    c Greater than 24 hours in a day is not possible.
5 a 10:35 am, 11:45 am, 12:50 pm, 1:50 pm,
       2:25 pm, 2:45 pm, 3:15 pm, 4:10 pm
    b 2:25 pm c 4:10 pm
    d i 11:10 pm ii 8:50 pm

EXERCISE 10E

1 a 7:21 am b 9:08 pm c 0.9 m, 3:20 am
    d 1.2 m, 1:46 pm
2 a 6 b 8:45 am c 5:00 pm
    d i 1 h 55 min ii 40 min e $9\frac{1}{2}$ h
    f any of the buses g bus B
3 a i arrival time ii departure time
    b 4:50 pm c 5:27 pm d 6:20 pm
    e i 4:11 pm ii 4:36 pm iii 5 min
    f i 45 min ii 51 min iii 44 min

There would be more trains on the track and more passengers for the 5:23 pm train (peak hour).

EXERCISE 10F

1 a 3 pm b 8 pm c 10 pm d 8 am
2 a 2:00 am Tuesday b 5:30 am Tuesday
    c 9:00 am Tuesday d 12:00 midnight Monday
3 a 5:00 pm Tuesday b 2:00 pm Tuesday
    c 8:00 am Wednesday
    d 12:00 midnight Tuesday
4 a 12:15 pm Sunday b 8:15 am Sunday

    c 10:45 pm Saturday d 8:45 pm Saturday
5 a 9:30 pm Friday b 8:00 pm Friday
    c 12:00 noon Friday d 4:00 am Friday
6 a 3:30 pm b 4:00 pm c 4:00 pm d 4:00 pm
7 a 3:50 am b 3:50 am c 2:20 am d 4:20 am
8

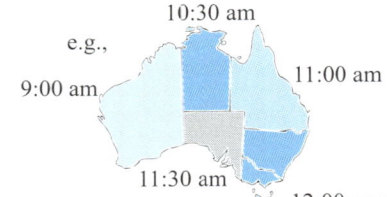

    a 12:30 pm b 2:00 pm c 2:30 pm
    d 3:30 pm e 3:30 pm
9 a 8:10 am b 6:10 am c 7:40 am d 8:10 am
10 a 8:30 am b 5:50 pm c 5:30 pm d 8:00 pm

EXERCISE 10G

1 a 90 km/h b 70 km/h c 83 km/h d 94 km/h
2 a 630 km b 450 km c 900 km d 315 km
    e 1026 km
3 a 255 km b 880 km c 441 km d 171 km
4 a 3 h b 6 h c $5\frac{1}{2}$ h d 8 h 20 min
    e 3 h 15 min

EXERCISE 10H

1 a 122°F b 176°F c 68°F
2 a 38°C b 10°C c 27°F
4 a 100°F ≑ 37.8°C, 50°F ≑ 10°C, 80°F ≑ 26.7°C
    b ≑ 32.2°C

REVIEW SET 10A

1 a hours b minutes c nanoseconds
    d years e centuries f seconds
2 a 49 days b 720 sec c 555 min
    d 1000 years
3 a i 6:45 am ii 0645 h
    b i 12:15 am ii 0015 h
    c i 9:30 pm ii 2130 h
4 a 20 h 41 min b 3 h 38 min
5 a 176 days b $2640 c $360
6 31st May
7 a i 2:00 pm Saturday ii 8:30 pm Saturday
    b i 10:00 pm Tuesday ii 1:30 am Wednesday
8 54 km **9** 3 km

REVIEW SET 10B

1 a 80 days b 730 days c 3652 days
2 53 **3** a 10th decade b 20th century
              c 2nd millennium
4 a 1001 years b 33 years c 152 years

5 a Yes (175 min) **b** No (195 min)
6 a 4:15 am **b** 1:00 pm **c** 11:35 pm
7 a 1194 min **b** 19 days 19 h
8 348 km **9** 1 h 15 min
10 a 15 min 1.07 sec, 15 min 5.42 sec
  b 3 hrs 1 min 1 sec **c** 14 h 19 min

REVIEW SET 10C

1 a 107 days **b** 61 h **c** 81 min **d** 300 sec
2 a 9th decade **b** 18th century
  c 2nd millennium
3 a 67 years **b** 151 years **c** 39 years
4 a 21/11/1963 **b** 17/10/2010
5 a fifty eight minutes after 2 o'clock in the afternoon
  b 2:58 pm **c** 1458 h
6 a 13 h 30 min **b** 6 days 1 h 3 min
  c 1 h 18 min
7 94 km/h **8** $5\frac{1}{2}$ h
9 a 8 days 3 h 19 min **b** Vostok 6
  c 97 h 35 min **d** 207 days **e** 8 yr 3 months

EXERCISE 11A

1 a i (diagram)
  ii
Unit no.	1	2	3	4	5	6	7
Matches	5	8	11	14	17	20	23

  b i (diagram)
  ii
Unit no.	1	2	3	4	5	6	7
Matches	4	9	14	19	24	29	34

  c i (diagram)
  ii
Unit no.	1	2	3	4	5	6	7
Matches	5	9	13	17	21	25	29

  d i (diagram)
  ii
Unit no.	1	2	3	4	5	6	7
Matches	3	7	11	15	19	23	27

2 a i 4, 7, 10, 13 **ii** 301
  iii (diagram)
  b i 2, 5, 8, 11 **ii** 299
  iii (diagram)
  c i 6, 10, 14, 18 **ii** 402
  iii (diagram)
  d i 1, 5, 9, 13 **ii** 397
  iii (diagram)

EXERCISE 11B

1 a 16, 19, 22; The next number is equal to the previous number plus 3.
  b 31, 35, 39; The next number is equal to the previous number plus 4.
  c 37, 44, 51; The next number is equal to the previous number plus 7.
  d 30, 36, 42; The next number is equal to the previous number plus 6.
  e 49, 58, 67; The next number is equal to the previous number plus 9.
  f 59, 72, 85; The next number is equal to the previous number plus 13.
2 a 28, 26, 24; The next number is equal to the previous number minus 2.
  b 17, 14, 11; The next number is equal to the previous number minus 3.
  c 33, 27, 21; The next number is equal to the previous number minus 6.
  d 88, 85, 82; The next number is equal to the previous number minus 3.
  e 218, 210, 202; The next number is equal to the previous number minus 8.
  f 45, 41, 37; The next number is equal to the previous number minus 4.
  g 32, 64, 128; The next number is equal to the previous number multiplied by 2.
  h 162, 486, 1458; The next number is equal to the previous number multiplied by 3.
  i 512, 2048, 8192; The next number is equal to the previous number multiplied by 4.
  j 2, 1, $\frac{1}{2}$; The next number is equal to the previous number divided by 2.
  k 5, $2\frac{1}{2}$, $1\frac{1}{4}$; The next number is equal to the previous number divided by 2.
  l 3, 1, $\frac{1}{3}$; The next number is equal to the previous number divided by 3.
  m 0.025, 0.0025, 0.000 25; The next number is equal to the previous number divided by 10.
  n 23, 30, 38; Each number is increased by one more than the previous number is increased.
  o 21, 34, 55; After the first 2 members, each number is the sum of the two previous numbers.
3 a 13, 19, 25 **b** 12, 21, 30 **c** $5\frac{1}{2}$, 7, $8\frac{1}{2}$
  d 45, 34, 23 **e** 125, 100, 75 **f** 3.3, 2.8, 2.3
  g 11, 25, 53 **h** 26, 256, 2556 **i** 49, 25, 13
  j 4, 16, 256

4 a □ = 15 **b** □ = 24 **c** □ = 45
d □ = 12 **e** □ = 15 **f** □ = 81
g □ = 8 **h** □ = 21 **i** □ = 120
j □ = 25 **k** □ = 23 **l** □ = 24

EXERCISE 11C

1 a i $M = 2 \times n + 1$, where M is the number of matchsticks and n is the unit number.

  ii △, △▽, △▽△, △▽△▽, ...

b i $M = 3 \times n + 2$, where M is the number of matchsticks and n is the unit number.

  ii ▯⌐, ▯▯⌐, ▯▯▯⌐, ▯▯▯▯⌐, ...

c i $M = 3 \times n - 1$, where M is the number of matchsticks and n is the unit number.

  ii ∟, ▯∟, ▯▯∟, ▯▯▯∟, ...

d i $M = 4 \times n + 3$, where M is the number of matchsticks and n is the unit number.

  ii △_△, △_△_△, △_△_△_△, ...

2 a i

n	1	2	3	4
M	2	4	6	8

  ii The number of matchsticks is two times the unit number.

  iii /\, /\/\, /\/\/\, /\/\/\/\, ...

b i

n	1	2	3	4
M	4	5	6	7

  ii The number of matchsticks is three more than the unit number.

  iii △_, △__, △___, △____, ...

c i

n	1	2	3	4
M	1	4	7	10

  ii The number of matchsticks is three times the unit number minus two.

  iii _, △_, △△_, △△△_, ...

d i

n	1	2	3	4
M	1	5	9	13

  ii The number of matchsticks is four times the unit number minus three.

  iii _, _△_, _△_△_, _△_△_△_, ...

EXERCISE 11D

1 a ▯▯▯▯, ▯▯▯▯▯, ▯▯▯▯▯▯, ...

b

n	1	2	3	4	5	6
M	4	6	8	10	12	14

c $M = 2 \times n + 2$ **d** 48

2 a △▽△▽, △▽△▽△, △▽△▽△▽, ...

b

n	1	2	3	4	5	6
M	3	5	7	9	11	13

c $M = 2 \times n + 1$ **d** 87

3 a ▯▯▯, ▯▯▯▯, ...

b

n	1	2	3	4	5
M	4	10	16	22	28

c $M = 6 \times n - 2$ **d** 340

4 a type 4, type 5, ...

b

t	1	2	3	4	5
M	7	12	17	22	27

c $M = 5 \times t + 2$ **d** 162

5 a type 4, type 5, ...

b

t	1	2	3	4	5
M	16	19	22	25	28

c $M = 3 \times t + 13$ **d** 70

EXERCISE 11E

1 a $60 **b** $100 **c** $140

2 a

Hrs of sunlight	0	1	2	3	4	5
Height (cm)	8	13	16	19	22	25
Hrs of sunlight	6	7	8	9	10	
Height (cm)	28	31	34	37	40	

b $H = 13 + (n-1) \times 3$ where n = hours of sunlight, H = height of bean

3 $C = 75 + 42 \times n$ where n = number of months, C = cost

a For $n = 7$, $C = \$369$
b For $n = 12$, $C = \$579$
c For $n = 18$, $C = \$831$
d For $n = 60$, $C = \$2595$

4 a 26 cumecs

b $F = 8 + 2 \times t$ where t = time in hours, F = flow in cumecs

c

Time (t hours)	0	1	2	3	4
Flow (F cumecs)	8	10	12	14	16
Time (t hours)	5	6	7	8	9
Flow (F cumecs)	18	20	22	24	26

5 a $C = 40 \times h + 30$ **b i** $950 **ii** $730

ANSWERS 437

6 a $T = 7 + (n-1) \times 7.2$ where
     n = number of km run
     T = elapsed time in minutes

Distance (n km)	1	2	3	4	5
Time (T min)	7	14.2	21.4	28.6	35.8
Distance (n km)	6	7	8	9	10
Time (T min)	43	50.2	57.4	64.6	71.8
Distance (n km)	11	12	13	14	
Time (T min)	79	86.2	93.4	100.6	

b $T = 7 + (n-1) \times 6.8$
   if $n = 14$, then $T = 95.4$
   i.e., the winner's time was 95 min and 24 sec
   which is 1 hour 35 min and 24 sec

Distance (n km)	1	2	3	4	5
Time (T min)	7	13.8	20.6	27.4	34.2
Distance (n km)	6	7	8	9	10
Time (T min)	41	47.8	54.6	61.4	68.2
Distance (n km)	11	12	13	14	
Time (T min)	75	81.8	88.6	95.4	

EXERCISE 11F

1 a i $17   ii $31   iii $37
  b The graph does not show values of n greater than 20.

2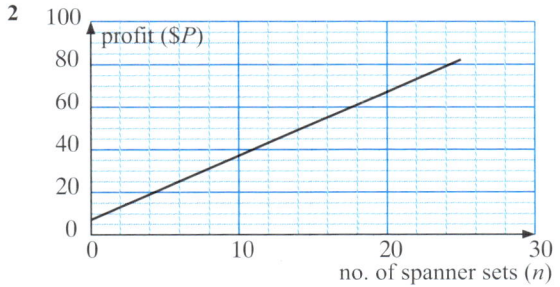
  a i $37   ii $61   iii $73   b iii $112
3 a i 8 cm   ii 14 cm   iii 32 cm
  b i 8 weeks   ii 12 weeks   iii 17 weeks

EXERCISE 11G

1 a $a = 3$ b $b = 5$ c $x = 21$ d $a = 15$
  e $b = 9$ f $x = 21$ g $a = 5$ h $b = 9$
  i $x = 20$ j $a = 25$ k $b = 24$ l $x = 7$
2 a $a = 12$ b $a = 5$ c $a = 2$ d $x = 10$
  e $x = 4$ f $x = 5$ g $y = 3$ h $y = 12$
  i $y = 0$
3 a $x = 7$ b $x = 12$ c $x = 4$ d $x = 2$
  e $x = 7$ f $x = 8$ g $x = 9$ h $x = 0$
  i $x = 3$
4 a $x = 6$ b $x = 11$ c $x = 10$ d $x = 7$
  e $x = 7$ f $x = 10$ g $x = 12$ h $x = 9$
  i $x = 13$

5 a $n - 5 = 16$ b $n - 8 = 30$ c $n + 3 = 31$
  d $n + 8 = 11$ e $7 \times n = 35$ f $2 \times n = 26$
  g $n \div 5 = 7$ h $n \div 3 = 9$ i $7 \times n - 6 = 64$
  j $8 \times n - 5 = 27$ k $3 \times n + 2 = 38$
  l $5 \times n + 12 = 72$
6 a $n - 10 = 11$, $n = 21$
  b $n + 3 = 17$, $n = 14$
  c $9 \times n = 63$, $n = 7$ d $n \div 9 = 6$, $n = 54$
  e $8 \times n - 6 = 50$, $n = 7$
  f $4 \times n + 3 = 23$, $n = 5$
  g $3 \times n + 1 = 64$, $n = 21$
  h $5 \times n - 11 = 54$, $n = 13$
7 a $465 = 45 \times x + 60$ b 9 hours
8 a $500 = 800 - 15 \times w$ b 20 weeks
9 a $21 = 3 \times d + 6$ b 5 days
10 a $320 = 360 - 4 \times x$ b 10 months

EXERCISE 11H

1 a An empty bath fills constantly for 1 minute. A person gets in and turns off the tap for 2 minutes. The water is turned on for another minute and then turned off. The person stays in the bath for another 3 minutes, gets out and lets out the water. It takes 1 minute to drain the bath.
  b An empty bath fills constantly for 2 minutes with a person in it from the start. The tap is turned off and the person soaks for 3 minutes and gets out. The bath is left for 2 minutes then the water is let out in 1 minute.

2 a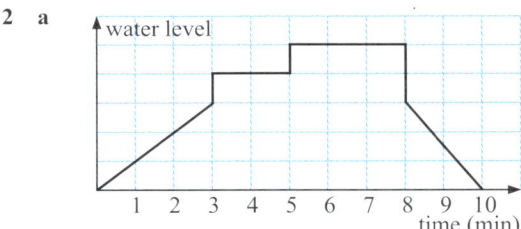

  b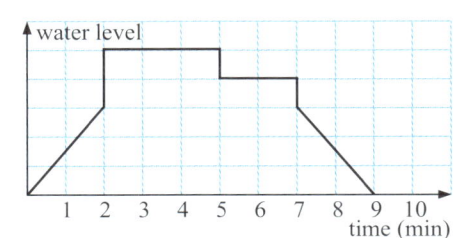

3 The graph begins at the end of spring when the lake has been filled by rain. Over summer and most of autumn the water level drops as it is used for irrigation. The lowest level is reached near the end of autumn. Then winter and spring rains fill the lake until the need for more water for irrigation occurs in early summer.

4 a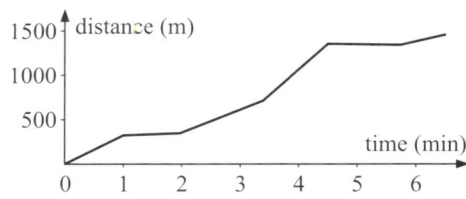

b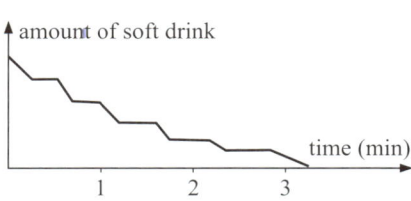

REVIEW SET 11A

1 a 29, 38, 47   **b** 160, 320, 640
  c $7\frac{1}{2}, 9\frac{1}{2}, 11\frac{1}{2}$ **d** $5, 2\frac{1}{2}, 1\frac{1}{4}$

2 a ▢▢▢▢ , ▢▢▢▢▢ , ...

  b
Unit no.	1	2	3	4	5
Matches	4	7	10	13	16

  c $M = 3 \times n + 1$ **d i** 22   **ii** 304

3
n	1	2	3	4	5	6
C	35	50	65	80	95	110

  a $C = 15 \times n + 20$ dollars   where C is the total cost and n is the number of rooms.
  b $425

4 a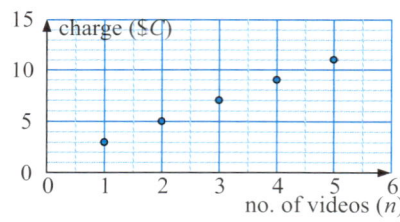

  b $C = 2 \times n + 1$ **c i** $19   **ii** $35

5 $6 \times n - 1 = 47$, $n = 8$
6 a $f = 35$ **b** $n = 42$ **c** $b = 7$

REVIEW SET 11B

1 a 91, 104, 117   **b** 64, 128, 256
  c 7.2, 9.0, 10.8   **d** 31, 25, 19

2 a
r	1	2	3	4	5
M	6	10	14	18	22

  b $M = 4 \times r + 2$
  c The number of matches is four times the number of rectangles plus two.
  d 122

3 a $58   **b** $160

4 a
n	0	1	2	3	4	5
E	400	480	560	640	720	800

  b $E = 80 \times n + 400$ **c** $1040
5 a $p = 6$ **b** $r = 32$ **c** $f = 9$
6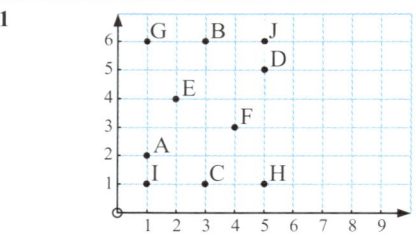

REVIEW SET 11C

1 a 11, 19, 35   **b** 59, 115, 227

2 a
n	1	2	3	4	5	6
M	6	11	16	21	26	31

  b $M = 5 \times n + 1$
  c The number of matchsticks is five times the number of units plus one.   **d** 401

3 a
n	0	1	2	3	4
C	150	190	230	270	310

  b $C = 40 \times n + 150$
  c i $230   **ii** $350   **iii** $390
4 a i $28   **ii** $52   **b** $C = 8 \times n + 4$ **c** $116
5 a $637 = 21 \times x + 532$ **b** 5 hours overtime
6 a $k = 35$ **b** $m = 3$ **c** $d = 15$

EXERCISE 12A.1

1

  a rectangle   **b** square   **c** yes

2 a B   **b** W   **c** Q   **d** P   **e** Y   **f** T
  g H   **h** A   **i** G   **j** O   **k** R   **l** U
  m S   **n** L   **o** I   **p** K   **q** E   **r** D
  s M   **t** N   **u** X   **v** C   **w** J   **x** V

3 a rectangle   **4** a parallelogram
5 C(6, 7), D(2, 7)   **6** R(4, 3), S(2, 2)
7 a i (7, 5)   **ii** (8.6, 1.7)   **iii** (6.5, 6.5)
    iv (2.3, 1.2) and (6.1, 6.2)
  b i Treasure Trove   **ii** Lion's Den
    iii Mt Ogre   **iv** Oasis
8 a i (1.5, 4)   **ii** (10.7, 0.3)   **iii** (11, 9.7)
    iv (8.4, 3.3)
  b i Kalgoorlie   **ii** Alice Springs   **iii** Mt Isa
    iv Brisbane

EXERCISE 12A.2

1 **a** A8 **b** B2 and B3 **c** G5 **d** G6 **e** B4
 f E8 **g** E6 **h** B6 and C6 **i** F7 **j** H7
2 **a** Vintage Machinery
 b Investigator Science & Technology Centre
 c Ridley Centre **d** Dairy Cattle
 e Police/Lost children **f** Horse Warm-up Area
3 **a** Main Entrance **b** Goodwood Rd Entrance

EXERCISE 12B.1

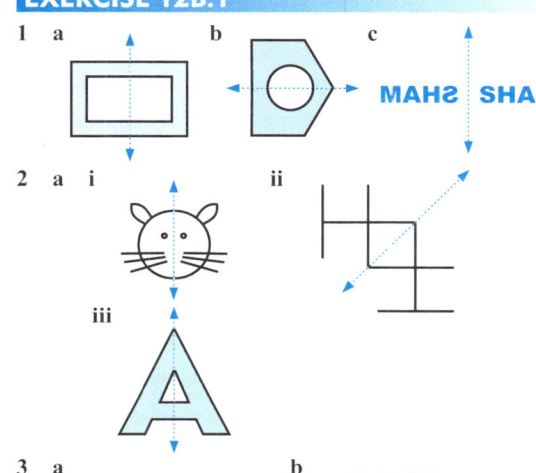

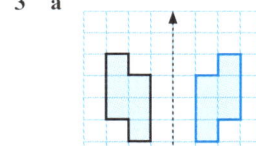

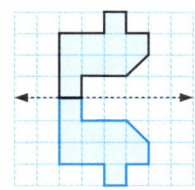

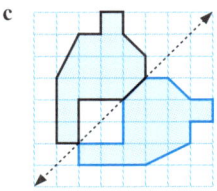

EXERCISE 12B.2

1 **a** B **b** D **c** A **d** C

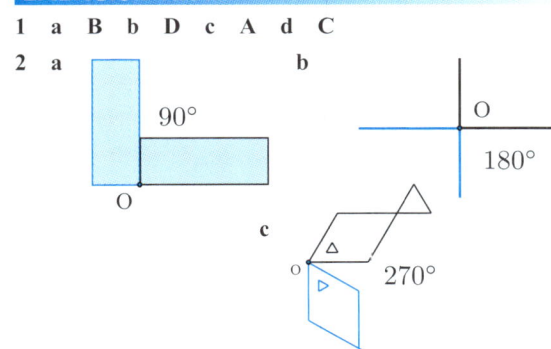

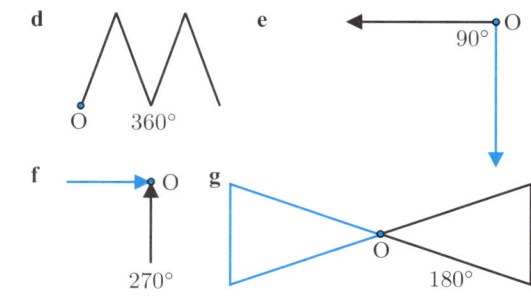

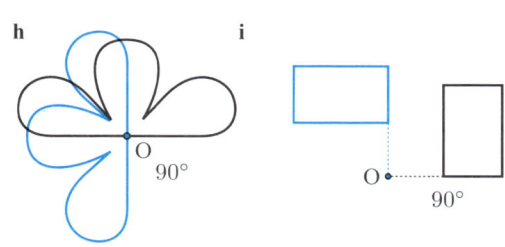

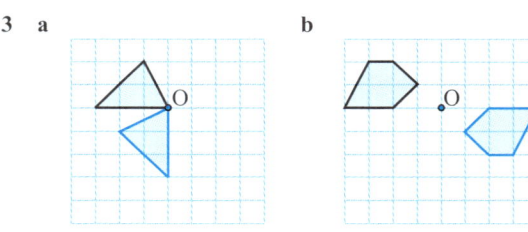

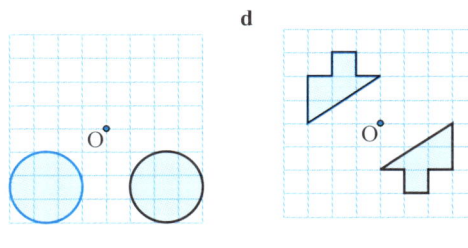

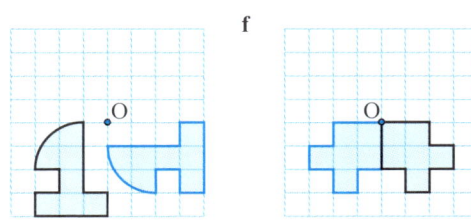

4 **a** 2 **b** 4 **c** 2 **d** 2 **e** 4 **f** 4 **g** 2
 h 6

EXERCISE 12B.3

1 **a** 7 units left, 1 unit up
 b 7 units right, 1 unit down
 c 3 units right, 4 units down
 d 3 units left, 4 units up
 e 4 units left, 3 units down
 f 4 units right, 3 units up

2 a 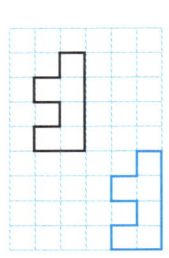 **b**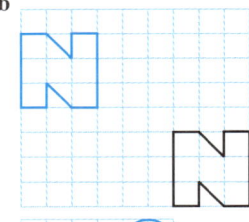

i 500 : 78 **j** 500 : 2000 **k** 300 : 1000
l 100 : 20

2 a i 2 : 3 **ii** 6 : 5 **iii** 6 : 9 : 5
  b i 7 : 5 **ii** 8 : 7 **iii** 5 : 7 : 8
  c i 2 : 3 **ii** 4 : 1 **iii** 1 : 3 : 1
  d i 18 **ii** 18 **iii** 18

3 a Tom : Tamara = 8 : 13
  b boys : girls = 3 : 1
  c blue eyes : hazel eyes = 3 : 5
  d cars : motorbikes = 15 : 1
  e books : software = 3 : 1
  f Power supporters : Crows supporters = 7 : 8
  g William's weight : Thomas' weight = 4 : 5

4 a 210 pkts **b** 540 pairs **c** 125 girls passed
  d 175 bring lunch **e i** 175 m **ii** 500 m

EXERCISE 12D

1 a N70°E **b** S30°W **c** N50°W **d** S60°W
  e S65°E **f** N75°E

EXERCISE 12B.4

1 a 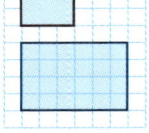 scale factor 2

b scale factor 3

c scale factor $\frac{1}{2}$

d 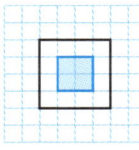 scale factor $\frac{1}{3}$

f  scale factor 2

e scale factor 4

2 a 3 **b** $1\frac{1}{2}$ **c** $\frac{1}{2}$ **3 a** 3 **b** $\frac{1}{3}$
4 a $\frac{1}{3}$ **b** 3

EXERCISE 12B.5

1 a 1 unit right, 1 unit down
  b 3 units right **c** 3 units down
  d 1 unit right, 1 unit down

EXERCISE 12C

1 a 9 : 7 **b** 5 : 3 **c** 14 : 5 **d** 8 : 7
  e 2 : 11 **f** 3 : 4 **g** 95 : 100 **h** 7 : 24

2 a 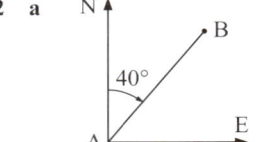 **b**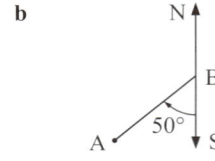

c 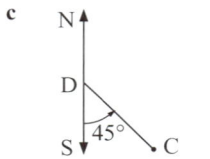 **d**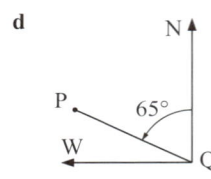

e 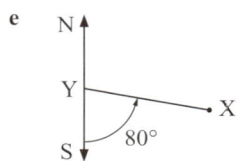 **f**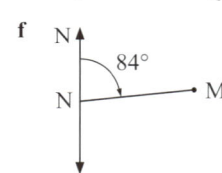

3 a 070°T **b** 210°T **c** 310°T **d** 240°T
  e 115°T **f** 075°T

4 a, b, c, d, e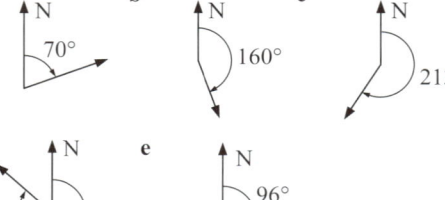

5 a West **b** True North
6 a 000°T **b** 045°T **c** 090°T **d** 135°T
  e 180°T **f** 225°T **g** 270°T **h** 315°T
7 a i H9 **ii** G5 **iii** K2 **iv** D2
  b i 068°T **ii** 127°T **iii** 307°T **iv** 349°T

8 **a** N **b** SE
 c **i** 041°T **ii** 333°T **iii** 096°T
9 **a** **i** 1560 km **ii** 3210 km **iii** 3060 km
 b **i** 022°T **ii** 299°T **iii** 133°T
10 **a** **i** 064°T **ii** 325°T **b** **i** 53 km **ii** 99 km

REVIEW SET 12A

1 **a** (1, 1) **b** (2, 5) **c** (5, 2) **d** (4, 4) **e** (3, 0)

2 a square

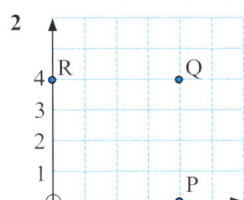

3 **a** 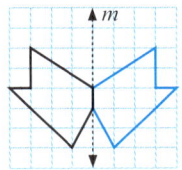 **b**

4 **a** 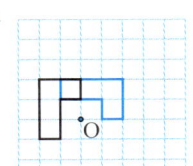 **b**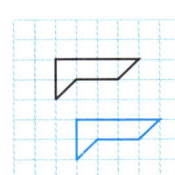

5 6

6 **a** **i** 244°T **ii** 299°T **b** 119 km

7 5.3 cm

8

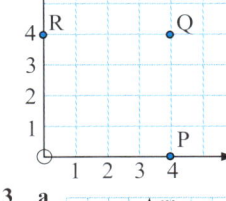

scale: 1 cm ≡ 5 m

REVIEW SET 12B

1 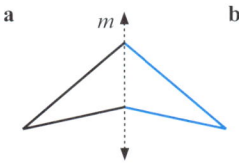 a parallelogram

2 **a** 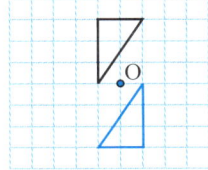 **b**

3 **a** 6 **b**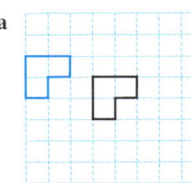

4 **a** **b**

5 88

6 **a** **i** 45°T **ii** 348°T **iii** 300°T
 b **i** 180 km **ii** ≑ 204 km

7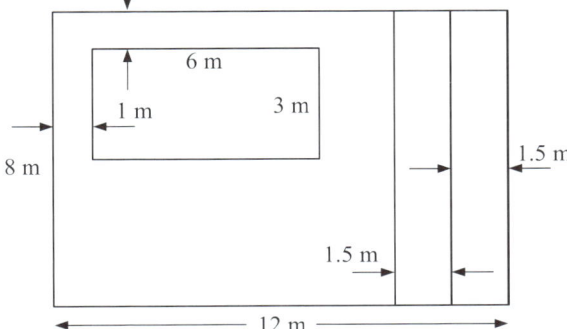

REVIEW SET 12C

1 **a** (6, 3)
 b (0, 2)
 c (5, 0)
 d (2, 6)
 e (3, 2)

2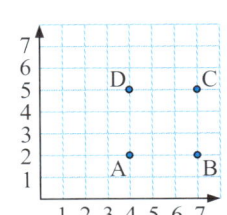

D(4, 5)

3 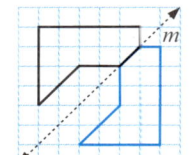 **4 a**  **b** 2

5 a 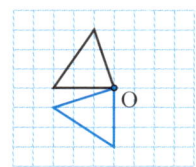 **b**

6 35 **7 a** 14 km, 180°T **b** 34 km, 298°T **c** 20 km, 038°T

8 1 cm ≡ 50 m

EXERCISE 13A

1 a highly unlikely **b** almost certain
c highly unlikely **d** highly unlikely
e unlikely **f** probably **g** highly unlikely
h certain **i** improbable

2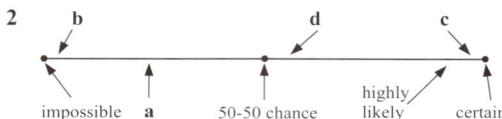

3 a very likely **b** no **c** true
4 a No, there is one more green disc. **b** green
c false
5 a possible **b** possible **c** possible
d possible **e** impossible **f** impossible
g i possible **ii** impossible

EXERCISE 13B

1 a 0.5 **b i** 1 **ii** 0

2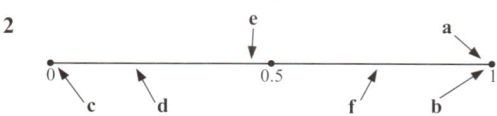

3 a i No, as some teams are better than others.
ii Yes **iii** Yes
iv No, as they can buy more than one ticket.

EXERCISE 13C

1 a i 3 blue, 2 white **ii** $\frac{3}{5}$ **iii** $\frac{2}{5}$
b i 4 blue, 3 white **ii** $\frac{4}{7}$ **iii** $\frac{3}{7}$
c i 6 blue, 2 white **ii** $\frac{3}{4}$ **iii** $\frac{1}{4}$

2 a $\frac{1}{2}$ **b** $\frac{1}{2}$ **c** $\frac{2}{3}$ **d** $\frac{5}{8}$ **3 a** $\frac{1}{2}$ **b** $\frac{1}{2}$

4 a No, as there are different sized sector angles.
b i white **ii** black **c** $\frac{1}{4}$ **d** 10 times

5 a $\frac{1}{4}$ **b** $\frac{1}{2}$ **c** 0 **d** 1

6 a $\frac{1}{8}$ **b** $\frac{1}{4}$ **c** $\frac{3}{8}$ **d** $\frac{5}{8}$ **e** 0

7 a $\frac{4}{9}$ **b** $\frac{1}{3}$ **c** $\frac{2}{9}$ **d** 0 **e** $\frac{5}{9}$ **f** $\frac{2}{3}$
g $\frac{7}{9}$ **h** $\frac{1}{3}$ **i** 1

8 a $\frac{1}{4}$ **b** $\frac{1}{52}$ **c** $\frac{1}{4}$ **d** $\frac{1}{26}$ **e** $\frac{1}{26}$ **f** $\frac{2}{13}$
g 0 **h** $\frac{1}{13}$ **i** $\frac{3}{13}$

9 a H1, H2, H3, H4, H5, H6,
T1, T2, T3, T4, T5, T6.
b 12 **c i** $\frac{1}{12}$ **ii** $\frac{1}{4}$ **iii** $\frac{1}{4}$ **iv** $\frac{1}{6}$

10 a A1, A2, A3, A4, B1, B2, B3, B4,
B1, B2, B3, B4, C1, C2, C3, C4,
b i $\frac{1}{16}$ **ii** $\frac{1}{4}$ **iii** $\frac{1}{2}$ **iv** $\frac{3}{16}$

EXERCISE 13D

1 a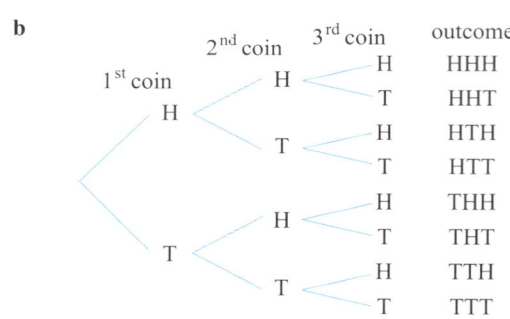

b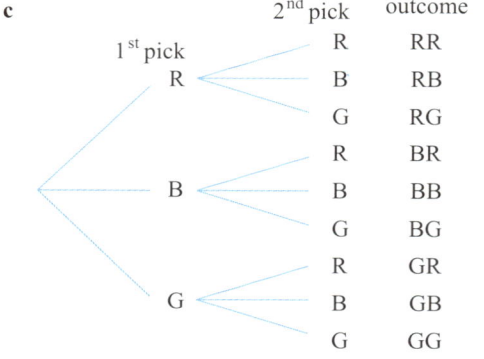

c

d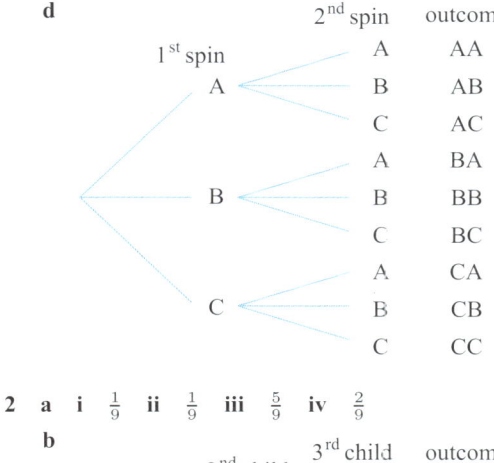

2 a i $\frac{1}{9}$ **ii** $\frac{1}{9}$ **iii** $\frac{5}{9}$ **iv** $\frac{2}{9}$

b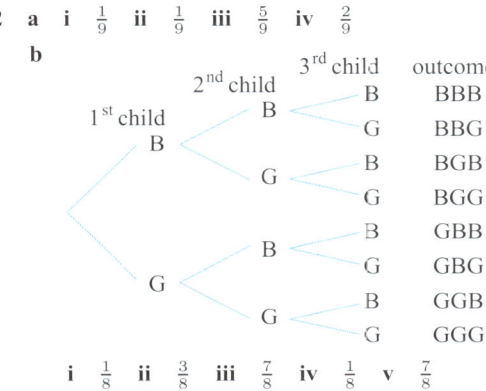

i $\frac{1}{8}$ **ii** $\frac{3}{8}$ **iii** $\frac{7}{8}$ **iv** $\frac{1}{8}$ **v** $\frac{7}{8}$

c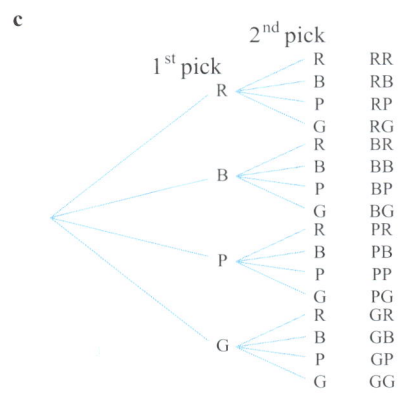

i $\frac{1}{16}$ **ii** $\frac{6}{16}$ **iii** $\frac{7}{16}$ **iv** $\frac{9}{16}$ **v** $\frac{2}{16}$

EXERCISE 13E

1 For example, coin with A on one side and B on the other *or* die with three faces A and three faces B.

2 A regular pentagonal spinner with two red and three blue parts. Five identically shaped objects in a hat with two red and three blue.

3 A die with one face marked A, two marked B and three marked C *or* six identically shaped objects in a hat with one marked A, two marked B and three marked C.

4 a a die

b A on one face, B on two faces, C on three faces

5 a Seven identically shaped objects in a hat with one labelled X, two labelled Y, four labelled Z

b i $\frac{1}{7}$ **ii** $\frac{2}{7}$ **iii** $\frac{4}{7}$

EXERCISE 13F

1 a 25 **b** B

2 a 15 times **b** 10 times **c** 5 times

3 5 days **4** 8 days

5 a 0.83 **b** 207 or 208

6 a i $\frac{1}{4}$ **ii** $\frac{3}{8}$ **iii** $\frac{1}{4}$ **iv** $\frac{1}{8}$

b 100 1s, 150 2s, 100 3s, 50 4s

REVIEW SET 13A

1 a little chance **b** some chance
c little chance **d** no chance

2 a 24 days **b i** 0.79 **ii** 395

3 a i $\frac{1}{2}$ **ii** $\frac{1}{2}$ **iii** $\frac{1}{8}$ **iv** $\frac{3}{8}$ **v** $\frac{1}{8}$
b i 20 **ii** 20 **iii** 5 **iv** 15 **v** 5

4 a i H : T = 8 : 2 = 4 : 1 **ii** H or T
b i O : E = 5 : 5 = 1 : 1 **ii** odd or even
c i R : B = 6 : 4 = 3 : 2 **ii** R or B

5 a S, P, R, Q **b i** $\frac{3}{8}$ **ii** $\frac{1}{4}$ **iii** $\frac{1}{8}$ **iv** $\frac{1}{8}$

REVIEW SET 13B

1 a 0 **b** 0.5 **c** 1 **d** 0.5

2 a 3 **b** $\frac{1}{2}$ **c** $\frac{5}{16}$ **d** $\frac{1}{2}$

3 a Pr[dark blue] = $\frac{1}{4}$, Pr[light blue] = $\frac{1}{4}$, Pr[black] = 0
b i D **ii** B **iii** A and E
c i C **ii** C **iii** A and E
d i C, likely; D, unlikely; E, unlikely
ii B, impossible; C, unlikely; D, unlikely
iii C, unlikely; D, impossible; E, impossible

4 a iv ($63) **b i** $127 **ii** $255

5 7, 8 and 5, 3, 12

INDEX

acute angle	82
algebra	338
angle	76, 81
ante meridiem (am)	323
anticlockwise	369
apex	112
approximately	18, 27
arc	114
area	252
ascending	17, 135
average	303
average speed	331
bar	121
base number	61
bearings	379
BEDMAS	51
billion	163
bisect	100, 101
boundary	266
capacity	277
cardinal points	379
categorical	290
Celsius	333
centimetre	224
centre	84, 114
centre of rotation	369
century	35, 317
certain	391
chance	390
circle	114
circumference	114
clockwise	369
column graph	295
common factor	55, 144
common fraction	122
common multiple	57
compass points	379
composite	54
cone	104, 107, 113
congruent	372
constant	343
construct	98
container	76
conversion diagram	228, 239, 257, 272
coordinates	363
counting numbers	16
cube	104
cube number	65
cubic	271
cubit	223
currency	150, 153
curved	76
cylinder	104, 112
daylight saving time	330
decade	317
decagon	93
decimal	150, 164
decimal currency	150, 153
decimal grids	156
degree	82
denominator	121, 122
descending	17, 135
diameter	114
difference	48
digits	16
directed number	42
direction	378
discount	215
distribution	292
divisibility rules	54, 59
divisible	54, 59
dot plot	290
East	379
edges	96, 105
Egyptian system	10
ellipse	112
enlargement	367, 372
equal	18, 125
equation	339
equilateral	91, 93
equivalent	125
estimate	27, 232
estimating	31, 123, 316, 322
Euler's rule	97
even	56
expanded form	17
expectation	402, 403
exponent	51, 61
face	105
factor	53
factorised	53
Fahrenheit	333
figure	77
flat	76
formula	343
fraction	120
frequency	292
front	110, 111
geoliner	83
geometry	76
GMT	328

gram	*224*	middle	*83*
GST	*216*	millennium	*35, 317*
hectare	*254*	milligram	*224*
height	*273*	millilitre	*277*
hexagon	*91*	millimetre	*224*
highest common factor	*55, 182*	million	*32, 163*
Hindu-Arabic system	*10*	millisecond	*317*
horizontal	*290*	mirror line	*368*
horizontal axis	*363*	mixed numbers	*137*
illusion	*113*	mode	*290*
image	*367*	modelling	*71*
impossible	*391*	multiples	*57*
improper fraction	*136*	nanosecond	*317*
index	*61*	natural numbers	*16*
inference	*286*	navigation	*378*
infinite	*16*	negative	*41*
instruments	*222*	net	*106*
interior	*266*	n-gon	*91*
intermediate points	*379*	North	*379*
International System of Units	*224*	number line	*166, 199*
intersecting	*78*	number plane	*363*
inverse	*353*	number system	*16*
irregular	*256*	numerator	*121, 122*
Islamic art	*104*	numerical data	*299*
isometric	*109*	object	*367*
isosceles	*93*	oblique	*108*
kilogram	*224*	obtuse angle	*82*
kilolitre	*277*	octagon	*91*
kilometre	*224*	odd	*56*
kite	*94*	opposites	*41*
lattice	*266*	order of operations	*51*
leap year	*317*	order of rotational symmetry	*370*
likelihood	*390*	ordered pair	*363*
likely	*391*	oval	*112*
line	*78*	pace	*223*
line graph	*307, 351*	pairs of factors	*53*
line segment	*78*	parallel	*78, 95*
line symmetry	*368*	parallelogram	*94*
litre	*277*	patterns	*338, 340*
location	*362*	pentagon	*91*
lowest common denominator	*135*	percent	*191*
lowest common multiple	*58*	percentage	*188, 190*
lowest terms	*129*	perimeter	*231*
MA blocks	*61, 154*	perpendicular	*95*
Megalitre	*277*	Pick's Rule	*266*
mass	*224, 239*	pie chart	*296*
Mayan system	*13*	pie graph	*296*
mean	*303*	place value	*10, 157*
measure	*222*	plan	*110*
median	*304*	point of intersection	*78*
metre	*224*	polygon	*91, 231*
microsecond	*317*	polyhedra	*104*

polyhedron	*104*	simplest numeral	*63*
population	*286*	solid	*76, 104*
positive	*41*	South	*379*
post meridiem (pm)	*323*	span	*223*
power	*23, 61*	speed	*331*
prime	*54*	sphere	*104*
prime meridian	*328*	square	*91, 94, 231, 258*
prism	*104, 105*	square number	*64*
probability	*395*	square root	*65*
product	*48*	square units	*253*
projection	*111*	standard time	*328*
pronumeral	*343*	standard time zones	*328*
proper fraction	*136*	stem-and-leaf plot	*299*
protractor	*83*	straight angle	*82*
pyramid	*104, 105, 112*	sum	*48*
quadrilateral	*91, 94*	surface	*76*
qualitative data	*241*	survey	*214, 306*
quotient	*48*	tally	*292*
radius	*114*	terminating	*179*
random	*286*	tessellation	*375*
ratings	*288*	tetrahedron	*105*
ratio	*376*	time line	*315*
rational number	*164, 181*	time series	*307*
ray	*78*	time zone	*328*
rectangle	*94, 231, 258*	timetable	*325, 327*
rectangular prism	*111, 273*	tonne	*224*
recurring	*180*	transformation	*367*
reduced	*372*	translation	*367, 372*
reduction	*372*	trapezium	*94*
reflection	*367*	tree diagram	*399*
reflex angle	*82*	trend	*307*
regions	*96*	trial and error	*68*
regular polygon	*91*	triangle	*91, 93, 231, 264*
revolution	*82*	triangular number	*67*
rhombus	*94*	true north	*380*
right angle	*82*	trundle wheel	*234*
risk	*392*	variable	*343*
Roman numerals	*11*	vertex	*77, 105*
rotation	*367, 369*	vertical	*290*
rotational symmetry	*369, 370*	vertical axis	*363*
rounding	*19, 160*	vertices	*96*
rule	*339*	volume	*271*
same units	*131*	West	*379*
sample	*286*	whole numbers	*16*
scale	*225, 299*	working backwards	*72*
scale diagram	*235*	yard	*224*
scale factor	*372*	year	*317*
scalene	*93*	zero	*13*
sector	*202, 296*		
sieve	*57*		
simple interest	*217*		
simplest form	*17, 129, 182*		

NOTES